*Place Names of the
Avalon Peninsula of the
Island of
Newfoundland*

magnifiquement surchargé de noms – PROUST

Published for
Memorial University of Newfoundland by
University of Toronto Press

Place Names of the Avalon Peninsula of the Island of Newfoundland

E. R. SEARY

MEMORIAL UNIVERSITY SERIES

1 *Christmas Mumming in Newfoundland: Essays in Anthropology, Folklore, and History*
Edited by HERBERT HALPERT and G.M. STORY

2 *Place Names of the Avalon Peninsula of the Island of Newfoundland*
By E.R. SEARY

© University of Toronto Press 1971
Toronto and Buffalo
Printed in Canada
Reprinted in 2018
ISBN 0-8020-3243-5
ISBN 978-1-4875-8246-3 (paper)
Microfiche ISBN 0-8020-0068-1
LC 73-151390

To Gwen

National Topographic Series,
Newfoundland, with Avalon Peninsula as inset

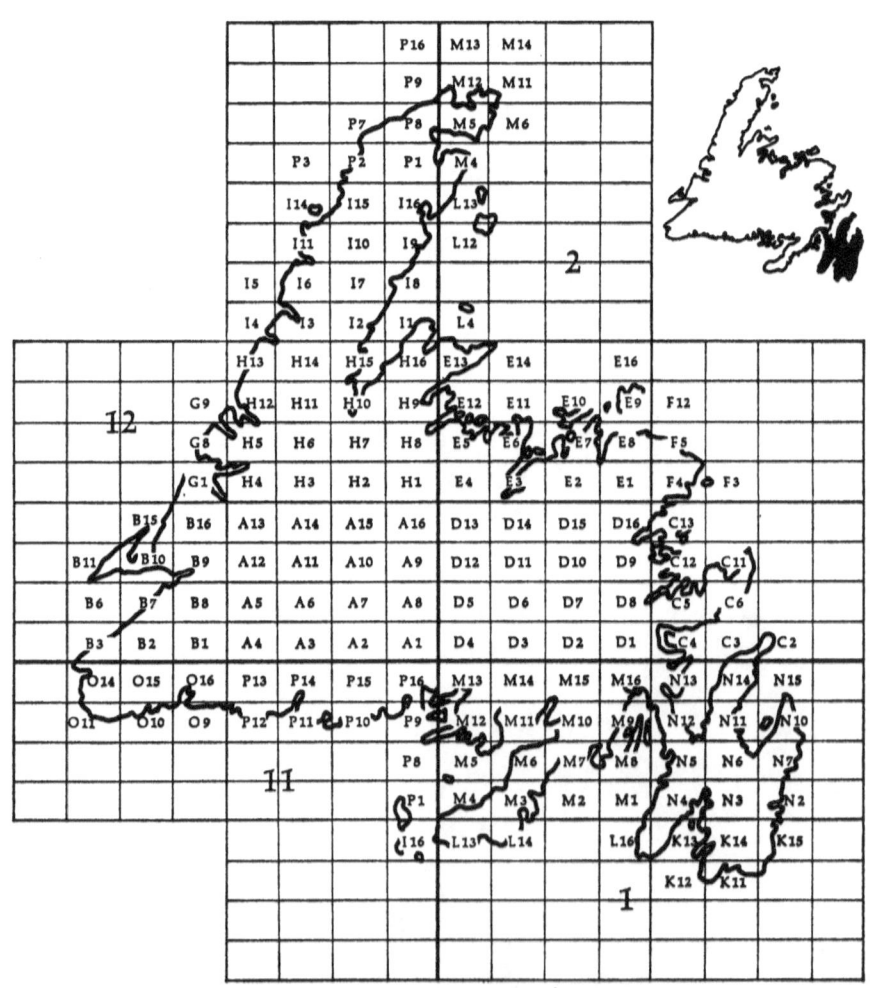

1K/ 11 Trepassey	2D/ 14 Mount Peyton	12A/ 10 Lake Ambrose
1K/ 12 St. Shotts	2D/ 15 Gander	12A/ 11 Star Lake
1K/ 13 St. Mary's	2D/ 16 Gambo	12A/ 12 Little Grand Lake
1K/ 14 Biscay Bay River	2E/ 1 Weir's Pond	12A/ 13 Corner Brook
1K/ 15 Renews	2E/ 2 Gander River	12A/ 14 Rainy Lake
1L/ 13 Lamaline	2E/ 3 Botwood	12A/ 15 Buchans
1L/ 14 St. Lawrence	2E/ 4 Hodges Hill	12A/ 16 Badger
1L/ 16 St. Bride's	2E/ 5 Roberts Arm	12B/ 1 Dashwoods Pond
1M/ 1 Ship Cove	2E/ 6 Point Leamington	12B/ 2 St. Fintan's
1M/ 2 Jude Island	2E/ 7 Comfort Cove	12B/ 3 Little Friars Cove
1M/ 3 Marystown	2E/ 8 Carmanville	12B/ 6 Cape St. George
1M/ 4 Grand Bank	2E/ 9 Fogo	12B/ 7 Flat Bay
1M/ 5 Harbour Breton	2E/ 10 Twillingate	12B/ 8 Main Gut
1M/ 6 Point Enragee	2E/ 11 Exploits	12B/ 9 Harry's River
1M/ 7 Baine Harbour	2E/ 12 Little Bay Island	12B/ 10 Stephenville
1M/ 8 Merasheen	2E/ 13 Nippers Harbour	12B/ 11 Mainland
1M/ 9 Harbour Buffett	2E/ 14 Cape St. John	12B/ 15 Shag Island
1M/ 10 Terrenceville	2E/ 16 Bishops Islands	12B/ 16 Serpentine
1M/ 11 Belleoram	2F/ 3 Cabot Islands	12G/ 1 Bay of Islands
1M/ 12 Gaultois	2F/ 4 Wesleyville	12G/ 8 Trout River
1M/ 13 St. Alban's	2F/ 5 Musgrave Harbour	12G/ 9 Skinner Cove
1M/ 14 Hungry Grove Pond	2F/ 12 Wadham Islands	12H/ 1 Gull Pond
1M/ 15 Gisborne Lake	2L/ 4 Horse Islands	12H/ 2 The Topsails
1M/ 16 Sound Island	2L/ 12 Grey Islands Harbour	12H/ 3 Deer Lake
1N/ 2 Ferryland		12H/ 4 Pasadena
1N/ 3 St. Catherine's	2L/ 13 Groais Island	12H/ 5 Lomond
1N/ 4 Placentia	2M/ 4 St. Julien's	12H/ 6 Cormack
1N/ 5 Argentia	2M/ 5 St. Anthony	12H/ 7 Sheffield Lake
1N/ 6 Holyrood	2M/ 11 Quirpon	12H/ 8 Springdale
1N/ 7 Bay Bulls	2M/ 12 Raleigh	12H/ 9 Kings Point
1N/ 10 St. John's	2M/ 13 Chateau Point	12H/ 10 Hampden
1N/ 11 Harbour Grace	2M/ 14 Belle Isle	12H/ 11 Silver Mountain
1N/ 12 Dildo	1I1/ 16 Ile de St. Pierre	12H/ 12 Gros Morne
1N/ 13 Sunnyside	1I0/ 9 La Poile	12H/ 13 St. Pauls Inlet
1N/ 14 Heart's Content	1I0/ 10 Rose Blanche	12H/ 14 Main River
1N/ 15 Pouch Cove	1I0/ 11 Port aux Basques	12H/ 15 Jackson's Arm
2C/ 2 Bay de Verde	1I0/ 14 Codroy	12H/ 16 Baie Verte
2C/ 3 Old Perlican	1I0/ 15 Grandys Lake	12I/ 1 Fleur de Lys
2C/ 4 Random Island	1I0/ 16 La Poile River	12I/ 2 Cat Arm River
2C/ 5 Sweet Bay	11P/ 1 Grande Miquelon	12I/ 3 Indian Lookout
2C/ 6 Trinity	11P/ 8 Pass Island	12I/ 4 Portland Creek
2C/ 11 Bonavista	11P/ 9 Facheux Bay	12I/ 5 Bellburns
2C/ 12 Eastport	11P/ 10 La Hune	12I/ 6 Blue Mountain
2C/ 13 St. Brendans	11P/ 11 Ramea	12I/ 7 Harbour Deep
2D/ 1 Tug Pond	11P/ 12 Burgeo	12I/ 8 Orange Bay
2D/ 2 Meta Pond	11P/ 13 Peter Snout	12I/ 9 Englee
2D/ 3 Mount Sylvester	11P/ 14 White Bear River	12I/ 10 Torrent River
2D/ 4 Twillick Brook	11P/ 15 Dolland Brook	12I/ 11 Port Saunders
2D/ 5 Burnt Hill	11P/ 16 D'Espoir Brook	12I/ 14 St. John Island
2D/ 6 Great Gull Lake	12A/ 1 Cold Spring Pond	12I/ 15 Castors River
2D/ 7 Kepenkeck Lake	12A/ 2 Pudops Lake	12I/ 16 Roddickton
2D/ 8 Port Blandford	12A/ 3 Burnt Pond	12P/ 1 Salmon River
2D/ 9 Glovertown	12A/ 4 King George IV Lake	12P/ 2 Brig Bay
2D/ 10 Dead Wolf Pond	12A/ 5 Puddle Pond	12P/ 3 Ferolle Point
2D/ 11 West Gander Rivers	12A/ 6 Howley Lake	12P/ 7 Flower's Cove
2D/ 12 Miguels Lake	12A/ 7 Snowshoe Pond	12P/ 8 Eddies Cove
2D/ 13 Grand Falls	12A/ 8 Great Burnt Lake	12P/ 9 Big Brook
	12A/ 9 Noel Pauls Brook	

National Topographic Series, Avalon Peninsula

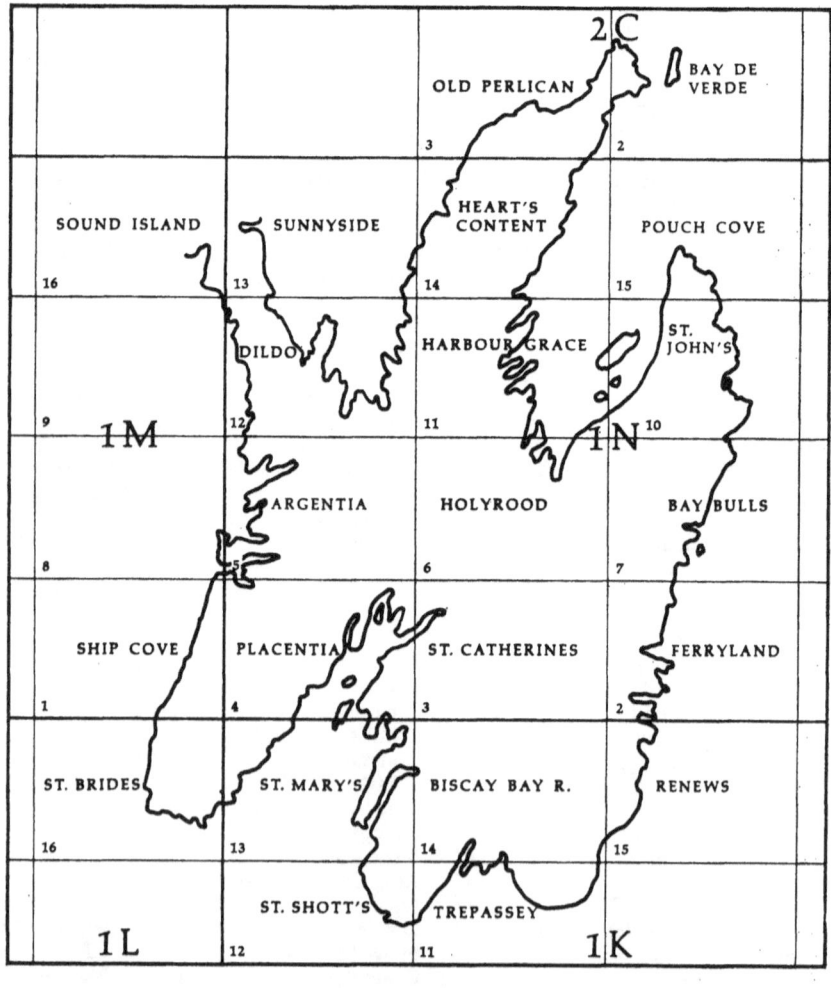

Preface

This study is a small part of a project conceived some twelve years ago by members of the Department of English Language and Literature of the Memorial University of Newfoundland in which the speech, dialect vocabulary, place names, and folklore of Newfoundland were to be subjected to a scrutiny worthy of their importance not only for Newfoundland but for the English-speaking world at large; for Newfoundland has preserved uniquely and almost intact until the present generation specimens, qualities, and characteristics of speech, vocabulary, nomenclature, and folklore from the cultures of which it has been compounded since the early years of the sixteenth century, though none had been studied with the rigour that contemporary scholarship demands.

In the distribution of the work, place names fell to me, speech to Mr Patrick Drysdale and later to Dr W. Kirwin, the dialect vocabulary to Dr G. M. Story, and in due course folklore to Dr H. Halpert, though we soon discovered that far from working in discrete fields we shared common concerns and common needs and were to be increasingly dependent on each other for special kinds of information. Other acknowledgements will be made later, but I should like to record here, however inadequately, my gratitude for the unflagging interest and unstinted help I have received from them, particularly in the exchange of ideas and information, the loan of books, and the reading of the manuscript.

The first need after the place names of the island had been collected and their descent broadly ascertained was for a pilot study of a limited area to establish a method of reference, citation, and commentary. For this purpose the Northern Peninsula of Newfoundland was chosen, and a check-list, consisting of a short history and analysis of the names and a descriptive and historical gazetteer, was published in mimeograph in 1959.

From the experience gained in the preparation of the check-list, it was felt that more profitable at this stage than a general study of the nomenclature of the whole island would be an intensive study of that part, the Avalon Peninsula, which had been first discovered and first settled, whose history was best documented, and which was most convenient for fieldwork. Further, it was decided that the historical and linguistic commentaries and the annotative and bibliographical apparatus should be as complete as possible since, as S. T. Rand had observed in 1872 of his gazetteer of Micmac place names in the Maritime Provinces, "To string together a lot of names in alphabetical order seems to be about as preposterous a thing as could well be done," since Newfoundland studies in the past, with few exceptions, have been notoriously deficient in documentation, and since many of the sources of information found useful for names on the Avalon Peninsula would be relevant to names elsewhere in the island.

For reasons given at the end of Chapter 1 the recording of the place names is not, and cannot be, complete; their exegesis is also deficient from the loss or unavailability of information about them. Much remains locked away in oral traditions. Little is known, for example, about pond names, and commentary on settlement names would have been richer had the minutes of the Nomenclature Board of Newfoundland, which from time to time has recommended changes to the government since its formation in 1902, been accessible. In other points, of course, I hold myself responsible for all those errors and omissions, unwarrantable surmises, inconsistencies, and shortcomings, which will be found in this study and go to my account with my readers "With all my imperfections on my head." But the burden would have been incomparably heavier had it not been for the many services, favours, and help I have received, and gratefully acknowledge here from: the President and Regents of the University, the Humanities Research Council, and the Canada Council, for generous financial assistance towards the cost of research and publication; Dr R. A. Skelton, formerly Superintendent of the Map Room of the British Museum, who placed his unrivalled knowledge of maps at my disposal and by his close reading of the manuscript obviated many errors; Dr W. Kaye Lamb, Mr T. E. Layng, Brigadier E. D. Baldock, Mr Gordon Delaney, Commander P. K. Kemp, Mr J. H. Burridge, the Hon. F. O'Dea, and the National Maritime Museum and the Hydrographic Department of the Admiralty for map-reading facilities, the provision of maps, photographs, and microfilms, and advice in cartographical matters; the Librarians and their staffs of the University Library, the Gosling Memorial Library, St. John's, the Public Archives of Canada, the British Museum Library, the Public Record Office, Lambeth Palace Library, and the Bodleian

Library, for professional help; Dean Leslie Harris, Dr D. G. Pitt, Miss Agnes O'Dea, Mrs K. R. Coldwell, Dr P. A. O'Flaherty, Dr W. Summers, Dr D. M. Baird, Dr C. R. Barrett, Dr Alan Wilshere, Mr G. Thomas, and Dr J. Hewson, among colleagues past and present, and the Hon. R. S. Furlong, Mr E. B. Foran, Mr David Webber, and Mr Gilbert Higgins, for information historical, geographical, geological, and linguistic; students of the University for help in the extraction of names from maps and in the preparation of work-cards, and for information about names in their communities; the late Mr A. Prince Dyke, who prepared the sketch maps; Mr B. Hansen for photographs of maps; Mrs D. G. Alexander for help in the preparation of the index; Mrs C. Rose, who typed the final draft; Miss Sheila Lynch who assisted in reading the proofs; and Miss Alison Adair of the Editorial Offices of the University of Toronto Press who transformed an often tortuous manuscript into "A bliss in proof."

Corrections and additions made after Chapters 1–9 were in print are marked in the Gazetteer by an asterisk.

Memorial University of Newfoundland
"the day of John the Baptist" 1970

E. R. S.

NOTE   In the following chapters, modern forms of place names on the Avalon Peninsula are given in small capitals and NTS signifies a map in the National Topographic Series.

Insula olim vocata Noua: Terrae by John Mason (1629)

Contents

PREFACE / ix

LIST OF MAPS AND TABLES / xv

1 Some General Considerations / 3

2 The Avalon Peninsula: Description, Indian Names, and European Discovery / 18

3 The French Place Names / 34

4 English Place Names of the Seventeenth Century / 56

5 English Place Names of the Eighteenth Century / 81

6 The Nineteenth Century / 99

7 The Irish Place Names / 121

8 Analysis of the Place Names / One: Distribution, Single-Element Names, Generics / 137

9 Analysis of the Place Names / Two: Specifics, Qualifiers, Composition / 149

Avalon Peninsula: GAZETTEER AND INDEX OF PLACE NAMES / 168

BIBLIOGRAPHY / ONE: Maps, Charts, and Atlases / 301

BIBLIOGRAPHY / TWO: A Selection of Manuscript and Printed Sources / 328

NOTES / 343

INDEX / 365

Maps and Tables

MAPS

National Topographic Series, Newfoundland, with Avalon Peninsula as inset	vi
National Topographic Series, Avalon Peninsula	viii
Insula olim vocata Noua: Terrae by John Mason (1626)	facing xii
Indian Place Names on the Avalon Peninsula	23
Portuguese Place Names on the Avalon Peninsula	29
French Place Names on the Avalon Peninsula	36
The Province of Avalonia by R. Robinson (1669) Reproduced by kind permission of the Keeper of Western Manuscripts, Bodleian Library, Oxford, from MS Rawlinson A. 183 fol. 101	facing 70

TABLES

1	Lane's Labrador and Newfoundland Surveys	14
2	Survey of Rocky River and Big Barren Brook by J. P. Howley, 1872	24
3	English Settlements in Newfoundland Captured in d'Iberville's Expedition 1696–7	79
4	English and Irish Inhabitants of the Avalon Peninsula 1732 and 1754	123
5	Place Names Associated with Irish Family Names	129
6	Avalon Peninsula: Names in NTS Maps	137
7	Place Names Associated with English Family Names	156

Place Names of the Avalon Peninsula of the Island of Newfoundland

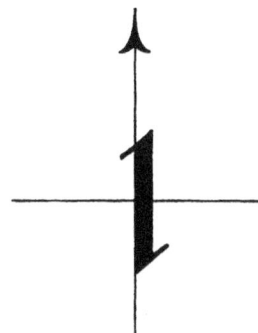

Some General Considerations

Toponymy, or the study of place names, is concerned with the origins, significance and interpretation of place names of all kinds and with the changes they have undergone, in form, spelling and pronunciation, whether they be names of natural features such as headlands, mountains, lakes, rivers, and bays, or of man-made places such as towns, villages, farms, fields, streets, and bridges, or even of arbitrary marine areas such as are designated by meteorologists.

Interest in place names is, of course, nothing new. The Authorized Version of the Bible, for instance, provides a number of examples of the interpretation of names, presumably on the grounds that to know the meaning of a name is to endow it with greater significance: "Therefore is the name of it called Babel; because the Lord did there confound the language of all the earth" (Genesis xi, 9); "a place called Golgotha, that is to say, a place of a skull" (Matthew xxvii, 33). But during the last sixty or seventy years, interest in place names has developed as never before. The pioneers of modern toponymy named by Mawer in his article in the *Encyclopaedia Britannica*, Föstermann in Germany, Rygh in Norway, Noreen in Sweden, Skeat in England, Longnon in France, have been followed by a host of successors in all parts of the world; organizations such as the English Place-Name Society, the American Name Society, la Commission Nationale de Toponymie et d'Anthroponymie, and the International Centre of Onomastics exist, wholly or in part, for the furtherance of toponymy; and its international character is attested by the work of the Swede Ekwall in English place names and of the German Gröhler in French place names.

From a mildly entertaining exercise for dilettante etymologists, toponymy has become a rigorous linguistic discipline, for, as Ekwall reminds us, "Place-names form a part of the vocabulary and deserve as much" – and we may add the same kind of – "attention as other words."[1] More particularly, Mawer has enunciated the two basic onomastic principles of toponymy: that no place name can be interpreted in the light of its present-day form alone, but must be traced back to its earliest recorded form; and that no explanation of a place name, however convincing as philology, can hold good if inconsistent with the known history and topography of the site, and, conversely, that no explanation based upon legend or topography is of value if inconsistent with philology.

Interesting as individual place names frequently are, they gain in significance when seen in some kind of association, and initially a national area tends to provide an association at once obvious and convenient. Hence the studies of English, French, German, Swiss, and other place names in such works as Ekwall's *The Concise Oxford Dictionary of English Place-Names* and Dauzat's and Rostaing's volumes on French place names. The refinement of national studies leads to regional and local studies, perhaps best exemplified in the county volumes of the English Place-Name Society. But within the national, regional or local frame, place names show rich variety. They may be of great antiquity or of recent imposition; the circumstances of their imposition may be known or unknown; they may be of diverse linguistic origin, reflecting periods of conquest and colonization by men of different races, though the original form of the name may have changed beyond recognition; they may be descriptive, commemorative of other places, people and incidents; occupational, metaphorical, fanciful; they may become obsolete; they may consist of a varying number of words in differing order; they may be widespread, or restricted to a particular region, or even unique. Part of the task of toponymists has been to evolve methodologies whereby this richness may be made readily apparent. One system, capable of general application, is that described by G. R. Stewart, author of a study of place names in the United States, *Names on the Land*, in his article "Names (In Linguistics) Place Names" in the *Encyclopaedia Britannica*, which has replaced the earlier one by Mawer.[2]

In this system, place names are seen to consist of two types: single-element names, with or without the definite article, such as BUTTER POT,

HARES EARS, THE BELL, THE KETTLE, in which no explicit indication is given of the kind of feature designated (BUTTER POT is in fact a hill, HARES EARS pinnacle rocks, THE BELL a rock, and THE KETTLE a point), and dual-element names in which a generic distinguishes different classes of place phenomena, such as rivers, bays and mountains, and a specific distinguishes one member of a class from others, such as SOUTH RIVER, SALMON RIVER, ROCKY RIVER. Usually in English, the specific precedes the generic, as in the examples given, but it may follow, as in BAY ROBERTS and MOUNT CARMEL, and even take the form not of a single word but of a phrase or clause, as in THE POND THAT FEEDS THE BROOK. The definite article may replace either the specific or the generic, as in Stewart's example of "the Ohio" or "the river" standing in different circumstances for the full name, "the Ohio river."

Both generics and specifics offer areas for exploration and investigation. Under generics fall such considerations as the differences in size denoted by brook, stream, and river; bight, gulf, bay, and cove; head and point; hill and mountain; lake and pond; and differences in usage in different places.[3] A noteworthy example of the study of generics of a special kind in a particular area is Donald B. Sands, "The Nature of the Generics in Island, Ledge, and Rock Names of the Maine Coast," *Names*, VII, 4 (December 1959).

Compared with generics, specifics are virtually unlimited in number, and of wide variety. Stewart makes a classification of specifics by usage under nine heads, though he recognizes that any specific may belong to more than one class. His classes are:

1 Descriptive names, which may indicate a long-standing quality of the generic (ROCKY RIVER, SERRATED HILL, RED HEAD),[4] identify by means of a possibly impermanent association (WOODY ISLAND, CASTLE HILL), or indicate a relation to something else (NORTH RIVER, SOUTH RIVER; SECOND POND, THIRD POND; HALFWAY BROOK; LEFT HAND POND, RIGHT HAND POND).

2 Incident names, which arise from an incident occurring at the place and making it memorable (SHIPWRECK POINT, DEADMANS POND). Names of persons and animals are often applied to natural features for this reason (ISLAND POND near NEW MELBOURNE is locally known as CHARLIE'S POND after Charlie Clarke of that community, whose horse and sled fell through the ice on the pond: MOSQUITO COVE, BEAR COVE, BEAVER POND). Names associated with occupations may also be taken as belonging to this class (ADMIRALS COVE, GUNNERS COVE, RINDERS POND).

3 Possessive names, which spring from the idea of ownership, whether legal or informal (CLARKE'S BEACH, TOM POWER LOOKOUT, MOUNT PEARL), and include most ethnic names (IRISHTOWN, FRENCHMANS COVE, PORTUGAL

COVE, JERSEYSIDE) and many mythological names derived from the names of gods and spirits.

4 Commemorative names, which are given consciously "in honour of" someone or something, as in religious (ST. MARY'S BAY, TRINITY BAY) and patriotic (VICTORIA, QUEEN'S RIVER, COCHRANE POND, PRINCE WILLIAM PLACE) names. This class includes most transfer names (KILBRIDE from Ireland, TORBAY from England, TREPASSEY from France, and NEW CHELSEA from the United States).

5 Euphemistic names, which are bestowed with the idea of making a good impression or establishing favourable auspices (PARADISE, FAIR-HAVEN, HEART'S CONTENT, HEART'S DELIGHT).

6 Manufactured names, which are constructed from recombined sounds or letters, out of fragments of old words, from initials, by backward spellings, etc. (Stewart cites Tesnus from Sunset).

7 Shift names, which result from the shift of the specific from one generic to another in the vicinity (DEER POND and RIVER, FOX MARSH and PONDS). The resulting group is called a name-cluster.

8 Folk-etymologies which "though they may be said merely to transform old names, really produce what are essentially new names, by the assumption that an obsolete or foreign word is something different from what it really is" (FERRYLAND from Port. *farelhão*, Fr. *ferillon*, or Eng. foreland; ST. SHOTTS from Fr. *chincette*).

9 Mistake names, which arise from failure in transmission, either oral or written (PEGWOOD for Pigweed Pond, WATERN for Watering Cove, POUNDEN for Pounding Cove).

A qualifier may be added to distinguish two features bearing the same specific (BIG OTTER POND, LITTLE OTTER POND; UPPER ISLAND COVE, LOWER ISLAND COVE; INSIDE ISLAND COVE POND, OUTSIDE ISLAND COVE POND).

Other essays in methodology, of special interest to Canadians, are by Armstrong, Kirkconnell, Lacourcière, Rudnyckyj, and Poirier.

Armstrong and Kirkconnell make a classification of Canadian place names on historical principles. Armstrong[5] recognizes five classes: Indian names, Names of the Period of exploration, Names of the French Period, Names of the British Loyalist Period, and Names of the modern or national period. Kirkconnell[6] sees successive chronological strata of cultures in Canada: the aboriginal Amerindian, the French (largely rural French colonists of the seventeenth century), the Anglo-Canadians (from England, Scotland and Ireland, partly by way of the American colonies at the time of the Revolutionary War), and the more recent European-Canadians (chiefly from Central and Eastern Europe), all of whom "have contributed something to the total and have left conspicuous marks on the place-names of the country."

Lacourcière[7] sees the three major linguistic groups of Indian, French and English place names and classifies the French names by their origins: Place names of France given to places in Canada; Names of historic personages (Governors, administrators, soldiers, bishops, noblemen, explorers, etc.) which have become place names; Religious names; Descriptive names; Foreign names, assimilated Indian or English names; Legendary, anecdotal and folkloristic names.

Rudnyckyj[8] classifies Canadian place names on historical principles after Armstrong, and independently on linguistic and onomastic principles. He finds six linguistic classes: Aboriginal Amerindian place names; Place names of Romance provenience, Portuguese, Spanish and French; Place names of Germanic origin, Anglo-Saxon, German, Icelandic, Scandinavian, other Germanic names; Place names of Celtic origin, Scotch and Irish; Place names of Slavic provenience, Ukrainian, Russian, Polish and other Slavic names; Other place names, of Hebrew origin, Grecized names, Latinized names, Names of other lingual origin, Artificial onomastic neologisms. His onomastic analysis reveals three classes: Autochthon (aboriginal) Amerindian names; Imported (mainly European) place names, which may be transplaced names or transferred names, originally personal names; and Canadian toponymic neologisms.

Poirier[9] discusses the origin, significance, modification and substitution of place names, which he sees as either spontaneous appellations or systematic impositions. He examines the kinds of documents, especially maps and archival materials, used in tracing the history of place names, and relates toponymical studies to national and local history, to physical and human geography, to dialectology and to phonetics. But the chief value of his work lies in his practical suggestions for research based largely on his own experiences as a toponymist in Quebec.

While each of these systems has its merits, it will be appreciated that, in the long run, the toponymist must be prepared to invent or to adapt a system best suited to demonstrate the characteristics of the region he is studying.

The main characteristic which distinguishes North American from European place names is age. Whereas certain elements in French place names, for example, have a pre-Indo-European, pre-Celtic, Gallic or Latin base, and some English place names can be traced back to Celtic, Latin and Scandinavian origins,[10] no North American place names, with the exception of Indian names, are more than four hundred years old. A second characteristic is that the circumstance of the imposition, or of the change, of a place name – its origin, date and authorship – are frequently known in North America, but rarely in Europe. The effect of these characteristics on toponymical research is that in North America the bias is towards history, tracing a name in records of one kind or another to its earliest citation, in Europe towards linguistics, especially in questions of identification and interpretation. Linguistic study in North America, except in Amerindian names, frequently has as its chief concern merely the changes that names of European provenance have undergone since their transfer.

Places receive names in one of two ways, described by Lacourcière as by deliberate imposition, that is by known persons who impose them with some measure of "authority", or by a process of spontaneous creation or collective usage. Stewart terms such names "bestowed" or "evolved." The origin of evolved names is regrettably "beyond all conjecture," but we know the authorship of many bestowed names from the author himself or from statements by historians and biographers. Newfoundland provides several illustrations of this kind of evidence.

Hakluyt, for instance, records the first naming of Newfoundland with a precision probably unsurpassed in the annals of toponymy, even if the "Island of S. John," in fact, does not exist:

In the yere of our Lord 1497 John Cabot ... discovered that land which no man before that time had attempted, on the 24 of June, about five of the clocke early in the morning. This land he called Prima vista, that is to say, First seene, because as I suppose it was that part whereof they had the first sight from sea. That Island which lieth out before the land, he called the Island of S. John upon this occasion, as I thinke, because it was discovered upon the day of John the Baptist.[11]

In John Guy's account of his explorations in TRINITY BAY in 1612, he writes that on 8 November "[We] came that nighte to the harbour ... which we call Flagstaffe Harbour, because we found theare the flagstaffe throwen by the savages away."[12] Cormack, who first crossed Newfoundland on foot from TRINITY BAY to St. George's Bay in 1822, informs us: "I have used the customary privilege of giving names to the lakes and mountains I met with in this hitherto unexplored route, and these are in compliment to distinguished individuals and private friends," though he named Mount Misery after an unpleasant night he spent there when stormbound on the 16–17 October.[13]

Evidence of the sometimes arbitrary and injudicious change of established names is also common, as when Fr Morris changed the name of the settlement at Gallows Harbour to St. Joseph's, with the result that Newfoundland had three St. Joseph's, a source of further confusion to a Post Office already embarrassed with a plurality of identical names;[14] when the Newfoundland Nomenclature Board re-named Silly (Scilly) Cove, a name recorded as early as 1675, WINTERTON in 1912, presumably out of deference to the susceptibilities of its inhabitants; and when the Canadian Board of Geographical Names, for reasons that only the bureaucratic mind can fathom, changed the name of the post office at Mann Point to Davidsville in 1956.

Place names occur in documents which vary from country to country and from period to period. In England, for example, names of great antiquity are to be found in chronicles and histories such as the *Anglo-Saxon Chronicle* and Bede's *Historia Ecclesiastica*, in charters of towns and boroughs, in rolls, deeds and records, some of which precede, and were used in, the compilation of *Domesday Book* as early as 1086. In North America, the oldest names, of major coastal features, are found in maps of the sixteenth and seventeenth centuries, by Italian, Portuguese, Spanish, Basque, Breton, Norman, French, Dutch, German, and English cartographers, compiled from not always accurate information received from explorers, fishermen and traders, either by word of mouth or from their portolans or sea-charts, and not infrequently eked out with their own conjectures and fancies. They were, it should be added, inveterate plagiarists and not least of their fellows' mistakes. "The maps," then, in Skelton's words, "used or drawn by explorers describe the borderland between the known and the unknown." He continues:

Their evidence may tell us what a traveller expected to find or what in fact he discovered. They may have the authority of a prophecy, of a prospectus, or of a chronicle. In early maps information derived from theory and from experience is often inextricably entangled, and for this reason they are important documents in the history both of geographical ideas and of geographical discovery. They illustrate the always shifting "relation of observation, theory, and practice" in this field of science.[15]

The exegesis of these maps since the publication of Kohl's *Documentary History of the State of Maine* in 1869 has provided most of the information we possess about the location and interpretation of the earliest names on the North Atlantic coast. The two classic studies are H. Harrisse, *Découverte et Évolution cartographique de Terre-Neuve et des Pays circonvoisins*, 1900, praised by Ganong as "not only the indispensable foundation for all future studies of its subject, but also well nigh a model of what such a work should be," and Ganong's own "Crucial Maps in the Early Cartography and Place-nomenclature of the Atlantic Coast of Canada," a series of nine papers published originally in the *Proceedings and Transactions of the Royal Society of Canada* from 1929 to 1937 and only recently brought within the covers of one volume, which presents both a comprehensive survey of previous cartographical work in the area and a scholarly elucidation of the nomenclature of the South Coast of Newfoundland.[16] A third study, *Cartological Material*, by G. R. F. Prowse (1860–1946), son of the Newfoundland judge and historian, D. W. Prowse, and friend and correspondent of Ganong, is little known.[17]

All three of these men made valuable contributions to Newfoundland toponymy, though none produced a complete survey, were such an achievement possible. They were primarily cartologists, to use Prowse's word, for whom the study of nomenclature was largely incidental to other interests. Their contribution lies in the identification, recording and interpretation of maps, but in not much more than the simple recording of the names they contain. Prowse, indeed, devoted the third volume of *Cartological Material* to Names, but he recorded names which had appeared for the most part only up to the mid-eighteenth century. He followed the usual practice of cartologists in arranging maps in what for him were related groups or traditions and recorded names in the same way, and hid the whole behind a baffling array of cryptic symbols and crabbed abbreviations.

Within their limits, Harrisse and Prowse remain the chief sources of information about names in the early maps. They differ from time to time in their ascriptions, identifications, and dates of maps, but show remarkable unanimity in their readings of names, the most common discrepancies being in initial capitals, raised letters, the retention and expansion of abbreviations, and such like *minutiae*. The introduction of more scientific ways of map-making by Cook, however, robbed cartology of much of its zest for them, and their treatment of later maps is often little more than perfunctory. Only occasionally does either offer historical or linguistic comment on the names he has extracted and, by the nature of their studies, both treat only of coastal names.

Harrisse, Ganong, and Prowse produced, of course, by no means the only commentaries on the early maps, for which a useful bibliography (of a voluminous and often contradictory and acrimonious literature) is B. G. Hoffman's *Cabot to Cartier*. But toponymists and cartologists do not look at maps with the same eyes – a map that is significant to the one on account of a numerous or rare nomenclature may hold little interest for the other – and the toponymist may often hold himself aloof from many of the theories, speculations, and controversies of the cartologists. His first need is for reliable information on the dates and provenance of the maps he uses, and for early maps an indispensable guide is *Sixteenth-Century Maps Relating to Canada*, a check-list and bibliography prepared and published by the Public Archives of Canada. How valuable this work is he quickly discovers when he enters the virtually uncharted seas of seventeenth- and eighteenth-century cartography.

The authoritative work on sixteenth-century Portuguese maps is *Portugaliae Monumenta Cartographica*, Volume v of which contains Cortesão's admirable analysis of the early representation of Newfoundland (pp. 157–69), with tables of the toponymy in forty-six maps before 1600. Though the collation of the names for this study was completed before *Portugaliae Monumenta Cartographica* was available, readings have been corrected where necessary after comparison with Cortesão's.

For over three hundred years after the discovery of Newfoundland, maps remain the principal source of names, though Prowse opens his account of the maps of Newfoundland with an estimate that "only about one per cent of the manuscript maps up to 1760 has survived" and adds that "It can be said, generally, that every manuscript and engraved map up to 1760 has features which show derivation from maps no longer extant."[18] Skelton states that, in contrast with the survival of many Spanish charts of the sixteenth and seventeenth centuries, "the maps of early French and English explorers suffered heavy mortality":

The pages of Richard Hakluyt abound in references to maps now lost – the 'Sea card' of John Cabot, Sebastian Cabot's world map ('the copye whereof was sette out by Mr Clemente Adams and is in many merchantes houses in London'), Jacques Cartier's maps, 'an olde excellent map which [Master John Verarzanus] gave to Henrie the eight, and is yet in the custodie of master Locke', a globe 'in the Queenes privie gallery at Westminster wch also semeth of Verarsanus making', and many others.[19]

The loss to cartography is undoubtedly heavy, but the loss to toponymy is perhaps not so serious though maps of the English surveys of the East and South Coasts of Newfoundland in 1497 and 1498, postulated by Prowse,[20] might have given an early incidence for such names as FLAMBRO HEAD (National Topographic Series[21] Bay de Verde) and Robin Hood Bay (NTS Trinity).

Recognizable names are to be found on maps as early as the first decade of the sixteenth century, such as Cabo de boa venture [Bonaventure] ("Cantino" 1502), Capo raso [CAPE RACE] ("King-Hamy" 1504–6), Cauo de la spera [CAPE SPEAR], Riuo de los Bacolaos [BACCALIEU] ("Oliveriana" 1505–8), but more often than not it would be rash to attempt a close identification of an early and a modern location. Early cartographers had but a hazy notion of the configuration of Newfoundland – its many bays and deep inlets led them to believe that it was an archipelago – and only after about a century of map-making did it come to be represented as an island having something of the shape we know, with names beginning to occupy fixed positions. The first map devoted exclusively to Newfoundland and showing a nomenclature (of some twenty-nine names) and details of the coast remarkable for the period was Langenes's *Terra Noua* of 1598.[22]

Whatever the provenance of maps made before 1600 – Spanish, Italian, Portuguese or French – the nomenclature is predominantly Portuguese, more or less corrupted, and generally restricted to the East and South Coasts between Fogo Island and ST. MARY'S BAY, which mark the limits of Portuguese exploration. The first French names to appear on a map are in Desceliers 1542 and extend as far north as Belle Isle, though Cartier records the imposition of French names during his voyages of 1534 and 1536.

Seventeenth-century cartography is marked by extended activity of the French in the number of maps produced, the accuracy of coastline delineated, and the number of names recorded. As early as 1601, Le Vasseur shows C raye, S Ioan, r dognon, R double on the West Coast; and by 1698 Chaviteau's *Carte de l'Isle de Terre Neuve* contains secondary names on the South Coast for the first time.[23] Henry Briggs's *The North Part of America conteyning Newfoundland*, 1625, inserted in Purchas, is perhaps the first extant English map to show English names and English forms of foreign names – Bell I, I of Beris, I of Bulls, Cape Race. John Mason's *Insula olim vocata Noua: Terrae*, 1626, contains more names than any of its predecessors: English versions of Portuguese names – C. S. Francis, Bay of Conception, Ferriland, Formosa, C. Race; of French names – C de Grote, Pettit harbour, Rhenus, Trepassa; names of contemporary plantations and settlements – North Favlkland, Avalonia, Bristol's Hope; names mostly Welsh imposed by Sir William Vaughan in whose *The Golden Fleece*, 1626, Mason's map was printed – Cambriola, Glamorgan, Pembroke, Cardigan, Colchos, Brechonia, all of which, as D. W. Prowse remarks, "with the exception of Baltimore's Avalon have disappeared from the maps";[24] and what is probably the first reference to an inland feature, *Lacus incognitus*,

"A great Lake or Sea unknowne, discouered by Captaine Mason." Mason was governor of Newfoundland from 1615 to 1621. The nomenclature of Fitzhugh's map of 1693 is almost entirely anglicized and is particularly rich in secondary names in the great fishing areas between Bonavista Bay and CAPE RACE. Two Basque maps, De Rotis 1674 and Detcheverry 1689, introduce the Basque element in the nomenclature of the West Coast in such names as Apphorportu [Port au Port], Portuichoa [Port au Choix] (De Rotis), and Annguachar [Ingornachoix] and B. ederra [Bonne Bay] (Detcheverry).

Eighteenth-century cartography shows few, if any, developments from that of the seventeenth century until it was transformed by Cook in the years after 1760. In contrast to the methods of his predecessors, Cook made his charts from his own surveys, adapting the techniques of land surveying by triangulation to marine surveys.[25] The range of Cook's surveys in Newfoundland waters, which not only gave him valuable experience for his later work in the Pacific but also possess great intrinsic value, has only recently been fully demonstrated in R. A. Skelton's *James Cook, Surveyor of Newfoundland*.

Cook made no surveys of the East and Southeast coasts of Newfoundland, except of a number of harbours on the AVALON PENINSULA in 1762, and some of these in fact may have been conducted by Gilbert in 1768. The authorities probably saw more urgency in the need to gain detailed knowledge of the South and West Coasts, the scene of rivalry between the English and French for fishing rights; and, of course, the navigational hazards of the East Coast were much better known to seamen from long familiarity.

The Journals of the *Grenville* from 1764 to 1767 have survived,[26] but not the field-books or private diaries in which Cook might have recorded names which he himself imposed. However, certain secondary names, mostly on the West Coast, not recorded before Cook, suggest his mark. Typical are names of ships employed in Newfoundland waters in his day (Lark I, Pearl I, Tweed I, Guernsey I, Grenville Rock, Solebay); of rivers particularly familiar to seamen (Humber, Thames, Medway); of his patron, the governor of Newfoundland (Graves's I); of his mate in the *Grenville* in 1764 (Parker's River); of eighteenth-century admirals (Hawke Bay, Port Saunders, Keppel Harbour). A note in *Directions for Navigating the West Coast of Newfoundland*, to accompany his chart of the West Coast, 1770, suggests Cook the navigator: "Portland – it makes not unlike Portland in the English Channel," as does another entry in *Directions for Navigating a Part of the N.E. Side of Newfoundland:* "a very remarkable Rock, called the Mewstone, like the Mewstone in Plymouth Sound." Occasionally the names are obscene and once at least invention failed (Nameless Cove). Such names as Hawkes Bay, C. Pallisser, C. Saunders, Bay of Islands, and River Thames in New Zealand recall Cook's surveys in Newfoundland.

On Cook's posting to the *Endeavour* for his work in the Pacific, the Newfoundland survey was continued by Michael Lane in the *Grenville*. Lane, who had been schoolmaster of the *Guernsey*, joined Cook in the *Grenville* as mate in 1767 for the charting of the West Coast from Cape Anguille to Point Ferolle and on 12 April 1768 was appointed "to act as Master of the brig *Grenville*" in Cook's absence on employment "elsewhere."[27] He commanded the *Grenville* until March 1775, when she was certified unfit for further service, and the *Lyon* brigantine from May 1775 to May 1776, still on the Newfoundland survey. From May 1776 to August 1777, he was master in the *Lyon* on two voyages for the Northwest Passage, the first under Lieut. Richard Pickersgill, the second under Lieut. Walter Young. On 27 October 1777, he was commissioned as Lieutenant. In July 1783, *Lyon*, under Lane's command, was commissioned for the Newfoundland survey and engaged in the survey under his command from May 1784 to September 1785. Thereafter, apart from the inclusion of his name in the list of lieutenants to the end of 1794 in Steel's *Navy List*, no further information about Lane has been found, though it may be presumed that he died either late in 1794 or early in 1795.

Table 1 shows Lane's Labrador and Newfoundland surveys under his own command.

TABLE 1

LANE'S LABRADOR AND NEWFOUNDLAND SURVEYS

Date	Area		Charts
[In *Grenville*]			
1768	Labrador:	Mecatina – Shecatica	
1769	"	Shecatica – Chateaux B.	
1770	"	C. Charles – Spotted I.	
1771	"	Spotted I. – Sandwich B.	
1772	Newfoundland:	Placentia B. (also St. John's)	BAHD* 402
1773	"	Pt. Lance – C. Spear	BAHD 403
1774	"	C. Spear – Bacaleau I.	BAHD 397
[In *Lyon*]			
1775	"	Baccalieu I. – C. Bonavista	Untraced
1784	"	Virgin Rocks	BAHD 339
1784	"	Fogo Harbour	BAHD B187
1785	"	Fogo Island	BAHD 401[28]

* British Admiralty Hydrographic Department

Another of Cook's contemporaries, Joseph Gilbert, conducted surveys in the Straights [sic] of Belle Isle 1767 and in Bay Despair 1769, and of various harbours in 1770, before he joined Cook as master of the *Resolution* on the second voyage to the Pacific, 1772–5.

The Hydrographic Department of the British Admiralty was established in 1795 and from the early years of the nineteenth century has made a series of intensive surveys of the coasts of Newfoundland. It has now published some ninety charts covering the whole coastline in great detail, which have served as models for charts subsequently issued by the hydrographic services of France, the United States, and Canada. In the various editions of the *Newfoundland and Labrador Pilot*, which is based on the charts, every coastal feature of any significance has its name.

Up to 1768 the cartography of Newfoundland had been restricted to coastal areas, with Mason's reference to the *Lacus incognitus*, the great inland "Lake or Sea unknowne," in 1626 perhaps unique. Commonly maps left the interior blank or, very rarely, bore a legend such as that on so late a map as Kitchin 1762, "The Inland parts of this Island are entirely unknown." Cook named a number of rivers, but the first record of the penetration of the interior is by John Cartwright in his *A Sketch of the River Exploits ... Taken on the spot by Lieutenant Ino. Cartwright of His Majesty's Ship* Guernsey: *1768*. This map, decorated with sketches of a wigwam and a canoe, bears a numerous and frequently imaginative nomenclature of lakes, ponds, brooks, and points, though much of it has been superseded. That Cartwright's Mount Labour-in-vain should degenerate into Hodges Hill must be a matter of regret. Other maps showing the interior came only in 1822 with Cormack's to illustrate his journey across Newfoundland on foot, and about 1840 with J. B. Jukes's, in which as the legend states "the interior [was] filled up partly from a rough personal survey and partly from oral information." Bonnycastle's map of 1842 names only the greater lakes.

During the present century, successive maps published by Newfoundland and Canadian government departments and other bodies have shown a steady increase in the nomenclature of inland features, and a notable step towards a comprehensive record of names was made in 1950 when the Geographic Branch of the Canada Department of Mines and Technical Surveys compiled *A List of the Place Names of the Island of Newfoundland* from the *Ten-Mile Map of Newfoundland*, which had been published by the Newfoundland Department of Natural Resources in 1941. The list contained some 3200 names of settlements and natural features and marked a great advance on any previous gazetteer, but its limitations became obvious with the publication of the maps in the National Topographic Series on a scale of 1.25 inches to 1 mile (1:50,000) between 1954 and 1959, which have provided the raw material for, and set the limits of, this toponymical study. E. Rouleau has published *A Gazetteer of the Island of Newfoundland*, containing over 9000 names, based on these maps. Completeness in the mere recording of names is, however, a distinct and perhaps unattainable goal, for the NTS maps, rich in nomenclature as they are, have left unnamed innumerable features and cannot, in the nature of things, contain such minor names as, for example, those of fishing berths.[29]

Other sources of nomenclature besides maps are documents such as Cartier's accounts of his voyages up the St. Lawrence, Hakluyt and Purchas, John Guy's journal of his voyage into Trinity Bay in 1612, the reports of the captains of the Newfoundland convoys to the Council of Trade and Plantations in the seventeenth and eighteenth centuries, and occasional Sailing Directions; but except for Cartwright's account of his expedition up the Exploits River in 1768, it is not until the nineteenth century that memoirs and reports of travellers, missionaries and geologists make any significant additions to names already known from maps, and even at this period the charts made by the Admiralty surveyors are still of first importance.

The recording of place names in a map, however, provides no direct evidence of their origin, age, and the circumstances in which they were imposed; it tells us nothing more than that the names were known and in use when the map or its prototype was made.

In this context, the mapmaker may be considered as filling his bucket from a pool of toponymy which was already there and into which other mapmakers, perhaps widely separated in time, may also have dipped their buckets. On the other hand, a chart or sailing directions prepared from a hydrographic survey will be a primary authority for names imposed by the surveyor.[30]

A distinction has to be made, that is, between the first recording of old names which have been lost or not previously recorded and the imposition of new names – a distinction valid, it need hardly be said, not only for maps but for any source of nomenclature.

Tracing the recorded history of place names is, however, only a preliminary step towards their fuller understanding, to be followed by attempts to interpret them and judge their significance. Different places will make different demands on the toponymist, but it may be taken for granted that he should know the topography and history of his chosen region, the names and origins of its families, their religious beliefs, their habits, their customs and occupations, their lore, legends and anecdotes, the kind of language they use. He will need to know the topography, toponymy and history of the places from which its explorers and settlers came. He must be able to recognize linguistic relationships and to perceive the name hidden under a more or less bizarre attempt at a phonetic spelling. He must be prepared to read everything about his region and to receive information from anyone who has special or local knowledge – a scholar in a university, a teacher in a school, the village priest, the oldest inhabitant. In Stewart's phrase, he must become "possessed by the fascination of names,"[31] but through them he will gain an insight not only into words but also into a history and culture that no other study can offer.

The Avalon Peninsula
Description, Indian Names, and European Discovery

The AVALON PENINSULA forms the southeast part of Newfoundland, bounded by TRINITY BAY to the northwest, by the Atlantic to the east and south, and by PLACENTIA BAY to the west. Its coastline includes the southern and eastern shores of TRINITY BAY, the whole of CONCEPTION BAY, the so-called SOUTHERN SHORE which is in fact the east coast, TREPASSEY BAY, ST. MARY'S BAY and the east coast of PLACENTIA BAY. It has an estimated length of some 785 miles, high in proportion to its area of 3690 square miles. The Peninsula is connected to the mainland of Newfoundland by an isthmus, the ISTHMUS OF AVALON, which is about twenty-five miles long and at its narrowest only two to three miles wide. Its main features are the two northerly peninsulas with their extremities at GRATES POINT and CAPE ST. FRANCIS, the PLACENTIA peninsula with its extremity in the south at POINT LANCE, and two lesser peninsulas, also pointing south, with their extremities at CAPE FREELS and MISTAKEN POINT.

Much of the coast is rugged and forbidding, with escarpments descending steep-to, as the *Newfoundland Pilot* so often has it, though they are broken by hundreds of bays and coves, which range in size from the magnificent almost landlocked harbour of ST. JOHN'S to shallow, unprotected bights. A river, though few of them are of any size, or a brook flows into almost every cove. Small areas of cultivable land usually lie at the head of the coves, their brilliant greens in contrast to the reds and grays of the hills and rocks on either side and to the browns of the barrens. Wherever a cove affords an anchorage for the fishing boats and the land will grow a few potatoes and cabbage, there a settlement, or the remains of one (for many of the smallest and most isolated have been abandoned over the years) will be found. Only a few favoured districts, some coastal, some inland, are able to support a more extensive farming. Where a harbour can accommodate larger craft – the schooners in the coastwise trade or the railway coastal boats – a small town will have grown which in former years was likely to have been the home of a sealing fleet.

Inland, the country is largely rough scrub covered with mosses and berry bushes or stands of spruce, the generally rugged monotony broken by intimidating bluffs or an isolated conical hill, a tolt; but most striking is the amount of water, the innumerable ponds and streams that are said to form about one-seventh of the total surface. Most of the few inland communities owe their existence to the building of the railway in the 1880s or to attempts at land settlement in selected areas in the 1930s, and J. P. Howley's statement made in 1876, that "There is scarcely a habitation anywhere situated five miles from the salt water"[1] is almost as true today as it was ninety years ago.

A policy of road-building, initiated by Sir Thomas Cochrane, governor of Newfoundland from 1825 to 1834, has linked together settlements formerly accessible only by sea by a system of roads which for the most part hug the coast, though in appropriate places they also traverse parts of the peninsula.

The original inhabitants of Newfoundland are believed to have been the Beothuck Indians, though recent investigation seems to suggest that they may have been preceded by other prehistoric people.[2] Evidence of their presence at the time of the earliest arrival of Europeans is attested in several documents.[3] John Guy encountered them on the ISTHMUS OF AVALON in 1612,[4] and their traces are still to be found on the Peninsula;[5] but by 1622, according to Whitbourne, they had deserted it to "liue altogether in the North and West part of the countrey, which is seldome frequented by the English."[6] They have left none of their nomenclature on the Peninsula and perhaps only three Beothuck names are to be found in the whole island. One was anglicized about 1840 by Jukes as Shannoc (Sheernock) Brook in Central Newfoundland. Jukes believed that Shannoc was the Beothuck name for the Micmac Indians,[7] but according to Speck, the American anthropologist, writing in 1914, it may be related to a tribal term applied to the Montagnais and the Beothucks by modern Newfoundland Indians.[8] The brook is now known as Noel Paul's Brook after a Micmac hunter.

Two Beothuck women, Mary March and Shanadithit, who were captured by white men in 1819 and 1823 and brought to ST. JOHN'S, are commemorated in brooks named after them in Central Newfoundland, Shanadithit thus providing the second Beothuck place name. She died in 1829, one of the last survivors of her race.

The third Beothuck name on the West Coast stands as an example of recent imposition, Aguathuna – "grindstone." The old name, Jack of Clubs Cove, is not found in maps or Sailing Directions but is believed to have been given by sailors in the late eighteenth or early nineteenth centuries after a supposed resemblance seen in the limestone rock eroded by the action of the sea. However, when a limestone quarry was developed at the cove in 1911, a petition was presented to the Postmaster General to have the name changed. Aguathuna was proclaimed on 23 June 1914 and happily displaced Limeville which somehow or other had received a temporary acceptance.*

English place names containing the specific "Indian" are not uncommon in Newfoundland – there are some fifty in all with two INDIAN PONDS (NTS Heart's Content and Holyrood) on the AVALON PENINSULA – and though some of them may refer to the Micmacs, others such as Indian Burying Place have Beothuck associations, as has Wigwam, the specific given to several brooks, coves, points and ponds. Incident names like Bloody Point and Rencontre Bay may have Indian associations. One name, OCHRE PIT COVE (NTS Heart's Content), Oker Pit Cove (Lane 1774), recalls Whitbourne's observation, "... it is well knowne,

---

* The petition, which was reprinted in the *Western Star*, Corner Brook, 19 May 1950, reads: TO THE HON. HENRY T. R. WOODS, POSTMASTER-GENERAL, St. John's, Newfoundland. The Petition of the undersigned inhabitants of Jack of Clubs Cove, in the Electoral District of St. George's, HUMBLY SHOWETH that there has lately been opened at Jack of Clubs Cove, by the Dominion Iron & Steel Company, Limited, a quarry of limestone which, it is hoped, may be worked on such a large scale as to inaugurate a new and profitable industry on the West Coast, give much employment to the people and render the settlement prosperous. THAT in the opinion of your petitioners, the present name of Jack of Clubs Cove, though perhaps picturesque, does not appear to be of any great antiquity, is not consecrated with any hallowed memories and is not suggestive of very elevated associations. It is certainly ludicrous when applied to a village whose energies are to be developed to the respectable, prosaic and useful industry of quarrying limestone.

THAT the continued association of its present name with a settlement which is expected to grow in population and respectability, must mitigate to its disad-

that the Natives of those parts have great store of red okar, wherewith they use to colour their bodies, Bowes, Arrowes and Cannowes,"[9] but ochre in recent times has had a more prosaic use among the white inhabitants as the colouring matter mixed with saltwater for painting houses and barns, and the cove, as well as Ochre, Ochre Pit Hill, Ochre Pit Island, Ochre Pit Pond and OCHRE PIT ROCK (NTS Heart's Content), elsewhere in the island, may well have been named as sources of ochre for this purpose. SALVAGE POINT (NTS Old Perlican) (Hack? 1677) and SALVAGE ROCK (NTS Harbour Grace), Salvage (Thornton 1689D), pronounced [sæl'veidʒ], recall T. S. Eliot's note to *The Dry Salvages*: "The Dry Salvages – presumably *les trois sauvages* – is a small group of rocks, with a beacon, off the NE coast of Cape Ann, Massachusetts. Salvages is pronounced to rhyme with assuages."[10]

According to Speck,[11] "the present Indian inhabitants [of Newfoundland], whose language is Micmac, are the mixed offspring of Montagnais hunters from Labrador and Micmac from Cape Breton Island. Immigration from both these neighbouring regions must have commenced at least several centuries ago, because our records from the early part of the nineteenth century show both the Micmac and the Montagnais to have been firmly established in Newfoundland at that time ... the successors, I believe in more than one sense, of the Beothuk." A name on the northwest coast, Passage des sauvages (Boissaie Le Bocage 1669), Passage of ye Savages (Moll 1709), The Path of the Indians (Cook 1764) and last recorded as Old Indian Path (Purdy 1814), identifies a track some forty miles long, apparently used by the Montagnais in their incursions into Newfoundland to avoid the harbourless stretch of the Straight Coast, as Cook calls it. "The Micmac," Speck continues, "claim to have had some knowledge of Newfoundland

> vantage, and your petitioners are desirous of having the name changed to a more appropriate one before the old one becomes identified with the new industry upon which the village relies for its development. It is felt that business correspondence emanating from a place called Jack of Clubs Cove will be hardly treated, at least by those unfamiliar with the place, and the writers, with that serious respect and confidence which it is the business of correspondents in mercantile matters to provoke.
>
> Your petitioners, therefore, pray that you may be pleased to submit to the Nomenclature Committee the expediency of considering whether the present name of "Jack of Clubs Cove" could not be changed to that of AGUATHUNA.
>
> And, as in duty, bound, your petitioners will ever pray.
>
> Signed at Jack of Clubs Cove, this 24th day of October A.D. 1911., A. HOUSE, B. J. BATES, P. S. HYNES, M. D. FINLAYSON, J. P. BURKE, M. J. JOY, M. F. ABBOTT
>
> The quarry ceased production in 1964.
>
> The interpretation of Aguathuna communicated by Dr J. Hewson.

22 / *Place Names of the Avalon Peninsula*

from remote times. They speak of a branch of their people called Sagawadgikik,[12] "ancients," who lived on the southern and western coasts before [those Micmac who accompanied the French in their invasions of Newfoundland in] the eighteenth century, and to corroborate this they give an old nomenclature of landmarks in various parts of this island in Micmac."[13]

In the absence of more precise information, Speck's references to "several centuries ago" and "remote times" offer some justification for a survey of Micmac nomenclature in Newfoundland as occurring in part at least before the imposition of place names by Europeans. Among these names, which are almost all descriptive of physical features, those on the South Coast have disappeared and have been replaced by European names,[14] but several in the interior have survived, among them: Ahwachanjeesh "little portage" Pond and Brook, Annieopsquotch "rocky" Mountains, Ebbegunbaeg "low bay" Lake, Kepenkeck "sandbar across the channel" Lake, Medonnegonix "village halfway" Lake, Kaegudeck "on the top" Lake, Meelpaeg "many bays" Lake, Mollyguajeck "low growth" Lake, and Pudops "whale" Lake. Some features have been named after Micmac chiefs and hunters: Matthews Pond, Lake Michel, Noel Paul's Brook, Joe Jeddore's Pond; and some are repeated in Micmac territory in Nova Scotia and New Brunswick.[15]

The few Micmac names on the AVALON PENINSULA are first recorded only in the 1870s by which time the Micmac were but rarely seen there; for as early as 1842 Bonnycastle had remarked that they "are seldom or never ... observed on the eastern shores, where their hunting would prove more precarious, where the white man chiefly dwells, and where the winter is extremely boisterous, uncertain, and severe."[16] That they had not entirely disappeared, however, may be deduced from a phrase in the *Geological Survey of Newfoundland, Report for 1872*: "The Dildo River, *according to the description given by the Indians*, rises within a little over 6 miles from the northern parts of St. Mary's Bay,"[17] though the reference appears to be unique. In that year, J. P. Howley,[18] later to be the authority on the Beothucks but then assistant to Alexander Murray, Director of the Geological Survey, undertook a survey of the ROCKY RIVER (NTS Placentia and Argentia) and its tributary BIG BARREN BROOK, from a starting-point at BRIGUS (NTS Harbour Grace) to its mouth in ST. MARY'S BAY. As may be seen in Table 2,[19] Howley introduced a number of Micmac names, none of which is given elsewhere, among the English names of ponds. Unfortunately he left no indication of their origin or interpretation, and the assumption would seem to be that he had Micmac guides who gave him a Micmac name when an

Indian Place Names on the Avalon Peninsula

English name was unknown. One such guide was John Stevens of JUNIPER STUMP, near CLARKES BEACH, who died about 1897, a well-known guide and trapper in Labrador and northern Newoundland and an associate of Captain R. A. ("Bob") Bartlett of BRIGUS.[20] No trace of any other recent Micmac inhabitant of the district has been discovered. In so far as the Micmac can be translated, the names appear to be entirely commonplace: NU-COOL-MINNI-GULOO GOSPEN "... islands ponds," TABOO-MINNIGU-GULOO GOSPEN "two islands pond," TSEIST-MINNIGU-GULOO GOSPEN "three islands pond," WAGEDIGULSIBOO GOSPEN "approach ... river

TABLE 2

SURVEY OF ROCKY RIVER AND BIG BARREN BROOK
By J. P. Howley, 1872

No.	Course	Distance		Height above high-water mark	Remarks
		mls	chs	feet	
1	S 61° W	4	40	45	From sea-level at Brigus to Mackinson's farm, upon the Telegraph line.
2	S 54° W	2	60	—	Along the Telegraph line to end of portage to Battin's Pond.
3	N 58° W	0	34	351	To Battin's Pond, head of Hodge Waters.
4	N 88° W	0	78	288	From Battin's Pond to inlet of Level Pond.
5	S 24° W	3	35	280	From Level Pond, along a suite of lakes to the outlet of Brigus Grand Pond, at the crossing of Telgraph line.
6	S 81° W	0	35	246	From outlet of Brigus Grand Pond to inlet of Hodge Water Pond.
7	N 87° W	0	40	246	Across Hodge Water Pond to the outlet.
8	N 82° W	0	40	—	From outlet of Hodge Water Pond, across Nu-cool-minni-guloo Gospen.
9	S 66° W	4	70	—	From outlet of Nu-cool-minni-guloo Gospen, along general course of Hodge Water River to inlet to Taboo-minnigu-guloo Gospen.
10	S 17° E	0	56	—	From inlet to Taboo-minnigu-guloo to outlet of Tseist-minnigu-guloo Gospen.
11	S 28° W	1	13	189	From outlet of Tseist-minnigu-guloo Gospen to outlet of Wagedigulsiboo Gospen. The big Barren River falls in on the south-east side of Wagedigulsiboo.
12	S 19° W	3	75	126	General course of river from outlet of Wagedigulsiboo Gospen to the forks of main brook of Rocky River.
13	South	7	37	—	To the falls of Rocky River. The top of the falls is from 20 to 25 feet above high-water mark. The average height of the cliffs below the falls is from 40 to 50 feet.

TABLE 2 (continued)

THE BIG BARREN BRANCH OF SAME RIVER, ASCENDING

No.	Course	Distance		Height above high-water mark	Remarks
		mls	chs	feet	
1	N 85° E	0	35	189	From outlet of Wagedigulsiboo to inlet of ditto from Big Barren Brook.
2	S 27° E	2	21	230	From mouth of Big Barren Brook, straight course up the stream, to outlet from Tusem Gospen.
3	N 45° E	1	70	233	From outlet of Tusem Gospen to inlet into Mestigue-gundaly Gospen; general course of river and ponds.
4	N 34° E	4	15	240	General course up Big Barren Pond to head, at end of portage to Hodge Water Pond.
		0	48	246	
5	N 11° E				Portage to south-west end of Hodge Water Pond.

* The courses given in the table are all from the true meridian, and indicate the straight directions and distances from one point to another without reference to roads, sinuosities of rivers or lakes, or irregularity of surfaces.

pond," TUSEM GOSPEN "... pond," MESTIGUE-GUNDALY GOSPEN ? "great land pond," now ROUND POND WEST (NTS Holyrood).

Admiralty Chart 232a, Newfoundland – Southern Portion, 1870,[21] contains several Micmac names of the interior of Newfoundland, but only one, QUEMO GOSPEN "loon pond" on the Peninsula.

M. F. Howley originally rejected one version of the popular belief associated with KITCHUSES (NTS Holyrood), a name recorded in the Census of 1869 as Ketchums and in that of 1874 as Kitchues: "The settlement ... is called Catchuses or Kitchuses, a name the origin of which is unknown. It has been suggested that it is a corruption of Kit Hughe's, for Christopher Hughe's, but this seems far-fetched, and I am not aware that any person of such name ever lived there."[22] But a correspondent soon led him to accept it in a somewhat modified form:

Dr Jones writes me from Avondale [a neighbouring community] concerning the name Kitchuses. I suggested, though with doubt, that it might be derived from a family of the name of Hughes. He says no family of that name ever lived there. "In olden times, however," he says, "there was a favorite meeting place, at the house of one Gushue, whose wife's name was Kate. Here young people used to gather of a Sunday evening for a gossip, a dance, or perhaps "a drop"! Hence the name Kit Gushue's which might very naturally in the course of time become changed to Kitchuses." This explanation seems very plausible and I willingly accept it. The name Gushue is quite common along that shore.[23]

Fay derives Gushue from the French Guizot, "a well-known Jersey family,"[24] and members of the family believe that it came to Newfoundland from Normandy *via* the Channel Islands, though a Breton form, Guiziou, would be a more satisfactory source. Goushon (with the final *n* a turned *u*) is recorded in 1785 at BRIGUS.[25]

Plausible as Howley found Dr Jones's explanation, there are difficulties in accepting the assimilation of Kit Gushue [kIt gU'ʒu:] to Kitchues [kI'tʃu:z], a pronunciation still heard, or of Kit Gushue's [kIt gU'ʒu:z] to Kitchuses [kI'tʃu:zIz], since [tg] to [tʃ] does not seem a convincing phonetic development. An alternative explanation, no less plausible on phonetic grounds and with almost identical social implications and an added topographical appropriateness, suggests an Indian source:

Quitouche, pour désigner une femme de moeurs douteuses, dérive de *toutouche* (sein, dans le dialecte mistassin). Le nom de lieu *Tadoussac*, de même origine, fait allusion aux mamelons du terrain. Cette appellation anatomique, accompagnée de l'adjectif possessif à la deuxième personne, se traduit par *kitoutouche* dans des dialectes algonquins. De là *quitouche*, emprunté par les coureurs des bois pour désigner les mêmes particulairités anatomiques. Tout en conservant ce sens aujourd'hui, il a acquis en outre l'autre acception."[26]

Two breast-like hillocks rise behind the settlement.

WABANA, on BELL ISLAND (NTS St. John's), which is almost the most easterly land in the American continent, was imposed about 1895 by Thomas Cantley, ? an official of the Nova Scotia Steel and Coal Company, which had secured a lease of the iron deposits on the island in 1893. WABANA seems to be an arbitrary formation from an Abnaki word "*Wâbuna'ki*, from *wâbun*, a term associated with 'light', 'white', and refers to the morning and the east; *a'ki* 'earth', 'land'; hence *wâbuna'ki* is an inanimate singular term signifying 'east-land', or 'morning-land', the elements referring to animate dwellers of the east being wanting."[27]

A final Indian name, PENETANGUISHENE (TANGUISHENE in NTS St. John's), the name of a modern settlement on the outskirts of ST. JOHN'S founded in the early 1950s, is also the name of a town in Simcoe County, Ontario, identified by Armstrong also as an Abnaki word meaning "the place of white falling sands" from "a great sandy cliff, pieces of which are continually breaking away."[28] The local name appears to be an arbitrary imposition.

European discovery of Newfoundland in the fifteenth century is traditionally associated with the voyage of John Cabot in 1497, as described by Hakluyt.[29] Newfoundland historians have been unanimous in asserting that Cabot's landfall was at Bonavista on the east coast of the island, though none seems to have been at all concerned to explain by what strange transformation Hakluyt's Prima vista became Bonavista. Others with no less insistence have stressed the claims of other places and particularly of Cape Breton. The most recent commentaries are by Hoffman,[30] Williamson and Skelton,[31] and Layng[32] and turn on the interpretations to be given to the John Day letter, discovered in the Archivo General de Simancas by Dr L.-A. Vigneras in 1956, which "must at least be tentatively accepted as a report on John Cabot's 1497 voyage,"[33] and to the La Cosa map, dated 1500, in the Museo Naval, Madrid, which "unambiguously illustrates John Cabot's voyage of 1497";[34] but no decisive conclusion has been, or perhaps can ever be, reached. As Layng puts it:

No doubt it would be a happy circumstance if a reconstruction of the John Day letter were forthcoming that could be reconciled with the form of the La Cosa map. Meanwhile if taken by itself the letter suggests two probabilities: first, the landfall was made at a southerly point along the east coast of Newfoundland and subsequent exploration was made to the north, and second the landfall was made at Cape Breton, and on the homeward voyage Cape Race was seen prompting a change in course northward leading to an entire ranging of the east coast of Newfoundland. Which takes us back almost to the place where Ganong and Prowse left off their life-long debate: was Cabot's landfall at Bonavista or on Cape Breton?[35]

There is, however, reason to believe that other explorers from England may have known the Newfoundland coast before Cabot, between 1480 and 1494.[36] If this were so, the argument that the Portuguese and French were later arrivals who were to use the harbours of the east coast of the AVALON PENINSULA as rendezvous for their fishing fleets is strengthened, and Blome's view, expressed in 1687, that the "Normands, Portugals and Brittanes of France resorted to Newfoundland and changed the names which had been given by the English to the Bays and Promontories,"[37] would seem to receive some support. G. R. F. Prowse, indeed, denied "a single Portuguese name on the American north east coast," maintaining that "It was not until about 1520 that England had a school of pilots-marine surveyors, so that all the primary English expeditions were mapped by Portuguese pilots and practically all the earlier maps were completed in Lisbon or were copies of such maps."[38] He is silent about the French.

In support of his assertion, Prowse says of FERRYLAND (NTS Ferryland), Port, Farilham (Verrazano 1529) – steep rock, that "this was properly called foreland, the common English name for a cape," though "undoubtedly there was a technical meaning for *farelhoam* and *forillon* in Portuguese and French ... and this made it easy for [the] Portuguese and French to corrupt the word foreland."[39] His interpretation of *farelhoam* and *forillon* as "a rock with a hole in it" is a trifle wide of the mark: *farelhão* is variously interpreted as steep rock, steep little island, reef, point; *forillon* as cape or point. Similarly he sees FERMEUSE (NTS Renews), Port. R. fermoso (Reinel 1519) – beautiful r[iver], as a "mistranslation of freshwater,"[40] which later became a common name on Newfoundland coasts for a place where ships could take on supplies of fresh water. However, Formosa (now Taiwan) in the western Pacific was so named by Portuguese navigators in 1590 for its beauty. He sees CAPE RACE (NTS Trepassey), Port. Capo raso "King-Hamy" 1504–6) – flat or barren cape, not as a development from the Portuguese, or from the Breton *raz* – tide race, but from English race with the same meaning, after The Race at Portland Bill.[41] He fails, not surprisingly, to provide an English origin for such a name as AQUAFORTE (NTS Ferryland), Port. ? R da aguea (Reinel c. 1519), anglicized as Agoforta ("Velasco" 1610) – strong water. The place seems to have been named after the waterfall on the north side of the harbour, though the ordinary Portuguese word for waterfall is *cascata*.

Lack of evidence obviates complete agreement with, or dissent from, Prowse's theories, but the fact remains that the earliest records of names of almost all the major features on maps showing the north, east and south coasts of the AVALON PENINSULA are in a Portuguese form; and Skelton advances three reasons, supported by evidence from the maps, why the names should be held to be of Portuguese, not English, origin.[42] First, he notices among the names that of an obscure Portuguese saint, St. Iria (or Eiria), which can hardly have been used by, or perhaps even known to, Englishmen. Secondly, he finds names on maps from *padrões*, the stone pillars set up on conspicuous features by Portuguese explorers claiming discovery. Thirdly, he suggests the extreme improbability of a Portuguese cartographer preferring names from an English source (if indeed he had them) to names from Portuguese expeditions whose presence on the Newfoundland-Labrador coasts is attested by other evidence. A not unwarranted conclusion is that the names are to be associated with the expedition of the Corte Reals to Newfoundland and Labrador in 1500–2, or with the subsequent rapid development of the cod-fishery in Newfoundland waters.

The following Portuguese names of features and harbours on the Avalon coasts are found in maps by 1534, though the precise location of the names is sometimes doubtful and some places received different names from different cartographers.

Cauo de ynglaterra (La Cosa 1500) – Cape England is perhaps CAPE

Portuguese Place Names on the Avalon Peninsula

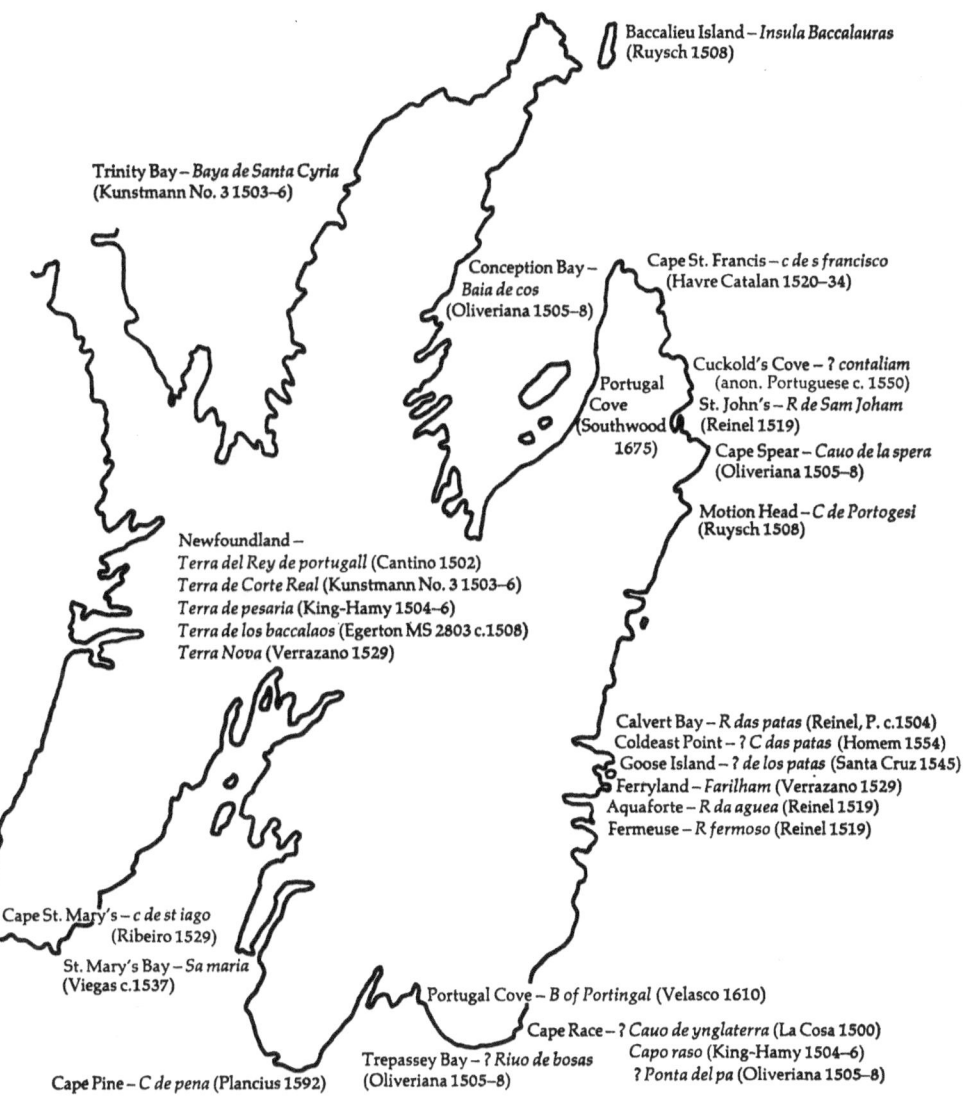

RACE (NTS Trepassey). Baya de Santa Cyria (for Iria or Eiria) ("Kunstmann no. 3" c. 1506) – Bay of St. Iria commemorates, according to Skelton, an "obscure seventh-century saint (Virgin and Martyr) [who] was apparently not well known even in Portugal ... if we may judge from the corruptions which her name suffered at the hands of later cartographers ... According to the *Grande Enciclopedia Portuguesa-Brasileira*, her cult was confined to some Portuguese dioceses only."[48] The modern name, TRINITY BAY, is first recorded in Whitbourne 1622. Capo raso ("King-Hamy" 1504–6) – the low, flat or barren cape, may be descriptive or transferred from the Cabo Raso at the mouth of the River Tagus, the last sight of Portugal for a voyager sailing west from Lisbon; it is now CAPE RACE (NTS Trepassey). In "Oliveriana" 1505–8 are five new names: Baia de cos[eicam], CONCEPTION BAY, named presumably in honour of the feast of the Conception, 8 December; Cauo de la spera – the cape of waiting, CAPE SPEAR (NTS St. John's),[44] and the shift name Riuo de la spera, SPEAR BAY (NTS St. John's); Riuo de bosas (for rosas) – river of roses, now perhaps TREPASSEY BAY; and Ponta del pa[drao] – the cape of the pillar, perhaps another name for CAPE RACE.

Insula Baccalauras (for Bacalhao) – island of cod, now BACCALIEU ISLAND (NTS Bay de Verde), and C de Portogesi – cape of the Portuguese, a name which persisted in a French form in maps until Buache 1736 and may be identified with MOTION HEAD (NTS Bay Bulls), are in Ruysch 1508. R. das patas (Reinel, P. c. 1504) – goose or auk river, is probably the present CALVERT BAY (NTS Ferryland).

In Reinel 1519 are R. de Sam joham – St. John's river, now ST. JOHN'S HARBOUR (NTS St. John's); R. da aguea – river of [?fresh]water, now AQUAFORTE (NTS Ferryland); R. fermoso – beautiful river, now FERMEUSE (NTS Renews); and P[orto] da cruz – harbour of the Cross, now HOLYROOD BAY (NTS St. Mary's). The last name persisted in this and similar Portuguese forms until the end of the sixteenth century (Sanches 1596, and other maps), to be restored almost one hundred and fifty years later in an English form, Hollyrood, in Lane 1773. In Bonnycastle 1842[45] it is English Cove and in Admiralty 2915, 1864 or later, it is St. Vincent Bay. The *Newfoundland and Labrador Pilot* 1951[46] cites Holyrood (Saint Vincent) bay. G. R. F. Prowse identified P. da cruz with HOLYROOD BAY,[47] Ganong with TREPASSEY BAY.[48] Its origin may be as a commemorative or an incident name, having reference to either the Exaltation of the Cross (14 September) or the Invention of the Cross (3 May). Bonnycastle's English Cove appears to be a shift name from CAPE ENGLISH (NTS St. Mary's), which forms its northern shore. St. Vincent may be commemorative of one of the saints of this name, or of the battle of Cape St. Vincent, Portugal, 1797, or of the English admiral John Jervis (1735–1823), victor of the battle and later earl of St. Vincent; or it may be a possessive, the French family name.[49] The occurrence of the French family name St. Croix – holy cross, holy rood, at ST. VINCENT'S (NTS St. Mary's) is probably fortuitous.[50]

c de s francisco ("Havre Catalan" 1520–34) is CAPE ST. FRANCIS (NTS Pouch Cove). Farilham (Verrazano 1529) – steep rock, steep little island, reef, point, is FERRYLAND (NTS Ferryland). c de st iago (Ribeiro 1529) – Cape St. James is now CAPE ST. MARY'S (NTS St. Brides); and Sa maria (Viegas 1537) is ST. MARY'S BAY.

Later additions to the names are de los patas (Santa Cruz 1545) – geese or auks, as in GOOSE ISLAND (NTS Ferryland) and C das patas (Homem 1554) – goose or auk cape, now probably COLDEAST POINT (NTS Ferryland), which occur in the vicinity of the R. das patas (Reinel 1519); the baffling contalian or contaliam (in Portuguese maps from c. 1550 to the end of the century, in variant forms), is perhaps CUCKOLDS COVE (NTS St. John's); and C de pena (Plancius 1592) – the cape of punishment or sorrow, now CAPE PINE (NTS St. Shotts).

Arenhosa (Plancius 1592), now RENEWS (NTS Renews), is apparently from the Portuguese *arenoso* – sandy, a quality which distinguishes the beach there from most beaches on the AVALON PENINSULA. Another explanation, however, would associate it with the Portuguese *ronhoso*, a word cognate with, and not improbably a translation of, Cartier's Rougnouse of 1536, the French *rogneux* – scabby, mangy, descriptive of the rock at the entrance to the harbour covered with kelp and shells, which was a sufficiently important feature to warrant mention by Jean Alfonse in his *Cosmographie* of 1544.

BAY DE VERDE (NTS Bay de Verde), which is Greene Bay in Guy's *Discourse* 1612, and POINT VERDE (NTS Ship Cove), Green Point in Gaudy 1715, alone appear to offer documentary evidence of translation from English to Portuguese, though in the latter *verde* may be a mistake in Lane 1772 for the French Pointe Verte (Buache 1736).

COLUMBINE POINT (NTS Bay Bulls) may be a shifted survival of I. Columbrina (Coronelli 1689) – Culverin island, after the kind of cannon.

The name Newfoundland may be traced in an embryonic form to a Privy Purse entry of 10 August 1497 in the phrase "to hym that found the new Isle," in which Isle is glossed by Ganong as "expressing, presumably, the belief that it was one of the islands in the Atlantic (most imaginary) shown on globes and maps of the time."[51] Ganong continues: "Cabot, however, believed he had found mainland leading towards Asia, which fact probably explains the use of 'land' in the phrase 'the londe and Isles of late founde by the said John' in Letters-Patent of the 3rd February 1498." The name first appears as "the newe founde launde" in an entry of 30 September 1502 in the Daybooks of King's Payments (Public Record Office E 101/415 3 [1 October 1499–30 September 1502];[52] and without the article in John Dee's statements on the date of the discovery of North America, composed in 1578 and written on the back of his map of the North Atlantic 1580: "Circa An. 1494. 2. Mr Robert Thorn his father, and Mr Eliot of Bristow discovered Newfownd Land."[53]

Four common Portuguese names for the general area of Newfoundland and Labrador occur in early maps and are repeated frequently in variant forms: Terra del Rey de portugall (Cantino 1502) – land of the king of Portugal; Terra de Corte Real ("Kunstmann no. 3" 1506); Terra de los bachalaos ("Egerton MS 2803" c. 1508) – land of the cod-fish; and Terra Nova (Verrazano 1529) – new land, though Terra Nova is found as a Latin name in Ruysch 1508. A less common name is Terra de peseria (for pescaria) ("King-Hamy" 1504–6) – land of fishing. One of a number of expanded forms is Terra nova dos bacalhaos (Velho 1561).

The French form, Terre-Neuve, is found by 1510, when Breton fishermen sold in Rouen "le poisson qu'ils avoient esté querir et pescher ès parties de la Terre Neufve,"[54] but it may date from the first appearance of the French on the fishing grounds about 1504.

Whether the English or the Portuguese were the first to discover Newfoundland, news of the abundance of cod off its coasts spread rapidly among the fishermen of Portugal, England, France and Spain, and before long venturers were fitting out ships to participate in the fishery. For cod, fresh, dried or salted, was a staple commodity in the diet of sixteenth century Catholic Europe when, it has been estimated, the church ordained no less than 153 days of abstinence in the year.[55] Its importance in the economy of both Europe and North America is attested by a voluminous literature of which two works are of outstanding significance: Harold A. Innis, *The Cod Fisheries*, and Ch. de la Morandière, *Histoire de la Pêche française*.

The Portuguese claim that by 1504 their ships were fishing in North American waters and a document of 15 October 1506 certainly refers to tithes to be collected from the fisheries of Newfoundland.[56] From some sources, the number of ships engaged as late as 1527 seems to be small, but by 1550 more than one hundred and fifty sailed from the port of Aveiro alone. From CAPE RACE (NTS Trepassey) northward at least as far as Bonavista (NTS Bonavista) they frequented the harbours of the east

Description, Indian Place Names, and European Discovery / 33

coast of Newfoundland to repair their ships, salt their cod and take on wood and water. Names of harbours such as FERMEUSE (NTS Renews) and AQUAFORTE (NTS Ferryland) derive from these early enterprises, as does BACCALIEU ISLAND (NTS Bay de Verde), here Frenchified but retaining its Portuguese form in another Bacalhao Island (NTS Twillingate), which seems, however, to be a modern imposition. BACCALIEU ISLAND, like Funk Island, off Fogo Island (NTS Fogo), according to Innis, was well-known for the sea-birds that nested there and served for fresh meat and bait for the fishermen,[57] as would also seem to be true of the places named R das patas, C das patas, and de los patas, mentioned above.[58]

A possessive name twice imposed by the English, PORTUGAL COVE, probably retains the memory of harbours occupied later as the Portuguese moved from congested areas where the English and French were in a hostile majority. One (NTS Trepassey) occurs as B[ay] of Portingal ("Velasco" 1610); the other (NTS St. John's) Portugal Cove (Southwood 1675) began to displace an older name, Abra Frade (Laet 1630 and other Dutch maps to Keulen 1682–4), seemingly a Portuguese name – friar's cove, but probably the Dutch cartographers' attempt at a phonetic rendering of the French Haure froid – cold harbour (Alemand 1687). Only after their expulsion from the harbours by the English in the seventeenth century did the Portuguese turn to fishing on the Banks of Newfoundland, as they still do.

The French Place Names

In comparison with the Portuguese contribution to the nomenclature of the AVALON PENINSULA, the number of places named by the French, English and Spanish in the period of discovery and early exploitation of the cod-fishery is small.

Innis believes "it is probable that the French arrived on the fishing grounds at about the same time as the Portuguese," that is, perhaps as early as 1504; and John Rut found "eleven saile of Normans and one Brittaine [Breton]" in ST. JOHN'S HARBOUR on 3 August 1527.[1] But Cartier's voyages and, Innis presumes, pressure from the Portuguese,[2] led to the extension of French, and especially Breton, interest first to the Northern Peninsula where many place names are of Breton origin,[3] then to the Gulf and River St. Lawrence, and eventually along the South Coast of Newfoundland.

No French names on the AVALON PENINSULA are recorded before Cartier, but a passage in the account of his voyage of 1536 suggests that RENEWS (NTS Renews) had been named previously: "vng hable, nommé Rougnouse, ou prinsmes eaues et boys, pour traverser la mer; et là laissames l'vne de noz barques".[4]

The French (or Portuguese) navigator Jean Alfonse, who accompanied Roberval to Canada in 1541, included ten French names on the Peninsula in his *Cosmographie* 1544, but of these nine were adaptations, shifts or replacements of names first recorded in Portuguese, and only one was new. Isle de Bacaillau, baie de Saincte Jehan, Cap d'espoir,

French Place Names / 35

cap de saincte Marie are French forms of the Portuguese names for BACCALIEU ISLAND, ST. JOHN'S HARBOUR, CAPE SPEAR, and CAPE ST. MARY'S. Cap de Ratz, CAPE RACE, is a French form of the Portuguese Capo raso, though perhaps not without overtones of the Pointe du Raz, Brittany. Isles d'Espoir, a collective name for the group now discriminated as SPEAR, FOX, PEBBLE and GOOSE ISLANDS (NTS Ferryland), appears to be a shift name from Cap d'espoir, Portuguese cauo de la spera, CAPE SPEAR (NTS St. John's). Baye de l'islet replaces Portuguese R. da aguea, AQUA-FORTE (NTS Renews). baie dicte Rogneuse repeats Cartier's Rougnouse, RENEWS (NTS Renews). saincte Christofle replaced the Portuguese riuo dos bosas, only to be superseded eleven years later by trepasses (Le Testu 1555B), from which developed the modern TREPASSEY (NTS Trepassey). Christofle (Christopher) is not only the name of the saint but also of two ships, both called *Xristofle*, of Ploumenac, Brittany, and La Rochelle, engaged in the Newfoundland fishery in 1533 and 1535.[5]

The specific in the one new imposition by Alfonse, cap de Chincete, appears to derive from O. Fr. *cince, chinche,* with the diminutives *cincette, chinchette* – little rag. Ragged is a common English specific in Newfoundland coastal names to denote features encumbered with shoals, as in Ragged Cove (NTS Nippers Harbour), Ragged Harbour (NTS Carmanville), Ragged Head (NTS Lamaline and Eastport), Ragged Islands (NTS Trinity and elsewhere), RAGGED POINT (NTS Bay Bulls and elsewhere) and RAGGED ROCKS (NTS Harbour Grace); and the same metaphorical usage may have obtained in French. But the name puzzled some later cartographers, both French and English, as the following citations show. In Courcelle 1675 and Detcheverry (a Basque) 1689 the name appears correctly as Chinchette, but others do little more than approximate to it, as Chavette (Robinson 1669); Sanshot (Hack c. 1690?), in which the genesis of the modern name is to be seen; Chincho (Chaviteau 1698); La chinette (Friend 1713); and Chinckhole (Gaudy 1715), Chink-hole (Senex 1728) and Chinkole (Bellin 1744), where the name seems to have acquired a relationship to the Norman and Picard family name Chincholle.[6] Cook and Lane 1770 [1775]B anglicizes the original name and produces a saint unknown to the Calendar, St. Shot, ST. SHOTTS (NTS St. Shotts), and also records Chink Hole as an alternative. But, as if one new saint were not enough, Lane 1773 also appears to canonize a neighbouring cove, originally perhaps Shores Cove *tout court,* as in the present SHORES COVE (NTS Ferryland), ST. SHORES (NTS St. Shotts), though St. is to be taken in this instance as an abbreviation for South, as it is recorded in South Shores (Mount and Page 1780). To the Newfoundlander, these apocryphal saints, Shott and Shore, are as

French Place Names on the Avalon Peninsula

1 Supersedes a previous Portuguese imposition

2 Supersedes a previous Spanish imposition

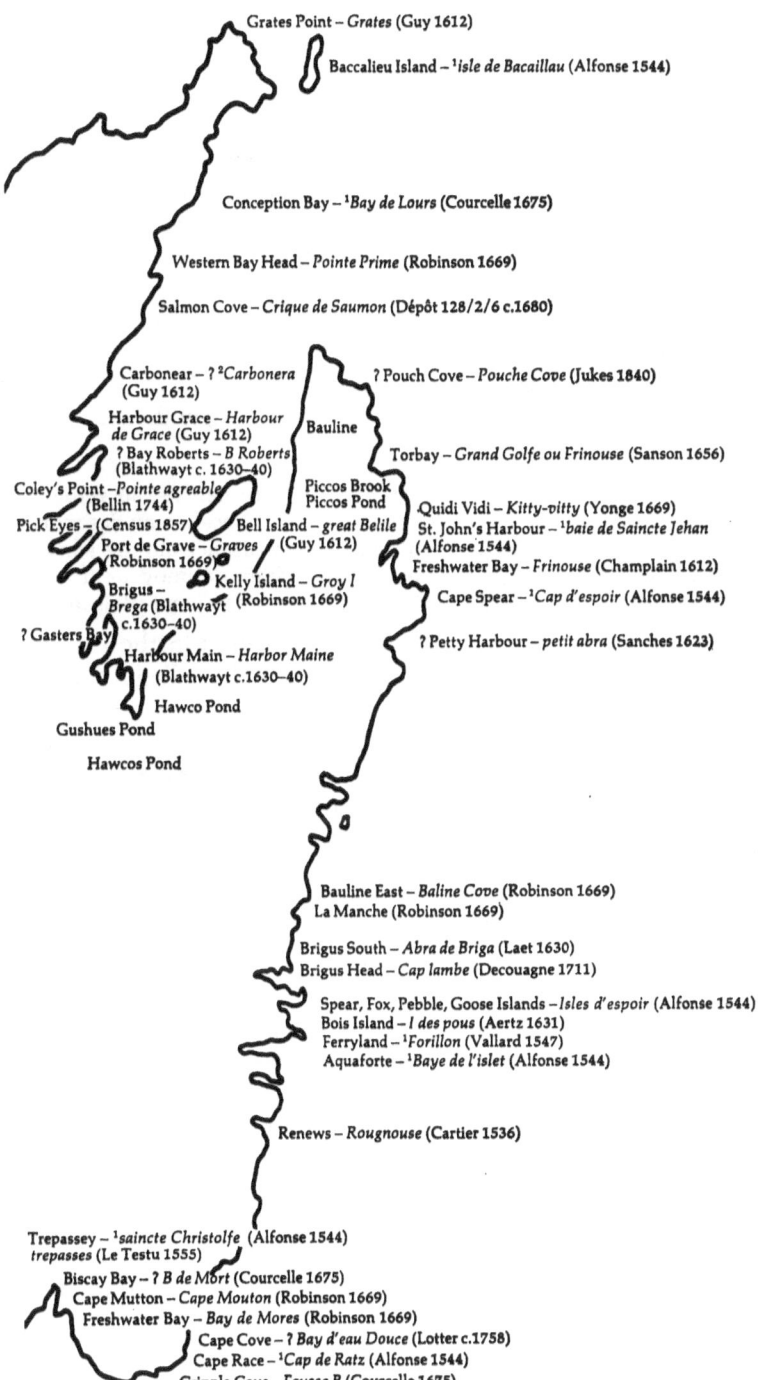

inseparable as Lamb's Simon and Jude, "clubbing (as it were) their sanctities together," unwarranted though they may be.

Somewhat surprisingly, Alfonse did not include FERRYLAND (NTS Ferryland), the Portuguese Farilham, among the places named in his *Cosmographie*, but within six years a French name, Forillon, occurs in two maps, "Vallard" 1547 and Desceliers 1550.[7] Godefroy defines *forillon* as cape, Huguet as point, and both give their earliest citation from Thevet, *Cosmographie*, 1558. It will be seen, however, that both Vallard and Desceliers anticipate Thevet.

The Vallard map first shows Ille de Plaisance, PLACENTIA (NTS Placentia), with island here as elsewhere in early maps of Newfoundland a common mistake for peninsula. Despite its French form in Vallard, Baron Lahontan writing about 1696 expressed the view that the Spaniards had first imposed the name:

Les espagnols ayant autrefois decouvert l'ile de terre neufve, au retour du lieu où est à present situé Kebec la nommèrent terre de Bacallao ou des morues par la quantité qu'ils en peschèrent dans la baye de plaisance qui tire son nom de plazencia que les espagnols luy donnèrent. ensuite de quoy les francois s'estant apropriés le lieu qu'ils ont fortifié depuis, le nommèrent plaisance.[8]

In view of the known early presence of the Basques in the Placentia area, the name was probably transferred from the village near San Sebastian.[9]

Shift names subsequently associated with PLACENTIA are: Bay of Plasentia (Wyet 1594) now PLACENTIA BAY, PLACENTIA HARBO[U]R (Mason 1626) (NTS Placentia), Little Plasentia (Robinson 1669) now ARGENTIA HARBOUR (NTS Argentia), Plasentia (Set.) (Visscher c. 1680) PLACENTIA (NTS Placentia), PLACENTIA SOUND (Lane 1772) (NTS Argentia), Little Placentia (Set.) (*Population Returns* 1836) now ARGENTIA (NTS Argentia), PLACENTIA ROAD (Imray 1862) (NTS Placentia), SOUTHEAST PLACENTIA (Set.) (*Census* 1869) (NTS Placentia), and PLACENTIA JUNCTION (c. 1888) (NTS Argentia).

The only other name of a possible Spanish origin found on the AVALON PENINSULA is Carbonera (Guy 1612), CARBONEAR (NTS Harbour Grace). This form of the name or approximations to it, but all with the final syllable in -a, persists throughout the seventeenth and eighteenth centuries: Carboneara (Seller c. 1671), Carbonera (*English Pilot. The Fourth Book* 1689, Mount and Page 1780), side by side with forms suggestive of a French origin: Carbonere (Robinson 1669, Southwood 1675 ... to Fitzhugh 1693), Carboniere (Popple 1733), Carbonere (Bellin 1744, 1754, Mount and Page 1755, Lotter c. 1758), Carboniere

(Kitchin 1758, 1762), Carbonere (Cook 1763), Carboniere (Cook and Lane 1770 [1775]A. Cook and Lane 1770 [1775]B records Carbonere or Carbonera Bay. Span. *carbonera* denotes variously wood prepared for burning into charcoal, a charcoal kiln, a female preparer of or dealer in charcoal; Carboneras is the name of a small town in Almeira, southern Spain. Carbonnier, a Norman or Picard form of the more common Charbonnier, is a French family name, La Carbonnière a Norman place name, and both are associated with the preparation or sale of charcoal.

Evidence for the origin of CARBONEAR, then, must remain inconclusive. The early occurrence and continuance of Carbonera and the nearby SPANIARD'S BAY (NTS Harbour Grace), though not recorded before Robinson 1669, lend support to a Spanish origin. On the other hand, D. W. Prowse's citation from the Records for 1614 that pirates or privateers "took a French ship fishing in Carbonier &c,"[10] the prevalence of the French form, and the common phenomenon of French family names and place names being transferred to Newfoundland, cannot be overlooked. If a Spanish origin is assumed, the name would seem to derive from the occupation; and Guy's letter to Slaney, 16 May 1611, tells how, among their many activities, his colonists at CUPIDS (NTS Harbour Grace) were engaged from October to May "in cutting wood for the collier, in coling of it,"[11] (that is, in cutting wood for the charcoal burner, [and] in preparing charcoal from it), for use in the smithy they had set up. A French origin would more likely be the family name or place name. COLLIERS (Blathwayt c. 1630–40) (NTS Holyrood), provides an English example of the same occupational name which is also a family name, and presents a similar insoluble problem of origin.

Le Testu's maps of 1555 include male baie – bad bay, unidentified precisely but near MISTAKEN POINT (NTS Trepassey), and trepasses (Fr. *trépassés* – the dead), TREPASSEY BAY (NTS Trepassey).[12] The name appears to have been transferred from the Baie des Trépassés, north of Pointe du Raz, Brittany: "On the coast of Brittany where Cap Raz stands out westward into the ocean, there is the "Bay of Souls" (trépassés), the launching place where the departed spirits sail off across the sea."[13] Imray, *Sailing Directory for the Island of Newfoundland 1873,* bears witness to the appropriateness of the name. Except for TREPASSY HARBOUR (NTS Trepassey) at the head of the bay, it is "exposed in every part to the full strength of south-westerly winds ... Between FRESHWATER POINT (NTS Trepassey) and PORTUGAL COVE (NTS Trepassey), the cliffs are 200 feet high, and the shore rocky and difficult of access; upon this shore many wrecks have occurred in foggy weather, caused doubtless by the indraught which sometimes runs 2 miles an hour on the east side of this bay."[14]

No other new French names have been found in maps or other documents before the end of the sixteenth century; but the imposition of three names[15] in CONCEPTION BAY and its immediate vicinity before 1612 may be deduced from Guy's references to them in the account of his voyage of exploration in that year.[16]

As de la Morandière rightly comments on the early French fishing settlements, it is difficult to be precise about the date of their establishment, since they were founded, not under the aegis of a body like the Compagnie de la Nouvelle France, but by a series of unrelated, individual acts of which archives have preserved no trace. He believes it possible that some of the French on the east coast may have abandoned such harbours as RENEWS (NTS Renews) and FERRYLAND (NTS Ferryland) before the English invasion, as he calls it, to find a quieter or calmer place ("*un lieu plus tranquille*"), and that these new settlements belong to the first half of the seventeenth century.[17] Such a settlement may have been HARBOUR GRACE (NTS Harbour Grace), a good harbour enjoying the shelter of CONCEPTION BAY, and sufficiently remote from the English until Guy established his colonies at CUPIDS (NTS Harbour Grace) in 1610 and at HARBOUR GRACE and BRISTOL'S HOPE within the next few years.[18]

There seems no reason to doubt that Guy's Harbor de Grace, HARBOUR GRACE, is a name transferred from Havre de Grâce, now Le Havre, Normandy, founded in 1517 by Francis I of France, which in time acquired much of the transatlantic trade previously conducted out of Harfleur and Rouen.[19] The abbé Jean Beaudoin, who accompanied d'Iberville's expedition into Newfoundland from Acadia in 1696–7, relates in his Journal a tradition then associated with the establishment of the settlement: "Ce havre est le premier estably par les Anglais en l'isle de Terre-Neuve. Il mourut icy un habitant, il y a trois ans, né en ce lieu, âgé de quatre-vingt-trois ans." A note adds: "Cet Anglais serait donc né à Terre-Neuve en 1600," meaning, of course, 1610.[20]

Beaudoin's first statement that HARBOUR GRACE was the first harbour established by the English in Newfoundland is of doubtful validity, if only because there is no reason why an English settlement should have been named after a French town. His second statement, that it was an Englishman who was born there, would suggest either that English and French were living together there in 1610, or that Guy's subsidiary colony of HARBOUR GRACE had been founded within a year of the first colony at CUPIDS and had usurped an earlier French settlement, knowledge of which had been forgotten by, or was unknown to, his informant in 1697.

In the absence of an acceptable English interpretation of the Grates (Guy 1612) GRATES POINT (NTS Bay de Verde), the name Guy and also later cartographers gave to the point at the northern extremity of the BAY DE VERDE PENINSULA (NTS Bay de Verde), M. F. Howley's identification of it with the French fishing term *dégrat* is probably correct.[21] Dégrat appears in the *Première Relation de Jacques Cartier de la Terre Neufve* 1534 as the name of a cape and a harbour on the Northern Peninsula, which have survived as Cape Degrat and Degrat Harbour (NTS Quirpon); as a shift name it is the modern name of an island and was formerly applied to Quirpon Island (NTS Quirpon). It occurs in combinative forms in De grat du cheval, now Cat Cove (NTS Englee), c degrat du pillier (both in Courcelle 1675), and Degrat de Ferolle (Lotter c. 1758), now New Ferolle Cove (NTS Ferolle Point); and as le Degrat (Bellin 1754), now Northeast Crouse (NTS Groais Island) – all on the Northern Peninsula.

En dégrat, according to Littré, is said of a boat leaving the harbour where the parent ship is anchored and going to find better fishing elsewhere; according to Loture,[22] it is the practice of fishing by the boats of a ship outside the harbour of which it held the fishing rights. The practice is discussed at some length in de la Morandière.[23] *Dégrat* itself seems to have meant stage or flake, terms somewhat confused in *OED* but distinguished in Newfoundland usage as the place where fish is landed and the platform on which it is dried, though the flake was frequently built over the stage as part of the same structure.

great Belile (Guy 1612), now BELL ISLAND (NTS St. John's and Harbour Grace), in CONCEPTION BAY, may also be a French imposition, transferred from Belle Isle off the coast of Brittany, as was Bell Island (NTS Grey Islands Harbour), off the coast of the Northern Peninsula. Throughout the seventeenth, eighteenth and nineteenth centuries, the name appears indifferently as Bell or Belle Isle. M. F. Howley tells of a ship's captain being sent to Bell Isle to load iron ore and proceeding mistakenly to the island in the Straits of Belle Isle (NTS Belle Isle). The tradition that the name of the island in CONCEPTION BAY derives from "a very remarkable rock, called the Bell, high, perpendicular, and cylindrical, standing almost close to its western side" has not been traced before 1819.[24] The form BELL ISLAND received official recognition in a proclamation of 26 April 1910.[25]

One other French name occurs in 1612, in Champlain's *Carte géo-*

graphique de la Novvele Franse: Frinouse, now FRESHWATER BAY (NTS St. John's). Neither Frinouse nor an alternative form Frinquise (Jansson 1636, Blaeu 1659), apparently a mistake for Frinouse, has any significance unless Frinouse itself is a mistaken or dialectal rendering of Freneuse, a place name in northern France[26] and a possible variant of a common family name, derived from *frêne* – ash or balsam. Frinouse is also an alternative name for TORBAY (NTS St. John's) in Grand Golfe ou Frinouse (Sanson 1656), which acquires a conflated form in Grand Golfe de Frinouse (Franquelin 1681).

Borrell (Whitbourne 1622), ? GOOSEBERRY COVE or SHIP COVE (NTS Ship Cove) is the French family name, Borel or Borrel.

petit abra (Sanches 1623), now PETTY HARBOUR (NTS Bay Bulls), is the small harbour compared with the great harbour of ST. JOHN's. Like Abra Frade (p. 33) and Abra de Brigas (p. 43), it has a quasi-Portuguese form, but originally it may have been either French or English. The specific occurs as Petit or Petty in both English and foreign maps, though the common generic is Harbo(u)r, giving such forms as Pettit harbor (Mason 1626), Petti Harbor (Blathwayt c. 1630–40, Laet 1630), Petty harbour (Robinson 1669) and Petit Harbour (Ogilby 1671).

A manuscript map ascribed to about 1630–40 in the *Blathwayt Atlas* in the John Carter Brown Library, so called after its compiler and first owner, William Blathwayt,[27] contains three new names of harbours in CONCEPTION BAY. The specific in Harbor Maine, HARBOUR MAIN (NTS Holyrood), is a French family name as well as the name of numerous hamlets.[28] M. F. Howley's identification of it with the Breton St. Mein (d. 617) – as in the old name for St. Anthony's Bight (NTS St. Anthony), St. Mein Bay – does not appear to be warranted.[29] The second name, B Roberts, BAY ROBERTS (NTS Harbour Grace), has the same construction as HARBOUR MAIN with the inversion of the specific and generic, BAY ROBERTS instead of Roberts Bay, HARBOUR MAIN instead of Main Harbour, as is not uncommon in French names; but the specific may be either English or French. It first appears in a succession of English maps (Blathwayt c. 1630–40, Robinson 1669, Southwood 1675, and Hack c. 1677) in the English form Roberts, which most later English cartographers retained. Exceptions are Bay Robards (Hack c. 1690?), Robert B (Popple 1733), and Bay Robert (Bowen 1747). Robert, the French form of the family name, is found in Dépôt 128.2.6 c. 1680, Bellin 1744, Robert de Vaugondy 1749, and Lotter c. 1758. A Dutch map records Roberts Bay (Visscher c. 1680); and Imray, *Sailing Directions for Newfoundland* 1862, has what may be taken as the English and French alternatives, Bay Robert, Robert's Bay.

The third name, Brega, BRIGUS (NTS Harbour Grace) in CONCEPTION BAY, coincides with the first recording of a similar name of a boat harbour on the SOUTHERN SHORE, Abra de Brigas (Laet 1630), BRIGUS SOUTH (NTS Ferryland).

Despite its apparently Portuguese form, Abra de Brigas – the harbour or roadstead of tumults, confusion, the late date of the first recording of the name on the SOUTHERN SHORE seems to obviate a Portuguese origin; indeed, as happened with Abra Frade (p. 33 above), it may have been yet another attempt by Laet to reproduce a French name. Moreover, Brega, as it occurs in CONCEPTION BAY, is an Old French word of southwestern France with the same meaning and, among several variants, some later cartographers record both names as the related Fr. *brigues* – intrigues, underhand work, corruption. Both names, too, occur in areas of French interest which contain other French names.

There does not appear to be any evidence to support identification of either BRIGUS with Brighouse, Yorkshire, England (Thoresby 1796), notwithstanding the identical pronunciation of the names [brIgəs]; or with the town at the foot of the northern slope of the Simplon Pass, Fr. Brigue, Ital. Briga; or with the Cornish St. Breage [brig] or with the village named after him.

The two BRIGUSes were formerly often distinguished by compound prepositions of a nautical turn, by South and more rarely by North, as in Brigus by South (Southwood 1675) and Brecast by North (*CSP* 1705), until the Canadian Board on Geographic Names changed the name of the post office at BRIGUS SOUTH to HILLDALE in 1959, though the innovation has not proved popular and BRIGUS SOUTH is still in common use.

Aertsz 1631 first records BOIS ISLAND (NTS Ferryland) as I des Pous – the island of wells (Fr. *pous* being a southwestern form of *puits* – wells) I Poiuz (Dudley 1646). Later cartographers record Bouy I. (Southwood 1675), Bony I (Thornton 1689B) with the -n- a turned -u-, I. Boi (L'Hermite 1695), Bouy Island (*English Pilot. The Fourth Book* 1716), Boy I (Senex 1728) and Bonny I (Popple 1733). Only with Cook 1763 and Lane 1773 does the specific achieve its modern form, I. Bois – wood island.

No name on the AVALON PENINSULA, with the possible exception of RENEWS (NTS Renews), occurs in so many variant forms, and none has generated so much speculation about its origin as QUIDI VIDI, the name of the lake and harbour on the outskirts of ST. JOHN'S (NTS St. John's).

The variants, of which the following are only a sample, may be taken as indicative of the uncertainty felt about an uncommon name by those

44 / Place Names of the Avalon Peninsula

who had occasion to record it in journals, maps and reports. The time of its first imposition is unknown, but its earliest recording seems to be in the Journal for 1669 kept by a surgeon with the Devon fishing fleet in St. John's in that year, James Yonge:

> I had forgot to mention that during our being here [St. John's] I went once to Petty Harbour, and twice to Kitty-vitty, of which place I forbear a description, intending to leave that to the figures by and by, to be made of all the harbours I have been in in this land.[30]

Thereafter it occurs as Quiteandy (Robinson 1669), Quilliwiddi (Seller c. 1671), Kitte Vitte (Southwood 1675) and Quide Vide (*Calendar of State Papers* 1677). Que de Vide Creek (*CSP* 1679) contains a rare generic in Newfoundland usage for the present Gut, the outlet of the lake into the harbour. Then follow Queue de Vide (*CSP* 1680), Kitivi ("Dépôt 128.2.6" c. 1680), Kitte Vitte (Visscher c. 1680), Cintee Wittee (*CSP* ?1682), Kitte Vitte (Thornton 1689B), Quidi Vidy or Kitty Vitty (*English Pilot. The Fourth Book* 1689), Kitty Vitty (Hack c. 1690?), Kitte Witte (L'Hermite 1695), Quirividy (Beaudoin 1697) the settlement, Quidi Vidy, Quidi Vidi (*CSP* 1705), Kitty Velle (Cook 1763), Kitty Ville (Mount and Page 1780), City Vety (Thoresby 1796) the settlement, Quiddibiddy (Bonnycastle, *Newfoundland in 1842*), Quiddy Viddy (Imray 1862, 1873) and Quidi Vidi or Kitty Vitty (M. F. Howley 1908).

The occurrence of the name in Kitiwiti or Kittee Wittee Shoals, off the coast of Nova Scotia, is recorded in Thomas J. Brown, *Place-Names of the Province of Nova Scotia*, p. 76, though without any indication of its origin or antiquity.

M. F. Howley advances a number of attempts at interpretation of the name only to dismiss them as lacking conviction.[31] The first, a child of the invention of the Rev. Moses Harvey,[32] that a "respectable widow woman" named Kitty Vitty kept a public house or inn there is, of course, of the same kind as the tradition associated with KITCHUSES (NTS Holyrood).[33] Others according to Howley see it derived from a quasi-Latin Quid[i] Vidi – what have I seen?, or from what is alleged to be Italian, Qui divide – here divide. He is contemptuous of an explanation known to H. W. LeMessurier, that it is a corruption of Guy's Divide, "a dividing line to protect St. John's against the encroachments of John Guy's people." Quidimiti and Quimiditi, found, he says, in French documents of 1704, suggest to him a Beothuck origin, which would make it "the unique example of a surviving Beothic name in the country."

In 1743, the Rev. Thomas Walbank, chaplain of HMS *Sutherland* at

ST. JOHN'S, recorded "Città Vecchià, commonly call'd Kitty Vitty," that is, the old town,[34] thus ascribing to it a second Italian origin. One Engleheart, a secretary to the Prince of Wales, later Edward VII, on his tour of America in 1860, seems to have confused QUIDI VIDI with Cabot's alleged cry of delight on sighting Newfoundland, "O Bona Vista," and thought the name "to be expressive of the surprise of the Portuguese on seeing so much beauty in so sterile a spot."[35] Yet another explanation, completely at odds with the preceding, finds the name a corruption of the French *Quittez, évitez* – leave, avoid, an interpretation which recalls the names da mirla and de farlla (Kunstmann No. 2 1503-06), glossed by Harrisse as a divided reading of C. de mirame et lexame – Cape Look at Me and Avoid Me, a reminder of the dangers Corte Real had experienced in his explorations.[36]

More probable than all the foregoing, in accord with the imposition of many French family and place names as place names in Newfoundland, and supported, if late, by the forms Kitty Velle (Cook 1763) and Kitty Ville (Mount and Page 1780), is a conjectural derivation of QUIDI VIDI from the French family name which occurs variously as Quédville in both Normandy and Picardy, Quidville in Picardy, Quiédeville in Normandy,[37] and Quetteville in Jersey,[38] or from the French place name Quetteville, near Honfleur.

The phonetic processes in the change from Quédville [ked 'vil], to take one of the above variants, to Quidi Vidi [ˌkIdi 'vIdi] or Kitty Vitty [ˌkIti 'vIti] are: [e] to [I] in the first syllable by raising; syllabification after the d in the first syllable, which corresponds with the existing medial unstressed syllable in the forms Quiédeville and Quetteville; and the change from [l] in -ville to [d] in Vidi or [t] in Vitty by reduplication or echo of the [d] in Quidi or the [t] in Kitty. The [d]s in Quidi Vidi and [t]s in Kitty Vitty are local variants, found elsewhere, for example, in Patrick ['pætrIk] and Paddy ['pædi], and in O. Fr. *jeu parti* [ʒø par'ti] and English jeopardy ['dʒɛpərdi].[39] The final unstressed syllable in French has been strengthened in English.

Captain (later Sir) Robert Robinson's manuscript map of 1669,[40] "An exact Mapp of Newfound-Land soe far as the English and French Fishing trade is concerned," is in fact a map of the AVALON PENINSULA, "The Province of Avalonia," as he calls it. Robinson (c. 1624–1705) seems to have known Newfoundland from at least as early as 1661 to 1680, as a commodore of the Newfoundland convoy and as an aspirant for the governorship. Despite allegations by the West of England merchants that at ST. JOHN'S in 1661 he had shown no more concern for good government than his predecessors, under whom "Laws [were] violated, and trees, woods, and stages destroyed by the inhabitants' increase," by 1668 he was first advocating the appointment of a civil governor both for the control of domestic affairs in the island and for its protection from the French:

Because Sir David Kirke's Government was careless or severe, it does not follow that if there be a bad Governor over a Plantation that therefore the Governor and the Plantation shall be removed, and so the country left to any other nation or people whatsoever, but rather that a better Governor be appointed and his Majesty's honour and interest still maintained. The destruction of stages, houses, woods, and harbours; the want of justice; breaking the Lord's day and having no offices of christianity, his Majesty being Defender thereof so that the very natives take notice of it, are some of the consequences of the want of a Governor. Arguments as to whether Newfoundland ought not to be kept from an enemy when it may be done at 1 per cent. on the fish. If the French should take it, whereas they now employ about 400 sail and 18,000 seamen, and the English 300 sail and 15,000 seamen, they would employ near 700 ships and 30,000 seamen, and the English be shut out of 700,000£. yearly, besides which the French would make double that sum. The great advantages of the Newfoundland fishery as a nursery for seamen. If the French should add what the English have planted there to what they possess already in Canada, Nova Scotia, and other places thereabouts, they would be bad neighbours to his Majesty's flourishing Plantations of New England, New York, and Virginia.[41]

His recognition of a *de facto* sphere of French influence in PLACENTIA BAY, however, is shown by the inscription on his map of the French arms near PLACENTIA (NTS Placentia), which the French had established as their chief port and seat of government in Newfoundland in 1662.[42] The English arms are shown on the SOUTHERN SHORE near FERRYLAND (NTS Ferryland).

As may be expected, Robinson's map is rich in both French and English names, with some twelve new French names on the Peninsula and others on the western side of PLACENTIA BAY.

Pointe Prime – first point, now ? WESTERN BAY HEAD (NTS Heart's Content), was presumably so named since it is the first important headland seen on rounding CAPE ST. FRANCIS (NTS Pouch Cove) to enter CONCEPTION BAY. This name is retained in Thornton 1689A, but eighteenth century cartographers record ? S. Williams Pt (Bowen 1747), Pte S. Guillaume (Bellin 1744 ... Lotter c. 1758), or Pt. William (Kitchin 1762), a survival, according to G. R. F. Prowse,[43] of a supposed early Yorkshire survey of Newfoundland which gave also FLAMB(O)RO(UGH) HEAD (NTS Bay De Verde) and Robinhoods Bay (NTS Trinity). William (d. 1154) was a Yorkshire saint. In Lane, *Directions* 1775, 1810, the headland received a shift name from the bay, Green or Western Bay Point. The modern form, WESTERN BAY HEAD, is apparently first recorded in Imray 1873. Similarly P Prime (Seller c. 1671), now BREME POINT (NTS St. Bride's), is the first important landmark for ships sailing south out of PLACENTIA. The voicing of [p] to [b], whereby Prime [prim] becomes Breme [brim], is found elsewhere, most notably in the change of the Irish family name Prunty to Brontë.

The names Graves, now BAY and PORT DE GRAVE (NTS Harbour Grace), and Groue [sc. Grave] de Navire, now? GREAT BARASWAY (NTS Ship Cove), refer to the French practice of drying cod on the beaches. Loture[44] notes that *grave* was used for *grève* – shoal, shingle in the Newfoundland fishery; Dauzat [45] defines Grave or Graves, a French family and place name, as the "forme occitane de grève, terrain sablonneux ou cailouteux." de la Morandière discusses the importance of the *grave* in the shore installations of the fishermen in some detail:

> Il faisait travailler également à remettre en état la grave, c'est-à-dire cette étendue plus ou moins vaste de rivage qui lui [le capitaine] était dévolue pour faire sécher son poisson. Cette étendue était limitée soit par la grave des autres bateaux, soit par la nature du terrain. On donnait à chaque navire une tendue de grave proportionnée au nombre de chaloupes qu'il équipait: on comptait 2 toises et demi par chaloupe ...
>
> L'organisation d'une grave était chose délicate. Si la plage était entièrement couverte de galets, comme le sont nos grèves d'Entretat, Dieppe, etc., le travail de remise en état était insignifiant. Il n'y avait qu'à vérifier si la couche de galets couvrait exactement tout le terrain, si elle ne présentait pas de trous, si elle n'avait pas été salie par les Anglais hivernants.
>
> Si la grave était de sable, il fallait la mettre en rances ou mieux en vignaux. L'organisation en rances était relativement simple: il suffisait de couvrir le sol d'une couche de branchages de sapin assez épaisse pour que la morue ne touche pas le sable dont l'humidité risquerait de la gâter. Les rances étaient surtout utilisées au Petit Nord.
>
> L'organisation en vignaux etait plus sûre, mais demandait beaucoup plus de travail. Pour faire des vignaux on enfonçait dans le sol, à la distance les uns des autres de deux mètres environ, des piquets de bois dont l'extrêmité supérieure devait s'élever à un pied et demi ou deux pieds au-dessus du sol. On réunissait la tête de cas piquets par de longues perches légères de façon à faire comme un quadrillage au-dessus du sable. Sur ce quadrillage on plaçait des branches de sapin qui étaient destinées à recevoir la morue.
>
> Une grave en vignaux était la meilleure des graves, supérieure même à la grave en galets parce que l'air, en passant sous le quadrillage, accélérait le séchage. Seulement il fallait de nombreuses journées de travail pour mettre en vignaux mille toises de terrain ou même simplement pour en réparer une que les intempéries, la pluie, la neige, sans compter les hivernants avaient plus ou moins détruite.[46]

The distinction between PORT DE GRAVE (NTS Harbour Grace), a small harbour, and BAY DE GRAVE (NTS Harbour Grace) as a whole is not made

48 / Place Names of the Avalon Peninsula

clear by cartographers until Lane, *Directions* 1775, 1810. Early citations after Robinson all include the generic P[ort], but since PORT DE GRAVE does not have a shingle beach, it seems evident that fishermen and cartographers identified the best harbour in the bay with the bay itself. The shingle beach in fact is found at the bottom of the bay at what is now CLARKES BEACH (NTS Harbour Grace).

If the identification of Robinson's Groue de navire – ship's beach with GREAT BARASWAY (NTS Ship Cove) is correct, the *grave* there is probably the shingle bar which separates the *barachois* from the open sea. Larousse[47] defines Fr. *barachois* as "petit port natural peu profond, entouré de rochers à fleur de l'eau," though in some localities the bar is a sand-bar; Jukes[48] as "a very common term for a shallow, marshy inlet or salt lake along the south coast of Newfoundland"; Bonnycastle[49] as a "boat-river in the French Newfoundland dialect." Lagoon or creek seems to be the nearest English equivalent. The name appears to be first recorded in Newfoundland by Lane in 1773 as G[reat] Barrysway and L[ittle] Barrysway, now BIG and LITTLE BARACHOIS (NTS Placentia), and presents an interesting example of a French name reverting to its French form after having been anglicized. A common name in Newfoundland, it occurs variously as Barachois, Barachoix, Barasway and Barrisway, but in Nova Scotia and New Brunswick, according to the gazetteers,[50] always as Barachois.

Robinson repeats the name Porche on the east coast of PLACENTIA BAY, once at ?LITTLE BARASWAY (NTS Ship Cove) and again at PERCH COVE (NTS St. Bride's), but in neither location was it acceptable to later cartographers. At LITTLE BARASWAY it becomes Porchet, a French family name,[51] probably of a fishing captain, consistently from Bowen 1747 to its last recording by Lotter c. 1758. At PERCH COVE it becomes La Perche in "Dépôt 128.2.6" c. 1680 and Chaviteau 1698, ?porchet ("Dépôt 132.5.10" 1706) probably through confusion with Porchet (LITTLE BARASWAY), thereafter la Perle until Lotter c. 1758, and finally PERCH COVE (Adm. 2915 1864). For some cartographers the neighbouring headland, CROSS POINT (NTS St. Bride's), was a more important feature. Bowen 1747 originally and uniquely recorded it as P. Perle, a name transferred from the cove. After an interval of over a hundred years it is CROSS POINT in Murray 1868,[52] Imray 1873,[53] and J. P. Howley 1907; M. F. Howley 1910[54] has Point La Perche; modern maps have CROSS POINT. Le Perche is a place name in northern France, whence the name *percheron* for the breed of horses; La Perche is a French family name derived from a nickname for one who was long and thin or who dealt in poles;[55] but la Morandière has drawn attention to the use of

French Place Names / 49

poles in building fishing-stages,[56] and the cove may have been known for a ready supply of poles. La Perche Harbour was also the name formerly given, as in Imray 1873,[57] to the bay north of Little Paradise (NTS Baine Harbour), on the west side of PLACENTIA BAY. La Perle – the pearl, is probably a cartographic error for La Perche, yet it is found as a place name originally given by the Huguenot settlers in South Africa to a district famous for its fertility and beauty, now known in the Afrikaans form, Paarl.

Other French names first recorded by Robinson are Collinet, now GREAT COLINET ISLAND (NTS St. Mary's), in ST. MARY'S BAY, the French family name Colinet;[58] Cape Mouton, now CAPE MUTTON (NTS Trepassey), with Mouton again a French family name.[59] but also the name of a cape and three rocks, Le Grand et Les Petits Moutons, at the entrance to the Bay of Morbihan, Brittany; Bay de Mores, that is of Moors, now ?FRESHWATER BAY (NTS Trepassey), which, like TURKS GUT (NTS Harbour Grace), retains a memory of the days when the coasts of Newfoundland were haunted by Barbary pirates;[60] LA MANCHE (NTS Ferryland) which, for want of a more satisfactory explanation, may be assumed to have been named after the English Channel; and Baline Cove, which appears twice, once at what is now BAULINE EAST (NTS Ferryland) and also two miles or so further north, south of MOBILE (NTS Ferryland), apparently now unnamed. Baline is Fr. *baleine* – whale, and was probably applied originally to the rock offshore, Whaleback (Southwood 1675), then to the cove and headland and finally to the settlement. But, whereas the rock retained its name in English, the cove and headland have been generally known by the French name. Both LA MANCHE and BAULINE are names repeated on the Peninsula: LA MANCHE (NTS Dildo) in PLACENTIA BAY, the site of a lead mine worked in the latter half of the nineteenth century; BAULINE (NTS St. John's), a small fishing settlement north of ST. JOHN'S. Groy I in CONCEPTION BAY, now KELLYS ISLAND (NTS Harbour Grace), repeats a name on the Northern Peninsula, Groais Island (NTS Groais Island), both transferred from the Ile de Groix off the coast of Brittany. BELL ISLAND (NTS St. John's, Harbour Grace) and Groy I, and Bell Island (NTS Groais Island, Grey Islands Harbour) and Groais Island have the same north-south relationship as Belle Ile and the Ile de Groix.[61] Groix is derived from the Breton *groac'h* – witch, sorceress.[62]

No single cartographer after Robinson recorded as many new French names on the Peninsula, but a number of isolated names, some not without passing interest, occur in the maps from time to time.

A direction in *The English Pilot. The Fourth Book* 1716[63] states:

"Before you come to CAPE ST. MARY, about five miles SE from it, lies several Rocks above Water, the two biggest of which the French call by the name of the BULL AND COW" (NTS St. Bride's). The name had been first recorded in French maps as vaches de S. Maria (Rotis 1674), Le beuf et la vache (Courcelle 1675) and La Vache et Le Bœuf ("Dépôt 128.2.6" c. 1680). Thereafter it generally appears in an English form, BULL AND COW (Gaudy 1715 ...); but a memory of another version of the French name persisted into the nineteenth century, as Anspach relates:

> In our coasting voyage round the island of Newfoundland we have had frequent opportunities of observing a copious mixture of English and French names, most of which may be traced either to the particular day on which those places were first discovered, or to some other striking incident or local circumstance. But now [in Labrador] we shall find it frequently difficult to indulge in such etymological speculations from the want of an Indian dictionary; for it does not appear probable that our researches should lead us here to the same fortunate result as was once the case when, at a loss to find out the meaning of the word *Washeltoraw*, it was, at last, after much study, discovered to mean "La Vache et le Taureau," the French name of some dangerous rocks near Cape St. Mary, on the south-east coast of Newfoundland, now more usually called "Cow and Bull Rocks."[64]

A sophisticated age has added Calf and Heifer to the original Bull and Cow.

A number of French maps of the last quarter of the seventeenth and the early years of the eighteenth century are generally rich in nomenclature for Newfoundland as a whole, though they add little to that of the AVALON PENINSULA. de Courcelle's map, compiled from a French naval survey of Newfoundland undertaken in 1675, records several shift names from earlier impositions and a few names that have not survived. Among them are a havre des cloches – harbour of bells, somewhere on the NORTH SHORE of CONCEPTION BAY in the vicinity of BACCALIEU ISLAND (NTS Bay de Verde), perhaps a shift name from BELL ISLAND; a unique designation, Bay de Lours – bay of bears, in place of the long-established name CONCEPTION BAY; Fausse B – false bay, for CRIPPLE COVE (NTS Trepassey), recorded in the same year by Southwood, with both names connoting a hazard to mariners; and B de Mort and C de Mort – bay and cape of the dead, in ?BISCAY BAY (NTS Trepassey), as well as Le Trepas – TREPASSEY.[65] But the most interesting entry on the map is at C. langlois – CAPE ENGLISH (NTS St. Mary's), which bears the legend "force serf [sc. cerf] et perdrix" – numerous deer and partridge.

The other French maps are in various portfolios formerly in the Dépôt Hydrographique de la Marine, Paris, now in the Bibliothèque

Nationale. "128.2.6" of about 1680 contains one new name, Crique de Saumon – SALMON COVE (NTS Heart's Content), "in which are store of salmon,"[66] which is repeated for another SALMON COVE (NTS Holyrood), first recorded in "Blathwayt" c. 1630–40. The *Carte basque de l'Isle de Terre Neuve* (128.2.3), as its inscription states, was made at PLACENTIA by Pierre Detcheverry of St. Jean de Luz for the French governor of PLACENTIA and Newfoundland, M. Parat, in 1689. It is valuable for its Basque names on the west coast of Newfoundland, but is oddly deficient in new names in the immediate vicinity of PLACENTIA, adding in fact only one, that of the small island off the entrance to PLACENTIA SOUND, I du renard – FOX ISLAND (NTS Argentia). An anonymous manuscript map, the *Carte de la coste de la Cadie De Baston et Partie de Terre Neuve* (132.2.10) of 1706, first names two more features north of PLACENTIA, haure long – LONG HARBOUR (NTS Argentia), and I gorichon, for Gorichon,[67] a French family name, now ?MERCHANT ISLAND (NTS Argentia), one of the IONA ISLANDS. Decouagne's *Carte du Canada* (124.1.2) 1711 appears to contain one of the rare new French impositions on the SOUTHERN SHORE at this late date, Cap lambe, now ?BRIGUS HEAD (NTS Ferryland). Since *lambe* does not exist in French, it may be an apocopated form of *lambel* or *lambeau* – ribbon, rags, which are also French family names.[68]

C. Crevecœur (Gaudy 1715) – Cape Heartbreak, CREVECŒUR POINT (NTS Argentia), repeats a place name which occurs in some sixteen *départements* in France. Longnon notes that "Plusieurs noms de lieu de base verbale tirent leur raison d'être d'événements militaires et de l'état d'esprit dans lequel ils furent accueillis par les populations. Ainsi l'on est fondé à croire que le nom Crèvecœur ... nom dont le sens est assez clair, puisque le mot *crève-cœur* est toujours d'un usage courant – a pris naissance à la suite d'un combat dont l'issue consterna les habitants de la région."[69] Rostaing attributes the name to the sterility of the district;[70] Dauzat cites it only as a family name after a locality.[71]

Newfoundland usage associates the name with steep cliffs, "difficult of being climbed or ascended."[72] In English it is Break Hart P (Visscher c. 1680), BREAKHEART POINT (NTS Bay de Verde) and elsewhere (NTS Marystown, Merasheen and Exploits). Once, as a mistake name, it becomes Breakfast Point (NTS Jackson's Arm). In ST. JOHN'S, the old name for CARTER'S HILL was Burst Heart Hill.[73] What appears to be a mistake name in French without any ascertainable signification is the shift name Privécœur Shoal, "almost half a mile westward of Crevecœur Point."[74]

M. F. Howley[75] suggests that GASKIERS BAY (NTS St. Mary's), Gaskers (Howley NQ XVII) and the settlement GASKIERS (NTS St. Mary's), Gaskier (Census 1857), Gaskier's (Smallwood 1940), Gascoigne (Newfoundland 1941, 1949), Gaskiers (Newfoundland 1955), and GASTERS BAY (NTS Holyrood), Gastries Bay (Murray 1868), Castries Bay (Imray 1873), Gasters Bay (*NLP* II 1953), and the settlement GASTERS (NTS Holyrood), Gasters (*Population Returns* 1836, Gastries (Adm. 296 1868), Gaskiers (*Electors* 1955), are English forms of a French *casse-cœur*, a synonym of *crève-cœur* – breakheart. *Casse-cœur*, however, appears to be unknown in its literal sense in French and is used only figuratively, meaning lady-killer! More probable is a derivation from either Gasquié, a French family name a variant of Gasquet[76] and related to the French and English family names Gascogne and Gascoigne, or from Castries, a village near Montpellier from which the Marquis de Castries (1727–1801) took his title. de Castries was Minister of Marine from 1780 to 1787 and in this office concerned himself with the reoccupation of St. Pierre and Miquelon by the French in 1783.[77] The interchange of initial [k] and [g], whereby Castries became Gastries, finds support in CLAM COVE (NTS Trepassey), recorded as Glam Cove (Yonge 1663), a form which anticipates the first citation of *glam* in OED in 1797.

Four French names of features are recorded between 1733 and about 1758. Popple 1733 has Marquess H[arbour], MARQUISE (NTS Argentia), which becomes a shift name for the narrow isthmus joining LITTLE PLACENTIA PENINSULA to the mainland. Marquès is a variant of the French family name,[78] of a village eight miles northeast of Boulogne. Cap Noir (Buache 1736) – Black C. (Bowen 1747), is now BLACK POINT (NTS Ship Cove), in contrast to GREEN POINT (NTS Ship Cove) a mile or so to the north. Pointe agreable (Bellin 1744, Robert de Vaugondy 1749) – pleasant point, is now ?COLEY'S POINT (NTS Harbour Grace). Bay d'Eau Douce (Lotter c. 1758) – Freshwater Bay, about half a mile north of CAPE RACE, has become ?CAPE COVE (NTS Trepassey), a shift name from the Cape.

Michael Lane's charts of his two surveys, of PLACENTIA BAY in 1772 and of the coast from POINT LANCE (NTS St. Bride's) to CAPE SPEAR (NTS St. John's), provide eight new French names, two of which, G[reat] and L[ittle] Barrysway, BIG and LITTLE BARACHOIS (NTS Placentia), have already been mentioned.[79]

Point Latina (Lane 1772), LATINE POINT (NTS Argentia), like Latin Point (NTS Groais Island), is apparently a descriptive name from the triangular sail, the "Latin" sail, so-called from its use in the Mediterranean. Despite M. F. Howley's objections that the local pronunciation is that of Latin and not lateen and that the derivation seems far-fetched,⁸⁰ the use of this kind of sail in the French Newfoundland fishery is attested by the inclusion of *voile latine* by Loture in his "Glossaire des Termes de Navigation et de Pêche": "Voile de forme triangulaire pouvant s'enverguer sur une antenne ou sur un étai, et se bordant de chaque côté d'une position intermédiaire située dans l'axe du navire."⁸¹

Point Roche (Lane 1772) – rock point, ROCHE POINT (NTS Argentia) probably derives from the "shingle spit, 9 feet high, surrounded by shoal water, [which] extends about one cable north-north-westward from Roche point."⁸² Roche is also an Irish family name, particularly associated with Co. Cork,⁸³ and found at FRESHWATER, PLACENTIA (NTS Argentia);⁸⁴ but no evidence has been found to connect the family name with the feature, especially at this early date.

Branch and Branch Head (Lane 1773), BRANCH COVE and BRANCH HEAD (NTS St. Mary's), is recorded as Branche by M. F. Howley⁸⁵ who states, without however citing any sources, that "the French maps give it as Les Branches." If the name is French, and no sense of English *branch* seems applicable to the cove or the headland, it may well be the French family name Branche.⁸⁶ Frapeau Pt (Lane 1773), FRAPEAU POINT (NTS St. Mary's), is French in appearance but of no obvious signification. Pt. la Haye (Cook 1762 or Gilbert 1768), LA HAYE POINT (NTS St. Mary's), is also a common French family and place name.

Howley⁸⁷ sees C Freels (Lane 1773), CAPE FREELS (SOUTH) (NTS St. Shotts), like the other Cape Freels (NTS Cabot Islands), as of Breton derivation, both transfers from Cap Fréhel, to the east of St. Brieuc Bay, Brittany. However, the names need to be discriminated and neither is necessarily Breton. Cape Freels (NTS Cabot Islands), in fact, is first recorded in Portuguese as Ilha de frey luis ("Kunstmann no. 3" c. 1506) – the island of Brother Lewis, whoever he was, and may have had associations with John Cabot.⁸⁸ The transition from frey luis to Freels is well attested; but to derive Freels from Fréhel takes no account of the final *s*, and one is tempted to find the origin of CAPE FREELS (NTS St. Shotts) not in a Breton place name but in a seventeenth century English word, *freel* or *frill* – cockle or scallop, the Cape of the Scallops.⁸⁹

PICK EYES (NTS Harbour Grace), a settlement near PORT DE GRAVE, is first recorded in the Census of 1874 but may have had its origin as early as the seventeenth century, contemporary with such other French settlements as PORT DE GRAVE itself, HARBOUR MAIN and BRIGUS. Picot (Picaud) is a French family name⁹⁰ which occurs as Piccott in the name of a property-owner, Elias Piccott, at PORT DE GRAVE in 1784.⁹¹ The transition to PICK EYES seems to be ['piko] > ['pikoI] > ['pIkaIz], with a geni-

54 / *Place Names of the Avalon Peninsula*

tive of association. Picco persists as a Newfoundland family name in several localities in the AVALON PENINSULA and is transferred to PICCOS BROOK and POND (NTS St. John's). Some members of the family, however, believe the name to be of Portuguese origin.

POUCH [puːtʃ][92] COVE (NTS Pouch Cove), the settlement, was served by a Methodist minister in 1821,[93] but the feature, as Pouche Cove, is apparently not recorded before Jukes 1840. Jukes's spelling, the absence of any obvious relevance of English pouch, and local pronunciation tend to suggest an origin in the French family name Pouche [puːʃ].[94] It may be noted that pouch in popular ST. JOHN's usage by analogy is also [puːtʃ], but elsewhere in Newfoundland [paUtʃ] is retained, as in Pouch Island (NTS Cabot Islands) and in the common noun.

ST. CROIX [sent 'krɔI] BAY (NTS Argentia), first recorded in Wix 1836, contains a common French family name[95] found at ST. VINCENT's and ST. MARY's (NTS St. Mary's).[96]

Harry Cove (*Population Returns 1836*), now HARRICOTT (NTS Placentia), may be the anglicized, popular form of the French family name Haricot.[97]

LANSECAN HILL and LANSECAN POINT (NTS St. Mary's), first recorded in Adm. 2915 1864, is Fr. *L'Anse à Cane*–Duck or Reed Cove, but folk etymology has produced a mistake name, still in popular use, Nancy Cann, paralleled on the South Coast of Newfoundland by Nancy Oh! or Nancyo, that is, *L'Anse à l'Eau* (NTS Marystown) – (fresh)water cove; Nancy Jobble, that is *L'Anse au Diable* (NTS St. Lawrence) – devil's cove; and Nancy Bark, that is, *L'Anse à Barque* – ship cove, now Lansey Bank Cove (NTS Lamaline).[98]

Apart from such names of features as PIERRES BROOK (NTS Bay Bulls), GUSHUES POND and HAWCO and HAWCOS PONDS[99] (NTS Holyrood), in which the specific is originally a French baptismal or family name, LANSECAN HILL is unique as an inland feature on the AVALON PENINSULA bearing a French specific.

Precise analysis of the seventy-odd names imposed by the French on the AVALON PENINSULA in some three hundred years is impossible,[100] but about twenty-five may be taken as descriptive, another twenty-five as possessive, and eleven as incident names. In the dozen commemorative names, only two are of religious significance and neither is an original French imposition. This general pattern of naming seems to have been followed also in French names on the Northern Peninsula and on the West and South Coasts of Newfoundland, except for the presence of religious names of French origin in the earliest impositions on the Northern Peninsula. Whatever the causes, which are to be found, of course, in the differing circumstances of the settlement of Newfoundland and Quebec, the paucity of French religious names in Newfoundland is in striking contrast with what amounts to a cult of religious nomenclature in Quebec.[101]

Most of the original French impositions on the AVALON PENINSULA are recognizable in the modern forms of the names, though some fifteen have become obsolete. Breton influence is less marked than on the Northern Peninsula.

English Place Names of the Seventeenth Century

The earliest place names on the AVALON PENINSULA recorded in an English form by voyagers to Newfoundland, the Haven of St John (Rut 1527),[1] St Johns and Cape Race (Parkhurst 1578),[2] and B of Conception, C St Francis and Placentia (Hayes 1583),[3] are all translations of previous impositions by the Portuguese, the Spanish and the French.[4] The first original English name, unique in a nomenclature otherwise seemingly Portuguese, is B of Bulls (Hood 1592), BAY BULLS (NTS Bay Bulls). The specific is puzzling, but may refer to a small sea-bird, the bull-bird or ice-bird, the Common Dovekie, *Plautus alle alle*, a common winter resident in Newfoundland, "occurring in countless numbers in the slob ice."[5]

Charles Leigh[6] in 1597 recorded the first of the many variants of CONCEPTION BAY, B of Assumption; Parlican, OLD PERLICAN COVE (NTS Old Perlican); and Caplen Bay, now CALVERT BAY (NTS Ferryland). Parlican or Perlican (sc. Pelican) is taken by M. F. Howley to be the bird, alleged by him to be "frequent on the coast,"[7] by G. R. F. Prowse to be a ship;[8] and it may be recalled that *The Golden Hind* in which Drake circumnavigated the globe in 1577–80 was originally called *The Pelican*. Whatever its significance, the name is noteworthy as the first known to have been recorded for a feature in TRINITY BAY.

Caplen Bay, which formerly had been usually recorded in Portuguese as R[io] das patas (Reinel c. 1504 ... Dee 1580), goose or auk river, received its new name after the caplin, "a fish much resembling Smeltes in forme and eating," as Mason described it in 1620.[9] According to *OED*, it is the same word as Fr. *capelan* or *caplan* and Span. *capelan*, though Parkhurst in 1578 in a marginal note on Smelt states that it is "Called by the Spaniards Anchovas, and by the Portugals Capelinas."[10] No less than fifteen Caplin Coves in Newfoundland to-day testify to its abundance on the coasts during its spawning season in June. The settlement of Leigh's Caplen Bay was re-named CALVERT by a proclamation of 30 January 1922, after Sir George Calvert, first baron Baltimore (1580?–1632), founder of the colony of AVALON in Newfoundland in 1621–23 and later of Maryland.

An anonymous English manuscript chart of the east coast of North America, the "Velasco" map of about 1610, contains three names of interest on the AVALON PENINSULA. The spelling S Jones, ST. JOHN'S (NTS St. John's), presumably attempts to capture a current pronunciation of the name in a form still preserved in St. Jones Within (NTS Random Island) and ST. JONES WITHOUT (NTS Sunnyside), though the latter name was first recorded by Lane only in 1775.[11] These names, with the qualifiers here denoting location inside and outside Random Sound, echo those of the twin parishes, St. John's Within and St. John's Without, of Waterford, Ireland. Agoforta, AQUAFORTE (NTS Ferryland), similarly appears to be the English phonetic version of a Portuguese name not previously recorded in this form.[12] B of Portingal, PORTUGAL COVE (NTS Trepassey), as was mentioned above,[13] probably marks the movement of the Portuguese from the proximity of the hostile French and English to less frequented fishing harbours.

With the single exception of John Cabot's naming of Newfoundland in 1497 as described by Hakluyt, there is no evidence of bestowed names on the island before 1612;[14] but in October and November of that year, John Guy, then governor of the colony at CUPIDS (NTS Harbour Grace), made a "voiadge of discoverie" from CONCEPTION BAY into TRINITY BAY and in his Journal of the voyage[15] recorded not only established names of places but also names of his own imposition. Some of the established names had been already recorded, Guy was to record others for the first time.

Of names already recorded, Guy cites bay of Conception, CONCEPTION BAY; Trinitie bay, TRINITY BAY; S. Catalinaes, Catalina (NTS Bonavista); Baccalean, BACCALIEU ISLAND (NTS Bay de Verde);[16] bay of Placentia, PLACENTIA BAY; Pernecam and Old Pernecam, OLD PERLICAN COVE (NTS Old Perlican);[17] Cape St. Lawrence, now Ferryland Head (NTS St. Lawrence); Bonaviste, Bonavista (NTS Bonavista); Renoose, RENEWS (NTS Renews);[18] Cape St Fraunces, CAPE ST. FRANCIS (NTS Pouch Cove);[19] and Cape Razo, CAPE RACE (NTS Trepassey).[20]

He is apparently the first to record Harbor de Grace, HARBOUR GRACE (NTS Harbour Grace) and the Pirates forte there;[21] Greene bay, BAY DE VERDE (NTS Bay de Verde);[22] the Grates, GRATES POINT (NTS Bay de Verde);[23] Hartes content, HEART'S CONTENT (NTS Heart's Content), possibly named after a ship;[24] an unidentified Avon "in the bay of Conception";[25] the Horselips, Horse Chops (NTS Trinity); Cape Broile, CAPE BROYLE (NTS Ferryland); Torrebay, TORBAY (NTS St. John's); great Belile, BELL ISLAND (NTS St. John's and Harbour Grace);[26] Cupers Cove, CUPIDS (NTS Harbour Grace); and Carbonera, CARBONEAR (NTS Harbour Grace).[27]

The Horselips, Horse Chops (NTS Trinity), a name found elsewhere in Newfoundland though not on the AVALON PENINSULA, usually denotes a headland resembling a horse's head. One such feature on the South Coast was known in the seventeenth century by its Breton equivalent Penmarc'h (Pensmark in Dudley 1646, Pemart in Courcelle 1675, Pesmarq in Detcheverry 1689), a transfer from the Pointe de Penmarc'h in Finistère, described by Harrisse as "une des curiosités du littoral breton."[28]

Cape Broile, CAPE BROYLE (NTS Ferryland) probably derives from broile – a confused disturbance, tumult or turmoil, or from brolle – to roar, to sound loud. The first of these interpretations is supported by the fact that "a ledge of sunken rocks extends about a cable" from CAPE BROYLE and that "On account of its complete exposure to south-easterly winds, which occasionally send in a very heavy sea, Broyle harbour is by no means recommended as an anchorage."[29]

Torrebay, TORBAY (NTS St. John's), which is recorded as Torbay in all later seventeenth century English sources except for a minor variant Tarr Bay in Robinson 1669, appears to be transferred from Torbay, Devonshire. However, a tradition touched on by Anspach, "Torbay, called in old books Thorne Bay,"[30] and given some support by Thorn(e) Bay (Blaeu c. 1630), associates the name with Robert Thorne the elder, who may have been one of the discoverers of Newfoundland.[31] M. F. Howley asserts, though without evidence, that "some of the first settlers in the place were a family of the name of Thorn, some of whose descendants are still living there."[32]

Cupers Cove, CUPIDS (NTS Harbour Grace), already recorded by Guy in 1611, may be a possessive name, a variant of the modern surname Cooper or Cowper, or of the tradesman, the maker of casks and tubs, indicative perhaps of an occupation followed there. M. F. Howley attributes the form CUPIDS to Sir William Alexander as early as 1630,[33] and Cupid's Cove occurs in "Orders sent by John Downing to the several Harbours of Newfoundland in 1677."[34] In the absence of any discernible relationship between Cupers and CUPIDS and such variants as Cupert's (Mason 1626) and Cubitts (Blathwayt c. 1630-40), the final dental consonant would appear to be intrusive.

Guy's own impositions relate to incidents and occasions on his voyage. Savage Harbour, either SPREAD EAGLE BAY (NTS Dildo) or CHAPEL ARM (NTS Dildo), was so called because "Heere we fownd some savage housen."[35] "ane harboure which now is called Alhallowes," RANTEM COVE (NTS Dildo), was entered on 31 October, All Hallow Eve, Hallowe'en.[36] "the headland which now is called 'the Elbow'" is descriptive of TICKLE HARBOUR POINT (NTS Dildo).[37] Passage harbour, COME BY CHANCE (NTS Sunnyside and Sound Island), was discovered by "a way cut into the woods, which being prosequuted, yt was fownd to lead directlie to a harborough in the bay of Placentia distant onlie two miles w, which harbour in Placentia Bay is now called 'Passage harbour'."[38] Flagstaffe Harbour, GREAT MOSQUITO COVE (NTS Sunnyside), was so called because "we fownd theare the flagstaffe [set up a few days previously] throwen by the savages away."[39] Truce sound, BULL ARM (NTS Sunnyside), celebrated the exchange of gifts between Guy's party and the "savages," described in the incidents of 6 November.[40]

None of Guy's impositions has survived the years, but the later names which superseded Guy's are not lacking in interest.

SPREAD EAGLE BAY (NTS Dildo), one of the two bays which may be identified with Guy's Savage Harbour, is a descriptive name, apparently first recorded by Jukes in 1840. Chapel Bay (Lane *Directions* 1775, 1810), now CHAPEL ARM (NTS Dildo), the alternative, may be an incident name from a nautical term *to chapel*, current in the eighteenth century: "*Chapeling a ship*, the act of turning her round in a light breeze of wind when ... close hauled, so as that she will lie the same way as she did before. This is commonly occasioned by the negligence of the steersman, or by a sudden change of wind."[41]

The specific in Rantem Cove (Imray 1862), Rantom Cove (Murray 1868), RANTEM COVE (NTS Dildo) is probably the same as in Random Head Harbour, Random Island and Random Sound (NTS Random Sound) with a variant of the final unstressed syllable, perhaps to be associated with, for example, *rantum-scantum*[42] – ?disorderly; *rant* – drink and riot, both as noun and verb; *randy* – any noisy fun, a boisterous spree;[43] and *randan* – riotous or disorderly behaviour, a spree.[44]

The use of *randan* is illustrated in the following extract from an account of festivities on the Labrador in the latter years of the nineteenth century:

Nor did the banquet end there; the committee in charge had a few bottles of stimulant hidden away, so the executive decided to have another night on the "randans" and clean up all the cakes and remaining stimulants.[45]

Rantem, then, may refer to some such incident or, by metaphor, be descriptive of turbulent weather or sea.

TICKLE HARBOUR POINT (NTS Dildo) is a shift name from Tickle Harbour ("Blathwayt" c. 1630–40), "in the south corner of Tickle Bay, at the entrance of a salt water lake, ... protected by a small islet and a reef of rocks. The entrance [-the Tickle-] is only a cable wide and is not more than 4 feet deep at low water."[46] Cartwright defines tickle, which occurs frequently in Newfoundland both as generic and specific, as "A passage between the continent and an island, or between two islands, when it is of no great width."[47]

COME BY CHANCE (NTS Sunnyside and Sound Island) is first recorded as Comby Chance in a despatch of 13 September 1706 from Major Lloyd, an officer prominent in the defence of Newfoundland against the French between 1703 and 1708, to ? Mr Secretary Hedges, which relates to a clash between the English and the French:

About 9 dayes since, I with 30 soldiers pursued a party of French of 21, who had plundered several inhabitants of Trinity Bay and carried yᵉ same to a place called Comby Chance in Plasintia Bay, where I overtook them ...[48]

A current tradition has it that the harbour was found "by chance" by fishermen in PLACENTIA BAY seeking shelter, but the likelihood of its being come upon unexpectedly by an overland route such as Guy followed is perhaps not to be discounted.

GREAT MOSQUITO COVE (NTS Sunnyside) does not seem to be recorded before Jukes 1842 in the form Mosquito Cove.[49]

BULL ARM (NTS Sunnyside) is B Bulls or some similar form from Southwood 1675 to about 1900, when it acquired the generic Arm. The specific may have the same value as in BAY BULLS (NTS Bay Bulls), the bull-bird.[50]

A second colonist in Newfoundland to provide a document of importance in the development of the nomenclature is Captain John Mason (?1586–1635),[51] governor of the colony founded by John Guy at CUPIDS[52] (NTS Harbour Grace) from 1615 to 1621, whose map, *Insula olim vocata Noua: Terrae. The Iland called of olde: Newfound Land*, prepared about 1620, was subsequently published in Sir William

Vaughan's *Cambrensium Caroleia* in 1625 and with some variants in Vaughan's *The Golden Fleece* of 1626.[53]

A lengthy Latin legend on the map recites the progress of colonization on the AVALON PENINSULA from Sir Humphrey Gilbert's Letters Patent of 1578 to the concession to the London and Bristol Company, Guy's colony, of 1610; to the purchase of land south of a line from PETTY HARBOUR (NTS Bay Bulls) to PLACENTIA BAY by Vaughan from the London and Bristol Company in 1616; and to Vaughan's subsequent sales of parts of his territory, first to Lord Falkland, who received a piece six miles wide between RENEWS (NTS Ferryland) and somewhat south of FERRYLAND (NTS Ferryland) and extending to PLACENTIA BAY, and then to Lord Baltimore, who received the remaining northern portion of Vaughan's land. Vaughan's own settlement was established at TREPASSEY[54] (NTS Trepassey).

The map, which has North at the bottom, is remarkable for a numerous older nomenclature, but its chief interest lies in those names on the AVALON PENINSULA associated with Vaughan and his contemporary colonists.

On the North Shore of TRINITY BAY is Lord Falkland's territory North Falkla[n]d, so called to distinguish it from the strip bought from Vaughan, South Falkland. None of the names known to Guy in TRINITY BAY is recorded, and only Belile, BELL ISLAND (NTS St. John's and Harbour Grace), Bristolshope, BRISTOL'S HOPE (NTS Harbour Grace) and Cupert's cove, CUPIDS (NTS Harbour Grace), in CONCEPTION BAY.[55] But the east coast of the Peninsula has twelve established names from CAPE ST. FRANCIS (NTS Pouch Cove) to CAPE RACE (NTS Trepassey), and the south coast has Trepassa, TREPASSEY (NTS Trepassey), C de pene, CAPE PINE (NTS St. Shotts), Bay S Maries, ST. MARY'S BAY, Fretum Placentiae, PLACENTIA BAY, and Placentia harbour, PLACENTIA (NTS Placentia).

Names first recorded by Mason are Bristolshope; Aualonia, with the ascription "Sr George Calvert Lord Baltimor de Baltimor"; South Falkland; and furthest south Cambriola – Little Wales or Little Britain, as that part of the south coast of the Peninsula was known to Bonnycastle as late as 1842,[56] the area of Vaughan's own settlement. Within Cambriola are a number of subsidiary names, mostly Welsh county names, undoubtedly transferred from South Wales by Vaughan himself. Between Formosa, FERMEUSE (NTS Renews), and Rhenus, RENEWS (NTS Renews), is Golden Groue, after the family seat of the Vaughans, an early Tudor mansion in the Vale of Tywi, near Llandeilo, Carmarthenshire.[57] Between a prominent hill, the Butter pots, BUTTER POT (NTS Biscay Bay River), and CAPE RACE (NTS Trepassey) are Vaughan's Coue, ?CAPPAHAY-

DEN (NTS Renews), Cardiffe and Glamorgan. Within TREPASSEY BAY is Colchos – ? the ethnic or adjectival form of Colchis, whence Jason recovered the Golden Fleece – a name symbolic of Vaughan's hopes for his colony and anticipating the title of his book, *The Golden Fleece ... Transported from Cambrioll Colchos, out of the Southermost Part of the Iland, commonly called the Newfoundland*; at the head of ST. MARY'S BAY, Carmarthe[n]; and on the southeast coast of PLACENTIA BAY, Pembrok[e], Cardigan and Brechonia (Brecknockshire).

To say with Howley that Vaughan "had a craze for new and fancy names for places,"[58] or to suggest with Prowse that the names imposed by the colonists were "fantastic"[59] is to do Vaughan and his fellow venturers less than justice. New his names may have been, but only Colchos and Cambriola in any degree qualify for the epithets "fancy" and "fantastic," and they are fanciful only in so far as such other latinized place names like Nova Scotia, Virginia and Hispaniola – common enough in an age not without classical learning and now accepted without question – may also be so styled. Three of the names first recorded by Mason have survived.

BRISTOL'S HOPE (NTS Harbour Grace) was a sub-settlement of John Guy's main settlement at CUPIDS (NTS Harbour Grace),[60] but the date and circumstances of its establishment are obscure. Estimates of the date vary from one to eight years after 1610. D. W. Prowse asserts that it was an offshoot of Guy's colony at HARBOUR GRACE; M. F. Howley and J. D. Rogers identify it with HARBOUR GRACE, Howley adding that Guy "endeavoured but unsuccessfully to oust the name of HARBOUR GRACE by substituting BRISTOL'S HOPE"; but Anthony à Wood, writing at the end of the seventeenth century, states that between 1620 and 1627 Robert Hayman was appointed "governor of the plantation of Harbor-Grace in Bristol-hope in Britaniola, anciently called Newfoundland,"[61] which suggests that HARBOUR GRACE was a subsidiary of BRISTOL'S HOPE. The historians, however, do not appear to have seen any significance in the element Hope, a generic with the meaning "valley" in a number of English place names, but also defined as "A piece of enclosed land e.g. in the midst of fens or marshes or of waste land generally" and as "An inlet, small bay, haven."[62] This last definition may be applied accurately to BRISTOL'S HOPE (a cove) in comparison with HARBOUR GRACE (a bay), and suggests that HARBOUR GRACE may originally have been Bristow *tout court* or "the Bristow Plantation," as in Wynne's letter of 17 August 1622 to Secretary Calvert,[63] and BRISTOL'S HOPE a nearby, lesser feature which gave its name to a settlement later than and distinct from Bristow or HARBOUR GRACE.

The transfer of the specific from Bristol, the merchants of which had joined with those of London in financing the venture of the London and Bristol Company, and of which Guy was an alderman, was not limited to this settlement. LONG COVE (NTS Trepassey) was formerly Bristoll Cove (Southwood 1675) and is still known locally as Bristy Cove, and another Brista Cove (not in NTS) is found on BACCALIEU ISLAND (NTS Bay De Verde). But the name of Guy's settlement was short-lived, to be replaced by Muscita – mosquito, as early as Blathwayt c. 1630–40, until BRISTOL'S HOPE was revived, first as the name of the cove as in Adm. 296 1868 (1929 edition), and afterwards, by a proclamation of 16 August 1910, as the official name of the settlement.

There seems no doubt that Mosquito as a specific refers to what Whitbourne called "a very little nimble Fly (the least of all other Flies),"[64] though Howley, in an uncommonly wild flight of toponymical fancy, ascribes it to the supposed presence of a "company of Musketeers here, as I have supposed the Carbineers to have been at Carbonear"![65] Despite Howley's rejection of a derivation from the "little nimble Fly," Mosquito occurs as a primary specific in at least five other localities in Newfoundland where there is no suggestion that musketeers were ever stationed, and the Basque Ulycillho – mosquito (Detcheverry 1689, the name of a harbour north of Cape Ray (NTS Port aux Basques), is interpreted as "trou à mouches, c'était un port infesté de moustiques."[66]

According to a seventeenth century biographer, Lord Baltimore, a devout Catholic, "obtained a charter for ... [his] colony under the name of the province of Avalon, so called in imitation of old Avalon in Somersetshire, where Glastonbury stands, the first-fruits of christianity in Britain, as the other was in that part of America,"[67] the allusion being to the foundation of the abbey of Glastonbury by Joseph of Arimathea, the leader of a group of disciples sent by St. Philip to convert the British. Historians have differed about the precise limits of Baltimore's colony, but the name seems to be that of the whole AVALON PENINSULA by Robinson 1669, which bears the inscription "The Province of Avalonia."[68]

BUTTER POT or Butter Pots, a name which appears in three places on the Peninsula (NTS Biscay Bay River, Bay Bulls and Holyrood), is applied to prominent, round-headed hills, two of which (NTS Biscay Bay River and Holyrood), according to Jukes in 1842, were popularly confused with each other:

> At each end of this range is a remarkable hummocky hill called the Butter pots; and so little is the country penetrated or known, that it is a common

belief ... that the Butter pots of Renews [NTS Biscay Bay River] is the same hill with the Butterpots of Holyrood, whence their common name. They are distant about twenty miles from each other, and ... neither can be seen from the summit of the other.[69]

In the absence of a lexical, or any other, citation for *butter pot*, M. F. Howley's deduction from *butter pat* is tempting: "The rounded peaks bear some resemblance to pats of butter. Hence the name Butter Pats given to them by the fishermen. It has been corrupted into Butter Pots!"[70] But he is apparently unaware of the antiquity of the name in the form in which it has survived and disregards its threefold occurrence.

In addition to three new French names, the Blathwayt map, c. 1630–40,[71] contains a number of new English names of minor features on the AVALON PENINSULA, of which TICKLE HARBOUR and COLLIERS have been discussed in other contexts.[72]

Samon Coue, SALMON COVE (NTS Holyrood), appears to have been applied originally to the whole of what is now GASTERS BAY,[73] later, as in Imray 1873, to the southwest arm of the bay, and most recently to the bight at the entrance to the bay. As early as Robinson 1669, a qualifier was added to the name, S[ou]t[h] Salmon Cove, to distinguish it from SALMON COVE (Heart's Content); and the settlements in these coves were similarly distinguished in the nineteenth century as Salmon Cove South and Salmon Cove North (Adm. 296 1868 or later). About 1906, however, the settlement at Salmon Cove (South) was re-named AVONDALE (NTS Holyrood) and the neighbouring community at Cats' Cove (*Population Returns* 1836), by a proclamation of 18 June 1906, became officially Avondale North, only to have its name changed again within a few months, it seems, to CONCEPTION HARBOUR (NTS Holyrood). A conjecture that AVONDALE is a transfer name from Avondale, Co. Wicklow, Ireland, near the scene of "The Meeting of the Waters" of Moore's *Irish Melodies*, receives confirmation in a document of 1891 which reveals yet another, if shortlived, name for the settlement, "Avoca (formerly Salmon Cove)."[74]

The origin of Hollyrude, HOLYROOD BAY (NTS Holyrood), is obscure. The absence of an earlier citation, in English or any other language, probably rules out the likelihood of its being a religious, commemorative name, unlike HOLYROOD BAY (NTS St. Mary's);[75] but a transfer from Holyrood House in Edinburgh is perhaps not implausible in view of John Mason's Scottish associates in the 1620s.[76]

Welles I, later Groy I (Robinson 1669)[77] and KELLY'S ISLAND (NTS Harbour Grace) (Lane, *Directions* 1775, 1810), is probably a possessive name, with the specific Kelly's either a mistake name for Welles or a new imposition. Local traditions associate the name with a seventeenth-century pirate, Captain Kelly, whose residence is said to have been on the mainland opposite to the island at Kelly's Grove, whence allegedly KELLIGREWS (NTS Harbour Grace).[78] KELLIGREWS, Killigrews (Wix 1836), a shift name for the settlement from Kelligrews Head (Lane 1774), KELLIGREWS POINT (NTS Harbour Grace), however, is more likely to be a possessive family name derived from a manor in Cornwall;[79] and another tradition alleges that a family of Kelligrews at PORT DE GRAVE (NTS Harbour Grace), whence Kelligrews Hill at that place, either settled permanently or had a summer plantation at KELLIGREWS for the shore fishery. A John Kelligrew died (? at ST. JOHN'S) on 9 April 1853.[80]

Flatt Rock, at FLAT ROCK POINT (NTS St. John's), is descriptive of one of the most noticeable features of the coast north of ST. JOHN'S: "Along the south side of this little cove, the thick red sandstone dips at a slight angle towards the sea, forming a long, smooth, sloping pavement, whence the name of the place."[81]

The four remaining new names in Blathwayt are all on the SOUTHERN SHORE.

Witless, WITLESS BAY (NTS Bay Bulls), according to G. R. F. Prowse,[82] is a name to be associated with an English survey of South Newfoundland, which he believed took place in 1497–8, and commemorates the Feast of the Holy Innocents, 28 December. Objections to this theory are that there is no proof that such a survey was ever conducted; that the name is not recorded before Blathwayt; and that *OED* does not cite Witless in this context. M. F. Howley considers the name "a corruption of Whittle's Bay, either from the name of a man, or from the prevalence of the shrub or osier which grows abundantly in our woods, the *viburnum nudum*, known in England as the withe-rod, and called by the West Countrymen wit-rod or wittle."[83] In support of the first of these conjectures, it may be noted that Whittle is an English family name particularly associated with Dorsetshire[84] and that the specific is cited as Witles (Yonge 1664), Whitley's, a settlement (*CSP* 1682), Whittles (Hack c. 1690?) and Witles (Fitzhugh 1693). Whittle is a family name current in various parts of Newfoundland to-day, from which WITLESS HEAD (NTS Argentia) in PLACENTIA SOUND also seems to be derived. WITHROD POND (NTS St. John's) affords limited support of the second conjecture. A third possibility is that Witless – crazy, lunatic, is used metaphorically of the seas: "Witless bay ... is open to south-eastward, and in every part too much exposed to southeasterly gales to be recommended as an anchorage."[85]

Presumptive reference to the exposed nature of the harbours on the SOUTHERN SHORE is found not only in CAPE BROYLE (NTS Ferryland)[86] and WITLESS BAY but also in Moueable B, MOBILE BAY (NTS Ferryland), which, too, is "exposed to south-eastward; [and] hence is safe only in summer, or while the wind is from the land."[87] The form MOBILE has not been found before *Population Returns 1836*, earlier forms being Mummable (Robinson 1669), Momable (Seller c. 1671), Momables (Southwood 1675), Movable (Thornton 1689A) and Mummale (Hack c. 1690?) which, with other variants, persisted until Momables (Imray 1862). Howley in 1908 has Moble.[88] Momable may be either a frequentative form of the English dialect verb and noun mumble or momble – jumble,[89] descriptive of a rough, confused sea, or a transfer from The Mumbles, a rocky peninsula near Swansea.

C Ballard, CAPE BALLARD (NTS Renews) may have been transferred from Cape Ballard near Poole, Dorsetshire, or it may be a possessive from the English family name associated especially with Worcestershire,[90] derived from M.E. *ballard* – a bald-headed man;[91] and "Cape Ballard ... has a bare round summit."[92] BALD HEAD for a similar feature is found in Seller c. 1671 (NTS Renews), Lane, *Directions 1775, 1810* (NTS Sunnyside) and *Newfoundland and Labrador Pilot 1951* (NTS Argentia). However, *ballard* is not cited in *OED* after 1485, and the name may be another descriptive, Bollard (Yonge 1663), Bollards (Howley 1909) – a round-headed post in a ship or on a dock for fastening ropes. G. R. F. Prowse associates the name with a seventh-century saint Baldred.[93]

Cro Iland, CROW ISLAND (NTS Ferryland), may have been a haunt of ravens rather than of crows.

The Journal of James Yonge (1647–1721),[94] a Plymouth doctor who as ship's surgeon with the West Country fishing fleet visited Newfoundland in 1663, 1664, 1669, and 1670, presents a unique view of Newfoundland and the fishery, and introduces in the text and in the maps which illustrate it a number of new place names. It is a matter of regret that Yonge's intention of leaving "figures" of all the harbours he had visited was unfulfilled, since his maps of FERRYLAND (NTS Ferryland), RENEWS and FERMEUSE (NTS Renews) contain a more detailed nomenclature than is to be found in any previous document.[95]

A new name on the SOUTHERN SHORE is Glam Cove, CLAM COVE (NTS Trepassey), "a little kind of harbour where the Renoose [RENEWS] boats, when put to leeward, use to shelter."[96] It is the outlet of a small stream which "swarms with clams."[97] Sir Joseph Banks describes, and notes the importance of, clams in his *Journal*, 1 June 1776:

specimens of shell fish call'd here Glams [are] of peculiar use in the fishery as the fishermen depend upon them for their baits in their first voyage to the Banks. At that time of the year the fish feed upon them & every fish they take has a number of them in his stomach which the fishermen take out & with them bait for others. The fish itself is remarkable as it is far too large for the shell which is so little adapted to cover its inhabitant that even when the fish is taken out, the sides will not close together.

In 1664, Yonge first described THE SPOUT (NTS Bay Bulls):

We intended for ST. JOHNS but the wind not permitting us, we bore away for BAY BULLS, and past by Spout Cove, lying between PETTY HARBOUR and BAY BULLS. It's a hollow rock, into which the sea squeezing in waves, the water and air spout out at a great hole that is over it, and make a noise, to be heard 2 or 3 mile and seen as many leagues.

"Here," he continues, "my father was cast away, about 20 years since. It was in the night, and the cliffs are steep and inaccessable. It pleased God that one nimble fellow climbed up, and carrying a line, drew up a rope, which he fastened to a tree, they all climbed up by it and were saved."[98]

A feature described briefly by Yonge in 1669, the Sugar Loaf, SUGARLOAF HEAD (NTS St. John's), "a high headland between ST. JOHN'S and TORBAY, resembling a sugar loaf,"[99] bears a name of considerable antiquity and of wide incidence in many parts of the world. It occurs on the AVALON PENINSULA at SUGARLOAF HEAD (NTS St. John's); SUGARLOAF (NTS Heart's Content), a headland; SUGARLOAF HILL and POINT (NTS Argentia); and SUGARLOAF PEAK (NTS Ship Cove), and in several other localities in Newfoundland, denoting, as elsewhere, a conical or conoidal hill or mountain, named after the shape in which crystallized sugar was commonly prepared for sale until well into the nineteenth century. The cone was usually wrapped in blue paper. The earliest citation of the word in *OED* is of 1422; "the oldest known reference to an orographic feature occurs in Richard Eden, *The Decades of the newe worlde or West India in 1555*: 'Teneriffa is a great hyghe pike lyke a sugar lofe.' "[100]

The specific in Cuckold's head, CUCKOLD HEAD (NTS St. John's), mentioned by Yonge in 1669, is found elsewhere in Newfoundland and also off the coast of Maine. The headland near ST. JOHN'S is described as "a round bare hill in the form of a hay-cock"[101] and as appearing "conical from seawards";[102] off the coast of Maine, however, The Cuckolds is the name of a different kind of feature, a ledge with a low flat surface.[103] No satisfactory explanation has been found for the name in either use. M. F. Howley suggests with reservations that Cuckold may be the fish "somewhat like the Bream ... common in our waters."[104]

Other possibilities are that it is another fish, the sculpin, also common around the shores of Newfoundland, the horns of which may perhaps be seen as conical; or that CUCKOLD COVE and HEAD are transfers from Cuckhold's Haven and Point on the Thames below Greenwich;[105] or that it is a changed survival of the sixteenth-century Portuguese name contalian or contaliam, last recorded as Conta Lion ("Velasco" 1610), for which, too, no meaning has been ascertained.[106]

"A list of the Planters and Interlopers" at ST. JOHN'S in 1669[107] includes a number of names subsequently identified with stages or coves in ST. JOHN'S HARBOUR: Mr Downing[108] – Downings (Visscher c. 1680), Goodman Bennet – Bennets (Thornton 1689B), Mr Furze – Mrs Fursey (Visscher c. 1680), and Mr. Dennis Loany – Dins Loneys (Visscher c. 1680).

Yonge's map of FERRYLAND[109] (NTS Ferryland) naturally includes the established major names in the vicinity, but it also has a number of minor names: Back side – the cove on the southern side of the peninsula which ends in Ferryland head, FERRYLAND HEAD, as distinguished from FERRYLAND HARBOUR on the northern side; Lady Kirk – a house on the peninsula;[110] Gull Iland – ? GOOSE ISLAND, though the bigger feature, BOIS ISLAND, is not named; North side – of FERRYLAND HARBOUR; barren Hill – rising behind the head of FERRYLAND HARBOUR; and Riverhead, now CALVERT, in Caplen Bay, CALVERT BAY (NTS Ferryland).

Riverhead is a name repeated by Yonge in RENEWS HARBOUR (NTS Renews), by Thornton 1689B in ST. JOHN'S HARBOUR (NTS St. John's), by Thornton 1689D in BAY BULLS (NTS Bay Bulls), and also found at HARBOUR GRACE (NTS Harbour Grace) and ST. MARY'S HARBOUR (NTS St. Mary's). In Newfoundland usage it denotes the mouth of a river (in English usage the source), at the place where it enters what again in Newfoundland usage is indiscriminately and contradictorily called the head or bottom of a harbour.

The map of Renooze,[111] RENEWS HARBOUR (NTS Renews), includes several minor names, not all recorded in NTS: Bever Pond; South Side; South poynt, now RENEWS HEAD; Riverhead; Amborals [Admiral's] Place; mo[unt] Faulcon; and Biscayn cove.

The map of Firmose,[112] FERMEUSE HARBOUR (NTS Renews), has Clowns cove – ? with the specific a possessive, though Clown does not seem to be a family name, repeated in Clounes Cove (Southwood 1675), CLOWNS COVE (NTS Heart's Content); Viceadmiralls place, now KINGMANS COVE (NTS Renews); northside; Amboralls [admiral's] place, now ADMIRAL'S COVE (NTS Renews); and clear-cove, here placed within FERMEUSE HARBOUR, though NTS shows CLEAR COVE on the northern side of the peninsula which ends in NORTHERN HEAD (NTS Renews). Clear may be descriptive, though M. F. Howley cites a tradition that it is a family name.¹¹³

Yonge's Biscayn cove – ? the cove frequented by the Basques, is the earliest recording of three such names. The second, BISCAY B[AY] (NTS Trepassey), is a contemporary recording in Southwood 1675; the third, Biscan Cove (*Population Returns* 1836), BISCAYNE BAY (NTS Pouch Cove), is first recorded much later. All three are probably survivals of French Basque interest in the Newfoundland fishery on the east coast before 1600; two of them, Yonge's Biscayn cove at RENEWS and Southwood's BISCAY B[AY] near TREPASSEY, are certainly in the close vicinity of harbours named by the French.¹¹⁴

Amborals Place in RENEWS HARBOUR and Amboralls¹¹⁵ place and Viceadmiralls place in FERMEUSE HARBOUR present the earliest references in place names to the rule of the Fishing Admirals in the harbours of Newfoundland, an old custom first described and regulated by the so-called First Western Charter of 1634, which was amplified in *An Act to Encourage the Trade to Newfoundland* of 1699:

> Fowerthly that accordinge to the aunciente custom everie Shipp or ffisher that first entreth a Harbour in behalf of the shipp, bee Admirall of the said Harbour wherein for the time beinge hee shall reserve only so much Beach and fflakes or both as is needefull for the number of Boates that he shall vse with an overplus only for one Boate more then hee needeth as a priviledge for his first cominge, And that everie Shipp cominge after, content himself wth what he shall have necessarie vse for, without keepinge or deteyninge any more, to the preiudice of others next cominge, And that any that are possessed of severall places in severall Harbours with intent to keepe them all before they can resolve upon wch of them to choose, shalbe bound to resolve, and send advise to such after comers in those places as expect his resolucon, And that w^thin forty eight howers if the weather so serve, that the said after comers may likewise choose their places, and so none receiue p^ruyduce by others delayes.¹¹⁶

> IV. And be it further enacted by the Authority aforesaid, That (according to the ancient Custom there used) every such Fishing Ship from England, Wales, or Berwick, of such Fishermen as shall, from and after the said twenty-fifth day of March, first enter any Harbour or Creek in Newfoundland, in Behalf of his Ship, shall be Admiral of the said Harbour or Creek during that Fishing Season, and for that Time shall reserve to himself only so much Beech or Flakes, or both, as are needful for the number of such Boats as he shall there use, with an Overplus only for the Use of one Boat more than he needs, as a Privilege for his first coming thither; and that the Master of every such second Fishing Ship, as shall enter any such Harbour or Creek shall be Vice Admiral of such Harbour or Creek during that Fishing Season; and that the Master of every such Fishing Ship next coming, as shall enter any such Harbour or Creek, shall be Rear Admiral of such Harbour or Creek during that Fishing Season; and that the master of every Fishing Ship there,

shall content himself with such Beech or Flakes, as he shall have necessary Use for, without keeping or detaining any more Beech or Flakes, to the Prejudice of any such other Ship or Vessell as shall arrive there; and that such Person or Persons as are possessed of several Places in several Harbours or Creeks there, shall make his or their Election of such Place as he or they shall choose to abide in; and shall also, within eight and forty Hours after any After-comer or After-comers into such Place or Places shall demand such his or their Resolution touching such his or their Election (if the Weather will so soon permit, or so soon after as the Weather will permit) give or send his or their Resolution to such After-comer or After-comers touching such his or their Election of such Place as he or they shall so choose to abide in for the Fishing Season, to the End that such After-comer or After-comers may likewise choose his or their Place or Places of his or their Abode there; and in case any Difference shall arise touching the said Matters, the Admirals of the respective Harbours where such Differences shall arise, or any two of them, shall Proportion the Place to the several Ships; in the several Harbours they fish in, according to the Number of Boats which each of the said Ships shall keep.[117]

Other place names containing the specific Admiral and presumably referring to the rule of the Admirals are Admiral Cove (NTS Grand Bank), Admiral Island (NTS Trinity), ADMIRALS BEACH (Lane 1773) (NTS Placentia) and ADMIRAL'S COVE (NTS Ferryland) in CAPE BROYLE HARBOUR. The rule, notorious for its many abuses,[118] was gradually superseded by the authority of the surrogates and naval governors in the first half of the eighteenth century.

Robinson 1669, which contains fewer new English place names than French,[119] records Little Pernocan, NEW PERLICAN (NTS Heart's Content); Cove Refused, ? the cove at NEW MELBOURNE (NTS Old Perlican), a name indicative of the inhospitable nature of the coast in this area; Greene Bay, now WESTERN BAY (NTS Heart's Content); Blackhead, BLACKHEAD (NTS Heart's Content), the first of some half dozen headlands on the AVALON PENINSULA to be so called; Trinity, midway between BLACKHEAD and CARBONEAR (NTS Harbour Grace), probably misplaced from Trinity (NTS Trinity), though Trinity also occurs in its correct position; Fromes, an unidentified feature, ? GREENLAND (NTS Harbour Grace), between PORT DE GRAVE (NTS Harbour Grace) and CUPIDS (NTS Harbour Grace), from the West Country family and place name, Fromes, of Dorset, Herefordshire and Somerset;[120] and Mistaken Point, MISTAKEN POINT (NTS Trepassey).

Greene or Green Bay now WESTERN BAY (NTS Heart's Content), (not to be confused with BAY DE VERDE (NTS Bay de Verde), called Greene bay by Guy 1612), was in common use until Lane 1774 and the cartographers of the nineteenth century generally gave the alternatives

The Province of Avalonia by R. Robinson (1669)

Reproduced by kind permission of the Keeper of
Western Manuscripts, Bodleian Library, Oxford, from
MS Rawlinson A. 183 fol. 101.

The French trading to and from Plasentia Bay

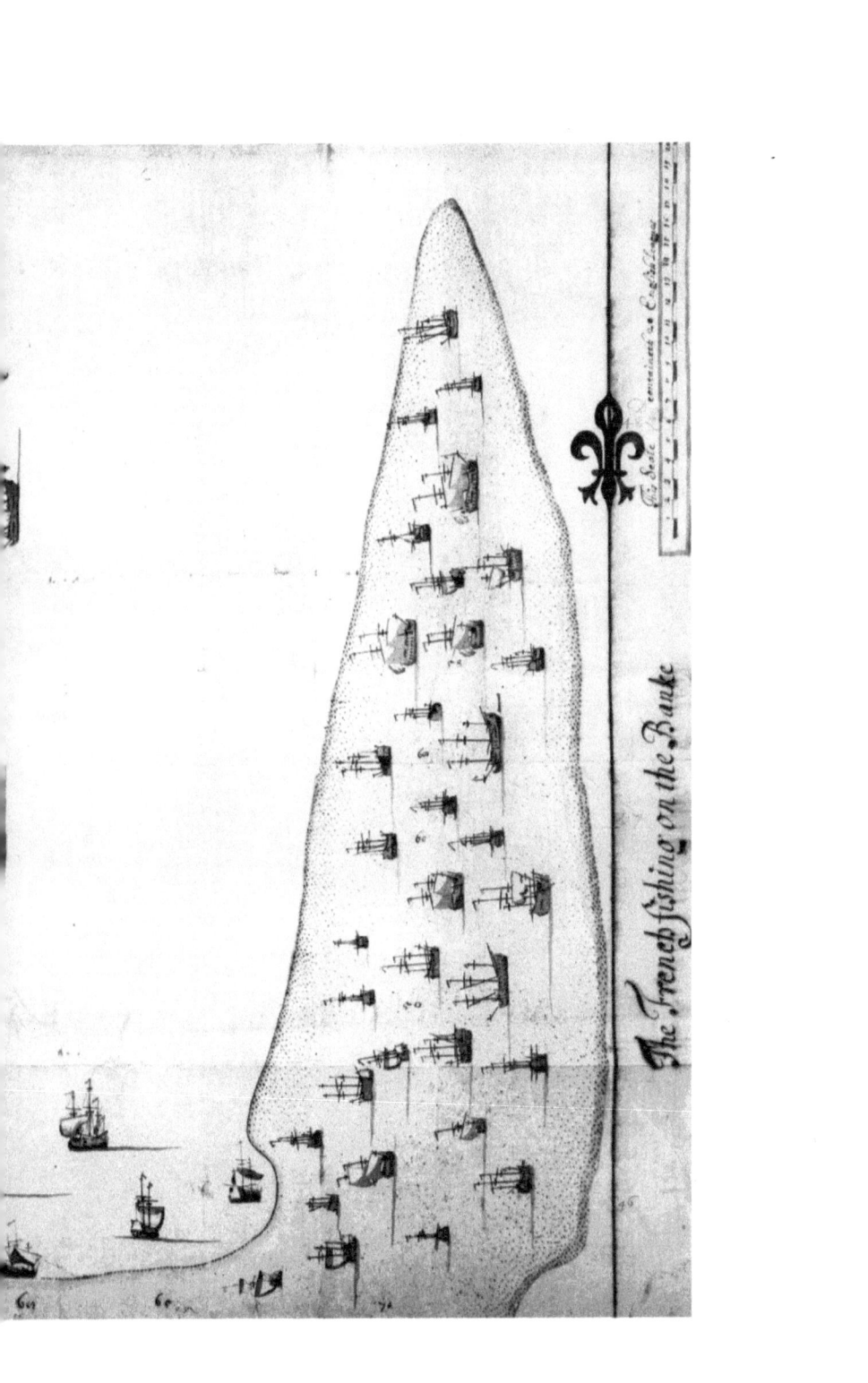

Green or Western Bay, ? since the bay is west of CAPE ST. FRANCIS (NTS Pouch Cove). In modern nomenclature, Western has completely ousted Green.

From Robinson 1669 to Cook 1763, cartographers recorded only one MISTAKEN POINT; thereafter they tended to name two points, French Mistaken Point and Mistaken or English Mistaken Point, for, in Anspach's words, "[two leagues] from this cape [RACE], to the westward, are two *points*, frequently *mistaken* for Cape-Race by mariners, when they first make the land from the southward."[121] However, modern cartographers no longer make the distinction and the tradition behind the names appears to be lost. Harrisse tentatively identified MISTAKEN POINT with Ponta del pa[drao] ("Oliveriana" 1505–8), the P de crux (Maggiolo 1527); it may even have been the original CAPE RACE (NTS Trepassey).[122]

The two maps of John Seller, of 1671 and c. 1671, add names of a number of minor features, especially on the SOUTHERN SHORE. Fres[h]- water Cove (Seller c. 1671), unnamed in NTS, lies between THE SPOUT (NTS Bay Bulls) and BULL HEAD (NTS Bay Bulls). Freshwater occurs at least eight times as a specific in names on the AVALON PENINSULA, signifying a source of fresh water for ships. Cook's Journals of the *Grenville*, 1764–7,[123] for instance, record frequent landings to replenish stores of wood and water and to brew, and repetition of the name is indicative of the importance of supplies of fresh water for small vessels with limited storage. Further south are Gul Isl (Seller c. 1671), GULL ISLAND (NTS Bay Bulls); Goose Isl (Seller c. 1671), GREAT ISLAND (NTS Ferryland), probably the de los patas of Santa Cruz 1545;[124] and C Neddick (Seller c. 1671), CAPE NEDDICK (NTS Ferryland), described in the *English Pilot. The Fourth Book* 1689 as "a high Point, flat at top, and streight down to the water." The Newfoundland English *nuddick* is "A hillock, generally with a level top of sufficient space for a house or small garden,"[125] from, or the same as, the English dialect word *niddick* – the "back of the neck, the nape; occasionally the back of the head; the whole head or skull."[126] Still further south are Bald head (Seller c. 1671), BALD HEAD (NTS Renews), and Bears coue (Seller c. 1671) and Sleepers Point (Seller 1671), now ?BEAR COVE HEAD (NTS Renews). Sleeper may be the English family name;[127] the presence of bears in Newfoundland had been noted as early as 1549.[128]

Split Point (Seller 1671), SPLIT POINT (NTS Bay de Verde), the southern extremity of the tip of BAY DE VERDE PENINSULA, "is named from the natural formation of the land which shows a great cleft or fissure."[129] Deadmans Bay (Seller 1671), DEADMANS BAY (NTS St. John's), and Deadmans point (Seller c. 1671), now ?CLIFF POINT (NTS St. John's), were so called from "several Men and Boats [being] formerly lost in that Bay" (*English Pilot. The Fourth Book* 1689). Crow Isl (Seller c. 1671) is Groy I (Robinson 1669), now KELLYS ISLAND (NTS Harbour Grace).[130] Black head (Seller c. 1671) at 47–45, 52–42 is now BLACK HEAD NORTH (NTS Pouch Cove), having received the qualifier to distinguish it from BLACK HEAD (*English Pilot, The Fourth Book* 1689) at 47–31, 52–39 (NTS St. John's).

Henry Southwood's maps of the east coast of Newfoundland, 1675, "The Coast of Newfoundland from Salmon Cove to Cape Bonavista" and "The Coast of Newfoundland from Cape Raze to Cape St. Francis," contain a numerous nomenclature with several new names which is repeated in Thornton 1689 with some additions,[131] in L'Hermite 1695 with some of Southwood's names translated into French,[132] and in Blaise Vion 1699 whose translations are notorious for their mangling of the original.[133]

The specific in Gorlob pt, GARLEP POINT (NTS Heart's Content), appears to be a prosthetic formation from C Orlop, with the initial letter of Cape misread as G and orlop – the lowest deck of a ship which covers the hold, giving the meaning of ? an overhanging cliff. The many variations of the specific – Corlab (Visscher c. 1680), Gorblob (Fitzhugh 1693), Garbab (after Moll 1711), Garbel (Popple 1733), Gortol (Bellin 1754), Garblo (Mount and Page 1755), Gorlot (Lotter c. 1758), and Gorlet (Kitchin 1762) – would seem to indicate that the cartographers found it unfamiliar and puzzling. With this interpretation, Point is tautological.

Smutty nose pt, now JEANS HEAD (NTS Heart's Content), is probably named after the sea-bird, the Smutty-nose Shearwater, now known as the Sooty Shearwater, *Puffinus griseus* (Gmelin).[134] The modern name, JEANS HEAD, was in use by Imray 1873.[135]

Sille Cove at Sugar loaf, now WINTERTON COVE (NTS Heart's Content), Scilly Cove in Popple 1733 and Kitchin 1762, may be a transfer from the Scilly Islands or a Cornish place name mentioned by Jonathan Couch in his *History of Polperro*: "We have a scoop in the cliff called Scilly Cove and Scilly Cove drang."[136] The change of the name of the settlement at Scilly Cove to WINTERTON, proclaimed on 13 August 1912, was made, not only in commemoration of Sir James S. Winter (1845–1911), Prime Minister of Newfoundland from 1898 to 1900, but also, it is alleged, in deference to the susceptibilities of its inhabitants.

Red head, RED HEAD (NTS St. John's), "of a deep red colour, and prominent,"[137] and Little red head, RED CLIFF HEAD (NTS St. John's), "formed of bold, steep, reddish cliffs,"[138] are descriptives in contrast with BLACK HEAD NORTH (Seller c. 1671) (NTS Pouch Cove).

The specific in Logy B, LOGY BAY (NTS St. John's), may mean "dull and heavy in motion or thought," a common Newfoundland usage illustrated by Captain R. A. ("Bob") Bartlett: "The radiator was so hot and my wet clothing so drenched with brine that the odor was terrific. I felt a little logy myself."[139] Kipling in *Captains Courageous* uses logy substantively of a heavy fish and M. F. Howley reports a tradition that "the fish caught at this cove are generally of a very large size and heavy weight."[140] But *OED* describes logy as of uncertain origin, limits its use to the United States and gives a first citation for 1859, nearly two hundred years later than Southwood's. In the circumstances, a more satisfactory interpretation of logy may be found by deriving it from the Cornish *lugh-ogo*, literally a cave-calf and hence a seal, giving the meaning Seal Cove. Logo Rock in Falmouth Harbour is believed to have the same origin.[141]

Small p., SMALL POINT at 47-36, 52-39 (NTS St. John's), is in contrast with the neighbouring SUGARLOAF HEAD (NTS St. John's). Freshwater B., FRESHWATER BAY (NTS St. John's), is Southwood's new English imposition for the bay previously recorded as Frinouse (Champlain 1612 ... Blaeu 1662).[142] He also has a second Freshwater B., FRESHWATER BAY (NTS Ferryland), and a third, now SEAL COVE (NTS Renews).

Among new names on the SOUTHERN SHORE, Southwood has Bull head, BULL HEAD (NTS Bay Bulls), a shift name from BAY BULLS; Whaleback,[143] which also anticipates the modern citation in *OED*; and Todes Cove, now TORS COVE (NTS Ferryland), ? from the English dialect word tod(e) – fox, of which the most likely interpretation is that it is a changed shift name from Foxes Island (*English Pilot. The Fourth Book* 1689), FOX ISLAND (NTS Ferryland), offshore. The name of the settlement was changed to TOR'S COVE by a proclamation of 18 January 1910, according to M. F. Howley in the mistaken belief that Tor(r)'s was the original specific and for its more pleasing connotations, though others maintain that Tors refers to the twin peaks there.[144]

Southwood's recording of Old Harry (not in NTS), "a rock with a depth of 2 fathoms over it ... half a mile eastward of NORTH POINT,"[145] CAPE BROYLE (NTS Ferryland), appears to be the first of at least six such impositions on the east and south coasts of Newfoundland, commonly for sunken rocks and shoals, though once for a pinnacle rock. The name appears as Old Harry, Old Harry Rock and Old Harry Shoals, and in one context with Young Harry.[146] It is probably a transfer from Old Harry, a sea-stack off the coast of Dorset south of Poole.

74 / *Place Names of the Avalon Peninsula*

OED does not give a citation for this usage of the familiar name of the devil. A variant is LONG HARRY, found at BELL ISLAND (NTS St. John's) and HARBOUR GRACE (NTS Harbour Grace), the latter in Thornton 1689c.

Other names on the SOUTHERN SHORE are Stone I., STONE ISLANDS (NTS Ferryland), Black head, BLACK HEAD (NTS Renews), Freshwater B., now SEAL COVE (NTS Renews),[147] and Chaine Cove, now CHANCE COVE (NTS Biscay Bay River). In the absence of a more satisfactory derivation, Chaine may perhaps be an anglicized form of the French family name Chêne or one of its variants, often from a place name, which occurs in the English family names Cheyney, Cheyne etc.[148] Chain Cove is found commonly as late as Purdy 1814 and is superseded permanently by CHANCE COVE only with Jukes 1840.

Beyond CAPE RACE, Southwood has Cripple Cove, CRIPPLE COVE (NTS Trepassey), probably a shift name from Cripple Rock, a small sunken pinnacle rock off CRIPPLE ROCK POINT;[149] Bristoll Cove, now LONG COVE (NTS Trepassey);[150] Biscay B., BISCAY BAY (NTS Trepassey);[151] and Powles, POWLES HEAD (NTS Trepassey) – [Saint] Paul, a commemorative name which occurs in early maps of the Atlantic and Newfoundland in various linguistic forms and different locations and refers to a cape, a bay and islands.[152]

In CONCEPTION BAY, Southwood records Clounes Cove, CLOWNS COVE (NTS Heart's Content);[153] Crokers Cove, CROCKERS COVE (NTS Harbour Grace); Carboner I., CARBONEAR ISLAND (NTS Harbour Grace);[154] Bryant's Cove, BRYANT'S COVE (NTS Harbour Grace); No[rth] Point, now COOPERS HEAD at SPANIARD'S BAY (NTS Harbour Grace); and Burat, i.e. Burnt head, BURNT POINT (NTS Harbour Grace), "so called, by reason the Trees that were on it are burnt down" (*English Pilot. The Fourth Book* 1689).

Crocker, an English family name especially associated with Devonshire and Dorsetshire,[155] is apparently one of the oldest family names still extant in Newfoundland, notably at VICTORIA, HEART'S CONTENT, HEART'S DELIGHT (all NTS Heart's Content) and GREEN HARBOUR (NTS Dildo). The forms Croker and Crocker are apparently analogous to ST. JONES and ST. JOHN'S.[156] Bryant is also a West Country name, common in Somerset and Wiltshire.[157]

Southwood was also the author of "A True Description of the Course and Distances of the Capes, Bayes, Coves, Ports, and Harbours in New-found-land; with Directions how to Sail in or out of any Port or Place between Cape Race and Cape Bonavista. By Henry Southwood", apparently compiled in 1675, which appeared in all editions of *The English Pilot. The Fourth Book*, from the first in 1689 to the last in 1794. It contains short commentaries on some of the places mentioned and adds six new names, including another shift name at RENEWS, Renowes-Point, now RENEWS HEAD (NTS Renews).

Southwood describes Shoe-Cove, SHOE COVE (NTS Pouch Cove), as a place "where Boats use to come a Tilting ... that is to split and salt the Fish they catch, and blowing hard and bad weather, cannot get to the places they belong to in time." More precisely "a Tilting" would mean to erect a tilt – a shelter or shack, as the word is found in Guy's *Journal*, 6 November 1612: "They [the Indians] had made a Tilte with a Sayle, that they got from some Christian."[158] Tilt occurs as an element in place names in various parts of Newfoundland, including TILT HILL GULLY (NTS Harbour Grace). The specific in SHOE COVE may be descriptive, although in the nineteenth century SHOE COVE was confused with BISCAYNE BAY (NTS Pouch Cove)[159] some four miles northeastward, as in Imray 1873: "a little inlet named Biscayne (and also Shoe) cove."[160]

Greens-Cove, or Green Cove (Mount and Page 1755, Imray 1862, 1873), which is not named in modern documents, is a small cove on the northwestern side of TORBAY (NTS St. John's), "the customary place where vessels anchor."[161] According to M.F. Howley, it takes its name from "a natural green sward [which] clothes the top over-hanging the sea."[162]

Black-Cove, "a cove ... on the East-side of Bay Verds Head," BAY DE VERDE HEAD (NTS Bay de Verde), is also not named in modern documents but is known locally as Back or Backside Cove, that is, the Cove "behind" BAY DE VERDE.

Sheeps Cove, now SHIP COVE (NTS Harbour Grace), is probably the Rock Cove of a document of 1755,[163] recorded as Sheep's or Ship Cove in Imray 1862. Although it is dismissed as "a little inlet but indifferently sheltered from eastward by [BLOW ME DOWN] head" (Imray 1873), some look on it as the best harbour in BAY DE GRAVE, a view which may account for its modern name.

Sherwink Point, SKERWINK POINT (NTS Old Perlican), occurs as Skerwick Pt (Mount and Page 1755), and Sherwick Pt (Cook 1763, Cook and Lane 1770 [1775]A and Imray 1862). The name is repeated in Skerwink Head (NTS Trinity). For G. R. F. Prowse, Skirwink was a Yorkshire name associated with FLAMBRO HEAD (NTS Bay de Verde) and ROBIN HOOD BAY (NTS St. John's and Trinity), from a supposed Yorkshire survey of Newfoundland undertaken in 1498;[164] but a first recording of the name as late as 1689 (or 1675) lends support to a conjectural derivation from either skirwink – to pare off turf for burning, an obsolete Devon dialect word,[165] or scurwink – a kind of sea-bird, a shearwater, also known as the haigdown or hagdown.[166]

None of the cartographers of the last quarter of the seventeenth century adds as many names to the nomenclature as Southwood, though all make contributions of some interest.

Hack ?1677 records Salvage, SALVAGE POINT (NTS Old Perlican), a name which is repeated in Salvage (Thornton 1689c), SALVAGE ROCK (NTS Harbour Grace);[167] Flambro head, FLAMBRO HEAD (NTS Bay de Verde);[168] Pt Verte, probably a mistake name for Southwood's Burnt head, BURNT POINT (NTS Harbour Grace); and Red head, now ? SCULPINS POINT (NTS St. John's), a recent imposition. SCULPINS POINT and LITTLE RED HEAD (Southwood 1675) appear to have been confused by cartographers from time to time.

Visscher c. 1680 records a number of new names in different parts of the AVALON PENINSULA. In TRINITY BAY are Break Hart P, BREAKHEART POINT (NTS Bay de Verde),[169] and Sciruy, i.e. Scurvy I, a small group unnamed in NTS but marked at 48–09, 52–58 (NTS Bay de Verde). Scurvy I.[170] denotes a feature covered with seaweed, kelp and shells, and persists until Imray 1862; but in Imray 1873 it becomes Sgeir islet or island, with *sgeir* the Gaelic form of *skerry*, a word in the Orkney dialect meaning "a rugged insulated sea-rock or stretch of rocks, covered by the sea at high water or in stormy weather."[171] The current local name is THE SKERRIES, found also in SKERRYS BIGHT (NTS St. John's). The imposition of Sgeir may perhaps be attributed to Admiralty surveyors who conducted a survey of the East Coast of Newfoundland between 1862 and 1871,[172] but the circumstances of the popular adoption of the anglicized form of this strangely exotic word are unknown.

On the NORTH SHORE of CONCEPTION BAY, Visscher has So[uth] W[est] Coue, now ?ADAMS COVE (NTS Heart's Content), the first important cove southwest of WESTERN BAY, and in PLACENTIA BAY Trinty, TRINNY COVE (NTS Argentia). From Lane 1772 to Imray 1873 the latter name is recorded as Tinny, but Howley 1911 has Trinny,[173] and Trinty and Trinny as ? syncopated forms of Trinity seem to support the local tradition that the cove was named after TRINITY BAY.

Visscher's most interesting additions to the nomenclature, however, are in ST. JOHN'S HARBOUR: No[rth] Ford, i.e. North Fort, a "Block-house on Signal Hill" (Lane, *Directions* 1775, 1810); One a Clock, Virginia and Magotts Cove, coves on the north side of the entrance to the harbour; Downings, Oxon, Oxfords, Hot Ioyner, Mrs Fursey, Dins Loneys, coves or stages, also on the north side but further in the harbour; and Ring, "a small Bay" (*English Pilot. The Fourth Book* 1689) on the south side, opposite to Virginia and One a Clock.

Of these names, Downings, Mrs Fursey and Dins Loneys are associated with planters known to Yonge.[174] Magotts Cove, now MAGGOTTY

COVE, appears from its form to be a possessive from the English family name Maggot,[175] though local tradition sees it as a descriptive from the fish refuse thrown into the cove. The name also occurs at BAY BULLS (NTS Bay Bulls) and elsewhere in Newfoundland and in MAGGOTTY POINT (NTS St. Mary's). One a Clock is a transfer name from a rock in the harbour, one O Clock Rock (Cook 1762 or Gilbert 1768), or vice versa, presumably a name of undetermined relative position. Virginia may have historical associations of some antiquity. Oxon and Oxfords, apparently designating different locations, Hot Ioyner, Hopping Joyner (Thornton 1689B), and Ring, Ring noone (Thornton 1689B), are not readily explicable. The last citation of Ring, as Ring-noon, is in the *English Pilot. The Fourth Book* 1716; One a Clock (the cove), Virginia, Downings, Oxon, Oxfords, Hot Ioyner, Mrs Fursey, Dins Loneys are in Mount and Page 1755.

John Thornton's *Trading Part of Newfoundland*, Thornton 1689B, contains only two new names on the Peninsula outside ST. JOHN'S. Clip Boney, ? LOW POINT (NTS Bay de Verde), is repeated as Chipbony in the *English Pilot. The Fourth Book* 1716 and copied in successive editions, after which it disappears from the records, except to reappear in part as a settlement name in Boney Brook (*Census* 1857), and in a local expression, still current, "to go for a walk over the Boney (or Bonny)." No meaning has been found for either Clip Boney or Chipbony. C[ape] Bay, now SPEAR BAY (NTS St. John's), had been recorded in the sixteenth century as Riuo de la spera ("Oliveriana" 1505–8), but Thornton first gave it an English name which persisted until at least as late as Imray 1873. In ST. JOHN'S HARBOUR and its vicinity, however, he adds Wash Ballocks, Bennets, Riverhead and So[uth] Forte to the names recorded by Visscher c. 1680.

Wash Ballocks, Wash-ball Rocks (Lane, *Directions* 1775, 1810) and Imray 1862, Wash-balls (Imray 1873 and *NP* 1952), lie one cable north-northeastward of NORTH HEAD (NTS St. John's).

Bennets, Bonnells (Mount and Page 1755), marks a stage apparently named after the planter, Goodman Bennet, who was known to Yonge in 1669.[176]

So[uth] Forte, ? the "Southside Castle" described by D. W. Prowse as "a substantial stone fort with a wooden block-house,"[177] was presumably erected as an additional defence to the harbour to complement the North Fort recorded in Visscher c. 1680.

Riverhead marks the head (or bottom) of ST. JOHN'S HARBOUR, where what is now called WATERFORD RIVER (NTS St. John's) enters the harbour.

Thornton also recorded three other new names on the Peninsula in his plan of BAY BULLS (NTS Bay Bulls), Thornton 1689D: Riverhead,[178] a name now obsolete in that locality, Bread and Cheese point and Joan Clays hill.

The specific in BREAD AND CHEESE POINT (NTS Bay Bulls) is repeated in the old name of BISHOP'S COVE (NTS Harbour Grace), still heard locally in popular usage and preserved in the shift name BREAD AND CHEESE COVE POND (NTS Harbour Grace). Lane recorded Bread and Cheese Islands, now Bread Island (NTS Harbour Buffett) in 1772 and Bread and Cheese Cove at BAY BULLS, a shift name from Thornton's Bread and Cheese Point, in 1773. Jukes 1840 also recorded Bread and Cheese (Hill) at the head of CALVERT BAY (NTS Ferryland). OED cites Bread and Cheese as "a child's name for the young leaves of the Hawthorn, the Wood-Sorrel or 'Cuckoo-bread,' and one or two other plants," which are plucked and eaten by children. Hawthorn and wood-sorrel are not indigenous to Newfoundland; but Bread and Cheese trees, believed to be cultivated hawthorn imported from Europe, are known in HARBOUR GRACE.[179] Children used to, and probably still do, eat the leaves.

Joan Clays hill, Ironclay hill (Imray 1873), JONCLAY HILL (NTS Bay Bulls), may similarly be a botanical name, changed from either the obsolete, rare juncary – land overgrown with rushes, cited uniquely in 1613 in OED, or Fr. *jonchaie* – rush-bed, ? after rushes growing in marshy land at the foot of the hill.

Chart 1, "Newfoundland, in Hack's *A Description of Coasts Islands &c. in the North Sea of America vizt Newfoundland* c. 1690? contains fifty-three place names previously recorded but no new names; Chart 2, *Terra Nova Pars*," adds one new name, Mary Gally Rock or the Griffith, ? MOLL ROCK, (NP 1952), a name later shifted to Pt. Moll (Lane 1772), MOLL POINT (NTS Argentia). Neither of Hack's names is explicable unless Mary Gally either derives from the anglicization of a unique combination of Fr. *morue* – cod and *galet* – pebble, ? rock, to form an unusual name, Morue Galet – cod rock, for which no analogue has been found, or, perhaps more likely, is a ship name. However, the specific of the later form, MOLL ROCK, is a common anglicization of the older alternative pronunciation of *morue* – *molue*.[180]

The nomenclature of Fitzhugh's manuscript map of 1693 which, according to Harrisse,[181] was intended specially to show the fishing districts exploited by the English, is numerous from CAPE RACE (NTS Trepassey) to Bonavista and contains no less than ninety-two names on the AVALON PENINSULA. The fact that, apart from Fourt, i.e. Fort, in BAY BULLS (NTS Bay Bulls), none is new may be taken as indicative that by

Seventeenth Century English Place Names / 79

the end of the seventeenth century all the major and many minor coastal features and settlements on the Peninsula had been designated.

The extent of settlement on the Peninsula at the end of the century is summarized in the *Journal* kept by the abbé Jean Beaudoin, who accompanied d'Iberville's expedition to Newfoundland in 1696–7.[182] No less interesting than his statistics of the soldiers and inhabitants at the settlements captured are his attempts to reproduce the names of the settlements in phonetic spelling. The names are identified in the last column of the following table:[183]

TABLE 3

ENGLISH SETTLEMENTS IN NEWFOUNDLAND
CAPTURED IN D'IBERVILLE'S EXPEDITION 1696–7

East coast	Soldiers	Inhabitants	Modern name
Rognouze (Rognousse p. 42)	120	7	RENEWS (NTS Renews)
Fremouse	40	7	FERMEUSE (NTS Renews)
Aigueforte	25	4	AQUAFORTE (NTS Ferryland)
Forillon	108	12	FERRYLAND (NTS Ferryland)
Caplan baye	12	2	Caplin Bay now CALVERT (NTS Ferryland)
Cap reüil	5	1	CAPE BROYLE (NTS Ferryland)
Brigue	15	3	BRIGUS SOUTH (NTS Ferryland)
Tothcove	30	3	Toads Cove now TORS COVE (NTS Ferryland)
Ouit lis baye	15	2	WITLESS BAY (NTS Bay Bulls)
Baye-Boulle			BAY BULLS (NTS Bay Bulls)
Le petit havre	80	14	PETTY HARBOUR (NTS Bay Bulls)
Saint-Jean	300	59	ST. JOHN'S (NTS St. John's)
Quirividi	40	9	QUIDI VIDI (NTS St. John's)
Conception Bay	Soldiers	Inhabitants	Modern name
Portugal-Cove	25	3	PORTUGAL COVE (NTS St. John's)
Havre vieu	12	1	? HARBOUR MAIN (NTS Holyrood)
Baye Quinscove	11	2	BACON COVE (NTS Holyrood)
Brige	70	11	BRIGUS (NTS Harbour Grace)
Port Grave	116	14	PORT DE GRAVE (NTS Harbour Grace)
Haylinscove	18	3	UPPER ISLAND COVE (NTS Harbour Grace)
Baye robert	10	3	BAY ROBERTS (NTS Harbour Grace)
Brianscove	30	4	BRYANT'S COVE (NTS Harbour Grace)
Havre-de-grâce	100	14	HARBOUR GRACE (NTS Harbour Grace)
Mousquit	35	3	BRISTOL'S HOPE (NTS Harbour Grace)

TABLE 3 (concluded)

Conception Bay	Soldiers	Inhabitants	Modern name
Carbonnière	220	22	CARBONEAR (NTS Harbour Grace)
Croquescove	30	4	CROCKERS COVE (NTS Harbour Grace)
Kelinscove	22	3	CLOWNS COVE (NTS Heart's Content)
Fraische oüatre	20	2	FRESHWATER (NTS Heart's Content)
Baye Ver	85	14	BAY DE VERDE (NTS Bay de Verde)
South coast of TRINITY BAY	Soldiers	Inhabitants	Modern name
Le vieux Perlican	130	19	OLD PERLICAN (NTS Old Perlican)
Lance arbre (Anse Arbe p. 57)	30	4	HANTS HARBOUR (NTS Old Perlican)
Celicove	40	4	Scilly Cove now WINTERTON (NTS Heart's Content)
New Perlican	60	9	NEW PERLICAN (NTS Heart's Content)
Havre-Content	20	4	HEART'S CONTENT (NTS Heart's Content)

Other features and settlements on the Peninsula mentioned elsewhere in the *Journal* are Plaisance (p. 38), PLACENTIA (NTS Placentia); baie de la Conception (p. 39), CONCEPTION BAY; Torbaye, TORBAY (NTS St. John's); cap Saint-Francois (p. 50), CAPE ST. FRANCIS (NTS Pouch Cove); l'isle de Carbonnière (p. 53), CARBONEAR ISLAND (NTS Harbour Grace); Saumon-Cove (p. 55), SALMON COVE (NTS Heart's Content); Baye de la Trinité (p. 60), TRINITY BAY; Baye-Boulle, "havre qui est au fond de la baie de la Trinité" (p. 60), BULL ARM (NTS Sunnyside). On the north coast of TRINITY BAY are Arcisse (p. 69), Heart's Ease Inlet (NTS Random Island) and La Trinité (p. 69), Trinity (NTS Trinity).

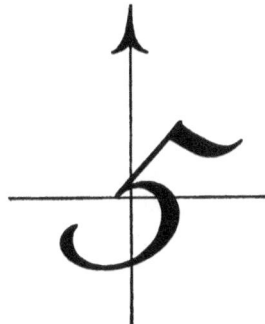

English Place Names of the Eighteenth Century

The recording of new place names on the AVALON PENINSULA proceeded but sluggishly until 1733, after which, for some forty years indeed, it seems to have ceased entirely. Only with the detailed surveys of the coasts of Newfoundland in the 1760s and 1770s by James Cook and Michael Lane and their associates, and especially with those of PLACENTIA BAY, from POINT LANCE to CAPE SPEAR, and from CAPE SPEAR to BACCALIEU ISLAND by Lane in 1772, 1773 and 1774, were significant additions made.[1]

A Chart Shewing Part of the Sea Coast of Newfoundland From ye Bay of Bulls to little Placentia exactly and Carefully lay'd down by John Gaudy Anno 1715, which first appeared in the English Pilot. The Fourth Book 1716, adds the shift name Renewes I., RENEWS ISLAND (NTS Renews); Black head, now SHOAL POINT (NTS St. Shotts); Sailing Cove, a name obsolete after the survey of TREPASSEY HARBOUR by either Cook in 1762 or Gilbert in 1768,[2] denoting a feature on the western shore of TREPASSEY BAY between BAKER HEAD (NTS Trepassey) and CAPE PINE (NTS St. Shotts); the first English citation of BULL AND COW [ROCKS] (NTS St. Bride's);[3] and the Virgins Rocks, VIRGIN ROCKS (Adm. 2915 1864), and Giberalter Rocks, GIBRALTAR ROCK (Adm. 2915 1864), which lie southwesterly of POINT VERDE (NTS Ship Cove). The VIRGIN ROCKS were probably named arbitrarily (the Newfoundland Pilot has ten features bearing the specific Virgin), though the name may have religious significance and date from the early French occupation of PLACENTIA. GIBRALTAR ROCK, however, doubtless commemorates the capture of Gibraltar by the British in 1704.

"An order by Commodore Cayley, *Dover*, at St. John's, 11th Oct. 1723, that John Masters and Phill. Wattson are to be allowed to prosecute their salmon fishery on Great and Little Salmonier ... Rivers,"[4] SALMONIER RIVER (NTS St. Catherine's) and LITTLE SALMONIER RIVER (NTS Placentia), introduces a specific which does not find a place in the dictionaries and does not seem to occur outside Newfoundland as a place name. It is composed of English salmon and what was originally a French suffix, later anglicized, -ier, to denote an occupation, a salmon-fisher. It is accented like bombardier and cavalier. The qualifier Great is replaced by Grand in a document of 1724.[5] A unique citation is in George Cartwright's *A Journal of Transactions and Events ... on the Coast of Labrador*, 13 July 1770: "When the Salmoniers visited their nets this morning, they found that the Indians had stolen our fleet."[6] By an oversight, perhaps, Cartwright omitted the word from the Glossary in the *Journal*. Salmonier occurs as a shift name at SALMONIER POINT (NTS Placentia) and in the names of a number of features on the South Coast of Newfoundland. The settlement, Great Salmon River (*Population Returns* 1836) is now ST. CATHERINE'S (NTS St. Catherine's).

Henry Popple's *A Map of the British Empire in America*, 1733, though rich in new names on the South Coast of Newfoundland, adds only three on the AVALON PENINSULA: Ship Harbour, SHIP HARBOUR (NTS Argentia), Marquess H[arbour],[7] MARQUISE (not in NTS Argentia), and Basin Cove, ? BURNT COVE (NTS Ferryland).

In contrast with Cook's later extensive surveys of the West and South Coasts of Newfoundland from 1764 to 1767, which made considerable additions to the nomenclature, his early limited surveys of PLACENTIA, the chart of which alone bears his name, and of TREPASSEY, ST. MARY'S, FERRYLAND, CARBONEAR and HARBOUR GRACE, and ST. JOHN'S, added little. All were conducted in 1762 unless, indeed, the last five were not the work of Gilbert in 1768.[8]

The Road and Harbour of Placentia adds Signal Hill, SIGNAL HILL (NTS Argentia), once used as "a place for signalling the approach of vessels";[9] Freshwater Bay, FRESHWATER COVE (NTS Argentia); Castle Hill, CASTLE HILL (NTS Argentia), where "a fort was erected by the French during their occupation of Newfoundland";[10] New Fort and Old Fort, the latter on what was later to be called TOWN POINT (Murray 1868)

(NTS Placentia), on the south side of the entrance to PLACENTIA HARBOUR, the former on the north side; Seven Islands, SEVEN ISLANDS (NTS Argentia) in the harbour; South East Arm, SOUTHEAST ARM (NTS Placentia); and a Block House.[11]

The Harbour of Trepassey with Mutton and Biscay Bays distinguishes a North West Arm and a North East Arm of TREPASSEY HARBOUR, and names Portland Point, now PORTUGAL POINT (NTS Trepassey). Portland here, like Portland Cove (NTS Portland Creek) on the West Coast of Newfoundland, named by Cook in 1767, is doubtless a transfer from Portland, the "peninsula or 'island' on the coast of Dorsetshire."[12]

St. Mary's Harbour first names the settlement at St. Mary's, ST. MARY'S (NTS St. Mary's); distinguishes North East Arm; names Browns Pond, now COOTE POND (NTS St. Mary's), and Ellis Point, now by metathesis LIZZY POINT (NTS St. Mary's);[13] and records Pt le Hays, LA HAYE POINT (NTS St. Mary's), a common French family or place name, which may have been an older imposition.

St. John's Harbour adds Signal Hill, SIGNAL HILL (NTS St. John's), North Head, NORTH HEAD (NTS St. John's), and South Head, SOUTH HEAD (NTS St. John's), at the entrance to the harbour; one O'Clock Rock,[14] Gibet Hill, The Old Fort, Kings Wharf and a Church on the north side; a Hospital and Watering Place at Riverhead;[15] a second Kings Wharf in the same area; and Stop Rock, ? now CAHILL POINT (NTS St. John's), and Chain Rock on the south side, though the modern CHAIN ROCK (NTS St. John's) is nearer the north side and the entrance to the harbour.

Gibet Hill is presumably not to be confused with the Gallows Hill whither it was suggested in a resolution of 1759 that the gallows should be removed from the site intended for a new church, ? the Church in the chart, near the present Anglican cathedral.[16] The Old Fort is that proposed by Sir Robert Robinson in 1680, destroyed by the French in 1697, and rebuilt between 1698 and 1708. The name Fort William appears to be first cited in 1708 in Charlevoix's account of the capture of ST. JOHN'S by the French in the same year;[17] it may date from 1702, the year of the death of William III, or somewhat earlier. Lane, *Directions*, 1775, 1810 refers to "the Old Garrison, called also Fort William." The Newfoundland Hotel was built on the site of the fort in 1926. CHAIN ROCK derives its name from one of the defences of the harbour prepared in 1705: "For better security of the harbour of St. John's a boom and chain has been placed at the entrance of the harbour on representation to Her Majesty."[18]

Carboniere and Harbour Grace adds Crockers Point, CROCKERS POINT

(NTS Harbour Grace), a shift name from CROCKERS COVE,[19] Bears Cove, BEARS COVE (NTS Harbour Grace), and Ships Head, SHIP HEAD (NTS Harbour Grace).

The Harbours of Ferryland and Aquafort with Caplin Bay adds only Freshwater Bay, now LANCE COVE (NTS Ferryland).

Cook's *A Sketch of the Island of Newfoundland Done from the latest Observations*, 1763, also adds only one new name on the Peninsula, Pt. Lance, POINT LANCE (NTS St. Bride's), ? descriptive of the long low promontory. The point, at the western extremity of ST. MARY'S BAY, was to mark a convenient *terminus ad quem* and *a quo* for Lane's surveys of PLACENTIA BAY and of the coasts from POINT LANCE to CAPE SPEAR.

Of the twelve new names recorded by Lane in *A Chart of Placentia Bay*, 1772, Point Roche, ROCHE POINT (NTS Argentia), and Point Latina, LATINE POINT (NTS Argentia), and the shift names Fox Harbour, FOX HARBOUR (NTS Argentia), Placentia Sound, PLACENTIA SOUND (NTS Argentia), and Pt. Moll, MOLL POINT (NTS Argentia), have been considered previously.[20] Lane also first records the generic in the form Keys at St. Mary's Keys, ST. MARY'S CAYS (*Newfoundland Pilot* 1952), the two small rocks about six and a half miles southward of CAPE ST. MARY'S (NTS St. Bride's).

Great South Harbour, GREAT SOUTHERN HARBOUR (NTS Sunnyside), and Little South Harbour, LITTLE SOUTHERN HARBOUR (NTS Dildo), form a cluster named in relation to North Harbour (NTS Sound Island). Little Harbour, LITTLE HARBOUR (NTS Dildo), appears to be a simple descriptive.

Pinchgut, GREAT PINCHGUT (NTS Dildo), denotes one who stints himself or others of food and is found as a sailor's word for a miserly purser.[21] Yonge in 1662 had an early reference to pinchgut money – pay received to compensate sailors for a short allowance of food.[22] Famishgut, now FAIR HAVEN (NTS Dildo), seems to have been imposed as a variation of, or companion name to, Pinchgut. Both names may refer to a period when Lane's crew was on short rations.

The name of the settlement at Famishgut, first recorded by Wix in 1836, was successively bowdlerized to become first Famish Cove, as in the Census of 1874, and eventually the euphonious, if not strictly exact, FAIR HAVEN, by a Proclamation of 29 June 1940. Shift names associated with Famishgut have also been changed, to FAIR HAVEN ISLAND (NTS Dildo) and FAIR HAVEN POINT (NTS Dildo), except that the Admiralty, conservative and not given to making concessions to squeamishness, still resolutely retains the vigorous, blunt old name.[23]

An attempt to refine the name PINCHGUT TICKLE (NTS Placentia) in ST. MARY'S BAY, first recorded in Admiralty Chart 2915, ?1864, and apparently descriptive of either the narrowness of the tickle as a whole or particularly of its extremities, came to nothing as M. F. Howley relates:

> The Rev. Dr O'Reilly's cultured ears were offended by this unpleasant name so he re-christened it Assumption Passage after the Religious Mystery of the Assumption of the Virgin. A rather amusing corruption crept in which somewhat spoiled the aesthetic idea of the learned clergyman for the people began to call it Consumption Passage, getting back somewhat to its original nomenclature.[24]

The same malapropism occurred for CONCEPTION BAY as early as Hood 1592 and persisted at least as late as Thornton 1689A.

Another attempt to remove the offensive Gut was partially successful in the change of the name of the settlement Turk's Gut to MARYVALE (NTS Holyrood), by a Proclamation of 7 November 1919; but the cove itself, TURKS GUT (NTS Harbour Grace), and a pond in the vicinity, TURKS GUT LONG POND (NTS Holyrood), have resisted the change and preserve not only Gut but also the memory of Turkish (or Barbary) pirates ravaging the coasts of Newfoundland in the seventeenth century.[25]

Ram Islands, now IONA ISLANDS (NTS Argentia), form two groups in which the old name is preserved, "Upper Ram and Lower Ram. The former and southern group consists of MERCHANT, KING, HOLE IN THE WALL, and BURKE ISLANDS; the latter and northern group consists of HARBOUR ISLAND, North and East Green islets [NORTH GREEN ISLAND and EAST GREEN ISLAND] and several other low islets and rocks."[26] M. F. Howley believed that Ram was "probably a corruption of the French Ramea," derived from *rameau* – bushy, adding that "the name was frequently given by the French, as our Englishmen were fond of Bushy or Woody Island, &c."[27] However, the possibility that Ram, like other names imposed by Lane, is a nautical term meaning "A solid point or beak projecting from the bows of a war-vessel, and enabling it to ram and batter in the side of an opponent," perhaps should not be overlooked, though the earliest citation of this usage in *OED* is as late as 1865. The appearance of HOLE IN THE WALL ISLAND may support this interpretation. However, the possibility that Ram is a transfer name should not be overlooked.

The renaming of the islands about 1911 is ascribed by Howley to the Rev. Father St. John, either "in view of the striking resemblance of the group to the more celebrated one on the west coast of Scotland ... or in compliment to the family of the Bruces who inhabit these islands, and who may have reminded Father St. John of the royal line of Scottish kings who lie buried beneath the sod on those distant 'isles of the West.' "[27]

Shalloway Pt, SHALLOWAY POINT (NTS Argentia), contains a specific not recorded in *OED* but described by D. W. Prowse:

> The fishing boats in the cod and seal fishery were formerly called shallops and shalloways ... The shallop was a large boat, decked at both ends and open in the centre, with moveable deck-boards and pounds; there were cuddies both fore and aft where the fishermen could sleep ... . The shalloways were open boats, what are now called punts.[28]

The name seems to suggest a boat for use in shallow waters. Lounsbury states that they were in use with shallops and sloops in the Bank Fishery after 1713.[29] Lane also records a Shalloway Island (NTS St. Lawrence and Marystown) in Burin Bay on this chart, and the name occurs elsewhere on the AVALON PENINSULA and in other parts of Newfoundland.

The results of Lane's second major survey in 1773, which added some fifty names to the previously known nomenclature, are recorded in the *Chart of Part of the Coast of Newfoundland, from Point Lance to Cape Spear*, with insets of four important areas, and *Directions* to accompany the chart. The survey was the most comprehensive of any part of the AVALON PENINSULA undertaken up to this time, equalled in its thoroughness only by Cook's surveys of the West and South Coasts of Newfoundland. Most of the newly recorded names are in ST. MARY'S BAY.

Some have been considered previously in other contexts: Branch, BRANCH COVE (NTS St. Mary's), and Branch Head, BRANCH HEAD (NTS St. Mary's);[30] the shift name L. Colinet Isld., LITTLE COLINET ISLAND (NTS Placentia);[31] G. Barrysway, BIG BARACHOIS (NTS Placentia), and L. Barrysway, LITTLE BARACHOIS (NTS Placentia);[32] Tickles, TICKLES (NTS Placentia), the settlement on PINCHGUT TICKLE;[33] Admirals Beach, ADMIRALS BEACH (NTS Placentia);[34] Frapeau Pt., FRAPEAU POINT (NTS St. Marys);[35] Cape English, CAPE ENGLISH (NTS St. Mary's), the first recording in English of the name that originated in a French form with de Courcelle in 1675;[36] Hollyrood, HOLYROOD BAY (NTS St. Mary's),[37] and the shift name Holly Rood Pond, HOLYROOD POND (NTS St. Mary's); St. Shotts, ST. SHOTTS COVE (NTS St. Shotts), and St. Shores, ST. SHORES COVE (NTS St. Shotts);[38] C Freels, CAPE FREELS (NTS St. Shotts);[39] the shift name Chain Cove Head, now CHANCE COVE HEAD (NTS Renews);[40] The Keys, THE KEYS (NTS Bay Bulls), now the name of a settlement;[41] and Magotty Cove, MAGGOTTY COVE (NTS Bay Bulls).[42]

Frequently the new names are commonplace and obvious requiring little comment, but a few, such as Mall Bay, Double Road Point and

Cold East Point, are more remarkable. The names as given below follow the course of Lane's survey from POINT LANCE to CAPE SPEAR.

Red Head, RED HEAD (NTS St. Mary's), derives its name from the red Brigus formation of the rock.

Hares Ears, HARE'S EARS (NTS St. Mary's and also NTS Ferryland), is a descriptive which occurs in at least seven localities in Newfoundland to describe two steep, adjacent, pinnacle-like rocks, standing offshore. *OED* does not record this meaning. M. F. Howley notes a local pronunciation, Hazures ?[heI'ʒUrz].[48]

Green Pt. now EAST HEAD (NTS St. Mary's) of JIGGING COVE, is descriptive.

Cape Dog, CAPE DOG (NTS Placentia), and Dog Bay, DOG COVE (NTS Placentia), may be either descriptive or incident names.

North Harbour, NORTH HARBOUR (NTS Placentia), is the northern arm of ST. MARY'S BAY. The name also occurs (NTS Sound Island) in PLACENTIA BAY. Little Harbour, LITTLE HARBOUR (NTS St. Catherine's), in SALMONIER ARM, also repeats the name in PLACENTIA BAY.

Muscle Pond Cove, MUSSEL POND COVE (NTS Placentia), is named after the pond, in fact a barachois, apparently noted for its mussels. The settlement Mussel Pond (*Population Returns* 1836) is now O'DONNELLS (NTS Placentia). There is a MUSSEL BED POND (NTS Harbour Grace) at NORTH RIVER.

Shoal Bay, SHOAL BAY, and Shoal Bay Point, SHOAL BAY POINT (NTS St. Mary's), were named, as the *Directions* state, from "there being several sunken Rocks lying off this Point."

NE Pt, at the entrance to ST. MARY'S HARBOUR, has been NORTH POINT (NTS St. Mary's) since Adm. 2915 ?1864.

M. F. Howley derives Mall Bay, MALL BAY (NTS St. Mary's), from Fr. *molue* – cod,[44] but Imray sees it in a sense rejected by Howley as Fr. *mal* – hurt, harm, or as the spelling may suggest from ? maul – to damage seriously, said, for example, of storms: "The anchorage in it (as its name implies) is not good, being exposed to sea winds which sometimes send in a very heavy swell."[45]

The specific in Double Road Point, DOUBLE ROAD POINT (NTS St. Mary's), variously spelled rode, road or rhode, is a term still current in Newfoundland for a rope, especially one attached to a boat anchor or trawl.[46] A Double Road might be used for extra security against a heavy swell such as is experienced in both MALL BAY and ST. MARY'S HARBOUR.[47] M. F. Howley, however, believed the word to be rote – the roaring of the sea or surf:

The fishermen are accustomed, in foggy weather, to find their bearings by carefully listening to the rout of the sea on the shore, which they (very correctly) call rote, or rut. According to the nature of the shore, whether sandy beach, gravel, rocky caves, and so forth, a different rote is made, and the fishermen are wonderfully expert in detecting their whereabouts by this sign. Sometimes the rote is deep and hollow, like the bellowing of distant thunder or of artillery, as the water rushes into deep caves, again sharp and shrill as it rolls over moving pebbly beaches; again hissing and seething as it creeps over a sandy shore. This point at ST. MARY'S has a sort of cave or gorge or split in the rock, so that after the sea strikes and makes its first rote, it then rushes into the fissure of the rock and again striking it produces a second rote.

Captain Fitzpatrick, of the S.S. *Portia*, has suggested to me another and very plausible reason for this name. In about the middle of the entrance to ST. MARY'S HARBOUR, half-way between DOUBLE ROTE POINT and Crapeau [FRAPEAU] Point on the north, there is a very good fishing "ground." It is called the Double Rote Ground, and the way to find it in a fog is to row out from the shore till you hear the two rotes, one from DOUBLE ROTE POINT on the south, and one from Crapeau [FRAPEAU] Point on the north, then you are on the "ground." The distance from point to point is about two miles.[48]

False Cape, FALSE CAPE (NTS St. Mary's), ? was likely to be mistaken for CAPE ENGLISH (NTS St. Mary's), two miles southward.

Peters River, PETERS RIVER (NTS St. Mary's), St. Peters River (Mount and Page 1780)!, appears to be a simple possessive, though M. F. Howley suggests, from Rivière de Pierre found by him in unidentified French maps, that Peter may be a mistranslation for Rocky. He admits, however, that he does not know if "the natural characteristics give any probability to such an interpretation."[49]

Shag Rocks, SHAG ROCK (NTS St. Shotts), a name common on all the coasts of Newfoundland, may be that of a number of species of cormorant[50] or describe a tangled mass of seaweed. The combination of shag with the generic roost, as in SHAG ROOST (NTS Dildo), suggests the former interpretation in some localities.

Gull Id, now GULL ISLAND POINT (NTS St. Shotts), retained the old name as late as M. F. Howley in 1909, though Adm. 2915 ?1864 added Point and *Newfoundland* 1920 recorded simply Gull Pt. The point is apparently connected to the mainland by a narrow isthmus and seems to have been taken for an island.

Broad Cove, BROAD COVE (NTS St. Shotts), correctly identified by Lane, has been confused with ST. SHORES COVE by some cartographers.

Eastern Hd, EASTERN HEAD (NTS St. Shotts), and Western Hd, WESTERN HEAD (St. Shotts), mark the extremities of ST. SHOTTS COVE (NTS St. Shotts).

Bakers Point, BAKER HEAD (NTS Trepassey), contains an unidentified possessive. The family name is common in Newfoundland, especially in settlements on the west coast of PLACENTIA BAY, but in this context it may be that of a member of Lane's crew.

Burnt Head, BURNT POINT (NTS Renews), and Sheeps Head Cove, as in the shift name SHEEP'S HEAD (NTS Renews), are descriptive, unless the latter is a transfer from Sheep Head, between Bantry Bay and Dunmanus Bay, Co. Cork, Eire.

Cold East Point, COLDEAST POINT (NTS Ferryland), ? the C das patas of Homem 1554 and 1558,[51] contains the name of a farm in Devonshire. OED cites three examples in poetic usage of cold prefixed to another adjective to indicate the combination of two qualities: cold-pale, cold-kind and cold-white, but notes that Shakespeare's cold-pale perhaps meant pale with cold (sb.) and that the later examples from Milton and Tennyson may be imitations.[52] Gover states that no parallel for such a compound is known [in place names], but observes that "the farm is in the east of the parish on land sloping down to the east."[53] Despite its rarity, the name occurs a second time in the nomenclature of the AVALON PENINSULA as Coldeast point (Imray 1873), now COLEY'S POINT (NTS Harbour Grace). An earlier name, ? Pointe agreable (Bellin 1744, Robert de Vaugondy 1749), is much at odds with Cold East. Cole Lees Point occurs as the name of the settlement in 1798.[54]

Scogins Hd, SCOGGINS HEAD (NTS Ferryland), contains an English family name of Norfolk and Suffolk.[55]

Saturdays Ledge, SATURDAY LEDGE (NTS Ferryland), in CAPE BROYLE HARBOUR, is probably for Satterlee, Satterley, Satterly or Saturley, an English family name "of Satterley or Satterleigh, a parish in Devonshire."[56] Although Jespersen[57] has no citation for l becoming d, the phenomenon may be explained by the laterally released alveolar consonant in a weakly stressed syllable being completely stopped in the same articulatory position, possibly influenced by the final riming weak syllable -day.

Horse Rock, HORSE ROCK (NP 1952), ? Horse Head (Cook 1794), lies off CAPE BROYLE HARBOUR (NTS Ferryland).

Great Island, GREAT ISLAND (NTS Ferryland), was originally Goose Isl (Seller c. 1671).[58] The alternative names are found in Great I. or Goose I. (Mount and Page 1780). The change was probably made to distinguish this Goose Island at 47–11, 52–48 from another at 47–02, 52–51.

Tinkers Point, TINKER POINT (NTS Ferryland), appears to be the Newfoundland name for the Northern Razor-bill, *Alca torda*, of which there is a colony on nearby GREEN ISLAND.[59]

Petty Harbour Point, now MOTION HEAD (NTS Bay Bulls), formerly ? C. de Portogesi (Ruysch 1508),[60] derived its latest name, in Adm. 296

1868, from THE MOTION, the heavy cross sea caused by the irregular and broken ground extending off the head.[61] Similarly the shift name Petty Harbour Bay (Jukes 1840) has become MOTION BAY (NTS Bay Bulls).

Lane's third survey of 1774, recorded in *A Chart of Part of the Coast of Newfoundland. from Cape Spear to Baceleau Island*, added thirty-one new names, including shift names, most of them on the NORTH SHORE of CONCEPTION BAY, the stretch of coast defined by Anspach 1819 as "From Carbonier to Point of Grates"[62] and by P. H. Gosse in 1828 as "from Carbonear to Point Baccalao."[63]

The shift names are Spear Bay, SPEAR BAY (NTS St. John's), Riuo de la spera ("Oliveriana" 1505–8), known in English as C[ape] Bay from Thornton 1689B to Imray 1873;[64] Moskito Pt., MOSQUITO POINT (NTS Harbour Grace);[65] Salmon Cove Head, SALMON COVE HEAD (NTS Heart's Content);[66] and Bay Verds Cove, unnamed in NTS, within BAY DE VERDE (NTS Bay de Verde).[67]

South Pt. Torbay, now TORBAY POINT (NTS St. John's), and North Pt. Torbay, now FLAT ROCK POINT (NTS St. John's), denote the extremities of TORBAY (NTS St. John's).

Brandys, THE BRANDIES, "three sunken rocks ... and a group of sunken and above water rocks, lie about three-quarters of a mile eastward and three-quarters of a mile east-southeastward, respectively, of the light-structure on CAPE ST. FRANCIS" (NTS Pouch Cove).[68] The name occurs variously as The Brandies, Brandies Rock(s), Brandies Shoal, Brandy Rock(s) in at least fourteen localities on the Newfoundland coast, and as The Brandies near the Saltee Islands off the southeast tip of Ireland. The name is apparently brandise – a trivet, an iron tripod for cooking over a fire, and probably referred originally to a group of three low pinnacle rocks, though subsequently it came to be applied to any low-lying rocks.[69] *OED* does not record this usage.

On BELL ISLAND (NTS St. John's and Harbour Grace), Lane records Grand Beach, now BELL BEACH (NTS St. John's), and Lance Cove, LANCE COVE (NTS St. John's). Two features associated with the island are Bell, THE BELL (NTS Harbour Grace), "a conspicuous conical rock, 122 feet high ... which lies near the western extremity of the island,"[70] from which in one tradition it is alleged to receive its name;[71] and the Clapper (unnamed in NTS), "a prominent rock 50 feet high [which] lies off the southern extremity."[72]

Along the shores of CONCEPTION BAY, Lane records Broad Cove, BROAD COVE (NTS St. John's). The name of the settlement there was changed to ST. PHILIPS (NTS St. John's) by a proclamation of 1 June 1905, through the efforts of the Rev. Canon Smith, rector of PORTUGAL COVE from 1886 to 1921.[73]

Topsail Head, at TOPSAIL (NTS St. John's), is a "bold height ... chiefly a mass of pure white quartz rock,"[74] so called, according to M. F. Howley, "on account of the very high land which stands out conspicuously to the view of vessels coming into the Bay. The sailors are accustomed to call high standing peaks of this kind by the name of Topsails." It occurs in the names of the inland features Gaff Topsail, Main Topsail and Mizzen Topsail (all in NTS The Topsails), to which Howley adds Fore Topsail, "well known since the Railway has been built across the country." "Seen at a distance across the vast plain of Patrick's Marsh, [? Patricks Pond (NTS Badger and Gull Pond) they] present a rude resemblance to the topmasts of a ship under sail and seen hull down in the horizon." Howley rightly rejects the tradition that TOPSAIL derives from Top's Hill after the family name "Top, or Tap, or Torp, or Thorp,' of "an old fisherman who in the beginning of the XIX Century used to go out from ST. JOHN's in winter to live in a tilt and cut hoops, staves and 'winter stuff.' He had his tilt on the side of this hill."[75]

Kelligrews Head, now KELLIGREWS POINT (NTS Harbour Grace), has been considered previously in relation to KELLY'S ISLAND (NTS Harbour Grace).[76]

Blowmedown Cove, BLOW ME DOWN (NTS Harbour Grace), in BAY DE GRAVE, contains a specific which occurs independently, or in conjunction with the generics Bluff, Head, Hill and Point, or as a shift name, seventeen times in the NTS maps of Newfoundland. BLOW ME DOWN HEAD (NTS Harbour Grace) is in BAY DE GRAVE; BLOW ME DOWN BLUFF (NTS Holyrood), ? a modern imposition, is in HOLYROOD BAY; Blow-me-down, a settlement near CARBONEAR (NTS Harbour Grace), was recorded in *Census 1857*. It is also found in the form Blomidon in Cape Blomidon and the shift name Blomidon Peninsula in Nova Scotia, and is said to occur in Labrador. W. F. Ganong,[77] who made an intensive study of the forms Blow me Down and Blomidon, comments:

> The charts and Sailing Directions fully confirm Patterson's statement[78] as to the kind of places called Blow-me-down in Newfoundland and Labrador, – *viz.*, abrupt and more or less isolated mountains, headlands, or bluffs, rising steeply from, or near, navigable waters, and therefore such places as render vessels under their lee especially liable to danger from squalls ... Accordingly it would seem sufficiently evident that Blow-me-down is a sailor's phrase half-humorously descriptive of what such places cause to befall one; and this catchy phrase, applied, as is the sailor's wont, wherever particularly appropriate, gradually acquires there the status of a place-name. Apparently the name originated among English sailors resorting to Newfoundland (for it

seems to occur nowhere else in the world apart from ten times in Newfoundland, [and] once each in Labrador and Nova Scotia) ... In summary, the evidence shows that Blomidon originated in Blowmedown, a sailor's phrase used as a place-name, shortened, apparently for cartographical convenience, to its present form.

Blowmedown is not cited in OED, though Blow-down, "a gust of wind and smoke down a chimney," is recorded in 1884.[79] Ganong dismisses Patterson's suggestions of a Portuguese or Micmac origin of the name.

Hibbs Hole, HIBBS HOLE (NTS Harbour Grace), had been recorded as the name of a settlement as early as 1745.[80] The English family name Hibbs[81] is no longer found at HIBBS HOLE, though it was that of a property-owner at [UPPER] ISLAND COVE in 1773[82] and is current in other communities in CONCEPTION BAY, including BELL ISLAND, KELLIGREWS and TOPSAIL. The generic hole, first cited in OED as a local United States [sic] usage in 1639, is steadily being ousted in favour of cove, a word in Roget's phrase less "offensive to ears polite."

Feather Rock and the shift name Feather Point (Lane, *Directions* 1810), FEATHER POINT (NTS Harbour Grace), and Mad Rock, MAD ROCKS (NTS Harbour Grace), denote two hazards to mariners, the first at one of the extremities of HARBOUR GRACE, the other at the entrance to SPANIARD'S BAY. MAD ROCKS are so called "from the circumstance that the sea breaks upon them with considerable violence when the wind sends in a swell from eastward."[83]

The settlement at Freshwater, FRESHWATER COVE (NTS Heart's Content), was among the places captured by d'Iberville in 1697.[84]

Perry's Cove, PERRY'S COVE (NTS Heart's Content), contains an English family name especially common in the West Country. It is still found at WESTERN BAY (NTS Heart's Content) and HEART'S DELIGHT (NTS Heart's Content).[85]

Mully's Cove, MULLEY'S COVE (*Electors* 1955, but unnamed in NTS Heart's Content), is adjacent to BROAD COVE SOUTH (*Census* 1884 – *Electors* 1955), an offshoot of Lane's Broad Cove, BROAD COVE (NTS Heart's Content. Mulley is a current family name (of unidentified origin) at BROAD COVE SOUTH and BLACKHEAD (NTS Heart's Content).[86]

Adams Cove, ADAMS COVE (NTS Heart's Content), ? So[uth] West Cove (Visscher c. 1680 ... *English Pilot. The Fourth Book* 1780), contains a common English family name particularly associated with Devonshire[87] and current in OLD PERLICAN (NTS old Perlican).[88] M. F. Howley, however, sees it as the baptismal name of Adam Clerke or Clarke, "who formerly carried on business here. He was the first settler."[89]

Bradleys Cove, BRADLEYS COVE (NTS Heart's Content), contains a widespread English family name found in many Newfoundland communities, though not on the AVALON PENINSULA.

Green or Western Bay, now WESTERN BAY (NTS Heart's Content), and Oker Pit Cove, OCHRE PIT COVE (NTS Heart's Content), have been considered previously.[90] Northern Bay, NORTHERN BAY (NTS Heart's Content), appears to have been named in relation to WESTERN BAY. Gull Island, GULL ISLAND (NTS Heart's Content), little more than a rock, is a resting-place for sea-birds.

The change of name of the settlement at Devils Cove to JOB'S COVE (NTS Heart's Content) was the subject of an "act" of piety by its inhabitants dated 29 May 1812, published in *The Royal Gazette and Newfoundland Advertiser*[91] on 11 June 1812 and subsequently. The "act" is equalled in interest only by the later proposal to re-name Jack of Clubs Cove, now Aguathuna (NTS Stephenville).[92]

An Act of the Inhabitants of Devil's Cove, *in Conception-Bay, altering said Name into the appellation* Job's Cove; *and that all said Bay, and its neighbouring Bays, may not be ignorant of said alteration, said Inhabitants do wish to insert this Act three different times in the St. John's News-paper.*

Devil's Cove, 29th May, 1812.

We the undersigned Inhabitants, conceiving the utility and benefits resulting from an early conception and sense of Religion instilled into the tender minds of our Children, and of the rising generation, do unanimously resolve to change and alter the barbarous, execrable, and impious name of *Devil's Cove*, into the ancient, venerable, and celebrated name of *Job's Cove*; and that the public News-paper of ST. JOHN's will publish these our resolutions three different times, so that every person in the Island may come to this knowledge, and none may plead ignorance, by saying, when they pronounce *Devil's Cove*, that it is from want of knowing better how to preclude any tergiversations, or vain excuses. After the publication of this Act we do declare, that our resolution is fixed, and that this Cove, which underwent the appellation of *Devil's Cove* these 50 years and upwards, to the scandal and detriment of God's honor and veneration, be altered and changed, and every one for the time to come, and always, will call it after the name we freely give it, to wit, *Job's Cove*. – And that all persons may hereafter take notice of these our resolutions, we sign our names.

1	Thos. English,	7	Edw. English,	13	Jos. Murphy,
2	Moses Sandy,	8	John Rilsom,	14	Jas. Walsh,
3	Rich. English,	9	Thos. English,	15	John Murphy,
4	Rich. Woodfine,	10	John Johnson,	16	J. Murphy, Jr.
5	Jas. English,	11	Ned English,	17	Geo. Johnson,
6	Wm. Bearns,	12	Wm. Johnson,	18	John English.

The original name of the feature doubtless arose from its being "exposed to easterly winds, and safe only during very fine weather."[93] There appears to be no evidence to link JOB'S COVE with either JOB'S POND (NTS Heart's Content), near CARBONEAR, perhaps a family name, or the family of merchants in ST. JOHN'S which gave its name to JOB'S COVE in ST. JOHN'S HARBOUR.

The settlement at Island Cove, now LOWER ISLAND COVE (NTS Heart's Content and Bay de Verde), had received the qualifier as early as Thoresby 1796 to distinguish it from UPPER ISLAND COVE (NTS Harbour Grace).

The chart of a fourth survey by Lane of the coast from BACCALIEU ISLAND to Bonavista has not been traced, but Lane, *Directions* 1775, 1810[94] doubtless includes the names recorded in the chart. It adds new names in ST. JOHN'S HARBOUR (NTS St. John's), at HARBOUR GRACE (NTS Harbour Grace) and elsewhere in CONCEPTION BAY, and especially on the west and south coasts of TRINITY BAY, an area almost entirely neglected previously.

Except for the Narrows, THE NARROWS (NTS St. John's), all the features in ST. JOHN'S HARBOUR are rocks or shoals: Pancake, PANCAKE SHOAL (*NP* 1952); the Vestal, VESTAL ROCK (*NP* 1952); and Prosser's Rock, PROSSER ROCK (*NP* 1952). The remaining names are of fortifications: Fort Amherst, FORT AMHERST (NTS St. John's), "the Old Garrison, called also Fort William,"[95] and Frederick's Battery, ? So[uth] Forte (Thornton 1689B).

THE NARROWS is obviously descriptive as Anspach makes clear: "[ST. JOHN'S] harbour is ... formed between two mountains, at a small distance from each other, the eastern points of which leave an entrance very appropriately called the Narrows."[96] PANCAKE SHOAL may be presumed also to be descriptive. Prosser is a Welsh and West Country family name. The signification of VESTAL ROCK has not been discovered.

FORT AMHERST "on SOUTH HEAD" is probably the South Head Battery in a *Plan of the Town and Harbour of St. John's*, 1765. It was named after Colonel William Amherst who retook ST. JOHN'S after its capture by the French in 1762.[97]

The old So[uth] Forte (Thornton 1689B),[98] on the South Side of ST. JOHN'S HARBOUR, had been destroyed by d'Iberville in 1696, rebuilt by Colonel John Gibson in 1697, and reduced again by d'Iberville in 1700. It withstood a three weeks' siege by Subercase in 1705, but was captured and destroyed again by St. Ovide in 1708, after which the site was abandoned. In 1744 the South Battery was built in a different location nearer the mouth of the harbour and captured in 1762. It was known as Fort Charles after its recapture by the British in September

1762, and as Frederick's Battery after it had been rebuilt in 1777, in honour of Captain Thomas Lenox Frederick, RN, governor of Newfoundland in the winter of 1777-8.[99]

At CARBONEAR (NTS Harbour Grace), Lane records Otterbury Point, of which the specific forms the name of settlements at that place (Census 1857), on the north side of HARBOUR GRACE (NTS Harbour Grace) (CO 199.18 1800), and on the north side of BAY DE GRAVE (NTS Harbour Grace). Although from its form OTTERBURY would seem to be a transfer from an English place name, in fact it does not occur in England except as the fictitious name of a fictitious town in Mr C. Day Lewis's novel, *The Otterbury Incident*, for which it was "invented, with a reminiscence of Ottery St. Mary."[100] J. B. Jukes, however, provides a clue to its origin: "Among the roots of these trees numerous otters have formed their burrows."[101] Otter-burrow, a compound not recorded in *OED*, has apparently changed to Otterbury on the analogy of a local pronunciation of narrow [narI] and follow [fɒlI].

In HARBOUR GRACE (NTS Harbour Grace), Lane records a shift name Feather Point, FEATHER POINT (NTS Harbour Grace), from Feather Rock (Lane 1774); Admiral's Beach;[102] the Bar, "a broad *spit of sand* [which] runs off from the southern shore ... what Mr Lane has called the bar";[103] and Point of the Bar, now ? POINT OF BEACH (NTS Harbour Grace); West Shore; and, as in ST. JOHN'S HARBOUR, the Narrows.

At BAY ROBERTS (NTS Harbour Grace), Lane records another shift name, Bay Roberts Point; and at CUPIDS COVE (NTS Harbour Grace), Spectacle Head, SPECTACLE HEAD (NTS Harbour Grace), to which he adds one of his rare explanatory comments: "The land on the north side of the entrance [to the cove] is remarkably high, and thence called Spectacle Head."[104] Brigus Head is now ? GREAT HEAD (NTS Harbour Grace).

The form of the specific in St. Jones's Harbour, ST. JONES HARBOUR (NTS Sunnyside), and in the shift name St. Jones's Island, ST. JONES ISLAND (NTS Sunnyside), has been mentioned previously.[105] Bald Head, BALD HEAD (NTS Sunnyside), is "a bold cliffy bluff"[106] presumably, like other headlands with the same name, bare of vegetation.

In Deer Harbour, DEER HARBOUR (NTS Sunnyside), Lane has Deer Island, now ? GRUB ISLAND; Scollop Cove, Shallop Cove in Imray 1862, which seems to be either SOUTHEAST ARM or a cove in the arm; and two unidentified features, Tickle Point, now ? TEA COVE POINT, and Harbour Island.

Bull Island, BULL ISLAND (NTS Sunnyside), is a shift name from Bay of Bulls, now BULL ARM (NTS Sunnyside).[107]

Chapel Bay, now CHAPEL ARM (NTS Dildo), has been discussed in the context of Guy's exploration of TRINITY BAY in 1612.[108]

Lane's Dildo Harbour appears to be a common name for the two features later distinguished as DILDO ARM (NTS Dildo) and DILDO COVE (NTS Dildo). In addition to the shift names in this area, DILDO (NTS Dildo) and SOUTH DILDO (NTS Dildo), two settlements, DILDO ISLANDS (NTS Dildo and Argentia), and DILDO POND (NTS Dildo and Argentia), Dildo also occurs as an element in Dildo Run (NTS Comfort Cove and Twillingate) (Jukes 1840) and Dildo Pond (NTS Gander River and Comfort Cove). OED gives two meanings for this obsolete word: first, as "a word of obscure origin, used in the refrains of ballads" and "also, a name of the penis or phallus, or a figure thereof"; and secondly, "A tree or shrub of the genus *Cereus* ... Also *Dildo-tree*, *Dildo-bush*, Dildo Pear Tree." A citation for the second meaning, taken from W. King's *The Transactioneer* 1700, brings together two words which in conjunction are interesting, if not significant, in the context of Newfoundland place names: "The Toddy-Tree, the Sower-Sop, the Bonavists, and the Dildoe," a juxtaposition repeated in a second citation from King for Bonavist: "The Dr resolves many Doubts and Difficulties ... relating to ... the Bonavists, and the Dildoe." Bonavists are a species of tropical pulse or kidney beans, Dildo(e)s a kind of cactus, and both are associated with the West Indies. The temptation to conjecture that some traveller saw in Newfoundland vegetation that reminded him of the West Indies and so named DILDO and Cape Bonavista (NTS Bonavista) is strong; but if vetch and beach-peas resemble bonavists, nothing like a cactus grows in Newfoundland. Moreover some two hundred and forty or fifty years separate the first recordings of these names.

M. F. Howley's assertion that dildo is a local form of the nautical term doldrum[109] seems to lack supporting evidence. A local tradition that suggests an incident name is hardly credible: "Two fishermen were out in TRINITY BAY fishing when a storm came up. They went into DILDO HARBOUR where it was lee. One man said to the other, 'Jack, will we stay here?' He replied, 'I guess 'twill do.' From this it later became DILDO."[110]

A more probable explanation of DILDO is to be found perhaps in a usage heard in the north of England in which it is a name not of the penis or phallus but of the vagina, applied here as a descriptive to a deep, narrow bay. Cook 1763 records, if he did not impose, a similar name in Cant [sic] Harbour in the vicinity of Cape Freels (NTS Cabot Islands and Musgrave Harbour). Conne River (Gilbert 1769) (NTS St. Albans etc) is an anglicization of the French equivalent, *le con*.

Tradition also suggests that New Harbour, NEW HARBOUR (NTS Dildo), derives from Newhook, the name of the first settlers.[111] According to Wix 1836,[112] the Nieuhooks were of Huguenot extraction and Charles Nieuhook jun. migrated to NEW HARBOUR from Trinity (NTS Trinity).

But the possibility that the name is to be seen in relation to another, earlier settlement elsewhere, perhaps Trinity itself, should not be overlooked.

Hope-all-head, HOPEALL HEAD (NTS Dildo), Hope-all-a-head (Imray 1862), may be an example of the loss of *w* between a consonant and any vowel in a weak syllable in the unidentified baptismal, ? family, or place name Hopewell,[113] as in the pronunciation [færəl] of the family name Farewell. HOPEWELL (NTS Holyrood), a settlement, is recorded in Census 1891.

Green's Harbour, now GREEN HARBOUR (NTS Dildo), contains a local family name but, despite the early possessive form still in common use, tradition has it that the specific refers to the forests around the hills and ponds when the first settlers arrived there.[114]

Witless Bay, now WHITEWAY BAY (NTS Dildo and Harbour Grace), recalls WITLESS BAY (NTS Bay Bulls) and presents similar problems of interpretation.[115] The name of the settlement was changed by a proclamation of 13 August 1912, ? to commemorate Sir William Vallance Whiteway (1828–1908), prime minister of Newfoundland in 1878–85, 1889–94 and 1895–97. The change of name of the feature followed.

Long Point, LONG POINT (NTS Dildo), is descriptive. King's Head, KING'S HEAD (NTS Heart's Content), may commemorate George III.

Heart's Content, HEART'S CONTENT (NTS Heart's Content), had been recorded by John Guy and l'Abbé Beaudoin, but then ignored or forgotten until Lane, who further recorded the associated names Heart's Delight, HEART'S DELIGHT (NTS Heart's Content), and Heart's Desire, HEART'S DESIRE (NTS Heart's Content).[116]

Hants Harbour, HANTS HARBOUR (NTS Old Perlican), is the first recording in English of Beaudoin's Lance arbe and Anse arbre in 1697.[117] Lane added the shift names Hants Head, HANTS HEAD (NTS Old Perlican), and Hants Harbour Rock. Hants may be a variant of the English family name Hand(s), though Hants County in Nova Scotia is said to be the abbreviation of Hampshire, England.[118]

Almost inevitably, after Lane's intensive recording of names on the AVALON PENINSULA, later charts of the eighteenth century could add little to the coastal nomenclature. An exception is the anonymous *A Chart of the South East Coast of Newfoundland*, printed for Mount and Page, 1780. The chart records Middle Rock in BRYANTS COVE (NTS Harbour Grace); Deepest Bay, now BAY ROBERTS HARBOUR (NTS Harbour Grace), and SW Bay of BAY ROBERTS (NTS Harbour Grace); South Bay on BELL ISLAND, the site of the settlement FRESHWATER (PARSONVILLE P.O.) (NTS Harbour Grace); High Ragged Pt,[119] now ? GREAT HEAD (NTS Harbour Grace), descriptive of the headland forming the southern extremity of BRIGUS BAY (NTS Harbour Grace); the alternative names Low Black Pt or Torbay North Pt for North Pt Torbay (Lane 1774, now FLAT ROCK POINT (NTS St. John's);[120] Low Pt., now SPRIGGS POINT (NTS St. John's); and the shift name Witless Bay Pt, now WITLESS POINT (NTS Bay Bulls).

Lane's general map, *The Island of Newfoundland 1790*, contains three names probably omitted from the *Directions* of 1775: Colliers Bay, COLLIER BAY (NTS Dildo), in which the specific is ? the English family name;[121] Shuffleboard, SHUFFLEBOARD (NTS Heart's Content), described in the *Newfoundland Pilot* as "a conspicuous hill," though the name would seem to be more appropriate to the long, flat escarpment north of HEART'S DESIRE (NTS Heart's Content), like the table on which the game is played; and Seal Cove, now NEW CHELSEA (NTS Old Perlican).

A Narrative of God's Love to William Thoresby,[122] an account of the work in Newfoundland from 1796 to 1798 of a Methodist missionary, contains a number of new names of settlements, mostly shift names from previously-named features: Adam's Cove,[123] ADAMS COVE (NTS Heart's Content); Blackhead,[124] BLACKHEAD (NTS Heart's Content); Muley's Cove,[125] MULL(E)Y'S COVE; Witson's Bay, ? WESTERN BAY (NTS Heart's Content);[126] Gull Island,[127] GULL ISLAND (NTS Heart's Content); Devil's Cove,[128] now JOB'S COVE (NTS Heart's Content), with an apposite if unconscious comment: "We found it sultry and disagreeable passing to Devil's Cove"; Lower Island Cove,[129] LOWER ISLAND COVE, (NTS Bay de Verde and Heart's Content); Broad Cove,[130] BROAD COVE (NTS Heart's Content); and Gawgel's Cove, ? JUGGLERS COVE (NTS Harbour Grace), near BAY ROBERTS. Wm. Earl had been recorded as a property-owner at Juglers Cove in 1760.[131] A local tradition maintains that the cove, "a small boat harbour formed by some rocks,"[132] derives its name from the dexterity needed to navigate it.

One other settlement name in the *Narrative*, Bareneed, BARENEED (NTS Harbour Grace), derives from a feature cited in a deed of 1787[133] as Bearing Head, a name which seems to imply that the head was known at any rate as a local navigational mark to sailors in BAY DE GRAVE, despite its absence from the *Sailing Directions* and M. F. Howley's inability to find a meaning for it. However, in the absence of more citations and precise information on the earlier pronunciation of the name, Howley's conjecture that BARENEED derives from an unauthenticated descriptive, Barren Head, cannot be completely ruled out.

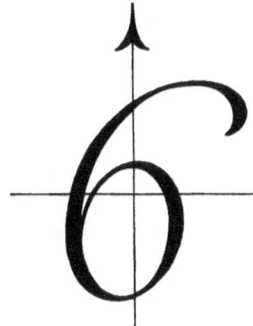

The Nineteenth Century

Up to the end of the eighteenth century, the chief sources of place names on the AVALON PENINSULA were maps compiled by what may be called external authorities. Only by inference is it possible for the most part to determine which names were obtained from local information or usage and which were imposed by the cartographers themselves. Cook, for example, introduced into his charts names used by local people and in his *A Chart of the Coasts, Bays and Harbours in Newfoundland between Griquet and Pt. Ferolle* compiled "A Table, of the Names of the Places in this Chart, as they are known to the English and French," though other names, as was shown in Chapter 1, bear the marks of his own imposition.

The problem of ascertaining the origin of names is by no means solved in the nineteenth century, but the work of external authorities is supplemented by local residents, officials, visitors and travellers who in their histories, reports and memoirs frequently throw light on the names they record. Moreover, with growing knowledge of the interior, names are no longer limited to coastal features, and names of settlements are recorded freely.

The circumstances of the imposition of one of the earliest names recorded in the century are recited in a news item which, not inappropriately in the year of Dickens's birth, suggests an expedition by members of the Pickwick Club:

On Tuesday, the 28th ... [January 1812], a large party of gentlemen

100 / *Place Names of the Avalon Peninsula*

appeared at the Merchant's Hall by appointment, and at ten o'clock set off for the head of Twenty Mile Pond, where they assembled agreeable to invitation at the house of Thomas Kearsey, and partook of a plentiful refreshment; the pleasure of which was much increased by the satisfaction of using excellent bread made from the wheat grown in the vicinity of St. John's. After regaling themselves and enjoying "the comforts of a clean room and a good fire," they took some excellent Old Madeira Wine, provided for the occasion, and pouring generous libations, called the village *Windsor*, with many good wishes for its prosperity and increase. They also named that noble and delightful piece of water adjoining (before called Twenty Mile Pond) WINDSOR LAKE [NTS St. John's]; and immediately proceeded over the immense sheet of ice which covered its romantic surface to the commencement of the New Road on the North side of it, and continued their journey to Mr. George Goff's at Portugal Cove, highly pleased with the New Road, and the varied and picturesque scenery which skirted its borders. They dined at Mr. Goff's with the greatest hilarity imaginable, and leaving his house at three o'clock returned over Windsor Lake, renewing their refreshments at Windsor, succeeded by the loyal song of "Hearts of Oak" reached St. John's at 5, much gratified with the amusements and occupations of the day.[1]

It is a matter for regret that the reporter of the event failed to say why the gentlemen chose the name WINDSOR, since its only contemporary association with Newfoundland – and that rather far-fetched – seems to lie in the fact that the father of the then governor, Sir J. T. Duckworth, was sometime Canon of Windsor. Indeed, a contemporary writer who celebrated the event in verse thought that the pond might well have been named after Kearsey himself:

> FOR THE ROYAL GAZETTE
> A PROPOSAL
>
> Ye muses celestial who favor this Isle,
> Enliven my numbers, embellish my style;
> Thalia, enchantress, inspire with thy wand
> Thy vot'ry who celebrates Twenty Mile Pond.
>
> When Sol's fervid beams proclaim Summer is near
> Its shores so romantic, its waters so clear,
> Have often induced the young lovers so fond
> To propose an excursion to Twenty Mile Pond.
>
> There nature profusely displays her rich stores
> Of all the ripe fruit which abounds on these shores;
> There marshberries, raspberries, strawberries, too,
> Give life to the scene and enrapture the view.
>
> And sure 'twould be strange when such treasures abound
> And Flora's productions enamel the ground,
> If a maiden fastidious this jaunt would refuse,
> Which affords such occasions to pick and to choose.

When winter with icy grip holds its control,
How rapture's sweet magic possesses the soul;
For then to the pond's frozen face we convey
Youth, beauty and elegance warm in a sleigh.

Glide on, lovely creatures, wherever you go,
Whether crossing deep waters or woods through the snow
May the Naiades and Dryades protect you from harm,
And remove for you even the shade of alarm.

On the banks of the pond, many years since was built
A hut which was known by the name of Snow's Tilt;
And many and oft times the gay and the fair
Found shelter and true hospitality there.

But jealous old Vulcan while ranging the grove,
Mistook a bright form for the sweet queen of love,
And out of revenge (as he thought) to the dame,
He involved the whole fabric in ruin and flame.

Now honest Tom Kersey's house peeps through the wood
And to man and to horse gives reception that's good;
And here weary travellers venture to stay,
Either going or coming to town from the bay.

A short time ago, a few friends to this spot,
Resolved upon change, and with zeal piping hot,
Cried "Fame take thy trumpet and loudly proclaim
That Twenty Mile Pond must adopt a new name."

Then pouring libations of wine on the earth,
All joy and hilarity, laughter and mirth,
They agreed its old title the pool should forsake,
And that Twenty Mile Pond should be called Windsor Lake.

But why should not Kersey's name stand on record,
Whose character's free from extortion and fraud?
And as his abode is upon the Lake's brim,
I think that the pond should be named after him.

In Westmoreland, Cumberland, also, we view
The sweet lake of Windermere, Buttermere too;
I therefore propose, ye sour critics don't sneer,
That Twenty Mile Pond should be called Kerseymere.[2]

The name Twenty Mile Pond, which is still current, derives from the traditional estimate of the length of the shoreline.

Lieutenant Edward Chappell's *Voyage of His Majesty's Ship* Rosamond *to Newfoundland* ... [in 1813] contains a few new names and some brief comments. A note on p. 27, "All the ports of *Newfoundland*, except that of the Capital, *St. John's*, are called Out-harbours," indicates a usage common in the nineteenth century but now obsolete. Outharbour (not cited in OED) has been universally superseded by outport, recorded in Newfoundland by Jukes in 1842[3] but cited in England as early as 1642.[4]

New names in ST. JOHN'S are the King's Dock-yard, "although it can scarcely be said to deserve this title," and Fort Townshend, a late recording of the name of the fortification built in 1777 and named after George Townshend (1724–1807), fourth viscount and first marquis Townshend, master-general of the ordnance.[5]

Chappell also mentions "a small battery perched on the top of a single pyramidal mount, which is called the Crow's Nest."[6] D. W. Prowse, however, maintains that "The existing memorial of Sir James Wallace [governor of Newfoundland in 1794] is the pointed rock often called Crow's Nest, but properly named Wallace's Battery; it is being gradually destroyed – being used by spoilers as a stone quarry."[7]

The *Map of Newfoundland* in the *Voyage* contains the name AVALON, which seems not to have been recorded since Robinson 1669.[8]

A map which contains only one new name on the AVALON PENINSULA, Copper I., COPPER ISLAND (NTS Sunnyside), is nevertheless of interest for its title: *A Map of Cabotia comprehending the Provinces of Upper and Lower Canada, New Brunswick, and Nova-Scotia with Breton Island Newfoundland &c. and including, also, the Adjacent Parts of the United States ... By John Purdy* (London, 1814) in which Cabotia is the unique use of this name, formed as in Tasmania and Rhodesia, by the addition of the suffix -ia to a personal name.

L. A. Anspach's *History of the Island of Newfoundland,* 1819, contains only three new names on the AVALON PENINSULA: Little Castor's River,[9] now ? WATERFORD RIVER (NTS St. John's), of which the specific, the old name for the beaver, is found also in Castors River (NTS Castors River) (Lotter c. 1758); Shoal-Bay, SHOAL BAY (NTS Bay Bulls), "which contains a mine of copper ore" worked by Cornish miners about 1775,[10] whence presumably MINER POINT (NTS Bay Bulls); and the Barrens, "a long rocky space ... which forms the communication between Fort William and Fort Townsend."[11]

Barrens, for the word is always used in the plural in Newfoundland though apparently in the singular in Nova Scotia, New Brunswick and parts of the United States, has been variously defined. The earliest citation for Newfoundland, which anticipates that in OED by eighteen years, is in Sir Joseph Banks's *Journal of a Voyage to Newfoundland and Labrador,* 1766: "We think it prudent to return upon the rocks and barrens (for so they call the places where wood does not grow),"[12] a description somewhat modified by George Cartwright in the Glossary in his *A Journal of Transactions and Events ... on the Coast of Labrador,* 1792: "Elevated lands, which will not produce timber."[13] Anspach is more explicit:

What is known of [the interior of Newfoundland] consists of a rocky and barren soil, steep hills covered with bad wood, some narrow and sandy valleys, and extensive plains covered either with heath, or with rocky surfaces, more or less extensive, where not a tree or shrub is to be seen, and which are from thence called *Barrens*;[14]

though J. B. Jukes was to provide the most exact definition in his "General Report of the Geological Survey of Newfoundland, during the Years 1839 and 1840," appended to his *Excursions in and about Newfoundland,* 1842:

The "barrens" of Newfoundland are those districts which occupy the summits of the hills and ridges, and other elevated and exposed tracts. They are covered with a thin and scrubby vegetation, consisting of berry-bearing plants and dwarf bushes of various species, and are somewhat similar in appearance to the moorlands of the north of England, differing only in the kind of vegetation, and in there being less of it. Bare patches of gravel and boulders, and crumbling fragments of rock, are frequently met with upon the barrens, and they are generally altogether destitute of vegetable soil.[15]

Barrens occurs as a specific in Barrens Pond (NTS Hodges Hill), and as a generic in Bateau Barrens (NTS Blue Mountain) and Browns Cove Barrens (NTS Hampden). It is not recorded in NTS on the AVALON PENINSULA, but is common in local usage as a generic associated with the name of a settlement, as in BRIGUS BARRENS, WITLESS BAY BARRENS and HEART'S CONTENT BARRENS.

Edward Wix's[16] *Six Months of a Newfoundland Missionary's Journal, from February to August 1835,* 1836, is the record of his archidiaconal visitations during a short period of his residence in Newfoundland from 1827 to 1837. His travels were almost entirely on foot or by boat from one settlement to the next, and he visited, and seems first to have recorded the names of, a number of the smaller outports and inland features.

With the exception of the shift names Topsail Beech [sic],[17] TOPSAIL (NTS St. John's), and Spaniard's Bay Beech [sic],[18] SPANIARD'S BAY (NTS Harbour Grace), all the new names on the AVALON PENINSULA are in TRINITY BAY, PLACENTIA BAY and the ISTHMUS OF AVALON (NTS Sunnyside).

Andrew's Cove[19] is an unidentified settlement between Dildo Cove, DILDO (NTS Dildo), and CHAPEL ARM (NTS Dildo). The specific is probably the family name Andrews, common in many localities on the AVALON PENINSULA and especially at WINTERTON (NTS Heart's Content). Norman's

Cove,[20] NORMAN'S COVE (NTS Dildo), also appears to bear a common family name, found especially at LONG HARBOUR (NTS Argentia). Both Andrews and Norman are English West Country family names: Andrews is particularly associated with Dorset and Norman with Somerset.[21]

Little Gut,[22] also unidentified, but in the neighbourhood of CHAPEL ARM (NTS Dildo), contains the first recording in Newfoundland of a generic used to identify both narrow coves and arms of rivers. The generic is not to be confused with gut as an element of the specific in Famishgut and PINCHGUT.[23]

The shift name Chapel Tolt,[24] not in NTS, contains a new generic, ? restricted to Newfoundland, not cited in OED, most satisfactorily defined as "a solitary hill, usually somewhat conical, rising by itself about the surrounding country."[25] Tolt occurs with the definite article, The Tolt (NTS Marystown, Harbour Breton, Merasheen and Port aux Basques); with a specific, Fortune Tolt (NTS Grand Bank), Garnish Tolt (NTS Marystown) and Snooks Tolt (NTS Terrenceville); and as a specific in Tolt Brook (NTS Gisborne Lake and Meta Pond) and Tolt Hill and Tolt Point (NTS Random Island).

Long Hill Deer country,[26] an area south of Wix's route from NORMAN'S COVE (NTS Dildo) to LONG HARBOUR (NTS Argentia), contains a generic illustrative of that "application of the word to a district having distinct physical or other characteristics,"[27] though commonly in Newfoundland usage it refers to a loosely-defined, uncultivated inland area such as that between CARBONEAR (NTS Harbour Grace) and HEART'S CONTENT (NTS Heart's Content). Country is used as a specific in COUNTRY POND (NTS Bay Bulls, Harbour Grace) and in the name of a small settlement inland from BAY ROBERTS, COUNTRY ROAD (NTS Harbour Grace). The form of the compound specific in Long Hill Deer country is unusual.

Long Harbour arm,[28] LONG HARBOUR (NTS Argentia), and Ship Harbour Point,[29] SHIP HARBOUR POINT (NTS Argentia), are shift names.[30] Martise Reach[31] is a mistake name for MARQUISE.[32] SE and NE guts[33] are alternative names for SOUTHEAST ARM (NTS Placentia)[34] and NORTHEAST ARM (NTS Argentia), the latter being here first recorded.

Bald Head, BALD HEAD (NTS Argentia), is descriptive.[35] St. Croix Bay,[36] ST. CROIX BAY (NTS Argentia), has been discussed previously.

The specific in Money's Cove,[37] Mooney's Cove (*Population Returns 1836*), now MOANY COVE (NTS Argentia), is the Irish family name still current at PLACENTIA (NTS Placentia). The modern form of the name has given rise to an expression used of one who is always complaining: "You must have come from MOANY COVE."

Corben's Head,[38] CORBIN HEAD (*NP* 1952), contains an English family name.[39] Tilley Cove,[40] which contains a common Newfoundland family name of Somersetshire origin, appears however to be a mistake name for TRINNY COVE (NTS Argentia).[41]

Red Cove,[42] RED COVE (*NP* 1952), is descriptive. Back Cove[43] is presumably "the pond at ... [the head of FAIR HAVEN (NTS Dildo)] into which boats pass, at high water, for shelter from onshore winds."[44]

The specific in Big Chance Cove[45] BIG CHANCE COVE (NTS Dildo), may be for mischance, that is, shipwreck, as also perhaps in CHANCE COVE (NTS Biscay Bay River).[46]

Bentham[47] is a mistake name for RANTEM (NTS Dildo).[48]

Master's Head,[49] MASTERS HEAD (NTS Dildo), contains an English family name particularly associated with Somerset and Dorset,[50] found in a number of communities in PLACENTIA BAY. Ram's Head,[51] RAM HEAD (NTS Dildo), may contain an English family name,[52] but may be descriptive. Stock or Stoke Cove,[53] STOCK COVE (NTS Sunnyside), may also contain an English family name. The generic in the shift name, Stock Cove Deer-look-out,[54] which is recorded some thirty times in Newfoundland, is usually applied to a coastal feature from which shipping is observed but is given here to a feature presumably used by hunters. Lookout is used as a specific in LOOKOUT POND (NTS Bay Bulls).

Frenchman's Island, ? MCKAY ISLAND (NTS Sunnyside), according to a tradition related to Wix, derived its name from the burning of an English brig in Bay Bulls Arm, BULL ARM (NTS Sunnyside), by the French who had come overland from PLACENTIA (NTS Placentia).[55]

Wix states that "From the top of Sainter's Hill, [CENTRE HILL (NTS Sunnyside)], a conspicuous object in this neighbourhood, the seven bays of Despair, Fortune, ST. MARY, TRINITY, Bonavista, CONCEPTION and PLACENTIA, may be seen at one time."[56] J. B. Jukes somewhat modifies Wix's statement and adds more information:

One remarkable hill at the head of TRINITY BAY deserves mention for the extensive view it commands. It is called, in TRINITY BAY, Sainters Hill; on the chart, CENTRE HILL; but is known in PLACENTIA BAY by the name of Powderhorn Hill. It is an isolated peak, upwards of 1000 feet above the sea, and overlooks nearly the whole of the BAYS OF PLACENTIA and TRINITY, as well as some of the high grounds about CONCEPTION, Bonavista, and Fortune Bays.[57]

The phonetic resemblance between Sainter ['sentər] and Centre ['sɛntər] is sufficiently close to suggest that Sainter is a mistake for Centre. However, Sainter is an English family name,[58] cited by both Wix and Jukes as a possessive, and Jukes apparently accepted both Sainter and Centre without questioning the likelihood that the names were identical. Powder-horn is descriptive of the conical shape of the hill.

Come-by-Chance River[59] marks the first recording of the shift name.

The year of the publication of Wix's *Journal*, 1836, was also the year of the first census taken in Newfoundland after the island had been granted a local legislature in 1832. The results are listed by districts in a document entitled simply *Population Returns*,[60] which contains more names of settlements, both old and new, than had ever been previously recorded. On the AVALON PENINSULA alone, in addition to fifty-five new shift names[61] (including seven recorded by Wix), are fifty-seven entirely new names (including five recorded by Wix). Most of these new names of settlements are in fact shift names from the names of previously unrecorded features, as the generics cove, gut, bay, point etc. show. When a settlement has been abandoned since 1836, its name has tended to be preserved in the name of the feature, giving a common historical sequence: unrecorded name of feature becomes name of settlement, which in turn becomes name of feature.

Two new names in the vicinity of ST. JOHN'S are Biscan Bay,[62] now BISCAYAN COVE (NTS Pouch Cove), a feature; and Outer Cove, OUTER COVE (NTS St. John's), named in relation to TORBAY (NTS St. John's), and MIDDLE COVE (NTS St. John's).

South Shore is still in common use for that part of CONCEPTION BAY defined by M. F. Howley as extending from TOPSAIL (NTS St. John's) to HOLYROOD (NTS Holyrood).[63]

Chapel's Cove, now CHAPEL COVE (NTS Holyrood), but still frequently CHAPEL'S COVE in popular usage, appears to contain an English family name, commonly spelt Chappell in Somerset and Chapple in Devonshire,[64] though a local tradition suggests a French origin.

Gasters,[65] GASTERS (NTS Holyrood), Cats' Cove,[66] now CONCEPTION HARBOUR (NTS Holyrood), and Turk's Gut,[67] now MARY(S)VALE (NTS Holyrood) have been considered previously.

Bull Cove,[68] BULL COVE (NTS Harbour Grace) and Caplin[69] Cove, CAPLIN COVE (NTS Harbour Grace), are now names only of the features, with the specific in the former probably the same as in BAY BULLS (NTS Bay Bulls).

Wm. Batton and Rich. Wells had been registered as property-owners at Salmon Cove, SALMON COVE (NTS Harbour Grace), in 1798,[70] though there is no evidence of a settlement there at that time.

South Gut, now SOUTH RIVER (NTS Harbour Grace), and Northern Gut, now NORTH RIVER (NTS Harbour Grace), are named after the two rivers which flow into BAY DE GRAVE (NTS Harbour Grace).

Other new names in CONCEPTION BAY are Sandy Cove, SANDY COVE (NTS Harbour Grace) and Bread and Cheese Cove,[71] now BISHOP'S COVE (NTS Harbour Grace). Upper Island Cove,[72] UPPER ISLAND COVE (NTS Harbour Grace) is the Haylinscove of Beaudoin 1697, with the qualifier Upper, in the sense of nearer the head of the bay, added to distinguish it from LOWER ISLAND COVE (NTS Heart's Content). Similar use of the qualifier is seen in UPPER GULLIES (NTS Holyrood) and Lower Gullies, now RIVERDALE (NTS Holyrood). The specific refers to the islet which fronts the cove. Low Point, LOW POINT (NTS Bay de Verde), replaces Clip Boney[73] (Thornton 1689B). Red Head Cove, RED HEAD COVE (NTS Bay de Verde), is a shift name from RED HEAD (NTS Bay de Verde), though RED HEAD itself is apparently not recorded before *Newfoundland 1941*.

In TRINITY BAY, Daniel's Cove, DANIELS COVE (NTS Bay de Verde) contains a family name common in Cornwall, Devonshire and Gloucestershire, though here it is a baptismal name.[74] Lance Cove was renamed BROWNSDALE (NTS Old Perlican) by a Proclamation of 8 August 1911, after the English family name found there. Since lance is not descriptive of any feature in the locality, it may refer to the lance or lawnce, "or sand-eel, a long thin fish which appears in June"[75] in Newfoundland waters with the caplin and is also used for bait. Caplin Cove, between HANTS HARBOUR (NTS Old Perlican) and Scilly Cove, now WINTERTON (NTS Heart's Content), has not been identified. The specific in Turk's Cove, TURKS COVE (NTS Heart's Content), ? Bay de Rose (Friend 1713), would seem to originate from the same source as in TURKS GUT (NTS Harbour Grace).[76]

According to a local tradition,[77] Old Shop, OLD SHOP (NTS Dildo), was formerly Old Chop, after a large tree trunk, a chopping-block, which stood outside a store there.

Norman's Cove, NORMANS COVE (NTS Dildo), and Chance Cove, BIG CHANCE COVE (NTS Dildo), were both recorded by Wix.[78] Gooseberry Cove has not been identified, but would seem to be in the neighbourhood of GOOSEBERRY ISLAND (NTS Sunnyside).

On the SOUTHERN SHORE, Soils Cove, between BAULINE EAST (NTS Ferryland and ST. MICHAELS (NTS Ferryland) has not been identified. Soil(e) is a Cornish dialect word, ? an irregular local variation of seal.[79]

Caplin Cove was re-named ST. MICHAELS by a Proclamation of 17 May 1904. Burn Cove appears to be a mistake name for BURNT COVE (NTS Ferryland), ? formerly Basin Cove (Popple 1733).

In ST. MARY'S BAY, Coote's Pond, now a feature COOTE POND (NTS St. Mary's), was formerly Browns Pond (Cook 1762 or Gilbert 1768).[80] Coote is both an English and an Irish family name not current in Newfoundland, a nickname from the coot, ? *Fulica americana americana.* "The expression 'silly as a coot' as applied to human beings probably originated from the peculiar appearance of a coot with its dark head, white bill and clumsy movements."[81]

River Head, RIVERHEAD (NTS St. Mary's), is at the head of ST. MARY'S HARBOUR (NTS St. Mary's).[82] Gleeson's Cove, between ADMIRALS BEACH (NTS Placentia) and Mussel Pond, now O'DONNELLS (NTS Placentia) has not been identified. Gleeson is an Irish family name,[83] found rarely in Newfoundland but not in this locality. Black Duck Gullies, now ? ST. JOSEPH'S (NTS Placentia)[84] appears to contain the first recording of the generic, used here perhaps in the sense of ravines. Black Duck, *Anas rubripes*, is "the common 'wild duck' of interior Newfoundland"[85] after which at least four ponds on the AVALON PENINSULA are named.

Rattling Brook, now MOUNT CARMEL (NTS St. Catherine's), contains a common specific in Newfoundland river-names, first cited by Cartwright in 1792: "... we arrived at the mouth of a strong, rattling brook." He defines rattle: "Where there is a succession of falls in a river (which are frequently to be met with in mountainous countries) the falling water makes a great noise; such a place is called a Rattle."[86] J. B. Jukes describes rattle simply as "the term used in Newfoundland for *rapid*."[87] Rattling Brook seems to have been known as Salmonier North before the most recent name MOUNT CARMEL, was proclaimed on 25 June 1930. In the first instance MOUNT CARMEL derives from Mount Carmel in Palestine, where a mendicant order of nuns and friars was founded in the twelfth century, but more immediately, like many of the commemorative names of religious significance on the AVALON PENINSULA, from the growth of Roman Catholicism in Newfoundland which followed the appointment of James Louis O'Donel as Prefect Apostolic in 1784 and as first bishop in 1796. The local church is dedicated to Our Lady of Mount Carmel.[88]

Cox's Point, COX POINT (NTS St. Catherine's), contains an English family name common in Dorset,[89] and still found in the area.

Harry Cove, now HARRICOTT (NTS Placentia), and Harry Cove Pt., now HARRICOTT POINT (NTS Placentia), probably contain the popular anglicization of the French family name Haricot.[90]

John's Pond, JOHN'S POND (NTS Placentia), now the name of a feature, is recorded as late as 1873 as the only settlement in COLINET HARBOUR.[91] Johns is an English family name, especially associated with Cornwall but found also in Devonshire, Monmouthshire and South Wales; John is restricted to Monmouthshire and South Wales.[92] Both forms occur in Newfoundland, though not locally.

The Nineteenth Century / 109

Beckford, now preserved only in the feature BECKFORD HEAD (NTS St. Mary's), is an English family name derived from Beckford, a parish in Gloucestershire.[93] It would appear to be the same as the Newfoundland family name Peckford, on the analogy of the change of initial b to p, observed by Bardsley in Beverley and Peverley, Beattie and Peattie, and Biddle and Peddell.[94]

Golden Bay, GOLDEN BAY (NTS St. Bride's), is said by M. F. Howley to be a "traditional site of hidden treasure," though the name may be descriptive and associated with Red Land, REDLAND POINT (NTS St. Bride's), "so called from the purple colour of the porphyritic rock of which the rocks are formed."[95]

In PLACENTIA BAY, Lear's Cove, LEARS COVE (NTS St. Bride's), contains a Devonshire family name,[96] found in Newfoundland especially at HIBBS HOLE (NTS Harbour Grace), whence LEARS COVE (NTS Harbour Grace), and at SEAL COVE (NTS Holyrood).[97]

Distress, now ST. BRIDE'S (NTS St. Bride's), though the feature is still DISTRESS COVE, is said by M. F. Howley to have been "On more ancient maps ... Le Stresse, apparently a French name,"[98] but no such citation has been traced. Support for the supposition that it is an English name, indicative of the notoriety and dangers of this part of the coast of PLACENTIA BAY from CAPE ST. MARY's to PLACENTIA, may be found in two widely-separated descriptions, the first by Jean Alfonse in 1544: "... a l'entour du cap [sainte Marie] et au long la coste y a des rochiers, qui boutent loing en la mer et sont dangereux,"[99] the second in the *Sailing Directory* 1873: "it is a most inhospitable shore, the headlands are steep, and the coves between only afford shelter to a few fishing stations."[100] Howley states that "The name of ST. BRIDE'S is quite modern, and was given from the titular Saint of the Church of St. Bridget."[101] Brigit or Bride (453–523) is one of the patron saints of Ireland.[102]

Cuslett, CUSLETT (NTS St. Bride's), is probably an unidentified family name. The features are named Curslett Brook and Curslett Cove (Adm. 2915 1864).

Features associated with Angel's Cove, ANGEL'S COVE (NTS Ship Cove), have received two mistake names: Angus Cove (Adm. 2915 1864 and Adm. 232a 1870) and Angles Cove (Howley NQ XXIX 1910), the latter occurring as early as 1868 in the shift name Angle's Brook (Murray 1868). There can be little doubt that Angel is the correct specific, since the neighbouring settlement bears a related name, Devil's Cove, now PATRICK'S COVE (NTS Ship Cove).

Gooseberry, GOOSEBERRY COVE (NTS Ship Cove), is ? Borrell (Whitbourne 1622).[103] M. F. Howley believed that it was "called no doubt

110 / *Place Names of the Avalon Peninsula*

from the prevalence of those wild fruit which grows [sic] numerously in certain parts of Newfoundland,"[104] but since no evidence has been found that gooseberries do grow wild in Newfoundland,[105] there is a likelihood that the original name of the feature was Goose Cove (as in Adm. 2915 1864), retained in Gooseberry (Goose) Cove (*NLP* 1951), ? a shift name from Goose Shoal, three-quarters of a mile northwest of the cove, to which the element berry has been arbitrarily added.

Ship Cove, SHIP COVE (NTS Ship Cove), is the alternative location of Borrell (Whitbourne 1622).[106]

Barrisways, now GREAT BARASWAY and LITTLE BARASWAY (NTS Ship Cove), and Green Point, GREEN POINT (NTS Ship Cove), have been discussed previously.[107]

NE Arm, NE gut in Wix,[108] is now DUNVILLE (NTS Placentia). Since Dunville, an English family name of French origin[109] has not been traced in Newfoundland, the place name, which dates from ? the late nineteenth or early twentieth century is perhaps the Irish family name Dunn(e), with what is in Newfoundland, if not elsewhere in North America, a somewhat rare suffix -ville, usually indicating a settlement.[110]

Seal's Cove, BIG or LITTLE SEAL COVE (NTS Argentia), is now the name only of the feature.

Crawley's Island, CRAWLEY ISLAND (NTS Argentia), contains an English or Irish family name,[111] current in Newfoundland but not locally. It is recorded as Harbour Island (Imray 1862, 1873), from its position at the mouth of LONG HARBOUR (NTS Argentia).

Mooney's Cove, now MOANY COVE (NTS Argentia), Bald Head, BALD HEAD (NTS Argentia), and La Manche, LA MANCHE (NTS Dildo), have been mentioned or discussed previously.[112]

Arnold's Cove, ARNOLD'S COVE (NTS Sunnyside), contains an English family name found elsewhere in Newfoundland but not locally, though the possibility that it is a baptismal name should not be overlooked. It is repeated in ARNOLD COVE (NTS St. Shotts), apparently first cited by M. F. Howley in 1909.[113]

J. B. Jukes's *Excursions in and about Newfoundland during the years 1839 and 1840*,[114] the record of his travels as Geological Surveyor of Newfoundland, together with his "Note on the Natural History of Newfoundland," his "General Report of the Geological Survey of Newfoundland," appended to fill out the *Excursions* to two volumes, and the map which accompanied the separate publication of the "General Report,"[115] contain more Newfoundland place names than any previous documents by one author. Besides names previously recorded, Jukes added several shift names and new names, though some of the new names have not received official recognition. His most valuable contribution to the toponymy is in the number of names of inland features.

Among the shift names and names first recorded by Jukes but referred to in earlier contexts are: the feature Pouche Cove,[116] POUCH COVE (NTS Pouch Cove); Cat's Cove Hills,[117] a shift name from Cats' Cove, now CONCEPTION HARBOUR (NTS Holyrood); and the province of Averlon,[118] which reintroduces the term province unused since Province of Avalonia (Robinson 1669) with the spelling suggesting perhaps that Jukes was unaware of the associations of the specific.

"Bay Verde, or, as the people call it, Bay of Herbs,"[119] BAY DE VERDE (NTS Bay de Verde), is glossed by Jukes: "This latter name is singularly inappropriate, as it is a wild desert place, composed entirely of bare red gritstone, like that on the coast near St. John's." BAY DE VERDE itself, Green Bay, would seem to be equally inappropriate.

Other names previously mentioned are: Centre Hill,[120] CENTRE HILL (NTS Sunnyside); Butterpots,[121] BUTTER POT (NTS Holyrood and Biscay Bay River); Bread and Cheese,[122] a hill at the head of CALVERT BAY (NTS Ferryland); Harrycove,[123] now HARRICOTT (NTS Placentia). Shift names are Colinet River and Arm,[124] COLINET RIVER (NTS Placentia); North Harbour Lookout[125] (unnamed in NTS Placentia); South-east Mountains and North-east Mountain[126] (unnamed in NTS), to be associated with SOUTHEAST RIVER (NTS Placentia) and NORTHEAST RIVER (NTS Argentia); and Spaniard's Bay Lookout[128] (unnamed in NTS). Turk's Head, TURKS HEAD (NTS Harbour Grace),[128] is apparently a shift name from TURKS GUT (NTS Harbour Grace), recorded in *Population Returns 1836.*

Mosquito Cove,[129] GREAT MOSQUITO COVE (NTS Sunnyside), is Flagstaffe Harbour (Guy 1612); and Spread Eagle Peak, SPREAD EAGLE PEAK (NTS Argentia), with its "conical shape," must be a shift name from the descriptive Spread Eagle (Jukes 1840), SPREAD EAGLE BAY (NTS Dildo), ? Savage Harbour (Guy 1612).[130] Spread Eagle, however, may have been transferred from Dorset where it is the name of a steep hill near Shaftesbury.

In the vicinity of ST. JOHN's Jukes records Branscombe Hill,[131] of which the specific, an English family name from Branscombe, Devonshire, is retained in the shift name, BRANSCOMBES POND (NTS St. John's). William Branscombe was a subscriber to *The Royal Gazette* in 1806.[132]

Jukes explains the seeming inexactitude of the name South Side Hill, SOUTH SIDE HILLS (NTS St. John's):

> My first impulse on landing was to ascend the ridge on the south-east side of the harbour, which, from the people all using compass bearings instead of the true, is called the south side, and the ridge the south side hill.[133]

114 / *Place Names of the Avalon Peninsula*

two leaps of about twenty or thirty feet each, over ledges of hard rock, with a foaming rapid of 100 yards in length between the falls. Above this spot the river is from sixty to eighty yards in breadth for some miles, but rapid, stony, and rarely more than knee-deep. About twelve miles up it forks, and the principal branch, called Hodge River, takes its rise from some ponds which are not more than five or six miles distant from Brigus in Conception Bay.[156]

Hodge River,[157] or Hodge Water River (Murray 1872) (unnamed in NTS), contains an English family name, found especially in Cornwall and Devonshire, preserved in HODGEWATER POND (NTS Holyrood).

Masterly as Jukes's whole "Sketch of the Physical Geography of Newfoundland"[158] is, it has particular value in its analysis of the hill formations of the AVALON PENINSULA in which he records for the first time the names of several features. He identified two principal ranges and a number of subordinate hills and ranges.

In the most easterly range, from the back of RENEWS (NTS Renews) to HOLYROOD (NTS Holyrood) he distinguished the two BUTTERPOTS (NTS Biscay Bay River and Holyrood),[159] at either end, and "eminences of nearly equal altitude ... at several parts of the range to which the local names of Bold Face, Bread and Cheese,[160] the Drop, the Flakey Downs, &c., have been attached." Hills associated with this range, if not part of it, are Hell Hill, north of CAPE BROYLE HARBOUR (NTS Ferryland), and the White Hills, "a range of high land [which] runs along the eastern side of CONCEPTION BAY" from TOPSAIL HEAD (NTS St. John's) ... to the neighbourhood of CAPE ST. FRANCIS (NTS Pouch Cove).

The other principal range runs from CAPE DOG (NTS Placentia) to the neighbourhood of CHAPEL ARM (NTS Dildo) and includes a number of elevations "for the most part rounded and flat-topped," such as Mount Sea-Pie, Cap Hill, the North Hill, Little Gut Lookout, the Tolt[161] and the Monument. Of these, only Mount Sea-Pie, now SEPOY HILL (NTS Placentia), is recorded in NTS. It is named after a fish-eating bird, the sea-pie or oyster-catcher, *Hæmatopus palliatus palliatus*, which used to breed on the Atlantic coast of North America as far north as the Southern Labrador Peninsula.[162] The rounding whereby [siːpaI] becomes [siːpoI] is common in Newfoundland speech.

Other hills mentioned by Jukes are the Sawyers' Hills, SAWYERS HILL (NTS Placentia), with "a peaked serrated outline." He writes: "The ground of this ridge [of which SAWYERS HILL is the southern extremity] had a singular appearance: it was utterly bare, and the sharp edges of the thin beds of slaty gritstone bristled up along it almost like the edges of a set of knives."[163] SERRATED HILL (Adm. 296 1863) (NTS Dildo) and La Scie (NTS Nippers Harbour) denote similar features.

Naked-man Ridge[164] (unnamed in NTS), "a rude pile of stones" between NORTHEAST ARM (NTS Argentia) and Northeast Mountain, bears a descriptive specific repeated by Jukes on Merasheen Island (NTS Merasheen and Harbour Buffett), and found also near CHANCE COVE (NTS Dildo), at Clarenville (NTS Random Island) and perhaps elsewhere in Newfoundland.

Chisel Hill,[165] (unnamed in NTS), "to the northeast of St. Mary's Bay," Long Point,[166] LONG POINT (NTS Bay Bulls), and The Red Ground[167] (unnamed in NTS), an area at the head of HOLYROOD POND (NTS Biscay Bay River), have descriptive specifics with an unusual generic in the last name.

Dixon's Hill,[168] DIXON HILL (NTS Placentia), is locally known as Cemetery Hill. A somewhat improbable tradition maintains that PLACENTIA (NTS Placentia) was originally called Dixon Island.

Jukes first notes the Newfoundland use of pond for lake: "The term pond is applied indiscriminately to all pieces of freshwater, whatever may be their size,"[169] one of the "peculiarities of the Colony," as D. W. Prowse puts it, "[which] can be traced back to our Devonshire forefathers. There are no lakes in the west of England, only ponds, so all our lakes are called ponds."[170] However, even if the *Lacus incognitus* the "great Lake or Sea unknowne discouered in Anno 1617 by Captaine Mason"[171] is disregarded, the gentlemen of ST. JOHN'S had renamed Twenty Mile Pond WINDSOR LAKE in 1812,[172] and W. E. Cormack had named no less than twenty-one Lakes in the course of his journey on foot across Newfoundland in 1822.[173] Bonnycastle, writing in the same year as Jukes, observes that not only are lakes called ponds, but that rivers are called brooks,[174] a statement that also needs qualification. Murray, in the Report of the Geological Survey for 1874, records a second use of pond: "Long stretches of still water, commonly called ponds by the trappers, constitute the greater part of the [Gander] river's course, and these are connected by gentle currents, which, but for the shallowness of the water, which sometimes spreads over an immense width, would be scarcely imperceptible."[175]

Sir Richard Bonnycastle's[176] *Newfoundland in 1842* records George's Pond, GEORGES POND (NTS St. John's), and Parson's Pond[177] (unnamed in NTS) both of unknown origin, are on SIGNAL HILL (NTS St. John's). Broad Cove Gastors,[178] BROAD COVE (NTS Holyrood), contains the qualifier Gastors, i.e. GASTERS (NTS Holyrood), to distinguish the feature from some half dozen other Broad Coves on the AVALON PENINSULA. The same construction is found in the popular form LONG POND MANUELS for MANUELS LONG POND (NTS St. John's). Turk's Gut,[179] TURKS GUT (NTS Harbour Grace), may be the first recording of the name of the feature, though the settlement had been recorded in *Population Returns 1836.* Lady Point, now NORTH HEAD (NTS Bay Bulls), and the shift name Deer Hd,[180] now DEER HARBOUR HEAD (NTS Sunnyside), occur in the map which accompanied the book.

The Census of 1857[181] was the last occasion in the nineteenth century on which new names in any number were to be recorded on the AVALON PENINSULA. The additions derived chiefly from distinguishing small settlements which had been enumerated as parts of larger communities in 1836.[182]

BECK'S COVE in ST. JOHN'S (NTS St. John's), which was taken to mark the division of the electoral districts of ST. JOHN'S EAST and ST. JOHN'S WEST, is one of a number of short side streets which link the main thoroughfare, WATER STREET, with the harbour front. The specific is probably the family name of an unidentified merchant; the use of the generic cove for street seems to be restricted to Newfoundland.[183]

Freshwater,[184] unnamed in NTS, is a settlement associated with MIDDLE COVE (NTS St. John's). Balline, BAULINE (NTS St. John's), has been discussed previously.[185]

The specific in Maddox Cove, MADDOX COVE (NTS Bay Bulls), between CAPE SPEAR (NTS St. John's) and PETTY HARBOUR (NTS Bay Bulls), is an English family name of Welsh origin, associated with Herefordshire in this form, and with Cheshire, Devonshire, and Shropshire in the form Maddock or Maddocks. According to M. F. Howley, it was well known in ST. JOHN'S in the nineteenth century; it is still found in a number of localities in Newfoundland.[186]

Several settlements in CONCEPTION BAY, which were enumerated simply as South Shore in *Population Returns 1836,* are identified individually. Horse Cove, HORSE COVE (NTS St. John's), of unknown origin, is retained as the name of the feature, though the settlement was somewhat clumsily renamed St. Thomas's, now ST. THOMAS (NTS St. John's), by a proclamation of 30 January 1922.

Chamberlain, now CHAMBERLAINS (NTS St. John's), is an English family name of Gloucestershire and other counties, rare in Newfoundland.[187] The form without the possessive is unusual. Manuels, MANUELS (NTS St. John's), is an English family name found at CARBONEAR (NTS Harbour Grace) and LOWER ISLAND COVE (NTS Heart's Content and Bay de Verde). M. F. Howley relates a tradition that the name "is derived from an old man-o'-war sailor, who deserted his ship in past time and took refuge in the locality where he lived for many years," but also conjectures elsewhere that Corte Real imposed the name in honour of Manuel I of Portugal.[188] Long Pond, unnamed in NTS but recorded in *Electors, Harbour Main* is descriptive.[189]

Local tradition maintains that Foxtrap, FOXTRAP (NTS St. John's), was so called when the settlement grew up in a previously unnamed district where only foxes were caught in the rabbit-snares. The earliest citation of the word in *OED* is Jonson's metaphorical use in *Volpone* (1605):

> To cozen him [Volpone-the fox] of all, were
> but a cheat
> Well placed: no man would construe it a sin:
> Let his sport pay for 't. This is called
> the Fox-trap.
> v, iii,

followed by a citation of its literal use only in 1856. But Wix had used it in 1836 in a context which may suggest that a foxtrap was an article of clothing:

A man had died in this neighbourhood [near La Poile (NTS La Poile) on the South Coast of Newfoundland] lately ... I found that a story of the appearance of his spirit, which was circulated by an illiterate drunken scoundrel, with the obviously interested motive, clumsily concealed, of influencing the distribution of the poor fellow's little effects, was very generally believed. More incredulity was expressed at my assurance that the distribution of a southwester, a foxtrap, or a pair of mockasins, was not a *dignus Deo vindice notus*, a matter for Divine interference, than had been excited by the whole story itself.[190]

Middle Bight, named after the slight indentation in the coastline between FOXTRAP (NTS St. John's) and KELLIGREWS (NTS Harbour Grace), was re-named CODNER (unnamed in NTS) after Samuel Codner, a nineteenth century philanthropist,[191] by a proclamation of 18 June 1906. The generic is unusual on the AVALON PENINSULA, occurring elsewhere only in SKERRYS BIGHT (NTS St. John's) with the same signification, and in TORBAY BIGHT (NTS St. John's) where it is used of the large cove at the bottom of TORBAY (NTS St. John's).

LOWER GULLIES, recorded in *Population Returns 1836*, re-named RIVERDALE (NTS Holyrood) by a proclamation of 3 January 1923, and Upper Gullies, UPPER GULLIES (NTS Holyrood), were so called after the gullies or small ravines formed by two rivers which ran into CONCEPTION BAY. Lance Cove, LANCE COVE (NTS Holyrood), and Seals Cove, now SEAL COVE (NTS Holyrood), are named after two minor features.[192] Three settlements are distinguished at HOLYROOD (NTS Holyrood): South Side Holyrood, South Arm of Holyrood, SOUTH ARM (NTS Holyrood), and North Side Holyrood.

Middle Arm, MIDDLE ARM (NTS Holyrood), is named after the major indentation in GASTERS BAY (NTS Holyrood) between CONCEPTION HARBOUR and AVONDALE.

In COLLIERS BAY (NTS Holyrood) are Colliers James Cove, JAMES COVE (NTS Holyrood), and Colliers English Cove, ENGLISH COVE (NTS Holyrood), now the names only of features, the first being an English family name widespread but especially common in the West Country, the second an Irish family name particularly associated with Co. Limerick and Co. Tipperary.[193] Both are found in Newfoundland, but not locally. Colliers Flat Rock is unnamed in NTS.

Turks Gut South is a shift name from Turk's Gut (Population Returns 1836), now MARYVALE (NTS Holyrood).

Rip Rap, near CUPIDS (NTS Harbour Grace), a name now obsolete, is a nautical term to denote a narrow submarine hill or the motion of the tide against the wind, cited in OED as a place name in the English Channel in 1669 and 1784. In the form Riff Raff, it is the name of a group of sunken rocks in HANTS HARBOUR (NTS Old Perlican) and SHOAL BAY (NTS Sunnyside).[194] Clarke's Beach, CLARKES BEACH (NTS Harbour Grace), has been discussed previously.[195]

Juniper Stump, JUNIPER STUMP (NTS Harbour Grace), a small inland settlement, may have been named after a hillock on which juniper, the Newfoundland name for larch,[196] used in boat-building, grew. The name also occurs, though unrecorded, at the junction of the roads from PORTUGAL COVE (NTS St. John's) and BAULINE (NTS St. John's).

Gullies, GULLIES (47-31, 53-14 NTS Harbour Grace), without a specific,[197] is joined with Goulds, now MAKINSON (GOULDS P.O.) (NTS Harbour Grace).[198]

According to a local tradition similar to that associated with MANUELS (NTS St. John's),[199] Hall's Town, HALLS TOWN (NTS Harbour Grace), is named after Isaac Hall, a deserter from a naval vessel, who made his home there in the early years of the nineteenth century. The family name is common in the settlement.

New names in the vicinity of PORT DE GRAVE (NTS Harbour Grace) are Dock, THE DOCK (NTS Harbour Grace), a place where vessels were hauled ashore for repairs, and Long Beach, a name preserved in the shift name, LONG BEACH POND (NTS Harbour Grace), and still in use locally.

Bishop's Cove, BISHOP'S COVE (NTS Harbour Grace), previously known as Bread and Cheese Cove (Population Returns 1836), contains an

English family name particularly associated with Dorset and found in the neighbouring community of UPPER ISLAND COVE (NTS Harbour Grace).[200]

In the immediate neighbourhood of BAY ROBERTS (NTS Harbour Grace) are Whitemonday Hill, ? commemorating an event of religious significance on a Whitmonday; Mercers Cove, MERCERS COVE (NTS Harbour Grace), after the English family name of BAY ROBERTS, known in 1765 when Jonathan Mercer was recorded as a property-owner, having received his property as a gift from his father;[201] Beachy Cove, BEACH COVE (NTS Harbour Grace); Centre Harbor, with the termination -or common throughout the Census; Dock Point; Coosh and Country Path, now COUNTRY ROAD (NTS Harbour Grace), and Coley's Point, COLEY'S POINT (NTS Harbour Grace), discussed previously.[202]

Three names, which have occurred elsewhere on the AVALON PENINSULA, are repeated on the NORTH SHORE of CONCEPTION BAY: Flat Rock, FLAT ROCK (NTS Heart's Content), Blow-me-down (unnamed in NTS), and Otterbury (unnamed in NTS), a shift name from Otterbury Point (Lane, *Directions* 1775, 1810).[203]

Marshall's Folly (unnamed in NTS) contains a generic unique, it is believed, in Newfoundland. Folly is used here, not in the English sense of "a popular name for any costly structure considered to have shown folly in the builder,"[204] but, according to a local tradition, as a comment on the foolishness of one Marshall, in moving his home ? from FRESHWATER (NTS Heart's Content). However, a second meaning of folly, "a clump of fir-trees on the crest of a hill," cited in Berkshire, Norfolk and Wiltshire, should not be overlooked.[205]

Upper Small Point, which is retained as the name of the feature though the settlement was renamed KINGSTON (NTS Heart's Content) by a proclamation of 27 August 1920, and Lower Small Point, LOWER SMALL POINT (NTS Heart's Content), now the name only of a feature, are at the southern and northern extremities of a small bay unnamed in NTS. Spout Cove, SPOUT COVE (NTS Heart's Content), appears to indicate the presence of a waterfall. Kettle Cove, unnamed in NTS, is perhaps descriptive. Caplin Cove,[206] CAPLIN COVE (NTS Bay de Verde), may have been Harbour Grande (Dudley 1646).

In TRINITY BAY, Island Cove is retained for the name of the feature, but the settlement was renamed ISLINGTON (NTS Heart's Content) by a proclamation of 8 August 1911.

On the SOUTHERN SHORE, the only new name is Goulds, GOULDS (NTS Bay Bulls), which has been discussed with MAKINSON (GOULDS P.O.).[207]

In ST. MARY'S BAY, the names Gaskier,[208] GASKIERS (NTS St. Mary's), and Mosquito,[209] MOSQUITO (NTS St. Mary's), on GREAT COLINET ISLAND (NTS St. Mary's and Placentia), have been discussed in other contexts; Middle House, ? between LITTLE SALMONIER RIVER (NTS Placentia) and LITTLE BARACHOIS RIVER (NTS Placentia), has not been identified; and Gull Cove, GULL COVE (NTS St. Bride's), contains a common specific.

One name, however, on GREAT COLINET ISLAND is remarkable for its bizarre form, still retained for the name of the feature in naval documents: Mother Ixx's (cove) officially renamed Regina by a proclamation of 27 October 1913 though the change had been introduced some years previously by the Rev. J. St. John, now REGINAVILLE (NTS Placentia). A unique citation, Mother Hicks Cove (Adm. 2915 1869 or later), makes the name intelligible and leads to the conjecture that it commemorates an inhabitant, perhaps of Cornish stock and a migrant from PETERS RIVER (NTS St. Mary's), where it is common. Loss of the initial aspirate in Hicks and an attempted phonetic spelling of the final consonantal group account for Ixx; but M. F. Howley knew the name as Mother Ex or Rex, and the latter form (with linking r) may have been the source of Father St. John's inspiration with its religious connotations.[210]

The Census does not appear to contain any new names on the AVALON PENINSULA in PLACENTIA BAY.

With the foregoing extraction of names from the Census of 1857, the linguistic and historical survey of the place names on the AVALON PENINSULA may be brought to a convenient, if arbitrary conclusion. Later censuses added a few more names of settlements, later Sailing Directions and Pilots added a few more names of coastal features, and the Survey of ROCKY RIVER (NTS Placentia) by J. P. Howley in 1872 was to reveal a group of Micmac lake names;[211] but by 1857, most place names on the Peninsula had been recorded.

Exceptions are the names of inland features, especially ponds, which often bear the names of inhabitants of neighbouring settlements, but very few of these names were recorded before detailed surveys of the interior were undertaken by government agencies in the present century, though many may well have been in existence for a hundred years or more.

The three following chapters discuss an important ethnic group of place names and make a toponymic analysis of most of the names on the AVALON PENINSULA in their modern forms.

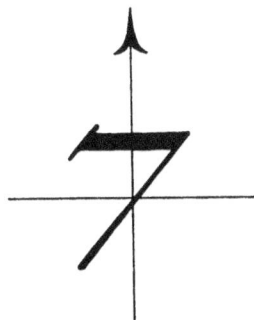

The Irish Place Names

Up to the present, no definitive study has been made of the Irish in Newfoundland despite the fact that people of Irish descent probably form a majority of the population and Irish influences on the culture are particularly evident in religion, education, lore, the spoken language, vocabulary[1] and idiom.

One tradition states that the first Irish immigrants reached Newfoundland about 1630:

The first arrival of emigrants from Ireland took place soon after the departure of Lord Baltimore [in 1629]. Viscount Falkland was then Lord-Lieutenant of Ireland. He sent out a body of settlers from that country to increase the small population of Newfoundland. These, at a later date, were followed by many more.[2]

The first documentary evidence, however, of the presence of the Irish seems to appear only in 1697 in Beaudoin's *Journal*.[3] He makes six references to them, mentioning eight Irish Catholics from BRIGUS (NTS Harbour Grace), "que les Anglais traitent icy comme des esclaves"; an Irishman who was in command at HEART'S CONTENT (NTS Heart's Content); three Irishmen who had joined the French and had been captured by the men of CARBONEAR (NTS Harbour Grace) and one who had escaped; and a further twenty who had also joined the French. He states that in a proposed exchange of prisoners, the English demanded one Englishman for one Frenchman, and three English for one Irishman. And he makes special mention of one Irishman who escaped (from the

English) by swimming from CARBONEAR ISLAND (NTS Harbour Grace) to find the French in the woods near HEART'S CONTENT (NTS Heart's Content), his feet frozen after spending three days without food or fire.[4]

John Roope's account of the French attack on ST. JOHN'S (NTS St. John's) under Subercase in 1705 states that "all ye Irish [at PLACENTIA (NTS Placentia)] are certainly entred" the French service.[5]

Neither Beaudoin nor Roope gives any indication of the total number of Irish in Newfoundland, but by October 1720, Commodore F. Percy could report somewhat incoherently to the Council of Trade and Plantations that

here are brought over every year by the Bristol, Biddeford and Bastable ships great numbers of Irish roman Catholic servants, who all settle to the southward in our Plantations; which if a warr with France etc. would be a direct means of loosing this country, who would joyne with any enemy, if some care be not taken to suppress the same, it may not be improbable that these very fellowes may turn pyrotts in a little time, especially, after a bad fishing voyage.[6]

The statement that the Irish "all settle to the southward in our Plantations," may be taken to mean that they were found not only at PLACENTIA (NTS Placentia) but also elsewhere in PLACENTIA BAY, in ST. MARY'S BAY and on the SOUTHERN SHORE, and that ST. JOHN'S (NTS St. John's) and the harbours of CONCEPTION BAY were by no means the main or only areas in which they congregated. Two groups may be distinguished: men who came as members of the crews of fishing vessels, but remained in Newfoundland at the end of the fishing season instead of returning home; and those who apparently came to seek permanent employment in the service of the planters and by-boatkeepers.

By 1729 their numbers had "considerably increased"; by 1731 "a majority of the male population of the island was Irish Catholic"; but in 1748 Governor Watson found that though "there was a considerable number in Newfoundland, ... they were not as numerous as circumstances made it appear":

They outbalanced the Protestants in ST. JOHN'S and the southern outports, but comprised only about a fifth of the population in the northern harbors, and the governor estimated that they proved about a quarter of the total population, although immigration from Ireland was proportionately larger than that from England.[7]

Information drawn from the Scheme of the Newfoundland Fishery for the years 1732 and 1754, though perhaps not wholly reliable, demonstrates the growth of the Irish population on the AVALON PENINSULA in the period:[8]

TABLE 4

ENGLISH AND IRISH INHABITANTS OF THE AVALON PENINSULA 1732 AND 1754

1732

Modern Name	Masters	Men Servants	Wives	Women Servants	Children	Masters	Men Servants	Wives	Women Servants	Children
	English					Irish				
NEW PERLICAN	9	70	5		18					
OLD PERLICAN	20	190	9		20					
BAY DE VERDE	20	100	16	2	60		12			
CARBONEAR-BRISTOL'S HOPE	60	248	53	53	137					
HARBOUR GRACE / BAY ROBERTS	22	74	16	4	93		26			
TORBAY / QUIDI VIDI / ST. JOHN'S	53	346	7	33	189					
PETTY HARBOUR / BAY BULLS / TORS COVE	29	80	14	1	76	4	166	7		
FERRYLAND	21	186	20	3	25			2		
FERMEUSE / RENEWS	32	267	1	1	40		35			
TREPASSEY	15	20		15	25					
ST. MARY'S	4	20	4		3		10			
PLACENTIA / ARGENTIA	15	60	19	2	34	4	46	4		16

1754

Modern Name	Masters	Men Servants	Wives	Women Servants	Children	Masters	Men Servants	Wives	Women Servants	Children
NEW PERLICAN										
OLD PERLICAN										
BAY DE VERDE										
CARBONEAR-BRISTOL'S HOPE	80	600	60	16	170		400		50	80
HARBOUR GRACE / BAY ROBERTS	170	1000	100	40	320		600		70	100
TORBAY / QUIDI VIDI / ST. JOHN'S	120	1000	100	50	230		700		50	100
PETTY HARBOUR	30	150	13	6	20		100		10	11
BAY BULLS / TORS COVE	30	424	38	20	80		282		12	
FERRYLAND	45	472	30	20	90		360		15	
FERMEUSE / RENEWS	27	285	10		26		180		1	
TREPASSEY	34	356	15	8	30		200		2	
ST. MARY'S	16	200	7	4	30		100		6	20
PLACENTIA / ARGENTIA	182	320	135	45	170		350		40	

Punitive measures introduced by Governor Dorrill in 1755 against the Irish included deportation, but this order does not seem to have been obeyed, since his successor, Governor Edwards, two years later "mentions a large number of Irishmen still living in Newfoundland";[9] and in 1764 "in consequence of the arrival from Ireland of poor and dissolute women who occasioned much disorder, [Governor] Palliser ... ruled that no woman could land unless security for good behaviour had first been lodged."[10] However, the flow of Irish immigrants continued so that between 1793 and 1815 the population increased from 20,000 to 40,000, and between 1811 and 1830 over 24,000 arrived. To try to meet the social and economic problems caused by the influx of such numbers, many of whom were destitute, the authorities in Newfoundland used to ship back many immigrants to Ireland,[11] but the situation was eased only when emigration to the United States, Canada and Australia became popular. In 1848 only 993 immigrants landed in Newfoundland, of whom 757 were Irish; and during the period 1842 to 1875 only 7642, of whom 4940 were Irish.[12] Nevertheless, Irish families in Newfoundland preserve a widespread tradition that their forbears came over during, or as a result of, the famine of 1845.

No evidence of Irish family names has been found before 1794–5, but a census of ST. JOHN'S (NTS St. John's) and neighbouring communities of that year[13] shows that most of the 2504 Roman Catholic inhabitants bore Irish names, with some eighteen having a history of forty or more years in Newfoundland. They include Morley 1739, King 1746, Fitzgerald 1749, Moreton 1750, Flaherty 1752, Butler 1754, and Shea, Fouleau, Hanrahan, Burke, Murphy, Bryan (? for Brien), White and Kenny all of 1755 in ST. JOHN'S (NTS St. John's); McManus 1745 and Welsh 1755 in PETTY HARBOUR (NTS Bay Bulls); Lanahan (? for Lerhinan or Lernihan) 1755 at QUIDI VIDI (NTS St. John's); and Power 1755 and King 1755 on BELL ISLAND (NTS St. John's and Harbour Grace).[14] The dates of the settlement of Irish families in the outports are generally unknown, though a Hearn is said to have escaped from a prison ship *en route* to Newfoundland in 1734 at FERRYLAND (NTS Ferryland) and subsequently settled at BAY BULLS (NTS Bay Bulls); the Connollys are said to have settled at NORTH RIVER (NTS Harbour Grace) about 1780; the Daltons at CONCEPTION HARBOUR (NTS Holyrood) in the early 1800s; the Whalens at ARGENTIA (NTS Argentia) about 1830; John Roach at COLEY'S POINT (NTS Harbour Grace) about 1832; a Thomey from County Cork at BRISTOL'S HOPE (NTS Harbour Grace) about 1835; and the Keatings from County Wexford at CONCEPTION HARBOUR (NTS Holyrood) about 1841.[15]

Except for part of the coast of the AVALON PENINSULA in TRINITY BAY,

Irish family names are found practically everywhere on the peninsula, frequently side by side with English names in CONCEPTION BAY and on the SOUTHERN SHORE as far south as CAPE BROYLE (NTS Ferryland), but virtually alone from CAPE BROYLE (NTS Ferryland) to CAPE RACE (NTS Trepassey), and in TREPASSEY BAY, ST. MARY'S BAY and PLACENTIA BAY as far north as LONG HARBOUR (NTS Argentia).

Certain names are associated particularly with certain places, such as O'Brien at CAPE BROYLE (NTS Ferryland), Ryan at MARYVALE (NTS Holyrood), Whelan at COLLIERS (NTS Holyrood), Wade at CONCEPTION HARBOUR (NTS Holyrood), Costello at AVONDALE (NTS Holyrood), and Power at several communities in ST. MARY'S BAY.

From these Irish family names derive many possessive specifics in the nomenclature of the AVALON PENINSULA, especially in the names of small coastal settlements and their neighbouring physical features. Table 5, at the end of this chapter, records in column one the place name; in column two, references to the Irish family name in E. MacLysaght's four volumes, *Irish Families (IF)*, *More Irish Families (MIF)*, *Supplement to Irish Families (SIF)* and *Guide to Irish Surnames (GIS)*, and occasionally in Sir Robert Matheson's *Surnames in Ireland*, with the locale of the name in Ireland; and in column three, the status of the family name on the AVALON PENINSULA, based for the most part on the *Official List of Electors 1955*.

The common combination of the Irish generic *bally* – town with a family name, as in BALLY HALY (not in NTS St. John's), suggests that Haly may be a changed form of Hall(e)y.[16] Lt. Col. W. Haly (?1772–1835), ADC to Governor Cochrane and member of the first Legislative Council in Newfoundland, developed the farm, now a golf course, in the early years of the nineteenth century.[17]

PADDYS POND (NTS Bay Bulls) contains the commonest of all Irish diminutives. ST. BRIDE'S (NTS St. Bride's) has been discussed previously.[18] The ethnic IRISHTOWN is used to denote parts of CARBONEAR (NTS Harbour Grace) and BAY BULLS (NTS Bay Bulls).

In contrast to the large number of possessive specifics recorded above, the Irish nomenclature of the AVALON PENINSULA contains few transfer names. AVONDALE (NTS Holyrood) has been discussed previously.[19]

SHEEP'S HEAD (NTS Renews) may be named after Sheep's Head, Co. Cork.

CAPPAHAYDEN (NTS Renews), a name imposed by a proclamation of 23 December 1913 to replace the older name Broad Cove, is believed locally to have been the choice of M. F. Howley after a Cappahayden, Co. Kilkenny, in which Ir. *ceapach* (anglicized as Cappagh and Cappa)

— meadow, plot of land, is combined with a family name to give the meaning Hayden's meadow. Hayden, a family name of Co. Carlow, is found at CAPE BROYLE (NTS Ferryland).[20]

SKIBBEREEN (NTS Holyrood), a small inland settlement, apparently first recorded in the Census of 1891, is named after Skibbereen, Co. Cork, "at the mouth of the river Ilen, on a little creek much frequented by small vessels, formerly – and still in some places – called *scibs* (Eng. skiff); and *Scibirin*, as the place is called in Irish, means a place frequented by *skibs* or boats."[21] SKIBBEREEN (NTS Holyrood), however, does not appear to have any connexion with sea or river.

BALLYHACK (NTS Holyrood), a settlement, and BALLYHACK POINT (NTS Holyrood) are probably named after Ballyhack, a village in Waterford Harbour.[22] The name is not recorded in Joyce.

DROGHEDA (not in NTS Harbour Grace) ?['drakəti], a small settlement on SOUTH RIVER (NTS Harbour Grace), named after Drogheda, Co. Louth, and known in the latter half of the nineteenth century for its small schooner-building industry, is now virtually abandoned.[23]

VINEGAR HILL (not in NTS Harbour Grace), near OTTERBURY (NTS Harbour Grace), may be named after Vinegar Hill, near Enniscorthy, Co. Wexford, "which figured very conspicuously in the Rebellion of Ninety-eight." Joyce continues:

This name has never been explained till now. There was formerly a wood round the hill which was well known by the name of *Fidh-na-gcaer*, represented exactly in sound in English letters by "Feenagare," with the very slight difference between broad *g* in the Irish form and slender *g* in the English form. This I have ascertained by hearing the name pronounced on the spot, as I did thirty years ago by several intelligent old natives independently. I have often heard it even in Dublin from natives. This name was retained by the old people down to recent times, and I believe it may still be heard if rightly searched for. Hence the hill was naturally named the "Hill of Feenagare" or "Feenagare Hill" as I often heard it called, which got easily corrupted to Vinegar Hill. *Fidh-na-gcaer* is perfectly plain, meaning the "hill of the berries." The word *caer* or *caor*, a berry, is found through all Ireland, used in the same way as here (in the gen. plur. with *c* changed to *g* by eclipsis after the article), examples will be found throughout this book, such as Kilnageer, *Coill-na-gcaor*, wood of the berries (vol. ii. p. 324), almost the same as our present Feenagare or *Fidh-na-gcaor*.

The conversion of "Feenagare" to "Vinegar" is a good example of the very general process called "Popular Etymology" (common in all countries), where a word in one language, whose meaning is lost, or obscured by mispronunciation, is converted into a word of a familiar language of nearly the same sound, whose meaning is quite obvious, affording a kind of satisfactory resting-place for an inquiring mind, uninformed in such matters and easily satisfied; as where "Bellerophon" (the name of a ship) was made "Billy

Ruffian"; "God encompasseth us" (on a tavern sign) was changed to "The Goat and Compasses;" Asparagus to "Sparrow-grass," &c.[24]

In the vicinity of ST. JOHN'S (NTS St. John's), KILBRIDE (NTS St. John's) and MOUNT CASHEL (not in NTS St. John's), an orphanage for boys, repeat two common Irish place names. KILBRIDE, Ir. *Cill-Bhrigde* – Brigid's or Bride's Church, is the name of some thirty-five townlands and parishes throughout Ireland.[25] MOUNT CASHEL, Ir. *caiseal* – circular stone fort, is the name of over fifty townlands.[26]

PARADISE (NTS St. John's) may be a transfer of the ironical name of a patch of very bad land in Kilclooney, Mothel Parish, Co. Waterford, though a local tradition maintains that the name was given because of the abundance of wood there.[27] It occurs once elsewhere on the AVALON PENINSULA at PARADISE POND (NTS St. Catherines) and as the specific in the name of several other features and settlements in Newfoundland where, however, it may sometimes reflect the genitive form of a common Newfoundland trisyllabic pronunciation of the disyllabic family name Pardy ['pardi].[28]

WATERFORD RIVER (NTS St. John's), ? Little Castor's River (Anspach 1819), and WATERFORD BRIDGE (Set.) (NTS St. John's), a centre of Irish settlement in ST. JOHN'S, are transfers from Waterford, one of the principal ports of Southern Ireland engaged in the Newfoundland trade:

It was to buy ... Irish woollens, "Frises, Bandel-cloths," "stockins," pork, beef, butter, and to engage Irish servants, that the West Countrymen first touched at Waterford and Cork on their way out to Newfoundland, and thus commenced the Irish Newfoundland trade in "youngsters and provisions,"[29]

which persisted from before 1690 to the middle years of the nineteenth century.

Riverhead (Thornton 1689B),[30] where WATERFORD RIVER enters ST. JOHN'S HARBOUR (NTS St. John's), is known as KERRYTOWN (not in NTS St. John's).

The remaining Irish place names on the AVALON PENINSULA, in the area covered by NTS Biscay Bay River, St. Catherines, Argentia and Placentia, are distinguished by their being in Irish or but partly anglicized.

TOCHER'S POND (NTS Biscay Bay River) is listed below tentatively as containing a family name, but an alternative origin may be found in Ir. *tochar* – causeway across a bog, made of "branches of trees, bushes, earth and stones, placed in alternate layers, and trampled down till they are sufficiently firm." Joyce comments:

These *tochars* were very common all over the country, our annals record the construction of many in early ages, and some of these are still traceable.

They have given names to a number of townlands and villages, several of them called Togher, and many others containing the word in combination.[31]

That the building of *tochars* was not unknown in Newfoundland may be inferred from Jukes:

In taking a road across a marsh, I observed that the simple expedient of laying a matting of boughs and branches across the road, before putting on the gravel, was frequently neglected. I can speak, from actual inspection, of the sound and durable nature of roads thus constructed in other localities.[32]

LADEN FIELD'S BROOK (NTS Biscay Bay River) appears to contain Ir. *leadan* – burdock, a plant name which forms an element in such Irish place names as Laddan, Co. Donegal, Tirlayden, Co. Donegal, and Turnalayden, Co. Sligo.[33] The plant is probably *Arctium minus* (Hill) Bernh. or *Arctium nemorosum* Lej. & Court, recorded by Rouleau.[34]

KNOCKHOUR HILL (NTS Placentia) contains Ir. *cnoc-odhartha* – pale-grey hill, as in "Knockoura in Cork and Galway."[35]

COVE NAN DRIOCH-CLOCHAN (NTS Argentia), with its shift name COVE NAN DRIOCH-CLOCHAN POINT (NTS Argentia), is perhaps the only unmistakably Irish place name, except for transferred names and family names. If *droich* is read for *drioch*, which is meaningless, the name contains two elements: *droich(ead)* – bridge and *clochan* – stepping-stones, giving a meaning on the lines of The Cove of the Stepping-Stone Bridge. Joyce has two relevant observations:

A row of stepping-stones across a ford on a river, is called in every part of Ireland by the name of *clochan*, pronounced *clackan* in the north of Ireland and in Scotland. This mode of rendering a river fordable was as common in ancient as it is in modern times; for in the tract of Brehon Laws in the Book of Ballymote, regulating the stipend of various kinds of artificers, it is stated that the builder of a *clochan* is to be paid two cows for his labour.

These stepping-stones have given names to places in all parts of Ireland, now called Cloghan, Cloghane, and Cloghaun, the first being more common in the north, and the two last in the south.[36]

Many places in Ireland have taken their names from bridges, and the word *droichead* is often greatly modified by modern corruption. It is to be observed that the place chosen for the erection of a bridge was very usually where the river had already been crossed by a ford; for besides the convenience of retaining the previously existing roads, the point most easily fordable was in general most suitable for a bridge. There are many places whose names preserve the memory of this, of which Drogheda is a good example. This place is repeatedly mentioned in old authorities, and always called *Droichead-atha* [Drohed-aha], the bridge of the ford; from which the present name was easily formed; pointing clearly to the fact, that the first bridge was built over the ford where the northern road along the coast crossed the Boyne.[37]

The name does not appear to have been recorded before the *Newfoundland and Labrador Pilot* 1929 and is not in popular use in the area.

Irish Place Names / 129

The generic Cosh, Ir. *cos* has been discussed previously.³⁸

Finally, the descriptive specific blue in Newfoundland place names, of which BLUE HILLS (NTS Holyrood) and the shift name BLUE HILL POND (NTS Heart's Content) are found on the AVALON PENINSULA, may suggest Irish influence, since *gorm* – blue "is often applied to mountains, and ... designates their blue colour when seen from a distance."³⁹

TABLE 5

PLACE NAMES ASSOCIATED WITH IRISH FAMILY NAMES

Place Name	Irish Family Name	Status of Family Name on the Avalon Peninsula
*? BAKER HEAD (NTS Trepassey)	MIF p. 281, GIS p. 23 Widespread	Not locally
? BAKER POINT (NTS Argentia)		In ARGENTIA area
? TIM BARRETT COVE (NTS Argentia)	IF p. 51 Cork, Galway, Mayo	At MARQUISE, ARGENTIA etc. Tim not identified.
BARRY POINT (NTS St. Mary's)	IF p. 52 etc., GIS p. 24 Cork, Munster	Not locally
BARRYS POND (NTS Harbour Grace)		At IRISH TOWN, CARBONEAR
? BLAKETOWN (NTS Argentia)	IF p. 54, GIS p. 28 Galway, but Sir Henry b. Limerick	After Sir Henry Blake, governor of Newfoundland 1887–8
? BOWES BROOK (NTS Harbour Grace)	MIF p. 36, GIS p. 30 Bowe(s) midland counties	Not current at CARBONEAR
? BOWES LONG POND (NTS Harbour Grace)		
? BOWES ROUND POND (NTS Harbour Grace)		
BRAZIL POND (NTS St. John's)	SIF p. 23 mainly Waterford	BELL I., ST. JOHN'S
BRAZILS POND (NTS Harbour Grace)		At SPANIARD'S BAY etc.
BREMIGENS (? for Branigan) POND (NTS St. John's)	MIF p. 39 E. Ireland	Not current
BRENNAN POINT (NTS Dildo)	IF p. 60 etc. especially Ossory, Galway, Kerry, Westmeath	At SHIP COVE, etc.
BRENNANS HILL (NTS Harbour Grace)		Not current at HARBOUR GRACE
BRIEN (Flag Stop CNR) (NTS Holyrood)	IF p. 62 Widespread	? O'Brien at HOLYROOD
BRIENS POND (NTS Holyrood)		
BURKE ISLAND (NTS Argentia)	IF p. 66, MIF p. 246 Widespread	At MT. ARLINGTON HEIGHTS
LITTLE BURKE ISLAND (NTS Argentia)		
BURKES COVE (NTS Holyrood)		At COLLIERS
BURNS (? for Byrnes) HEAD (NTS Ferryland)	IF p. 68, p. 305, MIF p. 282, SIF p. 156	Not current at FERRYLAND

130 / *Place Names of the Avalon Peninsula*

TABLE 5 *(continued)*

Place Name	Irish Family Name	Status of Family Name on the Avalon Peninsula
? BUTLER HEAD (NTS Dildo)		
? BUTLERS POND (NTS St. Catherine's)	IF p. 67 etc., MIF p. 247 etc. Kilkenny, Tipperary, Waterford, Dublin	At WITLESS BAY
? BUTLERS POND (NTS Holyrood)		At ROACHE'S LINE, BURNT HD., CLARKE'S BEACH
? BUTLERVILLE (NTS Harbour Grace)		At HARBOUR GRACE, BUTLERVILLE, SHEARSTOWN
CAHILL POINT (NTS St. John's)	IF p. 70 especially Tipperary, Cork, Kerry	At ST. JOHN'S etc.
CANTWELLS COVE (NTS St. John's)	MIF p. 50 Kilkenny, Tipperary	Cantwells lighthouse keepers at CAPE SPEAR since 1892
? CLEAR COVE (NTS Renews)	MIF p. 56, GIS p. 43 Wexford, Kilkenny	Yonge 1663–69
? COLLIER BAY (NTS Dildo)		? English name at COLLIER BAY
? COLLIERS (NTS Holyrood)	SIF p. 37, GIS p. 47 Carlow, Kilkenny, Wexford	"Blathwayt" c. 1630–40
CONNELLS POND (NTS Holyrood)	IF p. 85 etc. Kerry	O'Connell at HOLYROOD NORTH ARM (1)
CONNOR COVE (NTS Argentia) CONNOR COVE POINT (NTS Argentia)	IF p. 88, GIS p. 49 Cork, Wexford, Tipperary	Connors at ST. BRIDE'S, CUSLETT, PLACENTIA, JERSEYSIDE
CONWAY COVE (NTS Argentia) (2)	IF p. 92, p. 93, MIF p. 189 Mayo, Sligo	At ST. BRIDE'S
CONWAY BROOK (NTS Bay Bulls)		
? COOTE POND (NTS St. Mary's)	IF p. 320, MIF p. 84n., Dublin	
? CORBIN (for Corbane) HEAD (not in NTS Argentia)	MIF p. 65 ? Cork, Tipperary, Galway	Not locally. Wix 1836
? CRAWLEY (for Crowley) I. (NTS Argentia)	IF p. 100 Cork	Population Returns 1836
CULLEN COVE (NTS Argentia) CULLEN POINT (NTS Argentia)	IF p. 101 south-east Leinster	At ARGENTIA (1)
CURRENS (? for Curran) POND (NTS Holyrood)	IF p. 106 Waterford, Galway, etc.	At FOLEY'S HILL, ROACHE'S LINE
DALTON POINT (NTS Placentia)	IF p. 109 Westmeath etc.	At REGINAVILLE
DALTONS POND (NTS Holyrood)		At CAPE BROYLE and CONCEPTION HARBOUR

Irish Place Names / 131

TABLE 5 *(continued)*

Place Name	Irish Family Name	Status of Family Name on the Avalon Peninsula
? DAVIS POINT (NTS Placentia)	IF p. 290 Wexford	At COLINET
? DIXON HILL (NTS Placentia)	MIF p. 282, GIS p. 65	Not locally. Murray 1868
DONOVANS STA (NTS St. John's)	IF p. 124 Cork	At ST. JOHN'S and elsewhere not in immediate vicinity
DOYLES (Set) (NTS Bay Bulls) DOYLES BRIDGE (NTS Bay Bulls)	IF p. 128 Wickford, Wexford, Carlow	At PETTY HARBOUR
DOYLES BROOK (NTS Harbour Grace)		Police surgeon at HARBOUR GRACE C. 1850–60
DOYLES POND (NTS Holyrood)		At AVONDALE
? DRAKES POND (NTS Harbour Grace)	SIF p. 58, GIS p. 70 Wexford, Meath	Not locally
? DUFF's (NTS Holyrood)	MIF p. 89, GIS p. 71 ? Wexford	At this place
DUNVILLE (? for Dunn(e) + ville) (NTS Argentia)	GIS p. 72 Midland counties	Not common in area
? ENGLISH COVE (NTS Holyrood)	GIS p. 76 Limerick	Common in Nfld. but not locally. Murray 1868.
? FAIRYS POND (NTS Holyrood)	MIF p. 107 ? Kerry	Fary at HARBOUR MAIN. *(Directory 1877)*
? FENELONS POND (NTS Holyrood)	MIF p. 105 Carlow, Wexford	At ST. JOHN'S 1877
FERGUS ISLAND (NTS Harbour Grace)	MIF p. 107 Mayo	Fergus Islet (Imray 1873)
FINNIES (for Feeney) POND (NTS Holyrood)	IF p. 140 Feeney – Connacht MIF p. 105 Finny – Ulster	Not locally
FLINN RIVER (NTS Placentia)	IF p. 148, MIF p. 257 Widespread	At PLACENTIA, etc.
? FOX KNOB (NTS St. Mary's)	IF p. 151, p. 192, MIF p. 12	Not locally
KITTY GAULS BROOK (NTS St. John's)	MIF p. 222	At ST. JOHN'S
? GRACES GULLY (NTS Holyrood)	MIF p. 127 Kilkenny	At COLLIERS, AVONDALE
? GRANNY COVE (NTS Argentia)	SIF p. 82 Donegal, Derry	Not current in Newfoundland Adm. 2829 1877
? GRATTON (for Grattan) (NTS Harbour Grace)	IF p. 293, MIF p. 259, SIF p. 159 Tipperary, Dublin	Not locally
? HEALEYS (for Healy, Hely) POND (NTS St. John's)	IF p. 176, MIF p. 262 Cork	At ST. JOHN'S
HEALYS COVE (NTS Holyrood) HEALYS POND (NTS Holyrood)		At HOLYROOD NORTH ARM, CHAPEL COVE

132 / Place Names of the Avalon Peninsula

TABLE 5 (continued)

Place Name	Irish Family Name	Status of Family Name on the Avalon Peninsula
HENNESSEYS POND (NTS Bay Bulls)	IF p. 179 Cork, Limerick, Tipperary	At PETTY HARBOUR
HICKEYS POND (NTS St. John's)	IF p. 180 Clare, Limerick, Tipperary	At various localities on AVALON PENINSULA
HOGANS POND (NTS St. John's)	IF p. 182 Clare, Limerick, Tipperary	At ST. JOHN'S
HOLLIS (for Holly's) COVE (NTS Dildo)	SIF p. 90 Kerry, Ulster	Not current in Newfoundland
KEARNYS GULLIES (NTS Holyrood)	IF p. 192 Common	Not locally. At WITLESS BAY (1)
KEARNEY'S HILL (NTS Bay Bulls)		
KELLIS (for Kelly) POINT (NTS Bay Bulls)	IF p. 195 Widespread	Common in Newfoundland but not at BAY BULLS
KELLY POINT (NTS Argentia)		At FOX HARBOUR
KELLY POND (NTS Holyrood)		At HOLYROOD
KELLYS ISLAND (NTS Harbour Grace)		Lane, Directions 1810
KELLYS POND (NTS Harbour Grace)		At HARBOUR GRACE
KENNA'S HILL (St. John's)	IF p. 197 Clare, Kerry	Not current
KENNEDYS BROOK (NTS St. John's)	IF p. 198 Widespread	Not current at MIDDLE COVE
KENNEDYS POND (NTS Holyrood)		CONCEPTION HARBOUR
KENNYS POND (NTS St. John's)	IF p. 199, MIF p. 265 Clare, Kerry	At PORTUGAL COVE RD., ST. JOHN'S
KENTS POND (NTS St. John's)	IF p. 296 Cork	Family prominent in political life of ST. JOHN'S, 19th c.
KERWAN (for Kirwan) POINT (NTS St. Catherine's)	IF p. 203 Galway	Not locally
? KING ISLAND (NTS Argentia)	IF pp. 90, 91, 296 Galway, Limerick, etc.	At FOX HARBOUR
KINGSTON (NTS Heart's Content)		Kings at KINGSTON
PORT KIRWAN (formerly Admiral's Cove Fermeuse) (NTS Renews)		After a Mother Superior of the Convent
LAWLER BAY (NTS Renews)	IF p. 206 Kilkenny, etc.	At RENEWS, CAPPAHAYDEN
LEAHY POND (NTS Holyrood)	MIF p. 161 Cork, Tipperary, Kerry	Not locally
LEAMYS BROOK (NTS St. John's) } LEAMYS POND (NTS St. John's)	SIF p. 104 Tipperary	Not current locally, but previously at BLACKHEAD
LEARYS BROOK (NTS St. John's)	IF p. 207 Cork	Rare, and as Learie, in ST. JOHN'S

TABLE 5 (continued)

Place Name	Irish Family Name	Status of Family Name on the Avalon Peninsula
? LEONARDS POND (NTS Holyrood)	IF p. 289, GIS p. 137 Widespread	At CONCEPTION HARBOUR (1)
? LEONARDS WATERS (NTS Holyrood)		
LUCY (for Lucey) BEACH (NTS Holyrood)	MIF p. 168, GIS p. 141 Cork	Not current
? LUMLEY (for Rumley, local usage) COVE (NTS Renews)	GIS p. 241 Cork	Not current in Newfoundland
LYNCHS POND (NTS Heart's Content)	IF p. 213 etc., Kerry, Cork, Limerick, etc.	At HARBOUR GRACE, etc.
MCCARTHYS POND (NTS Harbour Grace)	IF p. 76 Cork etc.	At CARBONEAR (Directory 1877)
MACDONALD COVE (NTS Placentia)	IF p. 321 Mayo	McDonald's Cove (Murray 1868) At NEW BRIDGE
MCGRATH POND (NTS Holyrood)	IF p. 165 Waterford, Cork, Tipperary, Ulster, etc.	At COLLIERS, AVONDALE
MAHERS (NTS Holyrood)	Maher IF p. 223 Tipperary	Common, but not locally
? MAKER (for ? McCue) POINT (NTS Argentia)	IF p. 185, GIS p. 56 Galway, Fermanagh, etc.	At FOX HARBOUR; McHugh at JERSEYSIDE, FRESHWATER
MALONEYS (for ? Moloney) BEACH (NTS Holyrood) MALONEY'S RIVER (NTS Holyrood)	IF p. 226 Clare, Limerick, Tipperary	At HOLYROOD
MATURIN BROOK (NTS Argentia) MATURIN PONDS (NTS Argentia)	IF p. 35	Not current in Newfoundland
MOANY (for Mooney) COVE (NTS Argentia)	IF p. 227	Mooney at PLACENTIA and elsewhere
? MONDAY POND (NTS Bay de Verde) ? MONDAYS POND (NTS Holyrood)	MIF p. 123 Fermanagh, Derry	Mundy (1) at CARBONEAR
? MOORES GULCH (NTS Trepassey) ? MOORES POINT (NTS Trepassey)	IF p. 228, GIS p. 524	Not locally
MORIARTYS POND (NTS St. John's)	IF p. 230 Kerry	At ST. JOHN'S and elsewhere
? MULLEY'S COVE (Heart's Content)	IF p. 225	At BROAD COVE SOUTH and BLACKHEAD
? MUNDYS POND (NTS St. John's)	MIF p. 123 Fermanagh, Derry	
MURPHY COVE (NTS Dildo)	IF p. 235 Widespread espy. Cork, Kerry	At SHIP HARBOUR, LONG HARBOUR etc. (Lane 1774)
MURPHY POINT (NTS St. Mary's)		Not locally in MALL BAY
MURPHYS FIRST POND (NTS Heart's Content)		At JOB'S COVE

134 / Place Names of the Avalon Peninsula

TABLE 5 (continued)

Place Name	Irish Family Name	Status of Family Name on the Avalon Peninsula
MURPHYS RIVER (NTS St. Catherine's)		At MITCHELLS BROOK, MOUNT CARMEL
MURRAYS POND (NTS St. John's)	IF p. 236 etc. Widespread	At ST. JOHN'S
NAGLES HILL (St. John's)	IF p. 238, etc. Cork	At ST. JOHN'S (Directory 1877)
NEILS (? for O'Neill) POND (NTS Holyrood)	IF p. 241 etc. Ulster	At SPANIARD'S BAY, but not locally
NEILS (? for O'Neill) POND (NTS St. John's)		Not locally
NEVILLES POND	MIF p. 192 Limerick, Cork	At TOPSAIL
O'BRIENS BROOK (NTS Bay Bulls)	IF p. 62 etc., MIF p. 245 Widespread	At CAPE BROYLE
O'DONNELLS (NTS Placentia)	IF p. 120 etc. Clare, Galway, Donegal	Not locally
PATRICK POINT (NTS Placentia)	SIF p. 122, GIS p. 168 and baptismal name	Adm. 2915 1864
PATRICK'S COVE (NTS Ship Cove)		
? PEARCE PEAK (NTS Argentia)	IF p. 299	At ARGENTIA
PEYTONS BROOK (NTS Bay Bulls) PEYTONS POND (NTS Bay Bulls)	IF p. 307, SIF p. 123, GIS p. 169 Mayo	Not locally
? PEYTONS GULLIES (NTS Holyrood)		Not locally
? PEYTONS (? for Penton) POND (NTS St. John's)		Penton at POUCH COVE, SHOE COVE
? PHILLIPS POND (NTS Holyrood)	MIF p. 197, GIS p. 169 Mayo	At COLLIERS
? MAURICE POOLE COVE (NTS Argentia)	GIS p. 238 Rare	Common as English name in Newfoundland, but not locally
? POWELL POINT (NTS Argentia)	IF p. 160	Not locally
POWERS POND (NTS St. John's) LITTLE POWER POND (NTS St. John's)	IF p. 247 etc., GIS p. 171 Waterford etc.	Widespread in AVALON PENINSULA but not at ST. PHILLIPS or PORTUGAL COVE
TOM POWER LOOKOUT (NTS Argentia)		Tom, light keeper
RAYMOND HEAD (NTS Bay Bulls) RAYMOND BROOK RAYMONDS BRIDGE	GIS p. 176 Cork, Kerry	At LOWER GOULDS
? ROCHE POINT (NTS Argentia)	IF p. 258, MIF p. 274, GIS p. 179 Cork, Wexford (W. Kirwin)	At FRESHWATER, PLACENTIA Lane 1772

TABLE 5 (continued)

Place Name	Irish Family Name	Status of Family Name on the Avalon Peninsula
RYALLS POND (NTS St. John's)	SIF p. 132 Kerry	At ST. JOHN'S, KELLIGREWS (1) MANUELS (1)
RYANS BRIDGE (NTS Bay Bulls)	IF p. 260 etc., GIS p. 181 Limerick, Tipperary	At BAY BULLS
RYANS BROOK (NTS Harbour Grace)		At SPANIARDS BAY
RYANS HEAD (NTS Holyrood)		At COLLIERS, MARYVALE, etc.
RYANS POND (NTS Holyrood)		
? SALLS (? for Saul's) ISLAND (NTS Dildo)	MIF p. 212, GIS p. 181 Tipperary, Waterford	Not current in Newfoundland
SHANAHANS GULLY (NTS Harbour Grace)	IF p. 264, GIS p. 184 Cork, Kerry, etc.	At RIVERHEAD, HARBOUR GRACE. The gully was the site of the family's country home
SHEAS GULLY (NTS Harbour Grace)	IF p. 266, MIF p. 274, GIS p. 185 Kerry etc.	At CARBONEAR
? SLOANS GULLY (NTS Harbour Grace)	MIF p. 220, GIS p. 188 Ulster	At RIVERHEAD, HARBOUR GRACE (1)
? STEPHENS POND (NTS Bay Bulls)	MIF p. 224 Mayo (Matheson 72)	Not locally
SWEENEYS POND (NTS Heart's Content)	IF p. 271, GIS p. 192 Cork, Kerry, Ulster	At IRISH TOWN, CARBONEAR
TOBINS POND (NTS Holyrood)	IF p. 275 Tipperary, Kilkenny, Waterford, Cork	At WITLESS BAY
? TOCHER'S POND (NTS Biscay Bay River)	SIF p. 148 GIS pp. 196, 197 Tipperary, Offaly, Connacht	In Newfoundland as Tucker but not locally
? TRACES (? for Traceys) POINT (NTS Renews)	IF p. 277 Galway, Cork, Limerick, etc.	Current in Nfld. but not locally
? TUCKERS GULLY (NTS Harbour Grace)	See Tocher	Not locally
TOM WALDRONS POND (NTS Bay Bulls)	MIF p. 238, GIS p. 201 Connacht	Rare in Nfld.
WALLS POND (NTS Holyrood)	IF p. 280, GIS p. 201 Limerick, Waterford	At HARBOUR MAIN
TOM WALSH COVE (NTS Afgentia)	IF p. 281, GIS p. 201 Mayo, Galway, Cork, Wexford, etc.	Common in Nfld.
TOM WALSH LOOKOUT		Tom, light keeper
WHALENS (for Whelan) BROOK (NTS Holyrood)	IF p. 245 Waterford, Kilkenny, Wexford, Carlow	At COLLIERS etc.
WHALENS POND (NTS Holyrood) (2)		

TABLE 5 (concluded)

Place Name	Irish Family Name	Status of Family Name on the Avalon Peninsula
? WILLIAMS (Set) (NTS Bay Bulls) ? WILLIAMS COVE (NTS Bay Bulls) ? WILLIAMS HILL (NTS Bay Bulls) ? WILLIAMS HILL (NTS Bay Bulls) ? WILLIAMS POND (NTS Holyrood)	GIS p. 204 Widespread	At BAY BULLS At CONCEPTION HARBOUR
? WITLESS (? for Whittle's) HEAD (NTS Argentia)	GIS p. 203 Waterford etc.	In PLACENTIA area etc.

* A mark of interrogation before an entry indicates that the name may not be an Irish family name in its particular context. Names such as Baker, Butler, Davies and Dixon, for example, may be English, and Neil, Patrick, Sall and Stephen may be baptismal names.

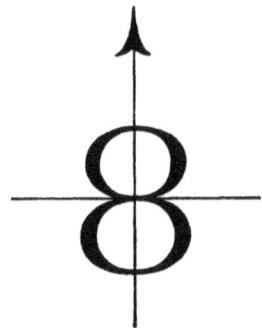

Analysis of the Place Names / One
Distribution, Single-element Names, Generics

1 DISTRIBUTION

With a few exceptions, the names studied in this survey were collected from the National Topographic Series of maps of the AVALON PENINSULA, in which they are distributed as follows.

TABLE 6

AVALON PENINSULA: NAMES IN NTS MAPS

Reference	Title	No. of Entries
1K/11 E	Trepassey	28
W		23
1K/12 E	St. Shotts	15
1K/13 E	St. Mary's	47
W		22
1K/14 E	Biscay Bay River	4
W		13
1K/15 W	Renews	34
1L/16 E	St. Bride's	27
1M/ 1 E	Ship Cove	17
1N/ 2 W	Ferryland	64
1N/ 3 E	St. Catherine's	6
W		15

TABLE 6 (continued)

Reference	Title	No. of Entries
1N/ 4 E	Placentia	52
W		25
1N/ 5 E	Argentia	9
W		93
1N/ 6 E	Holyrood	140
W		112
1N/ 7 E	Bay Bulls	47
W		110
1N/10 E	St. John's	100
W		141
1N/11 E	Harbour Grace	130
W		190
1N/12 E	Dildo	34
W		59
1N/13 E	Sunnyside	29
W		36
1N/14 E	Heart's Content	79
W		89
1N/15	Pouch Cove	15
2C/ 2 W	Bay de Verde	25
2C/ 3 E	Old Perlican	12
W		12
		1854

The average incidence of names is roughly 2 per square mile.

The following examination is limited for the most part to selected names in their contemporary, modern form.

2 SINGLE-ELEMENT NAMES[1]

Single-element names, that is, names without an explicit generic, refer to topographic features, hydrographic features and settlements. They may be shifted from features to become names of settlements, as in BLOW ME DOWN (NTS Harbour Grace) and GULLIES (NTS Harbour Grace). A generic is usually added if the name of a settlement becomes the name of a feature, as in MANUELS (NTS St. John's) and MANUELS RIVER (NTS Bay Bulls, St. John's); and conversely the generic in an original dual-element name of a feature may be dropped in the name of the settlement, so that Gastries Bay (Murray 1868) now GASTERS BAY (NTS Holyrood) becomes GASTERS (NTS Holyrood).

Examples of single-element names of topographic features are: BULL AND COW [Rocks] (NTS St. Bride's), BUTTER POT [Hill] (NTS Biscay Bay River, Bay Bulls, Holyrood), HARES EARS [Rocks] (NTS St. Mary's, Ferryland), OLD MAN [Hill] (NTS Sunnyside), SHUFFLE BOARD [Hill] (NTS Heart's

Content), SUGAR LOAF [Headland] (NTS Heart's Content) but elsewhere with the generic Head (NTS St. John's) and Hill (NTS Argentia), THE BELL [Rock] (NTS Harbour Grace), and THE KETTLE [Point] (NTS Bay Bulls).

Single-element names of hydrographic features are: LA MANCHE [Cove] (NTS Dildo), THE BIRCHIES [Ponds] (NTS Bay Bulls), THE SISTERS [Ponds] (NTS Harbour Grace), and THREE AUNT KATES [Ponds] (NTS Harbour Grace).

Single-element names of settlements, which number almost a hundred, contain many possessive or commemorative names, with and without an s suffix. The inclusion or exclusion of the apostrophe seems to be arbitrary, though convention has come to demand the form ST. JOHN'S (NTS St. John's), first recorded in *The English Pilot. The Fourth Book* 1689. Examples are: BRIENS (NTS Holyrood), CALVERT (NTS Ferryland), CAVENDISH (NTS Harbour Grace), CHAMBERLAINS (NTS St. John's), COLINET (NTS Placentia), ? COLLIERS (NTS Holyrood), ? CUPIDS (NTS Harbour Grace), DONOVANS (NTS St. John's), DOYLES (NTS Bay Bulls), DUFFS (NTS Holyrood), GOOBIES (NTS Sunnyside), HARRICOTT (NTS Placentia), IRVINE (NTS St. John's), KELLIGREWS (NTS Harbour Grace), KINGMAN'S (NTS Renews), MAHERS (NTS Holyrood), MAKINSON (NTS Harbour Grace), MANUELS (NTS St. John's), O'DONNELLS (NTS Placentia), ? PICKEYES (NTS Harbour Grace), ST. BRIDES (NTS St. Bride's), ST. CATHERINE'S (NTS St. Catherine's), ST. JOHN'S (NTS St. John's), ST. JONES (with the qualifier WITHOUT) (NTS Sunnyside), ST. JOSEPH'S (NTS Placentia), ST. MARY'S (NTS St. Mary's), ST. MICHAELS (NTS Ferryland), ST. PHILIPS (NTS St. John's), ST. STEPHEN (not in NTS St. Mary's), ST. THOMAS (NTS St. John's), ST. VINCENT'S (NTS St. Mary's), WHITBOURNE (NTS Argentia), WHITEWAY (NTS Harbour Grace), WILLIAMS (NTS Bay Bulls), and WOODFORD'S (NTS Holyrood).

Transferred single-element names include AVONDALE (NTS Holyrood), BALLYHACK (NTS Holyrood), CAPPAHAYDEN (NTS Renews), KILBRIDE (NTS St. John's), ? PARADISE (NTS St. John's), and SKIBBEREEN (NTS Holyrood) from Ireland; ? CARBONEAR (NTS Harbour Grace), ? GASKIERS (NTS St. Mary's), ? GASTERS (NTS Holyrood), LA MANCHE (NTS Ferryland and Dildo), ? QUIDI VIDI (NTS St. John's) and TREPASSEY (NTS Trepassey) from France; HOLYROOD (NTS Holyrood), and WOODSTOCK (NTS St. John's) from Britain.

Descriptive single-element names include BARENEED (NTS Harbour Grace), HARES EARS (NTS St. Mary's, Ferryland), SHUFFLE BOARD (NTS Heart's Content), ? SPREAD EAGLE (NTS Dildo), and SUGAR LOAF (NTS Heart's Content).

Single-element incident names appear to include BLOW ME DOWN (NTS

Harbour Grace), COME BY CHANCE (NTS Sunnyside) and ? BAULINE (NTS St. John's and Ferryland).

Despite the absence of an explicit generic, a number of single-element names in fact contain a suppressed generic sometimes concealed in an element in another language, as in BALLYHACK (NTS Holyrood), CAPPAHAYDEN (NTS Renews) and KILBRIDE (NTS St. John's), where Ir. *bally* = town, *cappa* = meadow, plot, and *kil* = church. Sometimes a generic is lost in a change of pronunciation, whereby, for example, ? Barren Head becomes BARENEED (NTS Harbour Grace), or tends to lose its identity in a weak form in an unstressed syllable, as in ISLINGTON (NTS Heart's Content), KINGSTON (NTS Heart's Content), ? TILTON (NTS Harbour Grace) and WINTERTON (NTS Heart's Content), where -ton = town. Sometimes a second element has become conventionally attached to a specific, so that the name is considered as a single element, as in AVONDALE (NTS Holyrood), GLENDALE (NTS St. John's), THORNLEA (NTS Dildo), REDLANDS (NTS Heart's Content) and SPRINGFIELD (NTS Harbour Grace). A mistake generic occurs in FERRYLAND (NTS Ferryland), from Port. *farelhão* or Fr. *forillon*.

Some single-element names with the definite article are substantially generics, as in THE DOCK (NTS Harbour Grace), though Dock in DOCK COVE (NTS Holyrood) is a specific, THE GORGE (NTS Bay Bulls), THE KEY (NTS Argentia) and THE KEYS (NTS Bay Bulls) cp. ST. MARY'S KEYS (Lane 1772) (not in NTS St. Mary's), THE LOOKOUT (NTS Heart's Content) cp. BRIGUS LOOKOUT (NTS Harbour Grace), THE BEACH (NTS St. John's) cp. CLARKES BEACH (NTS Harbour Grace), THE POND (NTS Argentia), and THE BROADS (NTS Harbour Grace). Others are substantially specifics, as in THE BIRCHIES (NTS Bay Bulls) and THE SISTERS (NTS Harbour Grace).

Some single-element names without the definite article are true generics, as in DROOK (NTS Trepassey) and GULLIES (NTS Harbour Grace).

3 GENERICS OF HYDROGRAPHIC FEATURES

Generics of hydrographic features refer to coastal and inland features.

The commonest coastal hydrographic generic is Cove which occurs some one hundred and thirty-six times on the AVALON PENINSULA, excluding repetitions. It follows the specific except in one instance, COVE NAN DRIOCH-CLOCHAN (NTS Argentia). It is tautological in BRISTOL'S HOPE COVE.[2]

Bay occurs fifty-two times and precedes the specific in BAY BULLS (NTS Bay Bulls), BAY DE GRAVE (NTS Harbour Grace), BAY DE VERDE (NTS Bay de Verde) and BAY ROBERTS (NTS Harbour Grace).

Harbour occurs thirty-five times and precedes the specific in HARBOUR GRACE (NTS Harbour Grace) and HARBOUR MAIN (NTS Holyrood). Haven occurs once, in FAIR HAVEN (NTS Dildo).

A specific of French origin is suggested where Bay and Harbour precede the specific.

Arm occurs eleven times and in six instances is associated with a specific denoting relative position, as in MIDDLE ARM (NTS Holyrood), NORTH ARM (NTS Holyrood), NORTHEAST ARM (NTS Ferryland, Argentia, Sunnyside), SOUTH ARM (NTS Holyrood), SOUTHEAST ARM (NTS Placentia, Sunnyside) and SOUTHWEST ARM (NTS Sunnyside).

Less frequent generics indicating coastal indentations are Bight: SKERRIES BIGHT (NTS St. John's), TORBAY BIGHT (NTS St. John's), and MIDDLE BIGHT, now CODNER (not in NTS St. John's); Gulch: BULL GULCH (POINT) (NTS Old Perlican), MOORES GULCH (NTS Trepassey) and SOLDIERS GULCH (NTS St. John's), though GREAT GULCH and LITTLE GULCH (NTS St. Bride's) are rivers flowing through ravines;[3] Hole: HIBBS HOLE (NTS Harbour Grace) and SALMON HOLE (NTS Argentia), though MUDDY HOLE (NTS Harbour Grace) is a pond; Hope: BRISTOL'S HOPE (NTS Harbour Grace); Gut: GREAT PINCHGUT (NTS Dildo), Famishgut (Lane 1772), now FAIR HAVEN (NTS Dildo), and TURKS GUT (NTS Harbour Grace), though NORTH RIVER and SOUTH RIVER (NTS Harbour Grace) were formerly known as North Gut and South Gut; Port: PORT DE GRAVE (NTS Harbour Grace) and PORT KIRWAN (not in NTS Renews); Road: PLACENTIA ROAD (NTS Placentia); and Sound: PLACENTIA SOUND (NTS Argentia). Head in RIVERHEAD (NTS St. Mary's and Harbour Grace) has been discussed previously.[4]

The generic Passage occurs once on the AVALON PENINSULA, in COLINET PASSAGE (NTS St. Mary's), but the common Newfoundland term for a strait is Tickle, as in BACCALIEU TICKLE (NTS Bay de Verde), BULL TICKLE (NTS Sunnyside), PINCHGUT TICKLE (NTS Placentia) and STRONG TICKLE (NTS Sunnyside).

Tickle, in the form Tickles,[5] is first cited in OED in Cook and Lane 1770 [1775]B, repeated in Lane 1773, for a locality at the head of ST. MARY'S BAY. It was first defined by Cartwright in 1792 as "A passage between the continent and an island, or between two islands, when it is of no great width,"[6] a definition modified and extended by J. P. Howley: "The word Tickle appears to refer to a narrow channel between two or more islands, or between islands and the mainland, through which the tide runs with considerable force."[7]

J. B. Jukes first raised the question of its origin, only to confess that he was at a loss,[8] though later commentators have been more daring.

G. Patterson, obsessed as he was with Portuguese influences on the nomenclature of the northeast coast of America, inevitably found a Portuguese origin:

> The first explorers of the coast ... were the Portuguese, who gave names to the leading places on these shores, a number of which remain to the present day. A large proportion of these were the names of places in Portugal or the Western Islands, from which they carried on much of their trade. Now on the coast of Portugal may be seen a point called Santa Tekla. It is a narrow projection some miles in length, inside of which is a lengthy basin, narrowed by an island. As there were few good harbors on the coast of that country, this formed a favorite resort particularly to her fishermen. What more natural than that they should give the name to places here of similar appearance and serving the same purpose? The slight change from Tekla to Tickle will not appear strange to any person who knows into what different forms foreign words have been changed when adopted by Englishmen.[9]

N. Peddel, a Newfoundland writer, probably invented the following uncorroborated, folksy version of its origin:

> In many other places the mode of capture [of seals] was "pounds" or "stoppers," so-called. At Indian Tickle, Venison Tickle, Chimney Tickle, and various other tickles, these appliances were used. A capstan was erected on each side of the tickle, with deep, strong nets attached. One of these were [sic] always hoist up with what was known as the "stopper." When the seals would come through those tickles and strike the "stopper," men on the other end would heave up the other net, and the seals were in the pound. The seals being entrapped would mesh in the nets, and those that would not mesh were shot, so the word tickle originated – "tickle them" with shot.[10]

M. F. Howley preferred a more prosaic, though no better authenticated, version:

> It has always been supposed that this name is a plain English word, implying a passage of some danger, from sudden squalls of wind or sunken rocks and shoals, so that it is a "ticklish" matter to get safe through. The word in this sense is properly applied, as a ticklish job means a difficult, critical job.[11]

OED follows Howley, but adds that "some would identify it with Eng[lish] dial[ect] *stickle* 'a rapid shallow place in a river.' "

None of these etymologies, however, is satisfactory and an acceptable one has still to be found. The name appears to be limited to Newfoundland and Labrador, though a form *tittle* is known in Nova Scotia.[12]

THE NARROWS (NTS St. John's) exemplifies a usage, chiefly in the plural, for "A narrow part of a sound, strait or river."[13]

Barachois and Cosh have been discussed previously.[14]

The commonest inland hydrographic generic is Pond which occurs over four hundred times, including a plural form fourteen times. This high incidence is in marked contrast to Lake which occurs only six times: BANNERMAN LAKE (NTS Harbour Grace), BROAD LAKE (NTS Dildo), LADY LAKE (NTS Harbour Grace), QUIDI VIDI LAKE (NTS St. John's), VIRGINIA LAKE (NTS St. John's) formerly Virginia Waters, and WINDSOR LAKE (NTS St. John's) formerly Twenty Mile Pond. The comments of Jukes and others on the prevalence of Pond have been discussed previously.[15]

Other terms used for expanses of inland water are Gully and Gullies, in all forty times, with Gully in twenty-two names and Gullies in eighteen. The application of the word appears to have been transferred from ravine to running water, especially seasonal "winter water" as Banks calls it,[16] in a ravine, thence to any long stretch of still water, until eventually it became synonymous with pond.

The use of the generic Waters for a succession of ponds linked by a stream, not recorded in OED, is confined to NTS Holyrood: COCOANUT WATERS, EASTERN WATERS, LEONARDS WATERS with LEONARDS POND nearby, LOCKYERS WATERS, PEDDLES WATERS, and the near-tautological OTTER POND WATERS.

Marsh occurs three times: FOX MARSH (NTS Holyrood), MAINS MARSH (NTS Harbour Grace) and ROACHES MARSH (NTS Bay Bulls).

The generics Sea in OLD SEA (NTS Holyrood) and Hole in MUDDY HOLE (NTS Harbour Grace) are apparently unique synonyms for Pond.

Bonnycastle's statement that rivers are called brooks in Newfoundland[17] is hardly supported on the AVALON PENINSULA, though the generic Brook outnumbers River by ninety-four to fifty-four.

Associated with brooks and rivers is Steady, defined by Cartwright as "A part [of a river] where the bed widens inclining to a pond, and there is no perceptible stream."[18] Later in the *Transactions* he writes,

> Keeping the eastern side of the lake, we rowed along it for a mile and an half, when we arrived at the mouth of a strong, rattling brook. We there landed ... and ... walked up by the side of it. We soon found ... three or four small ponds, or steadies ...[19]

Jukes described the course of a brook he explored as consisting of "a succession of small pools or steadies, shallows, rapids and shutes, for about two miles."[20] Murray defined Steady as "A common local term for still water"[21] in rivers. But P. K. Devine widened the definition: "A small lake or pond. A wide still brook where the current is not visible."[22]

Common as the term is in Newfoundland, it is recorded on the AVALON PENINSULA only in GOOSE STEADIES (NTS Holyrood) and as an element in the specific of STEADYWATER BROOK (NTS Bay Bulls and St. John's).

4 GENERICS OF TOPOGRAPHIC FEATURES

Generics of topographic features refer to coastal and inland features.

The commonest coastal topographic generic is Point which occurs some one hundred and thirty-four times, thus having an incidence practically identical with Cove. The specific always precedes the generic except in POINT LA HAYE (NTS St. Mary's) which, however, is a shift name from the feature LA HAYE POINT (NTS St. Mary's), POINT LANCE (NTS St. Bride's), POINT OF BEACH (NTS Harbour Grace), POINT OF THE GUT (NTS Argentia) and POINT VERDE (NTS Ship Cove).

Head occurs eighty-six times, once in the plural ISAAC HEADS (NTS Argentia); Cape eleven times, always preceding the specific; Peninsula three times: AVALON PENINSULA, BAY DE VERDE PENINSULA and POWLES PENINSULA (NTS Trepassey); and Isthmus once: ISTHMUS OF AVALON (NTS Sunnyside). Neck, meaning isthmus, occurs in THE NECK (NTS Argentia).

Lookout occurs six times, preceded by the definite article once, THE LOOKOUT (NTS Heart's Content), and once as the specific in LOOKOUT POND (NTS Bay Bulls). Its use for an inland feature has been discussed previously.[23] Cliff occurs three times: HORSESHOE CLIFF (NTS Bay Bulls) and in the specifics RED CLIFF HEAD and CLIFF POINT (NTS St. John's). Bluff occurs once as a generic in BLOW ME DOWN BLUFF (NTS Holyrood), and as the specific in BLUFF HEAD (NTS Renews, Placentia and St. Catherine's).

Beach occurs nine times but as a specific, including THE BEACH (NTS St. John's). It denotes a shore covered with shingle, as distinguished from Sands in, for example, NORTHERN BAY SANDS at NORTHERN BAY (NTS Heart's Content). Side, in the sense "A region, district, or the inhabitants of this,"[24] occurs in JERSEYSIDE (NTS Argentia) and SOUTHSIDE (NTS Harbour Grace). Shore, as in SOUTH SHORE and NORTH SHORE of CONCEPTION BAY, and SOUTHERN SHORE denotes a stretch of coast and the settlements on it.

Generics of off-shore features are Island which occurs sixty-five times, thirteen times in the plural; Rock, twenty-five times, fourteen in the plural; Islet twice; Keys or Cays, in ST. MARY'S KEYS,[25] THE KEY (NTS Argentia) and THE KEYS (NTS Bay Bulls); Roost once, in SHAG ROOST (NTS Dildo), where roost is perhaps used facetiously in the sense of perch.[26]

The commonest inland topographic generic is Hill which occurs forty-seven times, seven times in the plural and is also used as a street name in BARTER'S HILL, CARTER'S HILL etc. in ST. JOHN'S (NTS St. John's). Other orographical generics are Peak, which occurs ten times, three times, however, as a specific or part of a specific in PEAK POND (NTS

Holyrood), SOUTHERN PEAK POND (NTS Holyrood), and THREE PEAK HILL (NTS Bay Bulls); and Pinnacle in THE PINNACLES (NTS Argentia). Mount occurs in MOUNT CARMEL (NTS St. Catherine's), a settlement, MOUNT CASHEL (St. John's), an institution, MOUNT PEARL PARK (NTS St. John's), a settlement, MOUNT ARLINGTON HEIGHTS (NTS Argentia), a settlement, and MOUNT MISERY POND (NTS Biscay Bay River). In none of these names is Mount applicable to a feature, and Mountain does not occur on the AVALON PENINSULA. Heights occurs, as was just demonstrated, in MOUNT ARLINGTON HEIGHTS (NTS Argentia), and also in the street names, AMHERST HEIGHTS and CORNWALL HEIGHTS (St. John's), in the name of a housing development, APPLETON HEIGHTS (St. John's), and in the name of a settlement, WINDSOR HEIGHTS, overlooking WINDSOR LAKE (NTS St. John's). Ridge occurs three times, in CASTLE RIDGE (NTS Placentia), ROCKY RIDGE (NTS St. Mary's) and STONY RIDGE (NTS Bay Bulls). Tolt, which is not cited in NTS maps as the modern name of a feature on the AVALON PENINSULA, though Wix recorded Chapel Tolt, and Stump and Folly, have been discussed previously.[27] Knob occurs once in FOX KNOB (NTS St. Mary's). Jukes recorded Downs, in Flakey Downs.[28] Cairn occurs in CAPTAIN ORLEBARS CAIRN (NTS Bay Bulls) and as a specific in CAIRN HEAD (NTS Argentia).

Barrens and Country, used to denote land areas with certain characteristics, have been discussed previously.[29] Land itself occurred as an element in the names of two settlements Red Land (*Population Returns* 1836) and Redlands (*Census* 1874), but the former name has been shifted to REDLAND POINT (NTS St. Bride's) and the latter retained as the name of a cape, REDLANDS (NTS Heart's Content). It is also found in the names of two other settlements, GREENLAND (NTS Harbour Grace) now abandoned, and MARKLAND (NTS Argentia), established in 1934 as the first of the government of Newfoundland's land-settlement colonies, and named after one of the three areas in North America known to the early Scandinavian explorers as Vinland, Helluland and Markland.[30] Field occurs in SPRINGFIELD (NTS Harbour Grace), FOREST FIELD (NTS St. Catherine's), both settlements, and as an element in the specific of LADEN FIELD'S BROOK (NTS Biscay Bay River).

Lea, a tract of open ground, especially grass land, is an element in the settlement name THORNLEA (NTS Dildo), formerly Colliers Bay Cove, but renamed by a proclamation of 23 December 1913 "out of compliment to the Thorns, who are among the oldest settlers."[31] Thicket occurs in THE THICKET (NTS Harbour Grace).

Park was formerly rare in Newfoundland restricted to DEER PARK (not in NTS Holyrood), to MOUNT PEARL PARK (NTS St. John's), a settlement from which Park has been dropped officially, though it is still heard in popular speech, and to such areas as BOWRING PARK (NTS St. John's) and BANNERMAN PARK (St. John's) in the city of ST. JOHN'S. Recently the name has become common with the establishment of provincial and national parks, such as BUTTER POT PROVINCIAL PARK (not in NTS Holyrood) and SIGNAL HILL NATIONAL HISTORIC PARK (not in NTS St. John's).

Valleys are denoted by Vale, in EMERALD VALE (NTS Harbour Grace); Dale, in GLENDALE (NTS St. John's), an odd tautological compound, and RIVERDALE (NTS Holyrood); Gorge, in THE GORGE (NTS Bay Bulls); and Drook in DROOK (NTS Trepassey). All except THE GORGE have come to be settlement names, though Drook as the name of a feature not recorded in NTS maps occurs at CARBONEAR (NTS Harbour Grace) and JOB'S COVE (NTS Heart's Content).

Droke is recorded as a Cornish word for "A wrinkle, furrow; a passage, groove"; Drock as a West Country word for "A small watercourse, a ditch."[32] In Newfoundland, Droke, Drook or Drogue seems to bear four meanings: a wooded, narrow valley; a belt or clump of trees; a narrow valley or gulch; a steep path.[33] Newfoundland usage seems to represent an extension of English usage, except that the meaning "a steep path" suggests a possible confusion with drong or drang, a narrow lane or passage, another West Country word also in use in Newfoundland.[34]

Valley itself occurs as the specific in VALLEY PONDS (NTS Harbour Grace).

5 GENERICS OF MAN-MADE OBJECTS

Generics of man-made objects are in two main classes: names of buildings both in groups and individually, and names of objects associated with transportation.

Town occurs in HALLS TOWN (NTS Harbour Grace), NEWTON (NTS Holyrood), IRISHTOWN (NTS Bay Bulls) and as part of CARBONEAR (NTS Harbour Grace), and colloquially elsewhere as in Taylortown for part of SOUTH RIVER (NTS Harbour Grace); and as –ton in ISLINGTON (NTS Heart's Content), KINGSTON (NTS Heart's Content), TILTON (NTS Harbour Grace) and WINTERTON (NTS Heart's Content).[35] –ville occurs as an element in BUTLERVILLE (NTS Harbour Grace), DUNVILLE (NTS Argentia), GODDENVILLE (NTS Harbour Grace), REGINAVILLE (NTS Placentia), TALCVILLE (NTS St. John's) PARSONVILLE P.O. (NTS Harbour Grace), and PLEASANTVILLE (St. John's). VICTORIA (NTS Heart's Content) is recorded as Victoria Village (Census 1874, 1901), but the generic has since been dropped.

House occurs in the name of the settlement HALFWAY HOUSE (NTS Heart's Content) and Tilt, a shack, a hut, a temporary shelter, in ROGERS TILT POND (NTS St. John's) and TILT HILL GULLY (NTS Harbour Grace). The earliest citation of tilt in a Newfoundland document is in John Guy's *Journal* 1612.[36]

Room, the generic for a planter's or merchant's premises, except in colloquial speech, occurs on the AVALON PENINSULA only as the specific in LOW ROOM POINT (NTS Argentia). It is preserved elsewhere, however, as a generic, as in Spanish Room (NTS Marystown), and is usually preceded by a possessive specific. The usage of room is shown in Captain Crowe's Laws, 1711:

13th. Whosoever shall demolish, deface, or break down any stage, cooke room, house, or flakes by removing rafters, rinds, floorings, shoars, stakes, or layers, except to employ them on same room next year, shall forfeit £10 for repairing same to possessor of said stage and room.[37]

Special usages are in the combinative forms boats room and ship's room in the same document, but cooke room is found a hundred years earlier in Guy's Laws, 1611: "No person to destroy, deface, or spoile any stage cooke room flakes &c. – Penalty £10."[38]

Shop, of doubtful origin, occurs in OLD SHOP (NTS Dildo).[39]

Fort occurs in the names of military defences erected around ST. JOHN'S (NTS St. John's) in the eighteenth century: FORT AMHERST (NTS St. John's), FORT FREDERICK, FORT TOWNSHEND and FORT WILLIAM, Fort having superseded an earlier Battery in Frederick's Battery. Battery is also found in Wallace's Battery, alternatively called Crow's Nest. FORT WILLIAM was also known as the Old Garrison.

Highway is used of the major roads on the Peninsula: CONCEPTION BAY HIGHWAY, TRANS-CANADA HIGHWAY. Road itself is used of routes from one settlement to another, as in TORBAY ROAD, from ST. JOHN'S (NTS St. John's) to TORBAY (NTS St. John's), and PORTUGAL COVE ROAD, from ST. JOHN'S to PORTUGAL COVE (NTS St. John's), and in the names of thoroughfares in ST. JOHN'S: ALLANDALE ROAD, CIRCULAR ROAD, etc. It has been shifted to become the generic in names of settlements: BLACKHEAD ROAD (NTS St. John's), THORBURN ROAD (NTS St. John's), GOULDS ROAD (NTS Holyrood), COUNTRY ROAD (NTS Harbour Grace).

Line, a shortened form of what seems to have been a technical term in surveying in the nineteenth century, line of road, is used of a cross-country road linking a more important road with a settlement, the specific commonly denoting the terminus as in BAULINE LINE (NTS St. John's) and WITLESS BAY LINE (not in NTS Bay Bulls) or a family name as in HIGGINS LINE (not in NTS St. John's) and ROACH'S LINE (not in NTS Harbour Grace). This sense of line may be of Irish origin.[40]

Path, in the sense of country lane, occurs in MAJOR'S PATH (not in NTS St. John's).

Street is common in ST. JOHN'S (NTS St. John's) and larger settlements like HARBOUR GRACE (NTS Harbour Grace), but Kirwin draws attention to the use of square "to name a handful of short streets [in ST. JOHN'S] not noticeably different from dozens of other streets and lanes": ALLAN SQUARE, BRAZIL SQUARE, DICK'S SQUARE, etc., and of cove for the "short side streets running south from Water Street toward the harbour": JOB'S COVE, BAIRD'S COVE, etc.[41] Other synonyms for street in ST. JOHN'S are Avenue: HAMILTON AVENUE formerly Poke*mpath*, CASHIN AVENUE; Lane: JAMES LANE, COFIELDS LANE; Hill: FLOWER HILL, BARTERS HILL; and Place, a modern term usually given to a *cul-de-sac*: LARCH PLACE, PINEBUD PLACE, though BAIRD PLACE is a thoroughfare.

Bridge occurs as a generic in HODGEWATER BRIDGE (NTS Holyrood) and in the names of settlements: NEW BRIDGE (NTS St. Catherine's), RAYMONDS BRIDGE (NTS Bay Bulls), RICKETTS BRIDGE (NTS St. John's), RYANS BRIDGE (NTS Bay Bulls), and WATERFORD BRIDGE (NTS St. John's).

Also associated with transportation are Station: IRVINE STATION, TOPSAIL STATION (NTS St. John's), etc.; Siding: GOOBIES SIDING (NTS Sunnyside), LA MANCH SIDING (NTS Dildo), etc.; Junction: PLACENTIA JUNCTION (NTS Argentia); Crossing: CUPIDS CROSSING (NTS Harbour Grace). Airfield in ST. JOHN'S AIRFIELD (NTS St. John's) has been superseded by Airport. Lighthouse occurs in FORT AMHERST LIGHT HOUSE (NTS St. John's).

Post Office occurs as a generic in places where the name of a settlement and of the post office there differ, as in MAKINSON (GOULDS P.O.) (NTS Harbour Grace).

Pit occurs as part of the specific in OCHRE PIT COVE and OCHRE PIT ROCK (NTS Heart's Content).

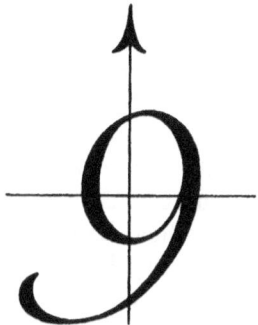

Analysis of the Place Names / Two
Specifics, Qualifiers, Composition

Four main kinds of specifics are evident in place names on the AVALON PENINSULA: Descriptive, Incident, Possessive and Commemorative, with of course numerous shift names and a sprinkling of Euphemistic specifics and examples of Folk Etymologies. Allocation of particular specifics to a class may often be arbitrary since many specifics of animal life, for instance, may well be incident specifics rather than specifics of impermanent association, and within a class a similar arbitrariness may be seen in the listing of Pumbly as a specific of composition rather than of formation.

Specifics are given in classes and sub-classes for the most part in alphabetical order, though relationships will frequently be observed within the groups, so that under the general title Animal Life will be found specifics drawn from the names of birds, fish and beasts, and under Man-made Objects are names relating to occupations, justice and buildings.

Interpretation of unusual and rare specifics may be found by reference to the Gazetteer.

1 DESCRIPTIVE SPECIFICS

Descriptive specifics, something over three hundred in all, fall into three main classes of which those indicating a long-standing quality of the generic account for roughly 46%, specifics of impermanent association for 38%, and specifics of relation or position for 16%.

Within the first class, distribution in the sub-classes is uneven. Specifics of colour are limited to Verde, Black, Blue, Emerald, Golden, Green, Red and White; and specifics of size to Big, Broad, ? Crossing Place, Grand, Great, ? Half, ? Jump, Little, Long, Ocean, Petty, Small and ? Squib. Specifics of quality, state or condition are more numerous: Bad, Bald, Barren as in Bareneed, ? Breakheart and its French equivalent Crevecœur, Burnt, ? Clear, Fermeuse, Freshwater, Level, Mad, Motion, Muddy, New, Old, Pounden, Ragged, Rattling, Ripple, Rocky, Rolling, Shoal, Smooth, Strong, ? Tochers, Warm and Wild. Specifics of composition, some of which must be regarded as fanciful, are somewhat fewer than the preceding: ? Beer, Bog, Brimstone, Brine, Chalk, ? Copper, ? Fleece, Fourteen Island, ? Grog, Holystone, ? Island, Lead, Nine Island, Pebble, Pumbly, Sandy, Shingle, Stone, Stony, Swamp, Talc and ? Whisky.

In contrast, more than half of this first class consists of specifics describing shape or formation: Angle, ? Aquaforte, The Arch, Banky, Bar, Beach, Beachy, Bell, Bluff, ? Breach, Butterpot, Cairn, Camels Back, Neddick, Castle, Cataract, Circle, Cliff, Crooked, ? Cross, Crown, Double, Feather, Flat, Four Corner, Funnel, ? Garlep, Half Moon, Hanging, Hares Ears, ? Hat, ? Heart, Hole in the Wall, Horsehead, Horseshoe, ? The Kettle, Kitchuses, ? Kite, Latine, Mizzen, Moon, The Neck, (Southern) Peak, Pierced ? Pinch, The Pinnacles, Pulpit, ? Rainbow, Round, Roundabout, Saddle, St. Shotts, Serrated, ? Shoe, Shuffle Board, Snowshoe, Spare, ? Spear, Split, Split Rock, Spoon, The Spout, Springfield, Steady water, Sugarloaf, Swamp Hill, – that Feeds the Brook, ? The Sisters, ? The Thicket, Three Arm, ? Three Aunt Kates, Three Corner, Three Island, Three Peak, Thumb, Tickle, (Tilt) Hill, Topsail, Triangle, Triangular, Twin, Two Island and Winging.

Specifics of impermanent association fall into three sub-classes, in which specifics of animal life outnumber vegetation specifics and specifics of man-made objects together. The preponderance of specifics of animal life over vegetation specifics reflects a common unfamiliarity of Newfoundlanders with names of plants.

Vegetation specifics include Birch, The Birchies, Bread and Cheese, Bois, ? Broom, (Burnt) Pine, Bushy, ? Cocoanut, ? Dildo, Forest, Goose-

Specifics, Qualifiers, Composition / 151

berry, Grassy, ? Jonclay, Juniper, Laden (Fields), Mint, Nut, Pea, Pegwood for Pigweed, Spruce, Tea, Whitewood, Witch Hazel, Wych Hazel, Withrod and Woody.

Specifics of animal life are Baccalieu, Bats, Bauline, Bull(s), Bear(s), Beaver, Black Duck, Boar, ? Brock, Caplin, Cat, Clam, Coote, Cow, Crow, ? Cuckold, Deer, Dog, Duck, Fox, Gander, Gannet, Goat, Goose, Grebe, ? Grub, Gull, Hare, Herring, Horse, ? Lance, ? Lansecan, ? Leech, Logy, Loo(n), ? Maggotty, Mall, Moll, Mosquito, Mouse, Muskrat, Mussel (Bed), Otter, Otterbury, Oxen, ? Perch, Pigeon, Quail, Ram, ? Robins, Salmon, Sculpin, Seal, Sepoy, Shag, ? Sharks, Sheeps, Skerwink, Old Sow, Sparrow, Spider, (Spread) Eagle, Spurwink, Squid, Stag, Tinker, Trout, Turtle, Whales.

Specifics of man-made objects are ? Bacon for Beacon, Chain, Church, Coalpit, ? Columbine, Cottage, nan Drioch-clochan, ? Dock, Gallows, Gibbet, Goldmine, Monument, Octagon, Ochre Pit, Quarry, (Rogers) Tilt, Salt Pit, Saw Pit, (Second) Junction, Shalloway, Ship, Signal, Skin Cabin, ? Sweetcake, Tilt and Town.

The final class of descriptive specifics denotes relation or position: Back, Backside, ? Cape, Centre, Coldeast, Coleys, Country, Cove, Downward, Drook, East, Eastern, First, Five Mile, Four Mile, Fourth, Halfway, ? Handy, Harbour, Inside, Left Hand, Left, Low, Lower, Middle, Ninth, ? Nord, North, Northeast, Norther, Northern, Northwest, Outer, Outside, ? Peak, – of Beach, – of the Gut, Right Hand, Second, Seven, South, Southeast, Souther, Southern, Southwest, Third, Third Junction, ? Twelve O'Clock, Upper, West, Western.

It will be seen below that many of these specifics may also act as qualifiers.

2 INCIDENT SPECIFICS

Incident specifics are much less easy to determine than descriptive specifics and appear to be much less common even if many specifics of animal life and of possession should in fact be regarded as incident specifics. The classes are events, names of persons, animals and objects, and occupations.

Specifics associated with events would seem to include: (Big) Chance, ? Blood, ? Bloody, Blow Me Down, ? Breach, Spear = waiting, Come by Chance, Cripple, Distress, ? Folly, Hard Weather, Mistaken, Misery, Newfound, Pinchgut, Shipwreck, Strayaway, Useless and Watern.

In addition to names of animals, the following names of persons and objects may be incident specifics: Deadmans, ? Devils, ? Heretic, Indian,

Old Mans, Old Womans, Salvage; Barking Kettle, Blast Hole, Burnt Pine, Coal Pit, Cottage, Dinnys, ? Empty Basket, Foxtrap, Freshwater, Goldmine, Gunridge, Hay Bag, Ochre Pit, Pothangers, Salt Pit and Saw Pit.

The third class of names, associated with occupations, includes Admiral, Bathers, ? Carrier, ? Chapel, ? Cooper, ? Fishers, ? Fitters, Grates, Graven, Gunners, ? Jugglers, Merchant, Miner, Molloys, (Little) Rinders, Salmonier, and Soldiers, though some of these may be personal names.

3 POSSESSIVE SPECIFICS

Possessive specifics which are personal names denoting ownership or association number about two hundred and eighty, of which about one hundred and ten are the Irish family names previously considered in Chapter VII. The remainder is made up of a handful of family names of French origin such as: ? Carbonear, ? Chapel, Colinet, Gushue, Harricott, Hawcos, ? La Haye, Piccos, Pierres, Pouch and St. Croix; of Scottish names: Bruce, Campbell, McKay, McLeod and Ohman; of baptismal or hypocoristic names without a family name: (Big) Johns, Charleys, Daves, ? Connys, Georges, ? Giles, Jacks, Jakes, ? Jeans, Johnnies, Johns, ? Jonas, Kate, Paddys, Patrick(s), Peggys, ? Pegs, ? Pierres, Sams and Sophia; and of about one hundred and seventy or more family names of English origin, though this number includes several of doubtful provenance.

Names in this last group are recorded in Table 7, at the end of this chapter. Column two quotes the reference to the English family name, which is probably the primary etymological source of the Newfoundland place name, and its locale, chiefly in H. B. Guppy, *Homes of Family Names in Great Britain*, though C. W. Bardsley, *A Dictionary of English and Welsh Surnames*, and P. H. Reaney, *A Dictionary of British Surnames* have also been consulted.

Without entering into a detailed analysis of these names, a somewhat futile exercise because of the lack of precise information about many of them, it will be seen that about a hundred are current on the AVALON PENINSULA, that about fifty have a local history of ninety years or more, though further research into the family names of Newfoundland would undoubtedly increase this number, and that the majority originated in the southwestern counties of England.

Ethnic names are Biscayne, ? English, French, Frenchmans, Indian,

Irish(town), Jersey(side), Langley, Portugal, Scotch, Spaniards and Turks.

4 COMMEMORATIVE SPECIFICS

The largest sub-class of Commemorative Specifics, about sixty, is composed of transferred names. It includes Avalon, ? Ballard, ? Beckford, ? Bethlehem, ? Brigus, Bristol, ? Coley's, Flambro, Islington, London, ? Long Harry, ? Longstone, ? Maker, Chelsea, ? Purbeck, ? Robin Hood, ? Springfield, Thames, Torbay, Virginia, Windsor and Woodstock from England; Avondale, Ballyhack, ? Cappahayden, Drogheda, Kilbride, Knock Hour, Cashel, ? Paradise, ? Sheep's (Head), Skibbereen, Vinegar (Hill) and Waterford from Ireland; ? Holyrood (NTS Holyrood) and Iona from Scotland; Crevecœur, ? Freels, (Harbour) Grace, La Manche, ? Marquise, ? Mutton, ? Quidi Vidi and Trepassey from France and ? Colinet and Jersey(side) from the Channel Islands; Biscay, Gibraltar, ? Pine and Placentia from Spain; Portugal and ? Race from Portugal; Carmel from Palestine; Mount Arlington and Niagara from the USA; and Penetanguishene from Canada.

Commemorative specifics of religious significance, about thirty, include Angel, Avalon, Conception, Devil, ? Holyrood (NTS St. Mary's), Jobs, Maria, Mary, Carmel, Paradise, Patrick's, Kirwan, Powles, Regina, St. Bride, St. Catherine, St. Francis, St. John, St. Joseph, St. Mary, St. Michael, St. Philip, St. Stephen, St. Thomas, St. Vincent, Trinity, and Virgin. St. Bernard has not survived as a new name for FOX HARBOUR (NTS Argentia). Vestal Rock (St. John's Harbour) appears to be the sole representative of non-Christian names.

Patriotic specifics, which may be taken to include specifics with historical associations, also number about thirty. They include Markland, Cabot, Whitbourne and Calvert from early Newfoundland history; Amherst, Frederick, Townshend, Wallace and William, names of seventeenth and eighteenth century fortifications in ST. JOHN'S (NTS St. John's) which commemorated military personages; and King's, ? Princes, Queens, and Victoria which commemorate royalty. Bannerman, Blake(town), Cavendish and Cochrane commemorate governors of Newfoundland, as do the following street names in ST. JOHN'S: Bannerman, Byron, Cochrane, Darling, Duckworth, Gambier, Gower, Graves, Hamilton, Harvey, LeMarchant, Maxse, Milbanke, Osbourne, Prescott, Rodney, Waldegrave, and Wallace. Statesmen and politicians are commemorated in Melbourne, Thorburn, and Whiteway.

Philanthropists, clergy and public benefactors are commemorated in Codner, Shears(town) and Bowring; a naval hydrographer in Captain Orlebar; and a former popular place of entertainment in Octagon.

5 MISCELLANEOUS SPECIFICS

Euphemistic specifics, with the term used somewhat loosely for want of a better to convey the idea of making a good impression or establishing favourable auspices, are Bellevue, Fair (Haven), Fermeuse, ? Harbour Grace, ? Heart's Content, Heart's Delight, Heart's Desire, Job's, Paradise, and Sunnyside.

Folk etymologies include Ferryland, ? Pick Eyes, Pine, St. Shores, St. Shotts, Sepoy, and Spear.

Mistake names include ? Bacon, Dinnys, ? Fairy, Gaskiers, Gasters, Graven, Kellis, ? Millers, ? Mollys, ? Ohmans, Otterbury, Pegwood, Polls, Pounden, Pusseys, Quidi Vidi, Salt Pit, Saturdays, Ship, ? Spices, ? Traces, Watern and Witless.

6 QUALIFIERS

The commonest qualifiers are Big and Little, each occurring about twenty times; in contrast Great occurs four times and Small once. The only other qualifier denoting size is Long (7). Qualifiers of relative position are South (4), East (3), Eastern (2), North (3), West (2), Western (4), Northeast (1), Northwest (1); First (3), Second (2), Third (1); Upper (3), Lower (4), Inside (1), Outside (1), Without (1), Middle (2) and Country (1). Relative age is denoted by Old (1) and New (3). Colour, state and shape are denoted by Blue (1) Rocky (1) and Round (2). In other contexts, all these qualifiers may occur as specifics.

7 COMPOSITION OF MULTIPLE-ELEMENT NAMES

The commonest method of forming multiple-element names is by the simple combination of SPECIFIC + GENERIC (as in Adams Cove, Admirals Beach and Andersons Brook) which occurs in some 1240 names, almost 67 per cent of the total names on the AVALON PENINSULA. This formula is elaborated but essentially unchanged in names in which the specific consists not of one word but of two or more inseparable elements: Barking Kettle Pond, Big John's Point, Black Duck Pond, Bob Ayles Pond, Bread and Cheese Hill, Burnt Pine Pond, Camels Back Pond,

Captain Orlebar's Cairn, Crossing Place River, Empty Basket Cove, George Norris Pond and the like.

The specific may be preceded by the definite article with suppression of a following generic, ARTICLE + SPECIFIC (+ GENERIC understood): The Bell (Rock), The Bower (Pond), The Birchies (Ponds), The Kettle (Point), The Sisters (Ponds), La Manche (Cove); though frequently the article precedes a generic: The Arch, The Beach, The Broads, The Dock, The Gorge, The Keys, The Lookout, The Motion, The Narrows, The Neck, The Pinnacles, The Pond, The Spout, and The Thicket.

Shift names are developed in about 190 names from the combination Specific + Generic by the addition of a second generic, (SPECIFIC + GENERIC) + GENERIC: Arnold's Cove Station, Back River Pond, Bacon Cove Head, Bald Head Bay, Beachy Cove Brook, etc.

A qualifier precedes a specific and a generic, QUALIFIER + (SPECIFIC + GENERIC), in fifty-eight names: Big Chance Cove, Blue Shag Island, East Green Island, Eastern Island Pond, Eastern Steady Pond, First Salmon Pond, Great Colinet Island, Little Bell Island, Long Island Pond, Lower Island Cove, Middle Gull Pond, North Green Island, Second Junction Pond, Third Junction Pond, Upper Back Cove, Western Gull Pond, etc.

Shift names are again developed by the addition of a generic, QUALIFIER + (SPECIFIC + GENERIC) + GENERIC, in Inside Island Cove Pond, Little Island Cove Pond, and Outside Island Cove Pond.

A medial qualifier, SPECIFIC + QUALIFIER + GENERIC, appears to occur in eighteen names unless the formation is in fact that of the preceding group with the family or place name the true qualifier: Bauline Long Pond, Bauline Rocky Pond, Bowes Long Pond, Bowes Round Pond, Brigus North Brook, Carbonear Long Pond, Colliers Big Pond, Cupids Big Pond, Cupids Long Pond, Flings Big Pond, Flings Long Pond, Goulds Big Pond, Holyrood Big Pond, Mobile Big Pond, Murphys First Pond, Riverhead Long Pond, and Topsail Round Pond. In Long Pond Manuels, the qualifier is obviously Manuels, giving SPECIFIC + GENERIC + QUALIFIER.

The formula is extended, (SPECIFIC + GENERIC = SPECIFIC) + QUALIFIER + GENERIC, in Gull Island South Head, Petty Harbour Long Pond, Pouch Cove Northeast Pond, Pouch Cove Northwest Pond, Seal Cove Rocky Pond, Turks Gut Long Pond, and Witless Bay Country Pond, and partly transposed, (GENERIC + SPECIFIC = SPECIFIC) + QUALIFIER + GENERIC, in Bay Bulls Big Pond.

A qualifier follows specific and generic, (SPECIFIC + GENERIC) + QUALIFIER, in Avondale Pond South, Black Head North, Five Mile Pond East,

Five Mile Pond West, Gull Pond East, Mitchells Pond North, Mitchells Pond South, Nine Island Pond South, Piccos Pond South, Portugal Cove South, and Round Pond West. The formula is extended, (SPECIFIC + GENERIC = SPECIFIC) + GENERIC + QUALIFIER, in Pouch Cove Brook West. It will be observed that the following qualifier is always a bearing.

Certain generics may precede the specific, GENERIC + SPECIFIC, as in Bay Bulls, Bay de Grave, Bay de Verde and Bay Roberts; Cape Ballard, Cape Broyle, Cape Dog, Cape Freels, Cape Mutton, Cape Neddick, Cape Pine, Cape Race, Cape St. Francis, Cape St. Mary's and Cape Spear; Cove nan Drioch Clochan; Harbour Grace and Harbour Main; Isthmus of Avalon; Mount Carmel; Point La Haye, Point Lance, Point of Beach, Point of the Gut, Point Verde; Port de Grave; Villa Maria. A unique formation, ARTICLE + GENERIC + SPECIFIC clause, is found in The Pond that Feeds the Brook.

Shift names are formed by the addition of a generic, (GENERIC + SPECIFIC) + GENERIC, in Bay Bulls River, Bay de Verde Head, Bay de Verde Peninsula, Bay Roberts Harbour, Cape Broyle Harbour, Cape Broyle River, Cove nan Drioch Clochan Point, Fort Amherst Lighthouse, Harbour Grace Islands, Harbour Main Island, Harbour Main Point, Harbour Main Pond, Mount Arlington Heights, Mount Carmel Pond, Mount Misery Pond, Mount Pearl Park, and Port de Grave Island.

The AVALON PENINSULA does not appear to possess such rich examples of agglutination as Lower Duck Island Cove Brook (NTS Baie Verte and Fleur de Lys), or East Side West Branch East River of Pictou, the name of a post office in Nova Scotia recorded in *Lovell's Gazetteer of British North America*, 1881.

TABLE 7

PLACE NAMES ASSOCIATED WITH ENGLISH FAMILY NAMES

Place Name	English Family Name	Status of Family Name on the Avalon Peninsula
ADAMS COVE (NTS Heart's Content)	Guppy, p. 23 etc. Bucks, Devon, Hants, Staffs	At OLD PERLICAN
ADAMS POND (NTS St. John's)		At ST. JOHN'S
ANDERSONS BROOK (NTS Harbour Grace)	Guppy, pp. 24, 449 N. England	Not locally
ANDERSONS POND (NTS Harbour Grace)		
ARNOLD COVE (NTS St. Shotts)	Guppy, pp. 24, 450 Warwicks, Leicester	Not current on AVALON PENINSULA Population Returns 1836
ARNOLD'S COVE (NTS Sunnyside)		

TABLE 7 *(continued)*

Place Name	English Family Name	Status of Family Name on the Avalon Peninsula
AXES († ? for Aske's) POND (NTS St. John's)	Bardsley, p. 63 – Rare	Not current in Newfoundland
BOB AYLES POND (NTS Heart's Content)	Guppy, pp. 205, 451 Hants	Not current on AVALON PENINSULA
? BAKER HEAD (NTS Trepassey) ? BAKER POINT (NTS Argentia)	Guppy, p. 25 Monmouth, Somerset, Sussex, Surrey	Lane 1773 At various communities in PLACENTIA BAY
HARRY BALDWINS POND (NTS Heart's Content)	Guppy, pp. 25, 197, 452 Gloucester etc.	At SIBLEY'S COVE, CARBONEAR, VICTORIA
? TIM BARRETT COVE (NTS Argentia)	Guppy, p. 26, Dorset etc.	MARQUISE, ARGENTIA etc.
BATTENS POND (NTS Harbour Grace)	Guppy, pp. 105, 146 Cornwall, Devon	At SOUTH RIVER, BARENEED, BAY ROBERTS etc. At PORT DE GRAVE 1768
? BECKFORD HEAD (NTS St. Mary's)	Bardsley, p. 90 Family and place name in Gloucester	Beckford (Set) *Population Returns* 1836. Cp. Newfoundland family name Peckford
BISHOP'S COVE (NTS Harbour Grace)	Guppy, pp. 27, 457 Dorset etc.	At UPPER ISLAND COVE
BISHOPS GULLY (NTS Harbour Grace)		At CARBONEAR (*Directory* 1877)
BISHOPS POND (NTS Harbour Grace)		At BURNT HEAD, CUPIDS etc.
BISHOPS PONDS (NTS Harbour Grace)		At BURNT HEAD, CUPIDS etc.
BOONE POINT (NTS Bay Bulls)	Boon – Guppy, pp. 360, 459 Staffs	At BAY BULLS
BRADLEYS COVE (NTS Heart's Content)	Guppy, p. 460 Widespread	Lane 1774
? BRIDGES POND (NTS Harbour Grace)	Guppy, pp. 395, 461 Wilts, Suffolk	Not current in Newfoundland
BRIERLY COVE (NTS St. Bride's)	Brierley – Bardsley, p. 133 Yorks	Adm. 232a 1870
? BROCKS POND (NTS St. John's)	Guppy, p. 461 Devon, Norfolk	Not current on AVALON PENINSULA
BROWNSDALE (NTS Old Perlican)	Guppy, p. 462 Widespread	At BROWNSDALE
BRUCE POND (NTS Heart's Content)	Guppy, p. 462 Durham	At LONG HARBOUR
BRYANTS COVE (NTS Harbour Grace)	Guppy, p. 463 Somerset, Dorset etc.	Southwood 1675
BUTLER HEAD (NTS Dildo)	Guppy, p. 464	
BUTLERS POND (NTS St. Catherine's)	Gloucester etc.	At WITLESS BAY

TABLE 7 (continued)

Place Name	English Family Name	Status of Family Name on the Avalon Peninsula
BUTLERS POND (NTS Holyrood)		At ROACHES LINE, BURNT HEAD, CLARKES BEACH
BUTLERVILLE (NTS Harbour Grace)		At HARBOUR GRACE, SHEARSTOWN, BUTLERVILLE. Buck (i.e. BACK). Jas. Butler property owner at Buck Cove i.e. BACK COVE ? now BLOW ME DOWN 1760
CHAMBERLAINS (NTS St. John's)	Guppy, pp. 28, 258, 466, Leicester, Rutland, etc.	Census 1857
? CHAPEL ARM (NTS Dildo)	Guppy, pp. 149, 323, 467 Notts, Somerset, Devon	Cook and Lane 1770 [1775]B
CHAPEL COVE (NTS Holyrood)		Chapel's Cove, Population Returns 1836
CLARKES BEACH (NTS Harbour Grace)	Guppy, pp. 28, 468 Widespread	Census 1857. At BRIGUS 1770
CLARKS BROOK (NTS Heart's Content)		At VICTORIA
CLARKS POND (NTS Holyrood)		Not locally
? CLEAR COVE (NTS Renews)	Guppy, pp. 83, 469 Cambridge	Yonge 1663–69
CLEMENTS COVE (NTS Heart's Content)	Guppy, p. 469 Leicester, Rutland, S. Wales, Devon	Not locally
CLEMENTS POND (NTS St. John's)		At BELL ISLAND, TORBAY etc.
? CLOWNS COVE (NTS Heart's Content)		Southwood 1675
? COLLIER BAY (NTS Dildo)	Guppy, p. 470 Surrey, Berks, Cheshire	Lane 1790
? COLLIERS (NTS Holyrood)		Blathwayt c. 1630–40
COOPER COVE (NTS Argentia)	Guppy, pp. 29, 88, 471 Widespread	At PLACENTIA, DUNVILLE, etc.
COOPER HEAD (NTS Argentia)		
COOPERS HEAD (NTS Harbour Grace)		CO 199.18 1780
? COOPERS POND (NTS Harbour Grace)		At SPREAD EAGLE, GREEN'S HARBOUR
COURAGES BEACH (NTS Harbour Grace)	Bardsley, p. 209, Reaney, p. 80	Not locally
COX POINT (NTS St. Catherine's)	Guppy, pp. 29, 473 Dorset, Somerset, etc.	Population Returns 1836 At ARGENTIA etc.
CROCKERS COVE (NTS Harbour Grace)	Guppy, pp. 150, 474 Dorset, Devon, Somerset	Southwood 1675. At VICTORIA, HEART'S CONTENT, HEART'S DELIGHT, etc.

Specifics, Qualifiers, Composition / 159

TABLE 7 *(continued)*

Place Name	English Family Name	Status of Family Name on the Avalon Peninsula
? CUSLETT (NTS St. Bride's)		*Population Returns* 1836
? DANIELS BROOK (NTS Holyrood)	Guppy, pp. 29, 476 Daniel: Cornwall, Devon, Worcester, Gloucester, etc. Daniels: Gloucester, etc.	Not locally
DAVIES HEAD (NTS Harbour Grace)	Guppy, pp. 30, 476 for Davey: Cornwall, Devon, etc.	? Among first settlers at COLEYS POINT
? DAVIS POINT (NTS Placentia)	Guppy, pp. 30, 476 Welsh Border	At COLINET
? DENNIS POINT (NTS Bay Bulls)	Guppy, pp. 107, 152, 477 Devon, Cornwall, etc.	Not locally
? DIXON HILL (NTS Placentia)	Guppy, pp. 31, 478 Chiefly Northern counties	Jukes 1842. ? An army officer.
DRAKES POND (NTS Harbour Grace)	Guppy, pp. 152, 171, 289, 479 Dorset, Devon etc.	Not locally
EZEKIEL'S COVE (NTS Holyrood)	*DNB* Jewish family of Devon	At HARBOUR MAIN
FISHERS POINT (NTS Trepassey)	Guppy, pp. 32, 485 Widespread	Not locally
FITTERS COVE (NTS Heart's Content)	Guppy, pp. 390, 485 Warwick	Vitters (Newfoundland 1955). Not current in Newfoundland.
FOWLERS BROOK (NTS St. John's)	Guppy, pp. 33, 486 Gloucester, Dorset, etc.	At CHAMBERLAINS
FRENCH COVE (NTS Harbour Grace)	Guppy, pp. 34, 154, 487 Devon, etc.	Ed. French at BAY ROBERTS 1775 where name still found.
GEAR POND (NTS Bay Bulls)	? Gare: Guppy, p. 488 Somerset	Not locally
? GENTLEMAN POINT (NTS Ferryland)	Bardsley, p. 314, Reaney, p. 133	Not current in Newfoundland
GILES POND (NTS Harbour Grace)	Guppy, pp. 396, 490 Wilts., Cornwall, Devon, etc.	Not locally
? GLADNEYS ARM (NTS St. John's)	Untraced	At ST. JOHN'S
GODDENS POND (NTS Heart's Content) GODDENVILLE (NTS Harbour Grace)	Guppy, pp. 229, 491 Kent	At HARBOUR GRACE. Thomas Godden shopkeeper there (*Directory* 1877)

160 / Place Names of the Avalon Peninsula

TABLE 7 (continued)

Place Name	English Family Name	Status of Family Name on the Avalon Peninsula
GOOBIES (NTS Sunnyside)	? Guppy: Guppy, pp. 172, 397, 494 Dorset	Gooby, Goobie formerly of HANTS HARBOUR, now at OLD PERLICAN, GOOBIES, ST. JOHN'S, Queens Cove (NTS Random Island)
? GREEN HARBOUR (NTS Dildo)		At GREEN HARBOUR
GREENS GULLY (NTS Harbour Grace)	Guppy, pp. 36, 493 Widespread except Devon and Cornwall	At CARBONEAR
HALLS GULLIES (NTS Holyrood) HALLS TOWN (NTS Harbour Grace)	Guppy, pp. 36, 495 Widespread	At HALLS TOWN, after Isaac Hall, a naval deserter *Census* 1857
HAWKE HILLS (NTS Holyrood, Bay Bulls)	Guppy, p. 498 Cornwall	Howley 1876. Not locally.
HIBBS HOLE (NTS Harbour Grace)	Bardsley, p. 381, Reaney, p. 176	1745. At BELL ISLAND, KELLIGREWS, etc. but not locally
HODGEWATER BRIDGE (NTS Holyrood) HODGEWATER POND (NTS Holyrood)	Hodge: Guppy, pp. 103, 109, 142, 502 Cornwall, Devon	Jukes 1842. Not locally
? HOPEALL (NTS Dildo)	? Hopewell: Bardsley, p. 396	Lane *Directions* 1775, 1810. Not current in Newfoundland
? HOPEWELL (NTS Holyrood)	Bardsley, p. 396	*Census* 1869. Not current in Newfoundland
HORTON ROCKS (NTS Heart's Content)	Guppy, pp. 95, 141, 390, 504 Devon, Shropshire, etc.	Not locally
HOSKINS POND (NTS Harbour Grace)	Guppy, pp. 102, 504 Cornwall, Devon	Site of house owned by John Hoskin(s), 19th century jam manufacturer of HARBOUR GRACE
HOWLETT POINT (NTS Ferryland)	Guppy, p. 505 Norfolk, Suffolk	At TORS COVE, WITLESS BAY
? HUGHS (? for HUGHES) POND (NTS St. John's)	Guppy, pp. 40, 505 Wales, Hereford, Shropshire	Not locally
IRVINE STATION (NTS St. John's)	Guppy, p. 590 Scottish Border	Not locally
? ISAAC HEADS (NTS Argentia)	Guppy, pp. 156, 507 Devon, Gloucester	Isaacs on Burin Peninsula

TABLE 7 *(continued)*

Place Name	English Family Name	Status of Family Name on the Avalon Peninsula
? JAMES COVE (NTS Holyrood)	Guppy, p. 41, 508	*Census* 1857
JAMES GULLY (NTS Harbour Grace)	South Wales, Dorset, Somerset, Cornwall	At CARBONEAR
? JOHN'S POND (NTS Placentia)	John: Guppy, p. 509 S. Wales, Monmouth	Murray 1868. Rare in Newfoundland and not locally
? JOHNS POND (NTS Holyrood)	Johns: Guppy, p. 509 Cornwall, Devon, S. Wales, Monmouth	
? JONAS POINT (NTS Placentia)	Guppy, p. 509 Cambridge	Adm. 2915 1864
JONES COVE (NTS St. John's)	Guppy, p. 509	At ST. PHILIPS etc.
JONES HEAD (NTS Harbour Grace)	Widespread	At BAY ROBERTS etc.
JONES POND (NTS St. John's)		Not locally
JOYS POINT (NTS Holyrood)	Guppy, pp. 187, 510 Essex	At HOLYROOD
KELLIGREWS (NTS Harbour Grace)	Killigrew: Cornwall	Wix 1836. Not current
? KELLIS (? for KELLY'S) POINT (NTS Bay Bulls)	Guppy, pp. 157, 510, 590 Cornwall, Devon	Not locally
? KELLY POINT (NTS Argentia)		At FOX HARBOUR
? KELLY POND (NTS Holyrood)		At HOLYROOD
? KELLYS ISLAND (NTS Harbour Grace)		Lane *Directions* 1775, 1810
? KELLYS POND (NTS Harbour Grace)		At HARBOUR GRACE
? KING ISLAND (NTS Argentia)	Guppy, p. 511 Widespread	At FOX HARBOUR
KINGMANS (NTS Renews)	Guppy, p. 512, Dorset	Not locally
? KINGS BEACH (NTS Harbour Grace)	Guppy, p. 511 Widespread	
KINGS COVE (NTS St. John's)		At BELL ISLAND
? KINGS HEAD (NTS Heart's Content)		Lane *Directions* 1775, 1810
KINGS HEAD (NTS Bay de Verde)		On BAY DE VERDE PENINSULA but not at DANIELS COVE
KINGS POND (NTS Harbour Grace)		At CARBONEAR
KINGSTON (NTS Heart's Content)		At KINGSTON
? LAWRENCE POND (NTS Holyrood)	Guppy, pp. 43, 344, 514, Somerset, Dorset, Gloucester	Not locally

162 / *Place Names of the Avalon Peninsula*

TABLE 7 *(continued)*

Place Name	English Family Name	Status of Family Name on the Avalon Peninsula
LEARS COVE (NTS St. Bride's)	Guppy, p. 514 Devon	Population Returns 1836
LEARS COVE (NTS Harbour Grace)		At HIBBS HOLE
LEES GULLY (NTS Holyrood) LEES POND (NTS Holyrood)	Guppy, pp. 43, 515 Widespread	Not locally
LEES POND (NTS St. John's)		At ST. JOHN's and elsewhere
LOADER (for LODER) POND (NTS Heart's Content)	Guppy, pp. 174, 516 Dorset	At HANTS HARBOUR
LOCKYERS WATERS (NTS Holyrood)	Guppy, pp. 345, 516 Somerset, Dorset	Not locally
NICK LONGS POND (NTS Heart's Content)	Guppy, pp. 44, 517 Monmouth, Wilts, Dorset	At CARBONEAR
? LOUIS (? for LEWIS) POND (NTS Holyrood)	Guppy, pp. 43, 515 Widespread	At HOLYROOD
LUTHERS GULLIES (NTS Harbour Grace)	Bardsley, p. 502, Reaney, p. 207	At CARBONEAR. Name of three planters there (*Directory* 1877)
MADDOX COVE (NTS Bay Bulls)	Guppy, pp. 88, 212, 444, 519 Cheshire, Hereford, Shropshire, Devon	Census 1857. At BAY BULLS
? MAIDEN ISLAND (NTS Heart's Content)	Maidens: Guppy, pp. 270, 519 Lincoln	Not current in Newfoundland
MAIDENS PONDS (NTS Harbour Grace)		
? MAINS MARSH (NTS Harbour Grace)	Guppy, p. 519 Northants	Not current in Newfoundland
MAKINSON (NTS Harbour Grace)	Liverpool	At MAKINSON
MANUELS (NTS St. John's)	Bardsley, p. 512	At ST. JOHN's, etc.
? MASTERS HEAD (NTS Dildo)	Guppy, pp. 353, 521 Somerset, Dorset	At Harbour Buffett, etc.
MERCERS COVE (NTS Harbour Grace)	Guppy, pp. 231, 522 Kent, Lancs	At BAY ROBERTS (1765)
MILES BROOK (NTS St. John's)	Guppy, pp. 45, 194, 523 Widespread	At ST. JOHN's
? MILLERS POND (NTS Biscay Bay River)	Guppy, pp. 46, 523 Widespread	Not locally
MITCHELLS POND NORTH (NTS St. John's) MITCHELLS POND SOUTH	Guppy, pp. 46, 524 Cornwall, Dorset, Devon etc.	At PORTUGAL COVE, BEACHY COVE
? MONDAY POND (NTS Bay de Verde)	Guppy, p. 526 Hants, etc.	Mundy (1) at CARBONEAR
? MONDAYS POND (NTS Holyrood)		Not locally

Specifics, Qualifiers, Composition / 163

TABLE 7 (continued)

Place Name	English Family Name	Status of Family Name on the Avalon Peninsula
? MOORES GULCH (NTS Trepassey) ? MOORES POINT (NTS Trepassey)	Guppy, pp. 46, 524 Widespread	Not locally
MOUNT PEARL PARK (NTS St. John's)		Residence of Sir James Pearl d. 1840
MUNDYS POND (NTS St. John's)	Guppy, p. 526 Hants, etc.	Not locally
? NEVILLES POND (NTS St. John's)	Reaney, p. 229	At TOPSAIL
NICHOLS POND (NTS Holyrood)	Guppy, pp. 48, 528 Cornwall, etc.	Not locally
NORMANS COVE (NTS Dildo)	Guppy, pp. 48, 528	At LONG HARBOUR
NORMANS POND (NTS Harbour Grace)	Somerset, Devon, etc.	At BAY ROBERTS 1802
GEORGE NORRIS POND (NTS Bay Bulls)	Guppy, p. 529 Somerset, Dorset, etc.	At WITLESS BAY
OLIVERS POND (NTS St. John's)	Guppy, pp. 48, 529 Widespread	At ST. JOHN'S
OXLEYS POND (NTS Holyrood)	Bardsley, p. 577 Yorks, etc.	Not locally
PACKS POND (NTS Heart's Content)	Bardsley, p. 578	Not locally
PARKERS POND (NTS St. John's)	Guppy, pp. 49, 531 Widespread	At ST. JOHN'S
PARSONS COVE (NTS Harbour Grace)	Guppy, p. 50 Wilts, etc.	At BRYANTS COVE
PARSONVILLE (NTS Harbour Grace)		At BELL ISLAND
? PEARCE PEAK (NTS Argentia)	Guppy, pp. 50, 210, 533 Cornwall, Devon, Somerset	At ARGENTIA
PEDDLES POND (NTS Harbour Grace)	Piddle: Bardsley 593	At HARBOUR GRACE, SPANIARDS BAY 1803
PEDDLES WATERS (NTS Holyrood)		At GEORGETOWN, BRIGUS, PORT DE GRAVE
PENNYS POND (NTS Holyrood)	Guppy, pp. 353, 534 Hants, Somerset	At AVONDALE, Penney at HOLYROOD
PERRY'S COVE (NTS Heart's Content)	Guppy, pp. 51, 344 Somerset, Gloucester, Cornwall, etc.	Lane 1774. At WESTERN BAY
? PEYTONS BROOK (NTS Bay Bulls) ? PEYTONS POND (NTS Bay Bulls)	Bardsley, p. 600 Devon	Not locally
PEYTONS GULLIES (NTS Holyrood)		Not locally
PEYTONS POND (NTS St. John's)		? For Penton at SHOE COVE, POUCH COVE

164 / *Place Names of the Avalon Peninsula*

TABLE 7 (continued)

Place Name	English Family Name	Status of Family Name on the Avalon Peninsula
PHILLIPS POND (NTS Holyrood)	Guppy, pp. 51, 535 Widespread	At COLLIERS
PIERCES (? for PEARCES or PIERCEYS) POND (NTS Heart's Content)	Guppy, pp. 161, 533 Devon	At WINTERTON, NEW PERLICAN, etc.
PIKES POND (NTS Harbour Grace)	Guppy, p. 535, Devon, Dorset, etc.	At CARBONEAR (*Directory* 1877)
? PINCHER (? for PINCH or PINCHES) GULLIES (NTS Heart's Content)	Guppy, p. 536 Cornwall, Shropshire	Not current in Newfoundland
PINHORNS POND (NTS Heart's Content)	London Postal Area Telephone Directory	At WINTERTON
PITCHERS POND (NTS Harbour Grace)	Guppy, p. 536 Bucks, Sussex	At WINTERTON
PITMANS POND (NTS Heart's Content and Old Perlican)	Guppy, pp. 174, 354, 536 Dorset, Somerset	At NEW PERLICAN
? POLLS (for PAULS) HEAD (NTS St. John's)	Guppy, pp. 174, 353, 532 Cornwall, Dorset, Somerset	At BAY ROBERTS, SPANIARDS BAY, etc.
MAURICE POOLE COVE (NTS Argentia)	Guppy, p. 536 Somerset, Gloucester, etc.	Not locally
? POUCH COVE (NTS Pouch Cove)	Reaney, p. 258	Not current in Newfoundland
? POWELL POINT (NTS Argentia)	Guppy, pp. 53, 537 Hereford, etc.	Not locally
POWELLS BROOK (NTS Harbour Grace)		At CARBONEAR
? PRINCES POND (NTS Bay Bulls)	Guppy, pp. 538 Staffs, Derby, Cheshire	Not locally
PROSSER ROCK (St. John's Harbour)	Guppy, p. 538 Hereford, Monmouth, etc.	Lane *Directions* 1775, 1810
PURBECKS POND (NTS Heart's Content)	In *DNB* as title of nobility	Not current in Newfoundland
? PUSSEYS (for PEARCEY or PIERCEY) BROOK (NTS Holyrood)	Guppy, pp. 161, 533 Devon	? Percy at BRIGUS
REDMANS HEAD (NTS St. John's)	Guppy, pp. 122, 431, 541 Wilts, Yorks, W.R.	At ST. JOHN'S (2)
RICKETTS BRIDGE (NTS St. John's)	Guppy, pp. 201, 542 Gloucester	At ST. JOHN'S
RIX HARBOUR (NTS Sunnyside)	Guppy, pp. 295, 543 Norfolk	Imray 1862
ROACHES LINE (Not in NTS Harbour Grace)	Guppy, p. 543 Gloucester, Cornwall;	
ROACHES MARSH (NTS Bay Bulls)	Roche in Barnstaple (W. Kirwin)	Not locally. ? for ROCHE

Specifics, Qualifiers, Composition / 165

TABLE 7 *(continued)*

Place Name	English Family Name	Status of Family Name on the Avalon Peninsula
ROBINS POND (NTS St. John's)	Guppy, p. 543 Cornwall, Devon, Herts, Warwick	At ST. JOHN'S
ROBINSON POINT (NTS Sunnyside)	Guppy, p. 543 Widespread	Imray 1873
ROBINSONS RIVER (NTS Pouch Cove)		Not locally
JOSEPH ROFF COVE (NTS Dildo)	Rolfe: Guppy p. 544 Herts	Roffe at Mortier (NTS Marystown)
ROGERS BROOK (NTS Harbour Grace)	Guppy, pp. 56, 101, 544 Hereford, Gloucester, Cornwall	Not locally
ROGERS GULLIES (NTS St. John's) ROGERS TILT POND (NTS St. John's)		At ST. JOHN'S
JIMMY ROWES POND (NTS Harbour Grace) MARTIN ROWES POND (NTS Heart's Content)	Guppy, pp. 102, 163, 544 Cornwall, Devon	At WHITEWAY, HEART'S CONTENT
SAMSON (for SAMPSON) POINT (NTS Argentia)	Guppy, p. 546 Cornwall, Devon, etc.	At FOX HARBOUR
SAUNDERS PONDS (NTS St. Catherine's)	Guppy, pp. 57, 546 Devon, Dorset, etc.	Not locally
? SAWYERS HILL (NTS Placentia)	Guppy, pp. 366, 546 Suffolk	Not locally
SCOGGINS HEAD (NTS Ferryland)	Bardsley, p. 672 Norfolk, Suffolk	Lane 1773
SEYMOURS GULLIES (NTS Harbour Grace)	Guppy, pp. 81, 548 Bucks, Berks	At BUTLERVILLE, SHEARSTOWN
? SHORE'S COVE (NTS Ferryland)	Guppy, pp. 98, 550 Cheshire	Not current in Newfoundland
SIBLEYS COVE (NTS Old Perlican)	Bardsley, p. 689, Reaney, p. 295	Not locally
SIMS POINT (NTS Trepassey)	Guppy, pp. 393, 550 Wilts, etc.	Not locally
? SKERRYS BIGHT (NTS St. John's)	London Postal Area Telephone Directory	Not current in Newfoundland
? SLOANS GULLY (NTS Harbour Grace)	Guppy, p. 594 Ayr	At RIVERHEAD, HARBOUR GRACE (1)
? SNAGGE HILL (NTS St. John's) ? SNAGGE POINT (NTS St. John's)	London Postal Area Telephone Directory	Not current in Newfoundland
SNOW'S POND (NTS Holyrood, Harbour Grace)	Guppy, pp. 164, 552 Devon, etc.	At CLARKES BEACH, HALLSTOWN
SOOLEYS GULLIES (NTS Heart's Content)	Sully – Guppy, pp. 355, 556 Somerset	At HEART'S CONTENT, HEART'S DELIGHT
SPARKS GULLY (NTS Holyrood)	Guppy, pp. 164, 386, 552 Devon, Somerset	At GEORGETOWN, BRIGUS

TABLE 7 (continued)

Place Name	English Family Name	Status of Family Name on the Avalon Peninsula
? SPARROW POINT (NTS Argentia)	Guppy, pp. 372, 552 Essex, Gloucester, Sussex	At SHIP HARBOUR, etc.
SPICES (? for SPICER) BROOK (NTS Heart's Content)	Guppy, pp. 175, 553 Dorset	At WINTERTON (1)
? SPRIGGS POINT (NTS St. John's)	Guppy, p. 553 Huntingdon	Not current in Newfoundland
? SQUIB (? for SQUIBB) POINT (NTS Sunnyside)	Bardsley, p. 710	At CARBONEAR
STANTON POINT (NTS Sunnyside)	Guppy, p. 554 Bedford	Imray 1862
? STEEL POINT (NTS Renews)	Guppy, pp. 554, 594 Cumberland, Westmorland	
? STEPHENS POND (NTS Bay Bulls)	Guppy, pp. 59, 554, 594 Cornwall, etc.	Not locally
? STICK POND (NTS St. John's)	Reaney, p. 307	At ST. JOHN'S
STICKLES POND (NTS St. John's)	Guppy, p. 555 Kent	Not current in Newfoundland
STILES (? for STOYLES) (NTS St. John's)	Stile(s): Reaney, p. 308; Stoyles: Reaney, p. 310	At BELL ISLAND
STOCK COVE (NTS Sunnyside)	Guppy, pp. 191, 555 Essex	Stock, Stoke. Wix 1836
SUTTONS POND (NTS Harbour Grace)	Guppy, pp. 60, 556 Cheshire, etc.	Not locally
? THOMAS POND (NTS Bay Bulls)	Guppy, pp. 60, 101, 559 S. Wales, Cornwall	At ST. JOHN'S
THORNLEA (NTS Dildo)	Guppy, pp. 142, 559 Devon, Dorset, etc.	Thorne at THORNLEA
? TICKLES (NTS Placentia)	Guppy, pp. 99, 560 Cheshire	Not current in Newfoundland
TRACES (for TRAC(E)Y) POINT (NTS Renews)	Bardsley, p. 761 Devon	Not locally. Adm. 2915 1864
? TUCKERS GULLY (NTS Harbour Grace)	Guppy, pp. 19, 62, 165, 562 Devon, Somerset, Cornwall, Dorset	Not locally
UPSHALL (NTS Dildo)	Upsall: Bardsley, p. 777	At CHANCE COVE, LITTLE HARBOUR
VIZARD HILL (NTS Bay Bulls)	Bardsley, p. 785	Fizzard at Creston and South Coast communities but not locally
VOISEYS BROOK (NTS St. John's)	Bardsley, p. 785, Reaney, p. 333	At ST. JOHN'S
? WALLS POND (NTS Holyrood)	Guppy, p. 565 Somerset, Shropshire, etc.	At HARBOUR MAIN

TABLE 7 (concluded)

Place Name	English Family Name	Status of Family Name on the Avalon Peninsula
WATTS POND (NTS St. John's)	Guppy, pp. 63, 141, 567 Somerset, Wilts, Gloucester, etc.	Not locally
WEBBERS POND (NTS Harbour Grace)	Guppy, pp. 19, 142, 568 Devon, Somerset	At CUPIDS
WELCH (? for WALSH) HILL (NTS Harbour Grace)	Welch – Guppy, p. 568; Walsh – Guppy, p. 566	Walsh at HARBOUR GRACE
WHITEWAY (NTS Harbour Grace)	Guppy, pp. 166, 570 Devon	At ST. JOHN'S and elsewhere
WHITEWAY POND (NTS St. John's)		
WIGMORE POND (NTS St. John's)	Bardsley, p. 812	Not locally
? WILLIAMS (NTS Bay Bulls)	Guppy, pp. 65, 572 Cornwall and widespread	At BAY BULLS
? WILLIAMS COVE (NTS Bay Bulls)		
? WILLIAMS HILL (NTS Bay Bulls)		
? WILLIAMS HILL (NTS Bay Bulls)		
? WILLIAMS POND (NTS Holyrood)		At CONCEPTION HARBOUR
WILLIAMS POND (NTS St. John's)		At POUCH COVE
JOHN WILLIAMS POND (NTS Harbour Grace)		At NEW HARBOUR
? WINTERTON (NTS Heart's Content)	Winter: Guppy, p. 573 Somerset, etc.	Not locally
WOODFORD'S (NTS Holyrood)	Bardsley, p. 824	At HARBOUR MAIN

* Based for the most part on the *Official List of Electors 1955*.
† A mark of interrogation before an entry indicates that the name may not be an English family name in its particular context.

Avalon Peninsula Gazetteer and Index of Place Names

Entries are in alphabetical order, both for individual names and within clusters. Hence the first name recorded in a cluster is not necessarily the earliest, as the historical citations show. Where the same name occurs in different places, entries follow in ascending degrees of latitude.

The aim, though often unfulfilled, has been to give the following for each name:

a Name – BAY ROBERTS, SEAL COVE.
b Pronunciation, where unusual, in phonetic script within square brackets.
c Description – Settlement, River, Cove.
d Latitude and longitude in degrees and minutes, but since all places are in latitude north and longitude west, N and W have been omitted – 47–32, 52–56. Positions of features have been plotted as follows:
Rivers – by the location of the mouth; Tributaries – at the point of junction with the main stream; Islands, Peninsulas, Expanses of water (arms, bays, bights, coves, harbours, inlets, lakes, ponds, and tickles) – by their central points. Where names in a cluster are in the same location, latitude and longitude of shift names are omitted.
e Reference to the map(s) in the National Topographic Series in which the name occurs – St. John's 1N/10W. See map on p. vi.
f Citations of the name in chronological order from the records, but restricted to the earliest recording except where variants are significant or interesting. Descriptions of most of the maps cited by author and year, e.g. Blathwayt c. 1630–40, are to be found in Bibliography I. Other works cited are to be found usually by authors' names or cue titles in Bibliography II. (H) and (P) indicate variant readings by H. Harrisse and G. R. F. Prowse.
g Cross references, in which Cp. is used to draw attention to associated names, and See usually indicates additional information.
h Older forms of names and obsolete names which differ significantly from modern forms are in lower case.
i Additional information, acquired after the historical introduction had been prepared.
j Linguistic, interpretative and other commentary. Page references are given to the commentary in Chapter I–IX. Main entries are in italics. A general commentary may precede a name common to a number of features.

Abra Frade (Laet 1630)
See PORTUGAL COVE (NTS St. John's).
P. 33.

ADAMS COVE 47–52, 53–05 (NTS
Heart's Content 1N/14E) ? So[uth]
W[est] Cove (Visscher c. 1680;
Mount and Page 1755), Adams Cove
(Lane 1774), Adam Cove (Jukes
1840).
— ADAMS COVE (Set.)
(Thoresby 1796; *Population Returns* 1836).
Pp. 76, 92, 156.

ADAMS POND 47–32, 52–53 (NTS St.
John's 1N/10W). P. 156.

ADMIRAL (Specific). Pp. 68–70.
Yonge, p. 63 notes: "1663. Mr
Waymouth, (who is Admiral and
always wore a flagstaff, Sundays a
flag, and is called my Lord, the vice-
admiral my Lady)."

ADMIRALS BEACH (Set.) 47–00, 53–39
(NTS Placentia 1N/4E) As feature:
(Lane 1773; Mount and Page 1780);
as set: (*Population Returns* 1836).
Pp. 70, 86, 108.

Admiral's Beach (Harbour Grace)
(Lane, *Directions* 1775, 1810).
P. 95.

ADMIRAL'S COVE 46–58, 52–55 (NTS
Renews 1K/15W)
In FERMEUSE HARBOUR.
Amboralls place (Yonge 1663–
1670), Admirals Cove (Lane 1773).
— ADMIRAL'S COVE (Set.)
"where lives a Planter" (*English
Pilot. The Fourth Book* 1689).
Pp. 5, 68. See PORT KIRWAN.

ADMIRAL'S COVE 47–06, 52–55 (NTS
Ferryland 1N/2W)
In CAPE BROYLE HARBOUR. P. 70.
— ADMIRAL'S COVE (Set.)
(Newfoundland 1941).
— ADMIRAL'S HEAD
(Imray, *Sailing Directory* 1873).

Admiral's Island (Adm. 297 1868)
See MOLLYS ISLAND (NTS Harbour
Grace). P. 113.

Agoforta ("Velasco" 1610)
See AQUAFORTE. Pp. 28, 57.

AIRFIELD (Generic). P. 148.

AIRPORT (Generic). P. 148.

Alhallowes (Guy 1612)
See RANTEM COVE. P. 59.

ALLAN SQUARE (St. John's). P. 148.

ALLANDALE ROAD (St. John's)
A ploughing match was held at
Allandale, 29 October 1864. (Devine
and O'Mara, (*Notable Events*, p.
204). P. 147.

Amborals Place (Renews Harbour)
(Yonge 1663–70). Pp. 68–9.

Amboralls Place (Fermeuse Harbour)
(Yonge 1663–70)
See ADMIRAL'S COVE 46–58, 52–55
(NTS Renews). P. 69.

AMHERST HEIGHTS (Street) (St. John's)
Cp. ? FORT AMHERST (NTS St.
John's). P. 145.

ANDERSONS BROOK 47–40, 53–18 (NTS
Harbour Grace 1N/11W)
(NDNR 1N/11 1948).
— ANDERSONS POND 47–41, 53–19
(NDNR 1N/11 1948).
P. 156.

Andrew's Cove (Trinity Bay) (Wix
1836). Pp. 103–4.

ANGEL'S COVE 47–00, 54–09 (NTS Ship
Cove 1M/1E)
Angus Cove (Adm. 2915 1864;
Adm. 232a 1870), Angles or Angels
Cove (M. F. Howley, xxix, NQ,
March 1910).
— ANGELS COVE (Set.)
(*Population Returns* 1836).
Angle's Brook (Murray and
Howley 1868) Cp. PATRICK'S
COVE.
P. 109.

ANGLE POND 47–23, 53–22 (NTS

Holyrood 1N/6W)
(NDNR 1N/6 1943).
? From the sharp peninsula forming part of the western bank.

Anse Arbe (Beaudoin 1697)
See HANTS HARBOUR. Pp. 80, 97.

APPLETON HEIGHTS (District) (St. John's). P. 145.

AQUAFORTE HARBOUR 47–00, 52–56 (NTS Ferryland 1N/2W)
? R da aguea (Reinel 1519; Ribeiro 1529), la baye de l'Islet (Alfonse 1544), Agafort (Whitbourne 1622), Agoforta ("Velasco" 1610), Agoforte (Briggs 1625), Ago forte (Speed 1626) Agoforte ("Blathwayt" c. 1630–40), Agua Fuerte (Laet 1630), Ago forte (Seile 1652), Agua Fuerte (Blaeu 1662), Agua Fuerta (Doncker 1667; Loon 1668), Aquaforte (Robinson 1669), Aquafort Harbour (Imray, *Sailing Directions* 1862).

— AQUAFORTE (Set.) 47–00, 52–58 Aigueforte (Beaudoin 1697), Aquafort (*Population Returns* 1836).
— AQUAFORTE RIVER 47–01, 52–59 N.W. Arm (USHO 0618 1941), Aquaforte River (Newfoundland 1941).
— AQUAFORTE ROCKS 46–59, 52–54 (Adm. 2915 1864).

la baye de l'Islet – after SPURWICK ISLAND, at the south side of the entrance to the harbour (Biggar, *Voyages of Jacques Cartier*, p. 279).

Aquaforte – "It takes its name ... from a pretty cascade on the northern side, where a brook shoots its waters over a cliff into the sea" (Jukes, *Excursions*, II, p. 8).
Pp. 28, 30, 33, 35, 57, 79.

THE ARCH 47–34, 53–12 (NTS Harbour Grace 1N/11E) (CHS 4572 1954).
A sea-arch formation.
Cp. The Arches 50–07, 57–39 (Portland Creek 12I/4E).

Arenhosa (Plancius 1592).
See RENEWS (NTS Renews). P. 31.

ARGENTIA (Set.) 47–18, 53–59 (NTS Argentia 1N/5W)
Little Placentia (*Population Returns* 1836 ... Census 1911), Argentia (? early 20th century).
"Little Placentia ... owing to the request of the Rev. Father St. John, has been named Argentia ... It was suggested by the opening of a silver mine in one of the cliffs, and though the mining enterprise proved a failure, the name has remained" (M. F. Howley, xxx, *NQ*, March 1911).

— ARGENTIA HARBOUR
Little Plasentia (Robinson 1669), Littel Plavsane (Seller c. 1671), p plesance (Courcelle 1675), Pettitt Plasentia (Hack 1677), Pt Plaisance ("Dépôt 128.2.6" c. 1680), Le Petit Plaisance ("Belle Carte du Dépôt" c. 1682) ... The Harbour of Little Placentia (Gaudy 1715), Little Placentia (*English Pilot. The Fourth Book 1716*) ... Little Placentia harbour (Imray *Sailing Directions* 1862, *Sailing Directory* 1873; NLP 1951), Argentia Harbour (CHS 4622 ?1953).

"Little Placentia harbour ... is known to the United States Naval Authorities as Argentia" (NLP I, 1951, p. 107).
Note: Argent Bay (Kitchin 1762) at the bottom of Placentia Bay; Argent Pt (Kitchin 1785) on the west coast of Placentia Bay.
See PLACENTIA.
Pp. 38, 123, 124, 129, 130.

ARM (Generic). P. 141.

ARNOLD (Specific). Pp. 110, 156.

ARNOLD COVE 46–37, 53–33 (NTS St. Shotts 1K/12E)

Arnold's Cove (M. F. Howley, xxviii, NQ, December 1909).

ARNOLDS COVE 47–45, 54–00 (NTS Sunnyside 1N/13W and Sound Island 1M/16E).
— ARNOLD'S COVE (Set.) (NTS Sunnyside 1N/13W) (*Population Returns* 1836).
— ARNOLD'S COVE STATION 47–47, 53–58

Assumption Passage
See PINCHGUT TICKLE (NTS Placentia). P. 85.

AVALON (Specific). P. 63.

Avalon (Plantation)
Avalonia (Mason 1626). P. 12.
— ISTHMUS OF AVALON 47–51, 53–58 (NTS Sunnyside 1N/13W) (Imray, *Sailing Directory* 1873). Pp. 18, 19, 103, 144.
— AVALON PENINSULA 47–30, 53–30 Avalon (Chappell 1813), peninsula of Avalon (Bonnycastle 1842).
— Avalon (Province)
province of Avalon (Lloyd 1665), Province of Avalonia (Robinson 1669), province of Averlon (Jukes 1842), province of Avalon (Bonnycastle 1842). P. 111.

AVENUE (Generic). P. 148.

Avoca (Insurance Policy 1891)
See AVONDALE (NTS Holyrood). P. 64.

Avon (Guy 1612). P. 58.

AVONDALE (Set.) 47–25, 53–12 (NTS Holyrood 1N/6E)
Salmon Cove (*Population Returns* 1836; Census 1857), Salmon Cove South (Adm. 296 1868), Salmon Cove (*Directory* 1877), Avoca (Insurance Policy 1891), Avondale (c. 1906).
Avondale North (Proclamation 18 June 1906)
See CONCEPTION HARBOUR (NTS Holyrood).

Cp. SALMON RIVER 47–25, 53–12. P. 64.
— AVONDALE POND SOUTH 47–19, 53–18 (NTS Holyrood 1N/6W) (NDNR 1N/6 1943).
— AVONDALE STATION 47–24, 53–12 (NTS Holyrood 1N/6E)
Salmon Cove Stn. (Adm. 296 1868).
Pp. 64, 125, 131, 139, 140.

AXES POND 47–41, 52–45 (NTS St. John's 1N/10W). P. 157.

BABOUL ROCKS
See BAY BULLS.

BACCALIEU ISLAND [bækə'luː] 48–08, 52–48 (NTS Bay de Verde 2C/2W)
Y. dos Bacalhas (H), y dos bacalhas (P) (Reinel c. 1504), Insula Baccalauras (Ruysch 1508), Illa dos bacalouz ("Havre Catalan" 1520–34) ... Baccallinu (Desliens 1541, Desceliers 1542) ... I des Molues ou Baccalaos (Coronelli-Tillemon 1689) ... I des Poissons (Cordier 1696), I coupe ("Dépôt 132.2.10" 1706) ... I. Bacaillo ou I des Morues (Bellin 1754) ... Baccalieu I. (Cormack 1822).
— Point Baccalao (Gosse 1828)
? C dos bachalaos (Viegas 1534).
? RED HEAD or SPLIT POINT (NTS Bay de Verde).
— BACCALIEU TICKLE 48–08, 52–50
? Riuo de los bacolaos ("Oliveriana" 1505–8).
Bacalao, a word not naturalized in English, is found in several variant spellings derived from Span. *bacallao* – cod-fish, though early navigators thought that it was of native Indian origin. As a place name, it seems to have been applied to the general area of Cabot's discoveries: "Cabot him selfe names those landes *Baccallaos*, bycause that in the seas ther about he found so great multitudes of certyne bigge fysshes ... which thin-

habitants caule Baccallaos."
(Richard Eden, *New World*, 1555, cited in OED, from which the preceding note is adapted.)

French cartographers glossed the apparently unfamiliar word with *molue, morue* – cod and *poisson* – fish, though the name I coupé presumably refers to the island "cut off" from the mainland by the tickle. For coves on the island, see BRISTA, FAMIT and LONDA. Pp. 12, 30, 33, 34–5, 50, 57, 63, 81, 90, 94, 141.

BACK as a specific is generally "Used to distinguish that one of two [features] ... which lies behind the main or front one, and is more or less subsidiary to it" (OED, Back. Adj. 1.2).

BACK BROOK (NTS Biscay Bay River) See BACK RIVER (NTS Trepassey).

BACK COVE 47–01, 53–41 (NTS Placentia 1N/4E) (Adm. 2915 1864). Of REGINA COVE.

BACK COVE 47–36, 53–11 (NTS Harbour Grace 1N/11E) (Adm. 297 1868). Of SHIP COVE.

BACK POINT 47–11, 53–35 (NTS Placentia 1N/4E) (NLP 1929).
Of PINCHGUT ISLAND.

BACK RIVER 46–45, 53–16 (NTS Trepassey 1K/11W)
As set: Back River (*Population Returns* 1836), Black R. (Jukes 1840), Back River (NDNR 1941), Back Brook (NTS Biscay Bay River 1K/14W).
In relation to BISCAY BAY RIVER. P. 113.

BACK RIVER 47–08, 53–24 (NTS St. Catherine's 1N/3W and Placentia 1N/4E)
(Newfoundland, Road Map of the Peninsula of Avalon 1931).
Tributary of LITTLE HARBOUR RIVER.

BACK RIVER 47–15, 53–29 (NTS Holyrood 1N/6W) Tributary of COLINET RIVER.

— BACK RIVER POND 47–16, 53–28 (NDNR 1N/6 1943).

Back side (Ferryland) (Yonge 1663–70). P. 68.

BACKSIDE POND 47–40, 53–30 (NTS Dildo 1N/12E and Harbour Grace 1N/11W) (NDNR 1N/11 1948).
Of GREENS HARBOUR.

BACON (Specific) ? Mistake name for Beacon.

BACON COVE 47–29, 53–10 (NTS Holyrood 1N/6E) (Murray and Howley 1868).

— BACON COVE (Set.)
Baye Quinscove (Beaudoin 1697), Bacon Cove (*Population Returns* 1836), Upper Beacon Cove (Census 1869).
P. 79.

— BACON COVE HEAD 47–29, 53–10 (CHS 4573 1953).

— BACON POINT
(CHS 4573 1953).

BACON COVE HEAD 47–53, 53–23 (NTS Heart's Content 1N/14W)
Bacon Cove unnamed in NTS.

BAD POND 47–16, 53–27 (NTS Holyrood 1N/6W) (NDNR 1N/6 1943).

Baia de cos[eicam] ("Oliveriana" 1505–8)
See CONCEPTION BAY. P. 30.

baie de Saincte Jehan (Alfonse 1544) See ST. JOHN'S HARBOUR (NTS St. John's). P. 34.

baie dicte Rogneuse (Alfonse 1544) See RENEWS (NTS Renews). P. 35.

BAIRD (Specific) After the family established in Newfoundland by James Baird (1828–1915) in 1873, subsequently prominent in the commercial life of St. John's. (Mosdell, p. 7.)

BAIRD PLACE (St. John's)
— BAIRD'S COVE (St. John's).
P. 148.

BAKER (Specific). ? English or Irish family name.

BAKER HEAD 46–40, 53–27 (NTS Trepassey 1K/11W)
Bakers Point (Lane 1773; Imray, *Sailing Directions* 1862), Baker Head (Adm. 2915 1864), Baker Point (M. F. Howley, XXVIII, *NQ*, December 1909). Pp. 81, *88–9*, 129, 157.

BAKER POINT 47–25, 53–54 (NTS Argentia)
(Adm. 3266 1939). Pp. 129, 157.

BALD (Specific) Bare, without vegetation; or ? mistake name for bold. P. 66.

BALD HEAD 46–58, 52–53 (Renews 1K/15W)
(Seller c. 1671), C de Bold (Hermite 1695), Cap de Blad (Bellin 1754), Cap Blad (Lotter c. 1758), Bald Head (Lane 1773). Pp. 66, 71.

BALD HEAD 47–27, 53–56 (NTS Argentia 1N/5W)
(Wix 1836), As set: (*Population Returns* 1836).
"Bald head is cliffy and rises to a conical mound, 120 feet high" (*NLP* I, 137).
— BALD HEAD BAY 47–27, 53–55 (Adm. 232A 1870).
Pp. 104, 110.

BALD HEAD 47–59, 53–38 (NTS Sunnyside 1N/13E)
(Lane, *Directions* 1775, 1810). P. 95.

BALLY HALY (St. John's). P. 125.

BALLYHACK (Set.) 47–26, 53–13 (NTS Holyrood 1N/6E)
(USHO, *Newfoundland Sailing Directions*, 1942).
— BALLYHACK POINT 47–27, 53–12 (CHS 4573 1953).
Pp. 126, 139.

Gazetteer and Index of Place Names: B / 173

BANKY POND 47–43, 53–21 (NTS Harbour Grace 1N/11W)
(NDNR 1N/11 1948)
? From a high bank on the eastern side.

BANNERMAN (Specific) ? After Sir Alexander Bannerman (1788–1864), governor of Newfoundland 1857–64.

BANNERMAN LAKE 47–41, 53–17 (NTS Harbour Grace 1N/11W)
(NDNR 1N/11 1948)
— BANNERMAN RIVER 47–40, 53–16
Dolly's Brook (CHS 4590 1943), Bannerman River
(NDNR 1N/11 1948).

BANNERMAN PARK (St. John's)
Opened 1 September 1891 (Mosdell, p. 7). P. 146.

the Bar (Harbour Grace) (Lane, *Directions* 1775, 1810). P. 95.

BAR POND 47–23, 53–26 (NTS Holyrood 1N/6W) (NDNR 1N/6 1943).
? After one of the two peninsulas that almost divide the pond.

BAR POND 47–32, 53–26 (NTS Harbour Grace 1N/11W) (NDNR 1N/11 1948).
In fact, two ponds divided by a narrow isthmus – the bar.

BARACHOIS ['bærə,ʃwa:]['bærə,sweɪ] (Generic), Pp. 48, 142.

BIG BARACHOIS 47–03, 53–47 (NTS Placentia 1N/4W)
G. Barrysway (Lane 1773, Mount and Page 1780), Big Barachois (Imray, *Sailing Directory* 1873).
"a shallow bay ... about a mile in extent and almost divided into two parts by a long narrow sandy bar that runs across it" (Imray, *Sailing Directory* 1873, p. 79).
— BARACHOIS POINT 47–02, 53–46 (Imray, *Sailing Directory* 1873).
— BIG BARACHOIS RIVER 47–03, 53–47
(DND 1942).

— LITTLE BARACHOIS 47-01, 53-48
L. Barrysway (Lane 1773, Mount and Page 1780), Little Barachois (Imray, *Sailing Directory* 1873).
"a creek 1½ miles south-westward from Big Barachois" (Imray, *Sailing Directory* 1873, p. 79.)
— LITTLE BARACHOIS RIVER (CHS 4622 ? 1953).
Pp. 52, 86, 120.

LITTLE BARACHOIS RIVER 47-11, 54-03 (NTS Ship Cove 1M/1E)
Lit. Barrasway Riv (Newfoundland 1949)
See LITTLE BARASWAY (Set.) 47-11, 54-03.

BARASWAY (Generic) See BARACHOIS.

GREAT BARASWAY (Set.) 47-07, 54-04 (NTS Ship Cove 1M/1E)
As feature: ? Groue [i.e. Grave] de Navire (Robinson 1669); as settlement, with Little Baraswey: Barrisways (*Population Returns* 1836); Big Barachois (Adm. 2915 1864), Great Barachois (Lovell 1881), Gt. Barasway (Newfoundland 1955).
— LITTLE BARASWAY (Set.) 47-11, 54-03
With Great Barasway: Barisways (*Population Returns* 1836).
P. 110.
The barachois after which the settlements are named is recorded as Porche (Robinson 1669), Porchet (Lotter c. 1758). Pp. 48, 110.

BARENEED (Set.) 47-35, 53-15 (NTS Harbour Grace 1N/11E)
As feature: Bearing Head (1787, Misc. Reg. pp. 48-9 cited in M. F. Howley, XIX, *NQ*, Oct. 1907); as settlement: Bareneed (Thoresby 1796), Bare Need (Wix 1836), Bareneed (*Population Returns* 1836, Census 1857). Pp. 98, 139, 140.

BARKING KETTLE POND 47-34, 52-51 (NTS St. John's 1N/10W)

Bark – "the tan which the fisherman applies to his net and sail." "I have been getting some juniper or black spruce rind to make tan bark" (Patterson, "Dialect of the People of Newfoundland," 1896, p. 36).
Barking-Kettle, bark-kettle, bark-pot – a container for "bark" in which nets are steeped to protect them against rot. The combinative forms are not recorded in *OED*; see Bark, oak-bark.
Cp. Oakbark Cove and Point (NTS St. John Island 121/14E).

BIG BARREN BROOK (Not in NTS Argentia 1N/5E)
Big Barren Brook, Big Barren River, Big Barren Branch (Murray and Howley 1872).
Tributary of ROCKY RIVER. P. 22.

barren Hill (Ferryland) (Yonge 1663-70). P. 68.

BARRENS (Generic), pp. 102-3, 145.
On the use of barrens in Kentucky, Stewart, *Names on the Land*, p. 153, writes: "... most of the newcomers looked at the open spaces and thought that they were treeless because the soil was too poor. So they called them *barrens*, and a whole region took that name, 'from there being little or no timber in it.'"

The Barrens (St. John's) (Anspach 1819). Pp. 102-3.

Barrisways (Sets.) (*Population Returns* 1836)
See GREAT BARASWAY, LITTLE BARASWAY (NTS Ship Cove) under BARACHOIS.

BARRY POINT 46-56, 53-33 (NTS St. Mary's 1K/13E)
(Adm. 3264 1902). P. 129.

BARRYS POND 47-45, 53-17 (NTS Harbour Grace 1N/11W). P. 129.

BARTER'S HILL (Street) (St. John's). Pp. 144, 148.

BATHERS POND 47–27, 52–42 (NTS Bay Bulls 1N/7E) (USHO 2139 1943).

Basin Cove (Popple 1733)
See ? BURNT COVE (NTS Ferryland).
Pp. 82, 107.

BATS POND 47–43, 53–22 (NTS Harbour Grace 1N/11W)
(NDNR 1N/11 1948).

BATTENS POND 47–33, 53–23 (NTS Harbour Grace 1N/11W)
Batten's Pond (Adm. 296 1868), Battens Pond (NDNR 1N/11 1948).
Not the same as Battin's Pond (not in NTS), "head of Hodge Waters" in Murray and Howley 1872. P. 157.

Battin's Pond 47–28, 53–21 (Not in NTS Holyrood 1N/6W)
See BATTENS POND (NTS Harbour Grace). Pp. 24, 157.

BATTERY (Generic). P. 147.

BAULINE (Specific) [bɔ:'li:n] French *baleine*-whale. P. 49.

BAULINE (Set.) 47–43, 52–50 (NTS St. John's 1N/10W).
Balline (Census 1857). Pp. 49, 116, 139.
— BAULINE BROOK
  (*NLP* I 1951).
— BAULINE LINE 47–38, 52–49
  Road from Portugal Cove to junction with Bauline Road at Juniper Stump (unnamed in NTS).
P. 147.
— BAULINE LONG POND 47–42, 52–49
— BAULINE ROCKY POND 47–42, 52–48

BAULINE EAST (Set.) 47–11, 52–51 (NTS Ferryland 1N/2W)
Baleen (*Population Returns* 1836), Bauline (Smallwood 1940, Newfoundland 1941), Bauline South (NTS Reference Sheet c. 1954, Bauline (Newfoundland 1955).
Rock: Whaleback (Southwood 1675, Thornton 1689B), Whales-Back (*English Pilot. The Fourth Book* 1689), Whaleback (Mount and Page 1755), Whales Back Breaker (Cook and Lane 1770 [1775]B).
Cove: Baline Cove (Robinson 1669 ... Thornton 1689B, *English Pilot. The Fourth Book* 1689), P aux Balaines (Hermite 1695), Baline B (Moll c. 1712), Baline Harbour (Moll 1715), Pt. aux Baleines (Bellin 1744, ... 1754), Po of Whales (Bowen 1747), Baline Cove (Mount and Page 1755), Baleine Cove (Cook and Lane 1770 [1775]B), Baline Cove (Lane 1773), Baleine Cove (Imray, *Sailing Directions* 1862), Bauline (Imray, *Sailing Directory*, 1873).
Headland: C de Balaine (Hermite 1695), Teste des balennes (Vion 1699), Baline H. (Moll 1709), Whale Pt. (Kitchin 1762), Baline Head (Lane 1773) ...
"A short distance off the Little Cove there is a rock which is just barely 'a-wash' ... so that as it appears and disappears alternately in the swell of the waves it presents a striking likeness of a whale breaching" (M. F. Howley, xxv, *NQ*, March 1909).
Pp. 107, 140.

BAY (Generic). P. 140.

BAY BULLS 47–18, 52–47 (NTS Bay Bulls 1N/7W)
B. of Bulls (Hood 1592) ... Bay Bulls ("Blathwayt" c. 1630–40), B Toru (Petavius 1659), B du Toreau ("Dépôt 128.2.6" c. 1680), B Bulls (Thornton 1689 B), B Buls ou des Taureaux (Hermite 1695), B. des beufs (Vion 1699).
— BAY BULLS (Set.) 47–19, 52–49
  Bayeboulle, Baye Boulle (Beaudoin 1697), Bay Bulls (*Population Returns* 1836).
— BAY BULLS BIG POND 47–24, 52–47 (Newfoundland 1941).
— BAY BULLS RIVER 47–19, 52–49
— BABOUL ROCKS 47–17, 52–46
  ? I of Bulls (Briggs 1625; Seile

178 / *Place Names of the Avalon Peninsula*

BEARS COVE 47–36, 53–15 (NTS Harbour Grace 1N/11W)
(CHS 4572 1954).

BEARS COVE 47–42, 53–12 (NTS Harbour Grace 1N/11E)
(Cook 1762 or Gilbert 1768).
— BEARS POINT 47–42, 53–12
Bear Point (Adm. 297 1933),
Ugly Head (Local name).

BEAVER (Specific) The occurrence of beavers in Newfoundland is recorded in Edward Hayes's "Report of the Voyage and success thereof, attempted in the yeare of our Lord 1583 by sir Humphrey Gilbert," in Hakluyt, *Voyages*, p. 263. The old name for beaver, castor, is the specific in Castors River (Pelegrin, 1735) 50–55, 56–57 (NTS Castors River 12I/15W) and Little Castors River (Anspach 1819) ? WATERFORD RIVER (NTS St. John's).

BEAVER BROOK 47–21, 52–55 (NTS Bay Bulls 1N/7W) (NDNR Bay Bulls 1943).

BEAVER POND occurs at 47–24, 52–49 (NTS Bay Bulls 1N/7W) (NDNR Bay Bulls 1943); 47–29, 53–17 (NTS Holyrood 1N/6W) (CHS 4573 1953); 47–32, 52–43 (NTS St. John's 1N/10E); 47–34, 53–17 (NTS Harbour Grace 1N/11W) (CHS 4572 1954); 47–35, 53–29, (NTS Harbour Grace 1N/11W) (NDNR 1N/11W 1948); 47–40, 53–24 (NTS Harbour Grace 1N/11W) (NDNR 1N/11 1948); 47–46, 53–13 (NTS Heart's Content 1N/14E) (NDNR 1N/14 1946), the site of VICTORIA (Set.); and 47–54, 53–22 (NTS Heart's Content) (NDNR 1N/14 1946).

BEAVER POND HILLS 47–04, 53–57 (NTS Placentia 1N/4W)
(CHS 4622 ?1953), Beaver Falls (Local name). Beaver Pond unnamed in NTS.

BECKFORD HEAD 46–54, 53–54 (NTS St. Mary's 1K/13W)

As set: Beckford (*Population Returns* 1836), Beckford's Point (Murray and Howley 1868). Pp. 109, 157.

BECK'S COVE (St. John's) (Census 1857). P. 116.

BEER POND 47–29, 52–44 (NTS Bay Bulls 1N/7E) (USHO 2139 1943).

THE BELL (Rock) (Bell Island) 47–37, 53–01 (NTS Harbour Grace 1N/11E) (Lane 1774).
— Bell Beach
See THE BEACH (NTS St. John's). P. 90.
— BELL COVE
(CHS 4566 1952)
— BELL ISLAND 47–38, 52–58 (NTS St. John's 1N/10W) and Harbour Grace 1N/11E)
great Belile (Guy 1612), Belile (Mason 1626), Bell Isle (Robinson 1669 ... Moll 1729), Belle I. (Popple 1733), Bell I. (Bowen 1747), Belle Isle (Bellin 1754), Bell Isle (Cook 1763) ... Cook and Lane 1770 [1775]B; Purdy 1814; set. *Population Returns* 1836; Jukes 1840), Belle Isle (Bonnycastle 1842), Great Belle Isle (Murray and Howley 1868), Bell Island (Imray, *Sailing Directory* 1873; Proclamation 26 April 1910).
— BELL POND 47–37, 53–00 (NTS Harbour Grace 1N/11E)
(CHS 4566 1952).
— LITTLE BELL ISLAND 47–34, 52–58 (NTS St. John's 1N/10W) (Thornton 1689B), L Belle I (Popple 1733 ... Imray, *Sailing Directions* 1862, Little Bell Island (Imray, *Sailing Directory* 1873).
Cp. The Clapper.
Pp. 5, 41, 49, 50, 58, 61, 74, 90, 92, 97, 124, 129.

BELL POND 47–39, 53–26 (NTS Harbour Grace 1N/11W) (NDNR 1N/11 1948).

BELLEVUE (Set.) 47–38, 53–44 (NTS Dildo 1N/12E)
Tickle Harbour (*Population Returns* 1836), ? Colliers Arm (Census 1874), Bellvue (Newfoundland 1941), Bellevue (Smallwood 1941).
  The settlement was named after Tickle Harbour ("Blathwayt" c. 1630–40 ... Fitzhugh 1693), H. chatouilleux (Vion 1699).
  The harbour is entered through a short, narrow tickle.
  See TICKLE BAY (NTS Dildo). P. 60.

Bennets (Cove or Stage) (St. John's Harbour) (Thornton 1689B). Pp. 68, 77.

Bentham (Wix 1836)
See RANTEM (NTS Dildo). P. 105.

BETHLEHEM POND 47–28, 53–16 (NTS Holyrood 1N/6E and W)
(CHS 4573 1953), Bedlam Gully (Local name).
  ? Bethlehem, a sophisticated rendering of bedlam; bedlam – from the cries of the gulls which frequent the pond. For the association between Bethlehem and Bedlam, see *OED* Bedlam.

Bever Pond (Renews Harbour) (Yonge 1663–70)
See BEAVER. P. 68.

BIG BARACHOIS, BIG BARACHOIS RIVER (NTS Placentia)
See BARACHOIS.

BIG BARREN BROOK (Unnamed in NTS Argentia)
See BARREN.

BIG BROOK 47–46, 53–16 (NTS Heart's Content)

BIG CHANCE COVE
See CHANCE COVE (NTS Dildo).

BIG GULL POND (NTS Holyrood, Holyrood and Harbour Grace, Heart's Content)
See GULL.

BIG GULLY (Pond) 47–22, 53–09 (NTS Holyrood) (NDNR 1N/6 1943).
Big – in comparison with GRASSY GULLY 47–21, 53–09. P. 143 for Gully.

BIG GULLY (Pond) 47–44, 53–20 (NTS Harbour Grace 1N/11W)
(NDNR 1N/11 1948). P. 143 for Gully.

BIG HEAD 47–26, 53–50 (NTS Argentia 1N/5W) (Adm. 3266 1939).

BIG HEAD (Bell Island) 47–37, 53–01 (NTS Harbour Grace 1N/11E)
(CHS 4566 1952).

BIG ISLAND 47–53, 53–43 (NTS Sunnyside 1N/13E)
(Imray, *Sailing Directory* 1873).

BIG ISLAND POND (NTS Holyrood, NTS Harbour Grace)
See ISLAND.

BIG JOHNS POINT 46–38, 53–06 (NTS Trepassey 1K/11E)
(CHS 4576 1950).

BIG NORTHERN POND
See NORTHERN POND (NTS Bay Bulls).

BIG OTTER POND (NTS Holyrood)
See OTTER.

BIG POND 46–40, 53–06 (NTS Trepassey 1K/11E) (CHS 4576 1950).
Third pond of river, unnamed in NTS, which enters the Atlantic ¼ mile west of CAPE RACE.

BIG POND also occurs at 47–16, 53–27 (NTS Holyrood 1N/6W) (NDNR 1N/6 1943); 47–28, 52–58 (NTS Bay Bulls 1N/7W) (NDNR Bay Bulls 1943); 47–29, 52–44 (NTS Bay Bulls 1N/7E (NDNR Bay Bulls 1943); 47–31, 53–28 (NTS Harbour Grace 1N/11W).

BIG POND 47–35, 52–46 (NTS St. John's 1N/10W)
The greater part of a pond divided by an isthmus into two parts, the smaller of which is MIDDLE POND 47–35, 52–46, q.v.

BIG POND 47–46, 53–59 (NTS Sunnyside 1N/13W)

180 / *Place Names of the Avalon Peninsula*

The bottom of GREAT SOUTHERN HARBOUR, almost a barachois.

BIG RATTLING BROOK (NTS Argentia)
See RATTLE, RATTLING.

BIG ROUND POND (NTS Harbour Grace)
See ROUND.

BIG SEAL COVE (NTS Argentia)
See SEAL.

BIG SUTTONS POND
See SUTTONS POND (NTS Harbour Grace).

BIG THREE CORNER POND 47–40, 52–46 (NTS St. John's 1N/10W)
Much smaller than many ponds in the vicinity.

BIG TRIANGLE POND (NTS Holyrood)
See TRIANGLE.

BIGHT (Generic). Pp. 117, 141.

BIRCH COVE 47–54, 53–42 (NTS Sunnyside 1N/13E)
(Imray, *Sailing Directory*, 1873).

THE BIRCHIES (Ponds) 47–24, 52–46 (NTS Bay Bulls 1N/7W)
(NDNR Bay Bulls 1943). Pp. 139, 140.

BISCAY BAY [bIskI] 46–53, 53–17 (NTS Trepassey 1K/11W)
(Southwood 1675).
— BISCAY BAY (Set.) 46–44, 53–18 (*Population Returns* 1836).
— BISCAY BAY RIVER 46–47, 53–17 (NTS Biscay Bay River 1K/E and W) Biscay Brook (Jukes 1840), Biscay Bay River (NDNR 1941). G. R. F. Prowse, *CM*, III, suggests that the Spanish arms were erected in BISCAY BAY c. 1540.
Pp. 50, 69, 74.

Biscayn cove (Renews Harbour) (Yonge 1663–70). P. 68.

BISCAYNE [bIsn] BAY 47–48, 52–47 (NTS Pouch Cove 1N/15W)
As set: Biscan Cove (*Population Returns* 1836); as feature: Biscayan Cove (Jukes 1840), Biskin or Biscayan Cove (Jukes 1842), Biscayne Cove (Imray, *Sailing Directory* 1873). Pp. 69, 75, 106.

BISHOP'S COVE 47–38, 53–13 (NTS Harbour Grace 1N/11E)
Formerly Bread and Cheese Cove; Bishops Cove (CHS 4572 1954).
— BISHOP'S COVE (Set.)
Bread and Cheese Cove (*Population Returns* 1836), Bishop's Cove (Census 1857).
Pp. 78, 107, 118, 157.

BISHOP'S GULLY (Pond) 47–43, 53–18 (NTS Harbour Grace 1N/11W) (NDNR 1N/11 1948). P. 157.

BISHOP'S POND 47–32, 53–27 (NTS Harbour Grace 1N/11W) (NDNR 1N/11 1948). P. 157.

BISHOPS PONDS 47–24, 53–24 (NTS Holyrood 1N/6W) (NDNR 1N/6 1943). P. 157.

BLACK COVE 47–14, 54–00 (NTS Placentia 1N/4W) (CHS 4622 ? 1953).
Black-Cove (Bay de Verde) (*English Pilot. The Fourth Book* 1689)
Back or Backside Cove (Local name). P. 75.

BLACK DUCK (Specific – Black Duck (*Anas rubripes*), "the common 'wild duck' of interior Newfoundland" (Peters and Burleigh, pp. 86, 61).

Black Duck Gullies (Set.) (*Population Returns* 1836)
See ST. JOSEPH'S (NTS Placentia). P. 108.

BLACK DUCK POND occurs at 47–25, 53–17 (NTS Holyrood 1N/6W) (NDNR 1N/6 1943); 47–34, 53–16 (NTS Harbour Grace 1N/11W), as set. (Census 1869); 47–39, 53–28 (NTS Harbour Grace 1N/11W); 47–48,

Gazetteer and Index of Place Names: B / 181

53–25 (NTS Heart's Content 1N/14W) (1N/NW E and 1N/NE W Avalon Peninsula 1942).

Black head (Gaudy 1715)
See SHOAL POINT (NTS St. Shotts).

BLACK HEAD 46–49, 52–56 (NTS Renews 1K/15W)
Small Point (Lane 1773), Black Head (Adm. 2915 1864). P. 74.

BLACK HEAD 46–59, 52–54 (NTS Renews 1K/15W)
Southwood 1675).

BLACK HEAD 47–18, 53–59 (NTS Argentia 1N/5W)
(CHS 4622 ? 1953).

BLACK HEAD 47–32, 52–39 (NTS St. John's 1N/10E)
(*English Pilot. The Fourth Book* 1689).
— BLACKHEAD (Set.)
(Census 1857).
— BLACKHEAD BAY
(Imray, *Sailing Directory* 1873).
— BLACKHEAD ROAD (Set.) 47–33, 52–43
(Census 1935).
Populated during the depression of the 1930s.
P. 72.

BLACK HEAD NORTH 47–46, 52–43 (NTS Pouch Cove 1N/15W)
Black head (Seller c. 1671). Pp. 72, 73.

BLACK HILL POND 47–30, 52–57 (NTS Bay Bulls 1N/7W) (CHS 4566 1952).

BLACK MOUNTAIN POND 47–26, 53–01 (NTS Holyrood 1N/6E)
(NDNR 1N/6 1943).
Cp. WHITE HILL POND 47–26, 53–03.

BLACK POINT 47–12, 54–03 (NTS Ship Cove 1M/1E)
Cap Noir (Buache 1736), Black C. (Bowen 1747), C. Noir (Robert de Vaugondy 1749; Bellin 1754); as set: Black Point (*Population Returns* 1836); Black Pt. (Adm. 2915 1864). P. 52.

BLACK POINT 47–41, 53–11 (NTS Harbour Grace 1N/11E) (Adm. 297 1899).

BLACK POINT 48–07, 53–00 (NTS Bay de Verde 2C/2W)
Black Head (Visscher c. 1680, Thornton 1689B, Fitzhugh 1693), Black C (Bowen 1747).

Black River (Jukes 1842)
See BACK RIVER (NTS Trepassey). P. 113.

BLACK RIVER 47–12, 53–22 (NTS St. Catherine's 1N/3W)
? (Murray and Howley 1862). Tributary of SALMONIER RIVER.

BLACKHEAD (Set.), BLACKHEAD BAY, BLACKHEAD ROAD (Set.) (NTS St. John's)
See BLACK HEAD 47–32, 52–39 (NTS St. John's 1N/10E).

BLACKHEAD (Set.) 47–51, 53–06 (NTS Heart's Content 1N/14E)
As feature: (Robinson 1669; Anspach 1819); as set: (Thoresby 1796), Black Head (*Population Returns* 1836).
— BLACKHEAD BROOK 47–51, 53–05
(NDNR 1N/14 1946).
Pp. 70, 92, 98.

BLAKETOWN (Set.) 47–29, 53–34 (NTS Argentia 1N/5E) (Census 1891).
After Sir Henry Arthur Blake (1840–1918), governor of Newfoundland 1887–8. (*Encyclopedia Canadiana*; Devine, *Ye Olde St. John's*, p. 105.)
Local tradition derives the name from By-the-Lake Town, the lake being DILDO POND (NTS Argentia and Dildo).
Cp. Blakestown, Co. Kildare, Eire.

BLAST HOLE PONDS 47–39, 52–51 (NTS St. John's 1N/10W)

? After a resemblance to holes caused by blasting, as seen by the iron-ore miners of BELL ISLAND (NTS Harbour Grace and St. John's).
Cp. ORE HEAD 47–42, 52–51 (*NLP* II 1953, p. 73, not in NTS).

Block House (Placentia) (Cook 1762). P. 83.

BLOOD HILL 47–30, 52–44 (NTS Bay Bulls 1N/7E) (USHO 2139 1943).

BLOODY POINT 47–55, 53–22 (NTS Heart's Content 1N/14W)

BLOW ME DOWN (Specific). Pp. 91–2.

BLOW ME DOWN BLUFF 47–26, 53–08 (NTS Holyrood 1N/6E)
(CHS 4573 1953).
"a bluff, 250 feet high" (*NLP* II, p. 85). P. 144.

BLOW ME DOWN (Set.) 47–36, 53–11 (NTS Harbour Grace 1N/11E)
? Buck (for Back) Cove (CO 199.18 1725), Blowmedown Cove (Lane 1774), Blow-me-down (Census 1857).
Amy Mugford, property-owner at Buck Cove, 1725 (CO 199.18 1725). Pp. 91, 138, 139–40.

— BLOW ME DOWN HEAD
(Lane 1774). P. 91. See BLUFF (Specific and Generic).

Blow-me-down (Set.) (Carbonear) (Census 1857). P. 119.

BLUE (Specific). P. 129.

BLUE HILL POND 47–47, 53–13 (NTS Heart's Content 1N/14E)
(NDNR 1N/14 1946).

BLUE HILLS 47–25, 53–15 (NTS Holyrood 1N/6E) (Adm. 296 1863).

BLUE SHAG ISLAND 47–28, 53–57 (NTS Argentia 1N/5W) (*NLP* 1951)
"is so named from the bluish-gray colour of its rock, which is unlike any other in the vicinity" (*NLP* I, p. 140).
See SHAG (Specific).

BLUFF (Specific and Generic). P. 144.
Adj. of a shore or coast-line: "Projecting almost perpendicularly into the sea, and presenting a bold front, rather rounded than cliffy in outline" (W. H. Smyth, *Sailor's Wordbook*, Blackie, London, 1867, p. 110).
Sb. A cliff or headland with a broad precipitous face. OED.

BLUFF HEAD occurs at 46–58, 52–55 (NTS Renews 1K/15W) (Adm. 376 1922); 47–01, 53–40 (NTS Placentia 1N/4E) (Adm. 2915 1864); 47–09, 53–27 (NTS St. Catherine's 1N/3W).

BOAR POINT 47–47, 53–29 (NTS Heart's Content 1N/14W)
(Newfoundland 1941).
Mistake name for Bore Point, after the strong tidal bore off the point.

BOB AYLES POND 47–48, 53–17 (NTS Heart's Content 1N/14W)
(NDNR 1N/14 1946). P. 157.

BOG POND 47–42, 53–13 (NTS Harbour Grace 1N/11E) (NDNR 1N/11 1948).
A shallow pond mostly bog.

BOIS ISLAND 47–02, 52–52 (NTS Ferryland 1N/2W)
I des Pous (Aertsz 1631), I. Potusa (H) I Poiux (P) (Dudley 1646), ? Bay Isl (Seller c. 1671), Bouy I. (Southwood 1675), Bouy I (Thornton 1689B), Bouy-Island (*English Pilot. The Fourth Book* 1689), I. Boi (Hermite 1695), ? Bay I. (Gaudy 1715), Bonny I (Popple 1733), Little Bog Island (Grant 1753; D. W. Prowse, p. 293), I. Bois (Cook 1763; Lane 1773), Isle aux Bois (Lane 1773 inset), Bois I (Imray, *Sailing Directions* 1862), Isle of Boys, Buoye Island (M. F. Howley xxv, *NQ* March 1909).
Pous – ? for Fr. *puits* – well; Lat. *potusa* – ? drinkable; Fr. *bois* – wood. Hence, an island on which water and wood might be found. Pp. 43, 68.

Bold Face (Hill) (Jukes 1842). P. 114.
Boney Brook (Set.) (Census 1857)
See ? LOW POINT (NTS Bay de
Verde). P. 77.

BOONE POINT 47–19, 52–46 (NTS Bay
Bulls 1N/7W)
(CHS 4586 1944). P. 157.

Borrell (Whitbourne 1588–1622)
See GOOSEBERRY COVE (NTS Ship
Cove), SHIP COVE (NTS Ship Cove). Pp.
42, 109.

THE BOWER (Pond) 47–43 53–19 (NTS
Harbour Grace 1N/11W)
(NDNR 1N/11 1948).

BOWES BROOK 47–42, 53–16 (NTS Harbour Grace 1N/11W)
(NDNR 1N/11 1948).
— BOWES LONG POND 47–41, 53–18
(NDNR 1N/11 1948).
— BOWES ROUND POND 47–42, 53–17
(NDNR 1N/11 1948).
P. 129.

BOWRING PARK 47–31, 52–45 (NTS St.
John's 1N/10W)
After Bowring Brothers Ltd.,
donors of the park to the city of ST.
JOHN'S in celebration of the centenary
of their business in Newfoundland,
1911.
For an account of the Bowring
family, see Keir, *The Bowring Story*.
P. 146.

BRADLEY'S COVE (Set.) 47–52, 53–04
(NTS Heart's Content 1N/14E)
As feature: (Lane 1774); as set:
(*Population Returns* 1836). Pp. 93,
157.

BRANCH (Set.) 46–53, 53–57 (NTS St.
Mary's 1K/13W)
(*Population Returns* 1836).
— BRANCH COVE 46–52, 53–56
(Lane 1773).
— BRANCH HEAD 46–52, 53–57
(Lane 1773).
— BRANCH RIVER 46–53, 53–57 (NTS
St. Mary's 1K/13W, Ship Cove
1M/1E, Placentia 1N/4W, St.

Bride's 1L/16E)
(Adm. 2915 1864).
Pp. 53, 86.

BRANDIES ROCKS 47–49, 52–46 (Not in
NTS Pouch Cove 1N/15W)
Brandys (Lane 1774).
"sunken rocks ... on which the sea
generally breaks" (Imray, *Sailing
Directions* 1862, p. 15). P. 90.

BRANSCOMBES POND 47–32, 52–47 (NTS
St. John's 1N/10W)
Branscombe Hill (Jukes 1842). P. 111.

BRAZIL [bræzəl] POND 47–32, 52–51
(NTS St. John's 1N/10W). P. 129.

BRAZIL SQUARE (Street) (St. John's).
P. 148.

BRAZILS POND 47–35, 53–24 (NTS
Harbour Grace 1N/11W)
(NDNR 1N/11 1948). P. 129.

BREACH HEAD 47–20, 52–44 (NTS Bay
Bulls 1N/7E)
(Adm. 296 1868).
? The head makes a break in the
coastal escarpment.

BREAD AND CHEESE (Specific). P. 78.
Note: "In Cornwall, Devon, Sussex,
and elsewhere I find the fruit of
the Mallow, and often the plant
itself, called Cheeses. Every boy and
girl who enjoys country life at all has
gathered them ... But other flowers
and plants bear this name, for the
Wood-Sorrel (*Oxalis Acetosella*) is
called Cuckoo's Bread-and-Cheese,
and the White Thorn is the Bread-
and-Cheese Tree. The leaves and
young shoots of these plants are
often eaten by young people" (Hilderic Friend, *Flowers and Flower
Lore*, 3rd ed. in 1 vol. ([Sonnenschein], London, 1886, p. 482).
Bread and Cheese Run is the name
of a small stream in Burlington
County, NJ, USA. (Communications
from H. Halpert).

Bread and Cheese (Hill) (Calvert

Bay) (Jukes 1840, 1842). Pp. 111, 114.

BREAD AND CHEESE (Set.) 47–19, 52–47 (NTS Bay Bulls 1N/7W) (CHS 4586 1944).
— Bread and Cheese Cove (Lane 1773).
— BREAD AND CHEESE POINT 47–18, 52–47 (Thornton 1689D).

Bread and Cheese Cove (Set.) (*Population Returns* 1836)
See BISHOP'S COVE (NTS Harbour Grace).
— BREAD AND CHEESE COVE POND 47–38, 53–16 (NTS Harbour Grace 1N/11W) (CHS 4572 1954).
Pp. 78, 107, 118–9.

BREAKHEART POINT 48–10, 52–58 (NTS Bay de Verde 2C/2W)
Break Hart P (Visscher c. 1680).
See CREVECŒUR POINT (NTS Argentia).
Pp. 51, 76.

Brechonia (Mason 1626). Pp. 12, 62.

BREME POINT 46–59, 54–10 (NTS St. Bride's 1L/16E)
P Prime (Seller c. 1671; Lotter c. 1758), Pt. Brim (Cook 1763), Point Breme (Lane 1772). P. 47.

BREMIGENS POND 47–31, 52–52 (NTS St. John's 1N/10W). P. 129.

BRENNAN POINT 47–37, 53–57 (NTS Dildo 1N/12W). P. 129.

BRENNAN'S HILL 47–42, 53–14 (NTS Harbour Grace 1N/11E) Brennan Hill (Imray, *Sailing Directory* 1873). P. 129.

Brianscove (Beaudoin 1697)
See BRYANTS COVE (NTS Harbour Grace). P. 79.

BRIDGE (Generic). P. 148.

BRIDGES POND 47–43, 53–21 (NTS Harbour Grace 1N/11W) (NDNR 1N/11 1948). P. 157.

BRIENS (Flag Stop CNR) 47–24, 53–07 (NTS Holyrood 1N/6E)
— BRIENS POND 47–23, 53–15 (NDNR 1N/6 1943). Pp. 129, 139.

BRIERLY COVE 46–51, 54–11 (NTS St. Bride's 1L/16E) (Adm. 232a 1870).
? Fr. *brulé* – burnt, or English family name. P. 157.

BRIGUS (Set.) 47–32, 53–13 (NTS Harbour Grace 1N/11E)
Brigass in the North (*CSP* 1677), Brige (Beaudoin 1697), Breckhouse (*CSP* 1705), Brecast by North (*CSP* 1705), Brigus, Brighouse (Thoresby 1796), Brigus (*Population Returns* 1836).
— BRIGUS BARRENS. P. 103.
— BRIGUS BAY 47–32, 53–11
Brega ("Blathwayt" c. 1630–40), Briggs (Robinson 1669), Brigues (Southwood 1675, Hack ? 1677, Visscher c. 1680, Thornton 1689B), Brigus (*English Pilot. The Fourth Book* 1689), Brigges (Hack c. 1690), Brigus (Fitzhugh 1693), Brigure (Bellin 1744, Robert de Vaugondy (1749), Brigues (Bellin 1754, Mount and Page 1755), Brigue (Cook 1763), Brigus (Cook and Lane 1770 [1775]A, B, Mount and Page 1780), Brigus Bay (Imray, *Sailing Directions* 1862).
— Brigus Grand Pond (Murray and Howley 1872)
See BRIGUS LONG POND.
— Brigus Head (Lane, *Directions* 1775, 1810)
See NORTH HEAD (NTS Harbour Grace). P. 95.
— BRIGUS JUNCTION (Sta.) 47–23, 53–18 (NTS Holyrood 1N/6W) (J. P. Howley 1907).
— BRIGUS LONG POND 47–30, 53–15 (NTS Harbour Grace 1N/11E and W) Brigus Grand Pond (Murray and Howley 1872, Brigus

Long Pond (CHS 4572 1954).
P. 24.
— BRIGUS LOOKOUT 47–33, 53–11
(Adm. 297 1868). P. 140.
— BRIGUS NORTH BROOK 47–32, 53–13 (CHS 4572 1954)
Brigus North refers to the settlement as distinguished from BRIGUS SOUTH, (NTS Ferryland) the next entry.
Pp. 22, 24, 26, 43, 53, 79, 113, 114, 121.

BRIGUS HEAD 47–06, 52–52 (NTS Ferryland 1N/2W)
? Cap lambe (Decouagne 1711), Brigus Head (Cook and Lane 1770 [1775]B; Lane 1773).
— BRIGUS SOUTH (Set.) 47–07, 52–53
Brigus by South (*English Pilot. The Fourth Book* 1689), Brigue (Beaudoin 1697), Brigus (*Population Returns* 1836), Brigus South (Newfoundland 1941, 1955), Hilldale (PO) (Canadian Board on Geographic Names 1959), Brigus South (Local name).
The headland and settlement were named after the boat harbour unnamed in NTS: Abra de Brigas (Laet 1630), Brittus (Ogilby 1671), Briggas (Seller c. 1671), Brigus by South (Southwood 1675), Brigues (Hack ? 1677), Breacas by South (Jones 1682 CSP 1681–5), Abra de Brigas (Coronelli-Tillemon 1689, Coronelli 1689), Briga (P) (Detcheverry 1689), Brigues by South (Thornton 1689B), Brigges (Hack c. 1690?), Briges by South (Fitzhugh 1693), Brecast by South (Sampson 1705 CSP 1705), Brigus by South (Mount and Page 1755), Brigus by Soth (Lane 1773), Brigus by South for Small Vessels (Mount and Page 1780), Brigus (Lane 1790; Purdy 1814), Brigus by S (Jukes 1840),

South Brigus (Bonnycastle 1842), Brigus-by-South (Imray, *Sailing Directory* 1873).
Pp. 43, 51, 79.

BRIMSTONE POND 47–48, 53–22 (NTS Heart's Content 1N/14W)
(NDNR 1N/14 1946).
Named after either sulphur pits said to have been found in the vicinity, or Brimstone Hill, yellow-brown in colour.

BRINE ISLANDS 47–27, 53–57 (NTS Argentia 1N/5W)
(Adm. 3266 1939).
"A group of many islets and rocks" (*NLP* I, p. 139), ? sometimes awash and whitened by spray.

BRISTA or BRISTO (Cove) (Baccalieu Island)
Local usage for Bristol.
One of three landing places on the island. The other two are Londa or Lunnon (London) and Famit or Farmint (Falmouth).
See LONG COVE (NTS Trepassey) and BRISTOL'S HOPE (NTS Harbour Grace).
P. 62.

Bristoll Cove (Southwood 1675)
See LONG COVE (NTS Trepassey). Pp. 63, 74.

BRISTOL'S HOPE (Set.) 47–43, 53–12 (NTS Harbour Grace 1N/11E)
? Bristol's hope (Mason 1626), Muskeets Bay (CSP 1677), Mousquit (Beaudoin 1697), Musketa-Cove (*English Pilot. The Fourth Book* 1689), Mosquito (*Population Returns* 1836), Bristol's Hope (Proclamation 16 August 1910).
— BRISTOL'S HOPE COVE 47–43, 53–11
Bristol's hope (Mason 1626), Muscita ("Blathwayt" c. 1630–40), Muskitto (Robinson 1669) and so with variant spellings to Bristol's Hope Cove (Adm. 296 1889 edn.), Mosquito cove, *NLP*

186 / *Place Names of the Avalon Peninsula*

1907), Bristol's Hope Cove
(Adm. 297 1933, CHS 4590
1943).
Cp. MOSQUITO BROOK, POINT,
POND (NTS Harbour Grace).
Pp. 12, 40, 61, 62–3, 79, 123, 124,
140, 141.

Britaniola (Hayman 1628). P. 62.

BROAD COVE 46–40, 53–38 (NTS St.
Shotts 1K/12E) (Lane 1773). P. 88.

BROAD COVE 46–41, 53–04 (NTS
Trepassey 1K/11E)
(CHS 4576 1950), Bear Cove (Local
name).

Broad Cove (Set.)
See CAPPAHAYDEN (NTS Renews).

BROAD COVE 47–03, 52–52 (NTS Ferryland 1N/2W)
(Imray, *Sailing Directory* 1873).

BROAD COVE 47–18, 53–58 (NTS
Argentia 1N/5W)
— BROAD COVE HEAD
— BROAD COVE POINT
    (Adm. 2829 1877).

BROAD COVE 47–26, 53–12 (NTS Holyrood 1N/6E)
Broad Cove Gastors (Bonnycastle
1842), Broad Cove (CHS 4573 1953),
? as set: Back Cove (Census 1955). P.
115.

BROAD COVE 47–36, 52–53 (NTS St.
John's 1N/10W) (Lane 1774).
For the settlement, see ST. PHILIPS
(NTS St. John's).
— BROAD COVE RIVER
— OLD BROAD COVE ROAD 47–35,
    52–50
    As set: (Census 1921).
P. 90.

BROAD COVE 47–50, 53–06 (NTS
Heart's Content 1N/14E)
(Lane 1774).
— BROAD COVE (Set.)
    Muley's Cove (Thoresby 1796),
    Broad Cove (Thoresby 1796 as
    separate settlement), Broad
    Cove *(Population Returns
    1836)*, ? Mulley Cove (Jukes
    1840), Broad Cove South
    (Census 1884 – Electors 1955),
    Mulley's Cove (Electors 1955).
— BROAD COVE BROOK
    (NDNR 1N/14 1946).
— BROAD COVE HEAD 47–50, 53–05
    (Lane 1774).
— BROAD COVE POND 47–50, 53–09
    (NDNR 17N/14 1946).
— Broad Cove South (Set.) (Census
    1884)
    See BROAD COVE (Set.) above.
Pp. 92, 98.

BROAD COVE POND 47–33, 53–32 (NTS
Dildo 1N/12E) (Newfoundland 1941).
Broad Cove (unnamed in NTS) is a
slight indentation on the east side of
DILDO ARM (NTS Dildo), which gives
its name to the settlement (Census
1884) on its shores.

BROAD LAKE 47–37, 53–46 (NTS Dildo
1N/12E and W)
(Adm. 296 1863). P. 143.

THE BROADS (Set.) 47–31, 53–16 (NTS
Harbour Grace 1N/11W)
Broads (Census 1884).
The settlement is near the part of
SOUTH RIVER (NTS Harbour Grace)
that widens into the Broads.
Broads – "In East Anglia, an extensive piece of fresh water formed by
the broadening out of a river"
(*OED*). P. 140.

BROCKS POND 47–40, 52–51 (NTS St.
John's 1N/10W)
Brock – Either the English family
name or the badger. *OED* notes a
former confusion between badger
and beaver. P. 157.

BROOK (Generic). P. 143.

BROOM COVE 46–42, 53–25 (NTS
Trepassey 1K/11W)
(USHO 0618 1941).
— BROOM RIVER
    (USHO 0618 1941).
"[From BAKER HEAD] to the

Gazetteer and Index of Place Names: B / 187

entrance to Trepassey harbour ... [the coast] is covered with brushwood" (*NLP* 1, 91).

Broom – "the earliest sense of the various forms appears to be 'thorny shrub', whence 'bramble', 'furze or gorse', and by confusion with the later 'broom' – a shrub bearing large handsome yellow papilonaceous flowers, – which seems to be the only Eng. sense." (*OED*). But *OED* has also Broom v. 2 – To bream a ship, cited in 1627. "The brooming of a ship meant in old time the burning of the filth from its side." 1707 *Glossogr. Nova*. The Brooming or Breaming of a Ship. Kersey 1708-21.

Browns Pond (Cook 1762 or Gilbert 1768)
See COOTE POND (NTS St. Mary's).
Pp. 83, 107.

BROWNSDALE (Set.) 48-02, 53-07 (NTS Old Perlican 2C/3E)
Lance Cove (*Population Returns 1836*), Brownsdale (Proclamation 8 August 1911).
Brownsdale "derived its present name from a young English lad of good family named Brown who, by a curious train of events became a Newfoundlander. Taken to Trinity on a friend's ship he was hauled ashore from the rocks at the mouth of that harbour. The lad never found his way back to the old land. After a time, in Old Perlican, he became the pioneer of this village" (Johnson, p. 288), "founded about 1830" (Smallwood 1941).

BRUCE POND 47-47, 53-18 (NTS Heart's Content 1N/14W)
(NDNR 1N/14 1946).
— BRUCE POND GULLY
(NDNR 1N/14 1946).
P. 157.

BRYANTS COVE 47-40, 53-11 (NTS Harbour Grace 1N/11E)
(Southwood 1675).

— BRYANT'S COVE (Set.)
Bryer's Cove (*CSP 1681*), Brians Cove (Beaudoin 1697; Bryan's Cove (*Population Returns 1836*).
— BRYANTS COVE POND 47-40, 53-12
(CHS 4572 1954).
P. 79.

BUCKET RIVER 46-53, 53-59 (NTS St. Mary's 1K/13W) (Adm. 2915 1864).

BULL AND COW (Rocks) 46-46, 54-06 (NTS St. Bride's 1L/16E)
Vaches de S Maria (Rotis 1674), Le beuf et la vache (Courcelle 1675), La Vache et Le Boeuf ("Dépôt 128.2.6" c. 1680), Bull and Cow (Gaudy 1715). Pp. 50, 81, 138.

BULL ARM 47-48, 53-51 (NTS Sunnyside 1N/13W)
? Truce sound (Guy 1612), B. Bulls (Southwood 1675 ... Popple 1733), Baye Butta (Lotter c. 1758), Bay of Bulls (Kitchin 1762, Cook 1763, Lane 1790), Bay Bulls Arm (Wix 1836), Bay of Bulls Arm (Jukes 1840).
— BULL ISLAND 47-46, 53-47
(Lane, *Directions 1775*, 1810, Cook and Lane 1770[1775]A).
— BULL TICKLE 47-47, 53-47
Bull island Tickle (Imray, *Sailing Directory 1873*), Bull Tickle (NP 1952). Between BULL ISLAND and the mainland.
Pp. 59, 60, 80, 95, 105, 141.

BULL COVE 47-30, 53-12 (NTS Harbour Grace 1N/11E)
As set: (*Population Returns 1836*); as feature: (Jukes 1840). P. 106.

BULL GULCH POINT 48-04, 53-03 (NTS Old Perlican 2C/3E) (USHO 73 1942). Bull Gulch unnamed in NTS. P. 141.

BULL HEAD
See BAY BULLS (NTS Bay Bulls).

BULL ISLAND POINT 48-47, 54-07 (NTS St. Bride's 1L/16E)

Bullisland point (Imray, *Sailing Directory* 1873).
? Shift name from BULL AND COW (NTS St. Bride's).

BULL POND 47–21, 53–22 (NTS Holyrood 1N/6W) (NDNR 1N/6 1943).

BULL POND 47–43, 53–14 (NTS Harbour Grace 1N/11E) (NDNR 1N/11 1948).

BULLS HEAD 47–36, 53–13 (NTS Harbour Grace 1N/11E) (CHS 4572 1954).
? Descriptive.

BURKE ISLAND 47–25, 53–58 (NTS Argentia 1N/5W) (Adm. 3266 1939).
— LITTLE BURKE ISLAND 47–25, 53–57
(Adm. 3266 1939).
Pp. 85, 129.

BURKES COVE 47–28, 53–12 (NTS Holyrood 1N/6E) (CHS 4573 1953).
Cp. Burke's Point (Murray and Howley 1868). P. 129.

BURNS HEAD 47–01, 52–52 (NTS Ferryland 1N/2W) (NLP 1951).
The name may have been originally applied to the Burnshead (rock), 1¼ cables south-southeastward of BURNS HEAD (Imray, *Sailing Directory* 1873, NLP 1951). P. 129.

BURNT (Specific)
The frequent occurrence of burnt, in French *Brulé*, as a specific in Newfoundland place names is indicative of the extent to which fire has ravaged the forests.

BURNT COVE (Set.) 47–12, 52–51 (NTS Ferryland 1N/2W)
As feature: ? Basin Cove (Popple 1733); as set: Burn Cove (*Population Returns* 1836). Pp. 82, 107.

BURNT HEAD 47–33, 53–55 (NTS Dildo 1N/12W)

BURNT HEAD 47–44, 53–11 (NTS Harbour Grace 1N/11E)
Gosse c. 1830).

BURNT PINE POND 47–24, 53–10 (NTS Holyrood 1N/6E) (CHS 4573 1953).

BURNT POINT 46–52, 52–56 (NTS Renews 1K/15W)
Burnt Head (Lane 1773), Burnt Pt. (Adm. 2915 1864). P. 89.

BURNT POINT 47–34, 53–11 (NTS Harbour Grace 1N/11E)
Burat [for Burnt] head (Southwood 1675), Pt Verte (Hack ?1677), Burnt Head (Visscher c. 1680 ... Popple 1733), C Brulet (Bellin 1754), Burnt Head (Cook and Lane 1770 [1775]B, Lane 1774); as set. (CSP 199.18 1790); Burnt Head (Imray, *Sailing Directions* 1862), Burnt Point (Imray, *Sailing Directory* 1873), Burnt Head (Local name).
"So called, by reason of the Trees that were on it are burnt down" (*English Pilot. The Fourth Book* 1689). P. 74.

BURNT POINT 47–58, 53–02 (NTS Heart's Content 1N/14E)
— BURNT POINT (Set.) 47–57, 53–02 (Census 1869).

Burst Heart Hill (Street) (St. John's)
See CARTER'S HILL (St. John's).

BUSHY HEAD 47–08, 53–37 (NTS Placentia 1N/4E)
Bushy Point (Imray, *Sailing Directory* 1873).

BUTLER HEAD 47–42, 53–58 (NTS Dildo 1N/12W). Pp. 130, 157.

BUTLERS POND 47–14, 53–02 (NTS St. Catherine's 1N/3E) (Newfoundland 1941). Pp. 130, 157.

BUTLERS POND 47–16, 53–18 (NTS Holyrood 1N/6W) (NDNR 1N/6 1943). Pp. 130, 158.

BUTLERVILLE (Set.) 47–35, 53–20 (NTS Harbour Grace 1N/11W) (NDNR 1N/11 1948). Pp. 130, 146, 158.

BUTTER POT (Hill) 46–58, 53–03 (NTS

Biscay Bay River 1K/14E)
Butter pots (Mason 1626; Yonge 1663; Jukes 1842). Pp. 61, 63–4, 111, 114, 138.

BUTTER POT (Hill) 47–20, 52–59 (NTS Bay Bulls 1N/7W)
(Newfoundland 1941). Pp. 63–4, 138.

BUTTER POT 47–24, 53–05 (NTS Holyrood 1N/6E)
Butterpots (Jukes 1842).
— BUTTER POT POND 47–24, 53–06 (CHS 4573 1953).
— BUTTER POT PROVINCIAL PARK 47–24, 53–03.
Pp. 63–4, 111, 114, 138, 146.

CABOT TOWER 47–34, 52–41 (NTS St. John's 1N/10E)
Erected to commemorate the quatercentenary of John Cabot's discovery of Newfoundland, 24 June 1497. The cornerstone was laid by Archbishop M. F. Howley on 22 June 1897, the tower was opened 20 June 1900. (Mosdell, p. 17).

CAHILL POINT 47–34, 52–42 (NTS St. John's 1N/10E)
? Stop Rock (Cook 1762 or Gilbert 1768). Pp. 83, 130.

CAIRN (Generic), P. 145.

CAIRN HEAD 47–18, 53–58 (NTS Argentia 1N/5W)
(Adm. 2829 1877). P. 145.

CALVERT (Set.) 47–03, 52–55 (NTS Ferryland 1N/2W)
Riverhead (Yonge 1663–70), Capelyn Bay (*CSP* 1674–5), Caplan Bay (Beaudoin 1697), Caplin Bay (*Population Returns* 1836), Calvert (Proclamation 30 January 1922).
— CALVERT BAY 47–03, 52–54
? R das patas (Reinel c. 1504, Reinel 1519, Ribeiro 1529 ... Jode 1593), Caplen Bay (Leigh 1597), R de Pescheurs (Hondius 1611), Capelin B (Whitbourne 1588–1622), Caplin bay (Mason 1626) ... Calvert Bay (after Proclamation of settlement as CALVERT 1922).
Port. *pata* – goose, auk; Fr. *pêcheur* – fisherman. See Caplin (specific).
Calvert – Sir George Calvert, 1st baron Baltimore (?1580–1632); educated Trinity Coll. Oxford, BA 1595; knighted 1617; MP 1609–11, 1621. Planted the colony of Avalon in Newfoundland 1621–3; professed Roman Catholicism 1625; created baron 1625; wintered in Avalon 1628–9; obtained grant of land for colony (Maryland) north of the Potomac River, 1632. *DCB.*
Pp. 30, 56–7, 68, 78, 79, 111, 139.

Cambriola (Mason 1626). P. 61.

CAMELS BACK POND 47–42, 53–26 (NTS Harbour Grace 1N/11W)
(NDNR 1N/11 1948).
? Descriptive of hump on north side.

CAMPBELL HILL 47–28, 53–12 (NTS Holyrood 1N/6E)
(Imray, *Sailing Directory* 1873), Phil[l]ips Hill (Local name).
Cp. PHILLIPS POND (NTS Holyrood).
Campbell – Scottish or Irish family name, not found locally.
Phillips – p. 164.

CAMPBELLS GULLY (Pond) 47–44, 53–22 (NTS Harbour Grace 1N/11W) (NDNR 1N/11 1948).
Campbell – not current in CARBONEAR (NTS Harbour Grace).

CANTWELLS COVE 47–32, 52–38 (NTS St. John's 1N/10E)
(NLP 1951). P. 130.

cap de Chincete (Alfonse 1544) See ST. SHOTTS (NTS St. Shotts). P. 35.

C de grote (Mason 1626), P. 12.

C de Mort (Courcelle 1675), P. 50.

190 / Place Names of the Avalon Peninsula

C de pena (Plancius 1592) C de pene (Mason 1626). Pp. 31, 61.

Cap de Ratz (Alfonse 1544)
See CAPE RACE (NTS Trepassey). P. 35.

Cap d'espoir (Alfonse 1544)
See CAPE SPEAR (NTS St. John's). P. 35.

Cap Hill (Jukes 1842). P. 114.

Cap lambe (Decouagne 1711)
See BRIGUS HEAD (NTS Harbour Grace). P. 51.

C. langlois (Courcelle 1675)
See CAPE ENGLISH (NTS St. Mary's). P. 50.

Cap Noir (Buache 1736)
See BLACK POINT (NTS Ship Cove). P. 52.

Cap reüil (Beaudoin 1697)
See CAPE BROYLE (NTS Ferryland), P. 79.

CAPE (Generic). P. 144.

CAPE BALLARD 46–47, 52–57 (NTS Renews 1K/15W)
C Ballard ("Blathwayt" c. 1630–40), Cape Bollard (Yonge 1663), Cape Ballard (Mount and Page 1780). See Old Harry (Rock). P. 66.

C[ape] Bay (Thornton 1689B)
See SPEAR BAY under CAPE SPEAR (NTS St. John's). Pp. 77, 90.

CAPE BROYLE 47–03, 52–52 (NTS Ferryland 1N/2W)
Cape Broile (Guy 1612), C. Brolle (Blaeu c. 1630), C. Broyle (Mason 1626; "Blathwayt" c. 1630–40), C Brolle (Laet 1630; Blaeu 1659), Cape Broyle (Yonge 1663; Robinson 1669; Ogilby 1671; Seller 1671, c. 1671), C brulé (Courcelle 1675), C Broyle (Southwood 1675).
— CAPE BROYLE (Set.) 47–06, 52–57
Cap reüil (Beaudoin 1697), Cape Broyle (Population Returns 1836).

— CAPE BROYLE HARBOUR 47–05, 52–54
(Robinson 1669).
— CAPE BROYLE RIVER 47–06, 52–58
(Newfoundland 1941).
Pp. 58, 66, 70, 73, 79, 89, 114, 125, 126, 130.

CAPE COVE 46–40, 53–04 (NTS Trepassey 1K/11E)
? Bay d'Eau Douce (Lotter c. 1758), Cape Cove (Adm. 2915 1864). P. 52.

CAPE DOG 47–05, 53–42 (NTS Placentia 1N/4E)
(Lane 1773); as set. (Population Returns 1836).
— DOG COVE 47–05, 53–43
Dog Bay (Lane 1773; Mount and Page 1780; Purdy 1814), Cape Dog Harbour (Murray and Howley 1868), Dog Cove (Imray, Sailing Directory 1873). Pp. 87, 114.

CAPE ENGLISH 46–47, 53–40 (NTS St. Mary's 1K/13E)
? Cauo de ynglaterra (Cosa 1500), ? Ponta del pa[drão] ("Oliveriana" 1505–8), C de cruz (Sanches 1618, 1623), C langlois (Courcelle 1675; Chaviteau 1698), C Mongloyi (Gaudy 1715), Cape Mouglois (Senex 1728), C Mongloyi (Popple 1733), English Cape (Bowen 1747), Cap a l'Anglois (Bellin 1744 ... Lotter c. 1758), C Monglog (Kitchin 1762), C Mongley (Cook 1763), Cape English (Lane 1773).
Cauo de ynglaterra – Cape of England. See CAPE RACE (NTS Trepassey).
Ponta del padrão – Point of the Padrão, a wooden post or cross, later stone, erected by the Portuguese to mark headlands, mouths of rivers and other prominent features and to establish their claim to the adjacent territory. G. R. F. Prowse, CM, III,

p. 136, however, associates the *padrão* with an English survey of South Newfoundland.
 C de cruz – Cape of the Cross, G. R. F. Prowse's identification (*CM*, III, p. 136).
 C langlois and variants – Cape of the Englishman.
See HOLYROOD BAY (NTS St. Shotts and St. Mary's).
Pp. 30, 50, 86, 88.

CAPE FREELS 46–37, 53–34 (NTS St. Shotts 1K/12E)
(Lane 1773), Cape Freels South (M. F. Howley, XXVIII, *NQ*, Dec. 1909). Pp. 18, 53, 86.

CAPE MUTTON 46–41, 53–21 (NTS Trepassey 1K/11W)
Cape Mouton (Robinson 1669), C. Mutton (Southwood 1675); thereafter Mouton in French maps and Mutton in English maps. Sheep Head (Local name).
— MUTTON BAY 46–42, 53–22 (Gaudy 1715).
P. 49.

CAPE NEDDICK 47–09, 52–51 (NTS Ferryland 1N/2W)
(Seller c. 1671). P. 71.

CAPE PINE 46–37, 53–32 (NTS St. Shotts 1K/12E)
C de pena (Plancius 1592), C de Pine (Seller 1671) C Pine (Southwood 1675), C de peine ("Dépôt 132.2.10" 1706), C Pine (Moll 1709). Pp. 31, 61, 81.

CAPE POND 47–12, 53–05 (NTS St. Catherine's 1N/3E)
(Newfoundland 1941).
 ? After the number of capes that project into the pond.

CAPE RACE 46–40, 53–05 (NTS Trepassey 1K/11E)
? Cauo de ynglaterra (Cosa 1500), Capo raso ("King-Hamy" 1504–6), cap de Raze (Cartier 1535–6), C de Raz (Desliens 1541), Cap de Ratz (Alfonse 1544), Cape Race (Parkhurst 1578).
— CAPE RACE (Set.) 46–39, 53–04 The settlement probably dates from the erection of the first lighthouse in 1853. The present inhabitants are all associated with the lighthouse and the radio station.
 Cauo de ynglaterra – Cape of England, "a very appropriate name for Cabot to give under the impression that it was the nearest point of the main new found land to England" (Ganong). Kohl, Dawson, Biggar and others take the name to apply to CAPE RACE, though Ganong identifies it with the southeastern angle of the Burin Peninsula and G. R. F. Prowse with CAPE ENGLISH (Ganong, *Crucial Maps*, pp. 28–9).
 Pp. 12, 27, 28–30, 32, 35, 52, 56, 58, 61, 71, 74, 78, 125.

CAPE ST. FRANCIS 47–49, 52–47 (NTS Pouch Cove 1N/15W)
 C. de S. francisco ("Havre Catalan" 1520–34), C St. Francis (Hayes 1583), c ste fresaye (Champlain 1612).
 M. F. Howley suggests that Corte Real was probably a member of the third order of St. Francis of Assisi, the tertiaries, and may have named the cape to commemorate the saint. (XX, *NQ*, March 1908). Pp. 12, 18, 31, 46, 56, 58, 61, 71, 80, 90, 114.

CAPE ST. MARY'S
See ST. MARY'S BAY.

CAPE SHORE
(Local name).
The coast roughly from PLACENTIA (NTS Placentia) to CAPE ST. MARY'S (NTS St. Mary's).

CAPE SPEAR 47–31, 52–37 (NTS St. John's 1N/10E)

192 / Place Names of the Avalon Peninsula

C da espera (Reinel c. 1504), Cauo de la spera ("Oliveriana" 1505–8), Co desperado (Freducci 1520–5), C despera ("Havre Catalan" 1520–34), C de spera (Maggiolo 1527), C despoir ("Harleian" 1542–3), Cap d'espoir (Alfonse 1544), C despoir (Desceliers 1546), C de Spera (Plancius 1592), C d'Espere (Wyet 1594), C Spere ("Blathwayt" c. 1630–40), C. Spear (Dudley 1646), Cape Despaire (Robinson 1669), C Spare (Seller c. 1671, Southwood 1675), C Speare (Hack ? 1677), Cap d'Espérance (Cordier 1696), C. Spear (Kitchin 1762). Pp. 12, 30 and note 44, 34–5, 52, 81, 84, 87, 90, 116, 130.
— SPEAR BAY 47–31, 52–38
Riuo de la spera ("Oliveriana" 1505–8), Rio de spera (Maggiolo 1527, Verrazano 1529), C[ape] Bay (Thornton 1689B, Cook and Lane 1770 [1775]B), Spear Bay (Lane 1774), Cape Bay (Imray, *Sailing Directory* 1873), Spear Bay (NLP I 1951). Pp. 30, 77, 90.
— SPEAR BAY BROOK
Port. *espera* – stay, waiting.
Fr. *espoir, espérance* – hope.

Caplen Bay (Leigh 1597, Yonge 1663–70)
See CALVERT BAY (NTS Ferryland) and CAPLIN (Specific) below.

CAPLIN ['keːplIn] (Specific) In a statement on the English, Spanish, Portuguese, French and Breton fishery by Anthony Parkhurst, 1578, a marginal note on Smelt reads: "Called by the Spaniards Anchovas, and by the Portugals Capelinas" (Hakluyt, *Principal Navigations*, VIII, p. 12).
"Caplin, capelin, capline, capling, capeling, capelan, caplein, capalan = Fr. *capelan, caplan*, Sp. *capelan*. A small fish very similar to a smelt, found on the coast of Newfoundland, and much used as a bait for cod. J. Mason 1620, *Newfoundland* p. 5, "June hath Capline a fish much resembling Smeltes in form and eating" (*OED*).
"But their greatest delicacy in the fish way is a small fish call'd here Capelin, in appearance not unlike a smelt, tho' scarce half as large. They come in very large shoals from the southward to deposit their spawn" (Banks, 9 August 1766).
Capelan is also a French family name (Dauzat, *Noms de Famille*, p. 85).

CAPLIN COVE 46–57, 53–36 (NTS St. Mary's 1K/13E) (Adm. 3264 1902).

Caplin Cove (Set.) (*Population Returns* 1836)
See ST. MICHAELS (NTS Ferryland) P. 107.

CAPLIN COVE 47–28, 52–41 (NTS Bay Bulls 1N/7E) (NDNR Bay Bulls 1943).

CAPLIN COVE 47–34, 53–14 (NTS Harbour Grace 1N/11E)
As set: (*Population Returns* 1836). P. 106.

CAPLIN COVE 47–42, 53–12 (NTS Harbour Grace 1N/11E)
(NDNR 1N/11 1948).

Caplin Cove (Set.) (*Population Returns* 1836). P. 107.

CAPLIN COVE (Set.) 48–02, 52–59 (NTS Bay de Verde 2C/2W)
As feature: ? Harbour Grande (Dudley 1646); as set: (Census 1857). P. 119.

Capo raso ("King-Hamy" 1504–6)
See CAPE RACE (NTS Trepassey).

CAPPAHAYDEN (Set.) 46–52, 52–57 (NTS Renews 1K/15W)
? Vaughan's Coue (Mason 1626), Broad Cove (former local name), Cappahayden (Proclamation, 23 December 1913). Pp. 61–2, 125, 139.

CAPTAIN ORLEBARS CAIRN (Hill) 47–19, 52–48 (NTS Bay Bulls 1N/7W) Cairn (Adm. 296 1868), American Man (CHS 4586 1944), Captain Olibars Cairn (USHO 2054 1947), American summit or Captain Orlebar's Cairn (NLP I 1951).

Orlebar – John Orlebar (1810– ?). Entered the Royal Navy, March 1824. Promoted to Lieutenant, September 1835 and became an Assistant Surveyor under Captain Bayfield on the survey of the Gulf and River St. Lawrence in 1836. Commander, February 1845, and continued as an Assistant Surveyor on the same station until February 1857 when he assumed charge of the Newfoundland survey. Post-Captain, 1 January 1861; Rear Admiral on retired list, August 1877; Vice-Admiral, May 1882. Retired in 1864 after 30 years' continuous employment in active surveying.

Admiralty Charts from Orlebar's surveys include: Cape Bonavista to Bay Bulls, Catalina Harbour, Trinity Harbour and Bays to English Head, Heart's Content, and New and Old Perlican Harbours, St. John's Harbour, Bay Bulls to Placentia, Broyle Harbour to Renewse Harbour, Barin [i.e. Burin] and St. Lawrence Harbours, Knife Bay to Cape Anguille, La Poile Bay, Duck Island to Ship Rock Shoal, including Port Basque, St. George Harbour and Codroy Road. (L. S. Dawson, *Memoirs of Hydrography*, II, p. 85). P. 145.

CARBONEAR (Set.) 47–44, 53–13 (NTS Harbour Grace 1N/11E) Carboneare (*CSP* 1674/5 1677), Carbonniere (Beaudoin 1697), Carbineer (*CSP* 1705), Carbonear (*CSP* 1705, Thoresby 1796), Carboniere (Imray, *Sailing Directions* 1862).

— CARBONEAR BAY 47–44, 53–12 Carbonera (Guy 1612), Carbonar ("Blathwayt" c. 1630–40), Carbonere (Robinson 1669), La Carboniere ("Dépôt 128.2.6" c. 1680), Carbonera Bay (Mount and Page 1780), Carbonear (Jukes 1840), Carbonear Bay (Imray, *Sailing Directory* 1873).

— CARBONEAR ISLAND 47–44, 53–10 Carbonere I (Southwood 1675). Pp. 74, 80, 121.

— CARBONEAR LONG POND 47–42, 53–19 (NDNR 1N/11 1948).

Longnon writes on the French place name: "Auxiliaire de la métallurgie, l'industrie charbonnière a donné naissance à un certain nombre des noms de lieu. Grégoire de Tours mentionne la Silva Carbonaria qui s'étendait, croit-on, sur une partie de la Belgique actuelle et du Hainaut français. La toponomastique actuelle comprend des communes appelées Charbonnière (Doubs), Charbonnières (Eure-et-Loire, Puy-de-Dôme, Rhône), – sans parler des écarts de même nom – et Cherbonnières (Charente – Inférieure); ces vocables ont pour équivalents Charbonniéras (Dordogne) et Carboniéras (Alpes-Maritimes). Précédés de l'article, le nom, fort répandu, la Charbonnière, sa variante, dans la langue d'oc et les dialectes du nord, la Carbonnière (Eure, Var), et son pluriel les Charbonnières (Cher, Loire) sont évidemment d'origine moins ancienne ... .

Bien entendu, parmi les localités visées dans l'énumération qui précède, il ne faut pas considérer ici celles dont le nom aurait été formé sur le nom de famille Charbonnier ou Carbonnier, et non pas sur le mot *charbon*; quant à celles qui doivent être retenues, elles doivent leur origine, les unes à des 'charbonnières' où l'on faisait le charbon de bois, les autres à des gisements houillers" (Longnon, pp. 558–9).

Le Messurier believed that the name was "given by the Jerseymen, as they had charcoal pits there at a very early period" (see Bibliography II). Pp. *38–9, 58, 63, 70, 80, 82, 90, 94, 95, 104, 116, 121 ,123, 129, 139.*

Cardiffe (Mason 1626). P. 62.

Cardigan (Mason 1626), Pp. 12, 62.

Carolinopole (Hayman 1630)
See HARBOUR GRACE (NTS Harbour Grace).

Carmarthe[n] (Mason 1626), P. 62.

CARRIER POINT 47–06, 52–56 (NTS Ferryland 1N/2W)
(Imray, *Sailing Directory* 1873).

CARTER'S HILL (Street) (St. John's)
Formerly Burst Heart Hill (Mosdell, p. 16).

The hill was renamed something over a hundred years ago after the Carters, a family prominent in the political life of Newfoundland in the nineteenth century, who had their residence, Hawthorn Cottage, on the hill. (Mosdell, p. 19; communication from E. B. Foran). Pp. 51, 144.

CASHIN AVENUE (Street) (St. John's)
The street was opened in May 1919 and named after Sir Michael Cashin then prime minister. Mosdell, p. 19; communication from E. B. Foran). P. 148.

CASTLE HILL 47–15, 53–58 (NTS Argentia 1N/5W (Cook 1762).
"upon this hill, a fort was erected by the French during their occupation of Newfoundland and we believe a few vestiges of the works can yet be traced" (Imray, *Sailing Directory* 1873, p. 84).

"On the summit of this hill are still to be seen the ruins of an old fort, or redoubt, which give[s] the modern name to the Hill. The fort occupied a most impregnable position. It commanded the whole range of the Roadstead as well as the great fort of St. Louis on the tongue of beach at the north or larbord side of the Gut on entering the harbour" (M. F. Howley, XXIX, NQ, March 1910). Pp. 5, 82.

CASTLE RIDGE 47–02, 53–56 (NTS Placentia 1N/4W)
(Adm. 2915 1864, Murray and Howley 1868).
? After the geographical formation. P. 145.

CAT HILL POND 47–38, 53–20 (NTS Harbour Grace 1N/11W)
(CHS 4572 1954).
Cat Hill unnamed in NTS.

CATARACT BROOK 47–13, 53–37 (NTS Placentia 1N/4E) (Newfoundland 1941).
Tributary of NORTH HARBOUR RIVER (NTS Placentia and Argentia).

Cat's Cove (Set.) (*Population Returns* 1836)
See CONCEPTION HARBOUR (NTS Holyrood).
— Cat's Cove Hills (Jukes 1842). Pp. 64, 106, 111.

C[auo] das patas (Homem 1554)
See COLDEAST POINT (NTS Ferryland). Pp. 31, 33, 89.

Cauo de la spera ("Oliveriana" 1505–8)
See CAPE SPEAR (NTS St. John's). Pp. 12, 30.

C[auo] de Portogesi (Ruysch 1508)
See MOTION HEAD (NTS Bay Bulls). Pp. 30, 89.

C[auo] de st iago (Ribeiro 1529)
See CAPE ST. MARY'S (NTS St. Bride's) under ST. MARY'S BAY. P. 31.

Cauo de ynglaterra (Cosa 1500)
See CAPE RACE (NTS Trepassey). Pp. 28–30.

CAVENDISH (Set.) 47–43, 53–29 (NTS Harbour Grace 1N/11W)
Formerly Shoal Bay; Cavendish (Proclamation 1 June 1905). "called Cavendish, after His Excellency Sir Cavendish Boyle" (Proclamation 1 June 1905).
Sir Cavendish Boyle (1849–1916), KCMG 1897; governor of Newfoundland, 1901–4; author of the "Ode to Newfoundland." (*Who Was Who 1916–28*). P. 139.
— CAVENDISH BAY 47–43, 53–30 Shoal Bay (Imray, *Sailing Directory* 1873), Cavendish Bay (Adm. 296 after 1899). "having in front of it a sunken patch of 1¾ fathoms" (Imray, *Sailing Directory* 1873, p. 39).
— CAVENDISH POND 47–43, 53–29 (NDNR 1N/11 1948).

Celicove (Beaudoin 1697)
See WINTERTON (NTS Heart's Content). P. 80.

Cemetery Hill
See DIXON HILL (NTS Placentia). P. 115.

Centre Harbor (Set.) (Census 1857). P. 119.

CENTRE HILL 47–53, 53–52 (NTS Sunnyside 1N/13W)
Sainter's Hill (Wix 1836), Centre Hill (Jukes 1840, Imray *Sailing Directory* 1873).
"an isolated cone and the highest land in this neighbourhood, separates the head of Deer harbour from that of Bull arm" (Imray, *Sailing Directory* 1873, p. 36). Pp. 105, 111.
— CENTRE BAY 47–51, 53–53

Chain Cove Head (Lane 1773)
See CHANCE COVE HEAD (NTS Renews). P. 86.

CHAIN ROCK 47–34, 52–41 (NTS St. John's 1N/10E)
(Cook 1762 or Gilbert 1768). P. 83.

Chaine Cove (Southwood 1675)
See CHANCE COVE (NTS Biscay Bay River). P. 74.

CHALK ROCKS 47–46, 53–48 (NTS Sunnyside 1N/13W)
(Imray, *Sailing Directions* 1862).

CHAMBERLAINS (Set.) 47–32, 52–57 (NTS St. John's 1N/10W)
Chamberlain (Census 1857), Chamberlain's (Census 1869). Pp. 116, 139, 158.
— CHAMBERLAIN'S POND

CHANCE BAY 46–58, 52–53 (NTS Renews)
(Imray, *Sailing Directory* 1873).

CHANCE COVE 46–45, 53–00 (NTS Biscay Bay River)
Chaine Cove (Southwood 1675, Visscher c. 1680), Chane cove (Thornton 1689A), Chaine Coue (Thornton 1689B), Chain Cove (*English Pilot. The Fourth Book* 1689), Chaine Cove (Fitzhugh 1695), Chain Cove (Gaudy 1715, Senex 1728, Popple 1733), P de Chiou (Bellin 1744), P de Chine (Robert de Vaugondy 1749), P de Chiou (Lotter c. 1758), Chain Cove (Cook 1763 ... Purdy 1814), Chance Cove (Jukes 1840). Pp. 74, 105.
— CHANCE COVE BROOK 46–46, 53–00
(Newfoundland 1941).
— CHANCE COVE HEAD 46–45, 52–59 (NTS Renews 1K/15W)
Chain Cove Head (Lane, *Directions* 1773, Imray *Sailing Directions* 1862)
— Chancecove Hd (Adm. 2915 1864). P. 86.

BIG CHANCE COVE 47–41, 53–49 (NTS Dildo 1N/12W)
(Wix 1836), Chance Cove (Jukes 1840), Big Chance Cove (Imray, *Sailing Directions* 1862).
— CHANCE COVE (Set.) 47–41, 53–50 Big Chance Cove (Wix 1836), Chance Cove (*Population Returns* 1836).

196 / Place Names of the Avalon Peninsula

— LITTLE CHANCE COVE
(Imray, *Sailing Directions* 1862).
Pp. 105, 107, 115.

CHAPEL ARM 47–32, 53–39 (NTS Dildo 1N/12E)
? Savage Harbour (Guy 1612, Powell *RGSJ* 1935), Chapel Bay (Cook and Lane 1770 [1775]A), Chapple Bay (Lane 1790), Chapel Bay (Lane *Directions* 1775, 1810, Anspach 1819), Chapple B. (Purdy 1814), Chapel Arm (Jukes 1840), Chapple Bay (Imray, *Sailing Directions* 1862), Chapple Arm (J. P. Howley 1907).
See SPREADEAGLE BAY (NTS Dildo).
Pp. 59, 95, 103, 114, 158.

— CHAPEL ARM (Set.) 47–31, 53–40 (Wix 1836), Chappel Arm (*Census* 1874).

— CHAPEL HEAD 47–35, 53–39
Chapel Tolt (Wix 1836).
Pp. 104, 145.

CHAPEL COVE 47–26, 53–08 (NTS Holyrood 1N/6E)
(Jukes 1840), Chapels cove (*NLP* II 1953).

— CHAPEL COVE (Set.) 47–26, 53–09
Chapel's Cove (*Population Returns* 1836).

— CHAPEL COVE POINT 47–27, 53–08
Chapels Cove head (*NLP* II 1953), Chapel Cove Point (CHS 4573 1953).
Pp. 106, 131, 158.

CHAPEL HEAD 47–17, 52–49 (NTS Bay Bulls 1N/7W) (NDNR Bay Bulls 1943).

CHARLEYS POND 47–25, 53–09 (NTS Holyrood 1N/6E) (CHS 4573 1953).
Chavette (Robinson 1669)
Chincete (Alfonse 1544)
Chinchette (Courcelle 1675)
Chincho (Chaviteau 1698)
Chinckhole (Gaudy 1715)
chinette, la (Friend 1713)
Chink-hole (Senex 1728)

Chinkhole (Bellin 1744)
See ST. SHOTTS (NTS St. Shotts). P. 35.

Chipbony (*English Pilot. The Fourth Book* 1716, 1780)
See ? LOW POINT (NTS Bay de Verde). P. 77.

Chisel Hill (Jukes 1842). P. 115.

CHURCH COVE 47–04, 52–52 (NTS Ferryland 1N/2W)
(Adm. 2915 ? 1864).
? Descriptive.

CHURCH POND 47–42, 52–50 (NTS St. John's 1N/10W)

CIRCLE POND 47–44, 53–23 (NTS Harbour Grace 1N/11W)
(NDNR 1N/11 1948).

CIRCULAR ROAD (St. John's)
Made before 1854. The name may have applied originally to what is now part of Bonaventure Avenue, the straight stretch which appears to be most inappropriately called Circular Road, part of Kingsbridge Road, and Military Road, the whole linking FORT TOWNSHEND and FORT WILLIAM by way of The Barrens. (Communication from E. B. Foran).
P. 147.

CLAM COVE 46–43, 53–03 (NTS Trepassey 1K/11E)
Glam Cove (Yonge 1663–70), Glame Cove (Southwood 1675), Glaine C (Hack ? 1677, Visscher c. 1680, Thornton 1689B), Glam Cove (*English Pilot. The Fourth Book* 1689, Hack c. 1690?), Glame Coue (Fitzhugh 1693), Po de Glome (Hermite 1695), Glane Cove (Gaudy 1715) Glame Cove (Senex 1728, Popple 1733), Port de Cheme (Buache 1736), P de Glome (Bellin 1744, Robert de Vaugondy 1749, Bellin 1754), Glame Cove (Mount and Page 1755), P de Glome (Lotter c. 1758), Clam Cove (Cook and Lane 1770 [1775])B, Glam Cove (Cook

and Lane 1770 [1775]A, Lane 1773, Mount and Page 1780, Lane 1790), Clam Cove (Purdy 1814, Jukes 1840), Glam or Clam Cove (Imray, *Sailing Directions* 1862).
Pp. *52, 66–7*.

CLAM RIVER 47–20, 53–26 (NTS Holyrood 1N/6W)
(NDNR 1N/6 1943).

Clapper, The (Rock) (Bell Island) 47–36, 53–01 (Lane 1774). P. 90.

CLARKES BEACH (Set.) 47–33, 53–17 (NTS Harbour Grace 1N/11W)
Clark's Beach (Census 1857).
Pp. *5, 24, 48, 113, 118, 130, 140, 158*.
— CLARKE'S BEACH POND (CHS 4572 1954).
— Clarke's Hill (Jukes 1842). P. 113.
— CLARKE'S POND 47–31, 53–19 (CHS 4572 1954).

CLARKS BROOK 47–46, 53–14 (NTS Heart's Content 1N/14E and W)
(NDNR 1N/14 1946). P. 158.

CLARKS POND 47–19, 53–19 (NTS Holyrood 1N/6W)
(NDNR 1N/6 1943). P. 158.

CLEAR COVE 46–58, 52–54 (NTS Renews 1K/15W)
clear-cove (Yonge 1663–70, but placed within FERMEUSE HARBOUR), Clears-Cove (*English Pilot. The Fourth Book* 1689, Cook and Lane 1770 [1775]B, Lane 1773, Mount and Page 1780), Clear's Cove (M. F. Howley, xxvi, *NQ*, July 1909), Clear Cove (Newfoundland 1941).
— CLEAR COVE ROCK (Adm. 2915 1864).
Pp. *68–9, 130, 158*.

CLEMENTS COVE 47–45, 53–11 (NTS Heart's Content 1N/14E)
(NDNR 1N/14 1946). P. 158.

CLEMENTS POND 47–38, 52–49 (NTS St. John's 1N/10W). P. 158.

CLIFF (Generic). P. 144.

CLIFF POINT 47–32, 52–40 (NTS St. John's 1N/10E)
? Deadmans point (Seller c. 1671), Cliff Point (*NLP* I 1951. "which shows a square face of cliff seaward" (*NLP* I 1951, p. 75). Pp. *71–2, 144*.

Clip Boney (Thornton 1689B) See ? LOW POINT (NTS Bay de Verde). Pp. *77, 107*.

Clowns Cove (Fermeuse Harbour) (Yonge 1663–70). P. 68.

CLOWNS COVE (Set.) 47–46, 53–11 (NTS Heart's Content 1N/14E)
As feature: Clounes Cove (Southwood 1675), Clouns Cove (Hack ? 1677), Clowns-Cove (*English Pilot. The Fourth Book* 1689). Clownes Cove (Fitzhugh 1693).
As settlement: Kelinscove (Beaudoin 1697), Clor's, Claur's, Clown's Cove (Thoresby 1796), Clown's Cove (*Population Returns* 1836).
Pp. *68, 74, 80, 158*.

COALPIT POINT 46–56, 53–33 (NTS St. Mary's 1K/13E)
(Adm. 3264 1902).
"Certain black rocks which show above water are called The Coal Pits" (M. F. Howley, xxvIII, *NQ*, December 1909).

COCHRANE (Specific) After Sir Thomas Cochrane, governor of Newfoundland 1825–34). "Sir Thomas Cochrane is now universally admitted to have been the best Governor ever sent to Newfoundland; everywhere are monuments erected to his memory. He inaugurated our system of roads, promoted agriculture, and laid out the beautiful grounds of Virginia as his country seat. Cochrane Street and the Military Road remind us of the great administrator. I cannot say much in praise of His Excellency's taste in the erection of Government House. The site is an admirable one, the grounds are well laid out, but the building itself looks more like a prison than a vice-regal residence; the ditch all round is a trap to catch snow, and in winter the north entrance is as cold as Siberia. I can give him credit for every other improvement, but am compelled to say that Government House is a huge pile of unredeemed ugliness" (D. W. Prowse, pp. 424–5). An account of Cocrane's governorship is in D. W. Prowse, pp. 424–36; of Cochrane and Government House in Fabian O'Dea, "Government House: its Construction and its History," in Smallwood (ed.), The Book of Newfoundland, IV, pp. 214–8. P. 6.

Cochrane Dale
See MAKINSON (GOULDS P.O.) (NTS Harbour Grace). Pp. 112–3.

COCHRANE POND 47–28, 52–51 (NTS Bay Bulls 1N/7W)
(NDNR Bay Bulls 1943).
— COCHRANE POND BROOK 47–27, 52–46

COCHRANE POND 47–33, 52–50 (NTS St. John's 1N/10W)

COCHRANE STREET (St. John's)

COCHRANE STREET (Harbour Grace)
One of four firebreaks made after the fire of 1832. (Barrelman, 27 March 1950).

Cochrane Racecourse (Harbour Grace)
Where races were held, 1 October 1833 (Barrelman, 1 October 1950).

COCOANUT WATERS 47–16, 53–25 (NTS Holyrood 1N/6W)
(NDNR 1N/6 1943). P. 143.

CODNER (Set.) 47–31, 53–00 (Unnamed in NTS St. John's 1N/10W)

Middle Bight (Census 1857), Codner (Proclamation, 18 June 1906). P. 117 and note 191, p. 141.

COFIELD'S LANE (St. John's). P. 148.

Colchos (Mason 1626). Pp. 12, 62.

COLDEAST POINT 47–02, 52–53 (NTS Ferryland 1N/2W)
? C das patas (Homem 1554), Cold East Point (Lane 1773).
See COLEY'S POINT (NTS Harbour Grace). Pp. 31, 87, 89.

COLEY'S POINT 47–35, 53–15 (NTS Harbour Grace 1N/11W)
? Pointe agreable (Bellin 1744, Robert de Vaugondy 1749), Coldeast point (Imray, Sailing Directory 1873, NLP 1907), Coley's Point (M. F. Howley, XIX, NQ, October 1907).
— COLEY'S POINT (Set.) 47–35, 53–16
Cole Lees Point (CO Misc. 199.18 1798), Coley's Point (Census 1857). See COLDEAST POINT (NTS Ferryland).
Pp. 52, 89, 119, 124.

COLINET (Specific) French family name (Dauzat, Noms de Famille, pp. 450–1 under Nicolas); place name Collinette, Sark, Channel Islands.

COLINET (Set.) 47–13, 53–33 (NTS Placentia 1N/4E)
Collonett (CSP 1680), Colinet (Population Returns 1836). Pp. 131, 139.
— COLINET HARBOUR 47–12, 53–35
? P. Colin (Courcelle 1675), Colinett (Hack ? 1677), Colinet Havre (Robert de Vaugondy 1749), Colinet Bay (Lane 1773, Purdy 1814). P. 108.
— GREAT COLINET ISLAND 47–00, 53–42 (NTS St. Mary's 1K/13E, Placentia 1N/4E).
Collinett (Robinson 1669), Colonet Isle (Seller 1671), Colonet I (Hack c. 1690?),

Collemot (Chaviteau 1698),
with LITTLE COLINET ISLAND, Les
Colinets (Gaudy 1715), G.
Colinet Isld (Lane 1773); as set:
Colinet Island (*Population
Returns* 1836).
Pp. 49, 120.
— LITTLE COLINET ISLAND 47–03,
53–40 (NTS Placentia 1N/4E)
(Lane 1773); as set: Little Island
(Census 1857). P. 86.
"The people from analogy with
the word colonel call these
islands by the name of Curnet
Islands" M. F. Howley, XXVIII,
NQ, December 1909).
— COLINET PASSAGE 46–59, 55–40
(NTS St. Mary's 1K/13E,
Placentia 1N/4E).
(Imray, *Sailing Directory* 1873).
P. 141.
— COLINET RIVER 47–13, 53–33 (NTS
Placentia 1N/4E, Argentia
1N/5E, Holyrood 1N/6W)
Colinet River and Arm (Jukes
1842). P. 111.

COLLIER BAY 47–36, 53–42 (NTS Dildo
1N/12E)
Colliers Bay (Lane 1790). Pp. 98,
130, 158.
— Colliers Bay Cove (Set.)
See THORNLEA (NTS Dildo). P. 145.
— COLLIERS POINT 47–36, 53–41

COLLIERS (Set.) 47–28, 53–13 (NTS
Holyrood 1N/6E)
(*Population Returns* 1836). Pp. 39,
64, 125, 129, 130, 131, 139, 158.
— COLLIERS BAY 47–29, 53–12 (NTS
Holyrood 1N/6E, Harbour Grace
1N/11E)
Colliers (Blathwayt c. 1630–40),
Colliers B (Southwood 1675).
P. 118.
— COLLIERS BIG POND 47–24, 53–19
(NTS Holyrood 1N/6W)
— Colliers English Cove (Set.)
(Census 1857)
See ENGLISH COVE (NTS

Holyrood). P. 118.
— Colliers Flat Rock (Set.) (Census
1857). P. 118.
— Colliers James Cove (Set.)
(Census 1857)
See JAMES COVE (NTS Holyrood).
P. 118.
— COLLIERS POINT 47–30, 53–10
(NTS Harbour Grace 1N/11E)
(Adm. 296 1868).
— COLLIERS RIVER 47–27, 53–15
NTS Holyrood 1N/6E and W)
— COLLIERS STATION 47–26, 53–16
(NTS Holyrood 1N/6W)
(NDNR 1N/6 1943).

COLUMBINE POINT 47–18, 52–45 (NTS
Bay Bulls 1N/7W)
? Pepperalley point (Imray,
Sailing Directory 1873), Columbine
Point (NDNR Bay Bulls 1943).
If, as suggested on p. 31, Columbine is a shifted survival of I.
Columbrina (Coronelli 1689),
probably one of the isles d'espoir
(See SPEAR ISLAND), it appears to
derive from Port. *colubrina* or Eng.
colubrine (1605) – culverin,
changed ? to the more familiar flower
name.
Pepperalley – "an alley in London,
hence allusively in pugilistic slang"
(*OED*). P. 31.

COME BY CHANCE (Harbour) 47–50,
54–00 (NTS Sunnyside 1N/13W,
Sound Island 1M/16E).
Passage harbour (Guy 1612),
Comby Chance (*CSP* 1706), Come
by Chance Harbour (Cook and Lane
1770 [1775]A ... Anspach 1819),
Chance Harbr (Purdy 1814, Bonnycastle 1842), Come-by-Chance
Harbour (Imray, *Sailing Directions*
1862).
Pp. 59, 60, 140.
— COME BY CHANCE (Set.) 47–51,
53–58 (NTS Sunnyside 1N/13W)
(*Population Returns* 1836, Wix
1836).

— COME BY CHANCE RIVER 47–51, 54–00 (Wix 1836). P. 106.
*Come by Chance is also a place name in New South Wales. The name was probably bestowed on the locality by an early squatter about 1840. (Communication from Professor R. B. Ward.)

CONCEPTION BAY 47–45, 53–00 (NTS Holyrood 1N/6E, Harbour Grace 1N/11E, Heart's Content 1N/14E, Pouch Cove 1N/15, Bay de Verde 2C/2W).
? Baia de cos[eicam] ("Oliveriana" 1505–8), Abaia de [con]cipicion (H) (Maggiolo 1527), Concepcion (Desliens 1541), Baia de s[anta] m[aria] (Cabot 1544), B de conception (Desceliers 1546), B da corybicion (Gutiérrez 1562), B of Conception (Hayes 1583), Conception Bay (Whitbourne 1588–1622), B de Consumption (Hood 1592), B of Assumption (Leigh 1597), B of Consumption ("Velasco" 1610), Bay Consumption (Robinson 1669), B. de Lours (Courcelle 1675), B. de la Cocepcion The Bay off Trinité (Coronelli-Tillemon 1689), Bay Conception alias Consumption (*English Pilot. The Fourth Book* 1689), Consomption bay (Thornton 1689A), Conception Bay (Thornton 1689B), The Bay of Consumtion (Hack c. 1690 ?), Consu[mption] Bay (Fitzhugh 1693), Baie de l'Assomption (Franquelin 1699), Conception B (Moll c. 1712).
Port. *conceição* – conception.
The arguments for the naming of CONCEPTION BAY with other major features on the AVALON PENINSULA by the Portuguese are given on pp. 28–30. G. R. F. Prowse, however, maintained that CONCEPTION BAY was entered and named on 8 December 1497, the feast of the Conception of the Blessed Virgin Mary, during an English survey of South Newfoundland, and that an earlier English survey had reached the bay on August 15, the feast of the Assumption. Sailors confused Conception and Assumption and produced the mistake name Consumption, recorded by Hood in 1592, by James Yonge in 1670: "the bay of Conception (called 'Consumption' by the people)," and according to M. F. Howley "so called by some of our people even at the present day [1907]." (G. R. F. Prowse, *CM*, III, p. 117; Yonge, p. 135; M. F. Howley, XVII, *NQ*, March 1907).
Fr. B. de Lours – Bear Bay.
Note the confusion with TRINITY BAY (Coronelli-Tillemon 1689).
See PINCHGUT TICKLE (NTS Placentia), pp. 84–5.
Pp. 18, 30, 40, 41, 42, 46, 49, 50, 56, 57, 61, 74, 76, 80, 85, 90, 92, 93, 94, 105, 107, 114, 116, 117, 122, 125, 144.

— CONCEPTION BAY HIGHWAY. P. 147.

CONCEPTION HARBOUR 47–26, 53–13 (NTS Holyrood 1N/6E)
Cat's Cove (Murray and Howley 1868), Cat Cove (Imray, *Sailing Directory* 1873), Conception [Harbour] (M. F. Howley, XIX, *NQ*, October 1907).

— CONCEPTION HARBOUR (Set.) Cats' Cove (*Population Returns* 1836), Avondale North (Proclamation 18 June 1906) Cat –
? the wild cat, "locally known as the wood cat," or the wood marten (M. F. Howley, XVI, *NQ*, October 1906). Avondale North See AVONDALE (NTS Holyrood).
Conception occurs in the vicinity in Friend 1713.
Pp. 64, 106, 111, 118, 124, 125, 130.

CONNELLS POND 47–24, 53–10 (NTS Holyrood 1N/6E)
(CHS 4573 1953). P. 130.

CONNOR COVE 47–19, 53–55 (NTS Argentia 1N/5W) (CHS 4622 ?1953).
— CONNOR COVE POINT
(CHS 4622 ?1953).
P. 130.

CONNS POND 47–17, 53–14 (NTS Holyrood 1N/6E)
(NDNR 1N/6 1943).

Consumption (Specific) See CONCEPTION.

Consumption Passage
See PINCHGUT TICKLE (NTS Placentia). P. 85.

contalian ("Anon. Portuguese" c. 1550)
See CUCKOLD HEAD (NTS St. John's). Pp. 31, 68.

CONWAY (Specific). P. 130.

CONWAY BROOK 47–31, 52–58 (NTS Bay Bulls 1N/7W)

CONWAY COVE 47–22, 53–54 (NTS Argentia 1N/5W) (CHS 4622 ?1953).

CONWAY COVE 47–26, 53–48 (NTS Argentia 1N/5W) (Adm. 3266 1939).

COOKS COVE 48–06, 53–00 (NTS Bay de Verde 2C/2W, Old Perlican 2C/3E) (Newfoundland 1941).
— COOKS POND 48–06, 52–59 (NTS Bay de Verde 2C/2W) (Provincial Representative CBGN).
Local tradition maintains that Captain Cook took observations from SKERWINK POINT (NTS Old Perlican), the western extremity of the cove. (Communication from C. R. Barrett).

COOPER COVE 47–18, 53–59 (NTS Argentia 1N/5W)
(NLP 1951). P. 158.

COOPER HEAD 47–20, 53–54 (NTS Argentia 1N/5W)
(NLP 1951). P. 158.

COOPERS HEAD 47–38, 53–13 (NTS Harbour Grace 1N/11E)
No[rth] Point (Southwood 1675); as set: Coopers Head (CO Misc. 199.18 1780). Pp. 74, 158.

COOPERS POND 47–39, 53–29 (NTS Harbour Grace 1N/11W)
(NDNR 1N/11 1948).
— LITTLE COOPERS POND 47–37, 53–30 (NTS Harbour Grace 1N/11W, Dildo 1N/12E), p. 158. However, men used to cut wood to make barrels near the pond (Communication from Miss K. George, New Harbour).

Coosh (Set.) (Bay Roberts) (Census 1857)
Cosh (Imray, *Sailing Directory* 1873). Cp. Cosh (North River). Pp. 112, 119.

COOTE POND 46–57, 53–31 (NTS St. Mary's 1K/13E)
Browns Pond (Cook 1762 or Gilbert 1768); as set: Coote's Pond (*Population Returns* 1836). Pp. 83, 107, 130.

COPPER ISLAND 47–51, 53–43 (NTS Sunnyside 1N/13E)
(Purdy 1814). P. 102.

CORBIN HEAD 47–29, 53–56 (Not in NTS Argentia)
Corben's Head (Wix 1836), Corbin head (*NP* 1952). Pp. 105, 130.

Corlab P. (Visscher c. 1680)
See GARLEP POINT (NTS Heart's Content). P. 72.

CORNWALL HEIGHTS (Street) (St. John's). P. 145.

Cosh (North River) (Jukes 1842)

Cp. Coosh (Bay Roberts). Pp. 112, 129, 142.

COTTAGE POND 47–31, 53–17 (NTS Harbour Grace 1N/11W)
(CHS 4572 1954).
Site of a cottage owned by a member of the Leamon family ? of BRIGUS.

COUNTRY (Generic and Specific).
Pp. 104, 145.

COUNTRY POND 47–20, 52–55 (NTS Bay Bulls 1N/7W)
(NDNR Bay Bulls 1943). P. 104.

COUNTRY ROAD (Set.) 47–35, 53–18 (NTS Harbour Grace 1N/11W)
Country Path (Census 1857), ? Jack Hill's Road (Local name).
— COUNTRY POND 47–34, 53–19
   (CHS 4572 1954).
Pp. 104, 119, 147.

COURAGES BEACH 47–41, 53–14 (NTS Harbour Grace 1N/11E)
Courage Beach (Adm. 297 1933), Courages Beach (CHS 4590 1943).
P. 158.

COVE (Generic = coastal inlet).
Pp. 140, 144.

COVE (Generic = Street). Pp. 116, 148.

COVE NAN DRIOCH-CLOCHAN 47–26, 53–54 (NTS Argentia 1N/5W)
(NLP 1929).
— COVE NAN DRIOCH-CLOCHAN POINT
   47–27, 53–55 (NLP 1929).
Pp. 128, 140.

COVE POND 47–43, 52–50 (NTS St. John's 1N/10W)
? After the small cove in the northwest corner of the pond. Cove Refused (Robinson 1669)
   See ? NEW MELBOURNE (NTS Old Perlican). P. 70.

COW POND 47–40, 53–19 (NTS Harbour Grace 1N/11W)
(NDNR 1N/11 1948).

— COW POND BROOK 47–40, 53–16
   (NDNR 1N/11 1948).

COX POINT 47–08, 53–29 (NTS St. Catherine's 1N/3W)
As set: Cox's Point (*Population Returns* 1836). Pp. 108, 158.

COXHILL COVE 47–18, 53–55 (NTS Argentia 1N/5W) (CHS 4622 ? 1953).
— COXHILL POINT
   (CHS 4622 ? 1953).

Crapeau Point (M. F. Howley, XXVIII, NQ, December 1909)
See FRAPEAU POINT (NTS St. Mary's).
P. 88.

CRAWLEY ISLAND 47–25, 53–52 (NTS Argentia 1N/5W)
As set: Crawley's Island (*Population Returns* 1836); Harbour island (Imray, *Sailing Directions* 1862, *Sailing Directory* 1873), Crawley Island (NLP 1929).
   Harbour – i.e. LONG HARBOUR (NTS Argentia). Pp. 110, 130.

CREVECŒUR POINT 47–15, 54–00 (NTS Argentia 1N/5W)
C Creve Coeur (Gaudy 1715), point Privecœur (Imray, *Sailing Directory* 1873). P. 51.

CRIPPLE COVE 46–38, 53–06 (NTS Trepassey 1K/11E)
? Fausse B. (Courcelle 1675), Cripple Cove (Southwood 1675)
— CRIPPLE ROCK
   (NLP 1951).
   "a small pinnacle rock situated 1 mile south-westward of Cape Race, and about 4 cables offshore" (NLP I, 90).
— CRIPPLE ROCK POINT
   (CHS 4576 1950).
Cripple – to disable (of ships).
Pp. 50, 74.

CRIPPLE COVE 47–49, 52–48 (NTS Pouch Cove 1N/15W)

CROCKERS COVE 47–45, 53–12 (NTS Harbour Grace 1N/11E)
Crokers Cove (Southwood 1675 ... Thornton 1689B), Crockers Cove (Hack c. 1690?); as set: Croquescove (Beaudoin 1697).
— CROCKERS GULLY 47–47, 53–15 (NDNR 1N/14 1946).
— CROCKERS POINT 47–44, 53–12 (Cook 1762 or Gilbert 1768).
Pp. 74, 80, 83–4, 158.

CROOKED POND 47–18, 53–15 (NTS Holyrood 1N/6W) (NDNR 1N/6 1943).

CROOKED POND 47–43, 53–23 (NTS Harbour Grace 1N/11W) (NDNR 1N/11 1948).

Croquescove (Beaudoin 1697) See CROCKERS COVE (NTS Harbour Grace). P. 80.

CROSS POINT 47–09, 53–28 (NTS St. Catherine's 1N/3W) (Adm. 2915 1864).
? A crossing place on SALMONIER ARM from MOUNT CARMEL to a point midway between NEW BRIDGE and FOREST FIELD. As a feature the Point is negligible.

CROSS POINT 47–14, 53–59 (NTS Placentia 1N/4W)

CROSS POINT 46–56, 54–11 (NTS St. Bride's 1L/16E)
P. Perle (Bowen 1747), Cross point (Murray and Howley 1868, Imray, *Sailing Directory* 1873, J. P. Howley 1907), Point La Perche (M. F. Howley, XXIX, *NQ*, March 1910), Cross Point (Newfoundland 1949).
Perche – ? Ancient district in the north of France (Mansion). Cross Point – ? Formerly the site of a cross. Cp. PERCH COVE. Pp. 48–9.

CROSS POND 47–25, 53–19 (NTS Holyrood 1N/6W) (NDNR 1N/6 1943).
? Fordable where opposite banks almost meet.

CROSS POND 47–38, 53–29 (NTS Harbour Grace 1N/11W) (NDNR 1N/11 1948).
Men from GREENS HARBOUR (NTS Dildo) used to cross this pond in winter on their slides laden with barrels of fish on their way to HARBOUR GRACE. (Communication from Miss K. George, New Harbour).

CROSSING (Generic). P. 148.

CROSSING PLACE RIVER 46–56, 53–28 (NTS Biscay Bay River 1K/14W and St. Catherine's 1N/3W). (Newfoundland 1941).
To avoid HOLYROOD POND (NTS St. Mary's and Biscay Bay River), the trail from the mouth of NORTHWEST BROOK (TREPASSEY HARBOUR) (NTS Trepassey) to ST. MARY'S HARBOUR (NTS St. Mary's) makes a northerly detour to the place where CROSSING PLACE RIVER enters HOLYROOD POND.

CROW ISLAND 47–01, 52–53 (NTS Ferryland 1N/2W)
Cro Iland ("Blathwayt" c. 1630–40), ? Bay Isl (Seller c. 1671), Crow I. (Southwood 1675). P. 66.

Crow Isl (Seller c. 1671) See KELLYS ISLAND (NTS Harbour Grace). P. 72.

CROWN HILL 47–30, 52–41 (NTS Bay Bulls 1N/7E) (Adm. 296 1868).

CROWN HILL 47–55, 53–46 (NTS Sunnyside 1N/13W) (Imray, *Sailing Directory* 1873).

CROWS NEST (St. John's) (Chappell 1813). P. 102.

CUCKOLD COVE 47–35, 52–40 (NTS St. John's 1N/10E)
Cuckhold's Cove (M. F. Howley, XVI, *NQ*, October 1906), Cuckold Cove (NLP 1951).

— CUCKOLD HEAD.
contalian ("Anon. Portuguese" c. 1550), cõtaliom ("Vallicelliana" c. 1550), confalcon (Desceliers 1550), comtaliom (Velho c. 1560), comtalion (Velho 1561), contalioni (Martines 1578), ceritaliam (Vaz Dourado 1580), antalioni (Martines 1583), Contaliã (Lopes c. 1583), Catalio (Hood 1592), Conta Lion ("Velasco" 1610), Cuckold's Head (Yonge 1668–9), C des Cocus (Hermite 1695), Cuckolds P[oint] (Popple 1733), Cuckolds Head (Mount and Page 1755).
Fr. *cocu* – cuckold, deceived husband.
"a round bare hill in the form of a hay-cock" (Lane, *Directions* 1775, 1810).
Pp. 31, 67–8.

CULLEN COVE 47–26, 53–51 (NTS Argentia 1N/5W)
(Adm. 3266 1939).
— CULLEN POINT
(Adm. 3266 1939).
P. 130.

Cupers Cove (Guy 1612)
— Cuperts coue (Mason 1626).
See CUPIDS (NTS Harbour Grace).
Pp. 58, 58–9, 61.

CUPIDS (Set.) 47–33, 53–14 (NTS Harbour Grace 1N/11E)
Cupers Cove (Guy 1612), Cupers coue (Mason 1626).
— CUPIDS BIG POND 47–30, 53–17 (NTS Holyrood 1N/6W, Harbour Grace 1N/11W)
(CHS 4572 1954).
— CUPIDS COVE 47–34, 53–13 (NTS Harbour Grace 1N/11E)
Cupert's coue (Mason 1626), Cubitts Cove ("Blathwayt" c. 1630–40), Coopers Cove (Robinson 1669, Seller 1671), Cupids Cove (Hack ? 1677), Coopers Cou[e] (Thornton 1689A), Cupids-Cove (*English Pilot. The Fourth Book* 1689).
— CUPIDS CROSSING (Set.) 47–31, 53–15. P. 148.
— CUPIDS LONG POND 47–28, 53–17 (NTS Holyrood 1N/6W) (CHS 4573 1953).
— CUPIDS POND 47–32, 53–14 (CHS 4572 1954).
— CUPIDS STATION (Set.) 47–32, 53–15
? c. 1884, from inception of railway.
Pp. 39, 40, 57, 58, 58–9, 60, 61, 62, 70, 139.

CURRENS POND 47–16, 53–23 (NTS Holyrood 1N/6W)
(NDNR 1N/6 1943). P. 130.

CUSLETT (Set.) 46–58, 54–10 (NTS St. Bride's 1L/16E)
(*Population Returns* 1836).
— CUSLETT BROOK 46–57, 54–10
Curslet Brk (Adm. 2915 1864).
— CUSLETT COVE 46–57, 54–10
Curslet Cove (Adm. 2915 1864)
— CUSLETT POINT 46–57, 54–11
Cp. Curslet Rock, 2 miles W by S from BREME POINT (NTS St. Bride's).
Cp. Cusslets Cove (Cook 1764) near Cape Onion (NTS Raleigh).
Pp. 109, 130, 159.

DALE (Generic). P. 146.

DALTON POINT 47–01, 53–41 (NTS Placentia 1N/4E)
(Adm. 2915 1864). P. 130.

DALTONS POND 47–16, 53–04 (NTS Holyrood 1N/6E)
(NDNR 1N/6 1943). P. 130.

DANIEL POINT 46–45, 53–23 (NTS Trepassey 1K/11W)
(USHO 0618 1941).
— DANIEL'S POINT (Set.) (NTS

Biscay Bay River 1K/14W)
(Smallwood 1940).
After Daniel Pennell, a squatter.
Pennell is a common family name at
DANIEL'S POINT. (Communication
from Miss D. O'Toole, Renews).

DANIELS BROOK 47–22, 53–10 (NTS
Holyrood 1N/6E). P. 159.

DANIELS COVE (Set.) 48–08, 52–58
(NTS Bay de Verde 2C/2W)
(*Population Returns* 1836). P. 107.

DAVES POND 47–49, 53–19 (NTS
Heart's Content 1N/14W)
(NDNR 1N/14 1946).

Davidson (Set.)
See SIBLEY'S COVE (Set.) (NTS Old
Perlican).

DAVIES HEAD 47–34, 53–16 (NTS
Harbour Grace 1N/11W)
Davey's Head (M. F. Howley, XIX,
NQ, October 1907).
The Daveys and Snows are said
to have been the first settlers at
COLEY'S POINT (NTS Harbour Grace).
(M. F. Howley, XIX, *NQ*, October
1907).
P. 159.

DAVIS POINT 47–13, 53–34 (NTS
Placentia 1N/4E)
(Adm. 2915 1864), Davies point
(Imray, *Sailing Directory* 1873).
Pp. 131, 159.

de los patas (Santa Cruz 1545)
See GOOSE ISLAND (NTS Ferryland),
COLDEAST POINT (NTS Ferryland),
CALVERT BAY (NTS Ferryland).
Pp. 31, 71.

DEADMANS BAY 47–32, 52–40 (NTS
St. John's 1N/10E)
Dedman Bay (Seller 1671),
Deadman B. (Hack ? 1677),
Dedmans Bay (Visscher c. 1680).
"several Men and Boats formerly
lost in that Bay" (*English Pilot. The
Fourth Book* 1716).

— Deadmans point (Seller c. 1671)
See CLIFF POINT (NTS St. John's).
P. 71–2.

DEADMANS POND 47–30, 52–45 (NTS
Bay Bulls 1N/7E and W)
(NDNR Bay Bulls 1943). P. 5.

Deepest Bay (Mount and Page 1780)
See BAY ROBERTS HARBOUR (NTS
Harbour Grace). P. 97.

DEER HARBOUR 47–54, 53–44 (NTS
Sunnyside 1N/13E and W)
(Lane, *Directions* 1775, 1810).
P. 95.
— DEER HARBOUR HEAD 47–54,
  53–42 (NTS Sunnyside 1N/13E)
  Deer Hd (Bonnycastle 1842),
  Deer Harbour head (Imray,
  Sailing Directory 1873). P. 116.
— Deer Island (Lane, *Directions*
  1775, 1810)
  See ? GRUB ISLAND (NTS
  Sunnyside). P. 95.

DEER PARK 47–16, 53–17 (Unnamed
in NTS Holyrood 1N/6W)
(Local name ? mid-19th century).
Formerly famous for its caribou
herds (Communication from J. H.
Gibbs).

DEER POND 46–49, 53–35 (NTS
St. Mary's 1K/13E)
(Newfoundland 1941).
— DEER RIVER 46–49, 53–36
  (Adm. 2915 1864).
P. 6.

DENNIS POINT 47–17, 52–50 (NTS
Bay Bulls 1N/7W)
(NDNR Bay Bulls 1943). P. 159, but
cp. DINNYS POND (NTS Harbour Grace).
Dennis and Dinnys are, of course,
almost identical in Anglo-Irish
pronunciation; cp. gintleman,
ginerally. (W. Kirwin).

Devil's Cove (Set.) (*Population
Returns* 1836)
See PATRICK'S COVE (NTS Ship
Cove).
P. 109.

Devils Cove (Lane 1774)
See JOB'S COVE (NTS Heart's Content). Pp. 93–4, 98.

DEVILS POINT 47–38, 52–40 (NTS St. John's 1N/10E) (*NLP* 1951).
"on its summit is a beacon of stones" (*NLP* 1951, p. 73) – ? the devil.

DICK'S SQUARE (St. John's). P. 148.

DILDO (Set.) 47–34, 53–33 (NTS Dildo 1N/12E)
Dildo Cove (Wix 1836, *Population Returns* 1836).
— DILDO ARM 47–33, 53–34 (J. P. Howley 1907, Newfoundland 1941). Formerly
— DILDO ARM and COVE were apparently undistinguished and given the common name DILDO HARBOUR as in Lane, *Directions* 1775, 1810).
— DILDO COVE 47–34, 53–34 (J. P. Howley 1907).
— Dildo Harbour (Lane, *Directions* 1775, 1810)
— DILDO ISLANDS 47–34, 53–35 *Dildo Island (Crowe's Laws 1711 in D. W. Prowse, p. 271).
— DILDO POND 47–29, 53–33 (NTS Argentia 1N/5E and Dildo 1N/12E)
— Dildo River (Murray and Howley 1872)
— SOUTH DILDO (Set.) 47–31, 53–33 (NTS Dildo 1N/12E).

Pp. 96, 103. For additional citations of Dildo see F. G. Cassidy and R. B. Le Page, *Dictionary of Jamaican English*, Cambridge, 1967, p. 149.
*Crowe's citation of Dildo anticipates Lane, *Directions*, 1775, 1810 (discussed on p. 96 above), and thus makes Dildo one of the earliest names recorded in the eighteenth century.

DINNYS POND 47–39, 53–25 (NTS Harbour Grace 1N/11W)
(NDNR 1N/11 1948), Denish Pond (Local name).
Denish = Dunnage, obs. dinnage. "Light material, as brushwood, mats and the like, stowed among and beneath the cargo of a vessel to keep it from injury by chafing or wet." Whitbourne 1623, p. 75 "Mats and dynnage under the Salt" (*OED*).
Men used to rind trees here to make denish for their schooners (Communication from Miss K. George, New Harbour).
Cp. ? DENNIS POINT (NTS Bay Bulls).
Cp. RINDERS POND (NTS Harbour Grace).

Dins Loneys (Stage or Cove) (St. John's Harbour) (Visscher c. 1680)
Denis Leucy (Mount and Page 1755). Pp. 68, 76–7.

DISTRESS COVE 46–55, 54–11 (NTS St. Bride's 1L/16E)
As set: Distress (*Population Returns* 1836), Distress Cove (Murray and Howley 1868).
Distress River (Murray and Howley 1868)
See ST. BRIDE'S (NTS St. Bride's). P. 109.

DIXON HILL 47–14, 53–57 (NTS Placentia 1N/4W)
Dixon's Hill (Jukes 1842), Cemetery Hill (Local name).
Dixon – ? an army officer. Pp. 115, 131, 159.

THE DOCK (Set.) 47–34, 53–15 (NTS Harbour Grace 1N/11W)
Dock (Census 1857).
Where vessels were hauled in for repairs.
On a use of dock as a place name in England: "Although Devonport, as a town, has grown up almost within the present century, the dockyard is more than two hundred years old. It was commenced in the reign of William the Third – a very

small affair, not one tithe the size of the present yard. Until 1823 both town and dockyard were known as 'Plymouth Dock' or simply as 'Dock' " (Page, p. 273). Pp. 118, 140.

DOCK COVE 47–28, 53–13 (NTS Holyrood 1N/6E)
(CHS 4573 1953). P. 140.

DOE HILLS 47–39, 53–49 (NTS Dildo 1N/12W) (Adm. 296 1863).

DOG COVE 47–05, 53–43 (NTS Placentia 1N/4E)
See CAPE DOG (NTS Placentia).

DOG HILL POND 47–50, 53–20 (NTS Heart's Content 1N/14W)
(NDNR 1N/14 1946).
Dog Hill, unnamed in NTS, is presumably the elevation (935 feet) east of the pond.

DOG POND 47–26, 52–57 (NTS Bay Bulls 1N/7W)
(NDNR Bay Bulls 1943).

DONNYS POND 47–21, 53–06 (NTS Holyrood 1N/6E)
(NDNR 1N/6 1943).

DONOVANS (Sta.) 47–32, 52–50 (NTS St. John's 1N/10W)
Anne's (1884), St. Anne's (both in M. Harvey 1900); Donovans.

Anne, St. Anne – "When our first railway was opened, in 1884, there was a station seven miles from St. John's, where there was only a solitary house. It seemed strange to have a station there, but there was a reason for it. The house belonged to Mrs Anne Fitzpatrick, a widow woman, who kept a very respectable place of entertainment for travellers and was much respected. It was long popular as a pleasure resort. The liquors were good, and the cooking unexceptionable. There were apartments where a game of cards could be enjoyed by evening parties and a hot supper served. The place was known simply as 'Anne's,' just like 'Kitty's' on the lake, and was much patronized by the young 'bloods' of St. John's. When it was said that anyone had gone to 'Anne's' for the afternoon, no further explanation was needed.

Thus it came to be important enough to have a station, and in the first time-tables it was entered as 'Anne's.' After a time, however, it was felt that the name was too short and meagre and did not sound well; and the conductor felt himself rather ridiculous in bawling out 'Anne's' as he thrust his head into the railway carriages. Frequently his announcement was greeted with peals of laughter and jokes innumerable.

Then some unknown person altered it to 'St. Anne's' in the timetable, and this was felt to be a distinct improvement. There was no intention of canonizing the respectable lady who conducted the establishment with much propriety. It was simply a matter of euphony in naming the station.

But now mark the trouble this simple, innocent change may give to the Judge Prowse's of a century hence, when they set to work to account for the name 'St. Anne's.' Very likely some of them will start the theory that there was a shrine and a holy well here, of which St. Anne was the patron saint, and that it was a place of resort for *pilgrims,* and that its well had healing virtues. This will be supported by many plausible arguments, and perhaps the early time-tables may be unearthed, proving how early it bore the name. But no one, unless this little paper should float down the stream of time so long – a most improbable event – will hit on the real origin of 'St. Anne's'; and yet how **simple and**

208 / *Place Names of the Avalon Peninsula*

natural it is once you know it." Harvey, "Etymology of the name 'Quidi Vidi'," communication from W. Kirwin).

Donovan – a former farmer in the locality. Pp. 131, 139.

DOUBLE BROOK 47–47, 53–15 (NTS Heart's Content 1N/14E and W)

DOUBLE POND 47–23, 53–21 (NTS Holyrood 1N/6W)
(NDNR 1N/6 1943).
Two parts of the pond are joined by a narrow channel.

DOUBLE ROAD POINT 46–56, 53–36 (NTS St. Mary's 1K/13E)
(Lane 1773). Pp. 86–88.

Downings (Stage or Cove) (St. John's Harbour) (Visscher c. 1680). Pp. 68, 76.

DOWNS (Generic). P. 145.

DOWNWARD HILL 47–20, 52–50 (NTS Bay Bulls 1N/7W) (CHS 4586 1944).
? Of the road leading into BAY BULLS.

DOYLES (Set.) 47–27, 52–46 (NTS Bay Bulls 1N/7W).
— DOYLES BRIDGE (Set.) 47–27, 52–47
(NDNR Bay Bulls 1943).
Pp. 131, 139.

DOYLES BROOK 47–42, 53–12 (NTS Harbour Grace 1N/11E)
(NDNR 1N/11 1948). P. 131.

DOYLES POND 47–25, 53–10 (NTS Holyrood 1N/6E)
(CHS 4573 1953). P. 131.

DRAKES POND 47–32, 53–12 (NTS Harbour Grace 1N/11E)
(CHS 4572 1954). Pp. 131, 159.

DROGHEDA ?['drakəti] 47–30, 53–18 (Unnamed in NTS Harbour Grace 1N/11W)
(Lovell 1881). P. 126.

DROOK (Generic). P. 146.

DROOK (Set.) 46–41, 53–15 (NTS Trepassey 1K/11E) (NDNR 1941).

— DROOK POINT 46–40, 53–15 (Adm. 2915 1864).
Pp. 140, 146.

DROOK (Unnamed in NTS Harbour Grace 1N/11E)
At CARBONEAR. P. 146.

DROOK 47–58, 53–01 (Unnamed in NTS Heart's Content 1N/14E)
At JOBS COVE. P. 146.

THE DROP (Hill) (Jukes 1842). P. 114.

DUCK ISLAND 47–44, 53–59 (NTS Dildo 1N/12W)

DUCK ISLANDS 47–46, 53–48 (NTS Sunnyside 1N/13W)
Duck Islets (*NP* 1952).

DUCK POND 47–27, 52–43 (NTS Bay Bulls 1N/7E)
(NDNR Bay Bulls 1943).

DUCK POND 47–34, 52–49 (NTS St. John's 1N/10W)
— LITTLE DUCK POND 47–35, 52–48

DUFF'S (CNR Stop) 47–27, 53–07 (NTS Holyrood 1N/6E)
(Census 1921). Pp. 131, 139.

DUNVILLE (Set.) 47–16, 53–54 (NTS Argentia 1N/5W)
? NE Arm (*Population Returns* 1836), NE gut (Wix 1836), Dunville (? c. 1888 with the opening of the railway).
Cp. SOUTHEAST ARM (NTS Placentia). Pp. 110, 131, 146.

EAST BROOK 47–32, 53–28 (NTS Harbour Grace 1N/11W)
(NDNR 1N/11 1948).

EAST GREEN ISLAND 47–26, 53–58 (NTS Argentia 1N/5W)
(Adm. 3266 1939). P. 85.

EAST HEAD 46–57, 53–51 (NTS St. Mary's 1K/13W)
Green Pt (Lane 1773), East Hd. (Adm. 2915 1864). P. 87.

EAST POND 47–24, 53–29 (NTS Holyrood 1N/6W)

Gazetteer and Index of Place Names: E / 209

(NDNR 1N/6 1943).
Cp. WEST POND.

EAST RIVER 47–20, 53–27 (NTS Holyrood 1N/6W)
(NDNR 1N/6 1943).
Tributary of COLINET RIVER. Cp. NORTH RIVER 47–20, 53–27.

EASTERN HEAD 46–37, 53–36 (NTS St. Shotts 1K/12E) (Lane 1773).
Cp. WESTERN HEAD. P. 88.

EASTERN HEAD 46–38, 53–08 (NTS Trepassey 1K/11E)
(Adm. 2915 1864).
Of LONG COVE 46–38, 53–08.
Adm. 2915 1864 has also Western Hd., unnamed in NTS.

EASTERN HEAD (Bell Island) 47–39, 52–55 (NTS St. John's 1N/10W)
(NLP 1951).
"the northeastern extremity of Bell Island" (NP 1952, p. 261).

EASTERN ISLAND POND 47–42, 53–18 (NTS Harbour Grace 1N/11W)
(NDNR 1N/11 1948).
Cp. WESTERN ISLAND POND.
Eastern, Western ? of BOWES LONG POND.

EASTERN ROCK 47–43, 53–08 (NTS Harbour Grace 1N/11E)
Easton's Rock (F. Page, Government Survey of Harbour Grace 1857), Eastern Rock (Imray, *Sailing Directory* 1873).
Easton – After the pirate, Peter Easton (fl. 1612–20), who made his headquarters at HARBOUR GRACE. DCB.
Cp. SHIP HEAD (NTS Harbour Grace).
Eastern – of HARBOUR GRACE ISLANDS.

EASTERN STEADY POND 47–31, 53–28 (NTS Harbour Grace 1N/11W)
(NDNR 1N/11 1948).
A Western Steady Pond is not named in NTS.

EASTERN WATERS 47–18, 53–25 (NTS Holyrood 1N/6W) (NDNR 1N/6 1943).
? East of COLINET RIVER. P. 143.

the Elbow (Guy 1612)
See TICKLE HARBOUR POINT (NTS Dildo). P. 59.

Ellis Point (Cook 1762 or Gilbert 1768)
See LIZZY POINT (NTS St. Mary's).
P. 83.

EMERALD VALE (Set.) 47–31, 53–18 (NTS Harbour Grace 1N/11W)
A farm, part of the estate of Charles Cozens (d. 1863), merchant of BRIGUS, who ? so named it.
(Census 1935).
Cp. MAKINSON, pp. 112–13. P. 146.

EMPTY BASKET COVE 47–29, 52–38 (NTS Bay Bulls 1N/7E)
(NDNR Bay Bulls 1943).
Cp. Vide Bidon Point 51–11, 55–42 (NTS St. Julien's 2M/4E).

English Cove (Bonnycastle 1842)
See HOLYROOD BAY (NTS St. Mary's) and CAPE ENGLISH (NTS St. Mary's).
Pp. 30–1.

ENGLISH COVE 47–29, 53–13 (NTS Holyrood 1N/6E)
As set: Colliers English Cove (Census 1857); (Murray and Howley 1868). Pp. 118, 131.

English Mistaken Point
See MISTAKEN POINT (NTS Trepassey).
Pp. 70–1.

EZEKIEL'S ['izikilz] COVE 47–26, 53–11 (NTS Holyrood 1N/6E)
(NDNR 1N/6 1943).
Family name at HARBOUR MAIN, borne by a Jewish family of Devon, the best-known members of which were Abraham (1757–1806), miniature-painter and scientific optician, and Solomon (1781–1867), writer. DNB.
P. 159.

FAIR HAVEN 47–31, 53–54 (NTS Dildo 1N/12W)

Famishgut (Lane 1772).
— FAIR HAVEN (Set.) 47–32, 53–54
  Famish Gut (Wix 1836,
  Population Returns 1836),
  Famish Cove (Census 1874),
  Fairhaven (Proclamation
  29 June 1940).
— FAIR HAVEN ISLAND 47–31, 53–55
— FAIR HAVEN POINT
Cp. GREAT PINCHGUT 47–36, 53–55
(NTS Dildo) under PINCHGUT.
Pp. 6, 84–5, 104, 105, 141.

FAIRYS POND 47–19, 53–14 (NTS
Holyrood 1N/6E)
(NDNR 1N/6 1943). P. 131.

FALSE CAPE 46–49, 54–11 (NTS
St. Bride's 1L/16E)
(Adm. 2915 1864).
"so named because before the
erection of the lighthouse on cape
St. Mary it was not infrequently
misaken for that point" (Imray,
Sailing Directory 1873, p. 81).

FALSE CAPE 46–49, 53–40 (NTS
St. Mary's 1K/13E) (Lane 1773).
? Likely to be mistaken for CAPE
ENGLISH 46–47, 53–40 (NTS
St. Mary's). P. 88.

Famish Cove (Set.) (Census 1874).
Famishgut (Lane 1772)
See FAIR HAVEN (NTS Dildo).

FAMIT or FARMINT (Cove) (Baccalieu
Island)
Local usage for Falmouth.
See BRISTA.

Farilham (Verrazano 1529)
See FERRYLAND (NTS Ferryland).
Pp. 27–8, 31, 38.

Fausse B[aie] (Courcelle 1675)
See CRIPPLE COVE (NTS Trepassey).
P. 50.

FEATHER POINT 47–42, 53–10 (NTS
Harbour Grace 1N/11E)
(Lane, *Directions* 1775, 1810).

? Shape of feature.
— Feather Rock
  (Lane 1774). Pp. 92, 95.

FENELONS POND 47–23, 53–07 (NTS
Holyrood 1N/6E) (NDNR 1N/6 1943).
? After Maurice Fenelon (1834–97)
b. Co. Carlow, Ireland; schoolmaster,
politician and bookseller in
ST. JOHN'S. (Mosdell, p. 40). P. 131.

FERGUS ISLAND 47–36, 53–13 (NTS
Harbour Grace 1N/11E)
Fergus Islet (Imray, *Sailing Directory*
1873). P. 131.

FERMEUSE (Set.) 46–59, 52–58 (NTS
Renews 1K/15W)
Fremouse (Beaudoin 1697), Fermeuse
(*Population Returns* 1836).
— FERMEUSE HARBOUR 46–58, 52–55
  R fermoso (Reinel 1519, "Havre
  Catalan" 1520–34), Rio
  fremoze ("Vallard" 1547),
  R. fremoso (Desceliers 1550,
  Homem 1568, Dee 1580),
  Fermous (Hayes 1583 in
  Hakluyt), Formosa
  (Whitbourne 1588–1622,
  Mason 1626), Firmoose (Yonge
  1663–70), Fermuse (Robinson
  1669, Detcheverry 1689),
  Frinouse ("Belle Carte du
  Dépôt" c. 1682), Frimouze
  (Chaviteau 1698), fermeuse
  ("Dépôt 132.2.10" 1706),
  Fremous (Bowen 1747),
  Fermowes Harbour (Cook and
  Lane 1770 [1775]B), Fermeuse
  Harbour (Imray, *Sailing
  Directory* 1873).
  Cp. Frinouse (Champlain 1612).
Pp. 28, 30, 33, 61, 66, 68–9, 79, 123.

FERRYLAND (Set.) 47–02, 52–53 (NTS
Ferryland 1N/2W) Forillon
(Beaudoin 1697), Ferryland
(Beauclerk *CSP* 1730).
— FERRYLAND HARBOUR
  Farrillon (Leigh 1597 in
  Hakluyt), Farillon or Fer-land

(Guy to Slany 1610 in Purchas), Feriland (Guy to Slany 1612 in Purchas), Ferryland (Yonge 1663-70, Robinson 1669), Freizeland (Robinson 1670 in *CSP*), Ferre Land (*CSP* 1674/5), Feryland (Southwood 1675, Hack ? 1677), Feriland (Visscher c. 1680, Thornton 1689B), Ferryland-Port or Harbour (*English Pilot. The Fourth Book* 1689), Fair Ellen (Campbell 1705 in *CSP*), Foreland H (Kitchin 1758), Ferryland Harbour (Lane 1773), Ferryland Port (Mount and Page 1780).

— FERRYLAND HEAD 47-01, 52-51 Farilham (Verrazano 1529), Farilhom (Freire 1546), Forillon ("Vallard" 1547, Desceliers 1550); thereafter Farilham and variants in Portuguese maps and Ferillon, Forillon and variants in French maps; Ferriland (Mason 1626), Ferryland heads (Yonge map c. 1663), Ferryland head (Southwood 1675), Ferriland des Anglois (Coronelli 1689), Foreland head (Popple 1733), Cap Foreland (Buache 1736), Foreland Hd (Kitchin 1762), Ferryland hd (Cook 1763).

— Ferryland Pool (*English Pilot. The Fourth Book* 1689).

Pp. 6, 27-8, 31, 38, 40, 46, 61, 66, 68, 79, 82, 84, 123, 124, 129, 140.

FIELD (Generic). P. 145.

FINNIES POND 47-22, 53-04 (NTS Holyrood 1N/6E) (NDNR 1N/6 1943). P. 131.

FIRST POND 46-40, 53-05 (NTS Trepassey 1K/11E) (CHS 4576 1950). Of river, unnamed in NTS, which enters the Atlantic Ocean ¼ mile west of CAPE RACE.

FIRST POND 47-26, 53-09 (NTS Holyrood 1N/6E) (CHS 4573 1953). First of three ponds south of CHAPEL COVE (Set.) 47-26, 53-09. Cp. SECOND POND 47-25, 53-09, THIRD POND 47-25, 53-09.

FIRST POND 47-28, 52-44 (NTS Bay Bulls 1N/7E) (NDNR Bay Bulls 1943). Of the river which enters PETTY HARBOUR.

FIRST POND 47-32, 53-23 (NTS Harbour Grace 1N/11W) (NDNR 1N/11 1948). Of a tributary, unnamed in NTS, of SHEARSTOWN BROOK. Cp. SECOND POND 47-32, 53-24.

FIRST SALMON POND 47-23, 53-15 (NTS Holyrood 1N/6E) (NDNR 1N/6 1943). Of SALMON RIVER 47-24, 53-13. Cp. SECOND SALMON POND 47-22, 53-14. See AVONDALE formerly Salmon Cove.

FISHER'S POINT 46-40, 53-04 (NTS Trepassey 1K/11E) (CHS 4576 1950). P. 159.

FITTERS COVE 47-55, 53-22 (NTS Heart's Content 1N/14W) (USHO no. 73 1942), Vitters Cove (Newfoundland 1955). The West Country voicing of an initial fricative [f] > [v] occurs, for example, in Newfoundland speech in such words as fir, far. P. 159.

FIVE MILE POND EAST 47-21, 53-04 (NTS Holyrood 1N/6E) (NDNR 1N/6 1943).

— FIVE MILE POND WEST 47-20, 53-04 (NDNR 1N/6 1943). Approximate distance from HOLYROOD on the WITLESS BAY

LINE. Cp. FOUR MILE POND 47–20, 53–06.

Flagstaffe Harbour (Guy 1612) See GREAT MOSQUITO COVE (NTS Sunnyside) under MOSQUITO. Pp. 8, 59, 111.

Flakey Downs (Hills) (Jukes 1842). Pp. 114, 145.

FLAMBRO HEAD 48–01, 52–58 (NTS Bay de Verde 2C/2W)
(Hack ? 1677).
"a black steep point" (*English Pilot. The Fourth Book* 1689).
Cp. Robinhood Bay (NTS Trinity 2C/6W), ? ROBIN HOOD BAY (NTS St. John's), ? SKERWINK POINT (NTS Old Perlican). Pp. 11, 46, 75–6.

FLAT HILL 47–42, 53–52 (NTS Dildo 1N/12W) (Adm. 296 1863).

FLAT POINT 47–19, 52–48 (NTS Bay Bulls 1N/7W)
(CHS 4586 1944).

FLAT ROCK 47–42, 52–42 (unnamed in NTS St. John's 1N/10E) ("Blathwayt" c. 1630–40).
— FLAT ROCK (Set.) 47–42, 52–42 (NTS St. John's 1N/10E) (*Population Returns* 1836).
— FLAT ROCK BAY
Flat Rock cove (*NLP* 1951).
— FLAT ROCK POINT
Low Black Pt or Torbay North Pt (Mount and Page 1780), North Point of Torbay (Flat Rock) (Lane, *Directions* 1775, 1810), Flat Rock Point (Imray, *Sailing Directions* 1862).
Pp. 65, 90, 98.

FLAT ROCK (Set.) 47–45, 53–11 (NTS Heart's Content 1N/14E) (Census 1857). Pp. 119.

FLAT ROCKS 47–47, 53–47 (NTS Sunnyside 1N/13W) (Imray 1862).

FLEECE COVE 47–26, 53–49 (NTS Argentia 1N/5W)
(Adm. 3266 1939).

FLINGS BIG POND 47–43, 53–18 (NTS Harbour Grace 1N/11W)
(NDNR 1N/11 1948).
? For Flinn.
— FLINGS LONG POND 47–44, 53–19 (NDNR 1N/11 1948).
— LITTLE FLINGS POND 47–43, 53–18
(NDNR 1N/11 1948).
Note transposition of Qualifier and Specific.

FLINN RIVER 47–10, 53–39 (NTS Placentia 1N/4E)
(*NLP* 1929). P. 131.

FLOWER HILL (Street) (St. John's). P. 148.

FOLLY (Generic). Pp. 119, 145.

FOLLY POINT 46–58, 52–54 (NTS Renews 1K/15W) (Adm. 376 1927).

FOLLY ROCKS 47–46, 53–09 (NTS Heart's Content 1N/14E)
(Adm. 296 1868).
Cp. MAD ROCK 47–45, 53–10.

FOREST FIELD (Set.) 47–09, 53–27 (NTS St. Catherine's 1N/3W). P. 145.

FOREST POND 47–27, 52–45 (NTS Bay Bulls 1N/7W)
(NDNR Bay Bulls 1943).
— FOREST POND HILL
(USHO 2139 1943).

FOREST POND 47–46, 53–12 (NTS Heart's Content 1N/14E)
(NDNR 1N/14 1946).

Forillon ("Vallard" 1547) See FERRYLAND (NTS Ferryland). P. 38.

Formosa (Mason 1626) See FERMEUSE (NTS Renews). Pp. 12, 61.

FORT (Generic). P. 147.

FORT AMHERST 47–33, 52–41 (NTS St. John's 1N/10E)

Fort Amherst on South Head
(Lane, *Directions* 1775, 1810).
Pp. 94, 147.
— FORT AMHERST LIGHTHOUSE.
P. 148.
Fort Charles (St. John's Harbour)
See Fort Frederick. Pp. 94–5.
Fort Frederick (St. John's Harbour)
? So[uth] Forte (Thornton 1689B),
Frederick's Battery (Lane,
Directions 1775, 1810; Imray
Sailing Directions 1862), Fort
Frederick (Tocque 1878). Pp. 77,
94–5, 147.
FORT TOWNSHEND (St. John's).
Pp. 102, 147.
FORT WILLIAM (St. John's)
(Charlevoix 1708), The Old Fort
(Cook 1762 or Gilbert 1768), "the
Old Garrison, called also
Fort William" (Lane, *Directions*
1775, 1810).
Pp. 83, 94, 102, 147.
FOUR CORNER POND 47–39, 53–15
(NTS Harbour Grace 1N/11E)
FOUR MILE POND 47–20, 53–06 (NTS
Holyrood 1N/6E) (NDNR 1N/6 1943).
Approximate distance from
HOLYROOD on the WITLESS BAY LINE.
Cp. FIVE MILE POND EAST, 47–21,
53–04, FIVE MILE POND WEST 47–20,
53–04.
Fourt (Bay Bulls) (Fitzhugh 1693)
i.e. Fort. P. 78.
FOURTEEN ISLAND POND 47–50, 53–15
(NTS Heart's Content 1N/14W)
(NDNR 1N/14 1946).
FOURTH POND 47–21, 53–27 (NTS
Holyrood 1N/6W)
(NDNR 1N/6 1943).
Of NORTH RIVER, tributary of
COLINET RIVER.
FOURTH POND 47–29, 52–46 (NTS
Bay Bulls 1N/7W)
(NDNR Bay Bulls 1943).

Of the river which enters PETTY
HARBOUR.
FOURTH POND 47–30, 53–13 (NTS
Harbour Grace 1N/11E)
(CHS 4572 1954).
Between BRIGUS and GEORGETOWN.
First and Second Ponds are
unnamed in NTS.
Cp. THIRD POND 47–31, 53–13.
FOWLERS BROOK 47–32, 52–57 (NTS
St. John's 1N/10W). P. 159.
FOX (Specific). In older place names
Fox is probably the animal, in
recent place names the family name.
The occurrence of foxes in
Newfoundland is recorded in
Edward Hayes's "Report of the
Voyage ... 1583 by Sir Humphrey
Gilbert," in Hakluyt, *Voyages and
Documents*, p. 263.
FOX COVE 47–44, 53–50 (NTS Dildo
1N/12W)
Fox Harbour (Jukes 1842). P. 113.
FOX HARBOUR 47–19, 53–55 (NTS
Argentia 1N/5W) (Lane 1772). P. 84.
— FOX HARBOUR (Set.)
(*Population Returns* 1836).
A Proclamation of 15 July 1918
renaming Fox Harbour
St. Bernard seems to have been
a dead letter.
? A shift name from FOX ISLAND
47–21, 54–00 below.
P. 132.
FOX ISLAND 47–13, 52–50 (NTS
Ferryland 1N/2W)
Foxes Island (*English Pilot The
Fourth Book* 1689), Fox Island
(Lane 1773). Pp. 35, 73.
FOX ISLAND 47–21, 54–00 (NTS
Argentia 1N/5W)
I. du Renard (Detcheverry 1689),
I au renard ("Dépôt 132.2.10"
1796), I aux Renards (Buache
1736), Foxes Isle (Bowen 1747),
Fox Island (Lane 1772). P. 51.

214 / *Place Names of the Avalon Peninsula*

FOX KNOB (Hill) 46–51, 53–59 (NTS St. Mary's 1K/13W)
Fox Nob (Adm. 2915 1864), Fox Knob (CHS 4622 ? 1953). The generic is perhaps unique in Newfoundland. Pp. 131, 145.

FOX MARSH (Flag Stop CNR) 47–24, 53–23 (NTS Holyrood 1N/6W) (CNR 1953).
— FOX PONDS 47–24, 53–24 (NDNR 1N/6 1943).
Pp. 6, 143.

FOX POINT 47–56, 53–04 (NTS Heart's Content 1N/14E)

FOX POND 47–40, 53–20 (NTS Harbour Grace 1N/11W) (NDNR 1N/11 1948).

FOX POND 47–41, 53–21 (NTS Harbour Grace 1N/11W) (NDNR 1N/11 1948).

FOX PONDS
See FOX MARSH.

FOXTRAP (Set.) 47–31, 52–59 (NTS St. John's 1N/10W) (Census 1857). Millais, p. 222 has an illustration of a foxtrap. P. 117.
— FOXTRAP RIVER 47–31, 53–00 (NTS St. John's 1N/10W, Bay Bulls 1N/7W)

Fraische oüatre (Beaudoin 1697)
See FRESHWATER (NTS Heart's Content). P. 80.

FRANKS POND 47–08, 53–12 (NTS St. Catherine's 1N/3E) (Newfoundland 1941).

FRAPEAU POINT 46–56, 53–38 (NTS St. Mary's 1K/13E)
(Lane 1773), Crapeaud (M. F. Howley XXVIII, *NQ*, December 1909).
For Crap(e)aud, toad, sc. frog, as a sailor's nickname for a Frenchman. "Well, d'ye see we were cruising off the Spanish coast, and we chased a whacking French privateer into a beautiful bay ... The skipper was determined to have Johnny Crapoh who ... presented his broadside of ten long brass nines right at us" ("Greenwich Hospital," in Barker, M. H. (ed.), *The Old Sailor's Jolly Boat* (London, 1844), pp. 68–9). Pp. 53, 86, 88.

Frederick's Battery (Lane, *Directions* 1775, 1810)
See Fort Frederick (St. John's Harbour). P. 94.

FRENCH COVE 47–37, 53–13 (NTS Harbour Grace 1N/11E)
French's Cove (Blackmore 1865). P. 159.

French Mistaken Point.
See MISTAKEN POINT (NTS Trepassey). Pp. 70–1.

FRENCHMANS COVE 46–45, 53–02 (NTS Trepassey 1K/11E, Biscay Bay River 1K/14E)
Frenchman Cove (Adm. 2915 1864).
"so called because a French vessel too stupid to go into Chance Cove [CHANCE COVE 46–45, 53–00] ... was lost there" (M. F. Howley, XXVI, *NQ*, July 1909). Pp. 5–6.

Frenchman's Island (Wix 1836)
See ? MC KAY ISLAND (NTS Sunnyside). P. 105.

FRESHWATER (Specific). Pp. 28, 71.

FRESHWATER (Set.) 47–15, 53–59 (NTS Argentia 1N/5W) (*Population Returns* 1836). P. 53.
— FRESHWATER COVE
Freshwater Bay (Cook 1762). P. 82.

FRESHWATER (PARSONVILLE P.O.) (Set.) (Bell Island) 47–36, 53–01 (NTS Harbour Grace 1N/11E)
As feature: South Bay (Mount and Page 1780); Freshwater (Census 1874). Pp. 97, 146, 150.

Freshwater (Set.) (Middle Cove) (Census 1857). P. 116.

FRESHWATER (Set.) 47–45, 53–11 (NTS Heart's Content 1N/14E) Fraische oüatre (Beaudoin 1697), Freshwater Cove (Thoresby 1796), Fresh water (*Population Returns* 1836).
— FRESHWATER COVE
Freshwater (Lane 1774).
Pp. 80, 92, 119.

FRESHWATER BAY 46–40, 53–15 (NTS Trepassey 1K/11E)
? Bay de Mores (Robinson 1669), Freshwater Bay (Newfoundland Highroads Commission, *Road Map of the Peninsula of Avalon* 1930). P. 49.

Freshwater B. (Southwood 1675) See SEAL COVE (NTS Renews). Pp. 73, 74.

Freshwater Bay (Cook 1762 or Gilbert 1768)
See LANCE COVE (NTS Ferryland). P. 84.

FRESHWATER BAY 47–08, 52–52 (NTS Ferryland 1N/2W)
(Southwood 1675). P. 73.

FRESHWATER BAY 47–33, 52–41 (NTS St. John's 1N/10E)
Frinouse (Champlain 1612), Frinquie (Laet 1625), Frinouse (Champlain 1632), Frinquise (Jansson 1636), Frinouse (Blaeu 1662), Freshwater B. (Southwood 1675), B d'eau douce (Robert de Vaugondy 1749), Freshwater B. (Lane 1774), Freshwater Cove (Bonnycastle 1842), Freshwater Bay (Imray, *Sailing Directions* 1862). Pp. 42, 73.
— FRESHWATER BAY POND 47–32, 52–41

Fres[h]water Cove (Seller c. 1671) ? 47–20, 52–44 (Unnamed in NTS Bay Bulls 1N/7E). P. 71.

FRESHWATER COVE (Bell Island) 47–39, 52–56 (NTS St. John's 1N/10W)

FRESHWATER POINT 46–38, 53–14 (NTS Trepassey 1K/11E) (Adm. 2915 1864).
"In the cove north of this point there is a waterfall 100 feet high" (Imray, *Sailing Directory* 1873).

FRESHWATER POINT 47–04, 52–54 (NTS Ferryland 1N/2W) (USHO 0618 1941).

FRESHWATER POND 47–41, 52–49 (NTS St. John's 1N/10W)

FRESHWATER POND 47–51, 53–26 (NTS Heart's Content 1N/14W)

FRESHWATER RIVER 46–39, 53–06 (NTS Trepassey 1K/11E) (CHS 4576 1950).

Fretum Placentiae (Mason 1626) See PLACENTIA BAY. P. 61.

Frinouse (Champlain 1612)
See FRESHWATER BAY (NTS St. John's), TORBAY (NTS St. John's). Pp. 42, 73.

Fromes (Robinson 1669). P. 70.

FUNNELL POND 47–41, 52–49 (NTS St. John's 1N/10W)
Funnell – ? English family name of Sussex (Guppy, p. 380), not found in Newfoundland.
? For funnel – after the outlet to FRESHWATER POND 47–41, 52–49.

GALLOWS (Specific) Captain Hugh Bonfoy, R.N., governor of Newfoundland 1752-5, "ordered outport J.P.s to erect gallowses on the public wharves in their districts, for the execution of persons found guilty of robbery or felony, October 12, 1754." (Devine and O'Mara, p. 193). For discussion and rejection of other meanings of gallows (i) braces, suspenders, (ii) "a sort of 'horse' or trestle made of rough rails or starrigans ... used for drying nets on," see M. F. Howley, xix, xx, NQ, October, December 1907.

GALLOWS COVE 47–16, 52–49 (NTS Bay Bulls 1N/7W)
(M. F. Howley, xxiv, NQ, December 1908).

GALLOWS COVE 47–27, 53–09 (NTS Holyrood 1N/6E)
(CHS 4573 1953).
Gallows Cove (Brigus)
(M. F. Howley, xix, NQ, December 1907).

GALLOWS COVE PONDS 47–41, 52–44 (NTS St. John's 1N/10E)
After Gallows Cove, unnamed in NTS: "Between FLAT ROCK and TORBAY is a small cove called Gallows Cove" (M. F. Howley, xxii, NQ, July 1908).

Gallows Hill (St. John's) (1759). P. 83.

GANDER POND 47–28, 53–27 (NTS Holyrood 1N/6W)
(NDNR 1N/6 1943).
Cp. GOOSE POND 47–26, 53–28.

GANNET POINT 47–48, 53–27 (NTS Heart's Content 1N/14W)
(USHO No. 73 1942).
Gannet – *Morus bassanus* (Peters and Burleigh, p. 65).

GARLEP POINT 47–55, 53–23 (NTS Heart's Content 1N/14W)
Gorlob pt (Southwood 1675, Thornton 1689B). Other citations p. 72.

GARRISON (Generic). P. 147.

GASKIERS (Set.) 46–53, 53–36 (NTS St. Mary's 1K/13E)
Gaskier (Census 1857), Gaskier's (Smallwood 1940), Gascoigne (Newfoundland 1941, 1949), Gaskiers (Newfoundland 1955).
— GASKIERS BAY 46–54, 53–37.
Pp. 51–2, 119, 139.

GASTERS (Set.) 47–27, 53–10 (NTS Holyrood 1N/6E)
(*Population Returns* 1836), Gasters (Bonnycastle 1842), Gasters (Census 1857), Gaskiers (Electors 1955).
— GASTERS BAY 47–27, 53–11
Gastries Bay (Murray and Howley 1868), Castries Bay (Imray, *Sailing Directory* 1873), Gasters bay (NLP II 1953).
— Gastries [point]
(M. F. Howley, xvii, NQ, 1907).
Pp. 52, 64, 106, 115, 118, 138, 139.

Gawgel's Cove (Thoresby 1796)
See ? JUGGLER'S COVE (NTS Harbour Grace). P. 98.

GEAR POND 47–27, 52–54 (NTS Bay Bulls 1N/7W)
(NDNR Bay Bulls 1943). P. 159.

GENTLEMAN POINT 47–05, 52–54 (NTS Ferryland 1N/2W)
(USHO 0618 1941). P. 159.

GEORGE NORRIS POND 49–19, 52–55 (NTS Bay Bulls 1N/7W)
(NDNR Bay Bulls 1943). P. 163.

GEORGES PEAK 47–23, 53–08 (NTS Holyrood 1N/6E) (CHS 4573 1953).

GEORGES POND 47–32, 52–47 (NTS St. John's 1N/10W)

GEORGES POND 47–34, 52–41 (NTS St. John's 1N/10E)
(Bonnycastle 1842). P. 115.

GEORGETOWN (Set.) 47–30, 53–14 (NTS Harbour Grace 1N/11E)
(Census 1891).
? After George Gushue, MHA

GIBBET HILL 47–41, 53–15 (NTS Harbour Grace 1N/11E)
(CHS 4590 1943).
Site of gibbet in early nineteenth century.

Gibet Hill (St. John's) (Cook 1762 or Gilbert 1768). P. 83.

GIBRALTAR ROCK 47–14, 54–03
Giberalter Rocks (Gaudy 1715), Gibraltar (Senex 1728), Gibralter Rock (Lane 1772).

"Gibraltar Rock, a one-fathom patch lies 1¼ miles west-southwestward of the light-tower on Verde Point [POINT VERDE (NTS Ship Cove)]" (*NP*, p. 49). P. 82.

GILES POND 47–39, 53–27 (NTS Harbour Grace 1N/11W) (NDNR 1N/11 1948). P. 159.

GLADNEYS ARM 47–36, 52–48 (NTS St. John's 1N/10W)
Part of WINDSOR LAKE
English family name. P. 159.

Glam Cove (Yonge 1663–70)
See CLAM COVE (NTS Trepassey). Pp. 66–7.

Glamorgan (Mason 1626). Pp. 12, 62.

Gleeson's Cove (Set.) (*Population Returns* 1836). P. 108.

GLENDALE (Set.) 47–31, 52–48 (NTS St. John's 1N/10W). Pp. 140, 146.

GOAT COVE 47–36, 52–53 (NTS St. John's 1N/10W)
As set: (Census 1911).
— GOAT COVE BROOK

GODDENS POND 47–48, 53–14 (NTS Heart's Content 1N/14E) (NDNR 1N/14 1946). P. 159.

GODDENVILLE (Set.) 47–36, 53–21 (NTS Harbour Grace 1N/11W) (Census 1901). Pp. 146, 159.

GOLDEN BAY 46–49, 54–09 (NTS St. Bride's 1L/16E)
As set: (*Population Returns* 1836). P. 109.

Golden Groue (Mason 1626). P. 61.

GOLDEN GULLIES 47–25, 53–22 (NTS Holyrood 1N/6W) (NDNR 1N/6 1943).
? From the presence of marsh-marigolds.
Cp. MAKINSON (GOULDS P.O.) (NTS Harbour Grace), pp. 112–13.

GOLDMINE HEAD 48–10, 52–55 (NTS Bay de Verde 2C/2W) (Newfoundland 1941).

Probably the site of small mining operations in the gold-bearing quartz veins in the area. See Murray and Howley 1868, 167 on gold in the AVALON PENINSULA.

the Golds (Jukes 1842)
See MAKINSON (GOULDS P.O.) (NTS Harbour Grace). P. 112.

GOOBIES (Set.) 47–56, 53–58 (NTS Sunnyside 1N/13W)
— GOOBIES SIDING (Set.) 47–57, 53–58 (Smallwood 1940).
Pp. 139, 148, 160.

GOOSE (Specific) Commonly ? the Eastern Canada Goose, *Branta canadensis canadensis*, described in Peters and Burleigh, pp. 82–5.

GOOSE COVE 47–52, 53–44 (NTS Sunnyside 1N/13E)

GOOSE ISLAND 47–02, 52–52 (NTS Ferryland 1N/2W)
? de los patos (Santa Cruz 1545), Goose I. (Southwood 1675).
Cp. COLDEAST POINT (NTS Ferryland, CALVERT BAY (NTS Ferryland). Pp. 31, 35, 68.

Goose Isl[and] (Seller c. 1671)
See GREAT ISLAND (NTS Ferryland). Pp. 71, 89.

GOOSE ISLAND 47–45, 54–00 (NTS Dildo 1N/12W, Harbour Buffett 1M/9E)

GOOSE POND 47–27, 53–28 (NTS Holyrood 1N/6W) (NDNR 1N/6 1943).
Cp. GANDER POND 47–28, 53–27.

GOOSE POND 47–27, 53–31 (NTS Argentia 1N/5E)
Quemo Gospen (Adm. 232a 1870), Goose Pond (Newfoundland 1941). P. 24.

GOOSE POND also occurs at 47–03, 53–56 (NTS Placentia 1N/4W) (Adm. 232a 1870), 47–21, 53–11 (NTS Holyrood 1N/6E) (CHS 4573 1953), 47–25, 52–46 (NTS Bay Bulls 1N/7W)

(NDNR Bay Bulls 1943), 47-30, 53-17
(NTS Holyrood 1N/6W) (CHS 4573
1953), 47-36, 53-19 (NTS Harbour
Grace 1N/11W) (CHS 4572 1954),
47-40, 52-45 (NTS St. John's
1N/10W).

GOOSE STEADIES 47-18, 53-27 (NTS
Holyrood 1N/6W)
(NDNR 1N/6 1943). P. 143.

GOOSEBERRY COVE 47-04, 54-06 (NTS
Ship Cove 1M/1E)
? Borrell (Whitbourne 1588-
1622), Goose Cove (Adm. 2915
1864), Gooseberry Cove (Murray
and Howley 1868), Gooseberry
(Goose) Cove (NLP I 1951).
— GOOSEBERRY COVE (Set.)
(Population Returns 1836).
Pp. 42, 109-10.

GOULDS (Set.) 47-29, 52-46 (NTS
Bay Bulls 1N/7W)
(Census 1857). Pp. 112, 119.

GOULDS P.O.
See MAKINSON (GOULDS P.O.) (NTS
Harbour Grace)
A suggestion that the settlement be
renamed Hueville was rejected by
the Nomenclature Board in 1910.
— GOULDS BIG POND 47-25, 53-21
(NTS Holyrood 1N/6W)
(NDNR 1N/6 1943).
— GOULDS BROOK 47-31, 53-18
(NTS Holyrood 1N/6W, Harbour
Grace 1N/11W)
(Murray and Howley 1872).
— GOULDS POND 47-25, 53-23 (NTS
Holyrood 1N/6W)
(NDNR 1N/6 1943).
— GOULDS ROAD (Set.) 47-30,
53-19

GRACES GULLY 47-25, 53-16 (NTS
Holyrood 1N/6W)
(NDNR 1N/6 1943). P. 131.

Grand Beach (Lane 1774).
See BELL BEACH (NTS St. John's).
P. 90.

Grand Golfe ou Frinouse (Sanson
1656)
See TORBAY (NTS St. John's). P. 42.

GRAND POND 47-27, 53-22 (NTS
Holyrood 1N/6W) (NDNR 1N/6 1943).
Grand = ? big.

GRANNY COVE 47-19, 53-58 (NTS
Argentia 1N/5W)
(Adm. 2829 1877). P. 131.

GRASSY (Specific) ? Indicative of good
pasture.

GRASSY GULLY 47-15, 53-21 (NTS
Holyrood 1N/6W) (NDNR 1N/6 1943).

GRASSY GULLY 47-21, 53-09 (NTS
Holyrood 1N/6E) (NDNR 1N/6 1943).

GRASSY ISLAND 47-30, 53-57 (NTS
Dildo 1N/12W)

GRASSY ISLAND 47-42, 53-58 (NTS
Dildo 1N/12W)

GRASSY ISLANDS 47-27, 53-57 (NTS
Argentia 1N/5W) (Adm. 232a 1870).
Of the BRINE ISLANDS group.

GRASSY POINT 47-26, 53-53 (NTS
Argentia 1N/5W) (Adm. 3266 1939).

GRASSY POND 47-35, 53-19 (NTS
Harbour Grace 1N/11W)
(CHS 4572 1954).

GRATES COVE (Set.) 48-10, 52-56 (NTS
Bay de Verde)
(Population Returns 1836).
"First founded probably 1790, by
three families from Lower Island
Cove and one from Old Perlican,
though undoubtedly it was
frequented by fishermen long before
this" (Smallwood 1941, p. 100).
— GRATES POINT 48-10, 52-57
the Grates (Guy 1612) ... Grates
P (Fitzhugh 1693), Point of the
Grates (English Pilot. The
Fourth Book 1689), Point of
Grates (Cook and Lane 1770
[1775]A).
Pp. 18, 41, 58, 90.

GRATTONS COVE (Bell Island 47–37, 53–00 (NTS Harbour Grace 1N/11E) (CHS 4566 1952). P. 131.

GRAVEN BEACH 46–58, 53–32 (NTS St. Mary's 1K/13E)
Graving Bank (M. F. Howley 1909.)
"It is a sandy spit on which the French in olden times beached their boats. The name is derived from the French word Grève (pronounced Grave or grahve)" (M. F. Howley XXVIII, *NQ*, December 1909).

Grave v.² from *grave* [of obscure origin; possibly from Fr. *grave* = *grève* – shore]. To clean (a ship's bottom) by burning off the accretions, and paying it over with tar or some composition, while aground on a beach, or placed in a specially-constructed dock. *OED*.

The form graven appears to be the cartographer's phonetic rendering of the local popular pronunciation of graving, found similarly in POUNDEN COVE (NTS Trepassey) and WATERN COVE (NTS Trepassey).
See PORT DE GRAVE, pp. 47–8.

GREAT BARASWAY (Set.) (NTS Ship Cove)
See BARACHOIS.

G[reat] Barrysway (Lane 1773)
See BIG BARACHOIS (NTS Placentia). under BARACHOIS. P. 86.

great Belile (Guy 1612).
See BELL ISLAND (NTS St. John's and Harbour Grace). P. 58.

GREAT COLINET ISLAND
See COLINET (NTS Placentia).

GREAT COVE 47–32, 53–11 (NTS Harbour Grace 1N/11E)
(CHS 4572 1954).
— GREAT HEAD 47–32, 53–12
? High Ragged Pt (Mount and Page 1780).
Pp. 97–8.

GREAT GULCH (River) 46–52, 54–04 (NTS St. Bride's 1L/16E)
(Adm. 2915 1864).
— LITTLE GULCH (River) 46–52. 54–03
(Adm. 2915 1864).
Tributaries of LANCE RIVER (NTS St. Bride's), each named from the ravine through which it flows.
P. 141.

GREAT GULL POND 47–06, 53–51 (NTS Placentia 1N/4W) (DND Placentia 1942.)
? After the Great Black-backed Gull, *Larus marinus*, known locally as the Saddle-back, a common resident in the ARGENTIA area. (Peters and Burleigh, pp. 224–5).

GREAT ISLAND 47–11, 52–49 (NTS Ferryland 1N/2W)
Goose Isl (Seller c. 1671) ... Great Island (Lane 1773), Great I or Goose I (Mount and Page 1780).
One of les isles d'espoir (Alfonse 1544). See SPEAR ISLAND.
Great – compared with the other islands in the group. Pp. 71, 89.

GREAT MOSQUITO COVE (NTS Sunnyside)
See MOSQUITO.

GREAT PINCHGUT (NTS Dildo)
See PINCHGUT.

GREAT POND 47–40, 52–46 (NTS St. John's 1N/10W)

Great Salmon River (Set.) (*Population Returns* 1836)
See ? ST. CATHERINE'S (Set.) (NTS St. Catherine's),
SALMONIER RIVER (NTS St. Catherine's).

GREAT SOUTHERN HARBOUR (NTS Sunnyside)
See SOUTHERN HARBOUR (Set.) NTS Dildo).

GREBE COVE 47–40, 53–12 (NTS

Harbour Grace 1N/11E)
(CHS 4572 1954).
? After one of the family of grebes, found occasionally in Newfoundland (Peters and Burleigh, pp. 49–51).

GREEN COVE 47–47, 53–47 (NTS Sunnyside 1N/13W) (NP 1952).

GREEN HEAD 47–37, 53–16 (NTS Harbour Grace 1N/11W) (Adm. 296 1868), Green point (Imray, *Sailing Directory* 1873).

GREEN HEAD 47–41, 53–48 (NTS Dildo 1N/12W)

GREEN HILLS 46–54, 54–07 (NTS St. Bride's 1L/16E) (Adm. 2915 1864).

GREEN ISLAND 47–15, 52–47 (NTS Ferryland 1N/2W)
Greene I ("Blathwayt" c. 1630–40), Green I. (Southwood 1675). French maps have I. Verte. P. 89.

GREEN ISLAND 47–53, 53–42 (NTS Sunnyside 1N/13E)
Green islet (Imray, *Sailing Directory* 1873).

GREEN ISLAND 48–12, 53–26 (NTS Old Perlican 2C/3W)
Green or Western Bay (Lane 1774) See WESTERN BAY (NTS Heart's Content). P. 92.
— Green or Western Bay Point (Lane, *Directions* 1775, 1810) See WESTERN BAY HEAD (NTS Heart's Content). Pp. 46–7.

Green Pt (Lane 1773)
See EAST HEAD (NTS St. Mary's). P. 87.

Green Point (Gaudy 1715)
See POINTE VERDE (NTS Ship Cove). P. 31.

GREEN POINT 47–13, 54–02 (NTS Ship Cove 1M/1E)
As set: (*Population Returns* 1836). Pp. 52, 110.

GREEN POINT 47–37, 53–10 (NTS Harbour Grace 1N/11E)
Point Roberts (Cook and Lane 1770 [1775]B), Bay Roberts Point (Lane, *Directions* 1775, 1810), Point Roberts (Mount and Page 1780), Green Point (Imray, *Sailing Directory* 1873).
Green – ? at the northern entrance to BAY DE GRAVE in contrast to BURNT POINT 47–34, 53–11 at the southern entrance.

Greene Bay (Robinson 1669)
See WESTERN BAY (NTS Heart's Content). Pp. 70–1.

Greene Bay (Guy 1612)
See BAY DE VERDE (NTS Bay de Verde). Pp. 31, 58.

GREENLAND (Set.) 47–34, 53–11 (NTS Harbour Grace 1N/11E)
? Fromes (Robinson 1669), Greenland (Census 1935), Northern Cove (Local name).
Greenland – descriptive of the lush sheep-pasture. Northern Cove – ? in relation to BRIGUS BAY 47–32, 53–11. Settlement abandoned c. 1938. Pp. 70, 145.

Greens-Cove (Torbay) (*English Pilot. The Fourth Book* 1689)
Green Cove (Mount and Page 1780, Imray, *Sailing Directions*, 1862, *Sailing Directory*, 1873, M. F. Howley, 1908). P. 75.

GREENS GULLY (Pond) 47–44, 53–20 (NTS Harbour Grace 1N/11W) (NDNR 1N/11 1948). P. 160.

GREENS HARBOUR 47–39, 53–31 (NTS Dildo 1N/12E)
Green's Harbour (Lane, *Directions* 1775, 1810), Green Hr. (Jukes 1840), Green's Hr (Bonnycastle 1842), Green Harbour (Imray, *Sailing Directions* 1862).
— GREENS HARBOUR (Set.) 47–39, 53–30

Greens Harbour *(Population Returns* 1836).
Pp. 74, 97, 160.

GROG POND 47–44, 52–46 (NTS St. John's 1N/10W)
? Resembling grog – rum and water; the water of the pond discoloured by peat.

Groue de Navire (Robinson 1669)
See GREAT BARASWAY (NTS Ship Cove) under BARASWAY. Pp. 47–48.

The Grove (Harbour Grace) (Jukes 1842). P. 112.

Groy I (Robinson 1669)
See KELLYS ISLAND (NTS Harbour Grace). Pp. 49, 64.

GRUB ISLAND 47–54, 53–44 (NTS Sunnyside 1N/13E)
? Deer Island (Lane, *Directions* 1775, 1810, Imray *Sailing Directions* 1862), Grub Isld (Imray, *Sailing Directory* 1873).
Cp. DEER HARBOUR (NTS Sunnyside). P. 95.

GULCH (Generic). P. 141.

GULL (Specific) See also BIG GULL, GREAT GULL, MIDDLE GULL, SMALL GULL.
For the varieties of gulls found in Newfoundland, see Peters and Burleigh.

GULL COVE 46–50, 54–00 (NTS St. Bride's 1L/16E, St. Mary's 1K/13W)
As set: (Census 1857); (Murray and Howley 1868). P. 120.

GULL ISLAND 47–02, 53–41 (NTS Placentia 1N/4E) (Adm. 2915 1864).

Gull Iland (Yonge 1663–70)
See GOOSE ISLAND (NTS Ferryland). P. 68.

GULL ISLAND 47–16, 52–46 (NTS Bay Bulls 1N/7W)
Gul Isl (Sellers c. 1671), Gull I. (Southwood 1675). P. 71.

GULL ISLAND 47–26, 53–58 (NTS Argentia 1N/5W) (Adm. 3266 1939).
One of the IONA ISLANDS.

GULL ISLAND 47–57, 53–03 (NTS Heart's Content 1N/14E) (Lane 1774).
Since the settlement GULL ISLAND is on the mainland, the island in popular, local usage is known as Gull Island Island. (Communication from P. A. O'Flaherty). Pp. 93, 98.

— GULL ISLAND (Set.)
(Thoresby 1796, *Population Returns* 1836). P. 98.

— GULL ISLAND BROOK 47–57, 53–04
(NDNR 1N/14 1946).

— GULL ISLAND POND 47–57, 53–03
(NDNR 1N/14 1946).

GULL ISLAND POINT 46–42, 53–39 (NTS St. Shotts 1K/12E)
Gull Island (Lane 1773 ... Imray, *Sailing Directions* 1862), Gull Island Pt. (Adm. 2915 1864), Gull Island (M. F. Howley xxvIII, *NQ*, December 1909), Gull Pt. (Newfoundland 1920), Gull island point (*NLP* I 1951).
P. 88.

GULL ISLAND SOUTH HEAD (Bell Island) 47–39, 52–56 (NTS St. John's 1N/10W)

GULL POND occurs at 47–04, 53–25 (NTS St. Catherine's 1N/3W) (Newfoundland 1941); 47–15, 53–20 (NTS Holyrood 1N/6W) (NDNR 1N/6 1943); 47–18, 52–52 (NTS Bay Bulls 1N/7W) (Newfoundland 1941); 47–28, 52–59 (NTS Bay Bulls 1N/7W) (CHS 4566 1952); 47–35, 52–50 (NTS St. John's 1N/10W); 47–35, 53–27 (NTS Harbour Grace 1N/11W) (NDNR 1N/11 1948); 47–40, 53–27 (NTS Harbour Grace 1N/11W) (NDNR 1N/11 1948); 47–45, 53–22 (NTS Harbour Grace 1N/11W, Heart's Content 1N/14W) (NDNR 1N/11 1948, 1N/14 1946).

BIG GULL POND 47–21, 53–29 (NTS Holyrood 1N/6W) (NDNR 1N/6 1943).

BIG GULL POND 47–30, 53–28 (NTS Holyrood 1N/6W, Harbour Grace 1N/11W) (NDNR 1N/11 1948).

BIG GULL POND 47–49, 53–15 (NTS Heart's Content 1N/14E and W) (NDNR 1N/14 1946).
Cp. SMALL GULL POND 47–48, 53–16. (NDNR 1N/14 1946).

GULL POND EAST 47–25, 53–03 (NTS Holyrood 1N/6E)
(NDNR 1N/6 1943).
Gull Pond West unnamed in NTS.

GULLIES, GULLY (Generic). P. 143.

GULLIES (Set.) 47–32, 53–14 (NTS Harbour Grace 1N/11E)
With GOULDS (Set.) (Census 1857). P. 118.

GULLIES (Set.) 47–39, 53–17 (NTS Harbour Grace 1N/11W)
(Census 1935). Pp. 138, 140.

GUNNERS COVE 47–33, 52–41 (NTS St. John's 1N/10E)
? From the days when ST. JOHN'S was a garrison town.
Cp. SOLDIERS GULCH, SOLDIERS POND.

GUNNERS POND 47–43, 53–18
(NTS Harbour Grace 1N/11W)
(NDNR 1N/11 1948).

GUNRIDGE (Set.) 47–19, 52–47 (NTS Bay Bulls 1N/17W) (CHS 4586 1944).
The site of a battery of artillery in the late eighteenth and early nineteenth centuries. (Communication from D. Webber.)

GUSHUES POND 47–24, 53–17 (NTS Holyrood 1N/6W)
(NDNR 1N/6 1943). Pp. 25–6, 54.

GUT (Generic). Pp. 104, 141.

HALF ISLAND 47–11, 53–35 (NTS Placentia 1N/4E)
(Imray, Sailing Directory 1873).
Peninsula in COLINET HARBOUR; "a low sandy islet, joined to the northwestern shore at the north end of Pinchgut island at low water" (Imray, Sailing Directory 1873, p. 79).

HALF MOON BROOK 47–44, 52–43 (NTS St. John's 1N/10E)
— HALF MOON POND 47–43, 52–45
Cp. MOON POND 47–42, 52–45.
HALF MOON POND is about half the size of MOON POND.

HALFWAY BROOK 47–59, 53–17 (NTS Heart's Content 1N/14W)
(NDNR 1N/14 1946).
? Between WINTERTON and HANTS HARBOUR, P. 5.

HALFWAY HOUSE (Set.) 47–48, 53–17
(NTS Heart's Content 1N/14W)
(NDNR 1N/14 1946).
Between HEART'S CONTENT and VICTORIA. P. 147.

HALFWAY POND 47–16, 53–16 (NTS Holyrood 1N/6W) (NDNR 1N/6 1943).
Between HOLYROOD and ST. CATHERINE'S on the SALMONIER LINE.

HALLS GULLIES 47–22, 53–27 (NTS Holyrood 1N/6W)
(NDNR 1N/6 1943). P. 160.

HALLS GULLIES 47–28, 53–28 (NTS Holyrood 1N/6W)
(NDNR 1N/6 1943). P. 160.

HALLS TOWN (Set.) 47–32, 53–20 (NTS Harbour Grace 1N/11W)
(Census 1857). Pp. 118, 146, 160.

HAMILTON AVENUE (St. John's)
Formerly Pokempath.
Hamilton – after a cobbler, Hamilton, who lived at the bottom of the street, c. ?1860.
(Communication from E. B. Foran). P. 148.

HANDY POND 47–30, 52–45 (NTS St. John's 1N/10E)
? Close to PETTY HARBOUR Road.

HANGING HILL 47–48, 53–24 (NTS

Heart's Content 1N/14W)
(Adm. 296 1868).
After an overhang on the hill.
(Communication from E. Bishop).
— HANGING HILL POND 47–48,
53–23
(NDNR 1N/14 1946).

HANTS HARBOUR 48–01, 53–16 (NTS Old Perlican 2C/3W)
(Lane, *Directions* 1775, 1810).
Pp. 97, 107, 118.
— HANTS HARBOUR (Set.)
Lance arbe, Anse arbre
(Beaudoin 1697), Hants
Harbour
(*Population Returns* 1836, Wix 1836). Pp. 80, 97.
— Hants Harbour Rock 48–03,
53–17
(Lane, *Directions* 1775, 1810).
P. 97.
— HANTS HEAD 48–01, 53–17
(Lane, *Directions* 1775, 1810).
P. 97.

HARBOUR (Generic). P. 141.

HARBOUR GRACE 47–41, 53–12 (NTS Harbour Grace 1N/11E and W)
Harbor de Grace (Guy 1612), Harborgrace ("Blathwayt" c. 1630-40), Carolinopole (Hayman 1630 in D. W. Prowse, p. 137), harbour grace (Robinson 1669), Harbour Grace (Southwood 1675).
Carolinopole – in honour of Charles I. Pp. 58, 62, 68, 74, 79, 82, 92, 94, 95, 141.
— HARBOUR GRACE (Set.) 47–42,
53–13
? the Bristow Plantation
(Wynne 1622), Haver de Grace
(*CSP* 1677), Havre de Grâce
(Beaudoin 1697), Harbour
Grace (*CSP* 1681). Pp. 40, 79,
112, 123, 129–35, 148.
— HARBOUR GRACE ISLANDS 47–42,
53–09
Harborgrace I (Visscher c. 1680).

— HARBOUR GRACE (SOUTHSIDE)
(Set.). 47–40, 53–13
(Census 1911). P. 144.

Harbour Grande (Dudley 1646)
See ? CAPLIN COVE (NTS Bay de Verde). P. 119.

Harbour Island (Imray, *Sailing Directions* 1862, *Sailing Directory* 1873)
See CRAWLEY ISLAND (NTS Argentia). P. 110.

HARBOUR ISLAND 47–25, 53–58 (NTS Argentia 1N/5W) (Adm. 3266 1939).
One of the IONA ISLANDS. P. 85.

Harbour Island (Deer Harbour)
(Lane, *Directions* 1775, 1810). P. 95.

HARBOUR MAIN 47–26, 53–09 (NTS Holyrood 1N/6E)
Harbor Maine ("Blathwayt" c. 1630–40). Pp. 42, 141.
— HARBOUR MAIN (Set.) 47–26,
53–10
Harbour Maine (*CSP* 1674–5).
Pp. 53, 79, 131.
— HARBOUR MAIN ISLAND 47–27,
53–09
(*NLP* 1952).
— HARBOUR MAIN POINT 47–26,
53–09
(*NLP* 1952).
— HARBOUR MAIN POND 47–22,
53–12
(NDNR 1N/6 1943).

HARBOUR ROCKS 47–52, 53–44 (NTS Sunnyside 1N/13E)
(Imray, *Sailing Directory* 1873).
At entrance to SHOAL BAY.

HARD WEATHER POND 47–47, 53–19
(NTS Heart's Content 1N/14W)
(NDNR 1N/14 1946).

HARE HILL occurs at 46–53, 53–35 (NTS St. Mary's 1K/13E) (Adm 2915 1864); 46–54, 53–58 (NTS St. Mary's 1K/13W (Adm. 2915 1864); 47–26, 52–45 (NTS Bay Bulls 1N/7E) (Adm. 296 1868).

224 / Place Names of the Avalon Peninsula

HARE'S EARS (Generic). Pp. 5, 87, 138, 139.

HARE'S EARS 46–52, 53–57 (NTS St. Mary's 1K/13W) (Lane 1773). "Two rocks, known as Hare's Ears, 40 feet high, lie close eastward of [Branch] head" (*NLP* I, p. 97).

HARE'S EARS 47–01, 52–51 (NTS Ferryland 1N/2W) (Lane 1773). "two high Rocks above Water lying close off ... [Ferryland] head" (Lane, *Directions*, 1773).

HARRICOTT (Set.) 47–11, 53–32 (NTS Placentia 1N/4E)
Harry Cove (*Population Returns* 1836, Census 1857, 1874), Harricot Cove (Census 1884), Harricot (Census 1891).
— HARRICOTT BAY 47–08, 53–33
  Harry Cove (Jukes 1840), Haricot bay (Imray, *Sailing Directory* 1873).
— HARRICOTT POINT
  As set: Harry Cove Pt. (*Population Returns* 1836); (Adm. 2915 1864).
— HARRICOTT POND 47–10, 53–32 (*NLP* 1929).
Pp. 54, 108, 111, 139.

HARRY BALDWINS POND 47–47, 53–19 (NTS Heart's Content 1N/14W) (NDNR 1N/14 1946). P. 157.

HAT POND 47–38, 53–20 (NTS Harbour Grace 1N/11W)
(CHS 4572 1954), Hat and Cuff Pond (Local name).

HAVEN (Generic). P. 141.
Haven of St. John (Rut 1527)
See ST. JOHN'S HARBOUR (NTS St. John's). P. 56.

Havre-Content (Beaudoin 1697)
See HEART'S CONTENT (NTS Heart's Content). P. 80.

havre des cloches (Courcelle 1675). P. 50.

Haure froid (Alemand 1687)
See PORTUGAL COVE (NTS St. John's). P. 33.

Havre vieu (Beaudoin 1697)
See HARBOUR MAIN (NTS Holyrood). P. 79.

HAWCO POND 47–24, 53–07 (NTS Holyrood 1N/6E)
(CHS 4573 1953). P. 54.

HAWCOS POND 47–18, 53–18 (NTS Holyrood 1N/6W)
(NDNR 1N/6 1943). P. 54.

HAWKE HILLS 47–20, 53–05 (NTS Holyrood 1N/6E, Bay Bulls 1N/7W)
Hawkes range (Murray and Howley 1876), Hawke Hills (Murray and Howley 1879). P. 160.

HAY BAG POND 47–44, 53–24 (NTS Harbour Grace 1N/11W)
(NDNR 1N/11 1948).
From the practice of taking bags of hay to the pond for winter feed for horses.

Haylinscove (Beaudoin 1697)
See UPPER ISLAND COVE (NTS Harbour Grace). Pp. 79, 107.

HEAD = hydrographic feature. Pp. 68, 141.

HEAD(s) = topographic feature. P. 144.

HEALEYS POND 47–25, 53–15 (NTS Holyrood 1N/6W)
See HEALYS COVE.

HEALEYS POND 47–35, 52–51 (NTS St. John's 1N/10W). P. 131.

HEALYS COVE 47–24, 53–09 (NTS Holyrood 1N/6E)
(CHS 4573 1953).
— HEALEYS POND 47–25, 53–15 (NDNR 1N/6 1943).
P. 131.

HEART COVE 48–09, 52–57 (NTS Bay de Verde 2C/2W)
See BREAKHEART POINT 48–10, 52–58.

HEART POINT 47–25, 52–42 (NTS Bay Bulls 1N/7E) (Newfoundland 1941). ? Descriptive.

HEART'S CONTENT (Inlet 47–52, 53–23 (NTS Heart's Content 1N/14W) Hartes content (Guy 1612), Hearts Content (Lane, *Directions* 1775, 1810). Pp. 6, 58 and Chap IV note 24, 97
— HEART'S CONTENT (Set.) 47–52, 53–22
  Havre-Content (Beaudoin 1697), Hearts Content (*Population Returns* 1836, Wix 1836). Pp. 74, 80, 97, 104, 121–2.
— HEART'S CONTENT BARRENS. P. 103.

HEART'S DELIGHT 47–47, 53–28 (NTS Heart's Content 1N/14W) (Lane, *Directions* 1775, 1810).
— HEART'S DELIGHT (Set.) (*Population Returns* 1836).
— HEART'S DELIGHT BROOK 47–46, 53–28
  (NDNR 1N/14 1946).
Pp. 6, 74, 92, 97.

HEART'S DESIRE (Cove) 47–49, 53–27 (NTS Heart's Content 1N/14W) (Lane, *Directions* 1775, 1810). Pp. 58 and Chap. IV note 24, 97, 98.
— HEART'S DESIRE (Set.) (*Population Returns* 1836).
— HEART'S DESIRE BROOK 47–48, 53–27
  (NDNR 1N/14 1946).

HEIGHTS (Generic). P. 145.

Hell Hill (Jukes 1842), P. 114.

HENNESSEYS POND 47–26, 52–57 (NTS Bay Bulls 1N/7W) (NDNR Bay Bulls 1943). P. 132.

HERETIC HILL 47–19, 52–47 (NTS Bay Bulls 1N/7W) (CHS 4586 1944).

HERRING COVE 47–29, 52–40 (NTS Bay Bulls 1N/7E) (?NDNR Bay Bulls 1943).
— HERRING COVE POND 47–29, 52–41 (NDNR Bay Bulls 1943).

HERRING COVE POND 47–45, 52–48 (NTS St. John's 1N/10W).

HIBBS HOLE (Set.) 47–36, 53–11 (NTS Harbour Grace 1N/11E) (*CSP* 1745); Hibbs Cove (Local name). Pp. 92, 109, 141, 160.

HICKEYS POND 47–41, 52–49 (NTS St. John's 1N/10W). P. 132.

HIGGINS LINE (St. John's)
After W. J. Higgins (1880–?), solicitor, politician and judge (Mosdell, p. 59). The road was built in the early 1920s as relief work, following the water line from WINDSOR LAKE to ST. JOHN'S. P. 147–8.

High Ragged Point (Brigus) (Mount and Page 1780)
See ? GREAT HEAD
(NTS Harbour Grace). Pp. 97–8.

HIGHWAY (Generic). P. 147.

HILL (Generic) = Feature. P. 144.

HILL (Generic) = Street. P. 148.

HILLDALE
See BRIGUS SOUTH (NTS Ferryland). P. 43.

Hodge River (Jukes 1842)
— Hodge Water River (Murray and Howley 1872).
— Hodge Waters
  See HODGEWATER POND.
— HODGEWATER BRIDGE 47–26, 53–23 (NTS Holyrood 1N/6W) (NDNR 1N/6 1943).
— HODGEWATER LINE
— HODGEWATER POND 47–27, 53–24
  Hodge Waters (Murray and Howley 1872).
Pp. 24, 114, 160.

HOGANS POND 47–35, 52–51 (NTS St. John's 1N/10W). P. 132.

226 / Place Names of the Avalon Peninsula

HOLE (Generic) = Cove. P. 141.

HOLE (Generic) = Pond. P. 143.

HOLE IN THE WALL ISLAND 47-23, 53-59 (NTS Argentia 1N/5W) (NLP 1929).
One of the IONA ISLANDS.
"It is 130 feet high and has a hole in the cliff on its north-eastern side" (NLP I, 138). P. 85.

HOLLISCOVE 47-36, 53-54 (NTS Dildo 1N/12W). P. 132.

Hollyrood (Lane 1773)
See HOLYROOD BAY (NTS St. Mary's). P. 30.

HOLYROOD BAY 46-46, 53-38 (NTS St. Shotts 1K/12E, St. Mary's 1K/13E) P[orto] da cruz (Reinel 1519 ... Sanches 1596), Hollyrood (Lane 1773), English Cove (Bonnycastle 1842 text, St. Vincent Bay (Adm. 2915 1864 or later), Holyrood Bay (Imray, *Sailing Directory* 1873), Holyrood (Saint Vincent) bay (NLP I 1951).
See ST. VINCENT'S (Set.)
Cp. HOLYROOD BAY (NTS Holyrood).
— HOLYROOD POND 46-52, 53-38 (NTS St. Mary's 1K/13E, Biscay Bay River 1K/14W)
Holly Rood Pond (Lane 1773), St. Vincent Pond (Adm. 2915 1864 or later), Holyrood (Saint Vincent) pond (NLP I 1951).
Pp. 30, 64, 86, 115.

HOLYROOD BAY 47-24, 53-08 (NTS Holyrood 1N/6E)
Hollyrude ("Blathwayt" c. 1630-40), Hollyrode (Southwood 1675). Pp. 64, 91, 139.
— HOLYROOD (Set.) 47-23, 53-08
Hollyrood (CSP 1705), Holyrood (*Population Returns* 1836).
— HOLYROOD BIG POND 47-21, 53-09
(NDNR 1N/6 1943).

— HOLYROOD NORTH ARM
See NORTH ARM 47-24, 53-09 (NTS Holyrood).

HOLYSTONE GULLIES (Ponds) 47-23, 52-55 (NTS Bay Bulls 1N/7W) (NDNR Bay Bulls 1943).
Holy stone, holy-stone – 1. A soft sandstone used ... for scouring the decks of ships. (*OED*).

HOPE (Generic). P. 141.

HOPEALL (Set.) 47-37, 53-31 (NTS Dildo 1N/12E)
(Census 1869).
— HOPEALL BAY 47-38, 53-32
— Hope all (Lane 1790).
— HOPEALL HEAD 47-38, 53-34
Hope-all-Head (Lane, *Directions* 1775, 1810),
Hope-all-a-head (Imray, *Sailing Directions* 1862).
— HOPEALL ISLAND 47-39, 53-33
Pp. 97, 160.

HOPEWELL (Set.) 47-29, 53-03 (NTS Sunnyside 1N/6E) (Census 1891).
Hopewell and *Chancewell* were armed ships equipped by Charles Leigh and Abraham van Herwick in 1597 for the Newfoundland voyage. (Anspach, p. 77).
The schooner *Hopewell* of Harbour Main was lost on Biscayan Rock, Cape St. Francis, 29 November 1875. (Mosdell, p. 60). Pp. 97, 160.

Hopping Joyner (Stage or Cove) (St. John's Harbour) (Thornton 1689B)
See Hot Ioyner. P. 77.

HORSE COVE 47-34, 52-54 (NTS St. John's 1N/10W)
As set: (Census 1857); St. Thomas Cove (Rouleau, *Gazetteer*, 1961).
See ST. THOMAS (NTS St. John's). P. 116.
— HORSE COVE BROOK 47-34, 52-54
— HORSE COVE LINE

HORSE GULLIES (Ponds) 47-23, 52-47

(NTS Bay Bulls 1N/7W)
(NDNR Bay Bulls 1943).
? Frequented by horses out at pasture during the summer months.

HORSE ROCK(S) (Cape Broyle) 47–04, 52–50 (*NP* 1952)
Horse Rock (Lane 1773), ? Horse Head (Cook and Lane 1770[1775]B).

HORSEHEAD POINT 47–03, 53–39 (NTS Placentia 1N/4E) (Adm. 2915 1864). See Horselips (Guy 1612) p. 58.

HORSESHOE CLIFF 47–27, 52–42 (NTS Bay Bulls 1N/7E) (USHO 2139 1943). "From the entrance to Petty harbour the coast is high and trends about half a mile south-eastward to a cove or gulch, shaped like a horseshoe, at Horseshoe cliff" (*NLP* I, p. 80), P. 144.

HORTON ROCKS 47–45, 53–11 (NTS Heart's Content 1N/14E) (NDNR 1N/14 1946). P. 160.

HOSKINS POND 47–43, 53–14 (NTS Harbour Grace 1N/11E) (NDNR 1N/11 1948). P. 160.

Hospital (Riverhead, St. John's Harbour) (Cook 1762 or Gilbert 1768). P. 83.

Hot Ioyner (Stage or Cove, St. John's Harbour) (Visscher c. 1680)
Hopping Joyner (Thornton 1689B; Mount and Page 1755). Pp. 76, 7.

HOUSE (Generic). P. 147.

HOWLETT POINT 47–00, 52–55 (NTS Ferryland 1N/2W)
(USHO 0618 1941). P. 160.

HUGHS POND 47–36, 52–51 (NTS St. John's 1N/10W). P.160.

Hundred Island Pond (Jukes 1842). P. 113.

Ille de Plaisance ("Vallard" 1547)
See PLACENTIA (NTS Placentia).
P. 38.

INDIAN MEAL LINE 47–38, 52–48 (NTS St. John's 1N/10W)
Road from PORTUGAL COVE to TORBAY, built as relief work in 1848. The workmen from MIDDLE COVE, OUTER COVE, TORBAY, FLAT ROCK and POUCH COVE were paid in Indian meal (meal made from Indian corn) [*Journal of the House of Assembly* (1848) Appendix, p. 328. Communication from W. Kirwin].

INDIAN POND 47–27, 53–06 (NTS Holyrood 1N/6E)
— INDIAN POND (Set.) (Census 1884).
P. 20.

INDIAN POND 47–57, 53–05 (NTS Heart's Content 1N/14E)
(NDNR 1N/14 1946). P. 20

INSIDE ISLAND COVE POND 47–44, 53–27 (NTS Harbour Grace 1N/11W) (NDNR 1N/11 1948).
The pond further inland from ISLAND COVE 47–46, 53–29 than OUTSIDE ISLAND COVE POND q.v. P. 6.

INSIDE POND 47–33, 52–52 (NTS St. John's 1N/10W)
Cp. OUTSIDE POND. The relationship is not obvious.

Insula Baccalauras (Ruysch 1508)
See BACCALIEU ISLAND (NTS Bay de Verde. P. 33.

IONA ISLANDS 47–24, 53–57 (NTS Argentia 1N/5W)
Ram Islands (Lane 1772 ... Imray, *Sailing Directory* 1873), Iona (M. F. Howley, xxx, *NQ*, March 1911). Pp. 51, 85.

Ironclay hill (Imray *Sailing Directory* 1873)
See JONCLAY HILL (NTS Bay Bulls). P. 78.

IRISHTOWN (Set.) 47–19, 52–49 (NTS Bay Bulls 1N/7W)
(CHS 4586 1944).

228 / *Place Names of the Avalon Peninsula*

Part of BAY BULLS (Set.). Pp. 5, 125, 146.

IRISHTOWN
Part of CARBONEAR (Set.) (NTS Harbour Grace). Pp. 125, 146.

*In Ireland, Irishtown is found as the name of a district in e.g. Clonmel, Kilkenny, and Dublin. It was originally imposed as a derogatory appellation for districts outside the city gates where the poor Irish, as opposed to the affluent English, lived. (Communicated by Dr. R. B. Walsh.)

IRVINE STATION 47–32, 52–52 (NTS St. John's 1N/10W)
Irvines (Local usage). Pp. 139, 148, 160.

ISAAC HEADS 47–20, 53–56 (NTS Argentia 1N/5W) (Adm. 2829 1877).
— ISAAC POINT 47–19, 53–57 (Adm. 2829 1877).
"two very peculiar hills of the haycock form, but very high ... are called The Isaacs" (M. F. Howley, xxx, *NQ*, March 1911). Pp. 144, 160.

ISLAND(s) (Generic). P. 144.

ISLAND COVE 47–06, 52–54 (NTS Ferryland 1N/2W)
(Imray, *Sailing Directory* 1873). From the small island, unnamed in NTS, in the cove.

ISLAND COVE 47–18, 52–46 (NTS Bay Bulls 1N/7W) (NDNR Bay Bulls 1943). "An islet 32 feet high ... lies in the middle of the cove" (*NLP* I, 82).

ISLAND COVE 47–43, 53–19 (NTS Harbour Grace 1N/11E) (Adm. 296 1868).

ISLAND COVE 47–46, 53–29 (NTS Heart's Content 1N/14W)
As set: (Census 1857).
See ISLINGTON (Set.) NTS Heart's Content). P. 119.

ISLAND COVE 47–40, 53–57 (NTS Dildo 1N/12W) (Adm. 296 1863).
? Opposite LONG ISLAND.
— ISLAND COVE HEAD (*NP* 1952).

Island Cove (Lane 1774)
See LOWER ISLAND COVE (NTS Heart's Content, Bay de Verde). P. 94.

ISLAND COVE POINT 46–55, 53–37 (NTS St. Mary's 1K/13E) (USHO 2275 1917).
Not named, apparently, after any island in the vicinity.

ISLAND COVE POINT 47–00, 52–55 (NTS Ferryland 1N/2W) (USHO 0618 1941).
The island seems to be a rock to the west of the cove; the cove is a shallow indentation of the coast.

ISLAND COVE POND
See UPPER ISLAND COVE (NTS Harbour Grace).

ISLAND COVE POND
See LOWER ISLAND COVE (NTS Heart's Content, Bay de Verde).

ISLAND HEAD 46–53, 54–12 (NTS St. Bride's 1L/16E) (Adm. 2915 1864).
? After Perch Rock, 3½ miles northwest from ISLAND HEAD. Cp. PERCH COVE.

Island of St. John (Hakluyt). P. 8.

BIG ISLAND POND 47–16, 53–06 (NTS Holyrood 1N/6E)

ISLAND POND occurs at 47–17, 53–17 (NTS Holyrood 1N/6W) (NDNR 1N/6 1943); 47–31, 53–29 (NTS Harbour Grace 1N/11W) (NDNR 1N/11 1948; 47–35, 53–30 (NTS Harbour Grace 1N/11W) (NDNR 1N/11 1948; 47–38, 52–43 (NTS St. John's 1N/10E); 47–59, 53–02 (NTS Heart's Content 1N/14E) (NDNR 1N/14 1946).

ISLAND POND 47–40, 53–21 (NTS
Harbour Grace 1N/11W)
(NDNR 1N/11 1948).
— ISLAND POND GULLY (Pond)
47–40, 53–22
(NDNR 1N/11 1948).
BIG ISLAND POND 47–43, 53–19 (NTS
Harbour Grace 1N/11W)
(NDNR 1N/11 1948).
— LITTLE ISLAND POND
(NDNR 1N/11 1948).
— ISLAND POND BROOK 47–44,
53–14 (NTS Harbour Grace
1N/11E and W) (CHS 4590 1943).

ISLAND POND 48–00, 53–10 (NTS
Heart's Content 1N/14E, Old
Perlican 2C/3E)
(NDNR 1N/14 1946). Charlie's Pond
(Local name). P. 5.

ISLAND POND BROOK 47–40, 52–44
(NTS St. John's 1N/10E)
Flows from WESTERN ISLAND POND
47–38, 52–46 (NTS St. John's
1N/10W).

ISLAND POND BROOK
See BIG ISLAND POND (NTS Harbour
Grace).

I[sle] Columbrina (Coronelli 1689)
See COLUMBINE POINT (NTS Bay
Bulls.) P. 31.

Isle de Bacaillau (Alfonse 1544)
See BACCALIEU ISLAND (NTS Bay de
Verde). P. 34.

I[sle] du Renard (Detcheverry 1689)
See FOX ISLAND (NTS Argentia).
P. 51.

I[sle] gorichon ("Dépôt 132.2.10"
1706)
See MERCHANT ISLAND (NTS
Argentia). Pp. 51, 85.

I[sle] of Bulls (Briggs 1625). P. 12.

Isles d'Espoir (Alfonse 1544)
See SPEAR, FOX, PEBBLE and GOOSE
ISLANDS (NTS Ferryland). P. 35.

Gazetteer and Index of Place Names: J / 229

ISLET (Generic). P. 144

ISLINGTON (Set.) 47–46, 53–29 (NTS
Heart's Content 1N/14W)
Island Cove (Census 1857);
Islington (Proclamation 8 August
1911).
Cp. ISLAND COVE (NTS Heart's
Content). Pp. 119, 140, 146.

ISTHMUS (Generic). P. 144.

ISTHMUS OF AVALON
See AVALON.

JACK POND 47–45, 53–57 (NTS
Sunnyside 1N/13W)
(Adm. 296 1952).

JACKS GULLIES (Ponds) 47–22, 53–22
(NTS Holyrood 1N/6W)
(NDNR 1N/6 1943).

JACKS POND 47–23, 53–20 (NTS
Holyrood 1N/6W)
(NDNR 1N/6 1943).

JAKES POND 47–26, 52–57 (NTS Bay
Bulls 1N/7W)
(NDNR Bay Bulls 1943).

JAMES COVE 47–29, 53–11 (NTS
Holyrood 1N/6E)
As set: Collier's James Cove
(Census 1857); (Imray, *Sailing
Directory* 1873). Pp. 118, 161.
— James's Point
(Murray and Howley 1868).

JAMES GULLY (Pond) 47–44, 53–22
(NTS Harbour Grace 1N/11W)
(NDNR 1N/11 1948). P. 161.

JAMES LANE (St. John's). P. 148.

JEANS HEAD 47–55, 53–22 (NTS
Heart's Content 1N/14W)
Smutty nose pt (Southwood 1675
... Imray, *Sailing Directions* 1862),
Jeans Hd. (Imray, *Sailing Directory*
1873). P. 72.

Jersey Point
See OLD SOW POINT (NTS Harbour
Grace).

JERSEYSIDE (Set.) 47–16, 53–58 (NTS Argentia 1N/5W)
(Census 1869). Pp. 6, 130, 144.

JIGGING COVE 46–58, 53–52 (NTS St. Mary's 1K/13W) (Adm. 2915 1864).
Jig. v. To catch (a fish) by jerking a hook into its body; to catch with a jig. *intr.* To fish with a jig. (*OED*, first citation 1883).
Jig, gig, jigger, gigger, sb. A contrivance of various kinds for catching fish. gig 1722, jig 1858. (*OED*).
Jigging. sb. Ib. The process of jerking the line and jigger up sharply, impaling a codfish on one of the three points. (*OED* 1886).
"As a matter of fact, jiggers have been in use from very early times. In 1716 complaints were made against their use by the French on the southern Labrador" [W. G. Gosling, *Labrador* (Alston Rivers London, 1910), pp. 415–6, but without documentation].
The French "began also to fish before us, by a method call'd here jigging, done by 2 large hooks each of them twice as large as those us'd for bait. These hooks are fasten'd together back to back, and a heavy lead plac'd upon their shanks which the French (wither of whim, or from any use they find in it I do not know) cast in the shape of a fish. These jiggs are fastn'd to the end of their lines & let down to the bottom from whence they are rais'd every half minute or theirabouts by a strong jerk of the fisherman's arm, in hopes of striking them into the fish who are accidentally swimming by. The jerk of the arms necessary in this fishing makes it so laborious that we can seldom or ever get any of our countrymen to do it." (Banks, *Journal*, 9 August 1766).

"The gigger or jigger consists of a pair of large hooks, fixed back to back, with some lead run upon the shanks, in the shape and colour of a fish." (Anspach, 1819, p. 408).
"A jigger is a plummet of lead, with two or three hooks stuck at the bottom, projecting on every side, and quite bare. This is let down by the line to the proper depth, and than a man, taking a hitch of the line in his hand, jerks it smartly in, the full length of his arm, then lets it down slowly and jerks it in again. The fish are attracted by seeing something moving in the water, and every now and then one is caught by one of the hooks. As soon as the man feels he has struck one, he hauls in upon the line, taking care to keep it tight till he heaves the fish into the boat." (Jukes, I, p. 29).

JIMMY ROWES POND 47–41, 53–29 (NTS Harbour Grace 1N/11W) (NDNR 1N/11 1948). P. 165.

Joan Clays Hill (Thornton 1699) See JONCLAY HILL (NTS Bay Bulls). P. 77.

JOB'S COVE (St. John's)
Job – Family of merchants in ST. JOHN'S since the eighteenth century. See R. B. Job, *John Job's Family* (Telegram Printing Co., St. John's, 1953). Pp. 94, 148.

JOB'S COVE 47–58, 53–02 (NTS Heart's Content 1N/14E)
Devils Cove (Lane 1774). Imray, *Sailing Directory* 1873, p. 44 discriminates JOB COVE and Devil's Point Cove.
— JOB'S COVE (Set.) 47–59, 53–01 Devil's Cove (Thoresby 1796), Job's Cove (Proclamation by inhabitants 1812).
— JOB'S COVE BROOK (NDNR 1N/14 1946).

— JOB'S COVE POINT 47–58, 53–01
Devils Cove Pt (Lane 1790).
Pp. 93–4, 98.

JOB'S POND 47–45, 53–16 (NTS
Heart's Content 1N/14W)
(NDNR 1N/14 1946). P. 94.
— JOB'S POND BROOK 47–46, 53–16

JOHN WILLIAMS POND 47–40, 53–28
(NTS Harbour Grace 1N/11W)
(NDNR 1N/11 1948). P. 167.

JOHNNIES POND 47–29, 52–58 (NTS
Bay Bulls 1N/7W) (CHS 4566 1952).

JOHN'S POND 47–08, 53–37 (NTS
Placentia 1N/4E)
As set: (*Population Returns* 1836).
? Same as Johns Point, "a fishing
settlement at the head of St. Mary's
Bay, Nfld., 6 miles from Salmonier"
(Lovell 1881); but cp. JONAS POINT
47–05, 53–41. Pp. 108, 161.

JOHNS POND 47–16, 53–25 (NTS
Holyrood 1N/6W)
(NDNR 1N/6 1943). P. 161.

JONAS POINT 47–05, 53–41 (NTS
Placentia 1N/4E)
(Adm. 2915 1864). P. 161.

JONCLAY HILL 47–19, 52–48 (NTS
Bay Bulls 1N/7W)
Joan Clays hill (Thornton 1689D,
Gaudy 1715), Ironclay hill (Imray
Sailing Directory 1873), Jonclay Hill
(CHS 4586 1944). P. 77.

JONES COVE 47–36, 52–53 (NTS
St. John's 1N/10W). P. 161.

JONES HEAD 47–36, 53–14 (NTS
Harbour Grace 1N/11E)
(CHS 4572 1954). P. 161.

JONES POND 47–39, 52–42 (NTS
St. John's 1N/10E). P. 161.

JOSEPH ROFF COVE 47–41, 53–57 (NTS
Dildo 1N/12W). P. 165.

JOYS POINT 47–24, 53–09 (NTS
Holyrood 1N/6E). P. 161.

JUGGLERS COVE 47–37, 53–12 (NTS
Harbour Grace 1N/11E)
As set: Juglers Cove (CO 199.18
1760), ? Gawgel's Cove (Thoresby
1796), Jugglers Cove (Census 1857);
as feature: (Imray, *Sailing Directory* 1873). P. 98.

JUMP GULLIES (Ponds) 47–47, 53–20
(NTS Heart's Content 1N/14W)
(NDNR 1N/14 1946).
Jump – ? because sufficiently narrow
to be leaped over.

JUNCTION (Generic). P. 148.

JUNIPER (Specific) D. W. Prowse
writing on the construction of
schooners in the early nineteenth
century states that "For the boat's
frame juniper was generally used"
(D. W. Prowse, p. 404). See WITCH
HAZEL.

JUNIPER PONDS 47–34, 52–47 (NTS
St. John's 1N/10W)

JUNIPER STUMP (Set.) 47–30, 53–18
(NTS Harbour Grace 1N/11W)
(Census 1857).
? Juniper used in boat-building at
DROGHEDA 47–30, 53–18. Pp.
24, 118.

Juniper Stump 47–37, 52–50
(Unnamed in NTS St. John's 1N/10W)

KATE POINT 47–18, 52–47 (NTS
Bay Bulls 1N/7W) (USHO 73 1942).

KEARNEY'S GULLIES (Ponds) 47–26,
53–22 (NTS Holyrood 1N/6W)
(NDNR 1N/6 1943). P. 132.

KEARNEYS HILL 47–17, 52–49 (NTS
Bay Bulls 1N/7W)
(CHS 4586 1944). P. 132.

Kelinscove (Beaudoin 1697)
See CLOWNS COVE (NTS Heart's
Content). P. 80.

232 / Place Names of the Avalon Peninsula

KELLIGREWS (Set.) 47–30, 53–01 (NTS Harbour Grace 1N/11E)
Killigrews (Wix 1836), Kellygrews (Bonnycastle 1842). Pp. 65, 92, 117, 139, 161.
— KELLIGREWS POINT
Kellygrews Head (Lane 1774). Pp. 65, 91.
— KELLIGREWS RIVER (NTS Holyrood 1N/6E, Harbour Grace 1N/11E) (CHS 4566 1952).

KELLIGREWS HILL (Port de Grave). P. 65.

KELLIS POINT 47–16, 52–49 (NTS Bay Bulls 1N/7W)
(NDNR Bay Bulls 1943). Pp. 132, 161.

KELLY POINT 47–19, 53–56 (NTS Argentia 1N/5W)
(CHS 4622 ? 1953). Pp. 132, 161.

KELLY POND 47–25, 53–01 (NTS Holyrood 1N/6E)
(NDNR 1N/6 1943). Pp. 132, 161.

KELLYS ISLAND 47–33, 53–01 (NTS Harbour Grace 1N/11E)
? Welles I ("Blathwayt" c. 1630–40), ? Groy I (Robinson 1669), Crow Isl (Seller c. 1671), Kelly's Island (Lane, *Directions* 1775, 1810); as set: (Census 1891). Pp. 49, 64–5, 72, 91, 132, 161.

KELLYS POND 47–38, 53–22 (NTS Harbour Grace 1N/11W)
(NDNR 1N/11 1948). Pp. 132, 161.

KENMOUNT HILL 47–32, 52–47 (NTS St. John's 1N/10W)

KENNA'S [kəˈnaːz] HILL (St. John's). P. 132.

KENNEDYS BROOK 47–39, 52–42 (NTS St. John's 1N/10E). P. 132.

KENNEDYS POND 47–21, 53–23 (NTS Holyrood 1N/6W)
(NDNR 1N/6 1943). P. 132.

KENNYS POND 47–35, 52–43 (NTS St. John's 1N/10E)

Robert Kenny was a subscriber to the *Royal Gazette and Newfoundland Advertiser* in 1806. (Mosdell, p. 163). P. 132.

KENTS POND 47–35, 52–43 (NTS St. John's 1N/10E)
Kent – a family prominent in commercial, government and legal circles in the nineteenth century in ST. JOHN'S. (Mosdell, pp. 69–70). P. 132.

KERRYTOWN (St. John's). P. 127.

KERWAN POINT 47–08, 53–29 (NTS St. Catherine's 1N/3W) (Adm. 2915 1869).
Cp. PORT KIRWAN (NTS Renews). P. 132.

THE KETTLE (Point) 47–25, 52–40 (NTS Bay Bulls 1N/7E)
(USHO 2139 1943).
Cp ? Kettle bottom – a name given to a hill with broad flat top and sloping sides. (*OED*). Pp. 5, 139.

Kettle Cove (Set.) (Census 1857). P. 119.

KEY(s) (Generic) "Key, Cay – Span. *cayo* – shoal, reef. A low island, sand-bank or reef, such as those common in the West Indies, or off the coast of Florida. Cp. the place-name Key West." (*OED*). P. 144.

THE KEY (Point) 47–25, 53–51 (NTS Argentia 1N/5W) (Adm. 3266 1939).
"A sharp point" (*NLP* 1951) in LONG HARBOUR. Pp. 140, 144.

THE KEYS (Set.) 47–18, 52–48 (NTS Bay Bulls 1N/7W)
As feature: Keys (Lane 1774).
Cp. ST. MARY'S KEYS. Pp. 86, 140, 144.

KILBRIDE (Set.) 47–32, 52–45 (NTS St. John's 1N/10E)
Roman Catholic church consecrated 1863 (Mosdell, p. 70). Pp. 6, 127, 139.

KING ISLAND 47–24, 53–58 (NTS Argentia 1N/5W) (CHS 4622 ? 1953). One of the IONA ISLANDS. Pp. 85, 132, 161.

KINGMAN'S (Set.) 46–58, 52–57 (NTS Renews 1K/15W)
— KINGMANS COVE 46–58, 52–56 Viceadmiralls cove (Yonge 1663–70), Kingmans Cove (19th century).
See ADMIRAL.
Pp. 68–70, 139, 161.

KING'S BEACH 47–40, 53–14 (NTS Harbour Grace 1N/11E)
? Admiral's Beach (Lane, *Directions* 1775, 1810), King's Beach (Adm. 297 1933), Long Beach (Local name). P. 161.

KING'S COVE 47–36, 52–53 (NTS St. John's 1N/10W). P. 161.

King's Dockyard (St. John's Harbour) (Chappell 1813). P. 102.

KING'S HEAD 47–59, 53–19 (NTS Heart's Content 1N/14W) (Lane, *Directions* 1775, 1810). King – ? George III. Pp. 97, 161.
— KING'S HEAD POND 48–00, 53–18 (NTS Heart's Content 1N/14W, Old Perlican 2C/3W) (NDNR 1N/14 1946).

KINGS HEAD 48–08, 52–58 (NTS Bay de Verde 2C/2W) Red Head (Newfoundland 1941), Kings Head (Provincial Representative CBGN). P. 161.

KINGS POND 47–43, 53–24 (NTS Harbour Grace 1N/11W) (NDNR 1N/11 1948). P. 161.

King's Wharf (St. John's Harbour at Riverhead) (Cook 1762 or Gilbert 1768). P. 83.

King's Wharf (St. John's Harbour – north side) (Cook 1762 or Gilbert 1768). P. 83.

KINGSTON (Set.) 47–49, 53–07 (NTS Heart's Content 1N/14E) Upper Small Point (Census 1857), Kingston (Proclamation 27 August 1920).
See UPPER SMALL POINT. Pp. 119, 132, 140, 146, 161.

KITCHUSES (Set.) 47–27, 53–11 (NTS Holyrood 1N/6E) Ketchums (Census 1869), Kitchues (Census 1874), Catchuses or Kitchuses (M. F. Howley, 1907). Pp. 25–6, 44.

KITE HILL 47–35, 53–47 (NTS Dildo 1N/12W)

KITTY GAULS BROOK 47–32, 52–45 (NTS St. John's 1N/10W) After Kitty Gaul who died ? about 1914 and is said to have kept some kind of inn or house of entertainment on the outskirts of ST. JOHN'S.
Cp. KITCHUSES (NTS Holyrood), DONOVANS (NTS St. John's). P. 131.

KLONDYKE (Causeway) (Bay Roberts Harbour) After the Klondyke River, Yukon, scene of the gold-rush of 1897–9. Presumably the causeway was built about this time. P. 112.

KNOB (Generic). P. 145.

KNOCK HOUR HILL 47–07, 53–57 (NTS Placentia 1N/4W) Knock Hour (Adm. 2915 1864, J. P. Howley, *Geography of Newfoundland* 1876). P. 128.

la baye de Plaisance (Lahontan c. 1696)
See PLACENTIA BAY. P. 38.

La chinette (Friend 1713)
See ST. SHOTTS (NTS St. Shotts). P. 35.

LA HAYE POINT 46–54, 53–37 (NTS St. Mary's 1K/13E) Pt le Hays (Cook 1762 or Gilbert 1768), Pt. La Haye (Lane 1773),

Pt la Hay (Mount and Page 1780),
Point la Haye (Imray, *Sailing Directions* 1862).
— POINT LA HAYE (Set.) 46–54, 53–36
   Point L'Haye (*Population Returns* 1836).
— LA HAYE POND 46–54, 53–36 (USHO 2275 1917).
Pp. 53, 83, 144.

LA MANCHE (Set.) 47–10, 52–52 (NTS Ferryland 1N/2W) (Census 1857).
   Settlement named after the cove: La Manche (Robinson 1669), La Mancha (Southwood 1675), Lamancha (Thornton 1689B), Lamanch (Hack c. 1690 ?), La Manche (Hermite 1695).
— LA MANCHE RIVER (NTS Ferryland 1N/2W, St. Catherine's 1N/3E) (Newfoundland 1941).
Pp. 49, 139.

LA MANCHE (Cove) 47–41, 53–57 (NTS Dildo 1N/12W)
— LA MANCHE (Set.) 47–42, 53–56 (*Population Returns* 1836).
— LA MANCHE HEAD 47–41, 53–57
— LA MANCHE SIDING (Set.) 47–52, 53–54

"La Manche [lead] vein said to have been discovered about 1855 by men in search of a landing place for the first Atlantic cable.
   "Mullock [Bishop Mullock, bishop of Newfoundland 1847–69] states that prior to the opening of the mine in 1857 'the fishermen in the lower part of Placentia Bay used to go to La Manche, take the pure galena, smelt it, and run jiggers out of it, and still the existence of the mine, though almost every pebble on the shore had specks of lead in it, was either unknown or disregarded.'" (Chute, p. 7).
   "The works were first commenced in 1857 by Messrs. Ripley and Co., under whose name and title the mine was carried on for the first few years of its existence, when it passed into other hands, who assumed the title of the Placentia Bay Lead Company; and finally it was once more transferred in 1863 to a third company, termed the La Manche Mining Company" (Murray and Howley, 1868, p. 172).
   Cp. JIGGING COVE.
Pp. 49, 110, 139, 148.

la Perle (Lotter c. 1758)
See PERCH COVE (NTS St. Bride's).
P. 48.

Lacus incognitus (Mason 1626).
Pp. 12–13, 15, 115.

LADEN FIELD'S BROOK 46–52, 53–25 (NTS Biscay Bay River 1K/14W) (Newfoundland 1941). Pp. 128, 145.

Lady Kirk (House at Ferryland) (Yonge 1663–70). P. 68.

LADY LAKE 47–41, 53–15 (NTS Harbour Grace 1N/11E and W)
Lady Pond (Jukes 1842).

Lady Point (Bonnycastle 1842).
See NORTH HEAD (NTS Bay Bulls).
P. 116.

LAKE (Generic). Pp. 115, 143.

LAKE VIEW (Set.) 47–25, 53–09 (Unnamed in NTS Holyrood 1N/6E) ? Formerly Wickalow (Census 1891).

LANCE (Specific) P. 107, except in POINT LANCE (NTS St. Bride's).

Lance arbe (Beaudoin 1697)
   See HANTS HARBOUR (NTS Old Perlican). Pp. 80, 97.

LANCE COVE
See POINT LANCE (NTS St. Bride's).

LANCE COVE 47–03, 52–53 (NTS Ferryland 1N/2W)
Freshwater Bay (Cook 1762 or

Gilbert 1768), Lance Cove (Adm. 2915 1864, Imray, *Sailing Directory* 1873). P. 84.

LANCE COVE 47–05, 52–53 (NTS Ferryland 1N/2W) (USHO 0618 1941).

LANCE COVE 47–29, 53–04 (NTS Holyrood 1N/6E) (CHS 4566 1952).
— LANCE COVE (Set.) 47–28, 53–04 (Census 1857). P. 117.
— LANCE COVE HEAD 47–29, 53–04 (CHS 4566 1952).

LANCE COVE (Set.) (Bell Island) 47–36, 52–59 (NTS St. John's 1N/10W) As feature: (Lane 1774); as set: (*Population Returns* 1836). P. 90.
— LANCE COVE POND 47–37, 52–59

Lance Cove (Set.) (*Population Returns* 1836)
See BROWNSDALE (NTS Old Perlican). P. 107.

LANCE RIVER
See POINT LANCE (NTS St. Bride's).

LAND(s) (Generic). P. 135.

LANE (Generic). P. 148.

LANGLEY COVE 46–56, 53–32 (NTS St. Mary's 1K/13E) (Adm. 2915 1864).
"Tradition has it that an old Englishman lived here many years ago, in the time of the French possession. They called him L'Anglais, the Englishman" (M. F. Howley, xxviii, *NQ*, December 1909).
Langley is also an English place name and family name, and an alternative name for Little Miquelon.
Cp. Englee (NTS Englee 12I/9E) and CAPE ENGLISH (NTS St. Mary's).

LANSECAN HILL 46–59, 53–49 (NTS St. Mary's 1K/13W) (Adm. 2915 1864).
— LANSECAN POINT (Adm. 2915 1864).
Hill and Point are named after the cove, recorded as Nancy Cann (M. F. Howley, xxviii, *NQ*, December 1909), unnamed in NTS, of which the point is the eastern extremity.
Fr. *L'Anse* – the cove.
P. 54.

LARCH PLACE (St. John's)
One of several streets, in an area of ST. JOHN'S developed in the 1940s and 50s, named after trees: Beech, Sycamore, Elm, Maple etc. P. 148.

LATINE POINT 47–19, 54–00 (NTS Argentia 1N/5W, Merasheen 1M/8E) Point Latina (Lane 1772).
Cp. Latin Point (NTS Groais Island 2C/13W). Pp. 52–3, 84.

LAWLER BAY 47–00, 52–54 (NTS Renews 1K/15W) (Adm. 376 1927). P. 132.

LAWRENCE POND 47–28, 53–03 (NTS Holyrood 1N/6E) (CHS 4566 1952). P. 161.

LEA (Generic). P. 145.

LEAD COVE (Set.) 48–03, 53–05 (NTS Old Perlican 2C/3E) (Census 1874).
? Site of lead deposits or mining.

LEAHY POND 47–17, 53–26 (NTS Holyrood 1N/6W) (NDNR 1N/6 1943). P. 132.

LEAMYS BROOK 47–32, 52–41 (NTS St. John's 1N/10E)
— LEAMYS PONDS 47–31, 52–42
"Mr. Leamy, from Blackhead, had a public house or liquor store [at Sclater's Corner, Water Street, St. John's] in the 'gas age' [i.e. after 1845]" (Devine, *Ye Olde St. John's*, p. 62).
P. 132.

LEARS COVE 46–52, 54–12 (NTS St. Bride's 1L/16E)
As set: Lear's Cove (*Population Returns* 1836). Pp. 109, 162.

LEARS COVE 47–36, 53–11 (NTS

Harbour Grace 1N/11E)
(CHS 4572 1954). Pp. 109, 162.

LEARYS BROOK 47–35, 52–42 (NTS
St. John's 1N/10E and W). P. 132.

LEECH POND 46–40, 53–04 (NTS
Trepassey 1K/11E)

LEES GULLY 47–23, 53–13 (NTS
Holyrood 1N/6E)
(*Road Map of the Peninsula of
Avalon* 1930).
— LEE'S POND 47–24, 53–12
   (*Road Map of the Peninsula of
   Avalon* 1930).
P. 162.

LEES POND 47–37, 52–50 (NTS
St. John's 1N/10W). P. 162.

LEFT HAND POND 47–28, 53–21 (NTS
Holyrood 1N/6W) (Adm. 296 1868).
On the left side of HODGEWATER
LINE going inland.
Cp. RIGHT HAND POND 47–28, 53–21.
P. 5.

LEFT POND 47–35, 52–46 (NTS
St. John's 1N/10W)
? Of MIDDLE POND 47–35, 52–46.

LEONARDS POND 47–20, 53–15 (NTS
Holyrood 1N/6E and W) (NDNR 1N/6
1943).
— LEONARDS WATERS 47–18, 53–16
(NDNR 1N/6 1943).
Pp. 133, 143.

LEVEL POND 47–28, 53–21 (NTS
Holyrood 1N/6W)
(Murray and Howley 1872). P. 24.

LIGHTHOUSE (Generic). P. 148.

LINE (Generic). P. 147-8.

LITTLE BARACHOIS (NTS Placentia)
— LITTLE BARACHOIS RIVER
See BARACHOIS.

LITTLE BARACHOIS RIVER (NTS Ship
Cove, Placentia)
See BARACHOIS.

LITTLE BARASWAY (Set.) (NTS Ship
Cove)
See BARACHOIS.

L[ittle] Barasway (Lane 1773)
See LITTLE BARACHOIS (NTS
Placentia) under BARACHOIS.

LITTLE BELL ISLAND
See BELL ISLAND (NTS St. John's).

LITTLE BROOK 47–18, 53–28 (NTS
Holyrood 1N/6W) (NDNR 1N/6 1943).
Tributary of COLINET RIVER (NTS
Placentia).

LITTLE BURKE ISLAND
See BURKE ISLAND (NTS Argentia).

Little Castor's River (Anspach 1819)
See ? WATERFORD RIVER (NTS
St. John's). Pp. 102, 112, 127.

LITTLE CHANCE COVE
See CHANCE COVE (NTS Dildo).

LITTLE COLINET ISLAND
See COLINET (NTS Placentia).

LITTLE COOPERS POND
See COOPERS POND (NTS Harbour
Grace).

LITTLE DUCK POND
See DUCK POND (NTS St. John's).

LITTLE FLINGS POND
See FLINGS BIG POND (NTS Harbour
Grace).

LITTLE GULCH
See GREAT GULCH (NTS St. Bride's.

Little Gut (Chapel Arm) (Wix 1836).
P. 104.
— Little Gut Lookout (Jukes
   1842). P. 114.

LITTLE HARBOUR 46–54, 53–53 (NTS
St. Mary's 1K/13W) (Adm. 2915
1864).

LITTLE HARBOUR 47–08, 53–29 (NTS
St. Catherine's 1N/3W) (Lane 1773).

— LITTLE HARBOUR POND 47–09, 53–18
(Newfoundland 1941).
— LITTLE HARBOUR RIVER 47–08, 53–29
(*Road Map of the Peninsula of Avalon* 1930).
See NEW BRIDGE (NTS St. Catherine's).

LITTLE HARBOUR 47–38, 53–56 (NTS Dildo 1N/12W)
(Lane 1772). P. 84.
— LITTLE HARBOUR (Set.) 47–39, 53–56
(*Population Returns* 1836), Little Harbour East (Census 1869).
— LITTLE HARBOUR HEAD 47–39, 53–58
— LITTLE HARBOUR ISLAND 47–37, 53–58
Harbour Island (Imray, *Sailing Directions* 1862).

LITTLE HARBOUR 47–55, 53–42 (NTS Sunnyside 1N/13E)

LITTLE ISLAND 47–24, 53–58 (NTS Argentia 1N/5W) (Adm. 3266 1939). One of the IONA ISLANDS.

LITTLE ISLAND COVE POND
See LOWER ISLAND COVE (NTS Heart's Content, Bay de Verde).

LITTLE ISLAND POND
See BIG ISLAND POND (NTS Harbour Grace) under ISLAND.

LITTLE MONUMENT POND
See MONUMENT POND (NTS Heart's Content).

LITTLE MOSQUITO COVE (NTS Sunnyside)
See MOSQUITO.

LITTLE OLIVER POND
See OLIVERS POND (NTS St. John's).

LITTLE OTTER POND
See BIG OTTER POND (NTS Holyrood) under OTTER.

Little Pernocan (Robinson 1669)
See NEW PERLICAN (NTS Heart's Content). P. 70.

LITTLE PINCHGUT (Cove) (NTS Dildo)
See PINCHGUT.

Little Placentia (Set.) (*Population Returns* 1836)
See ARGENTIA (Set.) (NTS Argentia). P. 38.

Little Placentia (Robinson 1669)
See ARGENTIA HARBOUR (NTS Argentia). P. 38.

LITTLE POND 47–27, 52–57 (NTS Bay Bulls 1N/7W)
(NDNR Bay Bulls 1943).

LITTLE POND 47–31, 53–15 (NTS Harbour Grace 1N/11E)
(CHS 4572 1954).

LITTLE POWERS POND
See POWERS POND (NTS St. John's).

LITTLE RATTLING BROOK (NTS Argentia)
See RATTLING.

Little Red head (Southwood 1675)
See RED CLIFF HEAD (NTS St. John's). Pp. 72, 76.

LITTLE RINDERS POND
See RINDERS POND (NTS Harbour Grace).

LITTLE SALMONIER POINT (NTS Placentia)
— LITTLE SALMONIER RIVER
See SALMONIER.

LITTLE SEAL COVE (NTS Argentia)
See SEAL.

LITTLE SOUTHERN HARBOUR
See SOUTHERN HARBOUR (Set.) (NTS Dildo).

LITTLE TRIANGLE POND (NTS Holyrood)
See TRIANGLE.

LIZZY POINT 46–57, 53–52 (NTS St. Mary's 1K/13E)
Ellis Point (Cook 1762 or Gilbert 1768), Ellis point, Lizzy point (Imray, *Sailing Directory* 1873). P. 83.

LOADERS POND 47–47, 53–18 (NTS Heart's Content 1N/14W) (NDNR 1N/14 1946). P. 162.

LOCKYERS WATERS 47–21, 53–17 (NTS Holyrood 1N/6W) (NDNR 1N/6 1943). Pp. 143, 162.

LOGY BAY 47–38, 52–40 (NTS St. John's 1N/10E) (Southwood 1675) ... Lugy Bay (Bonnycastle 1842), Logy Bay (Imray, *Sailing Directions* 1862). P. 73.
— LOGY BAY (Set.) (*Population Returns* 1836). "Here, in the summer only, live the fishers and their families, in huts and shanties of turf and boughs" (McCrea 1869, p. 219).

LONDA or LUNNON (Cove) (Baccalieu Island) Local usage for London. One of three landing places on the island. The other two are Brista or Bristo (Bristol) and Famit or Farmint (Falmouth).

LONDON POND 47–44, 53–16 (NTS Harbour Grace 1N/11W) (NDNR 1N/11 1948).

LONG BEACH 46–38, 53–08 (NTS Trepassey 1K/11E) (CHS 4576 1950). The beach, rather more than a mile in extent, between WATERN COVE and LONG COVE.
— LONG BEACH (Set.) (Newfoundland 1955).
— LONG COVE Bristoll Cove (Southwood 1675) ... Bristol Cove (Mount and Page 1755). The name is not recorded again, or the cove marked, until Long Cove (*Road Map of the Peninsula of Avalon* 1930), but the old name survives in local usage as Bristy Cove.
See BRISTOL'S HOPE (Set.) (NTS Harbour Grace).
Associated by G. R. F. Prowse, CM, III, with a South Newfoundland Survey of 1497–8.
Pp. 63, 74.

LONG BEACH (Set.) 47–57, 53–03 (NTS Heart's Content 1N/14E) (Census 1935).

LONG BEACH (Set.) 48–00, 53–49 (NTS Sunnyside 1N/13W) (Smallwood 1941).
Of SOUTHWEST ARM, Random Sound (NTS Sunnyside, Random Island).

Long Beach (Set.) (Census 1857)
— LONG BEACH POND 47–35, 53–16 (NTS Harbour Grace 1N/11W) (CHS 4572 1954). P. 118.

LONG COVE
See LONG BEACH (NTS Trepassey).

LONG COVE 47–35, 53–40 (NTS Dildo 1N/12E) (Jukes 1840).
— LONG COVE (Set.) 47–33, 53–40 (Census 1884).
P. 113.

LONG GULLIES (Ponds) 47–18, 53–07 (NTS Holyrood 1N/6E) (NDNR 1N/6 1943).

LONG GULLY 47–16, 53–12 (NTS Holyrood 1N/6E) (NDNR 1N/6 1943).

LONG GULLY (Pond) 47–25, 52–53 (NTS Bay Bulls 1N/7W) (NDNR Bay Bulls 1943).
A long, narrow pond between NORTHERN POND 47–27, 52–53 and BIG NORTHERN POND 47–25, 52–54.

LONG HARBOUR 47–25, 53–49 (NTS Argentia 1N/5W) haure long ("Dépôt 132.2.10" 1706), Long Harbour (Cook 1763).
— LONG HARBOUR (Set.) 47–26, 53–48 (Census 1857).
— Long Harbour arm (Wix 1836)

— LONG HARBOUR HEAD 47–23, 53–56
— LONG HARBOUR STATION 47–27, 53–43 (NTS Argentia 1N/5E) (*Road Map of the Peninsula of Avalon* 1930).
Cp. CRAWLEY ISLAND.
Pp. 51, 104, 110, 125.

LONG HARRY (Bell Island) (Point) 47–39, 52–55 (NTS St. John's 1N/10W)
See Old Harry. P. 73–4.

Long Harry (Harbour Grace) (Rock) (Thornton 1689c)
— LONG HARRY COVE 47–43, 53–11 (NTS Harbour Grace 1N/11E) (Adm. 297 1933).
See Old Harry. P. 73–4.

Long Hill Deer Country (Wix 1836). P. 104.

LONG ISLAND POND 47–43, 53–20 (NTS Harbour Grace 1N/11W)
(NDNR 1N/11 1948).
The composition of the name is Long + (Island Pond).

LONG POINT occurs at 46–41, 53–04 (NTS Trepassey 1K/11E) (CHS 4576 1950); 46–56, 53–37 (NTS St. Mary's 1K/13E) (Adm. 3264 1902); 47–16, 52–46 (NTS Bay Bulls 1N/7W) (CHS 4586 1944); 47–23, 52–43 (NTS Bay Bulls 1N/7E) (Jukes 1842); 47–45, 53–31 (NTS Dildo 1N/12E, NTS Heart's Content 1N/14W) (Lane, *Directions* 1775, 1810) p. 181.

LONG POND 47–22, 53–30 (NTS Holyrood 1N/6W)
Tusem Gospen (Murray and Howley 1872), Long Pond (NDNR 1N/6 1943). P. 25.

LONG POND (Set.) 47–31, 52–58 (Unnamed in NTS St. John's 1N/10W) (Census 1857), Long Pond Manuels (Local usage).
See MANUELS LONG POND (feature). Pp. 116, 117.

LONG POND 47–43, 53–28 (NTS Harbour Grace 1N/11W) (NDNR 1N/11 1948),
— LONG POND BROOK 47–43, 53–30 (NDNR 1N/11 1948).

LONG POND also occurs at 47–19, 52–51 (NTS Bay Bulls 1N/7W) (Adm. 296 1868); 47–21, 52–49 (NTS Bay Bulls 1N/7W) (Adm. 296 1868); 47–31, 53–26 (NTS Harbour Grace 1N/11W) (NDNR 1N/11 1948); 47–35, 52–44 (NTS St John's 1N/10E); 47–45, 53–18 (NTS Harbour Grace 1N/11W) (NDNR 1N/11 1948); 47–50, 53–21 (NTS Heart's Content 1N/14W) (NDNR 1N/14 1946); 47–57, 53–14 (NTS Heart's Content 1N/14E) (NDNR 1N/14 1946); 47–56, 53–18 (NTS Heart's Content 1N/14W) (NDNR 1N/14 1946).

LONGSTONE (Hill, Ridge) 46–54, 53–56 (NTS St. Mary's 1K/13W) (Adm. 2915 1864).
Longsdon, Longstone – English place names applied to ridges. (Ekwall, p. 289).

LOO (Specific). Local name for the Greater Common Loon, which nests on or near shores of inland ponds. (Peters and Burleigh, p. 46).

LOO POND 47–27, 52–55 (NTS Bay Bulls 1N/7W) (NDNR Bay Bulls 1943).

LOO POND 47–34, 53–28 (NTS Harbour Grace 1N/11W) (NDNR 1N/11 1948).

LOOKOUT (Specific and Generic). Pp. 105, 144.

THE LOOKOUT 47–45, 53–27 (NTS Heart's Content 1N/14W).
Pp. 140, 144.

LOOKOUT POND 47–16, 52–55 (NTS Bay Bulls 1N/7W) (NDNR Bay Bulls 1943). Pp. 105, 144.

240 / *Place Names of the Avalon Peninsula*

LOON POND 47–17, 53–20 (NTS Holyrood 1N/6W) (NDNR 1N/6 1943).
See LOO (Specific) above.

LORDS POND 47–23, 52–59 (NTS Bay Bulls 1N/7W)
(NDNR Bay Bulls 1943).
? Short for Lords' and Ladies' – Newfoundland name of the Eastern Harlequin Duck. (Peters and Burleigh, p. 111).

"The people here tell a remarkable fact, if it is a true one, of a kind of duck call'd here Lords and Ladies, who they say at times pursue the gulls whom they persecute till they make them dung which they catch with great dexterity before it reaches the water & immediately leave off the chase" (Banks, *Journal*, August 9, 1766). "those very beautiful birds, called by the people of Newfoundland 'lords and ladies' " (Wix, p. 138).

LOUIS POND 47–20, 53–11 (NTS Holyrood 1N/6E)
(NDNR 1N/6 1943). P. 162.

LOUSEY ROCK 47–53, 53–24 (NTS Heart's Content 1N/14W)
? for lousy – dirty, filthy.
The rock is covered with bird-droppings.

Low Black Pt. or Torbay North Pt. (Mount and Page 1780)
See FLAT ROCK POINT (NTS St. John's). P. 98.

Low Point (Mount and Page 1780)
See SPRIGGS POINT (NTS St. John's). P. 98.

LOW POINT 48–03, 52–57 (NTS Bay de Verde 2C/2W)
Clip Boney (Thornton 1689B), Chipbony (*English Pilot. The Fourth Book* 1716, 1780). P. 77.
— LOW POINT (Set.) 48–04, 52–57 (*Population Returns* 1836). P. 107.

LOW ROOM POINT 47–19, 53–58 (NTS Argentia 1N/5W) (CHS 4622 ? 1953).
Sc. the low point with a "room" on it. P. 147.

LOWER BACK COVE 47–36, 53–13 (NTS Harbour Grace 1N/11E)
(CHS 4572 1954).
Of PORT DE GRAVE. Cp. UPPER BACK COVE 47–35, 53–13.

LOWER COVE 47–25, 52–41 (NTS Bay Bulls 1N/7E) (NDNR Bay Bulls 1943).
The first cove south of MOTION BAY.

Lower Gullies (Set.) (*Population Returns* 1836)
See RIVERDALE (NTS Holyrood). Pp. 107, 117.
— LOWER GULLIES RIVER 47–30, 53–02 (NTS Holyrood 1N/6E) (CHS 4566 1952).
Cp. UPPER GULLIES (Set.) (NTS Holyrood).

LOWER ISLAND COVE (Set.) 48–00, 52–59 (NTS Heart's Content 1N/14E, Bay de Verde 2C/2W)
As feature: (Lane 1774); as set: (Thoresby 1796, *Population Returns* 1836).
Cp. UPPER ISLAND COVE (NTS Harbour Grace). Pp. 6, 94, 98, 107, 116.
— ISLAND COVE POND 48–00, 53–00 (NTS Heart's Content 1N/14E) (NDNR 1N/14 1946).
— LITTLE ISLAND COVE POND (NDNR 1N/14 1946).

LOWER POND 47–17, 52–49 (NTS Bay Bulls 1N/7W) (CHS 4586 1944).
Cp. UPPER POND 47–17, 52–50.

Lower Ram (Islands)
The northern group of the IONA ISLANDS (NTS Argentia). P. 85.

LOWER SMALL POINT 47–50, 53–06 (NTS Heart's Content 1N/14E)
As set: (Census 1857). P. 119.

LUCY BEACH 47–24, 53–08 (NTS Holyrood 1N/6E)
(CHS 4573 1953). P. 133.

LUMLEY COVE 46–58, 52–57 (NTS Renews 1K/15W)
Rumley's Cove (M. F. Howley, XXVI, *NQ*, July 1909, Census 1921, and local name), Lumley Cove (Adm. 376 1927). P. 133.

LUTHERS GULLIES (Ponds) 47–43, 53–22 (NTS Harbour Grace 1N/11W)
(NDNR 1N/11 1948). P. 162.

LYNCHS POND 47–48, 53–17 (NTS Heart's Content 1N/14W)
(NDNR 1N/14 1946). P. 133.

MCCARTHYS POND 47–42, 53–18 (NTS Harbour Grace 1N/11W)
(NDNR 1N/11 1948). P. 133.

MACDONALD COVE 47–15, 53–56 (NTS Placentia 1N/4W)
McDonald's Cove (Murray and Howley 1868). P. 133.

MCGRATH POND 47–19, 53–20 (NTS Holyrood 1N/6W)
(NDNR 1N/6 1943). P. 133.

MCKAY ISLAND 47–51, 53–56 (NTS Sunnyside 1N/13W)
? Frenchman's Island (Wix 1836). ? After A. M. McKay (1834–1905), born at Pictou, NS, who came to Newfoundland in 1857 as superintendent of the Anglo-American Telegraph Co. (Mosdell, p. 83; D. W. Prowse, pp. 496, 639, 641).
Cp. NIAGARA POINT (NTS Sunnyside). P. 105.

MCLEOD POINT 47–34, 53–38 (NTS Dildo 1N/12E)
McLeod Head (DND Rantem 1942).

MAD POINT 47–37, 53–12 (NTS Harbour Grace 1N/11E)
(Imray, *Sailing Directory* 1873).
— MAD ROCKS 47–38, 53–12

Mad Rock (Lane 1774), Mad Rocks (Imray, *Sailing Directory* 1873). P. 92.

MAD ROCK 47–46, 53–11 (NTS Heart's Content 1N/14E) (Adm. 296 1868).
Cp. FOLLY ROCKS 47–46, 53–09.

MADDOX COVE 47–28, 52–42 (NTS Bay Bulls 1N/7E)
(Adm. 296 1868). P. 162.
— MADDOX Cove (Set.) (Census 1857). P. 116.
— MADDOX COVE ROAD
— MADDOX POND 47–30, 52–42 (NDNR Bay Bulls 1943).

MAGGOTTY (Specific). Pp. 76–7.

MAGGOTTY COVE 47–18, 52–49 (NTS Bay Bulls 1N/7W)
Magotty Cove (Lane 1773).
— MAGGOTTY POND 47–18, 52–50 (NDNR Bay Bulls 1943).
P. 86.

MAGGOTTY COVE (St. John's Harbour) (Unnamed in NTS St. John's 1N/10E)
Magotts Coue (Visscher c. 1680).

MAGGOTTY POINT 46–58, 53–49 (NTS St. Mary's 1K/13W)
(Adm. 2915 1864).

Magotts Coue (Visscher c. 1680) See MAGGOTTY COVE (St. John's Harbour).

MAHERS (Set.) 47–24, 53–22 (NTS Holyrood 1N/6W)
(NDNR 1N/6 1943). Pp. 133, 139.

MAIDEN ISLAND 47–45, 53–11 (NTS Heart's Content 1N/14E)
(NDNR 1N/14 1946). P. 162.
Maiden occurs as an element in Devon place names (Gover et al., pp. 26, 460, 614, 647).

MAIDENS PONDS 47–42, 53–17 (NTS Harbour Grace 1N/11W)
(NDNR 1N/11 1948). P. 162.

MAINS MARSH 47–41, 53–14 (NTS Harbour Grace 1N/11E)
(CHS 4590 1943). Pp. 143, 162.

MAINTOP HILL 47–28, 52–45 (NTS Bay Bulls 1N/7W) (Adm. 296 1868).
Maintop – Top of the mainmast; a platform just above the head of the lower main-mast.
Cp. Foretop Hill (Adm. 296 1868), unnamed in NTS.
Cp. TOPSAIL 47–32, 52–56 (NTS St. John's).

MAKER POINT 47–19, 53–55 (NTS Argentia 1N/5W)
(CHS 4622 ? 1953).
? As transferred place name – after Maker, village in Cornwall, on west side of Plymouth Sound, where the old church is a well-known landmark.
? As family name – p. 133. Cp. KELLY POINT at southern entrance to FOX HARBOUR (NTS Argentia).

MAKINSON (GOULDS P.O.) (Set.) 47–31, 53–17 (NTS Harbour Grace 1N/11W) the Golds (Jukes 1842), the Goulds (Murray and Howley 1872), Mackinson's farm (Murray and Howley 1872).
"the beautiful farm called 'the Goulds', the property of Mr Makinson" (Murray and Howley 1872, p. 285).
See GOULDS. Pp. 24, 112–13, 118, 119, 139, 148, 162.

MALL BAY 46–58, 53–35 (NTS St. Mary's 1K/13E)
(Lane 1773), Mal Bay (Purdy 1828). Pp. 86–7.
— MALL BAY (Set.) 46–59, 53–35
Mal Bay (*Population Returns 1836*)
— MALL BAY BROOK 46–59, 53–34

MALONEYS BEACH 47–23, 53–08 (NTS Holyrood 1N/6E) (CHS 4573, 1953).
— MALONEY'S RIVER 47–26, 53–10 (CHS 4573 1953).
P. 133.

MANUELS (Set.) 47–31, 52–57 (NTS St. John's 1N/10W)

(Census 1857). Pp. 116–7, 118, 138, 139, 162.
— MANUELS LONG POND 47–31, 52–58
See LONG POND (Set.)
P. 116.
— MANUELS RIVER 47–32, 52–57
Manuels Brook (Murray and Howley 1868). P. 138.

MARKLAND (Set.) 47–23, 53–33 (NTS Argentia 1N/5E)
(1934).
See T. Lodge, "Land Colonisation and Markland" in Smallwood (ed.), *The Book of Newfoundland*, I, pp. 66–8; T. Lodge, *Dictatorship in Newfoundland* (Cassell, London, 1939), pp. 172–83. P. 145.

MARQUISE (Bight) 47–17, 53–59 (Unnamed in NTS Argentia 1N/5W)
Marquess H. (Popple 1733), Martise Reach (Wix 1836), Marquise (M. F. Howley, xxx, *NQ*, March 1911).
— MARQUISE (Isthmus) (*NLP* 1951).
The "name given to the narrow isthmus joining Little Placentia [ARGENTIA] peninsula to the mainland" (*NLP* I, p. 104).
— MARQUISE (Set.)
(Census 1857).
Pp. 52, 82, 104, 129

MARSH (Generic). P. 143.

Marshall's Folly (Set.) (Carbonear) (Census 1857). P. 119.

MARTIN ROWES POND 47–46, 53–27 (NTS Heart's Content 1N/14W)
(NDNR 1N/14 1946), Martin's Pond (Local name).
Martin Rowe was one of the first settlers at HEART'S DELIGHT from HEART'S CONTENT (Communication from E. Bishop). P. 165.

Martise Reach (Wix 1836)
See MARQUISE (unnamed in NTS Argentia). P. 104.

Mary Gally Rock or the Griffith

(Hack c. 1690 ?)
See ? MOLL ROCK, MOLL POINT (NTS Argentia). P. 78.

MARYVALE (Set.) 47–30, 53–12 (NTS Holyrood 1N/6E)
Turk's Gut (*Population Returns* 1836), Maryvale (Proclamation 7 November 1919).
Marysvale (Smallwood 1940).
  See TURKS GUT (NTS Harbour Grace). Pp. 85, 106, 118, 125.

MASTERS HEAD 47–43, 53–50 (NTS Dildo 1N/12W)
(Wix 1836). Pp. 105, 162.

MATTYS POND 47–42, 53–23 (NTS Harbour Grace 1N/11W)
(NDNR 1N/11 1948).

MATURIN BROOK 47–28, 53–48 (NTS Argentia 1N/5W)
— MATURIN PONDS 47–26, 53–49
  (Adm. 3266 1939).
P. 133.

MAURICE POOLE COVE 47–20, 53–55 (NTS Argentia 1N/5W)
(CHS 4622 ? 1953). Pp. 134, 164.

MEADOW POINT 46–44, 53–23 (NTS Trepassey 1K/11W)
(USHO 0618 1941), The Point Meadow (Local name).
Formerly a grassy area used for grazing, more recently the site of a fish plant.

MERCERS COVE 47–36, 53–14 (NTS Harbour Grace 1N/11E)
As set: (Census 1857).
See BAY ROBERTS. Pp. 119, 162.

MERCHANT ISLAND 47–24, 53–58 (NTS Argentia 1N/5W) (NLP 1951).
One of the IONA ISLANDS. Pp. 51, 85.

Mestigue-gundaly Gospen (Murray and Howley 1872)
  See ROUND POND WEST (NTS Holyrood). P. 25.

MIDDLE ARM 47–26, 53–12 (NTS Holyrood 1N/6E) (CHS 4573 1953).

Between CONCEPTION HARBOUR and AVONDALE. P. 141.
— MIDDLE ARM (Set.)
  (Census 1857). P. 118.

Middle Bight (Set.) Census 1857)
See CODNER (Unnamed in NTS St. John's). Pp. 117, 141.

MIDDLE COVE 47–39, 52–41 (NTS St. John's 1N/10E) (Jukes 1842)
Between TORBAY and OUTER COVE. P. 112.
— MIDDLE COVE (Set.)
  (Census 1857).
— MIDDLE COVE ROAD 47–38, 52–41

MIDDLE GULL POND 47–22, 53–18 (NTS Holyrood 1N/6W)
Gull Pond (Newfoundland 1941), Middle Gull Pond (NDNR 1N/6 1943), Gull Pond (Newfoundland 1949).

Middle Gut (Set.)
See ST. STEPHEN (Set.) 46–47, 53–37 (Unnamed in NTS St. Mary's).

Middle House (Set.) (Census 1857). P. 120.

MIDDLE POND 46–40, 53–05 (NTS Trepassey 1K/11E) (CHS 4576 1950).
Second pond of river, unnamed in NTS, which enters the Atlantic ¼ mile west of CAPE RACE.

MIDDLE POND 47–23, 52–48 (NTS Bay Bulls 1N/7W)
(Newfoundland 1941).
Between LONG POND 47–21, 52–49 and BAY BULLS BIG POND 47–24, 52–47.

MIDDLE POND 47–35, 52–46 (NTS St. John's 1N/10W)
The smaller part of a pond, the greater of which is BIG POND 47–35, 52–46. MIDDLE POND lies between BIG POND and LEFT POND 47–35, 52–46.

MIDDLE POND 47–42, 52–46 (NTS St. John's 1N/10W)
Between MOON POND and MIDDLE THREE ISLAND POND.

Middle Rock (Bryants Cove) (Mount and Page 1780). P. 97.

MIDDLE ROCKY POND 47–36, 52–46 (NTS St. John's 1N/10W)
? Associated with MIDDLE POND 47–35, 52–46.

MIDDLE THREE ISLAND POND 47–41, 52–46 (NTS St. John's 1N/10W)
Associated with NORTH THREE ISLAND POND 47–44, 52–45 and ? THREE ISLAND POND 47–31, 52–54.

MILES BROOK 47–45, 52–47 (NTS St. John's 1N/10W)
— MILES POND 47–44, 52–47. P. 162.

MILLER'S POND 46–46, 53–21 (NTS Biscay Bay River 1K/14W)
(*Road Map of the Peninsula of Avalon* 1930).
After a family once resident in the area. P. 162.

MINER POINT 47–24, 52–42 (NTS Bay Bulls 1N/7E) (Adm. 296 1868). See SHOAL BAY (NTS Bay Bulls). P. 102.

MINT COVE 47–37, 53–17 (NTS Harbour Grace 1N/11W)
(co Misc. 199.18 1783).
Mint is said to grow in the cove, as it does along the banks of many rivers in the area.

MISTAKEN POINT 46–37, 53–10 (NTS Trepassey 1K/11E)
? Ponta del pa[drao] ("Oliveriana" 1505–8), ? P de crux (Maggiolo 1527), ? Porto da cruz (Freire 1546), ? Port de X ("Vallard" 1547), ? P. de + (Desceliers 1550) ... ? P da cruz (Langenes 1598); Mistaken poynt (Robinson 1669), C Mistaken (Ogilby 1671, Seller c. 1671), Mistaken Point (Southwood 1675 ... Cook 1763); Mistaken Point, French Mistaken Point (Lane 1773), Mistaken Points (Cook and Lane 1770 [1775]A), English Mistaken Point, French Mistaken Point

(Imray, *Sailing Directions* 1862). Pp. 18, 39, 71.

MITCHELLS POND NORTH 47–36, 52–51 (NTS St. John's 1N/10W)
— MITCHELLS POND SOUTH 47–33, 52–52. P. 162.

MIZZEN HILL 47–52, 53–20 (NTS Heart's Content 1N/14W)
? Like a mizen sail. ? In relation to NORTHER POINT
— MIZZEN POND 47–52, 53–22. (NDNR 1N/14 1946).

MOANY COVE 47–27, 53–56 (NTS Argentia 1N/5W)
As set: Mooney's Cove (*Population Returns* 1836), Money's Cove (Wix 1836); Moany Cove (Adm. 3266 1939).
— MOANY COVE POINT (Adm. 3266 1939).
Pp. 104, 110.

MOBILE ['moːbəl] (Set.) 47–15, 52–51 (NTS Ferryland 1N/2W)
(*Population Returns* 1836).
— MOBILE BAY 47–15, 52–50
Moueable B ("Blathwayt" c. 1630–40), Mummable Bay (Robinson 1669) ? Barron Cove (Ogilby 1671), Momable B (Seller c. 1671), Momables B (Southwood 1675), Movable B (Thornton 1689A), Momables B (Thornton 1689B), Mummale Bay (Hack c. 1690 ?), Momables (Fitzhugh 1693), B de Momales (Hermite 1695), Momables Bay (Gaudy 1715, Popple 1733), B Manuale (Buache 1736), Bay Mouales (Bellin 1754), Momables Bay (Lane 1773 – Imray, *Sailing Directions* 1862), Mobile Bay (Imray, *Sailing Directory* 1873), Moble (M. F. Howley, XXIV, *NQ*, December 1908).
Pp. 49, 66.
— MOBILE BIG POND 47–16, 53–02

(NTS Holyrood 1N/6E, Bay Bulls 1N/7W) (Newfoundland 1941).
— MOBILE FIRST POND 47–15, 52–54 (NTS Bay Bulls 1N/7W) (NDNR Bay Bulls 1943).
— MOBILE RIVER 47–15, 52–51 (Newfoundland 1941).
— I. Momables (Franquelin 1699, 1708).

MOLL POINT 47–16, 54–00 (NTS Argentia 1N/5W, Merasheen 1M/8E) Pt. Moll (Lane 1772); as set: Point Maul (*Population Returns* 1836); Moll Point (Imray, *Sailing Directions* 1862).
— MOLL ROCK
? Mary Gally Rock or the Griffith (Hack c. 1690 ?), Moll Rock (*NP* 1952).
Pp. 78, 84.

MOLLYS ISLAND 47–32, 53–12 (NTS Harbour Grace 1N/11E) ? Sculpin Island (Cove) (Jukes 1842), Admirals island (Adm. 297 1868, Imray, *Sailing Directory* 1873, *Sailing Directions* 1905), Mollys Island (CHS 4572 1954). P. 113.

Momable B (Seller c. 1671)
See MOBILE BAY (NTS Ferryland).
P. 66.

MONDAY POND 48–03, 52–58 (NTS Bay de Verde 2C/2W) (Provincial Representative CBGN).
Cp. MUNDY POND (NTS Holyrood and Bay de Verde). Pp. 133, 162.

MONDAYS POND 47–29, 53–15 (NTS Holyrood 1N/6W) (CHS 4573 1953).
Cp. MUNDY POND (NTS Holyrood and Bay de Verde). Pp. 133, 162.

The Monument (Hill) (Jukes 1842). P. 114.

MONUMENT POND 47–49, 53–17 (NTS Heart's Content 1N/14W) (NDNR 1N/14 1946).
Local tradition maintains that a monument was erected in the vicinity of the pond in memory of a party of people who lost their lives while travelling from HEART'S CONTENT to CARBONEAR. (Communication from E. Bishop).
— LITTLE MONUMENT POND 47–49, 53–17 (NDNR 1N/14 1946).

MOON POND 47–42, 52–45 (NTS St. John's 1N/10E and W)
Cp. HALF MOON POND 47–43, 52–45.

Mooney's Cove (Set.) (*Population Returns* 1836)
See MOANY COVE (NTS Argentia).
P. 110.

MOORES GULCH 46–40, 53–04 (NTS Trepassey 1K/11E) (CHS 4576 1950). P. 141.
— MOORES POINT
(CHS 4576 1950).
Pp. 133, 163.

MORIARTYS POND 47–34, 52–51 (NTS St. John's 1N/10W). P. 133.

MOSQUITO (Specific). P. 63.

MOSQUITO (Set.) 46–59, 53–41 (NTS St. Mary's 1K/13E) (Census 1857). P. 120.
— MOSQUITO COVE
(USHO 2275 1917).
— MOSQUITO POINT 46–58, 53–41 (Adm. 3264 1902).

MOSQUITO BROOK 47–43, 53–12 (NTS Harbour Grace 1N/11E) (CHS 4590 1943).
— Mosquito Cove
See BRISTOL'S HOPE (NTS Harbour Grace).
— MOSQUITO POINT 47–44, 53–11 (Lane 1774).
P. 90.
— MOSQUITO POND 47–43, 53–12 (CHS 4590 1943).

GREAT MOSQUITO COVE 47–49, 53–53 (NTS Sunnyside 1N/13W)
Flagstaffe Harbour (Guy 1612), Mosquito Cove (Jukes 1842),

246 / *Place Names of the Avalon Peninsula*

Great Mosquito Cove (Imray, *Sailing Directions* 1862). Pp. 59, 60, 111.
— LITTLE MOSQUITO COVE 47–50, 53–54 (Imray, *Sailing Directions* 1862).

Mother Ixx's (Cove) (Set.) (Census 1857)
See REGINAVILLE (NTS Placentia). P. 120.

THE MOTION
(M. F. Howley, XXIV, *NQ*, December 1908).
"The sea off the south point of Petty Harbour is known to the fishermen as The Motion or Petty Harbour Motion. The name is quite expressive, as there is almost always a sort of 'under-tow' which causes the water to be somewhat rough" (M. F. Howley, XXIV, *NQ*, December 1908). P. 90.
— MOTION BAY 47–27, 52–40 (NTS Bay Bulls 1N/7E)
Petty Harbour Bay (Jukes 1840), Motion Bay (Adm. 296 1868), Petty Bay (Imray, *Sailing Directory* 1873), Motion Bay (NLP 1951).
— MOTION HEAD 47–26, 52–39
? C de Portogesi (Ruysch 1508), ? Cap du Portugaise (Verrier 1727), ? Cap des Portugais (Buache 1736), Petty Harbour Point (Lane 1773), Motion Head (Adm. 296 1868).
"C. de Portogesi ... has been taken for Cape Race, but ... I agree with [G. R. F.] Prowse in making [it] a cape farther north, no doubt the one called Cap des Portugals [sic], near St. John's on the Buache map of 1736" Ganong, *Crucial Maps*, p. 41). G. R. F. Prowse, *CM* III, p. 125, suggests that the Portuguese arms were erected in 1500 by Cortereal and must have been seen by some later explorer.
Pp. 30, 89–90.

THE MOTION (Set.) 47–31, 53–17 (NTS Harbour Grace 1N/11W)
Settlement near the tidal limit of SOUTH RIVER.

Moueable B ("Blathwayt" c. 1630–40)
See MOBILE BAY (NTS Ferryland). P. 66.

MOUNT (Generic). P. 145.

MOUNT ARLINGTON HEIGHTS (Set.) 47–26, 53–52 (NTS Argentia 1N/5W)
Formerly Sibley Cove; Mount Arlington Heights (DND Placentia 1942).
? Renamed by the Rev. Francis Cacciola.
Cp. SIBLEYS COVE (NTS Old Perlican). Pp. 129, 145.

MOUNT CARMEL (Set.) 47–09, 53–29 (NTS St. Catherine's 1N/3W)
? Rattling Brook (*Population Returns* 1836); Salmonier North; Mount Carmel (Proclamation 25 June 1930).
— MOUNT CARMEL POND 47–08, 53–06.
Pp. 5, 108, 145.

MOUNT CASHEL (St. John's). Pp. 127, 145.

mo[unt] Faulcon (Renews Harbour) (Yonge 1663–70). P. 68.

MOUNT MISERY POND 46–50, 53–25 (NTS Biscay Bay River 1K/14W) (Newfoundland 1949).
There is no mountain in the vicinity. W. E. Cormack named a Mount Misery in the interior of Newfoundland after spending an unpleasant night on 16–17 October 1822, when storm-bound while crossing the island on foot. (Cormack, p. 63). P. 145.

MOUNT PEARL (PARK) (Set.) 47–31, 52–47 (NTS St. John's 1N/10W)
One of a number of country residences and farms created during Sir Thomas Cochrane's governorship

of Newfoundland, 1825–34. See D. W. Prowse, p. 427.

Sir James Pearl, a retired naval officer, "was given by the Home Government in recognition of his good work 600 acres of land, ever since known as Mount Pearl" (Devine, p. 161). He died there in 1840. Pp. 5, 145–6, 163.

Mount Sea-pie (Jukes 1842)
See SEPOY HILL (NTS Placentia). P. 114.

MOUNTAIN (Generic). P. 145.

MOUSE ISLANDS 47–47, 53–47 (NTS Sunnyside 1N/13W)
Mouse Islets (NP 1952).

Mrs Fursey (Visscher c. 1680, Thornton 1689B), Mrs Furzey (*English Pilot. The Fourth Book* 1716) (Stage or Cove) (St. John's Harbour). Pp. 68, 76.

MUDDY HOLE (Pond) 47–39, 53–17 (NTS Harbour Grace 1N/11W) (CHS 4572 1954). Pp. 141, 143.

Mully's Cove
(Lane 1774); as set: Muley's Cove (Thoresby 1796), Mulley's Cove (*Population Returns* 1836); Mulloy Cove (Jukes 1840).
See BROAD COVE (NTS Heart's Content). Pp. 92, 98, 133.

Mummable Bay (Robinson 1669) See MOBILE BAY (NTS Ferryland). P. 66.

MUNDY POND 47–21, 52–52 (NTS Bay Bulls 1N/7W).
Cp. MONDAY POND (NTS Bay de Verde), MONDAYS POND (NTS Holyrood).

MUNDYS POND 47–33, 52–44 (NTS St. John's 1N/10E). Pp. 133, 163.
Cp. MONDAY POND (NTS Bay de Verde), MONDAYS POND (NTS Holyrood). Pp. 133, 163.

MURPHY COVE 47–36, 53–55 (NTS Dildo 1N/12W). P. 133.

MURPHY POINT 46–58, 53–35 (NTS St. Mary's 1K/13E) (Adm. 3264 1902). P. 133.

MURPHYS FIRST POND 47–54, 53–18 (NTS Heart's Content 1N/14W) (NDNR 1N/14 1946). P. 133.

MURPHYS RIVER 47–08, 53–24 (NTS St. Catherine's 1N/3W) (Newfoundland 1941). P. 134.

MURRAYS POND 47–37, 52–49 (NTS St. John's 1N/10W). P. 134.

Muscita ("Blathwayt" c. 1630–40)
See BRISTOL'S HOPE (NTS Heart's Content). P. 63.

MUSKRAT BROOK 46–54, 54–11 (NTS St. Bride's 1L/16E) (Adm. 2915 1864).

MUSSEL BED POND 47–33, 53–19 (NTS Harbour Grace 1N/11W) (CHS 4572 1954). P. 87.

Muscle Pond and Cove (Mount and Page 1780)
Mussel Pond appears to be the expanse of water behind the bar in the cove.
— Mussel Pond (Set.) (*Population Returns* 1836)
   See O'DONNELLS (Set.) (NTS Placentia).
Pp. 87, 108.
— MUSSELL POND COVE 47–04, 53–35 (NTS Placentia 1N/4E)
   Muscle Pond Cove (Lane 1773). P. 87.
— MUSSELL POND POINT 47–04, 53–36 (Adm. 2915 1864).

MUTTON BAY
See CAPE MUTTON (NTS Trepassey).

NAGELS HILL (St. John's)
John Neagle a butcher in ST. JOHN'S (*Directory* 1877). P. 134.

Naked Man Ridge (Jukes 1842). P. 115.

NARROWS (Generic), p. 94.

THE NARROWS 47–34, 52–41 (NTS St. John's 1N/10E)

(Lane, *Directions* 1775, 1810).
Pp. *94, 95*.
The Narrows (Harbour Grace)
(Lane, *Directions* 1775, 1810).
P. *95*.

NECK, THE (Isthmus) 47–20, 53–55
(NTS Argentia 1N/5W) (Adm. 2829 1877).
A short isthmus joining ISAAC HEADS to the mainland. P. *144*.

NEILS POND 47–21, 53–27 (NTS Holyrood 1N/6W)
(NDNR 1N/6 1943). P. *134*.

NEILS POND 47–32, 52–52 (NTS St. John's 1N/10W). P. *134*.

NEMOS POND 47–50, 53–15 (NTS Heart's Content 1N/14W)
(NDNR 1N/14 1946).
? For Scottish family name Nimmo untraced, however, in Newfoundland.
? After Captain Nemo, hero of Jules Verne's *Twenty Thousand Leagues under the Sea*, 1864, or Nemo, the law writer in Dickens's *Bleak House*.

NEVILLES POND 47–31, 52–53 (NTS St. John's 1N/10W, 2nd ed. 1953)
Same as OCTAGON POND q.v.
Pp. *134, 163*.

NEW BRIDGE (Set.) 47–08, 53–28 (NTS St. Catherine's 1N/3W)
Little Harbour (*Population Returns* 1836), New Bridge (Smallwood 1940).
At the site of a bridge erected in 1929 which crosses LITTLE HARBOUR RIVER to link ST. JOSEPH'S (NTS Placentia) and ST. CATHERINE'S (NTS St. Catherine's).
Cp. LITTLE HARBOUR (NTS St. Catherine's). P. *148*.

NEW CHELSEA (Set.) 48–02, 53–13 (NTS Old Perlican 2C/3E)
As feature: Seal Cove (Lane 1790, Purdy 1814); as set: (*Population Returns* 1836), New Chelsea (Proclamation August 8, 1911).
After Chelsea, part of metropolitan Boston, Mass., a favourite place of settlement by Newfoundlanders who emigrated to the United States in the latter years of the nineteenth century.
(Communication from C. R. Barrett).
Pp. *6, 98*.

NEW CHELSEA COVE 47–52, 53–25 (NTS Heart's Content 1N/14W)
See SEAL (NEW CHELSEA) COVE (NTS Heart's Content).

New Fort (Placentia) (Cook 1762). P. *82*.

NEW HARBOUR 47–36, 53–33 (NTS Dildo 1N/12E)
(Lane, *Directions* 1775, 1810).
— NEW HARBOUR (Set.) 47–35, 53–32
(Wix 1836, *Population Returns* 1836).
"The church of St. George's, New Harbour, ... opened for Divine Service in 1815" (Wix, p. 15).
"New Harbour is the oldest settlement at the bottom of Trinity Bay" (Johnson, p. 292).
Settled by Newhooks (Nieuhook in Wix) from Trinity, a family "of French Huguenot extraction" (Wix, p. 14). See N. C. Crewe, "The Newhooks of New Harbour," *Evening Telegram*, St. John's, 17, 18 June 1965.
New Harbour – ? a pun on Du. nieuwe hoek – new corner, nook; or in relation to other harbours in TRINITY BAY.

NEW MELBOURNE (Set.) 48–03, 53–09 (NTS Old Perlican 2C/3E)
? As feature: Cove Refused (Robinson 1669); as set: Russell's Cove (Lovell 1881), New Melbourne (Proclamation June 1, 1905).

Refused – ? Since the coast in this part of TRINITY BAY is rugged and encumbered with sunken rocks.

Russell – After Lord John Russell (1792–1878), prime minister 1846–52 and 1865–6, his first period of office being about the time the settlement was founded.
New Melbourne – following a petition from the inhabitants to change the name to Melbourne, after Viscount Melbourne, prime minister 1834 and 1835–41, to avoid confusion with Russell's Cove, Random Island, Trinity Bay. The Nomenclature Board, however, decided on New Melbourne to avoid confusion with Melbourne, Australia. (Communication from C. Button).
Pp. 5, 70.

NEW PERLICAN (Inlet) 47–55, 53–22 (NTS Heart's Content 1N/14W) Little Pernocan (Robinson 1669), New Parlican (Southwood 1675), New Perlican (Hack? 1677), New Pelican (Cook and Lane 1770 [1775]A), New Perlican (Lane, Directions 1775, 1810).
— NEW PERLICAN (Set.) 47–55, 53–21 (Beaudoin 1697).
— NEW PERLICAN POND 47–54, 53–22
(NDNR 1N/14 1946).
See OLD PERLICAN COVE (NTS Old Perlican).
Pp. 70, 80, 123.

NEWFOUND POND 47–37, 52–46 (NTS St. John's 1N/10W)

NEWFOUNDLAND HOTEL (St. John's). P. 83.

NEWTOWN (Set.) 47–22, 53–11 (NTS Holyrood 1N/6E)
(Census 1891). P. 146.

NIAGARA POINT 47–49, 53–46 (NTS Sunnyside 1N/13W)
(Imray, *Sailing Directory* 1873).

"the northern termination of a steep cliff" (Imray, *Sailing Directory* 1873, p. 36) ? with a waterfall; but the first Atlantic cable between Ireland and Newfoundland was landed in BULL ARM (NTS Sunnyside) on 5 August 1858 by the United States steamship, *Niagara* (D. W. Prowse, p. 642; Smallwood, *Book of Newfoundland*, IV, p. 562).
Cp. MCKAY ISLAND (NTS Sunnyside).

NICHOLS POND 47–23, 53–23 (NTS Holyrood 1N/6W)
(NDNR 1N/6 1943). P. 163.

NICK LONGS POND 47–48, 53–14 (NTS Heart's Content 1N/14E)
(NDNR 1N/14 1946). P. 162.

NINE ISLAND POND 47–26, 53–17 (NTS Holyrood 1N/6W) (NDNR 1N/6 1943).
— NINE ISLAND POND SOUTH 47–21, 53–15 (NTS Holyrood 1N/6E and W)
(NDNR 1N/6 1943).

NINE ISLAND POND 47–33, 53–26 (NTS Harbour Grace 1N/11W)
(NDNR 1N/11 1948).

NINTH POND 47–23, 53–25 (NTS Holyrood 1N/6W) (NDNR 1N/6 1943). Of NORTH RIVER, tributary of COLINET RIVER.

NORD POND 47–22, 53–14 (NTS Holyrood 1N/6E) (NDNR 1N/6 1943). ? For North. The pond is north of SOUTHWEST POND 47–20, 53–13.

NORMANS COVE (Set.) 47–33, 53–40 (NTS Dildo 1N/12E)
(Wix 1836, *Population Returns* 1836). Pp. 103–4, 104, 107, 163.

NORMANS POND 47–35, 53–22 (NTS Harbour Grace 1N/11W)
(NDNR 1N/11 1948).
Dan. Norman property-owner at BAY ROBERTS 1802. (CO Misc. 199.18). P. 163.

NORTH ARM 47–24, 53–09 (NTS Holyrood 1N/6E) (CHS 4573 1953). Of HOLYROOD BAY. Cp. SOUTH ARM, MIDDLE ARM. Pp. 130, 131, 141.
— NORTH ARM RIVER

NORTH COVE 47–38, 53–16 (NTS Harbour Grace 1N/11W)
Northern Cove (co Misc. 199.18 1785), North Cove (*NLP* 1953). Of SPANIARDS BAY.
Cp. NORTHERN COVE POND.

NORTH EAST See NORTHEAST.

North Favlkland (Mason 1626). Pp. 12, 61.

North Fort (St. John's Harbour) No. Ford (Visscher c. 1680), No. Fort (Thornton 1689B, *English Pilot. The Fourth Book* 1716), Block-house on Signal Hill (Lane, *Directions* 1775, 1810). Pp. 76, 77.

NORTH GREEN ISAND 47–26, 53–58 (NTS Argentia 1N/5W) (*NLP* 1951). One of the IONA ISLANDS, in relation to EAST GREEN ISLAND. P. 85.

NORTH HARBOUR 47–07, 53–40 (NTS Placentia 1N/4E)
(Lane 1773).
The northern arm of ST. MARY'S BAY. P. 87.
— NORTH HARBOUR (Set.) 47–09, 53–39
(*Population Returns* 1836).
— North Harbour Lookout 47–05, 53–41 (Unnamed in NTS Placentia) (Jukes 1842). P. 111.
— NORTH HARBOUR POINT 47–06, 53–40 (NTS Placentia 1N/4E) (Adm. 2915 1864).
— NORTH HARBOUR RIVER 47–11, 53–38 (NTS Placentia 1N/4E, Argentia 1N/5E) (Adm. 2915 1864).

NORTH HEAD 47–00, 52–54 (NTS Ferryland 1N/2W) (USHO 0618 1941).
Of AQUAFORTE HARBOUR.

NORTH HEAD 47–29, 52–38 (NTS Bay Bulls 1N/7E)
Lady Point (Bonnycastle 1842), North Head (Adm. 296 1868). Of MOTION BAY. P. 116.

NORTH HEAD 47–33, 53–11 (NTS Harbour Grace 1N/11E)
Brigus Head (Lane *Directions* 1775, 1810, Imray, *Sailing Directions* 1862), North Head (Adm. 297 1868).
Of BRIGUS BAY.

NORTH HEAD 47–34, 52–40 (NTS St. John's 1N/10E)
(Cook 1762 or Gilbert 1768).
Of ST. JOHN'S HARBOUR.
Cp. SOUTH HEAD 47–34, 52–41. Pp. 77, 83.

NORTH HEAD 47–55, 53–41 (NTS Sunnyside 1N/13E)
(Imray, *Sailing Directory* 1873).
Of ST. JONES HARBOUR.

North Hill (Jukes 1842), P. 114.

NORTH POINT 46–56, 53–35 (NTS St. Mary's 1K/13E)
N E Pt (Lane 1773, Mount and Page 1780), North Pt. (Adm. 2915 1864).
Of ST. MARY'S HARBOUR. P. 87.

NORTH POINT 47–04, 52–51 (NTS Ferryland 1N/2W)
Of the promontory of which CAPE BROYLE is the highest point. P. 73.

No[rth] Point (Southwood 1675) See COOPERS HEAD (NTS Harbour Grace). P. 74.

North Pt. Torbay (Lane 1774) See FLAT ROCK POINT (NTS St. John's). Pp. 90, 98.

NORTH POND 47–39, 52–45 (NTS St. John's 1N/10E and W)
Cp. SOUTH POND 47–39, 52–44.
— NORTH POND BROOK 47–40, 52–42.

NORTH RIVER 47–20, 53–27 (NTS

Holyrood 1N/6W) (NDNR 1N/6 1943). Tributary of COLINET RIVER. Cp. EAST RIVER 47-20, 53-27.

NORTH RIVER 47-33, 53-18 (NTS Harbour Grace 1N/11W)
northern gut (Jukes 1842), North Gut (Murray and Howley 1868), Northern Gut (J. P. Howley 1876, 1907), North River (M. F. Howley, XIX, NQ, October 1907). Cp. SOUTH RIVER 47-32, 53-17. Pp. 5, 87, 112, 141.
— NORTH RIVER (NORTH VALLEY P.O.) (Set.) 47-33, 53-19
Northern Gut (*Population Returns* 1836). Pp. 106, 124.

NORTH SHORE (Conception Bay)
"the western (or as it is called in Newfoundland the northern) shore of Conception Bay" (Jukes, *Excursions* I, p. 41). Pp. 50, 76, 90, 119, 144.

North side (Ferryland Harbour) (Yonge 1663-70). P. 68.

northside (Fermeuse Harbour) (Yonge 1663-70). P. 68.

North Side Holyrood (Set.) (Census 1857). P. 18.

NORTH THREE ISLAND POND 47-44, 52-45 (NTS St. John's 1N/10E and w) Cp. THREE ISLAND POND, MIDDLE THREE ISLAND POND.

NORTH WEST See NORTHWEST.

NORTHEAST

North East Arm (Trepassey Harbour) (Cook 1762 or Gilbert 1768)
Cp. North West Arm. P. 83.

North East Arm (St. Mary's Harbour) (Cook 1762 or Gilbert 1768). P. 83.

NORTHEAST ARM 47-00, 52-58 (NTS Ferryland 1N/2W) (USHO 0618 1941). At head of AQUAFORTE HARBOUR. P. 141.

NORTH EAST ARM 47-16, 53-56 (NTS Argentia 1N/5W) N E Gut (Wix 1836).
"Placentia harbour is also known as the North-east arm" (Imray *Sailing Directory* 1873, p. 85).
— North-east Mountain (Jukes 1842)
— NORTH EAST RIVER 47-16, 53-51 (NTS Argentia 1N/5E and w)
See DUNVILLE (NTS Argentia).
Pp. 104, 110, 111, 115, 141.

NORTHEAST ARM 47-55, 53-44 (NTS Sunnyside 1N/13E) (*NP* 1952). Of DEER HARBOUR.
Cp. SOUTHWEST ARM. P. 141.

NORTHEAST BROOK 46-46, 53-21 (NTS Biscay Bay River 1K/14W)
Trepassey River (Bonnycastle 1842), Northeast River (*Road Map of the Peninsula of Avalon* 1930), Northeast Brook (Newfoundland 1941).
Flows into TREPASSEY HARBOUR from the northeast. Cp. NORTHWEST BROOK 46-45, 53-23.

NORTHEAST COVE 47-21, 53-53 (NTS Argentia 1N/5W) (CHS 4622 ? 1953). Of SHIP HARBOUR.

NORTHEAST GULLY (Pond) 47-44, 53-22 (NTS Harbour Grace 1N/11W) (NDNR 1N/11 1948).
? Of CROOKED POND.

N[orth] E[ast] Pt. (Lane 1773)
See NORTH POINT (NTS St. Mary's). P. 87.

NORTHEAST POND 47-38, 52-50 (NTS St. John's 1N/10W)
Northeast of PORTUGAL COVE.

NORTHER HEAD 46-52, 54-12 (NTS St. Bride's 1L/16E) (Adm. 2915 1864).
The northern head of the bay formed by LEARS COVE and BRIERLY COVE.
Norther adj. Obs. 1. The more northerly of two places or things; situated or lying to the north. (*OED*).

252 / *Place Names of the Avalon Peninsula*

NORTHER POINT 47–53, 53–23 (NTS Heart's Content 1N/14W) (USHO 73 1942).
At entrance of HEART'S CONTENT (Inlet).
Cp. SOUTHER POINT.
See preceding entry.

NORTHERN BAY 47–56, 53–04 (NTS Heart's Content 1N/14E) (Lane 1774).
Cp. WESTERN BAY. Pp. 93, 144.
— NORTHERN BAY (Set.) 47–57, 53–04
    (*Population Returns* 1836)
— NORTHERN BAY BROOK 47–56, 53–05
    (*Newfoundland* 1941).
— NORTHERN BAY SANDS. P. 144.

NORTHERN COVE POND 47–38, 53–17 (NTS Harbour Grace 1N/11W) (CHS 4572 1954).
Cp. NORTH COVE 47–38, 53–16.

Northern Gut (*Population Returns* 1836)
    See NORTH RIVER (Set.) (NTS Harbour Grace).
P. 106.

NORTHERN HEAD 46–55, 52–55 (NTS Renews 1K/15W) (Adm. 376 1927).
Of RENEWS HARBOUR.
Pp. 68–9.

NORTHERN HEAD 46–58, 52–54 (NTS Renews 1K/15W) (Adm. 376 1927).
Of FERMEUSE HARBOUR.
Cp. BEAR COVE HEAD 46–57, 52–54.
P. 69.

NORTHERN POND 47–27, 52–53 (NTS Bay Bulls 1N/7W) (NDNR Bay Bulls 1943).
? North of WITLESS BAY LINE.
— BIG NORTHERN POND 47–25, 52–54
    (NDNR Bay Bulls 1943).

NORTHWEST

North West Arm (Trepassey Harbour) (Cook 1762 or Gilbert 1768)

Cp. North East Arm. P. 83.

NORTHWEST BROOK 46–45, 53–23 (NTS Biscay Bay River 1K/14W)
Northwest River (*Road Map of the Peninsula of Avalon* 1930), Northwest Brook (*Newfoundland* 1941).
  Flows into TREPASSEY HARBOUR from the northwest.
Cp. NORTHEAST BROOK 46–46, 53–21.
— NORTHWEST POND 46–51, 53–18
    (*Newfoundland* 1941).
    On NORTHWEST BROOK.

NORTH WEST POND 47–40, 52–50 (NTS St. John's 1N/10W)
? Northwest of BAULINE ROAD.

Nu-cool-minni-guloo Gospen (Murray and Howley 1872). P. 24.

NULMA HEAD 47–18, 52–46 (NTS Bay Bulls 1N/7W) (NDNR Bay Bulls 1943).

NUT BROOK 47–27, 53–00 (NTS Holyrood 1N/6E, Bay Bulls 1N/7W) (NDNR Bay Bulls 1943).
Tributary of KELLIGREWS RIVER.

O'BRIENS BROOK 47–24, 52–49 (NTS Bay Bulls 1N/7W) (NDNR Bay Bulls 1943). P. 134.

OCEAN POND 47–25, 53–27 (NTS Holyrood 1N/6W)
Big Barren Pond, Ocean Pond (Murray and Howley 1872).
"Big Barren Pond, known also to the coast settlers as Ocean Pond" (Murray and Howley 1872, p. 283).
Cp. BIG BARREN BROOK.
— OCEAN POND (Set.) 47–25, 53–25
    (NDNR 1N/6 1941).

OCEAN POND 47–41, 52–50 (NTS St. John's 1N/10W)
  From its size or proximity to the shores of CONCEPTION BAY.

OCEAN POND 47–41, 53–24 (NTS Harbour Grace 1N/11W) (NDNR 1N/11 1948).

The biggest pond in the area.

OCHRE PIT COVE 47–55, 53–04 (NTS Heart's Content 1N/14E)
Oker Pit Cove (Lane 1774). Pp. 20–1, 93, 148.
— OCHRE PIT BROOK 47–54, 53–04 (NDNR 1N/14 1946).
— OCHRE PIT COVE (Set.) 47–55, 53–05 *(Population Returns 1836)*.

OCHRE PIT ROCK 47–48, 53–08 (NTS Heart's Content 1N/14E). Pp. 20–1, 148.

OCTAGON POND 47–31, 52–53 (NTS St. John's 1N/10W)
Nevilles Pond (NTS St. John's, 2nd ed. 1955).
Octagon – After "Professor" Danielle's Octagon Castle, a place of entertainment formally opened by Sir W. Whiteway, prime minister of Newfoundland, on 18 June 1896, in which Danielle lived until his death in 1902.

Charles Henry Danielle was born in Baltimore, Md on 1 November 1830. He came to Newfoundland as a dancing-master in the late 1860s, but also kept a restaurant on Water Street, St. John's, which was destroyed by fire in 1892. He subsequently built the Pavilion on the banks of Quidi Vidi Lake, but dismantled it after two years and built the Octagon Castle on Topsail Road where for some years he exhibited his own coffin. Glass negatives showing the interior and exterior of the Castle and Danielle's coffin are in the Newfoundland Archives and a reproduction of a photograph of the exterior of the Castle is in Smallwood (ed.) *The Book of Newfoundland*, IV, p. 192. (Mosdell, p. 29; Devine, *Ye Olde St. John's*, pp. 101–3; Devine and O'Mara, p. 118; *Daily News*, St. John's, 31 July 1967; *Evening Telegram*, 13 October 1967, 29 March 1968).

O'DONNELLS (Set.) 47–04, 53–34 (NTS Placentia 1N/4E)
Mussel Pond *(Population Returns 1836)*, Muscle Pond (Census 1857), O'Donnell's (Electors 1955).
See MUSSEL POND COVE. Pp. 87, 108, 134, 139.

OHMAN'S POND 47–24, 53–29 (NTS Holyrood 1N/6W) (NDNR 1N/6 1943).
? For Oman – family name of Orkney and Shetland (Reaney *Surnames* p. 235) not found locally.

Old Fort (Placentia) (Cook 1762)
See TOWN POINT (NTS Argentia). Pp. 82–3.

Old Fort (St. John's) (Cook 1762 or Gilbert 1768)
See FORT WILLIAM. P. 83.

Old Garrison (St. John's) (Lane, *Directions* 1775, 1810)
See FORT WILLIAM. Pp. 83, 94, 147.

Old Harry (Rock) (Southwood 1675)
Cp. LONG HARRY.
"... it is the proud boast of Poole citizens that their forebears took a leading share in laying the foundations of this, our oldest colony. The very names of some of the physical features of the island bear eloquent testimony to this fact, as witness Purbeck Cove, Old Harry, Cape Ballard and Wadham Islands. I like to think, too, that the names Long Island, Round Island and Green Island, do not merely allude to shape or vegetation, but were given by some Poole seaman who had in mind the charming, similarly-named islets of his own picturesque Dorset Lakeland" (H. P. Smith, *History of the Lodge of Amity, No. 137, Poole*, (Poole, 1937), p. 129).

Dr. Kirwin, who presented the foregoing communication, also notes that southeast of Poole Harbour, near the Foreland or Handfast Point, are two chalk rocks, Old Harry and Old Harry's Wife, though the latter is almost washed away; and that in High Street, Poole, is an inn, Old Harry. Pp. 73-4.

OLD MAN (Hill) 47-55, 53-43 (NTS Sunnyside 1N/13E). P. 139.

OLD MAN'S POND 47-26, 53-20 (NTS Holyrood 1N/6W) (NDNR 1N/6 1943).

OLD PERLICAN (Set.) 48-05, 53-01 (NTS Old Perlican 2C/3E)
Le Vieux Perlican (Beaudoin 1697), Old Perlican (Thoresby 1796). Pp. 80, 92, 123.
— OLD PERLICAN COVE
Parlican (Leigh 1597), Pernecam, Old Pernecam (Guy 1612), Parlican ("Blathwayt" c. 1630-40), Pernocan (Robinson 1669), Old Parlican (Hack c. 1690?), Old Perlican (*English Pilot. The Fourth Book* 1689). Pp. 56, 57-8.
— PERLICAN ISLAND 48-05, 53-02
I du Vieux Perlican (Bellin 1754).
See NEW PERLICAN.

OLD POND 47-46, 52-47 (NTS Pouch Cove 1N/15W)

OLD SEA (Pond) 47-17, 53-13 (NTS Holyrood 1N/6E)
(NDNR 1N/6 1943). P. 143.

OLD SHOP (Set.) 47-32, 53-35 (NTS Dildo 1N/12E)
(*Population Returns* 1836).
Pp. 107, 147.

OLD SOW POINT 47-43, 53-10 (NTS Harbour Grace 1N/11E)
(Imray, *Sailing Directory* 1873), Old Sow Point (Jersey) (CHS 4590 1943), Jersey Point (NDNR 1N/11 1948), Old Sow point (NLP 1953).

? After Old Sow Rock close eastward of the point.
Jersey – Recalls Le Messurier's statement that Jerseymen had charcoal pits at CARBONEAR "at a very early period" (Le Messurier, "The Early Relations between Newfoundland and the Channel Islands").

OLD WOMAN'S BROOK 46-56, 52-57 (NTS Renews 1K/15W) Biscay Bay River 1K/14E)

OLIVERS POND 47-36, 52-50 (NTS St. John's 1N/10W)
— LITTLE OLIVER POND 47-36, 52-50.
P. 163.

One o'clock (Cove) (St. John's Harbour)
One a Clock (Visscher c. 1680, Thornton 1689B), One a Clocke (*English Pilot. The Fourth Book* 1716), One o'clock (Mount and Page 1755).
— One o'Clock (Rock) (St. John's Harbour)
one o'clock Rock (Cook 1762 or Gilbert 1768). Pp. 76-7, 83.

ORE HEAD 47-41, 52-51 (Unnamed in NTS St. John's 1N/10W)
(NLP 1953).

OTTER (Specific) "Otter (Sutra vulgaris). This species is tolerably common. (There are two species, one frequenting the freshwater and interior parts of the country, while the other keeps more to the coast and salt water. The latter animal is very much larger than the former. A[lexander] M[urray].)" (J. P. Howley, *Geography of Newfoundland*, 1876, p. 52).

OTTER COVE 47-17, 52-47 (NTS Bay Bulls 1N/7W) (CHS 4586 1944).

BIG OTTER POND 47-24, 53-03 (NTS Holyrood 1N/6E) (NDNR 1N/6 1943).
— LITTLE OTTER POND 47-24, 53-02

(NDNR 1N/6 1943).
P. 6.

OTTER POND WATERS 47–17, 53–25
(NTS Holyrood 1N/6W)
(NDNR 1N/6 1943).
Note the combination of the generics. P. 143.

OTTERBURY (Set.) 47–33, 53–16 (NTS Harbour Grace 1N/11W)
(CHS 4572 1954). Pp. 95, 126.
Otterbury (Set.) (Carbonear)
(Census 1857).
Otterbury Point
(Lane, *Directions* 1775, 1810; Imray, *Sailing Directions* 1862), Pp. 95, 119.

OTTERBURY (Set.) 47–40, 53–15 (NTS Harbour Grace 1N/11W)
? The Otterbury (CO Misc. 199.18 1800), Otterbury (Census 1935). P. 95.

Ouit lis baye (Beaudoin 1697)
See WITLESS BAY (NTS Bay Bulls). P. 79.

OUTER COVE 47–39, 52–41 (NTS St. John's 1N/10E)
(Bonnycastle 1842).
— OUTER COVE (Set.)
 (*Population Returns* 1836).
— OUTER COVE BROOK

OUTSIDE ISLAND COVE POND 47–45, 53–28 (NTS Harbour Grace 1N/11W, Heart's Content 1N/14W)
(NDNR 1N/11 1948).
The pond nearer to ISLAND COVE 47–45, 53–28 than INSIDE ISLAND COVE POND 47–44, 53–27.

OUTSIDE POND 47–34, 52–52 (NTS St. John's 1N/10W)
Cp. INSIDE POND. The relationship is not obvious.

OXEN POND 47–34, 52–46 (NTS St. John's 1N/10W)

Oxfords (Stage or Cove) (St. John's Harbour)
Oxon, Oxfords (Visscher c. 1680), Pxon, Oxfords (Thornton 1689B,

English Pilot. The Fourth Book 1716), Pxon, Oxfords (Mount and Page 1755), but denoting two places. P. 76.

OXLEYS POND 47–16, 53–19 (NTS Holyrood 1N/6W)
(NDNR 1N/6 1943). P. 163.

Oxon (Visscher c. 1680)
See Oxfords (Stage or Cove) (St. John's Harbour).

PACKS POND 47–48, 53–17 (NTS Heart's Content 1N/14W)
(NDNR 1N/14 1946). P. 163.

PADDYS POND 47–29, 52–53 (NTS Bay Bulls 1N/7W)
(NDNR Bay Bulls 1943). P. 125.

PANCAKE (Shoal) (St. John's Harbour) 47–34, 52–41
(Lane, *Directions* 1775, 1810; Imray, *Sailing Directions* 1862), Pancake Shoal (*NP* 1952).
Cp. LITTLE PANCAKE (Rock) (*NP* 1952). P. 94.

PARADISE (Set.) 47–32, 52–52 (NTS St. John's 1N/10W)
(Census 1911). Pp. 6, 127, 139.

PARADISE POND 47–14, 53–04 (NTS St. Catherine's 1N/3E)
(Newfoundland 1941). P. 127.

PARK (Generic). Pp. 145–6.

PARKERS POND 47–36, 52–47 (NTS St. John's 1N/10W). P. 163, but "absent or conspicuously rare in ... Devon and Cornwall" (Guppy, p. 49).

Parlican (Leigh 1597)
See OLD PERLICAN COVE (NTS Old Perlican). P. 56.

PARSONS COVE 47–41, 53–11 (NTS Harbour Grace 1N/11E). P. 163.

Parsons Pond (St. John's)
(Bonnycastle 1842). P. 163.

PARSONVILLE P.O. 47–36, 53–01 (NTS Harbour Grace 1N/11E)

See FRESHWATER 47–36, 53–01.
Pp. 146, 163.

PASSAGE (Generic). P. 141.

Passage harbour (Guy 1612)
See COME BY CHANCE (NTS Sunnyside). P. 59.

PATH (Generic). P. 148.

PATRICK POINT 47–08, 53–40 (NTS Placentia 1N/4E)
(Adm. 2915 1864). P. 134.

PATRICK'S COVE 47–02, 54–08 (NTS Ship Cove 1M/1E)
Patrick Cove (Adm. 2915 1864), Patrick's Cove (Murray and Howley 1868).
— PATRICK'S COVE (Set.) 47–03, 54–07
Devil's Cove (*Population Returns* 1836), Patrick Cove (Lovell 1881).
Cp. ANGELS COVE.
Pp. 109, 134.

PEA COVE 47–43, 53–10 (NTS Harbour Grace 1N/11E)
(NDNR 1N/11 1948).

PEAK (Generic). Pp. 144–5.

PEAK POND 47–19, 53–13 (NTS Holyrood 1N/6E)
(NDNR 1N/6 1943).
After the elevation between PEAK POND and SOUTHERN PEAK POND 47–19, 53–11. Pp. 144–5.

PEARCE PEAK 47–17, 53–58 (NTS Argentia 1N/5W)
(NLP 1951). Pp. 134, 163.

PEBBLE ISLAND 47–11, 52–50 (NTS Ferryland 1N/2W)
Pebble islet (Imray, *Sailing Directory* 1873), Peepy, Pebble, Peevet Island (M. F. Howley, xxv, NQ, March 1909). One of les isles d'Espoir (Alfonse 1544). See SPEAR ISLAND. P. 35.

PEDDLES POND 47–35, 53–23 (NTS Harbour Grace 1N/11W)
(NDNR 1N/11 1948). P. 163.

PEDDLES WATERS 47–21, 53–25 (NTS Holyrood 1N/6W)
(NDNR 1N/6 1943). Pp. 143, 163.

PEGGYS BAY 47–33, 52–40 (NTS St. John's 1N/10E)
Peggy's Bag (NLP 1951, NP 1952).

PEGS POND 47–42, 53–21 (NTS Harbour Grace 1N/11W)
(NDNR 1N/11 1948).
? For Peg, Pegge, English family name (Guppy, pp. 137, 534) of Derbyshire and Norfolk, not current in Newfoundland.

PEGWOOD POND 47–23, 53–05 (NTS Holyrood 1N/6E) (NDNR 1N/6 1943).
Mistake name for Pigweed, *Chenopodium album*. P. 6.

Pembroke (Mason 1626). P. 12, 62.

PENETANGUISHENE 47–36, 52–45
(TANGUISHENE in NTS St. John's 1N/10W). P. 26.

PENINSULA (Generic). P. 144.

PENNYS POND 47–16, 53–16 (NTS Holyrood 1N/6W)
(NDNR 1N/6 1943). P. 163.

PERCH COVE 46–56, 54–10 (NTS St. Bride's 1L/16E)
Porche (Robinson 1669), La Perche ("Dépôt 128.2.6" c. 1680, Chaviteau 1698), ? porchet ("Dépôt 132.2.10" 1706), la Perle (Bellin 1744, Robert de Vaugondy 1749, Bellin 1754, Lotter c. 1758), Perch Cove (Adm. 2915 1864).
Cp. CROSS POINT, LITTLE BARASWAY (NTS Ship Cove) under BARASWAY. Pp. 48–9.

PERLICAN ISLAND
See OLD PERLICAN (NTS Old Perlican).

Pernecam (Guy 1612)
See OLD PERLICAN (NTS Old Perlican). P. 57.

PERRY'S COVE 47–48, 53–09 (NTS

Heart's Content 1N/14E (Lane 1774).
— PERRY'S COVE (Set.) 47–47, 53–08 (*Population Returns* 1836).
Pp. 92, 163.

PETER'S RIVER 46–46, 53–37 (NTS St. Mary's 1K/13E)
(Lane 1773), St. Peter's Riv (Mount and Page 1780).
— PETER'S RIVER (Set.) (*Population Returns* 1836).
Pp. 88, 120.

petit abra (Sanches 1623)
See PETTY HARBOUR (NTS Bay Bulls). P. 42.

Pettit harbor (Mason 1626)
See PETTY HARBOUR (NTS Bay Bulls). P. 12.

PETTY HARBOUR 47–28, 52–42 (NTS Bay Bulls 1N/7E)
petit abra (Sanches 1623), Pettit harbor (Mason 1626), Petti Harbor ("Blathwayt" c. 1630–40), Petty harbour (Robinson 1669), Pitty harbour (Seller c. 1671), Petty harbor (Southwood 1675), Haure de Miséricorde (Vion 1699). Pp. 42, 44, 61, 67, 116.
— PETTY HARBOUR (Set.) 47–28, 52–43
Le petit havre (Beaudoin 1697).
Pp. 79, 123, 124, 131, 132.
— Petty Harbour Bay (Jukes 1840)
See MOTION BAY (NTS Bay Bulls).
Pp. 89–90.
— PETTY HARBOUR LONG POND 47–30, 52–45 (NTS Bay Bulls 1N/7E, St. John's 1N/10E)
Long Pond (Newfoundland 1941), (DND St. John's 1942).
— Petty Harbour Point (Lane 1773)
See MOTION HEAD (NTS Bay Bulls).
Pp. 89–90.
— PETTY HARBOUR PONDS 47–29, 52–43 (NTS Bay Bulls 1N/7E) (USHO 2139 1943).

The statement in G. R. F. Prowse, *CM*, III, p. 125, that "Pitty Harbour and Havre de Misericorde suggest that [the occasion of the naming] was the octave of Innocents Day Jan. 4 1498 [in an] English South Newfoundland Survey," shows the danger of trying to bolster an argument (in this case for the Survey) by drawing conclusions from arbitrarily chosen citations. Pitty harbour (Seller c. 1671) appears to be a unique form; its translation as Haure de Miséricorde (Vion 1699) shows that Vion was indebted to Seller as well as to Southwood for the nomenclature of his map, but in no way adds to the significance of Pitty. However, the pronunciation [pI'tI] is not infrequent locally.

PEYTONS BROOK 47–20, 52–56 (NTS Bay Bulls 1N/7W)
(NDNR Bay Bulls 1943), Pierres Brook (Newfoundland 1949).
— PEYTONS POND 47–21, 52–56 (NDNR Bay Bulls 1943).
Pp. 134, 163.

PEYTONS GULLIES 47–22, 53–19 (NTS Holyrood 1N/6W)
(NDNR 1N/6 1943). Pp. 134, 163.

PEYTONS POND 47–44, 52–45 (NTS St. John's 1N/10W)
? For Penton. Pp. 134, 163.

PHILLIPS POND 47–22, 53–23 (NTS Holyrood 1N/6W)
(NDNR 1N/6 1943).
Cp. CAMPBELL HILL 47–28, 53–12.
Pp. 134, 164.

PICCOS BROOK 47–43, 52–42 (NTS St. John's 1N/10E). P. 54.

PICCOS POND 47–40, 52–49 (NTS St. John's 1N/10W)
— PICCOS POND SOUTH 47–37, 52–51.
P. 54.

PICK EYES (Set.) 47-36, 53-11 (NTS Harbour Grace 1N/11E)
? Petyes (Robinson 1669), Pick Eyes (Census 1874). Pp. 53-4, 139.

PIERCED POINT 47-22, 52-44 (NTS Bay Bulls 1N/7E)
(Adm. 296 1868).

PIERCES POND 47-48, 53-22 (NTS Heart's Content 1N/14W)
(NDNR 1N/14 1946). P. 164.

PIERRES BROOK 47-17, 52-49 (NTS Bay Bulls 1N/7W)
(Newfoundland 1941).
Cp PEYTONS BROOK 47-20, 52-55. P. 54.

PIGEON ISLAND 47-48, 52-47 (NTS Pouch Cove 1N/15W)

PIKES POND 47-45, 53-16 (NTS Harbour Grace 1N/11W)
(NDNR 1N/11 1948). P. 164.

PINCH POINT 47-07, 53-32 (NTS Placentia 1N/4E) (USHO 2277 1937).
? Pinch – a hill or upgrade on a country road or woods path (Devine, *Folk-Lore*, p. 37).
The point is barely discernible.

PINCHER GULLIES 47-46, 53-16 (NTS Heart's Content 1N/14W)
(NDNR 1N/14 1946). P. 164.

Pinchgut (Lane 1772)
See GREAT PINCHGUT (NTS Dildo) under PINCHGUT. Pp. 84, 104.

PINCHGUT ISLAND 47-10, 53-35 (NTS Placentia 1N/4E)
(Adm. 2915 1864).
— PINCHGUT POINT 47-08, 53-36 (Adm. 2915 1864).
— PINCHGUT TICKLE 47-09, 53-34 (Adm. 2915 1864).
The tickle is particularly narrow at its extremities.
Pp. 84-5, 86, 141.

GREAT PINCHGUT (Bay) 47-36, 53-55 (NTS Dildo 1N/12W)

Pinchgut (Lane 1772); as set: Pinch Gut (Wix 1836, *Population Returns* 1836); Pinchgut cove (Imray, *Sailing Directory* 1873), Great Pinchgut (NP 1952).
— LITTLE PINCHGUT (Cove) 47-35, 53-54
(NP 1952).
— PINCHGUT POINT 47-36, 53-56 (NP 1952).
Cp. FAIRHAVEN 47-31, 53-54.
Pp. 84-5, 141.

PINEBUD PLACE (St. John's). P. 148.

PINHORNS POND 47-56, 53-15 (NTS Heart's Content 1N/14W)
(NDNR 1N/14 1946). P. 164.

PINNACLE (Generic). P. 145.

THE PINNACLES (Hills) 47-16, 53-59 (NTS Placentia 1N/5W)
(CHS 4622 ? 1953). P. 145.

Pirates forte (Harbour Grace) (Guy 1612). P. 58.

PIT (Generic). P. 148.

PITCHERS POND 47-41, 53-28 (NTS Harbour Grace 1N/11W)
(NDNR 1N/11 1948).
— PITCHERS POND BROOK 47-41, 53-27 (NDNR 1N/11 1948).
P. 164

PITMANS POND 48-00, 53-12 (NTS Heart's Content 1N/14E, Old Perlican 2C/3)
(Provincial Representative CBGN).
The Pittman family of NEW PERLICAN used to do logging in the vicinity. P. 164.

PLACE (Generic), P. 148.

PLACENTIA (Peninsula mistaken for an island)
Ille de plaisance ("Vallard" 1547), Ye de plaisance (Desceliers 1550), I. Plasasme (Velho c. 1560), Plesance (Parkhurst 1578 in Hakluyt),

Placentia (Hayes 1583 in Hakluyt), Plaisance (Vasseur 1601), Placentia (Guy 1611 in Purchas). Pp. *38, 56,* 115.

— PLACENTIA (Set,) 47–14, 53–58 (NTS Placentia 1N/4W)
Grand Placentia (*CSP* 1663), Plaisance (Beaudoin 1697), Great Placentia (*CSP* 1709, *Population Returns* 1836). Pp. *38, 46, 47, 51, 61, 80, 82, 105, 109, 122, 123, 130, 131, 133.*

— PLACENTIA BAY 47–00, 53–30 (NTS St. Bride's 1L/16E, Ship Cove 1M/1E, Argentia 1N/5W, Dildo 1N/12W, etc.)
Bay of Placentia (Wyet 1594 in Hakluyt), Bay of Pleasance (Whitbourne 1588–1622), Fretum Placentiae (Mason 1626), Plaisance (Blaeu c. 1630), Plasentia Bay (Visscher c. 1680), Placentia Bay (Hack c. 1690 ?), la Baye de Plaisance (Lahontan c. 1696). Pp. *18, 38, 46, 48–9, 52, 57, 59, 60, 61, 62, 76, 81, 84, 87, 89, 103, 105, 109, 120, 122, 125.*

— PLACENTIA HARBOUR 47–15, 53–57 (Mason 1626), The Harbour of Placentia (Gaudy 1715), R. de Plaisance (Buache 1736), Placentia Harbour (Lane 1772). Cp. NORTH EAST ARM (NTS Argentia). Pp. *38, 61.*

— PLACENTIA JUNCTION 47–23, 53–40 (NTS Argentia 1N/5E)
The railway was extended from WHITBOURNE to PLACENTIA in 1888. Pp. *38, 148.*

— PLACENTIA ROAD 47–15, 53–59 (NTS Placentia 1N/4W). (Imray, *Sailing Directions* 1862), Placentia roadstead (Imray, *Sailing Directory* 1873). Pp. *38, 141.*

— PLACENTIA SOUND 47–20, 53–56 (NTS Argentia 1N/5W)

(Lane 1772), Little Placentia Bay (Cook and Lane 1770 [1775]B), Little Placentia Harbour (Imray, *Sailing Directions* 1862; *Sailing Directory* 1873).
"The western part of Placentia sound, that which extends 1½ miles w. ¾ s. along the south side of point Roche, is known to the fishermen as Little Placentia harbour" (Imray, *Sailing Directory* 1873, p. 85).
See ARGENTIA HARBOUR (NTS Argentia). Pp. *38, 51, 65, 84, 141.*

— SOUTHEAST PLACENTIA (Set.) 47–13, 53–56
S.E. Arm (*Population Returns* 1836), Southeast Placentia (Census 1869).
See SOUTHEAST ARM (Feature). P. *38.*

PLATFORM HILLS 46–59, 54–03 (NTS St. Bride's 1L/16E)
(Murray and Howley 1868). A series of plateaux about 750 feet high.

PLEASANTVILLE (St. John's) 47–35, 52–41
Name, ? from 19th century, for meadowland north of QUIDI VIDI LAKE. It was known as Fort Pepperell 1941–65 whilst used by American forces as an Air Force base, after Sir William Pepperell (1696–1759), a Maine merchant, chief justice of the Massachusetts general court (1730), and head of the army that captured the French garrison at Louisburg (1745). "The King made him a baronet, and Massachusetts honored him with a town" (Stewart, *Names on the Land*, p. 143). P. *146.*

POINT (Generic). P. *144.*

Point Baccalo (Gosse 1828)
See BACCALIEU ISLAND (NTS Bay de Verde). P. *90.*

260 / Place Names of the Avalon Peninsula

POINT LA HAYE (Set.)
See LA HAYE POINT (NTS St. Mary's). Pp. 53, 83, 144.

POINT LANCE 46–47, 54–04 (NTS St. Bride's 1L/16E) (Cook 1763).
— POINT LANCE (Set.) 46–48, 54–05 (*Population Returns* 1836).
— LANCE COVE 46–48, 54–05 (Adm. 2915 1864).
— LANCE RIVER 46–48, 54–04 (Adm. 2915 1864).
Pp. 18, 52, 81, 84, 86, 144.

Point Latina (Lane 1772)
See LATINE POINT (NTS Argentia). Pp. 52–3, 84.

P[oin]t le Hays (Cook 1762 or Gilbert 1768)
See LA HAYE POINT (NTS St. Mary's). P. 83.

P[oin]t Moll (Lane 1772)
See MOLL POINT (NTS Argentia). P. 84.

POINT OF BEACH 47–41, 53–13 (NTS Harbour Grace 1N/11E)
? Point of the Bar (Lane, *Directions* 1775, 1810), Point of Beach (Imray, *Sailing Directory* 1873).
"a shingle point on the north side of ... Harbour Grace" (Imray, *Sailing Directory* 1873, p. 47). Pp. 95, 144.

Point of the Bar (Harbour Grace) (Lane, *Directions* 1775, 1810)
See ? POINT OF BEACH (NTS Harbour Grace). P. 95.

Point of the Grates (*English Pilot. The Fourth Book* 1689)
See GRATES POINT (NTS Bay de Verde). P. 90.

POINT OF THE GUT 47–25, 53–53 (NTS Argentia 1N/5W) (Adm. 3266 1939).
Headland which separates LONG HARBOUR from ST. CROIX BAY, at the entrance to the channel, the gut, between the mainland and CRAWLEY ISLAND. P. 144.

P[oint] Prime (Seller c. 1671)
See BREME POINT (NTS St. Bride's). P. 47.

Point Roche (Lane 1772)
See ROCHE POINT (NTS Argentia). P. 84.

POINT VERDE 47–14, 54–01 (NTS Ship Cove 1M/1E)
? Green Point (Gaudy 1715), P. Verte (Buache 1736), Pt. Verde (Cook 1762, Lane 1772).
"The summit or ridge of Pointe Verde is covered with a beautiful grassy sward" (M. F. Howley, xxix, *NQ*, March 1910).
— POINT VERDE (Set.) 47–14, 54–00 Point Verd (*Population Returns* 1836).
Pp. 31, 81, 144.

P[oin]t Verte (Hack ? 1677)
See ? BURNT POINT (NTS Harbour Grace). P. 76.

Pointe agreable (Bellin 1744)
See COLEY'S POINT (NTS Harbour Grace). Pp. 52, 89.

Pointe prime (Robinson 1669)
See WESTERN BAY HEAD (NTS Heart's Content). P. 46.

Pointe Verte (Buache 1736)
See POINT VERDE (NTS Ship Cove). Pp. 31, 144.

Pokempath (St. John's)
See HAMILTON AVENUE. P. 148.

POLLS HEAD (Bell Island) 47–39, 52–55 (NTS St. John's 1N/10W)
Cp. POWLES HEAD (NTS Trepassey). P. 164.

POND(s) (Generic). Pp. 115, 142–3.

THE POND 47–19, 54–00 (NTS Argentia 1N/5W)
Pond (Lane 1772).

"The Pond ... is a small salt water lagoon" (*NLP* I, p. 104).

THE POND THAT FEEDS THE BROOK 47–31, 53–23 (NTS Harbour Grace 1N/11W)
(NDNR 1N/11 1948).
The brook is NORTH RIVER (NTS Harbour Grace). P. 5.

P[onta] de crux (Maggiolo 1527)
See MISTAKEN POINT (NTS Trepassey). P. 71.

Ponta del pa[drão] ("Oliveriana" 1505–8)
See CAPE RACE (NTS Trepassey), MISTAKEN POINT (NTS Trepassey). Pp. 28–30, 71.

POOR BOY ISLAND 47–53, 53–43 (NTS Sunnyside 1N/13E)
(Imray, *Sailing Directory* 1873).
Cp. Poor Boy Ledge.

Porche (Robinson 1669)
See LITTLE BARASWAY (NTS Ship Cove), PERCH COVE (NTS St. Bride's). P. 48.

PORT (Generic). P. 141.

PORT DE GRAVE 47–34, 53–14 (NTS Harbour Grace 1N/11E and W)
Graves (Robinson 1669), P Graue (Southwood 1675), Pt Grave (Mount and Page 1755), Port Grave and Bay (Cook and Lane 1770 [1775]B), Portdegrave (Lane, *Directions* 1775, 1810), Port Grave and Bay (Mount and Page 1780), Port du Grave (Jukes 1842), Port de Grave (Bonnycastle 1842), Portgrave (Imray, *Sailing Directions* 1862).
Cp. GRAVEN BEACH (NTS St. Mary's). Pp. 47–8, 53, 65, 70, 141.
— BAY DE GRAVE 47–35, 53–13
  Portdegrave Bay (Lane, *Directions* 1775, 1810),
  Port Grave and Bay (Mount and Page 1780). Pp. 47–8, 75, 91, 95, 98, 140.
— PORT DE GRAVE (Set.) 47–35,
  53–13 (NTS Harbour Grace 1N/11E)
  Port Grave (*CSP* 1674/5), Porta Grave (*CSP* 1677), Port-Grave (Beaudoin 1697), Portegrave (*CSP* 1705), Port de Grave (Wix 1836).
  Pp. 79, 118.
— PORT DE GRAVE ISLAND 47–36,
  53–13 (CHS 1472 1954).
  The late intrusion of de may be seen as voicing of the final t in port.

PORT KIRWAN
See ADMIRAL'S COVE (Fermeuse) (NTS Renews).
Cp. KERWAN POINT (NTS St. Catherine's). Pp. 132, 141.

Portland Point (Trepassey Harbour) (Cook 1762 or Gilbert 1768)
See PORTUGAL POINT (NTS Trepassey). P. 83.

P[orto] da cruz (Reinel 1519)
See HOLYROOD BAY (NTS St. Mary's). P. 30.

PORTUGAL COVE 46–42, 53–16 (NTS Trepassey 1K/11W)
B of Portingal (Velasco 1610), B Portugall (Briggs 1625), B de St Portugas (Robinson 1669), Portugal Cove (Lane 1773).
Pp. 5–6, 33, 39–40, 57.
— PORTUGAL COVE BROOK 46–43,
  53–16 (NTS Trepassey 1K/11E and W, Biscay Bay River 1K/14E) (Newfoundland 1941)
— PORTUGAL COVE SOUTH (Set.)
  46–42, 53–16
  (*Population Returns* 1836); Portugal Cove South (Proclamation 30 August 1913), to distinguish from PORTUGAL COVE (NTS St. John's).
— PORTUGAL POINT 46–42, 53–17
  Portland Point (Cook 1762 or Gilbert 1768), Portugal Point (Adm. 2915 1864). P. 83.
  G. R. F. Prowse, CM, III, associates the cove and the point with the

262 / Place Names of the Avalon Peninsula

voyage of Corte Real and states that he erected the Portuguese arms at the point in 1500, marking the most westerly point he reached.
Cp. BISCAY BAY (NTS Trepassey), MOTION HEAD (NTS Bay Bulls).

PORTUGAL COVE 47–37, 52–52 (NTS St. John's 1N/10W)
Abra Frade (Laet 1630 ... Roggeven 1675), Portugal Cove (Southwood 1675, Hack ? 1677), Haure froid (Alemand 1687), Portugall Cove (Thornton 1689B).
Cp. PORTUGAL COVE (NTS Trepassey), MOTION HEAD (NTS Bay Bulls).
Pp. 5–6, 33.
— PORTUGAL COVE (Set.) 47–38, 52–51
 (Beaudoin 1697). Pp. 79, 90–1, 100, 147.
— PORTUGAL COVE ROAD (St. John's)
 " 'Whereas many of the inhabitants of St. John's and Conception Bay have expressed a wish that a good road may be made from St. John's to Portugal Cove; notice is hereby given that subscriptions for that purpose will be received by the Subscribers – Stepn. Knight. John Dunscomb.' (*The Royal Gazette*, 31 October 1811). At the same time tenders for the construction of said road were advertised for by Stephen Knight.
 "[A] lottery for the construction of this road, referred to as 'the Windsor Road,' advertised in *The Royal Gazette*, 6 February 1812, by David Tasker, R. Hutton, James Stewart, Wm. Thomas, Wm. Johnstone and Thos. Brooking. The prizes numbered 177, of a total value of $1200. Six hundred tickets were sold at $4 each." (Mosdell, p. 98).

See WINDSOR LAKE (NTS St. John's). P. 147.

POST OFFICE (Generic). P. 148.

POTHANGERS POND 48–00, 53–03 (NTS Heart's Content 1N/14E)
(NDNR 1N/14 1946), Penanger [pəˈnæŋgər] Pond (Local name). Local tradition maintains that the name derives from the loss of a family's pothangers in the pond when the ice broke during a move from a settlement in TRINITY BAY to a new home on the NORTH SHORE. (Communication from P. A. O'Flaherty).
 Pothanger – "I remember grandfather's old home, with the large, open fireplace, the flagstones surrounding it, the dog irons, the pot bars and hangers from which pots and kettles were suspended over the open fire ..." (Gillingham, *Evening Telegram*, St. John's, 11 August 1960).

POUCH COVE 47–46, 52–45 (NTS Pouch Cove 1N/15W)
Pouche Cove (Jukes 1840). Pp. 54, 111.
— POUCH COVE (Set.) 47–46, 52–46
 (*Minute Book*, Gower Street Church 1821; *Population Returns* 1836; Wix 1836).
 A suggestion that the name POUCH COVE be changed to Cape Town (after CAPE ST. FRANCIS) was rejected by the Nomenclature Board in 1910.
— POUCH COVE BROOK 47–46, 52–45
— POUCH COVE BROOK WEST 47–46, 52–46
— POUCH COVE N.E. POND 47–47, 52–47
— POUCH COVE N.W. POND 47–46, 52–47

POUNDEN COVE 46–41, 53–26 (NTS Trepassey 1K/11W)
(USHO 0618 1941).

"a rock, with a depth of less than 6 feet over it, [? on which the sea 'pounds'], lies in the middle of the Cove" (*NLP* I, p. 92).

The form pounden appears to be the cartographer's phonetic rendering of the local popular pronunciation of pounding, found similarly in GRAVEN BEACH (NTS St. Mary's) and WATERN COVE (NTS Trepassey). P. 6.

Powder-horn Hill (Jukes 1842)
See CENTRE HILL (NTS Sunnyside). Pp. 105–6.

POWELL POINT 47–18, 53–55 (NTS Argentia 1N/5W)
(CHS 4622 ? 1953). Pp. 134, 164.

POWELLS BROOK 47–44, 53–14 (NTS Harbour Grace 1N/11E and W)
(Adm. 297 1933). P. 164.

POWERS POND 47–34, 52–50 (NTS St. John's 1N/10W). P. 134.
— LITTLE POWERS POND 47–34, 52–52

POWLES HEAD 46–41, 53–24 (NTS Trepassey 1K/11W)
Powles (Southwood 1675), Powles (*English Pilot. The Fourth Book* 1689), The Poules (Gaudy 1715), Cap Poule (Bellin 1744, 1754), Cap de Poule (Lotter c. 1758), Powles (Lane 1773), Powles Head, Cape Powles (Imray, *Sailing Directions* 1862), Powles Hd. (Adm. 2915 1864), The Powles, Powell's Point (M. F. Howley 1909), Powles Point (Newfoundland 1955).

The name occurs in early maps of the Atlantic and Newfoundland in varying locations and refers to a cape, a bay and islands: C. de St. paulo ("Kunstmann no. 2" 1503–6), c de s palos (Ribeiro 1529) c dos palos (Ribeiro c. 1530), S. Paulo (Viegas 1534), Cabo de Sanct Pablo (Oviedo 1536), c de san palos (Santa Cruz 1545), c de s paulo (Freire 1546), B. de S. paulo (Homem 1558) Islas de S. paulo (Martines 1583), s paulo (Dirckx 1599), B de St. Paol (Boissaie le Bocage 1669), Powles Bay (Visscher c. 1680).

M. F. Howley, XXVII, *NQ*, September 1909, remarks: "The Powles, or Powell's Point, on some maps marked the Polls. This name is pronounced by the people as ow in howl, and is the Irish or Gaelic word for a hole. Whether it is really derived from this word or not I am unable to say. It is, however, rather a curious coincidence that the first Marconi Station should have been set up on this side of the ocean in a place near [?] the Powles, while the European end of the system was at a place called Powl dhu (black hole) in Cornwall."

Cp. POLLS HEAD (NTS St. John's). P. 74.
— POWLES PENINSULA 46–42, 53–23 (USHO 0618 1941). P. 144.

Prima vista (Hakluyt). P. 8.

PRINCE WILLIAM PLACE (St. John's)
Commemorates the visit of Prince William Henry (afterwards William IV) as captain of HMS *Pegasus* in 1786 (D. W. Prowse, pp. 365–7). P. 6.

PRINCES POND 47–20, 52–48 (NTS Bay Bulls 1N/7W)
(NDNR Bay Bulls 1943). P. 164.

Privécœur Shoal (*NLP* 1951). P. 51.

PROSSER ROCK (St. John's Harbour) 47–34, 52–42
Prosser's Rock (Lane, *Directions* 1775, 1810), Prosser Rock (*NP* 1952). ? after William Prosser, Lieutenant RN 1772 (*The Commissioned Sea Officers of the Royal Navy 1660–1815*, III, p. 747). Pp. 94, 164.

Prowsetown (Set.)
See SIBLEY'S COVE (Set.) (NTS Old Perlican).

PULPIT HEAD (Bell Island) 47–38, 52–55 (NTS St. John's 1N/10W)

PULPIT POND 47–19, 52–46 (NTS Bay Bulls 1N/7W)
(NDNR Bay Bulls 1943).

PUMBLY COVE 47–37, 53–56 (NTS Dildo 1N/12W)
Pumbly (of rock) – broken, ragged, thickly-spread. Not in *OED*, *EDD*, but perhaps to be associated with pumple – pimple, and pumple-stone – pebble-stone, a West Country usage (*EDD*).
Cp. Pumbly Cove (NTS Cat Arm River).

PURBECKS POND 47–47, 53–17 (NTS Heart's Content 1N/14W)
(NDNR 1N/14 1946).
? For Purbeck – a peninsula on the Dorset coast.
See Old Harry (Rock). P. 164.

PUSSEYS BROOK 47–29, 53–18 (NTS Holyrood 1N/6W)
(NDNR 1N/6 1943).
— PUSSEYS GULLY 47–29, 53–20 (NDNR 1N/6 1943). P. 164.

QUAIL POINT 47–18, 52–48 (NTS Bay Bulls 1N/7W)
(NDNR Bay Bulls 1943).

QUARRY BROOK 47–26, 53–06 (NTS Holyrood 1N/6E)
(CHS 4573 1953).

QUEEN'S RIVER 47–23, 52–43 (NTS Bay Bulls 1N/7E)
(Adm. 296, 1868), Queen river (*NLP* 1951).
? After Queen Victoria. P. 6.

Quemo Gospen ? 47–25, 53–37 (Unnamed in NTS Argentia 1N/5E) (Adm. 232a 1870). P. 25.

QUIDI VIDI (Set.) 47–35, 52–41 (NTS St. John's 1N/10E)
Quirividy (Beaudoin 1697), City Vety (Thoresby 1796). Pp. 79, 123, 124, 139.
— QUIDI VIDI HARBOUR 47–35, 52–40
Kitty-vitty (Yonge 1669), Quiteandy (Robinson 1669), Quilliwiddi (Seller c. 1671), Kitte Vitte (Southwood 1675), Kitty uity (Hack ? 1677), Quide Vide (*CSP* 1677), Que de Vide Creek (*CSP* 1679), Queue de Vide (*CSP* 1680), Kitivi ("Dépôt 128.2.6" c. 1680), Kitte Vitte (Visscher c. 1680, Thornton 1689B), Quidi Vidi or Kitty Vitty (*English Pilot. The Fourth Book* 1689), Kitty Vitty (Hack c. 1690?), Kitte Witte (Hermite 1695), Quidividi (*CSP* 1709), Quidividi (*CSP* 1722), Quidividy (*CSP* 1729, 1730), Città Vecchià (Walbanke 1743), Kitty Ville (Mount and Page 1755), Kitty Velle (Cook 1763), Quidy-Vidy (Cook and Lane 1770 [1775]A), Quidy-Vidy or Kitty Vitty (Cook and Lane 1770 [1775]B), Quid-Vidy (Mount and Page 1780), Kitty Vitty Cove (Bonnycastle 1842), Quiddybiddy (Bonnycastle, *Newfoundland in 1842*, I, p. 109 1842), Quiddy Viddy (Imray, *Sailing Directions* 1862, *Sailing Directory* 1873), Quidi vidi (J. P. Howley 1907), Quidi Vidi or Kitty Vitty (M. F. Howley 1908). Pp. 43–5.
— QUIDI VIDI LAKE 47–35, 52–41 (Tocque 1878). P. 143.
Cp. Kitty Vitty River (Amherst 1762 in D. W. Prowse, p. 412).

RACE POND 47–20, 53–23 (NTS Holyrood 1N/6W)
(NDNR 1N/6 1943).

RAGGED POINT 47–16, 52–49 (NTS Bay Bulls 1N/7W)
(NDNR Bay Bulls 1943). P. 35.

RAGGED ROCKS 47–42, 53–09 (NTS
Harbour Grace 1N/11E)
(Imray, *Sailing Directory* 1873),
Ragged Islands (Adm. 297 1933),
Ragged Rocks (CHS 4590 1933). P. 35.

RAINBOW GULLIES 47–34, 52–52 (NTS
St. John's 1N/10W)
— RAINBOW PONDS 47–33, 52–50

RAM HEAD 47–45, 53–50 (NTS Dildo
1N/12W)
Ram's Head (Wix 1836). P. 105.

Ram Islands (Lane 1772)
See IONA ISLANDS (NTS Argentia).
P. 85.

RANTEM (Set.) 47–42, 53–52 (NTS
Dildo 1N/12W)
Bentham (Wix 1836), Rantem
(Census 1869). P. 105.
— RANTEM COVE 47–42, 53–51
? Alhallowes (Guy 1612), Rantem Cove (Imray, *Sailing Directions* 1862), Rantom Cove
(Murray and Howley 1868).
P. 59.
— RANTEM STATION 47–39, 53–52
(Census 1911).

RATTLE, RATTLING (Specific and
Generic) "Where there is a succession of falls in a river ... the falling water makes a great noise; such a place is called a Rattle" (G. Cartwright, *Transactions*, 1792 Glossary).
"*rattle* ... the term used in Newfoundland for *rapid*" (J. B. Jukes, *Excursions* II, 1842, p. 136).
Not in *OED, EDD* in this sense.

Rattling Brook (Set.) (*Population Returns* 1836)
See MOUNT CARMEL (NTS St. Catherine's). P. 108.

BIG RATTLING BROOK 47–21, 53–52
(NTS Argentia 1N/5W)
(Adm. 2829 1877).
— LITTLE RATTLING BROOK 47–22,
53–51 (USHO 2375 1944).

RATTLING BROOK 47–25, 53–49 (NTS
Argentia 1N/5W)
(Adm. 3266 1939).
— RATTLING BROOK COVE
(Adm. 3266 1939).

RAYMOND BROOK 47–27, 52–46 (NTS
Bay Bulls 1N/7W)
(NDNR Bay Bulls 1943).
— RAYMOND HEAD 47–23, 52–43
(Adm. 296 1868).
— RAYMONDS BRIDGE (Set.) 47–26,
52–46
(NDNR Bay Bulls 1943).
Pp. 134, 148.

RED CLIFF HEAD 47–39, 52–40 (NTS
St. John's 1N/10E)
Little red head (Southwood 1675),
Little read head (Thornton 1689B),
Red-Head (*English Pilot. The Fourth Book* 1689), P[ointe] C[ap] Rouge
(Hermite 1695), Little red Head
(Popple 1733), Red P (Bowen 1747),
Pte Rouge (Robert de Vaugondy
1749), cap Rouge (Bellin 1754), Little
red Head (Mount and Page 1755),
Red Head (Kitchin 1762), Little red
Head (Cook and Lane 1770 [1775]B),
? Red Head (Bonnycastle 1842;
Imray, *Sailing Directory* 1873), Redcliff Head (*NLP* 1951; *NP* 1952).
RED CLIFF HEAD appears to have been
confused with SCULPINS POINT 47–38,
52–40 by cartographers from time to
time. Pp. 72–3, 144.

RED COVE 46–51, 53–58 (NTS
St. Mary's 1K/13W)
(Adm. 2915 1864).
From the red Brigus formation.

RED COVE (Fair Haven) (Wix 1836)
(*NP* 1952). P. 105.

RED COVE 47–17, 52–46 (NTS Bay
Bulls 1N/7W)
(CHS 4586 1944).
"Both SOUTH HEAD [47–17, 52–46]
and GULL ISLAND [47–16, 52–46] have
red cliffs" (*NLP* I, p. 83).

RED COVE HEAD 47–30, 53–55 (NTS Dildo 1N/12W)
The Red Ground (Jukes 1842).
P. 115.

RED HEAD 46–55, 53–53 (NTS St. Mary's 1K/13W)
(Lane 1773). Pp. 5, 87.
— RED HEAD RIVER 46–57, 53–52 (Murray and Howley 1869).

Red head (Hack ? 1677)
See ? SCULPINS POINT (NTS St. John's).
P. 76.

RED HEAD 47–43, 52–42 (NTS St. John's 1N/10E)
(Southwood 1675; Thornton 1689B). Pp. 5, 72–3.
— RED HEAD COVE

RED HEAD 48–09, 52–53 (NTS Bay de Verde 2C/2W)
(Newfoundland 1941).
— RED HEAD COVE (Set.) 48–08, 52–54
(*Population Returns* 1836).
P. 107.

RED HILL 46–53, 53–01 (NTS Biscay Bay River 1K/14E)
Red Hills (Adm. 2915 1864), Red Hill (Newfoundland 1941).

RED ISLAND POND 47–17, 53–27 (NTS Holyrood 1N/6W)
(NDNR 1N/6 1943).

Red Land (Set.) (*Population Returns* 1836)
See REDLAND POINT (NTS St. Bride's).
P. 145.

RED ROCK COVE 47–27, 53–09 (NTS Holyrood 1N/6E)
(CHS 4573 1953).

RED ROCKS 47–42, 53–31 (NTS Dildo 1N/12E)
(Adm. 296 1863).

REDLAND POINT 46–48, 54–08 (NTS St. Bride's 1L/16E)
As set: Red Land (*Population Returns* 1836); Redland Point (Adm. 2915 1864). P. 109.

REDLANDS (Cape) 47–59, 53–00 (NTS Heart's Content 1N/14E)
As set: (Census 1874). Pp. 140, 145.

REDMANS HEAD (Bell Island) 47–39, 52–55 (NTS St. John's 1N/10W)
(*NLP* 1951). P. 164.

REGINA COVE 47–01, 53–40 (NTS Placentia 1N/4E)
Mother Hicks Cove (Adm. 2915 1869), Mother Ixx cove (Imray, *Sailing Directory* 1873, *NLP* 1951), Mother Ex or Rex (M. F. Howley, XXVIII, *NQ*, December 1909).
— REGINAVILLE (Set.) 47–00, 53–41
Mother Ixx's (Census 1857), Mother Rex (Census 1891), Regina (Proclamation 27 October 1913, Smallwood 1940, Electors 1955), Reginaville (Canadian Board on Geographic Names 1951).
Pp. 120, 130, 146.

RENEWS (Set.) 46–56, 52–56 (NTS Renews 1K/15W)
Rognouze (Beaudoin 1697), Renewse (*Population Returns* 1836), though evidence of early settlement may perhaps be deduced from such a statement as "Soit faict memoire de la mercque de mes basteaux et barques, que je laisse en la Terre Noeufve, au havre de Jehan Denys, dict Rougnouse" (? 1544 Jehan Cordyer of Rouen. Bibliothèque Nationale, MS. fr. 24269, in Biggar, *Voyages of Jacques Cartier*, pp. 239–40). Pp. 40, 58, 61, 64, 69, 79, 114, 123.
— RENEWS HARBOUR 46–55, 52–56
Rougnouse (Cartier 1536), Rogneuse (Alfonse 1544), P. Rognoso (Agnese 1552–64), Rogneux (Hayes 1583 in Hakluyt), Renouze (Whitbourne 1588–1622), Bay of Rogneuse

(Fisher 1591), Arenhosa (Plancius 1592, Langenes 1598), Renoose (Guy 1612), Ranosa (Sanches 1618), Rhenus (Mason 1626), Renosa ("Blathwayt" c. 1630–40), B Arenosa – Rognose (P) (Dudley 1646), Renoose (Yonge 1663), Urrupnus (Rotis 1674), Ranowes (Southwood 1675), Renows (Hack ? 1677), Roigneuse ou Reneuse Port (Coronelli-Tillemon 1689), Ranowes (Thornton 1689B), Renewes (Gaudy 1715), Renowes (Cook 1763), Renews (Chappell 1813, Jukes 1840).

"Renowes is but a bad Harbour, by reason of sunken rocks going in" (*English Pilot. The Fourth Book* 1716).

"an indifferent harbour, having several rocks in the entrance, and the south-east winds heave in a very great sea" (Lane, *Directions* 1775, 1810). Pp. *31, 34, 35, 40, 43, 66, 68, 69*.

For a conjectural Basque origin: "Rognouse is supposed to be a corruption of Orrougne, near Saint Jean de Luz" (J. Reade, "The Basques in America," *TRSC*, 1888, II, II, p. 22).

— RENEWS HEAD 46–54, 52–55 South poynt (Yonge 1663–70), Renowes Point (*English Pilot. The Fourth Book* 1689), Renews Pt (Bonnycastle), Renewse Hd. (Adm. 2915 1864), Renews Head (Newfoundland 1941). Pp. 68, 75.

— RENEWS ISLAND 46–54, 52–55 Renewes I. (Gaudy 1715), Renowes I. (Senex 1728), Renouse I (Mount and Page 1780), Renewse Islet (*NLP* 1929), Renews Island (Newfoundland 1941). P. 81.

— RENEWS ROCKS 46–53, 52–54 Ranows rocks (Southwood 1675), Renowes Rock (Hack ? 1677, *The English Pilot. The Fourth Book* 1689), Ranows Rock (Visscher c. 1680; Fitzhugh 1693), Renewes Rock (Gaudy 1715), Renous Rocks (Kitchin 1762).

"There is a rock off the coast of Brittany having the same name, and right in the entrance of the harbour of Renews, there is a large rock of precisely the same description" (M. F. Howley, XXVI, *NQ*, July 1909).

"Et à la mer de la baye de Rogneuse, environ vne lieue et demye en la mer, y a vng mauvais rochier, qui semble à vng basteau" (J. Alfonse, *Cosmographie*, 1544, in Biggar, *Voyages of Jacques Cartier*, p. 279).

Rennie's Mill (St. John's) (Jukes 1842)
— RENNIE'S RIVER (St. John's) 47–35, 52–41. P. 112.

Rhenus (Mason 1626)
See RENEWS HARBOUR (NTS Renews). Pp. 12, 61.

RICKETTS BRIDGE (Set.) 47–36, 52–44 (NTS St. John's 1N/10E). Pp. 148, 164.

RIDGE (Generic). P. 145.

Riff Raff (Rocks) (Shoal Bay) 47–52, 53–45 (NTS Sunnyside) (*NLP* 1953). P. 118.

Riff Raff (Rocks) (Hants Harbour) 48–03, 53–14 (NTS Old Perlican) (*NLP* 1953). P. 118.

RIGHT HAND POND 47–28, 53–21 (NTS Holyrood 1N/6w) (NDNR 1N/6 1943).
On the right side of HODGEWATER LINE going inland.
Cp. LEFT HAND POND 47–28, 53–21. P. 5.

RINDERS POND 47–40, 53–26 (NTS Harbour Grace 1N/11W)
(NDNR 1N/11 1948).
Rind – "To strip the rind or bark from (a tree, etc.) (*OED*).
"There have bin rinded this yere not so few as 50,000 trees" (Wynne in Whitbourne, p. 110, cited in *OED*).
— LITTLE RINDERS POND 47–39, 53–25
(NDNR 1N/11 1948).
Cp. DINNYS POND (NTS Harbour Grace).
P. 5.

Ring (Cove, St. John's Harbour) (Visscher c. 1680), Ring noone (Thornton 1689B), Ring-noon (*English Pilot. The Fourth Book* 1689).
"a small Bay" in St. John's Harbour (*English Pilot. The Fourth Book* 1689).
P. 77.

R[io] da aguea (Reinel 1519)
See AQUAFORTE (NTS Ferryland). Pp. 28, 30, 35.

R[io] das patas (Reinel c. 1504, 1519)
See CALVERT BAY (NTS Ferryland). Pp. 30, 31, 33.

R[io] fermoso (Reinel 1519)
See FERMEUSE (NTS Renews). Pp. 28, 30.

Rip Rap (Set.) (Census 1857). P. 118.

RIPPLE POND 47–19, 53–28 (NTS Holyrood 1N/6W)
(NDNR 1N/6 1943).
? From the confluence of EAST and NORTH RIVERS.

Riuo de bosas [for rosas] ("Oliveriana" 1505–8)
See TREPASSEY BAY (NTS Trepassey). P. 30.

Riuo de la spera ("Oliveriana" 1505–8)
See SPEAR BAY (NTS St. John's). Pp. 30, 77, 90.

Riuo de los Bacolaos ("Oliveriana" 1505–8). P. 12.

RIVER (Generic). P. 143.

RIVERDALE (Set.) 47–30, 53–01 (NTS Holyrood 1N/6E)
Lower Gullies (*Population Returns* 1836), Riverdale (Proclamation 3 January 1923).
Cp. UPPER GULLIES (NTS Holyrood).
Pp. 107, 117, 146.

RIVERHEAD (Set.) 46–58, 53–31 (NTS St. Mary's 1K/13E)
River Head (*Population Returns* 1836).
At the head of ST. MARY'S HARBOUR.
Pp. 68, 108, 141.

Riverhead (Calvert Bay) (Yonge 1663–70)
See CALVERT (NTS Ferryland). P. 68.

Riverhead (Renews Harbour) (Yonge 1663–70). P. 68.

Riverhead (Bay Bulls) (Thornton 1689D). Pp. 68, 78.

Riverhead (St. John's Harbour) (Thornton 1689B). Pp. 68, 77, 83, 112; as set: 112.

Riverhead (Bay Roberts) (Blackmore 1865)
See BAY ROBERTS (NTS Harbour Grace), Cosh.

RIVERHEAD (Set.) 47–40, 53–16 (NTS Harbour Grace)
(Adm. 296 1868).
Of HARBOUR GRACE (NTS Harbour Grace). Pp. 68, 141.
— RIVERHEAD LONG POND 47–39, 53–18
(CHS 4572 1954).

RIX HARBOUR 47–47, 53–48 (NTS Sunnyside 1N/13W)
(Imray, *Sailing Directions* 1862).
P. 164.

ROACHES LINE (Road and Set.) 47–30,

53–19 (Unnamed in NTS Harbour Grace). Pp. 130, 148, 164.

ROACHES MARSH 47–18, 52–49 (NTS Bay Bulls 1N/7W) (CHS 4586 1944). Pp. 143, 164.

ROAD (Generic) As hydrographic feature. P. 141.
As topographic feature. P. 147.

ROBIN HOOD BAY 47–37, 52–39 (NTS St. John's 1N/10E)
Robin Hood's Cove (M. F. Howley, XXII, NQ, July 1908), Robin Hood Bay (NLP 1951).
In this location apparently a modern imposition, as opposed to Robinhood Bay (NTS Trinity), recorded in Laet 1625, though G. R. F. Prowse, CM, III, p. xxiii, would associate both names with a Yorkshire Survey of Newfoundland in 1498. Cp. Robin Hood Cove (NTS Gaultois 1N/12W).
? After Robin Hood's Bay, Yorkshire. P. 75

ROBINS POND 47–39, 52–46 (NTS St. John's 1N/10W). P. 165.

ROBINSON POINT 47–54, 53–44 (NTS Sunnyside 1N/13E)
(Imray, Sailing Directory 1873). P. 165.

ROBINSONS RIVER 47–46, 52–46 (NTS Pouch Cove 1N/15W). P. 165.

ROCHE POINT 47–19, 53–58 (NTS Argentia 1N/5W)
Point Roche (Lane 1772).
Fr. *roche* – rock, boulder, any hard stone or stony mass.
"a shingle spit, 9 feet high, surrounded by shoal water, extends about one cable north-north-westward from Roche point" (NLP 1951, p. 104).
Roche is a frequent name in Barnstaple and Wexford. New Ross and Waterford ships landed annually in Placentia in the nineteenth century (Communication from W. Kirwin). Pp. 53, 84, 134.

ROCK(S) (Generic). P. 144.

Rock Cove (CO Misc. 199.18 1755)
See SHIP COVE (NTS Harbour Grace). P. 75.

ROCKY BROOK 47–41, 52–47 (NTS St. John's 1N/10W)
— ROCKY POND 47–44, 52–48.

ROCKY GULLY 47–44, 53–23 (NTS Harbour Grace 1N/11W) (NDNR 1N/11 1948).

ROCKY POND occurs at 46–54, 54–02 (NTS St. Bride's) (Adm. 2915 1864); 47–18, 53–05 (NTS Holyrood 1N/6E) (NDNR 1N/6 1943); 47–29, 52–44 (NTS Bay Bulls 1N/7E) (NDNR Bay Bulls 1943); 47–31, 52–53 (NTS St. John's 1N/10W); 47–34, 53–17 (NTS Harbour Grace 1N/11W) (CHS 4572 1954); 47–36, 53–21 (NTS Harbour Grace 1N/11W) (NDNR 1N/11 1948); 47–37, 53–25 (NTS Harbour Grace 1N/11W) (NDNR 1N/11 1948); 47–39, 53–25 (NTS Harbour Grace 1N/11W) (NDNR 1N/11 1948); 47–47, 53–15 (NTS Heart's Content 1N/14E and W) (Newfoundland 1941).

ROCKY POND 47–42, 53–14 (NTS Harbour Grace 1N/11E)
? Associated with Rocky Drong (Gosse c. 1830); (NDNR 1N/11 1948).

ROCKY RIDGE 46–59, 53–55 (NTS St. Mary's 1K/13W) (Adm. 2915 1864).
The western extremity of the ridge is named Granderose, i.e. *Grande Roche* – big rock. (Adm. 2915 1864). P. 145.

ROCKY RIVER 47–13, 53–35 (NTS Placentia 1N/4E, Argentia 1N/5E) (Jukes 1842). Pp. 5, 22–5, 113–4, 120.

ROCKY RIVER 47–26, 53–25 (NTS Holy-

270 / *Place Names of the Avalon Peninsula*

rood 1N/6W)
(NDNR 1N/6 1943).

ROGERS BROOK 47–32, 53–14 (NTS Harbour Grace 1N/11E and W) (CHS 4572 1954). P. 165.

ROGERS GULLIES 47–42, 52–49 (NTS St. John's 1N/10W)
— ROGERS TILT POND 47–42, 52–49.
Pp. 147, 165.

ROLLING COVE 47–42, 53–10 (NTS Harbour Grace 1N/11E) (NDNR 1N/11 1948).
The slight indentation offers no shelter.

ROOM (Generic). P. 147.

ROOST (Generic). P. 144.

Rougnouse (Cartier 1536)
See RENEWS (NTS Renews). Pp. 31, 34.

ROUND HARBOUR 47–58, 53–39 (NTS Sunnyside 1N/13E)
? Haleford (Laet 1625), Round Harbour (Imray, *Sailing Directory* 1873).

ROUND POND occurs at 47–24, 53–01 (NTS Holyrood 1N/6E) (NDNR 1N/6 1943); 47–36, 52–49 (NTS St. John's 1N/10W) and WESTERN ROUND POND 47–36, 52–50; 47–38, 53–18 (NTS Harbour Grace 1N/11W) (CHS 4572 1954); 47–40, 53–29 (NTS Harbour Grace 1N/11W) (NDNR 1N/11 1948); BIG ROUND POND 47–41, 53–25 (NTS Harbour Grace 1N/11W) (NDNR 1N/11 1948); 47–42, 53–18 (NTS Harbour Grace 1N/11W) (NDNR 1N/11 1948); 47–44, 53–29 (NTS Harbour Grace 1N/11W) (NDNR 1N/11 1948).

ROUND POND WEST 47–23, 53–28 (NTS Holyrood 1N/6W)
Mestigu-gundaly Gospen (Murray and Howley 1872), Round Pond West (NDNR 1N/6 1943). P. 25.

ROUNDABOUT POND 47–22, 52–50 (NTS Bay Bulls 1N/7W) (NDNR Bay Bulls 1943).

Russell's Cove (Lovell 1881)
See NEW MELBOURNE (NTS Old Perlican).

RYALLS POND 47–33, 52–52 (NTS St. John's 1N/10W). P. 135.

RYANS BRIDGE (Set.) 47–26, 52–46 (NTS Bay Bulls 1N/7W) (NDNR Bay Bulls 1943). Pp. 135, 148.

RYANS BROOK 47–36, 53–18 (NTS Harbour Grace 1N/11W). P. 135.

RYANS HEAD 47–28, 53–13 (NTS Holyrood 1N/6E) (CHS 4573 1953). P. 135.

RYANS POND 47–22, 53–21 (NTS Holyrood 1N/6W) (NDNR 1N/6 1943). P. 135.

SADDLE HILL 47–27, 52–43 (NTS Bay Bulls 1N/7E) (Adm. 296 1868).
"Saddle-hill – a saddle-back hill." According to *OED* obsolete, with citation from Cook 1773.

SADDLE HILL 47–43, 53–13 (NTS Harbour Grace 1N/11E) (Adm. 297 1868).
See preceding item.

Sailing Cove (Trepassey Bay) (Cook 1762 or Gilbert 1768). P. 81.

saincte Christofle (Alfonse 1544)
See TREPASSEY (NTS Trepassey). P. 35.

ST. BRIDES (Set.) 46–55, 54–10 (NTS St. Bride's 1L/16E)
Distress (*Population Returns* 1836), St. Brides (M. F. Howley, xxix, *NQ*, March 1910).
See DISTRESS COVE (NTS St. Bride's).
Pp. 109, 130, 125, 139.

ST. CATHERINE'S (Set.) 47–11, 53–24 (NTS St. Catherine's 1N/3W)
Great Salmon River (*Population*

Returns 1836), St. Catherine's (Smallwood 1940).
See SALMONIER RIVER (NTS St. Catherine's). Pp. 82, 139.

ST. CROIX BAY 47–26, 53–51 (NTS Argentia 1N/5W)
(Wix 1836).
— ST. CROIX POINT 47–26, 53–55 (*NLP* 1929).
Pp. 54, 104.

ST. JOHN'S (Set.) 47–34, 52–43 (NTS St. John's 1N/10E)
Sam Joham (Freire 1546), sainct Johan (Le Testu 1555A), St. John's (Parkhurst 1578), S Jones ("Velasco" 1610), Saint Iohns (Mason, *Discourse* 1620), St. Johns (Whitbourne 1588–1622). Pp. 18, 20, 43, 44–5, 49, 51, 54, 56, 57, 65, 67, 68, 74, 77, 79, 82, 83, 91, 93, 94–5, 100, 101–2, 111, 112, 115, 116, 122, 123, 124, 127, 129–35, 139, 144, 146, 147, 148, 153.
— ST. JOHN'S AIRFIELD (TORBAY) 47–37, 52–44 (NTS St. John's 1N/10E and W). P. 148.
— ST. JOHN'S BAY 47–34, 52–38 (NTS St. John's 1N/10E)
Baie de St-Jean (Alfonse 1544), Bay de St. John (Popple 1733).
— ST. JOHN'S EAST (Electoral District). P. 116.
— ST. JOHN'S HARBOUR 47–34, 52–42 (NTS St. John's 1N/10E)
R de Sam joham (Reinel 1519), Haven of St. John (Rut 1527), St Ieans Harbour (Visscher c. 1680), St. Johns Harbor (Thornton 1689B), St. John's Harbour (*English Pilot. The Fourth Book* 1689). Pp. 18, 30, 34–5, 42, 56, 68, 76, 77, 82, 83, 94–5, 95, 113, 127.
— St. John's Island
Island of S. John (Hakluyt ? 1589), Ille St Jean (Champlain 1612) ...
I s Iean (Keulen 1682–4). P. 8.

— ST. JOHN'S WEST (Electoral District). P. 116.
S Jones ("Velasco" c. 1610)
See ST. JOHN'S (NTS St. John's).
P. 57.

ST. JONES HARBOUR 47–55, 53–43 (NTS Sunnyside E & W)
St. Jones's Harbour (Lane, *Directions* 1775, 1810), Jones Hr (Purdy 1814), St. Johns Hr (Jukes 1840), Jones' Harbour (Imray, *Sailing Directions* 1862), St. Jones Harbour (Imray, *Sailing Directory* 1873). P. 95.
— ST. JONES HEAD 47–58, 53–40 (NTS Sunnyside 1N/13E) (Imray, *Sailing Directory* 1873).
— ST. JONES ISLANDS 47–55, 53–40
St. Jones's Island (Lane, *Directions* 1775, 1810), Jones' Island (Imray, *Sailing Directions* 1862), St. Jones islet (Imray, *Sailing Directory* 1873, NP 1952).
— ST. JONES WITHOUT (Set.) 47–55, 53–42
Founded in 1858 by a family named Green from WINTERTON (Smallwood, *Newfoundland* 1941, p. 136).
Pp. 57, 74, 139.

ST. JOSEPH'S (Set.) 47–07, 53–31 (NTS Placentia 1N/4E)
? Black Duck Gullies (*Population Returns* 1836), St. Josephs (Census 1911).
   The local church is dedicated to St. Joseph. Pp. 108, 139.

ST. MARY'S (Set.) 46–55, 53–34 (NTS St. Mary's 1K/13E)
(Cook 1762, *Population Returns* 1836). Pp. 54, 83, 88, 123, 139.
— ST. MARY'S BAY 46–50, 53–45 (NTS St. Shotts 1K/12E, St. Mary's 1K/13E and W, St. Bride's 1L/16E, Placentia 1N/14E and W)

S Maria (Viegas 1534), Sa maria (Viegas c. 1537), B St marie ("Harleian" 1542-3), Bay S Maries (Mason 1626), St. Marys Bay (Moll 1709), St Martyre Bay St Marys Bay (after Moll 1711). Pp. 6, 12, 18, 22, 31, 49, 61, 62, 84, 85, 86, 87, 105, 107, 115, 119-20, 122, 125, 141.

— CAPE ST. MARY'S 46-49, 54-12 (NTS St. Bride's 1L/16E)
? C de s tiago (Ribeiro 1529), C da tromenta (H) c da tromta (P), (Viegas 1534, c. 1537), Cabo de Sancta Maria (Oviedo 1536), Cap cazamello (H) c caramello (P) (Rotz 1542), C de S Maria (Santa Cruz 1542), C caramello ("Harleian" 1542-3), cap de saincte Marie (Alfonse 1544); thereafter the forms Maria or Marie are general, though caramello and santiago also occur, and a variant Varie is found in C de Varie (Hondius 1607; Jansz 1610; Langren 1625, Blaeu 1648; Visscher c. 1669); C de Golfo (P) (Dudley 1646), C. S. Mirie (Seller 1671), C S Mary (Friend 1713), Cape St. Mary's (Mount and Page 1780), Cape St. Mary (Purdy 1814).
"C Destiago, that is, C de St. Iago (i.e. St. James) on the Spanish map of Ribero, seems applied to C. St. Mary, though it appears on the Santa Cruz map ... as if alternative to Cape Race" (Ganong, Crucial Maps, p. 54).
tromenta — i.e. Port. tormenta — storms.
Port. caramelo — ice. Pp. 31, 35, 50, 84, 109.

— ST. MARY'S HARBOUR 46-56, 53-35 (NTS St. Mary's 1K/13E)
St. Mary (Whitbourne 1588-1622), St. marie port (Leigh 1597), St Maries (Robinson 1669). Pp. 68, 82, 83, 87, 88, 108.

— ST. MARY'S KEYS 46-43, 54-13
b[aixo] de Santa Maria (Santa Cruz 1545), Cases de St Maria (Robinson 1669), Basse Ste Marie (Courcelle 1675), Caises de St Maria (Thornton 1689A), Rocks Mary (Friend 1713), St Maries Rocks (Senex 1728), St. Mary's Rock (Popple 1733), St. Mary's Keys (Lane 1772).
"Saint Mary's cays are two small rocks, about one cable apart ... situated about 6¾ miles southward of Cape Saint Mary" (NLP I, p. 100).
"Santa Cruz makes the name [St. Mary] apply to a shoal (baxa), and so it appears on later maps, surviving on our charts as St. Mary's Cays, when apparently the name was extended to Cape and Bay [and Harbour and settlement]" (Ganong, Crucial Maps, p. 54.)
Port. baixo, Span. cayo, Fr. basse, OFr. cay, caye — shoal, reef, sunken rock. See OED, Cay, Key. P. 84, 140, 144.

ST. MICHAELS (Set.) 47-11, 52-51 (NTS Ferryland 1N/2W)
Caplin Cove (Population Returns 1836), St. Michael's (Proclamation 17 May 1904).
"a neat little chapel has been erected there dedicated to the Archangel" (M. F. Howley, xxv, NQ, March 1909). Pp. 107, 139.

St. Peters Riv[e]r (Mount and Page 1780)
See PETERS RIVER (NTS St. Mary's). P. 88.

ST. PHILIPS (Set.) 47-36, 52-53 (NTS St. John's 1N/10W)

Broad Cove (*Population Returns 1836*), St. Phillips (Proclamation 1 June 1905).
See BROAD COVE Pp. 90–1, 139.
ST. SHORES COVE 46–40, 53–38 (NTS St. SHOTTS 1K/12E)
Sth Shores (Mount and Page 1775), South Shores (Cook and Lane 1770 [1775]B), St. Shores (Lane 1773), South Shores (Mount and Page 1780). Pp. 35–8, 86, 88.
— ST. SHORES RIVER

ST. SHOTTS (Set.) 46–38, 53–35 (NTS St. Shotts 1K/12E)
(*Population Returns 1836*).
— ST. SHOTTS COVE 46–38, 53–36
The specific has been applied to a cape or island as well as to the cove: cap de Chincete (Alfonse 1544), Chavette (Robinson 1669), C chuchette (H) C Chinchette (P) (Courcelle 1675), Chinchette (Detcheverry 1689), Sanshot (Hack c. 1690?), C. Chincho (Chaviteau 1698), Lachinette (Friend 1713), Chinckhole (Gaudy 1715), Chinkhole (Senex 1728), C chinche (Maurepas 1733), Chinkole (Bellin 1744), St. Shot or Chink Hole (Cook and Lane 1770 [1775]B), St. Shotts (Lane 1773, I Sth Shot or Chink Hole (Mount and Page 1780), St. Shotts (Jukes 1840), St. Shotts Bay (Bonnycastle 1842).
Pp. 6, 35–8, 86, 88.
— ST. SHOTTS RIVER (NTS Trepassey 1K/11W, St. Shotts 1K/12E, Biscay Bay River 1K/14W) (Newfoundland 1941).

ST. STEPHEN (Set.) 46–47, 53–37 (Unnamed in NTS St. Mary's).
? Formerly Middle Gut;
St. Stephen (Newfoundland 1955), St. Stephen's (Electors 1955). P. 139.
Renamed on the suggestion of Fr G. W. Battcock, parish priest of ST. VINCENT'S, to commemorate the late Fr Stephen O'Driscoll who served the community before the parish was established.

ST. THOMAS (Set.) 47–34, 52–54 (NTS St. John's 1N/10W)
Horse Cove (Census 1857), St. Thomas's (Proclamation 30 January 1922).
See HORSE COVE. Pp. 116, 139.

St. Vincent Bay (Adm. 2915 1864 or later)
See HOLYROOD BAY (NTS St. Mary's).
— ST. VINCENT'S (Set.) 46–48, 53–58 (NTS St. Mary's 1K/13E)
Holyrood (*Population Returns 1836*), Holyrood or Holyrood South (M. F. Howley, XXVIII, NQ, December 1909), St. Vincent (Proclamation 15 November 1910).
Pp. 30–1, 54, 139.

S. Williams Point (Bowen 1747)
See WESTERN BAY HEAD (NTS Heart's Content). P. 46.

Sainter's Hill (Wix 1836)
See CENTRE HILL (NTS Sunnyside).
Pp. 105–6.

SALLS ISLAND 47–39, 53–57 (NTS Dildo 1N/12W). P. 135.

Great Salmon River (Set.)
(*Population Returns 1836*)
See ST. CATHERINE'S (NTS St. Catherine's). P. 82.

SALMON COVE 47–25, 53–10 (NTS Holyrood 1N/6E)
Samon Cove ("Blathwayt" c. 1630–40), St. Salmon Cove (Robinson 1669), Salmon Cove (Thornton 1689 B), Salmon Cove sometimes called Salmon Pool (*English Pilot. The Fourth Book* 1716), Salmon Cove (Anspach 1819), Salmon Cove South (Adm. 296 1868).
— Salmon Cove South – Cp.

SALMON COVE 47–47, 53–09.
See AVONDALE.
Pp. 51, 64.
— SALMON COVE POINT 47–28,
53–09 (CHS 4573 1953).
SALMON COVE (Set.) 47–33, 53–16
(NTS Harbour Grace 1N/11W)
(CO Misc. 199.18 1798, *Population Returns* 1836).
At SOUTH RIVER (NTS Harbour Grace). P. 106.

SALMON COVE 47–47, 53–09 (NTS Heart's Content 1N/14E)
Crique de Saumon ("Dépôt 128.2.6" c. 1680), Salmon Cove (Visscher c. 1680) ... Salmon Cove North (Adm. 296 1868).
"a River in the said Cove runs up, in which are store of Salmon" (*English Pilot. The Fourth Book* 1689).
"a cove which affords an abundant supply of salmon, but only shelter for boats" (Imray, *Sailing Directions* 1862, p. 17).
— Salmon cove North – cp. SALMON COVE 47–25, 53–10. Pp. 51, 64, 80.
— SALMON COVE (Set.) 47–47, 53–10
Saumon-cove (Beaudoin 1697), Salmon Cove (*Population Returns* 1836).
— SALMON COVE BROOK (NTS Heart's Content 1N/14E and W)
— SALMON COVE HEAD 47–47, 53–09 (NTS Heart's Content 1N/14E)
(Lane 1774). P. 90.
— SALMON COVE POND 47–47, 53–11
(NDNR 1N/14 1946).
— SALMON COVE RIVER 47–47, 53–10 (NTS Heart's Content 1N/14E and W)
SALMON HOLE 47–26, 53–49 (NTS Argentia 1N/5W)
(Adm. 3266 1939).

The mouth of MATURIN BROOK. P. 141.

SALMON RIVER 47–24, 53–13 (NTS Holyrood 1N/6E and W)
(CHS 4573 1953).
Cp. AVONDALE.
Cp. FIRST (47–23, 53–15) and SECOND (47–22, 53–14) SALMON PONDS. P. 5.

SALMONIER ARM 47–08, 53–30 (NTS St. Catherine's 1N/3W, Placentia 1N/4W)
(*Road Map of the Peninsula of Avalon* 1930). P. 87.
— SALMONIER LINE
— Salmonier North (Set.)
See MOUNT CARMEL (NTS St. Catherine's). P. 108.
— SALMONIER POINT 47–07, 53–33 (NTS Placentia 1N/4E)
(Adm. 2915 1869). P. 82.
— SALMONIER RIVER 47–11, 53–24 (NTS St. Catherine's 1N/3W)
Great Salmonier (*CSP* 1723), Grand Salmonier (*CSP* 1724), Great Salmon River (Lane 1773), Salmonier River (Adm. 2915 1869).
In comparison with LITTLE SALMONIER RIVER 47–02, 53–45 (NTS Placentia 1N/4W) on the west side of ST. MARY'S BAY. Pp. 82, 113.
— Great Salmon River (Set.) (*Population Returns* 1836)
See ST. CATHERINE'S (NTS St. Catherine's). P. 82.

SALMONIER POINT 47–17, 53–59 (NTS Argentia 1N/5W)
(M. F. Howley, xxx, *NQ*, March 1911).

LITTLE SALMONIER POINT 47–02, 53–45 (NTS Placentia 1N/4W)
(Adm. 2915 1864).
— LITTLE SALMONIER RIVER 47–02, 53–45

(CSP 1723), L. Salmon River (Mount and Page 1780). In contrast with SAMONIER RIVER 47–10, 53–24 (NTS St. Catherine's 1N/3W) on the east side of ST. MARY'S BAY. Cp. L. Salmon I. (Cook and Lane 1770 [1775]B). Pp. 82, 120.

SALT PIT POND 47–46, 53–23 (NTS Heart's Content 1N/14W) (NDNR 1N/14 1946). One tradition maintains that the water is brackish; another that Salt Pit is a mistaken name for Saw Pit, from the practice of cutting wood in the vicinity of the pond. Cp. SAW PIT GULLY 47–44, 53–21.

SALVAGE [sæl'veIdʒ] POINT 48–04, 53–10 (NTS Old Perlican 2C/3E) Salvage (Hack ? 1677), Salvage Pt (Lane, *Directions* 1775, 1810 ... Purdy 1814), Salvage Hd (Jukes 1840), Salvage Pt. (Bonnycastle 1842). Pp. 21, 76.

SALVAGE ROCK 47–42, 53–11 (NTS Harbour Grace 1N/11E) Salvage (Thornton 1689C), Salvages (*English Pilot. The Fourth Book* 1689), Salvage (Lane 1774), Salvage Rock (Adm. 296 1899). "in Harbour Grace channel" (*English Pilot. The Fourth Book* 1716). Pp. 21, 76.

SAMS BROOK 46–42, 53–31 (NTS St. Shotts 1K/12E, St. Mary's 1K/13E) (Newfoundland 1941). Maps apply the name to two streams, one of which enters ST. SHOTTS RIVER approximately six miles upstream, the other about half a mile upstream.

SAMSON POINT 47–19, 53–56 (NTS Argentia 1N/5W) (CHS 4622 ? 1953). P. 165.

SANDS (Generic). P. 144.

SANDY COVE 47–17, 54–00 (NTS Argentia 1N/5W) (CHS 4622 ? 1953).

SANDY COVE 47–35, 53–13 (NTS Harbour Grace 1N/11E) As set: (*Population Returns* 1836); (CHS 4572 1954). P. 107.

SANDY POINT 47–26, 53–48 (NTS Argentia 1N/5W) (Adm. 3266 1939).

SANDY POND 47–28, 53–00 (NTS Holyrood 1N/6E) (NDNR 1N/6 1943).

Sanshot (Hack c. 1690?) See ST. SHOTTS (NTS St. Shotts). P. 35.

S[ant]a Maria (Viegas c. 1537) See ST. MARY'S BAY. P. 31.

SATURDAY LEDGE 47–06, 52–55 (unnamed in NTS Ferryland 1N/2W) Saturdays Ledge (Lane 1773). "6 feet under water, lies off the western shore of Admiral's cove [CAPE BROYLE HARBOUR]" (Imray, *Sailing Directory* 1873, p. 61). P. 89.

SAUNDERS PONDS 47–07, 53–09 (NTS St. Catherine's 1N/3E) (Newfoundland 1941). P. 165.

Savage Harbour (Guy 1612) See SPREADEAGLE BAY (NTS Dildo), CHAPEL ARM (NTS Dildo). Pp. 59, 111.

SAW PIT GULLY 47–44, 53–21 (NTS Harbour Grace 1N/11W) (NDNR 1N/11 1948). Cp. SALT PIT POND (NTS Heart's Content).

SAWYERS HILL 47–11, 53–52 (NTS Placentia 1N/4W) Sawyer's Hills (Jukes 1842). Pp. 114, 165.

Scilly Cove (Popple 1733) See WINTERTON COVE (NTS Heart's Content). Pp. 9, 72, 107.

Sciruy (Visscher c. 1680)

See SCURVY ISLAND (Unnamed in NTS Bay de Verde). P. 76.

SCOGGINS HEAD 47–02, 52–53 (NTS Ferryland 1N/2W)
Scogins Hd (Lane 1773), Scougings (Deed 1798 cited in M. F. Howley xxv, *NQ*, March 1909), Scogins Hd (Imray, *Sailing Directions 1862*), Scroggins (M. F. Howley, loc. cit.). Pp. *89, 165.*

Scollop Cove (Lane, *Directions 1775*, 1810)
See ? SOUTHEAST ARM (NTS Sunnyside). P. 95.

SCOTCH POND 47–38, 53–30 (NTS Harbour Grace 1N/11W, Dildo 1N/12E) (NDNR 1N/11 1948).

SCULPIN (Specific)
"A name for various small worthless fish having a spiny appearance" (*OED*). See Leim and Scott, pp. 344–64.

Sculpin Island Cove (Jukes 1842)
See MOLLYS ISLAND (NTS Harbour Grace). P. 113.

SCULPIN POINT 46–55, 52–55 (NTS Renews 1K/15W)

SCULPINS POINT 47–38, 52–40 (NTS St. John's 1N/10E)
? Red head (Hack ? 1677), Red Head (*English Pilot. The Fourth Book 1689*), Pointe rouge (Bellin 1744), Red Head (Imray, *Sailing Directions 1862*).
Cp. RED CLIFF HEAD (NTS St. John's) P. 76.

SCURVY ISLAND 48–09, 52–59 (Unnamed in NTS Bay de Verde)
Sciruy I. (Visscher c. 1680), I Sciruy (Thornton 1689 B), Scurvy Island (*English Pilot The Fourth Book 1689*), Scuruy I (Fitzhugh 1693), I des galeaux (Vion 1699), Scurvey I. (after Moll 1711), Scurvy Island (Imray *Sailing Directions 1862*), Sgeir island, islet (Imray *Sailing Directory 1873*), The Skerries (Local name). P. 76.

SEA (Generic) = Pond. P. 143.

SEAL COVE 46–51, 52–57 (NTS Renews 1K/15W)
Freshwater B. (Southwood 1675 ... Bonnycastle 1842), Seal Cove (Adm. 2915 1864). Pp. 73, 74.

BIG SEAL COVE 47–21, 53–55 (NTS Argentia 1N/5W) (Adm. 2829 1877).
— LITTLE SEAL COVE 47–23, 53–55 (CHS 4622 ? 1953).
— Set: Seal's Cove (*Population Returns 1836*).
P. 110.
— SEAL COVE HEAD 47–22, 53–55 (CHS 4622 ? 1953).
SEAL COVE HEAD divides BIG SEAL COVE from LITTLE SEAL COVE.

SEAL COVE 47–27, 52–41 (NTS Bay Bulls 1N/7E)
(NDNR Bay Bulls 1943).

SEAL COVE (Set.) 47–28, 53–05 (NTS Holyrood 1N/6E)
Seals Cove (Census 1857).
Pp. 109, 117.
— SEAL COVE POND (Adm. 296 1868).
— SEAL COVE RIVER 47–27, 53–05 (CHS 4573 1953).
Flows into SEAL COVE POND.
— SEAL COVE ROCKY POND 47–25, 53–02
(NDNR 1N/6 1943).

SEAL (NEW CHELSEA) COVE 47–52, 53–25 (NTS Heart's Content 1N/14W)
Seal Cove (Newfoundland 1941), New Chelsea Cove (Seal Cove) (USHO 0584 1943), New Chelsea Cove (Adm. 296 1952), Seal (New Chelsea) Cove (USHO 73 1942, *NP* 1952).
The alternative name, New Chelsea, appears to be the result of confusion with NEW CHELSEA 48–02, 53–12 (NTS Old Perlican 2C/3E),

formerly Seal Cove.
— SEAL COVE BROOK
(NDNR 1N/14 1946).
— SEAL COVE HEAD 47–52, 53–26
(USHO 73 1942).
— SEAL COVE POND 47–50, 53–24
(NDNR 1N/14 1946).
SEAL HEAD 47–31, 53–11 (NTS
Harbour Grace 1N/11E)
(*NLP* 1907).
SEAL ISLAND 47–57, 53–40 (NTS
Sunnyside 1N/13E)
Seal islet (Imray, *Sailing Directory*
1873).
SEA ISLET 47–44, 53–58 (NTS Dildo
1N/12W)
SEAL LOOKOUT 47–33, 53–12 (NTS
Harbour Grace 1N/11E)
(*NLP* 1953).
SEAL POINT 47–09, 54–03 (NTS Ship
Cove 1M/1E)
(Adm. 2915 1864).
SEAL POND 47–47, 53–15 (NTS Heart's
Content 1N/14W)
(NDNR 1N/14 1946).
Seal's Cove (Set.) (*Population
Returns* 1836). P. 110. See BIG SEAL
COVE, LITTLE SEAL COVE (NTS Argentia)
under SEAL.
SECOND JUNCTION POND 47–23, 53–18
(NTS Holyrood 1N/6W)
(NDNR 1N/6 1943).
After BRIGUS JUNCTION (Sta.)
Cp. THIRD JUNCTION POND. A First
Junction Pond is not recorded in NTS.
SECOND POND 47–25, 53–09 (NTS
Holyrood 1N/6E)
(CHS 4573 1953).
The second of three ponds south
of CHAPEL COVE (Set.).
Cp. FIRST POND 47–26, 53–09, THIRD
POND 47–25, 53–09. P. 5.
SECOND POND 47–27, 52–44 (NTS Bay
Bulls 1N/7E)
(Adm. 296 1868).

Of the river which enters PETTY
HARBOUR.
SECOND POND 47–32, 53–24 (NTS
Harbour Grace 1N/11W)
(NDNR 1N/11 1948).
On a tributary, unnamed in NTS,
of SHEARSTOWN BROOK.
Cp. FIRST POND 47–32, 53–23.
SECOND SALMON POND 47–22, 53–14
(NTS Holyrood 1N/6E)
(NDNR 1N/6 1943).
From the mouth of SALMON RIVER
47–24, 53–13.
Cp. FIRST SALMON POND 47–23, 53–15.
See AVONDALE.
SEPOY HILL 47–04 53–44 (NTS
Placentia 1N/4E)
Mount Sea-Pie (Jukes 1842),
Sepoy hill (Adm. 2915 1864, Imray,
Sailing Directory 1873). P. 114.
SERRATED HILL 47–40, 53–52 (NTS
Dildo 1N/12W)
(Adm. 296 1863).
Pp. 5, 114.
SEVEN ISLANDS 47–16, 53–55 (NTS
Argentia 1N/5W)
(Cook 1762).
A group of small islands in NORTH
EAST ARM (NTS Argentia).
SEYMOURS GULLIES 47–33, 53–28
(NTS Harbour Grace 1N/11W)
(NDNR 1N/11 1948). P. 165.
Sgeir I. (Imray, *Sailing Directory*
1873)
See SCURVY ISLAND (Unnamed in
NTS Bay de Verde). P. 76.
SHAG (Specific) 1. Rough, matted
hair, wool, etc. e. A mass of shrubs,
trees, foliage, etc. (*OED*). Hence a
tangle of seaweed, kelp, etc.
2. The Newfoundland name for
the Atlantic Common Cormorant
and Northern Double-Crested Cor-
morant, the latter being a fairly

common summer resident on inland ponds and the coast. (Peters and Burleigh, p. 69). P. 88.

SHAG ISLANDS 47–46, 53–51 (NTS Sunnyside 1N/13W)
(NP 1952).

SHAG PONDS 47–17, 54–00 (NTS Argentia 1N/5W)
(CHS 4622 ? 1953).

SHAG ROCK 46–43, 53–39 (NTS St. Shotts 1K/12E)
Shag Rocks (Lane 1773). P. 88.

SHAG ROCK 47–23, 53–58 (NTS Argentia 1N/5W)
(Adm. 3266 1939).

SHAG ROCK POINT 47–04, 52–52 (NTS Ferryland 1N/2W)
(USHO 0618 1941).

SHAG ROCKS 47–25, 53–54 (NTS Argentia 1N/5W)
(NLP 1951).

SHAG ROOST 47–34, 53–55 (NTS Dildo 1N/12W). Pp. 88, 144.

Shallop Cove (Imray, *Sailing Directions* 1862)
See ? SOUTHEAST ARM (NTS Sunnyside). Pp. 86, 95.

SHALLOWAY (Specific). P. 86.

SHALLOWAY COVE 47–18, 53–54 (NTS Argentia 1N/5W)
(CHS 4622 ? 1953).
— SHALLOWAY PONDS 47–18, 53–53 (CHS 4622 ? 1953).

SHALLOWAY POINT 47–17, 54–00 (NTS Merasheen 1M/8E, Argentia 1N/5W)
(Lane 1772).

SHANAHANS GULLY 47–38, 53–21 (NTS Harbour Grace 1N/11W)
(CHS 4572 1954). P. 135.

SHARKS COVE 47–34, 53–13 (NTS Harbour Grace 1N/11E)
(CHS 4572 1954).
— SHARKS COVE (Set.) (Census 1935).

See W. Templeman, *Distribution of sharks in the Canadian Atlantic (with special reference to Newfoundland waters)*, Fisheries Research Board of Canada, Bulletin no. 140, 1963.

SHEARSTOWN (Set.) 47–35, 53–19 (NTS Harbour Grace 1N/11W)
Originally Spaniards Bay Pond; Shearstown (Census 1901). After the Rev W. C. Shears (1839– ?), b. Trinity, T. B., Newfoundland. Anglican priest at BAY ROBERTS 1868–1903, who also served St. Mark's church at Spaniard's Bay Pond. He left Newfoundland in 1903 to reside in the United States. (Mosdell, p. 117).
— SHEARSTOWN BROOK 47–36, 53–18 (CHS 4572 1954).

SHEAS GULLY 47–44, 53–24 (NTS Harbour Grace 1N/11W)
(NDNR 1N/11 1948). P. 135.

Sheeps Cove (*English Pilot. The Fourth Book* 1716)
See SHIP COVE (NTS Harbour Grace). P. 75.

SHEEP'S HEAD 46–58, 52–57 (NTS Renews 1K/15W)
Sheep Head (Adm. 376 1927).
— Sheep's Head Cove (Lane 1773, Imray, *Sailing Directions* 1862). Pp. 89, 125.

Sherwick Pt (Cook 1763)
See SKERWINK POINT (NTS Old Perlican). P. 75.

SHINGLE HEAD 46–38, 53–07 (NTS Trepassey 1K/11E)
(Imray, *Sailing Directory* 1873). "with slate cliffs" (Imray, *Sailing Directory* 1873, p. 71).

SHIP COVE 47–06, 54–05 (NTS Ship Cove 1M/1E)
? Borrell (Whitbourne 1588–1622), Ship Cove (Adm. 2915 1864). Pp. 42, 110, 129.

— SHIP COVE (Set.)
(*Population Returns* 1836).

SHIP COVE 47–25, 53–08 (NTS Holyrood 1N/6E) (CHS 4573 1953). "a slight indentation, at the head of which is a remarkable gravel bank" (*NLP*, II, p. 85), presumably suitable for careening ships.

SHIP COVE (Set.) 47–36, 53–12 (NTS Harbour Grace 1N/11E)
As feature: Sheeps Cove (*English Pilot. The Fourth Book* 1689); as set: Rock Cove (co Misc. 199.18 1755); as feature: Ship Cove (Lane, *Directions* 1775, 1810), Sheep's or Ship Cove (Imray, *Sailing Directions* 1862), Ship Cove (Imray, *Sailing Directory* 1873.) P. 75.

SHIP HARBOUR 47–21, 53–55 (NTS Argentia 1N/5W)
(Popple 1733). P. 82.
— SHIP HARBOUR (Set.) 47–22, 53–53
(*Population Returns* 1836).
— SHIP HARBOUR BROOK 47–21, 53–52
(DND Placentia 1942).
— SHIP HARBOUR POINT 47–21, 53–56
(Wix 1836).
P. 104.

SHIP HEAD 47–41, 53–14 (NTS Harbour Grace 1N/11E)
Ships Head (Cook 1762 or Gilbert 1768), Ship Head (Imray, *Sailing Directory* 1873).
The reputed site of the Pirates forte (Guy 1612) or Pirate's Lair, where the pirate Easton's prize, the *San Sebastian*, was beached. (Barrelman, 30 November 1949).
See EASTERN ROCK. Pp. 58, 84.

SHIPWRECK POINT 47–04, 52–53 (NTS Ferryland 1N/2W)
(Adm. 2915 1864). P. 5.

SHOAL (Specific) "A place where the water is of little depth, a shallow, a sand-bank or bar" (*OED*).

SHOAL BAY 46–59, 53–38 (NTS St. Mary's 1K/13E)
(Lane 1773). P. 87.
— SHOAL BAY POINT 46–59, 53–39
(Lane 1773). P. 87.
— SHOAL BAY POND 47–00, 53–37
(NTS St. Mary's 1K/13E, Placentia 1N/4E)
(USHO 2275 1917).

SHOAL BAY 47–23, 52–43 (NTS Bay Bulls 1N/7E)
(Jukes 1842). Pp. 102, 112.

Shoal Bay (Set.)
See CAVENDISH (Set.) (NTS Harbour Grace).

SHOAL BAY 47–52, 53–45 (NTS Sunnyside 1N/13 E and W)
(Imray, *Sailing Directory* 1873). P. 118.
— SHOAL HARBOUR 47–51, 53–45
(Jukes 1840); as set: (Census 1857). P. 112.

SHOAL POINT 46–37, 53–35 (NTS St. Shotts 1K/12E)
Black head (Gaudy 1715 ... Imray, *Sailing Directions* 1862), Shoal point (Imray, *Sailing Directory* 1873). P. 81.

SHOAL POINT (Set.) 46–46, 53–21 (NTS Biscay Bay River 1K/14W)
(Smallwood 1940).

SHOAL POINT 47–41, 53–12 (NTS Harbour Grace 1N/11E)
(CHS 4590 1943).
The end of the bar across HARBOUR GRACE.

SHOE COVE 46–47, 52–59 (NTS Renews 1K/15W)
(Adm. 2915 1864).

SHOE COVE 47–46, 52–44 (NTS Pouch Cove 1N/15W)
(*English Pilot. The Fourth Book* 1689).

See BISCAYNE BAY 47–48, 52–47.
P. 75.
— SHOE COVE BROOK 47–46, 52–44
(NTS St. John's 1N/10 E and W,
Pouch Cove 1N/15W)
— SHOE COVE ISLAND (NTS Pouch
Cove 1N/15W)
Referred to, but not named, in
Imray, *Sailing Directory* 1873,
p. 54.
— SHOE COVE POND 47–45, 52–44
(NTS St. John's 1N/10E)

SHOP (Generic). P. 147.

SHORE (Generic). P. 144.

SHORE'S COVE (Set.) 47–06, 52–56
(NTS Ferryland 1N/2W)
Electors 1911), Shore Cove (Newfoundland 1941).
Cp. ST. SHORES COVE (NTS
St. Shotts). Pp. 35–8, 165.

SHUFFLE BOARD (Hill) 47–50, 53–26
(NTS Heart's Content 1N/14W)
(Lane 1790). Pp. 98, 138–9, 139.

SIBLEY'S COVE (Set.) 48–02, 53–06
(NTS Old Perlican 2C/3E)
"Sibley's Cove ... has been settled about forty years [i.e. c. 1855] by people from Old Perlican" (Johnson, p. 288).
The settlement was renamed Prowsetown after the judge and historian, D. W. Prowse (d. 1914) (Proclamation, 22 September 1914), later, ? unofficially, Davidson after Sir W. E. Davidson, governor of Newfoundland 1913–8, only to revert to SIBLEY'S COVE.
Cp. MOUNT ARLINGTON HEIGHTS (NTS Argentia). P. 165.

SIDE (Generic). P. 144.

SIDING (Generic). P. 148.

SIGNAL HILL 47–15, 54–00 (NTS
Argentia 1N/5W)
(Cook 1762). P. 82.

SIGNAL HILL 47–34, 52–41 (NTS
St. John's 1N/10E)
(Cook 1762 or Gilbert 1768). Pp. 76, 83, 115.
— SIGNAL HILL NATIONAL HISTORIC
PARK. P. 146.

Sille Cove at Sugar loaf (Southwood 1675)
See WINTERTON COVE (NTS Heart's Content). Pp. 9, 72.

SIMS POINT 46–45, 53–22 (NTS Trepassey 1K/11W)
(USHO 0618 1941). P. 165.

THE SISTERS (Ponds) 47–44, 53–25
(NTS Harbour Grace 1N/11W)
(NDNR 1N/11 1948). Pp. 139, 140.

THE SKERRIES
See SCURVY ISLAND (Unnamed in NTS Bay de Verde). P. 76; but Skerries is also the name of a seaport and rocks, Dublin, Eire.

SKERRYS BIGHT 47–36, 52–40 (NTS
St. John's 1N/10E)
Skerries (Skerry's) bight (*NLP* 1951). Pp. 76, 117, 141, 165.

SKERWINK POINT 48–06, 53–01 (NTS
Old Perlican 2C/3E)
Sherwink Point (*English Pilot. The Fourth Book* 1689), Skerwick Pt (Mount and Page 1755), Sherwick Pt (Cook 1763, Cook and Lane 1770 [1775]A), Sherwick Point (Imray, *Sailing Directions* 1862). P. 75.

SKIBBEREEN (Set.) 47–23, 53–11 (NTS
Holyrood 1N/6E)
(Census 1891). Pp. 126, 139.

SKIN CABIN POND 47–10, 53–51 (NTS
Placentia 1N/4W)
(Adm. 2915 1864).
After a cabin built by trappers for use when stretching pelts. (Communication from Miss J. Linegar).

Sleepers Point (Seller 1671)
See BEAR COVE HEAD (NTS Renews).
P. 71.

SLOANS GULLY 47–44, 53–23 (NTS
Harbour Grace 1N/11W)
(NDNR 1N/11 1948). Pp. 135, 165.

SMALL GULL POND (NTS Heart's Content)
See BIG GULL POND under GULL.

SMALL POINT 47–36, 52–39 (NTS St. John's 1N/10E)
(Southwood 1675 ... *English Pilot. The Fourth Book* 1689), Small Head (Popple 1733), Small Pt (Lane 1774). Small – In comparison with SUGARLOAF HEAD 47–37, 52–39. P. 73.

SMALL POINT 47–45, 52–43 (NTS St. John's 1N/10E)

SMALL POND 47–26, 53–08 (NTS Holyrood 1N/6E)

SMOOTH COVE 47–55, 53–04 (NTS Heart's Content 1N/14E)
As set: (Census 1891); (NDNR 1N/14 1946).
Smutty nose pt (Southwood 1675) See JEANS HEAD (NTS Heart's Content). P. 72.

SNAGGE HILL 47–31, 52–39 (NTS St. John's 1N/10E)
(NLP 1951). P. 165.

SNAGGE POINT 47–40, 52–42 (NTS St. John's 1N/10E)
(NP 1952). P. 165.

SNOWS POND 47–28, 53–23 (NTS Holyrood 1N/6W, Harbour Grace 1N/11W)
(Murray and Howley 1872). P. 165.

SNOWSHOE POND 47–15, 53–22 (NTS Holyrood 1N/6W)
(NDNR 1N/6 1943).

Soils Cove (Set.) (*Population Returns* 1836). P. 107.

SOLDIERS BROOK 47–39, 52–43 (NTS St. John's 1N/10E)
— SOLDIERS BROOK POND 47–38, 52–43

SOLDIERS GULCH 47–35, 52–40 (NTS St. John's 1N/10E)
? A bathing place for soldiers stationed at the North Fort (Thornton 1689B) on SIGNAL HILL. P. 141.

SOLDIERS POND 47–24, 53–00 (NTS Holyrood 1N/6E, Bay Bulls 1N/7W)
(NDNR 1N/6 1943, NDNR Bay Bulls 1943).

SOLDIERS POND 47–33, 52–41 (NTS St. John's 1N/10E)

SOOLEYS GULLIES 47–50, 53–16 (NTS Heart's Content 1N/14W)
(NDNR 1N/14 1946). P. 165.

SOPHIA HEAD 47–54, 53–44 (NTS Sunnyside 1N/13E)
(Imray, *Sailing Directory* 1873). A *Sophia* was engaged in the seal fishery in 1861 (D. W. Prowse, p. 707).

SOUND (Generic). P. 141.

SOUTH ARM 47–23, 53–08 (NTS Holyrood 1N/6E)
As set: South Arm of Holyrood (Census 1857); Holyrood South Gut (Murray and Howley 1868), South Arm (CHS 4573 1953). Cp. NORTH ARM, MIDDLE ARM. Pp. 117–8, 141.

South Battery (St. John's Harbour) See Fort Frederick. P. 94.

South Bay (Bell Island) (Mount and Page 1780)
See FRESHWATER (PARSONVILLE P.O.) (NTS Harbour Grace). P. 97.

SOUTH BROOK 47–31, 52–45 (NTS Bay Bulls 1N/7W, St. John's 1N/10E and W)
Tributary of WATERFORD RIVER.

SOUTH DILDO
See DILDO (NTS Dildo).

South Falkland (Mason 1626). P. 61.

So[uth] Forte (St. John's Harbour) (Thornton 1689B)
See Fort Frederick. Pp. 77, 94–5.

South Gut (Set.) (*Population Returns* 1836)
See SOUTH RIVER (Set.) 47–32, 53–16 (NTS Harbour Grace). P. 106.

282 / *Place Names of the Avalon Peninsula*

SOUTH HEAD 47–00, 52–54 (NTS Ferryland 1N/2W)
(USHO 0618 1941).
Of AQUAFORTE HARBOUR.

SOUTH HEAD 47–17, 52–46 (NTS Bay Bulls 1N/7W)
(Lane 1773).
Of BAY BULLS.

SOUTH HEAD 47–34, 52–41 (NTS St. John's 1N/10E)
(Cook 1762 or Gilbert 1768).
Of ST. JOHN'S HARBOUR.
Cp. NORTH HEAD. Pp. 83, 94.
South Head Battery (Plan 1765)
See FORT AMHERST. P. 94.

SOUTH HEAD 47–58, 53–39 (NTS Sunnyside 1N/13E)
(Imray, *Sailing Directory* 1873).
Of ROUND HARBOUR.

SOUTH POINT 46–57, 55–43 (NTS St. Mary's 1K/13E)
(Adm. 2915 1864).
Of GREAT COLINET ISLAND.

SOUTH POINT 47–32, 53–11 (NTS Harbour Grace 1N/11E)
? Brigus South Head (Murray and Howley 1868), South Point (Imray, *Sailing Directory* 1873).
Of BRIGUS BAY

South Pt. Torbay (Lane 1774)
See TORBAY POINT (NTS St. John's).
P. 90.

SOUTH POND 47–31, 53–16 (NTS Harbour Grace 1N/11W)
(CHS 4572 1952).
South – ? of THE BROADS.

SOUTH POND 47–39, 52–44 (NTS St. John's 1N/10E)
Cp. NORTH POND 47–39, 52–45.

SOUTH RIVER 47–22, 53–07 (NTS Holyrood 1N/6E)
(CHS 4573 1953).
Flows into SOUTH ARM, HOLYROOD BAY.

SOUTH RIVER 47–32, 53–17 (NTS Harbour Grace 1N/11W)
Southern Gut (Jukes 1842), South Gut (Murray and Howley 1868), Southern Gut (J. P. Howley 1876, 1907), South River (M. F. Howley, XIX, *NQ*, October 1907).

"[Brigus] is a wild rocky little place; but about three miles inland from it is a fertile valley, through which runs a brook forming occasional ponds, and emptying itself into the sea on the southern side of Port de Grave. It is accordingly called the Southern Gut" (J. B. Jukes, *Excursions* I, p. 44).
Cp. NORTH RIVER 47–33, 53–18.
Pp. 5, 112, 126, 141.

— SOUTH RIVER (Set.) 47–32, 53–16
South Gut (*Population Returns* 1836), but according to D. W. Prowse, p. 98, Guy's colonists settled there in 1610–1: "On Southern River they erected mills, houses, and farm buildings ... Early in the [nineteenth] century the remains of these buildings were found, together with mill stones, coins, &c."
P. 106.

SOUTH RIVER 47–40, 53–15 (NTS Harbour Grace 1N/11W)
(NDNR 1N/11 1948).

S[ou]t[h] Salmon Cove (Robinson 1669)
See AVONDALE (NTS Holyrood).
P. 64.

SOUTH SHORE (Conception Bay)
As set: (*Population Returns* 1836).
"when we hear people speaking of the 'South Shore' one immediately understands that the South Shore of Conception Bay is meant, and especially the portion extending from Topsail to Holy Rood" (M. F. Howley, xx, *NQ*, March 1908).
Cp. SOUTHERN SHORE, ST. SHORES, NORTH SHORE. Pp. 106, 116, 144.
South Side (Renews Harbour)
(Yonge 1663–70). P. 68.

SOUTH SIDE (Set.)
See HARBOUR GRACE (NTS Harbour Grace). P. 144.

SOUTH SIDE HILLS 47–32, 52–42 (NTS St. John's 1N/10E)
(Jukes 1842). P. 111.

South Side Holyrood (Set.) (Census 1857). Pp. 117–8.

SOUTH WEST
See SOUTHWEST.

SOUTHEAST

SOUTHEAST ARM 47–13, 53–57 (NTS Placentia 1N/4W)
(Cook 1762).
A branch of PLACENTIA HARBOUR.
Pp. 83, 104, 141.
— South east mountains (Jukes 1842). P. 111.
— SOUTHEAST RIVER 47–13, 53–55 (NTS Placentia 1N/4E and W)
Cp. DUNVILLE (Set.).

SOUTHEAST ARM 47–54, 53–43 (NTS Sunnyside 1N/13E)
? Scollop Cove (Lane, *Directions* 1775, 1810), ? Shallop Cove (Imray, *Sailing Directions* 1862), Southeast Arm (*NP* 1952).
Of DEER HARBOUR.
Cp. NORTHEAST ARM 47–55, 53–44.
Pp. 95, 141.

SOUTHEAST PLACENTIA
See PLACENTIA.

SOUTHER POINT 47–53, 53–24 (NTS Heart's Content 1N/14W)
(USHO No. 73 1942).
At the entrance of HEART'S CONTENT inlet.
Souther adj. obs. The more southerly of two things or places, situated or lying to the south. (*OED*).
Cp. NORTHER POINT.

SOUTHERN COVE POND 47–51, 53–22 (NTS Heart's Content 1N/14W)
(NDNR 1N/14 1946).
South of HEART'S CONTENT.

SOUTHERN HARBOUR (Set.) 47–43, 53–58 (NTS Dildo 1N/12W)
(*Population Returns* 1836).
In LITTLE SOUTHERN HARBOUR.
— SOUTHERN HARBOUR STATION 47–44, 53–54
— GREAT SOUTHERN HARBOUR 47–45, 53–59 (NTS Sunnyside 1N/13W)
South Harbr (Cook and Lane 1770 [1775]A), Great South Harbour (Cook and Lane 1770 [1775]B, Lane 1772, Mount and Page 1780), Sth Harbr (Anspach 1819), Great South Harbour (Imray, *Sailing Directions* 1862).
P. 84.
— LITTLE SOUTHERN HARBOUR 47–43, 53–58 (NTS Dildo 1N/12W)
South Harbr (Cook and Lane 1770 [1775]A), Little South Harbour (Cook and Lane 1770 [1775]B, Lane 1772, Mount and Page 1780), South Hr. (Purdy 1814), Little South Harbour (Imray, *Sailing Directions* 1862), Little Southern Harbour (Murray and Howley 1868).
P. 84.

SOUTHERN PEAK POND 47–19, 53–11 (NTS Holyrood 1N/6E)
(NDNR 1N/6 1943).
? Southern for Southeastern.
Peak – after the unnamed elevation between PEAK POND and SOUTHERN PEAK POND. P. 145.

SOUTHERN ROCK 47–42, 53–09 (NTS Harbour Grace 1N/11E)
(Adm. 297 1933).
Of HARBOUR GRACE ISLANDS.

SOUTHERN ROCKS 47–37, 53–10 (NTS Harbour Grace 1N/11E)
Southern Rock (*NLP* 1953), Southern Rocks (CHS 4572 1954).
At the entrance to BAY ROBERTS.

SOUTHERN SHORE
"the line of shore ... which lies to the southward of St. John's as far as

Cape Race" (M. F. Howley, xx, *NQ*, March 1908). Pp. 18, 43, 46, 51, 65, 66, 71, 74, 107, 119, 122, 125, 144.

SOUTHWEST

SOUTHWEST ARM 48-00, 53-45 (NTS Sunnyside 1N/13W, Random Island 2C/4E and W)
Of Random Sound.
Cp. LONG BEACH (NTS Sunnyside). P. 141.

S[outh] W[est] Bay (Bay Roberts) (Mount and Page 1780). P. 97.

SOUTH WEST BROOK 47-31, 53-30 (NTS Harbour Grace 1N/11W)
(NDNR 1N/11 1948).
? Mistake name for Northwest, since the brook flows in a north-westerly direction into ISLAND POND (NTS Harbour Grace).

S[outh] W[est] Coue (Visscher c. 1680)
See ADAMS COVE (NTS Heart's Content). Pp. 76, 92.

SOUTHWEST POND 47-21, 53-14 (NTS Holyrood 1N/6E) (NDNR 1N/6 1943).
? Southwest of HARBOUR MAIN POND 47-22, 53-12.

SPANIARD'S BAY 47-38, 53-13 (NTS Harbour Grace 1N/11E and W)
(Robinson 1669). Pp. 39, 74, 92.
— SPANIARD'S BAY (Set.) 47-37, 53-17
Spaniard's Bay Beech (Wix 1836), Spaniards' Bay (*Population Returns* 1836).
Since the settlement is not named in early co records or, for example, in Beaudoin 1697, it must either have been founded later or have been of less importance than its neighbours, HARBOUR GRACE and BAY ROBERTS.
P. 103.
— Spaniard's Bay Lookout (Jukes 1842). P. 111.
— Spaniard's Bay Pond (Set.)
See SHEARSTOWN.

SPARE POINT 47-41, 53-11 (NTS Harbour Grace 1N/11E)
(Imray, *Sailing Directory* 1873).
Spare – ? of land, ground, etc.: Uncultivated, unoccupied, vacant. Obs. (*OED*), rather than mistake name for Spear, which would appear to be inappropriate.

SPARKS GULLY 47-28, 53-20 (NTS Holyrood 1N/6W)
(NDNR 1N/6 1943). P. 165.

SPARROW POINT 47-21, 53-55 (NTS Argentia 1N/5W)
(*NLP* 1951). P. 166.

SPEAR BAY
— SPEAR BAY BROOK
See CAPE SPEAR (NTS St. John's).

SPEAR ISLAND 47-12, 52-50 (NTS Ferryland 1N/2W)
les isles d'Espoir (Alfonse 1544) comprised SPEAR, FOX, PEBBLE and GREAT ISLANDS (Biggar, *Voyages of Jacques Cartier*, p. 279), Ille despoir ("Vallard" 1547), Illes despoier (Le Testu 1555A, B), Ilhas despera (Mercator 1569), Y des pera (Lopes c. 1583), I de Spera (Plancius 1592), I despera (Jode 1593), I despoir (Hondius 1608), I D'Espoir (Jansz 1610), I de Espera ("Velasco" 1610), Illes des poirs (Champlain 1612), I of Spere ("Blathwayt" c. 1630-40), jlla di jspirit (Oliva 1650A), I de L'Espere (Blaeu 1659), I de Spere (Visscher c. 1660), Isle Despair (Robinson 1669), Isle of Spears (Ogilby 1671), I Spear (Hack ? 1677), I de Spear (Thornton 1689B), Isles de Spear (*English Pilot. The Fourth Book* 1689), Spear I. (Gaudy 1715), Ship Island (Local name in M. F. Howley, xxv, *NQ*, March 1909).

Ship Island – "I asked the fishermen why it is so called, and they said that under the lee of it is the best anchorage ground for large ships,

but no ships come here now, nor for many years past" (M. F. Howley, ibid.).He cites Taverner's *Pilot* (1755): "Isle de Spear, a mile within the greatest of the said islands uses a ship every year to fish there, on which island is a stage on the inside, ... and good riding in the summer season, the island being pretty large."
Cp. CAPE SPEAR (NTS St. John's).
P. 35.

SPECTACLE HEAD 47–34, 53–14 (NTS Harbour Grace 1N/11E)
(Lane, *Directions* 1775, 1810).
"a remarkable bluff 330 feet high" (Imray, *Sailing Directory* 1873).
P. 95.

SPICES BROOK 47–48, 53–16 (NTS Heart's Content 1N/14W)
(NDNR 1N/14 1946). P. 166.

SPIDER POND 47–40, 53–20 (NTS Harbour Grace 1N/11W)
(NDNR 1N/11 1948).

SPLIT POINT 48–06, 52–51 (NTS Bay de Verde 2C/2W)
(Seller 1671). P. 71.

SPLIT ROCK POND 47–19, 53–13 (NTS Holyrood 1N/6E) (NDNR 1N/6 1943).

SPOON COVE 47–39, 53–12 (NTS Harbour Grace 1N/11E)
(CHS 4572 1954).
Descriptive (Local interpretation).
— SPOON COVE (Set.)
(CO Misc. 119.18 1770).
Nick Dobbin recorded as property owner at SPOON COVE (CO Misc. 119.18 1770).

THE SPOUT 47–22, 52–44 (NTS Bay Bulls 1N/7E)
Spout Cove (Yonge 1664), Spout (Seller c. 1671).
Descriptions after Yonge are: "a hollow place which the Sea runs into, and having a vent on the top of the Land near the Water side, spouts up the Water in that manner that you may see it a great way off, especially if there be any Sea which causes the greater Violence" (*English Pilot. The Fourth Book* 1689).

"Immediately opposite to the ship, appeared a remarkable natural curiosity, called the *Spout*, which is visible at a great distance from the shore. We had no opportunity of examining this phenomenon minutely; but could easily perceive that the *spout* in question was occasioned by a column of water forcing itself through a fissure in the rock; and being impelled to an amazing height, it assumed the appearance of volcanic smoke. In this state it admirably answers the purpose of a landmark, for those who are otherwise unacquainted with the coast" (Chappell 1818, p. 23).

"About midway between the Bay of Bulls and Little Bay is a cavern, having an opening at the summit, through which the water spouts whenever the sea runs high, thus presenting a remarkable object, visible a considerable distance off; it is hence called the Spout" (Imray, *Sailing Directions* 1862, p. 13).

"... the Spout, a remarkable natural phenomenon caused by the successive rush of the sea wave into an underwater cavern, from which a fissure in the rock allows its escape in jets of foam. It is most remarkable at high water, and when there is much ocean swell. It makes a roaring noise and may be seen distinctly 3 miles from the land" (Imray, *Sailing Directory* 1873, p. 59). Pp. 67, 71.

SPOUT BROOK 47–47, 53–12 (NTS Heart's Content 1N/14E)

SPOUT COVE 47–06, 52–56 (NTS Ferryland 1N/2W)
(Imray, *Sailing Directory* 1873).

"water can be obtained here from the waterfall in Spout cove" (*ibid.*).

SPOUT COVE (Set.) 47–49, 53–08 (NTS Heart's Content 1N/14E) (Census 1857). P. 119.
— SPOUT COVE BROOK (NDNR 1N/14 1946).

SPREAD EAGLE (Set.) 47–32, 53–37 (NTS Dildo 1N/12E) (Census 1869).
— SPREAD EAGLE BAY 47–33, 53–36 ? Savage Harbour (Guy 1612, D. W. Prowse, p. 133), Spread Eagle (Jukes 1840). See CHAPEL ARM.
— SPREAD EAGLE PEAK 47–27, 53–38 (NTS Argentia 1N/5E) (Jukes 1842).
Pp. 59, 111, 139.

SPRIGGS POINT 47–33, 52–40 (NTS St. John's 1N/10E)
Low Point (Mount and Page 1780), Small Point (Lane 1774, Imray, *Sailing Directions* 1862), Spriggs Point (*NP* 1952). Pp. 98, 166.

SPRINGFIELD (Set.) 47–31, 53–17 (NTS Harbour Grace 1N/11W) (Census 1869).
? After a spring in a field, but also an Essex place name. (Stewart, *Names on the Land*, p. 49). P. 145.

SPRUCE POND 47–39, 53–24 (NTS Harbour Grace 1N/11W) (NDNR 1N/11 1948).

SPRUCE POND 47–42, 53–22 (NTS Harbour Grace 1N/11W) (NDNR 1N/11 1948).

SPURWINK ISLAND 47–00, 52–54 (NTS Ferryland 1N/2W)
? ylet (Guérard 1631), Spurwink Island (Imray, *Sailing Directory* 1873), Spurawinkle (M. F. Howley, xxv, *NQ*, March 1909).
Spur-wing, spurwing. A spur-winged water-hen, goose, etc. (*OED*).

SQUARE (Generic) = Street. P. 148.

SQUIB POINT 47–48, 53–46 (NTS Sunnyside 1N/13W) (*NP* 1952).
Squib – ? insignificant (after *OED* 4) in comparison with NIAGARA POINT; or for squid by assimilation. P. 166.

SQUID POND 47–46, 53–17 (NTS Heart's Content 1N/14W) (NDNR 1N/14 1946).

STAG POND 47–50, 53–20 (NTS Heart's Content 1N/14W) (NDNR 1N/14 1946).

STANTON POINT 47–47, 53–50 (NTS Sunnyside 1N/13W) (Imray *Sailing Directions* 1862). P. 166.

STATION (Generic). P. 148.

STEADY (Generic). P. 143.

STEADYWATER BROOK 47–31, 52–59 (NTS Bay Bulls 1N/7W, St. John's 1N/10W). P. 143.

STEEL POINT 46–58, 52–56 (NTS Renews 1K/15W) (Adm. 376 1927). P. 166.

STEPHENS POND 47–21, 52–51 (NTS Bay Bulls 1N/7W) (NDNR Bay Bulls 1943). Pp. 135, 166.

STICK POND 47–38, 52–42 (NTS St. John's 1N/10E). P. 166.
— STICK POND BROOK 47–38, 52–41

STICKLES POND 47–41, 52–49 (NTS St. John's 1N/10W)
Stickle – ? West Country name for a shallow in a river (*OED*). The area of the pond is marshy. P. 166.

STILES COVE 47–45, 52–43 (NTS St. John's 1N/10E). P. 166.

STOCK COVE 47–46, 53–52 (NTS Sunnyside 1N/13W)
As set: Stock Cove, Stoke Cove

(Wix 1836).
Stock Cove Deer-lookout
 (Wix 1836). Pp. 105, 166.

STONE ISLANDS 47–03, 52–52 (NTS Ferryland 1N/2W)
Stone I. (Southwood 1675 Thornton 1689B); Stone Isl. (Lane 1773).
P. 74.

STONY RIDGE 47–20, 52–47 (NTS Bay Bulls 1N/7W)
(USHO 2054 1947). P. 145.

Stop Rock (St. John's Harbour) (Cook 1762 or Gilbert 1768)
See ? CAHILL POINT (NTS St. John's).
P. 83.

STRAYAWAY POND 47–28, 53–31 (NTS Holyrood 1N/6W, Argentia 1N/5E)
(DND 1942).

STREET (Generic). P. 148.

STRONG TICKLE 47–54, 53–43 (NTS Sunnyside 1N/13E)
Strong – ? of the current through the tickle. P. 141.

STUMP (Generic). Pp. 118, 145.

SUGARLOAF (Specific). P. 67.

SUGARLOAF (Headland) 47–57, 53–21 (NTS Heart's Content 1N/14W)
(Southwood 1675, Thornton 1689B).
"a conspicuous conical hill rising steeply from the coast to an elevation of 415 feet" (*NP*, p. 271). Inset view on Adm. 296. Pp. 67, 139.

SUGARLOAF HEAD 47–37, 52–39 (NTS St. John's 1N/10E)
Sugar Loaf (Yonge 1668–9).
"a high headland between St. Johns and Torbay, resembling a sugar loaf" (Yonge 1668–9, p. 117).
Pp. 67, 73, 139.
— SUGARLOAF POND 47–37, 52–40

SUGARLOAF HILL 47–22, 53–53 (NTS Argentia 1N/5W)
(NLP 1951).

— SUGARLOAF POINT 47–21, 53–53 (NLP 1951).
Pp. 67, 139.

SUGARLOAF PEAK 47–03, 54–01 (NTS Ship Cove 1M/1E)
Sugar loaf (Adm. 2915 1864).
P. 67.

Sunday's Hill (North River C.B.) (Jukes 1842). P. 112.

SUNNYSIDE (Set.) 47–51, 53–55 (NTS Sunnyside 1N/13W)
Bay Bulls Arm (Wix 1836), Sunnyside (Proclamation 25 June 1930).
"The section of Bay Bulls Arm, now inhabited" (Proclamation 25 June 1930).
On the north shore of BULL ARM, i.e. facing south.
See BULL ARM.

SUTTONS POND 47–35, 53–28 (NTS Harbour Grace 1N/11W)
(NDNR 1N/11 1948). P. 166.
— BIG SUTTONS POND 47–37, 53–26 (NDNR 1N/11 1948).

SWAMP HILL BROOK 47–45, 53–17 (NTS Heart's Content 1N/14W)

SWEENEYS POND 47–46, 53–17 (NTS Heart's Content 1N/14W)
(NDNR 1N/14 1946). P. 135.

SWEET CAKE POND 47–48, 53–21 (NTS Heart's Content 1N/14W)
(NDNR 1N/14 1946).

Taboo-minnigu-guloo Gospen (Murray and Howley 1872). P. 24.

TALCVILLE (Set.) 47–31, 52–58 (NTS St. John's 1N/10W)
Pyrophyllite deposits, which resemble talc, were first worked at this place in 1903.
(NDNR, Bulletin no. 7, 1937). P. 146.

TANGUISHENE (Set.) 47–36, 52–45 (NTS St. John's 1N/10W)
See PENETANGUISHENE. P. 26.

288 / *Place Names of the Avalon Peninsula*

Taylortown (South River C.B.).
P. 146.

TEA COVE 47–53, 53–44 (NTS Sunnyside 1N/13E)
— TEA COVE POINT
? Tickle Point (Lane, *Directions* 1775, 1810, Imray, *Sailing Directions* 1862), Tea cove point (Imray, *Sailing Directory* 1873, NP 1952).
Tea – ? for Indian Tea, *Ledum groenlandicum* Retz., *Rhododendron canadense* (L.) Torr. (E. Rouleau, p. 32); ? changed name from Tickle.
P. 95.

THAMES HARBOUR POINT 47–52, 53–44 (NTS Sunnyside 1N/13E)
(Imray, *Sailing Directory* 1873).

THICKET (Generic). P. 145.

THE THICKET (Set.) 47–39, 53–15 (NTS Harbour Grace 1N/11W)
(Census 1935). P. 145.

THIRD JUNCTION POND 47–23, 53–18 (NTS Holyrood 1N/6W)
(NDNR 1N/6 1943).
After BRIGUS JUNCTION.
Cp. SECOND JUNCTION POND. A First Junction Pond is not recorded in NTS.

THIRD POND 47–25, 53–09 (NTS Holyrood 1N/6E)
(CHS 4573 1953).
The third of three ponds south of CHAPEL COVE (Set.) 47–26, 53–09.
Cp. FIRST POND 47–26, 53–09, SECOND POND 47–25, 53–08. P. 5.

THIRD POND 47–27, 52–46 (NTS Bay Bulls 1N/7E and W)
(Adm. 296 1868).
Of the river which enters PETTY HARBOUR.

THIRD POND 47–31, 53–13 (NTS Harbour Grace 1N/11E)
(CHS 4572 1954).
Between BRIGUS and GEORGETOWN.
First and Second Ponds are not named in NTS.
Cp. FOURTH POND 47–30, 53–13.

THIRD POND 47–35, 53–26 (NTS Harbour Grace 1N/11W)
(NDNR 1N/11 1948).
Relationship to unnamed First and Second Ponds is doubtful.

THOMAS POND 47–27, 52–55 (NTS Bay Bulls 1N/7W). P. 166.

THORBURN HILLS 47–27, 52–44 (NTS Bay Bulls 1N/7E)
(Adm. 296 1868 or later edn).
? After Sir Robert Thorburn (1836–1906); born at Juniper Brook, Peebleshire, Scotland; came to ST. JOHN'S 1852; MLC 1870–85, Prime Minister of Newfoundland 1885–9; KCMG 1887. (Mosdell, p. 129).
— THORBURN ROAD (Set.) 47–35, 52–51 (NTS St. John's 1N/10W)
Formerly Thorburn Line. The road, from Freshwater Road, ST. JOHN'S, to Broad Cove, now ST. PHILIPS (Set.), was built in 1886 (Mosdell, *ibid.*).
P. 147.

THORNLEA (Set.) 47–36, 53–43 (NTS Dildo 1N/12E)
Colliers Bay Cove (Census 1874), Thornlea (Proclamation 23 December 1913).
Pp. 140, 145, 166.

THREE ARM POND 47–30, 52–54 (NTS Bay Bulls 1N/7W, St. John's 1N/10W) (CHS 4566 1952).

THREE AUNT KATES (Ponds) 47–43, 53–24 (NTS Harbour Grace 1N/11W)
(NDNR 1N/11 1948).
Three of four connected ponds.
P. 139.

THREE CORNER POND 47–27, 53–29 (NTS Holyrood 1N/6W)
(NDNR 1N/6 1943).
Not obviously triangular, but cp. the adjacent TRIANGULAR POND 47–27, 53–28.

THREE CORNER POND 47-34, 53-27
(NTS Harbour Grace 1N/11W)
(NDNR 1N/11 1948).

THREE CORNER POND 47-48, 53-14
(NTS Heart's Content 1N/14E)
(NDNR 1N/14 1946).

THREE ISLAND POND 47-29, 53-14
(NTS Holyrood 1N/6E)
(CHS 4573 1953).

THREE ISLAND POND 47-31, 52-54 (NTS
St. John's 1N/10W)

THREE PEAK HILL 47-29, 52-41 (NTS
Bay Bulls 1N/7E)
(Adm. 296 1868). P. 145.

THUMB PEAK 47-31, 53-16 (NTS
Harbour Grace 1N/11W)
(Adm. 296 1868).

TICKLE (Generic and Specific). Pp. 60, 141–2.

TICKLE BAY 47-39, 53-46 (NTS Dildo 1N/12E and W)
Tickle Harbour Bay (Imray, *Sailing Directions* 1862).
— Tickle Harbour ("Blathwayt" c. 1630–40)
　　Tickle Harbour (Set.)
　　(*Population Returns* 1836)
　　See BELLEVUE (Set.) 47-38, 53-44 (NTS Dildo 1N/12E).
— TICKLE HARBOUR POINT 47-42, 53-42 (NTS Dildo 1N/12E)
the Elbow (Guy 1612, Powell's identification *RGSJ* 1935), Tickle Point (Cook and Lane 1770 [1775]A, Lane, *Directions* 1775, 1810), Tickle Hr. Pt. (Lane 1790, Purdy 1814), Tickle Pt (Bonnycastle 1842), Tickle Harbour Point (Imray, *Sailing Directions* 1862). Pp. 59, 60, 64.
— TICKLE HARBOUR (Set.) 47-35, 53-50 (NTS Dildo 1N/12W)
Variously TICKLE HARBOUR and TICKLE HARBOUR STATION in modern documents.

TICKLE POINT 47-08, 53-34 (NTS Placentia 1N/4E)
(*NLP* 1929).
At the southern extremity of PINCHGUT TICKLE.

TICKLE POINT 47-33, 53-55 (NTS Dildo 1N/12W)
Tickle Point (Lane, *Directions* 1775, 1810)
See ? TEA COVE POINT (NTS Sunnyside). P. 95.

TICKLE PONDS 47-42, 53-27 (NTS Harbour Grace 1N/11W)
(NDNR 1N/11 1948).
Tickle – ? After the long, narrow shape of the ponds or the short streams which join them.

TICKLES (Set.) 47-09, 53-34 (NTS Placentia 1N/4E)
As feature: (Lane 1773); as set: (*Population Returns* 1836).
The settlement is in PINCHGUT TICKLE. Pp. 86, 166.

Tilley Cove (Wix 1836)
See TRINNY COVE (NTS Argentia). P. 105.

TILT. P. 147.
Tilt sb. 4. In Labrador and Newfoundland: A fisherman's or wood-cutter's hut. (*OED* with first citation 1895).
"temporary log houses, which they erect in the woods to pursue there their winter occupations" (Anspach, p. 468).
　"This [tilt] was formed of trunks of trees placed upright on the ground close together, with larger ones for the corner pieces, and a good strong gable-end roof formed of a frame of roughly squared beams. The corner pieces and beams were nailed together, and the rest driven in tight with wooden wedges wherever necessary. The interstices of those trunks which formed the walls were

filled up with moss tightly rammed between them; and the roof was covered by long strips or sheets of birch bark, laid tile-like over one another, and kept down by poles or sticks laid across them. A space for a door is left in the middle of one side, and a fire-place is built up with stones and boulders against one end, over which is a space in the roof, and some boards nailed together for a chimney. In this way a tolerable room, twelve or fourteen feet by eight or ten, is formed, sufficiently compact to keep out wind and weather to a certain extent. A "crew" of men, say six or eight, go off in the beginning of winter with a stock of provisions to the head of some of the largest and least-frequented arms of the sea they can find, where the wood has been least cut up, and, building one of these huts, employ themselves either in cutting fire-wood to be hauled out over the snow and ice, or in making oars or staves, building punts, fishing-boats, or even in some cases small schooners. The house which we had thus lighted upon had been occupied by a party the preceding winter building a large boat, which was the reason of the pile of chips we saw on the shore, being the spot where they had built and launched her. The roof had suffered a little, some of the bark or "rinds" having been stripped off by the winds. This, however, was soon repaired; and in a quarter of an hour we had one end of the roof water-proof, and a blazing fire lighted. We then brought the sails and provisions out of the boat, and one of the men "rinding" a few more trees, we completed the roof, and commenced cooking our dinners." Jukes, *Excursions* I, pp. 69–71.

For verbal use see SHOE COVE (NTS Pouch Cove). Pp. 75, 147.

TILT HILL GULLY 47–44, 53–25 (NTS Harbour Grace 1N/11W) (NDNR 1N/11 1948).

TILTON (Set.) 47–38, 53–18 (NTS Harbour Grace 1N/11W) (Census 1884).
At a meeting of the Nomenclature Board in the early 1900s, the Rev. Dr. Pilot asserted that he himself had given the name to the settlement, which had formerly been called the Tilts. (Barrelman, 4 May 1950). Pp. 140, 146.
— TILTON POND
(CHS 4572 1954).

TIM BARRETT COVE 47–24, 53–52 (NTS Argentia 1N/5W) (Adm. 3266 1939). Pp. 129, 157.

TINKER ISLET 47–35, 53–54 (NTS Dildo 1N/12W)
Tinker – the Northern Razor-bill, *Alca torda torda* L. Nests in colonies on rocky sea islands or isolated cliffs. (Peters and Burleigh, p. 250).

TINKER POINT 47–13, 52–50 (NTS Ferryland 1N/2W)
Tinker's Point (Lane 1773).
There is a colony of the birds on GREEN ISLAND 47–14, 56–46. Peters and Burleigh, pp. 250–1). P. 89.

Tinny Cove (Lane 1772)
See TRINNY COVE (NTS Argentia). P. 76.

TOBINS POND 47–18, 53–15 (NTS Holyrood 1N/6E) (NDNR 1N/6 1943). P. 135.

TOCHER'S POND 46–47, 53–28 (NTS Biscay Bay River 1K/14W)
Tocher Pond (Newfoundland 1941), Tochers Pond (Newfoundland 1949), Tucker's Pond (Local name). Pp. 135, 127–8.

Todes Cove (Southwood 1675)
See TORS COVE (NTS Ferryland).
P. 73.

TOLT (Generic). Pp. 19, 104, 145.
the Tolt (Jukes 1842). P. 114.

TOM POWER LOOKOUT 47-26, 53-53
(NTS Argentia 1N/5W)
(Adm. 3266 1939).
A landmark, 562 feet high, for
shipping entering LONG HARBOUR.
Tom Power attended the light.
Pp. 5, 134.

TOM WALDRONS POND 47-22, 52-47
(NTS Bay Bulls 1N/7W)
(NDNR Bay Bulls 1943). P. 135.

TOM WALSH COVE 47-24, 53-54 (NTS
Argentia 1N/5W)
(Adm. 3266 1939).
— TOM WALSH LOOKOUT
A landmark for shipping
entering LONG HARBOUR.
Tom Walsh attended the light.
P. 135.

-TON (Generic). P. 146.

TOPSAIL (Set). 47-32, 52-56 (NTS
St. John's 1N/10W)
Topsail Beech (Wix 1836), Topsail
(Jukes 1842).
— TOPSAIL HEAD 47-33, 52-55
(*NP* 1952)
Topsail Heads (Lane, *Directions*
1775, 1810), Topsail Head
(Jukes 1842).
Pp. 91, 92, 103, 106, 114.
— TOPSAIL HIGHROAD
the Bay Road (Murray and
Howley 1868).
— TOPSAIL POND 47-31, 52-54
— TOPSAIL RIVER 47-32, 52-55
— TOPSAIL ROUND POND 47-31,
52-55
— TOPSAIL STATION 47-31, 52-55.
P. 148.

TORBAY 47-40, 52-42 (NTS St. John's
1N/10E)
Torrebay (Guy 1612), Thorne Bay
(H) Thorn Bay (P), (Blaeu c. 1630),
Torbay (Whitbourne 1588-1622),
Torbay (Mason 1626), Enseada
Grande (Laet 1633), Grand Golfe
ou Frinouse (Sanson 1656), Tarr
Bay (Robinson 1669), Torbay (Seller
1671, Southwood 1675, Hack ?1677,
Thornton 1689B, *English Pilot. The
Fourth Book* 1689), Grand Golfe de
Frinouse (Franquelin 1681), Grande
Baye (Cordier 1696), Torbay (Moll
1709).
— TORBAY (Set.) 47-40, 52-44
(*English Pilot. The Fourth Book*
1689; *Population Returns* 1836)
"There live two planters at
Torbay" (*English Pilot. The Fourth
Book* 1689).
— TORBAY BIGHT 47-40, 52-43
(*NLP* 1951).
— TORBAY POINT 47-40, 52-40
South Pt. Torbay (Lane 1774),
Torbay South Pt (Cook and
Lane 1770 [1775]B, Mount and
Page 1780), Tor Bay point
(Imray, *Sailing Directory*
1873).
Cp. FLAT ROCK POINT.
— TORBAY ROAD.
Pp. 6, 42, 58, 67, 75, 90, 106, 117,
123, 147.

TORS COVE 47-13, 52-51 (NTS
Ferryland 1N/2W)
Todes Cove (Southwood 1675),
Toad Cove (Hack ?1677), Todes
Cove (Visscher c. 1680, Thornton
1689B), Toads-Cove (*English Pilot.
The Fourth Book* 1689), Todes Cove
(Fitzhugh 1693).
— TORS COVE (Set.) 47-13, 52-51
Tothcove (Beaudoin 1697),
Toad's Cove (*Population Re-
turns* 1836), Tor's Cove
(Proclamation 18 January 1910).
— TORS COVE POND 47-13, 52-53
Pp. 73, 79, 123.

292 / *Place Names of the Avalon Peninsula*

TOWN (Generic). P. 146.

TOWN POINT 47–15, 53–58 (NTS
(Placentia 1N/4W)
Murray and Howley 1868).
The southern entrance point of
PLACENTIA HARBOUR. Pp. 82–3.

TRACES POINT 46–58, 52–54 (NTS
Renews 1K/15W)
(Adm. 2915 1864). Pp. 135, 166.

TRANS-CANADA HIGHWAY. P. 147.

TREPASSEY (Set.) 46–44, 53–22 (NTS
Trepassey 1K/11W)
Settled by Sir W. Vaughan in
1617 (*DCB*).
— TREPASSEY BAY 46–37, 53–30
(NTS Trepassey 1K/11E and W,
St. Shotts 1K/12E)
? Riuo de bosas ("Oliveriana"
1505–8), ? sainct Christofle
(Alfonse 1544), trepasses (Le
Testu 1555B), Trepassa (Hayes
1583), Trepassey (Whitbourne
1588–1622), trépasés
(Champlain 1612), Trepassa
Colchos (Mason 1626), B de
Trepasser (Blaeu c. 1630),
Trepassey ("Blathwayt" c.
1630–40).
— TREPASSEY HARBOUR 46–43,
53–24 (NTS Trepassey 1K/11W)
Abra Trepassa (Laet 1630 ...
Roggeveen 1675), Port des
Trepassez (Bellin 1754),
Trepassey Harbour (Cook
1763).
Cp. NORTHEAST BROOK 46–46,
53–21.
Pp. 6, 39, 61, 81, 82, 83, 123, 129.

TRIANGLE BROOK 47–42, 52–49 (NTS
St. John's 1N/10W)

BIG TRIANGLE POND 47–20, 53–12 (NTS
Holyrood 1N/6E)
(NDNR 1N/6 1943).
— LITTLE TRIANGLE POND

TRIANGLE POND 47–34, 52–48 (NTS
St. John's 1N/10W)

TRIANGULAR POND 47–27, 53–28 (NTS
Holyrood 1N/6W)
(NDNR 1N/6 1943).
Cp. THREE CORNER POND 47–27,
53–29.

Trinity (Robinson 1669). P. 70.

TRINITY BAY 48–00, 53–30 (NTS Dildo
1N/12E and W, Sunnyside 1N/13E
and W, Heart's Content 1N/14W,
Bay de Verde 2C/2W, Old Perlican
2C/3W, etc.).
Baya de Santa Cyria ("Kuntsmann
no. 3" c. 1506) baya de santa ana
(Reinel 1519), Rio santo (Maggiolo
1527), Baia de s ciria (Verrazano
1529), Baya de cotebirion (H) baya
de cotebi (P) (Cabot 1544), Abaia de
Sta ciria (Freire 1546 ... Lopes
c. 1583), b de sta anna (Homem
1554), Trinity Bay (Whitbourne
1588–1622), B S Clara (Laet 1625),
S Clare (Aertsz 1631), B Ste Claire
(Champlain 1632), Trinity Bay
(Dudley 1646).
G. R. F. Prowse, *CM*, III, notes
confusion on maps up to 1700
between Bonavista and Trinity Bays,
whence he assumes that St. Claire,
? French reading of clear, refers to
Bonavista Bay, in contrast with a
Bay of Foggs (Blaeu c. 1530,
Kitchin 1785), ? Sir Charles
Hamilton Sound. Coronelli 1689
appears to confuse TRINITY BAY with
CONCEPTION BAY. Sta anna is
probably a mistake name for Santa
Cyria (for Iria or Eiria). Trinity may
be a transfer name from either of
the harbours, Trinity (NTS Trinity)
or Trinity (NTS St. Brendans). Pp. 6,
8, 16, 18, 30, 56, 57, 60, 61, 76,
80, 94, 95, 96, 103, 105, 107, 124–5.

TRINNY COVE 47–29, 53–55 (NTS
Argentia 1N/5W)

Trinity (Visscher c. 1680), Tinny
Cove (Lane 1772, Cook and Lane
1770 [1775]B, as set: Tilley Cove
(Wix 1836); Tinny Cove
(*Population Returns* 1836), Tinny
Cove (Imray, *Sailing Directions*
1862, *Sailing Directory* 1873),
Trinny Cove (Adm. 232a 1870,
M. F. Howley, xxx, *NQ*, March
1911). Pp. 76, 105.

TROUT POND 47–27, 52–57 (NTS
Bay Bulls 1N/7W)
(NDNR Bay Bulls 1943).

TROUT POND 47–45, 52–49 (NTS Pouch
Cove 1N/15W)

TROUT POND 47–58, 53–05 (NTS
Heart's Content 1N/14E)
(Newfoundland 1941).

Truce sound (Guy 1612)
See BULL ARM (NTS Sunnyside).
P. 59.

Tseist-minnigu-guloo Gospen
(Murray and Howley 1872). P. 24.

TUCKERS GULLY 47–44, 53–20 (NTS
Harbour Grace 1N/11W)
(NDNR 1N/11 1948).
Cp. TOCHER'S POND (NTS Biscay Bay
River). Pp. 135, 166.

TURKS COVE 47–56, 53–21 (NTS
Heart's Content 1N/14W)
? B de Rose (Friend 1713).
— TURKS COVE (Set.)
(*Population Returns* 1836).
P. 107.
— TURKS HEAD 47–57, 53–21

TURKS GUT (Cove) 47–30, 53–12 (NTS
Harbour Grace 1N/11E)
(Bonnycastle 1842).
Cp. FRESHWATER BAY (NTS
Trepassey).
— Turks Gut (Set.) (*Population
Returns* 1836)
See MARYVALE (NTS Holyrood).
— TURKS GUT LONG POND 47–28,

53–16 (NTS Holyrood 1N/6E and W)
(CHS 4573 1953).
— Turks Gut South (Set.) (Census
1857). P. 118.
— Turks Head 47–30, 53–11
(Jukes 1842).
Pp. 49, 85, 106, 107, 111, 116, 141.

TURTLE HILL 47–29, 52–45 (NTS
Bay Bulls 1N/7W)
(Adm. 296 1868).

Tusem Gospen (Murray and Howley
1872). P. 25.

TWELVE O'CLOCK HILL 47–18, 52–48
(NTS Bay Bulls 1N/7W)
(Adm. 296 1868).

Twenty Mile Pond (St. John's)
(*Royal Gazette* 1812)
See WINDSOR LAKE (NTS St. John's).
Pp. 99–101, 115.

TWIN PEAK 47–31, 53–12 (NTS
Harbour Grace 1N/11E)
(Adm. 296 1868), the Twins
(Imray, *Sailing Directory* 1873).
"a double peak 542 feet high"
(Imray, *Sailing Directory* 1873,
p. 51).

TWO ISLAND POND 47–21, 53–10 (NTS
Holyrood 1N/6E)
(NDNR 1N/6 1943).

UPPER BACK COVE 47–35, 53–13 (NTS
Harbour Grace 1N/11E)
(CHS 4572 1954).
Of PORT DE GRAVE.
Cp. LOWER BACK COVE 47–36, 53–13.

UPPER GULLIES (Set.) 47–29, 53–02
(NTS Holyrood 1N/6E)
(Census 1857).
Cp. RIVERDALE, LOWER GULLIES RIVER.
Pp. 107, 117.

UPPER ISLAND COVE 47–39, 53–12 (NTS
Harbour Grace 1N/11E)
Island Cove (Imray, *Sailing
Directory* 1873).

"a small rocky bight fronted by an islet" (Imray 1873).
Cp. LOWER ISLAND COVE (NTS Heart's Content).
— UPPER ISLAND COVE (Set.) Haylinscove (Beaudoin 1697), Island Cove (co Misc. 199.18 1773), Upper Island Cove (*Population Returns* 1836).
Pp. 6, 79, 92, 94, 107, 119.
— ISLAND COVE POND 47–39, 53–14 (CHS 4572 1954).

UPPER POND 47–17, 52–50 (NTS Bay Bulls 1N/7W)
(CHS 4586 1944).
Cp. LOWER POND 47–17, 52–49.

Upper Ram (Islands)
The southern group of the IONA ISLANDS (NTS Argentia). P. 85.

UPPER SMALL POINT 47–49, 53–06 (NTS Heart's Content 1N/14E)
As set: (Census 1857).
See KINGSTON. P. 119.

UPSHALL (Set.) 47–40, 53–54 (NTS Dildo 1N/12W). P. 166

USELESS BAY 47–19, 52–46 (NTS Bay Bulls 1N/7W)
(NDNR Bay Bulls 1943).

VALE (Generic). P. 146.
VALLEY (Generic). P. 146.

VALLEY PONDS 47–44, 53–25 (NTS Harbour Grace 1N/11W)
(NDNR 1N/11 1948). P. 146.

Vaughan's Cove (Mason 1626)
See ? CAPPAHAYDEN (NTS Renews). Pp. 61–2.

VELVET HEART POND 47–19, 53–10 (NTS Holyrood 1N/6E)
(NDNR 1N/6 1943).
? For Velvet Hart – ? a (caribou or moose) stag in velvet, i.e. before "the soft downy skin which covers a deer's horn while in growing stage" has been shed. (*OED*. Velvet. sb. 2).
Cp. *Velvet Horn*, name of a restaurant at HOLYROOD.

VESTAL ROCK (St. John's Harbour) 47–34, 52–41
the Vestal (Lane, *Directions* 1775, 1810), Vestal Rock (Imray, *Sailing Directions* 1862, *Sailing Directory* 1873, NP 1952). P. 94.

Viceaúmiralls place (Fermeuse Harbour) (Yonge 1663–70)
See KINGMANS COVE (NTS Renews). P. 69.

VICTORIA (Set.) 47–46, 53–14 (NTS Heart's Content 1N/14E)
Victoria Village (Census 1874 ... 1901), Victoria (Census 1911).
? Presumably after Queen Victoria.
"Victoria is a comparatively new community its whole history lying within the past fifty years. Its settlement [at BEAVER POND] was due to people moving back [from CARBONEAR] to the slightly better farming land and nearness to wood for firing. At first a collection of winter tilts then a few 'liveyers' and at last a large community with fine church and three room school" (Johnson, 1925, p. 278). However, since the population was recorded as 265 in Census 1874, the foundation of the settlement would seem to have been much earlier than Johnson states. Pp. 6, 74, 146.

VILLA MARIA (Set.) 47–18, 53–51 (NTS Argentia 1N/5W)
Ville Marie Stn. (Stanford 1898), Villa Maria (Newfoundland 1941).
Place names in France of the same form and with a religious value are Villedieu, Villejésus and Ville-St. Jacques. (Dauzat, *Dictionnaire des Noms de Lieux*, p. 720).

VILLAGE (Generic). P. 146.

-VILLE (Generic). P. 146.

VINEGAR HILL 47–33, 53–16 (unnamed in NTS Harbour Grace 1N/11E). Pp. 126–7.

VIRGIN POINT 47–19, 53–58 (NTS Argentia 1N/5W) (*NLP* 1951).

VIRGIN ROCKS 47–09, 54–06 Virgins Rocks (Gaudy 1715), Virgin rocks (Senex 1728), Virgins (Popple 1733), Virgins Rocks (Kitchin 1762), Virgin Rs (Cook 1763). "Virgin Rocks and Girdle Rock, about 1¾ miles offshore, lie 6½ and 7½ miles, respectively, south-southwestward of Verde Point [i.e. POINT VERDE (NTS Ship Cove)]" (*NP*, 1952, p. 49). Pp. 81–2.

Virginia (Cove) (St. John's Harbour) (Visscher c. 1680). P. 76.

VIRGINIA LAKE 47–37, 52–42 (NTS St. John's 1N/10E) Downing's Pond, Virginia Waters, Virginia Water (McCrea 1869). ? After Virginia Water, an artificial lake near Windsor, Bucks, excavated for William, Duke of Cumberland, who commanded the English army at Culloden, after 1746. "the present Virginia Lake, known to the old settlers, and called on old maps 'Downing's Pond' " after the Downing family, settled in Newfoundland since 1640. (D. W. Prowse, pp. 195, 205). A cove on the north side of ST. JOHN'S HARBOUR is named Downings (Visscher c. 1680, Thornton 1689B, *English Pilot. The Fourth Book* 1716, 1780). "the former summer residence of the governors of Newfoundland"

(McCrea 1869, 217). See COCHRANE. Pp. 142–3.

VIZARD HILL 47–25, 52–42 (NTS Bay Bulls 1N/7E) (Adm. 296 1868). P. 166.

VOISEYS BROOK 47–38, 52–49 (NTS St. John's 1N/10W). P. 166.

WABANA (Set.) (Bell Island) 47–38, 52–57 (NTS St. John's 1N/10W). P. 26.

Wagedigulsiboo Gospen (Murray and Howley 1872). Pp. 24–5.

Wallace's Battery (St. John's). P. 102.

WALLS POND 47–25, 53–09 (NTS Holyrood 1N/6E) (CHS 4573 1953). Pp. 135, 166.

WARM GULLIES 47–43, 53–25 (NTS Harbour Grace 1N/11W) (NDNR 1N/11 1948).

WASHBALLS (Rocks) St. John's Harbour) 47–34, 52–40 Wash Ballocks (Thornton 1689B, *English Pilot. The Fourth Book* 1716, 1780), Wash-ball Rocks (Lane, *Directions* 1775, 1810; Imray, *Sailing Directions* 1862), Wash-balls (Imray, *Sailing Directory* 1873), Washballs (*NP* 1952). P. 77.

WATCH HILL 47–26, 52–42 (NTS Bay Bulls 1N/7E) (Adm. 296 1868). ? A lookout.

— WATCH HILL POND 47–26, 52–43 (NDNR Bay Bulls 1943).

WATER STREET (St. John's) The specific is found in the names of streets on the waterfront in ST. JOHN'S, HARBOUR GRACE and CARBONEAR, Halifax, N.S. and elsewhere in North America, but has not been traced in Britain or Eire.

WATERFORD BRIDGE (Set.) 47–32,

296 / *Place Names of the Avalon Peninsula*

52–45 (NTS St. John's 1N/10E)
As feature: (Jukes 1842). Pp. 127, 148.
— WATERFORD RIVER 47–33, 52–43
? Little Castor's River (Anspach 1819).
Pp. 77, 102, 112, 127, 148.

Watering Place (Riverhead, St. John's Harbour) (Cook 1762 or Gilbert 1768)
A place for ships to take on fresh water. P. 83.

WATERN COVE 46–38, 53–09 (NTS Trepassey 1K/11E)
(CHS 4576 1950).
The form watern appears to be the cartographer's phonetic rendering of the local popular pronunciation of watering, found similarly in GRAVEN BEACH (NTS St. Mary's) and POUNDEN COVE (NTS Trepassey).
Cp. FRESHWATER (Specific).

WATERS (Generic)
It may be noted that though Derwentwater and Ullswater, Cumberland, for example, are lakes, Dawlish Water, Devonshire, is a brook. Page, p. 383). P. 143.

WATTS POND 47–40, 52–44 (NTS St. John's 1N/10E). P. 167.

WEAVERS POND 47–27, 53–12 (NTS Holyrood 1N/6E)

WEBBERS POND 47–34, 53–16 (NTS Harbour Grace 1N/11W)
(CHS 4572 1954). P. 167.

WELCH HILL 47–42, 53–13 (NTS Harbour Grace 1N/11E)
(Adm. 297 1933, CHS 4590 1943).
P. 167.

Welles I. (Blathwayt c. 1630–40)
See KELLY'S ISLAND (NTS Harbour Grace). Pp. 64–5.

WEST BROOK 47–33, 53–14 (NTS Harbour Grace 1N/11E)
(NDNR 1N/11 1948).

WEST POND 47–23, 53–28 (NTS Holyrood 1N/6W)
(NDNR 1N/6 1943).
Cp. EAST POND.

West Shore (Harbour Grace) (Lane, *Directions* 1775, 1810). P. 95.

WESTERN BAY 47–53, 53–04 (NTS Heart's Content 1N/14E)
Greene Bay (Robinson 1669), Green B (Hack ?1677, *English Pilot. The Fourth Book* 1689), Greene Bay (Thornton 1689B), Green or Western Bay (Lane 1774), Western Bay (Jukes 1840), Green or Western Bay (Imray, *Sailing Directions* 1862).
Cp. NORTHERN BAY.
— WESTERN BAY (Set.) 47–53, 53–05
(*Population Returns* 1836).
— WESTERN BAY BROOK
(Newfoundland 1941).
— WESTERN BAY HEAD 47–53, 53–03
? Pointe Prime (Robinson 1669), Pt Prine (Thornton 1689A), Pte S. Guillaume (Bellin 1744), ? S. Williams Pt (Bowen 1747), Pte S. Guillaume (Robert de Vaugondy 1749; Bellin 1754; Lotter c. 1758), Pt. William (Kitchin 1762), Green, or Western Bay Point (Lane, *Directions* 1775, 1810, Imray, *Sailing Directions* 1862).
Pp. 46–7, 70–1, 76, 93, 98.

WESTERN GULL POND 47–25, 53–27
(NTS Holyrood 1N/6W)
(NDNR 1N/6 1943).
An Eastern Gull Pond is not named in NTS.

WESTERN HEAD 46–38, 53–37 (NTS St. Shotts 1K/12E)
(Lane 1773).
Cp. EASTERN HEAD. P. 88.

WESTERN HEAD 47–42, 53–50 (NTS Dildo 1N/12W)
(Adm. 296 1863).
Of RANTEM COVE.

WESTERN ISLAND POND 47–38, 52–46 (NTS St. John's 1N/10W)
Cp. ISLAND POND.

WESTERN ISLAND POND 47–41, 53–19 (NTS Harbour Grace 1N/11W)
(NDNR 1N/11 1948).
Cp. EASTERN ISLAND POND.

WESTERN POND 47–28, 52–54 (NTS Bay Bulls 1N/7W)
(NDNR Bay Bulls 1943).
? West of COCHRANE POND.

WESTERN POND 47–37, 52–51 (NTS St. John's 1N/10W)
West of PORTUGAL COVE ROAD.

WESTERN POND 47–57, 53–17 (NTS Heart's Content 1N/14W)
(NDNR 1N/14 1946).
? On the western side of the peninsula.

WESTERN ROUND POND 47–36, 52–50 (NTS St. John's 1N/10W)
West of ROUND POND 47–36, 52–49.
52–49.

Whaleback (Southwood 1675)
See BAULINE EAST (NTS Ferryland).
Pp. 49, 73.

WHALENS BROOK 47–28, 53–14 (NTS Holyrood 1N/6E)
(CHS 4573 1953). P. 135.

WHALENS POND 47–15, 53–24 (NTS Holyrood 1N/6W)
(NDNR 1N/6 1943). P. 135.

WHALENS POND 47–23, 53–21 (NTS Holyrood 1N/6W)
(NDNR 1N/6 1943). P. 136.

WHALES POND 47–21, 52–58 (NTS Bay Bulls 1N/7W)
(NDNR Bay Bulls 1943).

WHISKY POND 47–15, 53–17 (NTS Holyrood 1N/6W)
(NDNR 1N/6 1943).

WHITBOURNE (Set.) 47–25, 53–32 (NTS Argentia 1N/5E)
Harbour Grace Junction (c. 1889), Whitbourne (52 Vict. c. 16 1 June 1889, Census 1891).
Named after Sir Richard Whitbourne, (fl. 1579–1628), sailor, merchant, writer, governor of Sir William Vaughan's colony at TREPASSEY, 1618–20, (*DCB*), by Sir Robert Bond, prime minister of Newfoundland, 1900-8, who had his home there. P. 139.

WHITE HILL 47–19, 52–46 (NTS Bay Bulls 1N/7W)
(CHS 4586 1944).

WHITE HILL POND 47–27, 53–03 (NTS Holyrood 1N/6E)
(NDNR 1N/6 1943).
Cp. BLACK MOUNTAIN POND 47–26, 53–01.

White Hills (Jukes 1842). P. 114.

WHITE HILLS 47–36, 52–40 (NTS St. John's 1N/10E)
? (McCrea 1869).

WHITE POINT 47–18, 53–55 (NTS Argentia 1N/5W)
(CHS 4622 ? 1953).

WHITE POINT 48–03, 53–12 (NTS Old Perlican 2C/3E)

WHITEHILL POND 47–38, 53–26 (NTS Harbour Grace 1N/11W)
(NDNR 1N/11 1948).

Whitemonday Hill (Set.) (Bay Roberts) (Census 1857)
Whit Monday Hill (Blackmore 1865).
See BAY ROBERTS (NTS Harbour Grace). P. 119.

WHITEWAY ['waɪtə,weɪ] (Set.) 47–41, 53–29 (NTS Harbour Grace 1N/11W)

Formerly Witless Bay, Whiteway (Proclamation 13 August 1912). ? After Sir William Vallance Whiteway (1828–1908), born near Totnes, Devonshire; came to Newfoundland, 1843; prime minister of Newfoundland 1878–85, 1889–94, 1895–7; K.C.M.G. 1880. The pronunciation of the name in Newfoundland seems to derive from an alternative spelling, Whiteaway. (Guppy p. 145). Pp. 139, 167.
— WHITEWAY BAY 47–41, 53–30 (NTS Harbour Grace 1N/11W, Dildo 1N/12E)
Witless Bay (Lane, *Directions* 1775, 1810; *NLP* 1907), Whiteway Bay (*NLP* 1953).
Pp. 97, 139, 167.

WHITEWAY POND 47–39, 52–46 (NTS St. John's 1N/10W). P. 167.

WHITEWOOD POND 47–37, 53–28 (NTS Harbour Grace 1N/11W) (NDNR 1N/11 1948).
Whitewood – white maple, *Acer spicatum* Lam., *Viburnum trilobum* Marsh; whitewood berry or ironwood berry, *Viburnum trilobum* Marsh. (Rouleau, pp. 32, 40).

Whittle's Bay (M. F. Howley XXIV, *NQ*, December 1908)
See WITLESS BAY (NTS Bay Bulls). P. 65.

WIGMORE POND 47–34, 42–46 (NTS St. John's 1N/10W). P. 167.

WILD COVE 46–57, 53–42 (NTS St. Mary's 1K/13E) (Adm. 2915 1864).
— WILD HEAD (Adm. 2915 1864).

WILD COVE 46–59, 53–49 (NTS St. Mary's 1K/13W, Placentia 1N/4W)
(Adm. 2915 1864, Imray, *Sailing Directory* 1873).

"a dangerous place affording no shelter" (Imray, *Sailing Directory* 1873, p. 80).

WILD COVE, 47–26, 53–53 (NTS Argentia 1N/5W) (Adm. 3266 1939).
— WILD COVE HEAD (Adm. 3266 1939).

WILLIAMS (Set.) 47–26, 52–46 (NTS Bay Bulls 1N/7W) (USHO 2139 1943). Pp. 136, 139, 167.

WILLIAMS COVE 47–18, 52–47 (NTS Bay Bulls 1N/7W) (CHS 4586 1944).
— WILLIAMS HILL 47–19, 52–49 (CHS 4586 1944).
Pp. 136, 167.

WILLIAMS HILL 47–24, 52–45 (NTS Bay Bulls 1N/7E) (Adm. 296 1868), William hill (*NLP* 1951). Pp. 136, 167.

WILLIAMS POND 47–20, 53–19 (NTS Holyrood 1N/6W) (NDNR 1N/6 1943). Pp. 136, 167.

WILLIAMS POND 47–43, 52–48 (NTS St. John's 1N/10W). P. 167.

WIND GAP ROAD 47–41, 52–43 (NTS St. John's 1N/10E)
"Gaps ... in which the depression in the ridge is not sufficiently deep to give passage to a watercourse are known as 'wind-gaps'" (J. D. Whitney, *United States* (Little and Brown, Boston, 1889), p. 223, cited in *OED* gap 5b). Here, however, wind gap would seem to refer to a break in the escarpment through which easterly winds blow vigorously, unless, as a local pronunciation ['waɪnd,gæp] would suggest, it refers to the tortuous nature of the road.
*However, a communication from Mr Burnham Gill, Provincial Archivist, suggests a transfer name:

"Michael Allen. Administrator to the Estate & Effects of Richard Keef. of Wind Gap. County of Kilkenny Ireland. But late of St. John's Newfoundland Labourer." "In the Probate Court," St. John's, 16 March 1825.

Windsor (*Royal Gazette* 1821).
— WINDSOR HEIGHTS (Set.) 47–36, 52–49.
— WINDSOR LAKE 47–36, 52–48 (NTS St. John's 1N/10W)
Twenty Mile Pond, Windsor Lake (*Royal Gazette* 1821).
Pp. 100–101, 115, 143, 145.

WINGING ROCKS 47–42, 53–59 (NTS Dildo 1N/12W)
(*NP* 1952).
Winging – ? as if flying or sailing.

WINTERTON (Set.) 47–58, 53–20 (NTS Heart's Content 1N/14W)
Celicove (Beaudoin 1697), Scilly Cove (*Population Returns* 1836), Winterton (Proclamation 13 August 1912).
— WINTERTON COVE
Sille Cove at Sugar loaf (Southwood 1675), Sille cove (Thornton 1689B), Sillee Cove (*English Pilot. The Fourth Book* 1689), Scilly Cove (Popple 1733), Sillee Cove (Jukes 1840; Imray, *Sailing Directions* 1862, *Sailing Directory*, 1873). P. 72.
Pp. 9, 72, 80, 103, 107, 140, 146, 167.

WITCH HAZEL PEAK 47–26, 53–15 (NTS Holyrood 1N/6E)
Witch hazel or Newfoundland oak, *Betula lutea* Michx f. "The schooners [of the early nineteenth century] all had deep, heavy keels; both the bottom planking and keel were made of birch and witch hazel" (D. W. Prowse, p. 404).

Cp. WYCH HAZEL POND (NTS Bay Bulls).

WITHROD POND 47–30, 52–45 (NTS St. John's 1N/10E)
Withrod – Thrasher-wood berry, *Virburnum cassinoides* L. (Rouleau, pp. 39, 40).

WITLESS BAY 47–16, 52–48 (NTS Bay Bulls 1N/7W)
Witless ("Blathwayt" c. 1630–40), Witless Bay (Yonge 1664), Witless Bay (Robinson 1669), ? Whitburns Bay (Ogilby 1671), Witless Bay (Thornton 1689B, *English Pilot. The Fourth Book* 1689), Whittles Bay (Hack c. 1690?), Witles B (Fitzhugh 1693), Witles Bay (Gaudy 1715), Witles B (Popple 1733), Wittelit (Robert de Vaugondy 1749), Bay Wittelit (Bellin 1754), Witless Bay (Cook 1763).
— WITLESS BAY (Set.) 47–16, 52–50 (*CSP* 1677), Whittley's Bay (*CSP* 1682), Ouit lis baye (Beaudoin 1697), Witless Bay (*Population Returns* 1836).
Pp. 65–6, 79, 97, 130, 132.
— WITLESS BAY BARRENS. P. 103.
— WITLESS BAY BROOK 47–17, 52–50
— WITLESS BAY COUNTRY POND 47–17, 52–54
(NDNR Bay Bulls 1943).
— WITLESS BAY LINE. P. 147.
— WITLESS POINT 47–15, 52–48 (NTS Ferryland 1N/2W)
Witless Bay Pt. (Cook and Lane 1770 [1775]B, Mount and Page 1780), Witless Pt (Adm. 2915 1864).

Witless Bay (Lane, *Directions* 1775, 1810)
See WHITEWAY BAY (NTS Dildo, Harbour Grace). P. 97.

WITLESS HEAD 47–18, 53–53 (NTS Argentia 1N/5W)
(CHS 4622 ? 1953). Pp. 65, 136.

Witson's Bay (Thoresby 1796)
See ? WESTERN BAY (NTS Heart's
Content). P. 98.

WOODFORD'S (Set.) 47–24, 53–09 (NTS
Holyrood 1N/6E)
Woodford Stn (Adm. 232a ? 1886
edn), Woodford's (CHS 4573 1953).
Pp. 139, 167.

WOODSTOCK (Set.) 47–32, 52–54 (NTS
St. John's 1N/10W)
(3/55 Crown Grants No. 1020,
18 October 1851 to Henry Winton)
(Communication from Mr P.
Vavasour).

? Transferred name from Woodstock, Oxfordshire.
Cp. Woodstock (NTS Nipper's
Harbour 2E/13W). P. 139.

WOODY ISLAND 47–27, 53–57 (NTS
Argentia 1N/5W)
(Adm. 3266 1939).
One of the BRINE ISLANDS. Pp. 5, 85.

WOODY ISLAND 47–41, 53–58 (NTS
Dildo 1N/12W)

WYCH HAZEL POND 47–29, 52–56 (NTS
Bay Bulls 1N/7W)
See WITCH HAZEL PEAK (NTS
Holyrood).

Bibliography / One
Maps, Charts and Atlases

For a short account of the significance of maps in the study of place names in Newfoundland, see Chapter 1.

The list that follows contains only important or representative maps of toponymical value and interest for this study. They are arranged in chronological order, with conjectural dates in square brackets. Admiralty charts are entered under the date of publication, but maps based on other surveys are entered under the date of the survey, if it is known. The name following the date is generally that of the cartographer (stated, known or inferred), but where a map is known by a commonly accepted appellation, the name is put in inverted commas, as the "Cantino" chart. When a cartographer has more than one map in the same year, A, B, C etc. follow his name to distinguish them. The surname of the cartographer or the name of the map plus the date form the cue-title in the Gazetteer and elsewhere. Any map not indicated as a manuscript is printed.

The list does not include a number of contemporary charts and maps, such as those issued by the Canadian Hydrographic Service (CHS) and the United States Hydrographic Office (USHO).

The following short forms of reference have been used:

Harrisse, *Découverte* – H. Harrisse, *Découverte et Évolution cartographique de Terre-Neuve*, 2 vols. (London, Paris 1900).

Prowse, CM I, III – G. R. F. Prowse, *Cartological Material*, I Maps (Winnipeg 1936); III *Names* (Winnipeg 1942).

MCV – R. Almagià, *Monumenta Cartographica Vaticana*, 4 vols. (Città del Vaticano 1944–55).

PAC – *Sixteenth-Century Maps relating to Canada: A Check-List and Bibliography* (Public Archives of Canada, Ottawa 1956).

PMC – A. Cortesão and A. Teixeira da Mota. *Portugaliae Monumenta Cartographica*, 6 vols. (Lisbon 1960).

BN – M. Foncin, M. Destombes, and M. de la Roncière. *Bibliothèque Nationale: Catalogue des cartes nautiques sur vélin* (Paris 1963).

Ganong – W. F. Ganong, *Crucial Maps in the Early Cartography and Place-Nomenclature of the Atlantic Coast of Canada* (reprint) (Toronto 1964).

Where no acknowledgement of the source of the nomenclature is made, readings are by E. R. Seary.

1500 LA COSA, JUAN DE
Manuscript world map, signed and dated, in the Museo Naval, Madrid. PAC 5. Ganong, pp. 8–43, 469–73. Some writers ascribe the map to a later date (1508–10, G. E. Nunn; after 1524, B. G. Hoffman).

La Cosa, a Basque, was a member of Columbus' crew on his second and third voyages.

Names which seem to correspond to lands near Newfoundland after Harrisse, *Découverte*, pp. 18, 215, 359, and Prowse, *CM* III, p. 19.

[1502] "CANTINO" PLANISPHERE
Carta da nauigar per le Isole nouam^{te} tr ... in le parte de l'India: dono Alberto Cantino Al S. Duca Hercole ...

Manuscript world map of Portuguese authorship, unsigned and undated, in the Biblioteca Estense, Modena. Completed in Lisbon, September to October 1502, and sent to Duke Ercole d'Este by his agent Cantino. PAC 6. PMC, I, pp. 7–13, pl. 4–5.

Names after Harrisse, *Découverte*, p. 359.

[1503–6] "KUNSTMANN NO. 2"
Manuscript chart of the North Atlantic, unsigned and undated, probably of Italian authorship, in the Bayerische Staatsbibliothek, Munich. So named from its reproduction in F. Kunstmann, *Atlas zur Entdeckungsgeschichte Amerikas*, 1859.

Names after Harrisse, *Découverte*, pp. 49, 359.

[1504–6] "KING-HAMY" PLANISPHERE
Manuscript world map, unsigned and undated, of Italian authorship, in the Huntington Library, San Marino, California. PAC 8. The map is known by the names of two previous owners, Richard King and E. T. A. Hamy.

Names after Harrisse, *Découverte*, pp. 39, 359.

[ABOUT 1504] REINEL, PEDRO
Manuscript chart of the North Atlantic, known as "Kunstmann no. 1," signed "Pedro Reinel a fez," but undated, in the Bayerische Staatsbibliothek, Munich (Cod. icon. 132). The date is that assigned by Cortesão, though "some authorities date it two or three years later, while Ganong believes it to be as late as 1516–20." PAC 58. *PMC*, I, pp. 25–7, pl. 8. Ganong, pp. 47–8, 61–5.

Harrisse, *Découverte*, p. 75, notes that the nomenclature is exclusively Portuguese and such as we shall find, scarcely changed, in all the maps, not only Portuguese, but Spanish, Catalan, Italian and French.

Names after Harrisse, *Découverte*, p. 360, and Prowse, *CM* I [1143], pp. 137–8.

[1505–8] "OLIVERIANA" or "PESARO"
Manuscript world map, unsigned and undated, of Italian authorship, in the Biblioteca e Musei Oliveriana, Pesaro, Italy. PAC 16. Ganong, pp. 174–5.

Names after Harrisse, *Découverte*, pp. 53, 359, and Prowse, *CM* III, p. 19.

[ABOUT 1506] "KUNSTMANN NO. 3"
Manuscript chart of the North Atlantic, unsigned and undated, of Portuguese authorship, formerly in the Hauptconservatorium der Armee, Munich, now lost. PAC 11. *PMC*, I, pp. 15–6, pl. 6.

Names after Harrisse, *Découverte*, pp. 53, 359, and Prowse, *CM* I, p. 15.

[ABOUT 1508] "EGERTON MS. 2803"
Manuscript portolan atlas of 13

charts, including one of the Atlantic Ocean, unsigned and undated, of Italian authorship, in the British Museum (Egerton MS. 2803). Commonly ascribed to Vesconte Maggiolo and the year 1508. PAC 22. Harrisse, *Découverte*, p. 70.

1508 RUYSCH, JOHANNES
Universalior Cogniti Orbis Tabula Ex Recentibus Confecta Observationibus
World map in the Rome edition of Ptolemy's *Geographia*, 1508. PAC 21.
Names after Harrisse, *Découverte*, pp. 56, 360, and Prowse *CM* I, [2059], p. 236.

[1519] [REINEL, PEDRO, and JORGE] "MILLER ATLAS"
Manuscript chart of the North Atlantic, forming the tenth and last chart in the so-called "Miller Atlas," in the Bibliothèque Nationale, Paris (Rés. Ge. DD. 683). The atlas, of Portuguese authorship, is unsigned and undated (except the world map, in private ownership, signed by Lopo Homem 1519). The regional charts are ascribed by Cortesão to Pedro and Jorge Reinel. PAC 59. *PMC*, I, pp. 55–61, pl. 24. *BN*, no. 23. Ganong, pp. 48–55.
Names after Harrisse, *Découverte*, pp. 85, 360, who notes that the nomenclature is that of Pedro Reinel [about 1504] with additions, and Prowse, *CM* I, [2252], p. 291.

[1520–25] FREDUCCI, CONTE OTTOMANNO
"Manuscript chart of the Atlantic ... in the Archivio di Stato, Florence. The map is signed 'Conte de Hectomanno Freducci de Anchona la facta in Anchona nella ... ', but unfortunately the date is obliterated. The 'Conte' in the signature is a proper name, not a title." PAC 80.
Harrisse, *Découverte*, p. 82, notes that the Newfoundland nomenclature is Portuguese, but with Spanish influences and less numerous than in Reinel, and comments on a number of bizarre forms.
Names after Harrisse, *Découverte*, pp. 82, 360.

[1520–34] "HAVRE CATALAN" ATLAS
"Atlas of thirteen maps ... preserved in the Bibliothèque municipale, Havre. Five of the maps relate to America." PAC 81.
Names after Harrisse, *Découverte*, p. 131, and Prowse, *CM* I, [2551], p. 291.

1527 MAGGIOLO, VESCONTE
Manuscript world map, signed and dated, formerly in the Biblioteca Ambrosiana, Milan, destroyed during World War II. PAC 107. Ganong, pp. 104–24.
Names after Harrisse, *Découverte*, p. 97, who considers that the Newfoundland nomenclature is from a Portuguese prototype, and Prowse, *CM* I, [1150], pp. 139–41.

[1529] VERRAZANO, GIROLAMO DA
Manuscript world map, signed but undated, in the Biblioteca Apostolica Vaticana (Borgiano I). PAC 119. *MCV*, I, pp. 53–55, pl. XXVII–XXIX. Ganong, pp. 104–24.
Names after Harrisse, *Découverte*, pp. 94, 361, who notes that the Newfoundland nomenclature is from a Portuguese prototype, and Prowse, *CM* I, [1165], pp. 139–41.

1529 RIBEIRO, DIOGO
Carta Universal en que se contiene todo lo que del mundo se ha descubierto fasta agora ...
Manuscript world map, signed and

304 / *Place Names of the Avalon Peninsula*

dated from Seville, in the Biblioteca Apostolica Vaticana (Borgiana III). PAC 121. *PMC*, I, pp. 101–3, pl. 39. *MCV*, I, pp. 50–2, pl. XXI–XXIII. Ganong, pp. 53–9, 149–52, 210–4.

Names after Prowse, *CM* I, [2653], p. 291.

[ABOUT 1532] [RIBEIRO, DIOGO]
Manuscript map of America and the Far East, forming part of a world map, unsigned and undated, known as "Wolfenbüttel B," in the Herzog August Bibliothek, Wolfenbüttel. PAC 135. *PMC*, I, pp. 107–9, pl. 41. The attribution of authorship and date is made by Cortesão.

Names after Prowse, *CM* I, [2655], p. 291.

1534 VIEGAS, GASPAR
Manuscript chart of the Atlantic, signed and dated, in the Bibliothèque Nationale, Paris (Rés. Ge. B. 1132). PAC 160. *PMC*, I, pp. 115–6, pl. 44.

Names after Harrisse, *Découverte*, p. 106, and Prowse, *CM* I, [1493], p. 187.

[ABOUT 1537] [VIEGAS, GASPAR]
"Portuguese manuscript atlas of 26 maps, beautifully coloured, anonymous and undated, in R. Archivio di Stato, Biblioteca Riccardiana, Florence [Cod. Ricc. 1813] ... Two of the sheets, xvii and xviii, form a detailed map of our eastern coastline." PAC 157. *PMC*, I, pp. 117–21, pl. 45–57. The atlas, formerly known as the "Riccardiana Homem," is ascribed to Gaspar Viegas by Teixeira da Mota.

Names after Harrisse, *Découverte*, pp. 107, 362, and Prowse, *CM* I, [1491], p. 187.

1541 DESLIENS, NICOLAS
Manuscript world map, signed "faicte à Dieppe par Nicolas Desliens, 1541," in the Sächsische Landesbibliothek, Dresden. The earliest dated example in a series of large world maps drawn by Norman cartographers at or near Dieppe from a Portuguese model and incorporating information from Cartier's first two voyages. Termed by Harrisse "cartes lusitano-françaises." (See below 1547 "Vallard Atlas"). PAC 210. Ganong, pp. 226–9, 331–5.

Names after Harrisse, *Découverte*, p. 204, and Prowse, *CM* I, [2057], p. 233.

1541 MERCATOR, GERARD
"Terrestrial globe, 16.5" in diameter, consisting of twelve engraved gores and two polar caps covering a hollow wooden ball." PAC 211. Ganong, pp. 168–9, 205–6, 245–6.

Names after Harrisse, *Découverte*, p. 141, who notes that the Newfoundland nomenclature, short as it is, indicates very old Portuguese sources which have not yet been recovered.

[1542] [DESCELIERS, PIERRE]
"Manuscript portolan atlas, containing six double-page maps ... in the Pierpont Morgan Library, New York." Unsigned and undated; of Dieppe authorship. PAC 240. Ganong, pp. 229–30.

The ascription of authorship and date was made by Ganong. Names after Prowse, *CM* I, [1346], p. 167.

1542 ROTZ, JEAN
"Boke of Idrography ... made be me Johne Rotz," dedicated to King Henry VIII and dated 1542. Manuscript atlas of twelve charts, in the British Museum (Royal MS. 20. e. IX). PAC 233, 234, 235. *PMC*, V, pp. 139–40, pl. 625. Ganong pp. 221–4, 292–5.

Harrisse, *Découverte*, pp. 206–8, notes that Rotz was a Dieppois in the service of Henry VIII, but the nomenclature is almost entirely Portuguese or translated from Portuguese by a cartographer who did not know the language well, and that the map bears an inscription, but in another hand than Rotz's, "The new fonde londe whar men goeth fisching."

Names after Harrisse, *Découverte*, pp. 207–8, and Prowse, *CM* I, [1344], p. 167.

1542 SANTA CRUZ, ALONSO DE
Nova Verior Et Integra Totius Orbis Descriptio ...
Manuscript world map, signed and dated, in the Royal Library, Stockholm. PAC 232. Ganong, pp. 156–7.

Names after Prowse, *CM* I, [728], pp. 97–9.

[1542–3] "HARLEIAN" MAP
Manuscript world map, unsigned and undated, of Dieppe authorship, in the British Museum (Add. MS. 5413); known as the "Harleian" or "Dauphin" mappe monde. Formerly attributed to Pierre Desceliers; more probably (as suggested by Ganong) the work of Jean Rotz. "Certain names on this map ... first appeared in Cartier's journal of 1542." PAC 241. Ganong, pp. 224–6, 293–5.

Harrisse, *Découverte*, p. 209, notes that the Newfoundland nomenclature is Portuguese, but more comprehensible and complete than in Rotz.

Names after Harrisse, *Découverte*, pp. 209–10, 222, 363, and Prowse, *CM* I, [1345], p. 167.

1544 ALFONSE, JEAN
"Sketch maps in an elaborate manuscript, *Cosmographie*, by the French navigator Jean Alfonse, who accompanied Roberval to Canada in 1541. The manuscript is in the Bibliothèque Nationale, Paris, MS français 676." PAC 261, 264. *PMC*, I, pp. 149–50, pl. 72–73. Ganong, pp. 197–9, 364–80.

Cortesão considers the author, "João Afonso," to have been Portuguese.

Harrisse, *Découverte*, p. 225, notes that the nomenclature is limited, even when the names cited in the descriptive text are added. Prowse, *CM* I, [155], p. 48, states: "These names ... were not taken from a map, but were from Alfonse's knowledge of the coasts."

Names after Harrisse, *Découverte*, pp. 225, 363, and Prowse, *CM* I, [155], pp. 46–8.

1544 CABOT, SEBASTIAN
"Elliptical map of the world ... engraved in copper, probably at Antwerp." Only known copy in the Bibliothèque Nationale, Paris. PAC 259. Ganong, pp. 18–20, 230–2, 335–7.

Harrisse, *Découverte*, p. 209, ascribes the faulty nomenclature to bad readings by Cabot or by the Flemish engraver.

Names after Harrisse, *Découverte*, pp. 205, 364, and Prowse, *CM* I, [2044], p. 231.

1545 SANTA CRUZ, ALONSO DE
"Islario General: Manuscript atlas of 109 maps in the Biblioteca Nacional, Madrid (MS. J. 92) ..." Four maps relate to Canada. PAC 274, 275, 276. Ganong, pp. 52–3, 154–6.

Names after Harrisse, *Découverte*, pp. 118–21, and Prowse, *CM* I, [727], p. 97, from the *Islario* text.

1546 DESCELIERS, PIERRE
Manuscript world map, signed "faictes à Arques par Pierre Desceliers, presb^{re} 1546," in the John Rylands Library, Manchester. A

306 / *Place Names of the Avalon Peninsula*

map of Dieppe type. PAC 293. Ganong, pp. 232–3, 294–5, 328–31.

Harrisse, *Découverte*, pp. 210–1, notes that the nomenclature is uniformly that of the "Harleian" Map [1542–3], but it is less numerous, even if the names on the west coast are included.

Names after Harrisse, *Découverte*, pp. 211–2, 222, from a facsimile in Jomard, *Monuments de la Géographie*, and Prowse, *CM* I, [1347], p. 167.

1546 FREIRE, JOÃO
"Manuscript atlas of seven maps [signed and dated] in [the] Huntington Library, San Marino (HM 35). Map no. 7 relates to Canada." PAC 294. *PMC*, I, pp. 153–4, pl. 75–8.

Names after Harrisse, *Découverte*, p. 241, and Prowse, *CM* I, [1142], pp. 136, 140–1.

1547 "VALLARD ATLAS"
Manuscript atlas of 15 charts, unsigned and undated, with the owner's inscription "Nicolas Vallard de Dieppe 1547," in the Huntington Library, San Marino, California (HM 29). The ninth chart depicts the east coasts of North America. PAC 306. *PMC*, V, pp. 136–9, pl. 621–4. Ganong, pp. 234–5, 337–41.

The origin and authorship of this atlas have been much debated. Teixeira da Mota (in *PMC*, V, 136–9) takes the view, now generally accepted, that the atlas "was very probably drawn by a Portuguese cartographer living in France, possibly the same who, some years earlier [c. 1538], drew the atlas in The Hague," and who thus supplies the missing link between Portuguese cartography and the Dieppe maps.

Harrisse, *Découverte*, p. 228, describes the nomenclature as Portuguese with several Frenchified additions, but Prowse, *CM* I, [71], p. 31, declares that "the names are predominantly Spanish."

Names after Harrisse, *Découverte*, pp. 228–9, from Kohl, *History ... of Maine*, and Prowse, *CM* I, [71], p. 31.

[ABOUT 1550] ["ANONYMOUS PORTUGUESE"]
Manuscript chart of the Atlantic, unsigned and undated, of Portuguese authorship, in the Bodleian Library, Oxford (MS. K1 (111)). *PMC*, I, p. 162, pl. 82.

[ABOUT 1550] "VALLICELLIANA" PLANISPHERE
Manuscript world map, unsigned and undated, of Portuguese authorship, in the Biblioteca Vallicelliana, Rome. *PMC*, I, pp. 157–9, pl. 80.

1550 DESCELIERS, PIERRE
Manuscript world map, signed "faicte A Arques par Pierres Desceliers Pbre: Lan 1550," in the British Museum (Add. MS. 24065). PAC 323. Ganong, pp. 233–4, 243–5.

Harrisse, *Découverte*, p. 230, describes the nomenclature as more complete than in "Vallard" 1547 and to a great extent Frenchified.

Names after Harrisse, *Découverte*, pp. 222, 230, and Prowse, *CM* I, [73] pp. 32–3.

1550 GUTIÉRREZ, DIEGO (the elder)
Manuscript chart of the Atlantic, signed and dated from Seville, in the Bibliothèque Nationale, Paris (Dépôt Rés. 110, p. 1; S.H. Archives no. 2). PAC 324. *BN*, no. 134. Ganong, pp. 395–8.

Names after Harrisse, *Découverte*, pp. 124, 240, and Prowse, *CM* I, [722], pp. 98–9.

[1552–1564] [AGNESE, BATTISTA?]
"Atlas of eighteen maps in the Biblioteca Universitaria, Bologna, Cod. 997. Wagner LXV. These maps do not conform to any of the usual Agnese types, and ... are listed by Wagner as 'doubtful'." PAC 371.

Harrisse, *Découverte*, p. 255, remarks that the nomenclature is short but interesting, containing two names, *Carpont* and *Rognose*, which go back to the earliest times of French explorations but are given here for the first time on a map. A note adds that a manuscript of the first half of the sixteenth century reads: "Soict faict mémoire de la mecque (marque) de mes basteaux et barques que je laisse en la terre neufue au havre de Jehan denys dicte Rongnousi." Bibl. Nat. MS. français, 24 209 recto du dernier f.

Names after Harrisse, *Découverte*, p. 255, and Prowse, *CM* I, [1488], p. 184.

1554 HOMEM, LOPO
Manuscript world map, signed: "Lopo Homē cosmographo caualero fidalgo delrei nosso snōr me fēzē lixboa Era de 1554 Annos," in the Museo di Storia della Scienza, Florence. PAC 385. *PMC*, I, pp. 67–8, pl. 27.

Names after Prowse, *CM* I, [2087], p. 244.

1555 LE TESTU, GUILLAUME (A)
Cosmographie universelle selon Les navigateurs tant anciens que modernes ...
Manuscript atlas of 55 charts, signed and dated from Le Havre, in the Bibliothèque Nationale, Paris. PAC 393–403. Ganong, pp. 398-401. Charts 7 and 9 relate to Newfoundland. Chart 9: "Map showing the coastline between the 13th and the 51st degrees of latitude, including that of Bacaillaux." PAC 403.

Names in PAC 403 after Prowse, *CM* I, [730], pp. 98–9.

1555 LE TESTU, GUILLAUME (B)
Cosmographie universelle ...
As above Chart 7: "Map of the North Atlantic region from the 26th to the 66th degree of latitude, including the coasts of Labrador and Newfoundland." PAC 399.

Names in PAC 399 after Prowse, *CM* I, [2056], p. 232.

1558 HOMEM, DIOGO
Manuscript atlas of nine charts, signed and dated, in the British Museum (Add. MS. 5415A). Charts 4 and 10 are of Canadian interest. No. 10 shows the eastern coast of North America. PAC 423. *PMC*, II, pp. 13–5, pl. 100–8.

Harrisse, *Découverte*, p. 243, notes that the nomenclature is fairly complete without being in all respects free from faulty or unintelligible readings.

Names after Harrisse, *Découverte*, p. 243, Prowse, *CM* I, [2063], p. 244.

1559 HOMEM, ANDRÉ
Universa ac navigabilis totius terrarum orbis descriptio ...
Manuscript world map, signed and dated from Antwerp, in the Bibliothèque Nationale, Paris (Rés. Ge. cc. 2719). PAC 429. *PMC*, II, pp. 69–71, pl. 187–91.

Names after Harrisse, *Découverte*, p. 245, and Prowse, *CM* I, [2093], p. 242.

[ABOUT 1560] [VELHO, BARTOLOMEU]
Manuscript chart of the North Atlantic, of Portuguese authorship, unsigned and undated, in the Bibliothèque Nationale, Paris (Rés. Ge. B 1148. PAC 344. *PMC*, I, p. 165, pl. 84; V, p. 185. The attribution of

authorship and date is by Cortesão.

Harrisse, *Découverte*, p. 233, states that the nomenclature includes a few new names.

Names after Harrisse, *Découverte*, p. 233, and Prowse, *CM* I, [54], p. 27.

1561 GASTALDI, GIACOMO
Tierra Nueva
Map in Ptolemy's *Geografia*, Italian edition by Ruscelli, Venice 1561 (and in later editions to 1574). PAC 462.

Names after Harrisse, *Découverte*, p. 254.

1561 VELHO, BARTOLOMEU
Four manuscript maps constituting a world map, that of the New World being dated 1561, in the Accademia di Belle Arti, Florence. PAC 452. *PMC*, II, pp. 95–101, pl. 202. Harrisse, *Découverte*, pp. 234–6.

1562 GUTIÉRREZ, DIEGO (the younger)
Americae Sive Quartae Orbis Partis Nova Et Exactissima Descriptio (Hieronymous Cock, Antwerp). PAC 461. Ganong, p. 362.

Names after Harrisse, *Découverte*, p. 241, and Prowse, *CM* I, [729], pp. 98–9.

1564 ORTELIUS, ABRAHAM
Nova Totius Terrarum Orbis Iuxta Neotericorum Traditiones Descriptio (Gerard de Jode, Antwerp). PAC 473.

Names after Prowse, *CM* I, [2090], p. 244.

1568 HOMEM, DIOGO
Manuscript atlas of 22 charts, signed "Diegus Homē Cosmographus Lusitanus fecit venettis año apartu virginis 1568," in the Sächsische Landesbibliothek, Dresden (Mscr. F. 59^a). PAC 303. *PMC*, II, pp. 31–2, pl. 128–43.

Names after Prowse, *CM* I, [2074], p. 240.

1569 MERCATOR, GERARD
Nova et aucta orbis terrae descriptio ad usum navigantium emendate accommodata (Gerard Mercator, Duisburg). PAC 507.

Names after Harrisse, *Découverte*, p. 265, and Prowse, *CM* I, [1597], p. 210.

1570 ORTELIUS, ABRAHAM
Americae Sive Novi Orbis, Nova Descriptio. In Ortelius, *Theatrum* (Antwerp 1570). PAC 522. Ganong, pp. 443–4.

Names after Prowse, *CM* I, [1731], p. 198.

1575 THEVET, ANDRÉ
Le Nouveau Monde Descouvert Et Illustre De Nostre Temps or *Quarte Partie Du Monde*. In Thevet, *La Cosmographie universelle* (Paris 1575).

Names after Prowse, *CM* I, [1858], p. 202.

1578 MARTINES, JOAN
"Manuscript atlas of eighteen maps ... [signed and dated from Messina] in the British Museum, Harleian MS 3450 ... No. 15 embraces part of the east coast of North America showing 'Tierra Del Bacalaos'." PAC 593.

Martines's period of activity, represented by 34 maps or atlases, extended from 1556 to 1591 (J. Rey Pastor and E. García Camarero, *La Cartografía mallorquina* (Madrid 1960), pp. 101–18.

Names after Prowse, *CM* I, [1486], p. 181.

1580 DEE, JOHN
"Manuscript map, on a ... polar projection, comprising North America, and the Atlantic north of the equator, [signed and dated] ... in the British Museum (Add. MS. 5414)." PAC 603.

John Dee (1527–1608), the cele-

brated astrologer, wrote several works on navigation.
Names after Harrisse, *Découverte*, p. 302, and Prowse, *CM* I, [2094], p. 244.

1580 VAZ DOURADO, FERNÃO
Manuscript atlas of 12 charts, signed and dated, in the Bayerische Staatsbibliothek, Munich (cod. icon. 137). Map no. 4 relates to Canada. PAC 604. *PMC*, III, pp. 27–8, pl. 314–28. *PMC* describes six atlases by or attributed to Vaz Dourado, 1568–80.
Names after Harrisse, *Découverte*, p. 247.

1581 POSTEL, GUILLAUME
Pola aptata nova charta universi
Woodcut world map, published at Paris by Jean de Gourmont, 1581; republished from the same blocks, but with French legends substituted for Latin, by Denis de Mathonière, 1586, and by Nicolas de Mathonière, 1621.
Names (from the 1621 edition) after Prowse, *CM* I, [2091], p. 242.

[ABOUT 1583] [LOPES SEBASTIÃO?]
Manuscript planisphere, of Portuguese authorship, unsigned and undated, in the Bibliothèque Nationale, Paris (Dépôt Rés. 1.0.4; S.H. Archives no. 38). PAC 342. *PMC*, IV, pp. 17–21, pl. 408. *BN*, no. 136. Ganong, pp. 401–3, 495. The attribution of authorship and date is by Cortesão.
Styled "Carte Portugaise du Dépôt" by Harrisse, p. 234, who notes that the nomenclature is numerous and interesting, though it reproduces in a servile fashion certain names which must have been as incomprehensible to the Portuguese cartographer as they are to us.
Names after Harrisse, *Découverte*, p. 234, and Prowse, *CM* I, [76], p. 33.

1583 MARTINES, JOAN
"Manuscript atlas of seven maps ... known as the "Miller Martines," in the Bibliothèque Nationale, Paris. Map 1 is an oval map of the world; map 2 is of the North Atlantic region; and map 4 is of North America from 60° N to 7° s latitude." PAC 628. *BN*, no. 47. See above 1578 Martines, Joan.
Names after Harrisse, *Découverte*, p. 259, and Prowse, *CM* I, [1861], p. 202.

1592 HOOD, THOMAS
"Manuscript map in the British Museum (Add. MS. 17938). This map is neither signed nor dated, but according to Harrisse its relationship to ... [a manuscript map found in the Dudley manuscript atlas, in the Bayerische Staatsbibliothek, Munich, with the inscription: 'Thomas Hood made this platte, 1592'] is obvious." PAC 696. Ganong, pp. 442–3.
Names after Harrisse, *Découverte*, p. 304, and Prowse, *CM* I, [79], p. 35.

1592 PLANCIUS, PETRUS
Nova et exacta terrarum orbis tabula geographica ac hydrographica
(Cornelis Claesz, Amsterdam). PAC 691.
Plancius's representation of North America is derived from a manuscript Portuguese chart by Bartholomeu Lasso, 1590 (*PMC*, III, pl. 370).
Names after Prowse, *CM* I, [825], pp. 107–8.

1593 JODE, CORNELIS DE
Americae Pars Borealis, Florida, Baccalaos, Canada, Corterealis. In De Jode, *Speculum Orbis Terrae* (Antwerp 1593). PAC 707.
Names after Prowse, *CM* I, [1864], p. 210.

310 / *Place Names of the Avalon Peninsula*

1595 MERCATOR, MICHAEL
Americae sive India Nova. In Mercator's *Atlas* (Duisburg 1595). PAC 644.
  Names after Prowse, *CM* I, [1616], p. 194.

1596 SANCHES, CIPRIANO
Manuscript chart of the Atlantic, signed and dated, in the British Museum (Cotton Roll XIII. 46). *PMC*, III, p. 109, pl. 387.

1597 WYTFLIET, CORNELIUS
Nova Francia et Canada. In Wytfliet, *Descriptionis Ptolemaicae Augmentum* (Louvain 1597). PAC 749.
  Names after Prowse, *CM* I, [1873], p. 210.

1598 LANGENES, BARENT
Terra Nova, &c. Map in *Caertthresoor* ... , Middelburg, Barent Langenes, 1598, and in subsequent editions to 1618, with text by Petrus Bertius. PAC 815. Derived, through a map by Plancius engraved by Jan van Dentecum c. 1592–4, from Lasso's map of 1590 (*PMC*, III, pl. 370, 381A). See above 1592 Plancius, Petrus.
  Harrisse, *Découverte*, p. 283, notes that this is the first map devoted exclusively to Newfoundland and shows a nomenclature and details of the coast remarkable for the period.
  Names after Harrisse, *Découverte*, pp. 283–4.

1599 DIRCKX, JAN
Manuscript chart of the North Atlantic, embracing the Gulf of St. Lawrence region, signed and dated from Edam, in the Bibliothèque Nationale, Paris (Dépôt Rés. 116, p. 5; S.H. Archives no. 4). PAC 784. *BN*, no. 137.
  Names after Harrisse, *Découverte*, pp. 282–3, who observes that the nomenclature is corrupted Portuguese without a trace of French names, and Prowse, *CM* I, [1194], pp. 143, 146–7.

1601 LE VASSEUR, GUILLAUME
Manuscript chart of the Atlantic, signed and dated from Dieppe, in the Bibliothèque Nationale, Paris (Dépôt Rés. 116.0.6; S.H. Archives no. 5). *BN*, no. 138.
  Names after Harrisse, *Découverte*, p. 292, and Prowse, *CM* I, [855], pp. 109–10.

[1606–8] "THE VIRGINIA COMPANY CHART"
Manuscript chart of the Atlantic, by an English cartographer, unsigned and undated, in the Phelps-Stokes Collection, New York Public Library. Facsimile in Phelps-Stokes, *Iconography of Manhattan Island*, VOL. II, pl. 21A.
  Names after Prowse, *CM* I, [1938], p. 218.

1607 HONDIUS, "ATLAS MINOR"
America noviter delineata.
  Map by Jodocus Hondius in various Amsterdam editions of his *Atlas Minor* from 1607 to 1621; subsequently published in *Purchas His Pilgrimes* (London 1625), and in *Historia Mundi* or *Mercator's Atlas* (London 1635).
  Names after Prowse, *CM* I, [946], pp. 115–7.

1608 HONDIUS, JODOCUS
Nova et exacta totius orbis terrarum descriptio geographica et hydrographica
  Engraved map in 12 sheets. Unique copy is in the Royal Geographical Society, London.
  Names after Prowse, *CM* I, [731], p. 100.

1609 LESCARBOT, MARC
Figure de la Terre Neuve ... In
Lescarbot, *Histoire de la Novelle
France* (Paris 1609).
Names after Prowse, *CM* I, [1932],
p. 217.

[1610] "VELASCO" MAP
Anonymous English manuscript
chart of the east coast of North
America from Cape Fear to Newfoundland, drawn in colours on four
sheets of paper pasted together, in
the Archivo General de Simancas,
Estado.
Don Alonso
de Velasco, Spanish Ambassador in
London, to the King of Spain, together with a letter in cipher dated
22 March, 1611. In this letter Velasco
calls it a copy of the English province
in America, presented to King James
by a surveyor sent out by the English
King, in the preceding year, to survey
that province, and adds that it contains all that could be discovered by
this surveyor, who had returned
three months before Velasco wrote
the letter. The surveyor has not been
identified, though Prowse ascribes
the map to John Daniel. According
to Prowse, it is known variously as
the Virginian, Velasco or Simancas
map. (Communication from T. E.
Layng, PAC.)
Names after Prowse, *CM* I, [167],
p. 53.

1610 JANSZ, HARMEN and MARTEN
*Nova orbis terrarum geografica ac
hydrogr. tabula* ...
Manuscript planisphere, signed
and dated from Edam, in the Bibliothèque Nationale, Paris (Rés. Ge. A.
1048). *BN*, no. 66. Phelps-Stokes,
Iconography of Manhattan Island,
p. 38.
Names after Prowse, *CM* I, [856],
pp. 110, 116–7.

Bibliography: Maps, Charts, and Atlases / 311

1611 HONDIUS, JODOCUS
*Nova et exactissima totius orbis
terrarum descriptio* ...
Reproduced in facsimile by E. L.
Stevenson and J. Fischer (New York
1907), from the unique copy in
Schloss Wolfegg, Wurtemberg.
Names after Prowse, *CM* I, [860],
p. 112.

1612 CHAMPLAIN, SAMUEL DE
*Carte géographique de la Novvelle
France* ... 1612. Map in *Les Voyages
dv sievr de Champlain Xaintongeois*
(Paris 1613).
Harrisse, *Découverte*, p. 294, notes
that the nomenclature contains
numerous French names, but that
they are as unintelligible as badly
spelled.
Names after Harrisse, *Découverte*,
p. 294, and Prowse, *CM* I, [961],
pp. 122, 124–5.

1613 OLIVA, JOAN
Chart of the Atlantic in a manuscript
atlas in the British Museum (Egerton
MS 819), signed "Joannes Oliva fecit
in civitate Marsiliae, Año 1613."
Names after Prowse, *CM* I,
[1213], pp. 143, 146.

1613 VAULX, PIERRE DE
Manuscript chart of the Atlantic,
signed "Ceste carte a Este faiste Au
havre de Grace par Pierre deuaulx.
Pilote Geographe pour le Roy lan
1613," in the Bibliothèque Nationale, Paris (Dépôt Rés. 116, p. 7;
S. H. Archives no. 6). *BN*, no. 139.
Names after Prowse, *CM* I, [106],
p. 40.

1618 SANCHES, DOMINGOS
Manuscript chart of the Atlantic in
the Bibliothèque Nationale, Paris
(Rés. Ge. AA. 568). *PMC*, v, p. 15,
pl. 526.

Prowse, *CM* I, p. 49, believes it to be the latest map to give *Tera dos Cortereas* on the Nova Scotia-New England coast.

Names after Prowse, *CM* I, [1224], pp. 149-50.

1623 SANCHES, ANTÓNIO
Manuscript world map, signed and dated, in the British Museum (Add. MS. 22874). *PMC*, V, pp. 17-8, pl. 527A.

Names after Prowse, *CM* I, [1229], pp. 149-50.

1625 BRIGGS, HENRY
The North Part of America conteyning Newfoundland.
The map was published in Lib. IV, Chap. XX, of *Purchas His Pilgrimes* (London 1625), entitled "A brief discourse of the probabilitie of a passage to the Westerne or South Sea, illustrated with testimonies and a brief Treatise and Mappe by Master Briggs."

Names after Harrisse, *Découverte*, p. 306, and Prowse, *CM* I, [169], p. 53.

1625 DUPONT, JEAN
Manuscript chart of the Atlantic, signed and dated from Dieppe, in the Bibliothèque Nationale, Paris (Dépôt Res. 116, p. 8; S. H. Archives no. 9). *BN*, no. 143.

Names after Prowse, *CM* I, [948], pp. 118-9.

1625 GUÉRARD, JEAN
Novvelle description hydrographique de tout le monde.
Manuscript planisphere, signed and dated from Dieppe, in the Bibliothèque Nationale, Paris (Dépôt Rés. 1.0.4; S. H. Archives no. 10). *BN*, no. 144.

Names after Prowse, *CM* I, [949], p. 119.

1625 LAET, J. DE
Nieuwe Wereldt, ofte Beschrijvinghe van West-Indien.
Since of the ten maps in this (the first) edition, none shows Newfoundland, Prowse took his names from the text of the work, which has a chapter on Nova Francia.

Names after Prowse, *CM* I, [205], p. 57.

[1625] LANGREN, HENDRIK VAN
A large engraved terrestrial globe in the Bibliothèque Nationale, Paris. Phelps-Stokes, *Iconography of Manhattan Island*, II, p. 139.

Names after Prowse, *CM* I, [864], pp. 113, 116-7.

1626 MASON, JOHN
Insula olim vocata Noua: Terrae. The Iland called of olde: Newfovnd. land. described by Captaine Iohn Mason an industrious Gent: who spent seuen yeares in the Countrey.
Map in Sir William Vaughan, *The Golden Fleece* (London, 1626).

Mason was governor of Newfoundland from 1615 to 1621.

Harrisse, *Découverte*, p. 308, notes that, up to this date, no map of Newfoundland had contained so many names, either English or translated from the French.

Names collated with Harrisse, *Découverte*, p. 308, and Prowse, *CM* I, [2060], p. 236.

1626 SPEED, JOHN
America with those known parts in that unknowne world ... Ano 1626.
Published in Speed, *A Prospect of the most Famous Parts of the World* (London 1627). Reprinted in later editions up to 1676.

Names after Prowse, *CM* I, [174], p. 68.

[ABOUT 1630] BLAEU, WILLEM JANSZOON
West Indische Paskaert ...
Engraved chart of the Atlantic. Copies, with content substantially unchanged, were engraved for other Amsterdam publishers c. 1640–90. Harrisse, *Découverte*, pp. 284–6, describes the copy published by Anthony Jacobsz, c. 1650, to which (following his source) he ascribes the incorrect date 1621.

Harrisse, p. 284–5, notes that the nomenclature is essentially French and contains some new names. He also notes the occurrence of names that are wholly English and others that are composed of both French and English elements. These last are the first of the kind that he has encountered.

Names after Harrisse, *Découverte*, pp. 285–6, and Prowse, CM I, [1963], pp. 324–5.

[ABOUT 1630–40] "BLATHWAYT"
Manuscript map of English authorship, unsigned and undated; no. 7 in a collection of maps known as the "Blathwayt Atlas," in the John Carter Brown Library, Providence, R.I. The atlas was assembled between 1680 and 1685 "as a reference atlas for the Office of Trade and Plantations," of which William Blathwayt was then secretary.

Names after Prowse, CM I, [48], p. 24.

1630 LAET, JAN DE
Nova Francia et regiones adiacentes. Map in *Beschrijvinghe van West-Indien ... IIe druk* (Leiden 1630); also in *Novus Orbis* (Leiden 1633), and *L'Histoire du Nouveau Monde* (Leiden 1640).

Names after Prowse, CM I, [205], pp. 60–1.

1631 AERTSZ
Map in the Bibliothèque Nationale, Paris (S.H. 116.0.9).
Names after Prowse, CM I, [956], p. 121.

1631 GUÉRARD, JEAN
Manuscript chart of the Atlantic, signed and dated from Dieppe, in the Bibliothèque Nationale, Paris (Dépôt Rés. 116, p. 10; S.H. Archives no. 14). BN, no. 148.
Names after Prowse, CM I, [2058], p. 234.

1632 CHAMPLAIN, SAMUEL DE
Carte de la nouuelle france. Map in *Les Voyages de la Novvelle France Occidentale, dicte Canada, faits par le Sr. de Champlain ...* (Paris 1632). Harrisse, *Découverte*, p. 298, notes that the nomenclature of Newfoundland in this map differs little from that adopted by Champlain in 1612, except in the spelling, number, and position of the names [!]

Names after Harrisse, *Découverte*, p. 298, and Prowse, CM I, [973], pp. 123–5.

1636 JANSSON, JAN
America Septentrionalis.
First published in the *Atlas Novus* of Jansson and Henricus Hondius, Latin edition (Amsterdam 1636); republished in editions of the *Atlas Novus* and of Jansson's *Atlas Major* to 1658.

Names after Prowse, CM I, [2021], pp. 224–5.

1646 DUDLEY, Sir ROBERT
Terra Nova.
Map engraved by Antonio Lucini in Robert Dudley, *Dell'Arcano del Mare* (Florence 1646–7). Phelps-Stokes, *Iconography of Manhattan Island*, II, pp. 145–7.

Harrisse, *Découverte*, p. 310, notes that the nomenclature is an amalgam of French and Italianized English names.

Names after Harrisse, *Découverte*, p. 310, and Prowse, *CM* I, [1928], p. 214.

[1648] BLAEU, JOAN
Nova totius terrarum orbis tabula, Amsterdam, Joan Blaeu.

Large hemispheric world map, with dedication to Gasparo de Bracamonte e Guzman, Spanish plenipotentiary to the Peace Congress at Münster in 1648.

Names after Prowse, *CM* I, [905], p. 114.

1650 OLIVA, FRANCISCO (A)
Manuscript atlas of five charts, signed and dated from Marseille, in the British Museum (Add. MS 17276). Chart 1: the North Atlantic.

Names after Prowse, *CM* I, [1231], p. 151.

1650 OLIVA, FRANCISCO (B)
As above. Chart 2: North America.

Names after Prowse, *CM* I, [1235], p. 152.

1652 SEILE, HENRY
Americae nova descriptio. Will. Trevethen sculp. In Peter Heylyn, *Cosmographie* (London 1652).

Names after Prowse, *CM* I, [173], p. 68.

1656 SANSON, NICOLAS
Le Canada, ou Nouvelle France, &c. (Pierre Mariette, Paris).

1659 BLAEU, JOAN
America Septentrionalis. (Joan Blaeu, Amsterdam).

Large engraved map on six sheets with marginal descriptive text. Copies are in the British Museum and Bibliothèque Nationale, Paris.

Names after Prowse, *CM* I, [1939], pp. 224–5.

1659 PETAVIUS, DIONYSIUS
A New and Accurate Map of the World. World map in *The History of the World* (London 1659).

Names after Prowse, *CM* I, [2024], pp. 224–5.

1662 BLAEU, JOAN
Extrema Americae versus Boream, ubi Terra Nova, Nova Francia, adjacentiaque. Map in *Atlas Maior*, vol. XI (Amsterdam 1662).

Names after Prowse, *CM* I, [995], pp. 123–5.

1667 DONCKER, HENDRIK
Pas Caert van Terra Nova.

Chart in *L'Atlas de Mer ou Monde aquatique, remontrant toutes les costes de la mer* (Amsterdam 1667).

Names after Prowse, *CM* I, [121], p. 41.

1667 TEIXEIRA ALBERNAZ, JOÃO (II)
Manuscript planisphere, signed and dated, in the Bibliothèque Nationale, Paris (Dépôt Res. 116, p. 11; S.H. Archives no. 18). *BN*, no. 154. *PMC*, V, p. 33, pl. 548.

Names after Prowse, *CM* I, [1230], pp. 149–50.

1668 LOON, JOHANNES VAN
Pas-caerte van Terra Nova ...

Chart in *Klaer lichtende Noortster ofte Zeeatlas* (Amsterdam 1668).

[ABOUT 1669] VISSCHER, NICOLAES
America quarta pars orbis ...
Map in the Bibliothèque Nationale, Paris, (Cartes C5150).

Names after Prowse, *CM* I, [857], pp. 111, 116–7.

1669 BLOME, RICHARD
A New Mapp of America Septentrionale... Designed by M. Sanson...

and rendred into English... by
Richard Blome... Francis Lamb sculp.
... 1669.
Dedicated to the "Rt. Hon.
Caecilius Calvert, Baron Baltemore ...
absolute Lord and Proprietor of the
Provinces of Maryland and Avalon,"
and published in R. Blome, A Geographical Description of the Four
Parts of the World (London 1670).
Names after Prowse, CM I, [2034],
p. 227.

1669 BOISSAIE LE BOCAGE
Manuscript chart of the North
Atlantic by Boissaie Le Bocage,
"Idrographe et Professeur Roial en
la nauigation du haure de Grace,"
1669, in the Bibliothèque Nationale,
Paris (Dépôt Res. 116.0.12).
Names after Harrisse, Découverte,
p. 321, and Prowse, CM I, [44], p. 23.

1669 ROBINSON, ROBERT
The Province of Avalonia.
Manuscript map bearing the
inscription: "An exact Mapp of
Newfound-Land soe far as the
English and French Fishing trade is
concerned. By Capt. Robert Robinson. Anno Dom: 1669," in the
Bodleian Library (MS Rawlinson
A 183, [f. 101]).
Names after Prowse, CM I, [2574],
pp. 311–2.

1671 OGILBY, JOHN
Novissima et accuratissima totius
Americae descriptio ... F. Lamb sculp.
Engraved map, dedicated to
Anthony, Lord Ashley, and issued in
Ogilby, America (London 1671).
Names after Prowse, CM I, [2662],
p. 293.

[ABOUT 1671] SELLER, JOHN
A Chart of the Northerne Sea.
Included in a preliminary version
of The English Pilot. The Fourth
Book, printed for Seller about 1671
(British Museum, Maps 22.d.2).
Names after Prowse, CM I, [2672],
pp. 294–6.

1671 SELLER, JOHN
A Chart of the Coast of America
from New found land to Cape Cod.
In Seller, The English Pilot. The
Fourth Book (London 1671).
Names after Harrisse, Découverte,
p. 310, and Prowse, CM I, [2670],
p. 294.

1674 ROTIS, DENIS DE
Manuscript chart of the North
Atlantic, "Faict à Saint Jean de luz
par moi Denis de Rotis, 1674," in
the Bibliothèque Nationale, Paris
(Dépôt Rés. 116, p. 19; S.H.
Archives no. 21). BN, no. 155.
Harrisse, Découverte, p. 316, notes
that the nomenclature contains
several unintelligible and badly
spelled names. It may be added that
some are of Basque origin.
Names after Harrisse, Découverte,
p. 316, and Prowse, CM I, [2100],
pp. 248–51.

1675 COURCELLE, Sieur DE
Manuscript chart of Newfoundland
and Labrador, "Faite à Breste le 14^e
janvier 1676 par le Sr de Courcelle,
lieutenant de vaisseau du Roy entretenue en la marine ayant fait le tour
de lille de Terre neufue et Niganisse
l'este de l'année 1675", in the Bibliothèque Nationale, Paris (Dépôt Rés.
128.2.1; S.H. Archives no. 23). BN,
no. 157.
Harrisse, Découverte, p. 319, notes
that the nomenclature is not the
work of a pilot or cartographer more
or less illiterate, but of an officer of
the [French] Royal Navy. He adds
that, indeed, many of the designations are spelled in a singular and
unintelligible manner, but that was

the custom.
　Names after Harrisse, *Découverte*, p. 319, and Prowse, *CM* 1, [2096], pp. 248–51.

1675 ROGGEVEEN, ARENT
Pascaert van Terra Nova, Nova Francia, Neiuvw Engeland en de groote revier van Canada.
　Chart in Roggeveen, *Het eerste deel van het Brandende Veen, verlichtende alle de vaite kusten ende eylanden van geheel West-Indien ofte rio Amasones ...* (Amsterdam [1675]).
　Names after Prowse, *CM* 1, [136], p. 42.

1675 SOUTHWOOD, HENRY
The Coast of Newfoundland from Salmon Cove to Cape Bonavista. The Coast of Newfoundland from Cape Raze to Cape St. Francis. Described by Henry Southwood Anno 1675. Ia. Clark sculp.
　Two sectional charts, from different plates, mounted together. The charts were reprinted, with the date erased, in editions of *The English Pilot. The Fourth Book*, 1716 to 1749. Prowse, *CM* 1, p. 297, notes that the names correspond practically with those in Thornton, *Trading Part of Newfoundland*, 1689. Thornton, however, has a number of names not recorded by Harrisse for Southwood.
　Names after Harrisse, *Découverte*, pp. 312–3, and Prowse, *CM* 1, [2689], p. 297.

[1677?] HACK, WILLIAM
Terra Nova.
　Manuscript chart in the British Museum (Add. MS 13972).
　Names after Prowse, *CM* 1, [2752], pp. 310–1.

1678 BOISSAIE LE BOCAGE
Partie de terre neuue.

Manuscript chart in the Ministère des Affaires Étrangères, Paris.
　Names after Harrisse, *Découverte*, p. 322, and Prowse, *CM* 1, [1013], pp. 127–8.

[ABOUT 1680] "BM Add. MS 5414.2"
Manuscript map of the Northern Hemisphere, on a spherical projection, 3 feet 8 inches in diameter, drawn on vellum.
　Names after Prowse, *CM* 1, [183], p. 68.

[ABOUT 1680] "DÉPÔT HYDROGRAPHIQUE DE LA MARINE 128.2.6"
One of the several manuscript maps in Portfolio 128 hitherto undescribed. Now in the Bibliothèque Nationale, Paris (Dépôt Res. 128.2.6).
　Names after Prowse, *CM* 1, [2101], pp. 253–4.

[ABOUT 1680] VISSCHER, NICOLAES
Carte Nouvelle contenant la Partie d'Amerique la plus Septentrionale ... et l'ile de Terre Neuve ...
　Prowse *CM* 1, pp. 303–6, dates this map about 1690.
　Names collated with Prowse, *CM* 1, [2718], pp. 303–6.

1681 FRANQUELIN, JEAN-BAPTISTE LOUIS
Carte de la Nouvelle France et des Terres qui s'estendent depuis 44 jusqu'à 61 degrez de Latitude.
　Map in the Bibliothèque Nationale, Paris (Dépôt Res. 125.1.3).
　Names after Harrisse, *Découverte*, p. 330, and Prowse, *CM* 1, [290], p. 69.

[ABOUT 1682] "LA BELLE CARTE DU DÉPÔT"
Carte de l'Amérique septentrionale ...
　Manuscript map, unsigned and undated, in the Dépôt Hydrographique de la Marine, known to

Harrisse as *La Belle Carte du Dépôt*. Now in the Bibliothèque Nationale, Paris.

Harrisse, *Notes sur la Nouvelle France*, no. 219, states that the map has no author's name and no date, but is evidently the work of a French cartographer and of a date before 1682.

Names after Harrisse, *Découverte*, p. 337, and Prowse, *CM* I, [1937], p. 217.

1682–4 KEULEN, JOHANNES VAN
Pas-Kaart, vande Zee-Kusten, van Terra Nova.

Chart published in van Keulen, *Zee Atlas*, Amsterdam, 1682–4.

1687 ALEMAND, PIERRE
Cartes des costes de l'Amérique septentrionale et des terres nouvellement découvertes.

Manuscript chart in the Bibliothèque Nationale, Paris (Dépôt 124.1.1.).

Names after Harrisse, *Découverte*, pp. 339–40, and Prowse, *CM* I, [144], p. 43.

1688 FRANQUELIN, JEAN-BAPTISTE LOUIS
Carte de l'Amerique Septentrion ...

Manuscript map in Bibliothèque Nationale, Paris (Dépôt Res. 4040.10).

Prowse dates the map 1699.
Names after Prowse, *CM* I, [405], pp. 77–8.

1689 CORONELLI-TILLEMON
Partie orientale du Canada ... Dressée sur les Mémoires les plus nouveaux par Coronelli ... Corrigée et augmentée Par le Sr Tillemon ... (Nolin, Paris 1689).

Names after Harrisse, *Découverte*, p. 338, and Prowse, *CM* I, [212], p. 58.

1689 CORONELLI, V. M.
Tera nuova.

Map in the Bibliothèque Nationale, Paris, CPf 202 (5335).
Names after Prowse, *CM* I, [210], pp. 60–1.

1689 DETCHEVERRY, PIERRE
Carte Basque de l'Isle de Terre-Neuve ...

Manuscript chart, "Faix a plaisance par pierre detcheuerry dorre de St. Jan de luz pour monsr Parat gouuerneur de plaisance et lisle de Terre Neufe," in the Bibliothèque Nationale, Paris (Dépôt 128.2.3). A copy on vellum (Dépôt 125.1.2) reproduced by Harrisse, *Découverte*, pl. XXIV.

Harrisse, *Découverte*, p. 324, notes that the nomenclature is unusual and often unintelligible. It may be added that some of the forms are Basque.

Names after Harrisse, *Découverte*, pp. 324–5, and Prowse *CM* I, [2097], pp. 248–51.

1689 THORNTON, JOHN (A)
A New Chart of the Sea Coast of Newfoundland, Nova Scotia ... In *The English Pilot. The Fourth Book* (W. Fisher and J. Thornton, London 1689). Also in later editions to 1706.

Names after Prowse, *CM* I, [2074], p. 299.

1689 THORNTON, JOHN (B)
A New Chart of the Trading Part of Newfoundland. In *The English Pilot. The Fourth Book* [London 1689 (as above)], with inset plan of St. John's. Also in later editions to 1706.

Names after Prowse, *CM* I, [2705], pp. 299–300.

1689 THORNTON, JOHN (C)
Harbour Grace. Plan in *The English Pilot. The Fourth Book* [London 1689 (as above)]. Also in later editions to 1760.

1689 THORNTON, JOHN (D)
Bay Bulls. Plan in *The English Pilot. The Fourth Book.* [London 1689 (as above)]. Also in later editions to 1760.

[ABOUT 1690?] HACK, WILLIAM
A Description of Coasts Islands &c. in the North Sea of America vizt Newfoundland ...
Manuscript atlas of 39 charts of the Atlantic coasts of North America and the West Indies, including one of Newfoundland, in the British Museum (K. Mar. VII.3).

1693 FITZHUGH, AUGUSTINE
Manuscript chart of Newfoundland, signed and dated from London, in the British Museum (Add. MS. 5414.30).
Harrisse, *Découverte,* pp. 313–4, notes that the nomenclature is exclusively English and very numerous, but only from Bonavista Bay to Cape Race. This is explained by the fact that the purpose of the map was to show the fishing districts exploited by fishermen. It is for this reason that the whole of the eastern coast, between 45° 30' and 48° 30', as well as the Grand Banks, is decorated with numerous fishing boats. Several men-of-war are to be seen in echelon from Cape Race to Placentia.
Names from the reproduction of the map in Harrisse, *Découverte,* Plate 22, facing p. 314, and after Prowse, *CM* I, [2748], pp. 310–1.

1695 L'HERMITE, Sieur
Carte de Terre-Neuve depuis le cap de Bonavista jusqu'à Plaisance ...
Manuscript chart in the Bibliothèque Nationale, Paris (Dépôt 128.3.1).
Harrisse, *Découverte,* p. 340, notes that L'Hermite was major at Placentia in 1695. The map is a copy of Southwood 1675 from which L'Hermite also took the nomenclature.
Names after Harrisse, *Découverte,* pp. 340–1.

1696 LE CORDIER, SIMON
Carte de la baye de Canadas, de la Riviere de Kebec, du banc de Terreneuue, et autre haures, rades et batures où se fait d'ordinaire la pêche des Morües ...
Engraved map published at Havre de Grace, 1696.
Names after Harrisse, *Découverte,* pp. 341–2, and Prowse, *CM* I, [147], p. 43.

1698 CHAVITEAU, JACQUES
Carte de l'Isle de Terre Nevue [sic].
Manuscript chart in the Bibliothèque Nationale, Paris (Dépôt 128.2.2).
Harrisse, *Découverte,* p. 344, notes that the nomenclature is in a relatively intelligible orthography and contains a number of new names.
Names after Harrisse, *Découverte,* pp. 344–5, and Prowse, *CM* I, [2102], pp. 254–5.

1699 VION, BLAISE
Carte particulière des costes de L'île de Terre-Neuve...
Manuscript chart in the Bibliothèque Nationale, Paris (Dépôt 128.3.2).
Harrisse, *Découverte,* p. 345, notes that Vion, like L'Hermite 1695, borrowed his nomenclature from Southwood 1675.
Names after Harrisse, *Découverte,* pp. 345–6, and Prowse, *CM* I, [2717], p. 301.

1699 FRANQUELIN, JEAN-BAPTISTE LOUIS
Partie de L'Amérique Septentrionale.
Manuscript map (copies after Franquelin's death), in the Bibliothèque Nationale, Paris (Dépôt 4040-12).

Harrisse, *Découverte*, p. 333, notes that the nomenclature is numerous, with some new names.
Names after Harrisse, *Découverte*, p. 334, and Prowse, *CM* I, [408], pp. 77–8.

1706 "DÉPÔT HYDROGRAPHIQUE DE LA MARINE 132.2.10"
Carte de la coste de la Cadie De Baston et Partie De Terre Neuve.
Manuscript chart, unsigned, in the Bibliothèque Nationale, Paris (Dépôt 132.2.10).
Names after Prowse, *CM* I, [2098], pp. 249–51.

1708 FRANQUELIN, JEAN-BAPTISTE LOUIS
Carte Générale de la Nouvelle France dans l'Amérique Septentrionale.
Manuscript map in the Bibliothèque Nationale, Paris.
Names after Prowse, *CM* I, [409], pp. 76–8.

1709 MOLL, HERMAN
A New Map of Newfoundland ... In *Atlas Manuale* (London 1709).

1711 DECOUAGNE, —
Carte du Canada ...
Manuscript chart, signed and dated, in the Bibliothèque Nationale, Paris (Dépôt 124.1.2).
Names after Prowse, *CM* I, [2103], p. 255.

1711 [after MOLL]
Chart of the Coast of Newfoundland ...
Manuscript map in the British Museum (Add. MS. 33231 HH).
Names after Prowse, *CM* I, [2854], pp. 321–4.

[AFTER 1711] "ANONYMOUS ANGLO-GERMAN"
A New Fovndland od. Terra Nova ...
Engraved coloured map in the Bibliothèque Nationale, Paris (Dépôt 125.1.7).
Harrisse, *Découverte*, p. 289, notes that although the map was made for the use of English sailors, as may be seen from the English versions of most of the names, it is, despite its [German] title, the work of a Dutch cartographer.
Names after Harrisse, *Découverte*, p. 290.

[ABOUT 1712] MOLL, HERMAN
North America according to ye Newest and most Exact Observations. B. Lens delin. G. Vertue sculp.
Names after Prowse, *CM* I, [2792], pp. 314–5.

1713 FRIEND, JOHN
A chart of Newfoundland ... by I^{no}. Friend Hydrographer. (British Museum, Maps 13.e.8.(36)).
Names after Prowse, *CM* I, [2062], p. 238.

1715 GAUDY, JOHN
A Chart Shewing Part of the Sea Coast of Newfoundland from ye Bay of Bulls to little Placentia exactly and Carefully lay'd down by John Gaudy 1715. S. Parker sc.
In *The English Pilot. The Fourth Book* (Mount and Page, London 1716). Also in later editions to 1778.
This appears to be the same chart as listed in Prowse, *CM* I, [2685], p. 297, though Prowse's item bears the date c. 1750.

1715 MOLL, HERMAN
A New and Exact Map of the Dominions of the King of Great Britain on ye Continent of North America containing Newfoundland...
Names after Prowse, *CM* I, [2809], pp. 321–4.

1725 DU COULOMBIER, —
Manuscript chart, signed and dated, in the Bibliothèque Nationale, Paris (Dépôt 128.4.4).
Names after Prowse, CM I, [2105], p. 256.

1727 VERRIER Fils
Carte de l'île Royale et des principaux caps de l'île de Terre Neuve
Map in the Bibliothèque Nationale, Paris (Cartes c. 3713).
Names after Prowse, CM I, [2322], p. 270.

1728 SENEX, JOHN
The Coast of Newfoundland from Placentia to Cape Bonavista.
Map no. 50 in Atlas maritimus & commercialis ... (London 1728).

1729 MOLL, HERMAN
Newfoundland St Laurence Bay, The Fishing Banks ... In Moll, Atlas Minor ... (London 1729).

1733 MAUREPAS, Comte DE
Manuscript chart of Newfoundland in the Bibliothèque Nationale, Paris (Dépôt 128.2.7).
Names after Prowse, CM I, [2208], pp. 261–2.

1733 POPPLE, HENRY
A Map of the British Empire in America, With the French and Spanish Settlements adjacent thereto. W. H. Toms sculp. (London).
Names after Prowse, CM I, [2895], pp. 321–4.

1735 PELEGRIN, G.
A Chart of the Streights of Belisle. Taken ... in the Year 1735.
Manuscript chart in the British Admiralty, Hydrographic Department (B 5804).

1736 BUACHE, PHILIPPE
Carte des cotes meridionales de l'isle de Terre Neuve ...
Names collated with Prowse, CM I, [2166], p. 260.

[1744] SEALE, R. W.
A Map of North America. In P. Rapin, The History of England. Continued by N. Tindal, Vol. III (London 1744).
Names after Prowse, CM I, [2378], p. 274.

1744 BELLIN, JACQUES NICOLAS
Carte de l'Isle de Terre-Neuve. In P. F. X. de Charlevoix, Histoire et Description de la Nouvelle France, vol. IV (Paris 1744).
Names after Prowse, CM I, [2112], p. 267, and [2272], pp. 265–6.

[1747] BOWEN, EMANUEL
A New & Accurate Map of the Islands of Newfoundland, Cape Briton ... In Bowen, A Complete System of Geography, vol. II (London 1747); republished in A Complete Atlas (London 1752).

1749 ROBERT DE VAUGONDY, GILLES
Isle de Terre-Neuve Par le S^r. Robert de Vaugondy Fils de M^R. Robert Geog ord. du Roi Avec Privilege. 1749.

1754 BELLIN, JACQUES NICOLAS
Carte Réduite du Golphe de St Laurent Contenant l'Isle de Terre Neuve ... MDCCLIV. In Bellin, Hydrographie Française (Paris 1737–76).

1755 [MOUNT and PAGE]
A New and Correct Chart of the Coast of New Foundland from Cape Raze to Cape Bonavista ... Done from the latest Observations. Sold by W.

Bibliography: Maps, Charts, and Atlases / 321

and I. Mount & T. Page on Tower Hill. In *The English Pilot. The Fourth Book.* (Mount and Page, London 1755). Also in later editions to 1794.

[ABOUT 1758] LOTTER, TOBIAS CONRAD
Partie Orientale de la Nouvelle France ou du Canada avec l'Isle de Terre-Neuve ... (A. C. Seutter, Augsburg).
Names collated with Prowse, CM I, [2272], pp. 265–6.

[1758] KITCHIN, THOMAS
A Map of New England and Nova Scotia ... & the adjacent Islands of Newfoundland, Cape Breton, &c (London).
Names after Prowse, CM I, [2357], p. 272.

[1762] ROCQUE, JOHN
A General Map of North America ... (M. A. Rocque and A. Dury, London [1762]).
Names after Prowse, CM I, [2376], p. 273.

1762 COOK, JAMES
The Road and Harbour of Placentia. By James Cook.
Engraved chart published in 1769–70 and subsequently in editions of *The North-American Pilot* from 1775 to 1806. Reproduced in R. A. Skelton, *James Cook, Surveyor of Newfoundland* (San Francisco 1965).

1762 COOK, JAMES or 1768 GILBERT, JOSEPH
The Harbour of Trepassey with Mutton and Biscay Bays
See above: 1762 Cook, James.

1762 COOK, JAMES or 1768 GILBERT, JOSEPH
St. Mary's Harbour
See above: 1762 Cook, James.

1762 COOK, JAMES or 1768 GILBERT, JOSEPH
St. John's Harbour
See above: 1762 Cook, James.

1762 COOK, JAMES or 1768 GILBERT, JOSEPH
Carboniere and Harbour Grace
See above: 1762 Cook, James.

1762 COOK, JAMES or 1768 GILBERT, JOSEPH
The Harbour of Ferryland and Aquafort with Caplin Bay
See above: 1762 Cook, James.

[1762] KITCHIN, THOMAS
A New Map of the only useful and frequented part of New Found Land (London).

1763 COOK, JAMES
A Sketch of the Island of Newfoundland. Done from the latest Observations. By James Cook 1763.
Manuscript map in the Naval Library, Ministry of Defence, London (Vv 2: "America, MS charts and maps," vol I, no. 21). A compilation by Cook from previous maps, with notes on the dates of English settlement (before 1660, before 1729 and before 1735) and a colour code indicating English fisheries, fishing grounds allowed to the French, and (by yellow outline) "Doubtfully described" coasts. The only coasts not "doubtfully described" are sections of Placentia Bay, St. Mary's Bay, the Avalon Peninsula (East coast), Conception Bay and the Bonavista Peninsula.

1764 BELLIN, JACQUES NICOLAS
Carte du Golphe de St Laurent et Pays Voisins ... In *Le Petit Atlas Maritime* (Paris 1764).

[1764] COOK, JAMES
A Chart of the Coasts, Bays and Harbours in Newfoundland between Griquet and Pt. Ferolle. Survey'd by order of Hugh Pallisser Esqr Commodr &c &c by James Cook.

Manuscript charts in the National Maritime Museum, Greenwich, and British Admiralty, Hydrographic Department (c 54/7).

1767 COOK, JAMES
A Chart of the West Coast of Newfoundland, from Cape Anguille to Point Ferolle Surveyed by Order of Commodore Palisser Governor of Newfoundland &c. &c. By James Cook Surveyor 1767.

Manuscript chart in the British Museum (Add. MS 17963d).

1768 CARTWRIGHT, JOHN
A Sketch of the River Exploits, the east end of Lieutenants Lake and parts adjacent in Newfoundland. Taken on the spot by Lieutenant Ino. Cartwright of His Majesty's Ship Guernsey: 1768.

Sketch map published in *The Life and Correspondence of Major [John] Cartwright. Edited by his niece, F. D. Cartwright* ... vol. I (Henry Colburn, London 1826), p. 33.

1770 [1775] COOK and LANE (A)
A General Chart of the Island of Newfoundland with the Rocks and Soundings. Drawn from Surveys taken by Order of the Right Honourable the Lords Commissioners of the Admiralty. By James Cook and Michael Lane Surveyors and Others. London. Publish'd according to Act of Parliament. 10th May 1770. By Thomas Jefferys Geographer to the King. Printed for Robt. Sayer and Jno. Bennett. No. 53 in Fleet Street.

Published in this state, incorporating Lane's surveys of the Avalon Peninsula in 1772–3, in *The North-American Pilot* (London 1775); and subsequently, with change of imprint only, to 1806.

1770 [1775] COOK and LANE (B)
A Chart of the South-East Part of Newfoundland containing the Bay of Placentia, St. Mary, Trepassey and Conception from Actual Surveys. London. Printed for R. Sayer and I. Bennett ... 10 May 1770.

Published in this state, incorporating Lane's surveys of the Avalon Peninsula in 1772–3, in *The North-American Pilot* (London 1775); and subsequently, with change of imprint only, to 1806.

1770 GILBERT, JOSEPH
Manuscript chart without title, inscribed "Part of the Island of Newfoundland" and with inset plans of Harbour Grace & Carbonier, Trepassy Bay, Placentia Bay, Port St. Mary's, St. John's, Plan of the Coast from Sauker Head to Bad Bay, Hearts Content, Croque Harbour, signed "Joseph Gilbert, Master of his Majesty's Ship the Pearl, fect. 1770."

Chart in the British Admiralty, Hydrographic Department (x 58).

1771 SEALE, R. W.
A New and Accurate Map of North America, drawn ... and engraved by R. W. Seale (Carington Bowles, London 1771).

Names after Prowse, CM I, [2321], p. 270.

1772 LANE, MICHAEL
A Chart of the Bay of Placentia ... Surveyed by Order of Commodore Shuldham Governor of Newfoundland Labradore &c. by Michael Lane, 1772. (Jefferys and Faden, London 1773).

The MS original is in the British

Admiralty, Hydrographic Department (402).

1773 LANE, MICHAEL
A Chart of Part of the Coast of Newfoundland, from Point Lance to Cape Spear. Survey'd by Order of Commodore Shuldham Governor of Newfoundland, Labradore &c. by Michael Lane in 1773 (Jefferys and Faden, London 1774).

The MS original is in the British Admiralty, Hydrographic Department (403). A second edition, revised by J. F. Dessiou, was published in 1809.

1774 LANE, MICHAEL
A Chart of Part of the Coast of Newfoundland from Cape Spear to Bacaleau Island. Surveyed by Order of Commodore Shuldham, Governor of Newfoundland, Labrador etc. etc. by Michael Lane 1774.

Manuscript chart in the British Admiralty, Hydrographic Department (397).

1780 [MOUNT and PAGE]
A Chart of the South East Coast of Newfoundland. In *The English Pilot. The Fourth Book* (Mount and Page, London 1780). Also in later editions to 1794.

1780 BONNE, RIGOBERT
Isle et Banc de Terre-Neuve ... In Bonne, *Atlas de toutes les parties connues du Globe terrestre* (Paris 1780).

1785 KITCHIN, THOMAS
A Map of New England, Newfoundland ...
  Map not traced.
  Newfoundland names after Prowse, CM I, [2373], p. 273.

1790 LANE, MICHAEL
The Island of Newfoundland, laid down from Surveys taken by order of the Right Honourable the Lords Commissioners of Admiralty, by Lieut. Michael Lane Principal Surveyor of the said Island. 1790. London: Published by Wm. Faden Geographer to the King, Charing Cross Jany. 1st 1791.

This chart, published separately, was also included in George Cartwright, *A Journal of Transactions and Events, during a Residence of nearly Sixteen Years on the Coast of Labrador* ... vol. I (Newark 1792), facing p. [ix].

1807 CARY, JOHN
A New Map of Nova Scotia, Newfoundland, &c. (London).
  Names after Prowse, CM I, [3008], p. 331.

1813 CHAPPELL, EDWARD
Map of Newfoundland and the South Coast of Labrador, Shewing the Author's Track In Edward Chappell, *Voyage of His Majesty's Ship* Rosamond *to Newfoundland ... [in 1813]* (London 1818).

1814 PURDY, JOHN
Island of Newfoundland. Inset of *A Map of Cabotia ... Compiled ... by John Purdy, London. Published 12th October 1814 by Ja^s Whittle and Richd Holmes Laurie. N°. 53, Fleet St.*

Second and third editions were published in 1828 and 1838.

[1819] "ANSPACH"
A Chart of the Island of Newfoundland ... Rowe fc. Change Alley. Drawn and engraved expressly for the Revd. L. A. Anspach's History of Newfoundland.

Map in Anspach, *A History of the*

Island of Newfoundland (London 1819).

[1840] JUKES, JOSEPH BEETE
Map of the Island of Newfoundland.
Map in the Public Archives of Canada, Ottawa (D 100), reproduced in J. B. Jukes, *General Report of the Geological Survey of Newfoundland* (London 1843).
"Note. The Coast Lines compiled from the most recent Admiralty Charts. The interior filled up partly from a rough personal survey and partly from oral information, by J. B. Jukes, M.A., F.G.S., etc. Geological Surveyor of Newfoundland in the years 1839–40."

1842 BONNYCASTLE, Sir RICHARD HENRY
Newfoundland in 1842.
Manuscript map in the Public Archives of Canada, Ottawa.

1859 ADMIRALTY CHART 2649
Bull Arm.
Survey by H. C. Otter, 1858.

1859 PAGE, FREDERICK R.
A Hand Map of the Island of Newfoundland. Published by Frederick R. Page Land Surveyor, St. John's, Newfoundland. June 1859. In *A Concise History and Description of Newfoundland, being a Key to the Chart of the Island just published.* By F. R. Page, Land Surveyor, St. John's, Newfoundland. (R. H. Laurie, 53 Fleet Street, London 1860).

1864 ADMIRALTY CHART 2915
Bay Bulls to Placentia.
Survey by J. Orlebar, 1863.

1864 ADMIRALTY CHART 376
Broyle Harbour to Renewse Harbour.
Survey by J. Orlebar, 1863.

1865 ADMIRALTY CHART 619
Hearts Content and New Perlican.
Survey by J. Orlebar, 1862.
Inset *Old Perlican.* Survey by J. H. Kerr, 1866.

1868 ADMIRALTY CHART 296
Cape Bonavista to Bay Bulls, including Trinity and Conception Bays.
Surveys by J. Orlebar and J. H. Kerr, 1862–71.

1868 ADMIRALTY CHART 297
Carbonear to Brigus Bay, including Harbour Grace.
Survey by J. H. Kerr, 1866.

1870 ADMIRALTY CHART 232a
Newfoundland – Southern Portion ... From the surveys of Cook, Lane, & Bullock.

1876 ADMIRALTY CHART 290
Placentia to Burin Harbour
Surveys by J. Orlebar 1860–3 and W. F. Maxwell 1874–8.

1877 ADMIRALTY CHART 2829
Placentia and Ship Harbours ...
Surveys from J. Orlebar 1860 to W. F. Maxwell 1874.

1878 ADMIRALTY CHART 2666
St. John's to Halifax ...
Inset *The Virgin Rocks & Eastern Shoals.* Survey by W. F. Maxwell 1879.

1886 ADMIRALTY CHART 292
Harbours and anchorages in the southern portion of Newfoundland.
Surveys by W. F. Maxwell 1882–5.

1897 ADMIRALTY CHART 2902
Motion Head to Flat Rock ... Survey by Lockyer 1897.

1899 ADMIRALTY CHART 1702
Plans on the South Coast of Newfoundland.
  Trepassey Harbour. Survey by H. W. Bayfield 1847, revised to date.
  Lamaline Harbour and Road... Survey by W. F. Maxwell 1884, revised to date.

1899 ADMIRALTY CHART 3046
Bay Bulls and Cape Spear.
  Survey by Lockyer 1898.

1902 ADMIRALTY CHART 3266
Long Harbour and Ste. Croix Bay ...
  Survey by W. F. Maxwell 1874, revised to date.

1902 ADMIRALTY CHART 3263
Salmonier River and Colinet Harbour
  Survey by J. Orlebar 1862, revised to date.

1902 ADMIRALTY CHART 3264
St. Marys Harbour ...
  Survey by J. Orlebar 1862, revised to date.

1903 HALIFAX MORNING CHRONICLE
Map of the Island of Newfoundland
  Names after Prowse, CM 1, [3050], p. 333.

1903 WHITE, RICHARD
Map showing position of wrecks around the coast. Compiled by R. White. April 1903
  Manuscript map by R. White, Superintendent of Lighthouses, in the possession of Dr G. M. Story, St. John's, Nfld. It is corrected to December 1903 and to April 1924.
  A second map, without title, shows the south-east coast from Bay Bulls to Cape English on a larger scale. It is corrected to December 1924.

[1907] HOWLEY, JAMES PATRICK
Geological Map of Newfoundland compiled from the most recent and authentic sources. The coast line corrected to date from the Admiralty Surveys, the Interior chiefly from the work of the Geological Survey. By James P. Howley, F.G.S. Director. Reprinted 1925.

1914 ADMIRALTY CHART 298
St. John's Harbour
  Survey by J. W. F. Combe 1912.

1920 NEWFOUNDLAND. DEPARTMENT OF AGRICULTURE AND MINES
Newfoundland. 12 miles to 1 inch.

1922 [SPECK, FRANK G.]
Hunting Territories of the Micmac Indians in Prince Edward Island and Newfoundland In Hodge, F. W. (ed.), *Indian Notes and Monographs: Beothuk and Micmac*, by Frank G. Speck. (New York, 1922)

1927 LABRADOR BOUNDARY.
CANADIAN ATLAS
Atlas of fifty-two maps to accompany *In the Privy Council. In the Matter of the Boundary between the Dominion of Canada and the Colony of Newfoundland in the Labrador Peninsula* [London 1927].

1933 GANONG, WILLIAM FRANCIS
Newfoundland (Terreneuve) Gtagamgog
  Inset of map at p. 108, *Ancien District Micmac de Esgigeoagig-Acadie avec Terreneuve*, accompanying "Gtagamgog-Newfoundland Sag Megoetjiteoagig", *Bulletin de la Société de Géographie de Québec*, vol. 28 (Jan. 1934), pp. 137–47.

1941 NEWFOUNDLAND. DEPARTMENT OF NATURAL RESOURCES
Ten Mile Map of Newfoundland. 10 miles to 1 inch.

1949 CANADA. DEPARTMENT OF MINES AND RESOURCES
Province of Newfoundland. 10 miles to 1 inch.

1953 IMPERIAL OIL LIMITED
Newfoundland. 11.75 miles to 1 inch.

1955 NEWFOUNDLAND. DEPARTMENT OF MINES AND RESOURCES
Province of Newfoundland. 10 miles to 1 inch.

1954–1959 NATIONAL TOPOGRAPHIC SERIES (NTS)
Maps of Canada, 1.25 inches to 1 mile, published by the Map Distribution Office, Surveys and Mapping Branch, Department of Energy, Mines and Resources, Ottawa, Ontario.

Gazetteers of Newfoundland based on these maps are E. Rouleau, *A Gazetteer of the Island of Newfoundland* (Montreal 1961) [Mimeograph], and *Gazetteer of Canada, Newfoundland and Labrador* (Canadian Permanent Committee on Geographical Names, Ottawa 1968).

The maps listed on the facing page have been used in this study:

AVALON PENINSULA: INDEX OF NTS MAPS BY NAMES
(With year of publication and edition)

Name	Code	Direction	Year-Edition
Argentia	1 N/5	E & W	1954–1
Bay Bulls	1 N/7	E & W	1955–1
Bay de Verde	2 C/2	W	1954–1
Biscay Bay River	1 K/14	E & W	1955–1
Dildo	1 N/12	E & W	1954–1
Ferryland	1 N/2	W	1954–1
Harbour Grace	1 N/11	E & W	1954–1
Hearts Content	1 N/14	E & W	1955–1
Holyrood	1 N/6	E & W	1956–1
Old Perlican	2 C/3	E & W	1954–1
Placentia	1 N/4	E & W	1955–1
Pouch Cove	1 N/15		1953–2
Renews	1 K/15	W	1954–1
St. Brides	1 L/16	E	1954–1
St. Catherine's	1 N/3	E & W	1955–1
St. John's	1 N/10	E & W	1959–3
St. Mary's	1 K/13	E & W	1954–1
St. Shotts	1 K/12	E	1954–1
Ship Cove	1 M/1	E	1954–1
Sunnyside	1 N/13	E & W	1955–1
Trepassey	1 K/11	E & W	1954–1

AVALON PENINSULA: INDEX OF NTS MAPS BY CODE NUMBERS
(With year of publication and edition)

Code	Direction	Name	Year-Edition
1 K/11	E & W	Trepassey	1954–1
1 K/12	E	St. Shotts	1954–1
1 K/13	E & W	St. Mary's	1954–1
1 K/14	E & W	Biscay Bay River	1955–1
1 K/15	W	Renews	1954–1
1 L/16	E	St. Brides	1954–1
1 M/1	E	Ship Cove	1954–1
1 N/2	W	Ferryland	1954–1
1 N/3	E & W	St. Catherine's	1955–1
1 N/4	E & W	Placentia	1955–1
1 N/5	E & W	Argentia	1954–1
1 N/6	E & W	Holyrood	1956–1
1 N/7	E & W	Bay Bulls	1955–1
1 N/10	E & W	St. John's	1959–3
1 N/11	E & W	Harbour Grace	1954–1
1 N/12	E & W	Dildo	1954–1
1 N/13	E & W	Sunnyside	1955–1
1 N/14	E & W	Hearts Content	1955–1
1 N/15		Pouch Cove	1953–2
2 C/2	W	Bay de Verde	1954–1
2 C/3	E & W	Old Perlican	1954–1

Bibliography / Two
A Selection of Manuscript and Printed Sources

WITH CUE-TITLES

Census 1857

Abstract Census and Return of the Population, &c. of Newfoundland, 1857. [St. John's 1857].

Act 10 & 11 William III, Cap. 25 (Imperial) An Act to Encourage the Trade to Newfoundland.

ADAMS, WILLIAM FORBES. Ireland and the Irish Emigration to the New World from 1815 to the Famine (Yale University Press, New Haven 1932; reissued Russell, New York 1967).

MCV

ALMAGIÀ, R. Monumenta Cartographica Vaticana, 4 vols. (Città del Vaticano 1944–55).

ANDERSON, WILLIAM P. Geographic Board of Canada. Micmac Place-Names in the Maritime Provinces and Gaspé Peninsula between 1852 and 1890 by Rev S[ilas] T[ertius] Rand. Collected, arranged and indexed by W. P. Anderson (Surveyor General's Office, Ottawa 1919).

ANDREWS, CHARLES M. and FRANCES G. DAVENPORT. Guide to the Manuscript Materials for the History of the United States to 1783, in the British Museum in Minor London Archives and in the Libraries of Oxford and Cambridge (Carnegie Institution, Washington 1908).

Anspach

ANSPACH, LEWIS AMADEUS. A History of the Island of Newfoundland (London 1819).

ANTHIAUME, A. Cartes marines, Constructions navales, Voyages de Découverte chez les Normands 1500–1650, 2 vols. (Dumont, Paris 1916).

ARMSTRONG, G. H. Origin and Meaning of Place Names in Canada (Macmillan, Toronto 1930).

AYRE, AGNES MARION. Newfoundland Names [St. John's 1939]. A series of articles published in the Daily News, St. John's, in eleven parts during August and September 1938.

BAGROW, LEO. Die Geschichte der Kartographie (Safari-Verlag, Berlin 1951).

— History of Cartography. Revised and enlarged by R. A. Skelton. (Watts, London 1964).

BAIRD, DAVID M. *Rocks, Minerals and Scenery of Newfoundland* (Department of Education, [St. John's] 1957).

Banks
BANKS, JOSEPH. *Journal of a Voyage to Newfoundland and Labrador commencing April the seventh and ending November the 17th. 1766.* MS. Original in Adelaide, Australia. Copy by Sophia Sarah Banks in British Museum (Natural History Museum, South Kensington) Folio 1772.

Bardsley
BARDSLEY, CHARLES WAREING. *A Dictionary of English and Welsh Surnames* (Oxford University Press, London 1901).

"BARRELMAN," pseudonym of JOSEPH RAMSAY SMALLWOOD, q.v.

BARTLETT, ROBERT A. *The Log of Bob Bartlett* (Putnam, London, New York 1928).

BEAUDOIN, JEAN. See GOSSELIN, A.

BN
Bibliothèque Nationale. See FONCIN, M. etc.

BIGGAR, HENRY PERCIVAL. *The Precursors of Jacques Cartier 1497–1534* (Canadian Archives Publications, no. 5, Ottawa 1911).

— *The Voyages of Jacques Cartier* (Public Archives of Canada, Publication no. 11, Ottawa 1924).

BLACKMORE, MARTIN. Lecture on the History of Bay Roberts, 29 January 1865, in *The Fisherman's Advocate* (24 February 1950) (Port Union, Newfoundland).

Bonnycastle
BONNYCASTLE, RICHARD HENRY. *Newfoundland in 1842*, 2 vols. (Colburn, London 1842).

BRAZÃO, EDUARDO. *La Découverte de Terre-Neuve* (Les Presses de l'Université de Montréal, Montréal 1964).

— *The Corte-Real Family and the New World*. (Agencia-Geral do Ultramar, Lisbon 1965).

BREBNER, JOHN BARTLET. *The Explorers of North America 1492–1806* (Black, London 1933; reprinted Doubleday, Garden City, NY 1955).

BRITTEN, NATHANIEL LORD and ADDISON BROWN. *An Illustrated Flora*, 2nd edition, 3 vols. (Scribner's, New York 1913).

BROWN, THOMAS J. *Place-Names of the Province of Nova Scotia* (n.p. 1922).

BROWN, VERA LEE. "Spanish Claims to a Share in the Newfoundland Fisheries in the Eighteenth Century," *The Canadian Historical Association, Report of the Annual Meeting 1925* (Canadian National Parks Branch of the Department of the Interior, Ottawa 1926).

BROWNE, P. W. *Where the Fishers Go: The Story of Labrador* (Cochrane, New York 1909).

BUCHANAN, M. A. "Early Canadian History," *Transactions of the Royal Society of Canada*, XLII, series III, section 2 (May 1948), pp. 31–57.

BURRILL, MEREDITH F. "Toponymic Generics," *Names* IV, 3 and 4 (September and December 1956), pp. 129–37, 226–40.

CSP

Calendar of State Papers. Colonial Series [1574–1736]. America and West Indies, vols. I, V, VII, IX, X, XI, XIII–XVII, edited by W. N. Sainsbury, et al (Public Record Office, London 1860–).

CAMERON, KENNETH. *English Place Names* (Batsford, London 1961).

CARTIER, JACQUES. See BIGGAR, H. P.

Cartwright, *Transactions*

CARTWRIGHT, GEORGE. *A Journal of Transactions and Events ... on the Coast of Labrador*, 3 vols. (Newark 1792).

CARTWRIGHT, JOHN. *The Life and Correspondence of Major Cartwright*. Edited by his niece, F. D. Cartwright, 2 vols. (Colburn, London 1826).

CASSIDY, F. G. and R. B. LE PAGE. *Dictionary of Jamaican English* (Cambridge University Press, Cambridge, 1967).

Catalogue of the Manuscript Maps, Charts, and Plans, and of the Topographical Drawings in the British Museum, vol. III (London 1861).

Catalogue of the Maps, Plans and Charts in the Library of the Colonial Office, 1910. Now in Public Record Office, co 700.

Census 1794–95 (Colonial Secretary's Office, [St. John's 1795]). MS Copy of the Census in the Gosling Memorial Library, St. John's.

Census 1836. See *Population Returns*.

Census 1857. See *Abstract Census ... of Newfoundland 1857*.

Census of Newfoundland and Labrador, 1869, [1874, 1884, 1891, 1901] (The Queen's Printer, St. John's 1869 etc.).

Census of Newfoundland and Labrador 1911, [1921] (The King's Printer, St. John's 1911, 1921).

Census of Newfoundland and Labrador 1935 (Department of Public Health and Welfare, St. John's 1937).

Census of Newfoundland and Labrador 1945 (Government of Newfoundland, St. John's 1945).

CHAPPELL, EDWARD. *Voyage of His Majesty's Ship* Rosamond *to Newfoundland ... [in 1813]* (Mawman, London 1818).

CHAPUY, PAUL. *Origine des Noms patronymiques français* (Dorbon-Ainé, Paris [1934]).

CHUTE, N. E. *Mineral Deposits of the Placentia Bay Area*. (Newfoundland Geological Survey, Bulletin no. 18, St. John's 1939).

CLARK, J. S. *Micmac Dictionary* compiled by S. T. Rand, edited by J. S. Clark (Patriot Publishing Co., Charlottetown, PEI 1902).

CO

Colonial Office. "Return of Possessions held in Conception Bay." Misc. 199.18.

— "Scheme of the Newfoundland Fishery." 194/9, 194/13.

The Commissioned Sea Officers of the Royal Navy 1660–1815, 3 vols. [National Maritime Museum, Greenwich 1954]. Mimeograph.

COMPTON, F. C. B. *Lahontan* (Nelson, Toronto 1928).

COOK, JAMES. See SKELTON, R. A.

CORMACK, WILLIAM EPPS. *Narrative of a Journey across the Island of Newfoundland in 1822* edited by F. A. Bruton (Longmans, London 1929). The original account was published in the *Edinburgh Philosophical Journal*, x (October–April 1823–4).

PMC

CORTESÃO, ARMANDO and AVELINO TEIXEIRA DA MOTA. *Portugaliae Monumenta Cartographica* 6 vols. (Lisboa 1960).

COTTLE, BASIL. *The Penguin Dictionary of Surnames* (Penguin Books, Harmondsworth 1967).

Daily News, St. John's, 1860–. [Daily].

Dauzat, *Noms de Famille*

DAUZAT, ALBERT. *Dictionnaire étymologique des Noms de Famille et Prénoms de France.* (Larousse, Paris 1951).

Dauzat, *Noms de Lieux*

— *Les Noms de Lieux*, 15th edition (Delagrave, Paris 1957).

— *La Toponymie française*, revised edition (Payot, Paris 1960).

— et CH. ROSTAING. *Dictionnaire étymologique des Noms de Lieux en France* (Larousse, Paris 1963).

DAVIES, ARTHUR. "The last Voyage of John Cabot and the Rock at Grates Cove," *Nature*, vol. 176 (26 November 1955), pp. 996–9.

— "The 'English' Coasts on the Map of Juan de la Cosa," *Imago Mundi*, XIII (1956), pp. 26–9.

DAWSON, L. S. *Memoirs of Hydrography*, 2 parts: Part I 1750–1830; Part II 1830–1885. (Keay, Eastbourne Part I n.d., Part II 1885).

DEVINE, M. A. and M. J. O'MARA. *Notable Events in the History of Newfoundland* (St. John's 1900).

DEVINE, P. K. *Ye Olde St. John's, 1750–1936* (Newfoundland Directories, St. John's 1936).

— *Devine's Folk Lore of Newfoundland in old Words, Phrases and Expressions.* (Robinson, St. John's 1937).

DCB

Dictionary of Canadian Biography, I, 1000 to 1700, edited by George W. Brown (University of Toronto Press, Toronto 1966).

EKWALL, EILERT. *The Concise Oxford Dictionary of English Place-Names* (Clarendon Press, Oxford 1936).

Electors. See *Official List of Electors.*

ENGLAND, GEORGE ALLEN. "Newfoundland Dialect Items," *Dialect Notes*, V (1925), pp. 322–46.

The English Pilot. The Fourth Book (London, 1st edition 1689; 37th edition 1794), See VERNER, COOLIE. The editions used in this study were the 1st (1689); 6th (1716); and 33rd (1780).

Evening Telegram, St. John's, 1879– [Daily].

FAY, C. R. *The Channel Islands and Newfoundland* (Heffer, Cambridge 1961).

FISHER, RICHARD. See HAKLUYT, *Voyages.*

BN

FONCIN, MYRIEM, MARCEL DESTOMBES, and MONIQUE DE LA RONCIÈRE. *Bibliothèque Nationale: Catalogue des cartes nautiques sur vélin* (Paris 1963).

GANONG, WILLIAM FRANCIS. "The Origin of the East-Canadian Place-names Gaspé, Blomidon, and Bras d'Or," *Proceedings and Transactions of The Royal Society of Canada*, third series, vol. XXII, section II The Royal Society of Canada, Ottawa 1928), pp. 249–70.

Ganong, *Crucial Maps*

— *Crucial Maps in the early Cartography and Place-Nomenclature of the Atlantic Coast of Canada*, with an introduction, commentary and map notes by Theodore E. Layng (University of Toronto Press, Toronto 1964). A series of papers which appeared from 1929 to 1937, Parts I to IX, in *Transactions of the Royal Society of Canada*, 3rd series.

Gazetteer of Canada, New Brunswick (Canadian Board on Geographic Names, Ottawa 1956).

Gazetteer of Canada, Newfoundland and Labrador. (Canadian Permanent Committee on Geographical Names, Ottawa 1968).

Gazetteer of Canada, Nova Scotia (Canadian Board on Geographic Names, Ottawa 1961).

GODEFROY, F. *Dictionnaire de l'ancienne langue française* (Librairie des Sciences et des Arts, Paris 1938).

GOSSE, EDMUND. *The Life of Philip Henry Gosse* (Kegan Paul, London 1890).

GOSSELIN, A. *Les Normands au Canada. Journal d'une Expédition de D'Iberville* [par l'abbé Jean Beaudoin] (Évreux 1900).

GOVER, J. E. B., A. MAWER, and F. M. STENTON. *The Place-Names of Devon.* English Place-Name Society. Part I, vol. VIII (Cambridge 1931); Part II, vol. IX (Cambridge 1932).

Gower Street Church, St. John's, Minute Book (United Church Conference Archives, St. John's) MS.

GROSSETÊTE, J. M. *La grande Pêche de Terre-Neuve et d'Islande* (Rennes 1921).

GUDDE, ERWIN G. "Sugarloaf," *Names*, IV, 4 (December 1956), pp. 241–3.

GUPPY, HENRY BROUGHAM. *Homes of Family Names in Great Britain* (Harrison, [London] 1890).

GUTSELL, B. V. *An Introduction to the Geography of Newfoundland* (Canada Department of Mines and Resources, Geographical Bureau, Information Series no. 1, Ottawa 1949). Appendix A, "Place Names of Newfoundland," pp. 78–9.

HAKLUYT, *Voyages*

HAKLUYT, RICHARD. *The Principal Navigations Voyages Traffiques & Discoveries of the English Nation.* 1st edition 1589, enlarged 1598–1600, 12 vols. (MacLehose, Glasgow 1903–4).

— *Voyages and Documents*, selected by Janet Hampden (World's Classics, London 1958; reprinted 1963).

Harrisse, *Découverte*

HARRISSE, HENRY. *Découverte et évolution cartographique de Terre Neuve* (London, Paris 1900).

HARVEY, MOSES. *Text Book of Newfoundland History*, 2nd edition (Collins, London and Glasgow 1890).

— "Etymology of the Name 'Quidi Vidi'," *Tribune*, Christmas Number, VII ([St. John's] 1900).

HAYES, EDWARD. See Hakluyt, *Voyages*.

HIPPEAU, C. *Dictionnaire topographique du Département du Calvados* (Imprimerie Nationale, Paris 1883).

HOBBS, J. S. *Sailing Directions for the Island and Banks of Newfoundland* (Wilson, London [1865]).

HODGE, FREDERICK WEBB. *Handbook of American Indians* (Pageant Books, New York 1959).

HOFFMAN, BERNARD G. *Cabot to Cartier* (University of Toronto Press, Toronto 1961).

HOWLEY, JAMES P. *Geography of Newfoundland* (Stanford, London 1876).

— *The Beothucks or Red Indians, the Original Inhabitants of Newfoundland* (Cambridge University Press, Cambridge 1915). See also MURRAY, ALEXANDER.

HOWLEY, MICHAEL FRANCIS. *Ecclesiastical History of Newfoundland* (Doyle and Whittle, Boston 1888).

Howley, M. F., *NQ*

— "Newfoundland Name-Lore," *The Newfoundland Quarterly* (St. John's, October 1901–December 1914). A series of forty-one papers.

HUGUET, E. *Dictionnaire de la Langue française du XVIe siècle* (Champion, Paris 1925).

Hutchinson's Newfoundland Directory, for 1864–5 (McConnan, St. John's 1864).

IMRAY, JAMES F. *Sailing Directions for Newfoundland* (Imray, London 1862).

— *Sailing Directory for the Island of Newfoundland* (Imray, London 1873).

In the Privy Council. In the Matter of the Boundary between the Dominion of Canada and the

334 / Place Names of the Avalon Peninsula

Colony of Newfoundland in the Labrador Peninsula. 9 vols. and atlas [London 1927].

INNIS, HAROLD A. The Cod Fisheries. The History of an International Economy, revised edition (University of Toronto Press, Toronto 1954).

Irish Coast Pilot (London 1941).

JESPERSEN, OTTO. A Modern English Grammar, 7 vols. (Allen and Unwin, London ed. 1954).

JOHNSON, D. W. History of Methodism in Eastern British America. (Tribune Printing Co., Sackville, NB [1925]).

JORDAN, JOHN. "Induction to Dialect," The New Newfoundland Quarterly, LXV, 3 (February 1967), pp. 23–6.

JOYCE, PATRICK WESTON. English as we Speak it in Ireland (Longmans, London; Gill, Dublin 1910).

— The Origin and History of Irish Names of Places, 1st edition 1869. 3 vols. (Dublin and London, vol. I n.d; vol. II 1922; vol. III 1920).

Jukes, Excursions

JUKES, JOSEPH BEETE. Excursions in and about Newfoundland, during the years 1839 and 1840, 2 vols. (Murray, London 1842).

— General Report of the Geological Survey of Newfoundland during the years 1839 and 1840 (Murray, London 1843).

KEENLEYSIDE, H. L. "Place-Names of Newfoundland," Canadian Geographical Journal, XXIX, 6 (December 1944), pp. 255–63.

KEIR, DAVID. The Bowring Story. (The Bodley Head, London 1962).

KIRKCONNELL, WATSON. "Canadian Toponymy and the Cultural Stratification of Canada," Onomastica, no. 7 (1954).

KIRWIN, WILLIAM. "Lines, Coves, and Squares in Newfoundland Names," American Speech, XL, 3 (October 1965), pp. 163–70. See also SEARY, E. R.

KOHL, JOHANN G. "A History of the Discovery of the East Coast of North America." Collections of the Maine Historical Society, 2nd Series: Documentary History of the State of Maine (Portland, 1869).

LACOURCIÈRE, LUC. Toponymie canadienne. (Les Presses de l'Université Laval, Quebec 1956).

— "Bibliographie raisonnée de l'Anthroponymie canadienne," Mémoires de la Société généalogique canadienne-française, IX, 3–4 (Montréal, juillet-octobre 1958).

LAHONTAN, LOUIS ARMAND. The Oakes Collection. New Documents by Lahontan concerning Canada and Newfoundland, edited by G. Lanctot (King's Printer, Ottawa 1940).

LAMBERT, R. S. Exploring the Supernatural (McClelland and Stewart, Toronto 1955).

LA MORANDIÈRE, CHARLES DE. Histoire de la Pêche française de la Morue dans l'Amérique septentrionale, 3 vols. (Maisonneuve et Larose, Paris 1962, 1966).

Lane, *Directions* 1773, 1810

LANE, MICHAEL. *Directions for Navigating Part of the Coast of Newfoundland from Point Lance to Cape Spear. Surveyed ... by Michael Lane, in 1773.* (William Faden, London 1774). Second edition, revised by J. F. Dessiou (William Faden, London 1810).

Lane, *Directions* 1775, 1810

— *Directions for Navigating Part of the Coast of Newfoundland, from Cape Spear to Cape Bonavista. Surveyed by ... Michael Lane, in 1775* (William Faden, London 1776). Second edition, revised by J. F. Dessiou (William Faden, London 1810).

LA RONCIÈRE, CHARLES DE. "Le premier routier-pilote de Terre-Neuve (1579)," *La Bibliothèque de l'École des Chartes*, vol. 64 (Paris, 1904), pp. 116–25.

LEIM, A. H. and W. B. SCOTT. *Fishes of the Atlantic Coast of Canada.* Fisheries Research Board of Canada, Bulletin no. 155 (Ottawa, 1966).

LE MESSURIER, HAROLD W. "The Early Relations between Newfoundland and the Channel Islands," *The Geographical Review* (December 1916).

List of Maps, Plans, &c: Belonging to the Right Honble: The Lords Commissioners for Trade and Plantations, under the care of Francis Ægidius Assiotti, Draughtsman. 1780. Public Record Office. CO 326/15 (Ind. 8315). MS.

A List of the Place Names of the Island of Newfoundland ... Compiled from the 10-Mile Map of Newfoundland published by The Department of Natural Resources, Newfoundland, 1941. Canada, Department of Mines and Technical Surveys. Geographical Branch (Ottawa, 1950). Mimeograph.

LONGNON, AUGUSTE. *Les Noms de Lieu de la France* (Librairie Ancienne Honoré Champion, Paris 1920–9).

LOTURE, ROBERT DE. *Histoire de la Grande Pêche de Terre-Neuve* (Gallimard, [Paris] 1949).

LOUNSBURY, RALPH GREENLEE. *The British Fishery at Newfoundland 1634–1763* (Yale University Press, New Haven 1934).

Lovell's Gazetteer of British North America. (Lovell, Montreal 1881).

McAlpine's Maritime Provinces Directory for 1870–71 (David McAlpine, Halifax, NS 1870).

MCATEE, W. L. *Folk-Names of Canadian Birds*, National Museum of Canada, Bulletin no. 149, Biological Series No. 51 (Ottawa, 1957).

MCCREA, ROBERT B. *Lost amid the Fogs: Sketches of Life in Newfoundland* (Sampson Low, London 1869).

MCLINTOCK, A. H. *The Establishment of Constitutional Government in Newfoundland 1783–1832. A Study in Retarded Colonization* (Longmans, London 1941).

MacLysaght IF

MACLYSAGHT, EDWARD. *Irish Families* (Hodges Figgis, Dublin 1957).

MacLysaght MIF

— *More Irish Families* (O'Gorman, Galway and Dublin 1960).

MacLysaght SIF

— *Supplement to Irish Families* (Genealogical Book Company, Baltimore [1964]).

MacLysaght GIS

— *A Guide to Irish Surnames* (Genealogical Book Company, Baltimore [1964]).

MASON, JOHN. *A Briefe Discourse of the New-found-land* (Edinburgh 1620), printed in *Capt. John Mason* (Prince Society, Boston 1887).

MATHESON, ROBERT E. *Special Report on Surnames in Ireland.* (His Majesty's Stationery Office, Dublin 1909).

MAWER, ALLEN. "English Place-Names and their Pronunciation," *Essays and Studies by Members of the English Association,* XVII (Oxford 1932), pp. 90–105.

— "Place Names," *Encyclopaedia Britannica,* 1951 edition, XVII, pp. 987–9.

MENCKEN, HENRY LOUIS. *The American Language,* 4th edition (Knopf, New York 1949).

— *The American Language,* Supplement II (1952).

MIFFIN, ROBERT JAMES. "Some French Place Names of Newfoundland," *American Speech,* XXXI (February 1956), pp. 79–80.

MILLAIS, J. G. *Newfoundland and its Untrodden Ways* (Longmans, London 1907).

Minutes of the Newfoundland District of the Wesleyan Methodist Church, 1829–1850 (United Church Conference Archives, St. John's), MS.

Minutes of the St. John's District of the Newfoundland Methodist Conference, 1877–1895 (United Church Conference Archives, St. John's), MS.

MCV

Monumenta Cartographica Vaticana. See ALMAGIÀ, R.

Mosdell

MOSDELL, H. M. *When was That?* (Trade Printers, St. John's 1923).

Murray and Howley

MURRAY, ALEXANDER and J. P. HOWLEY. *Geological Survey of Newfoundland* [Reports of 1864–1880] (Stanford, London 1881). See also HOWLEY, J. P.

MUSSET, PAUL LOUIS E. G. *Les Rochelais à Terre-Neuve, 1500–1789* (Chez l'auteur, La Rochelle 1899).

NANCE, R. MORTON. "Cornish Names of the Seal," *Old Cornwall,* III, 2 (Winter 1937), p. 85.

— "Killigrew," *Old Cornwall,* V, 1 (Summer 1951), p. 41.

— *A Guide to Cornish Place-Names*, 4th edition (The Federation of Old Cornwall Societies, Marazion 1963).

The New World. A Catalogue of an Exhibition of Books, Maps, Manuscripts and Documents held at Lambeth Palace Library between 1 May and 1 December 1957. (Lambeth Palace Library, [London] 1957). Appendix 1: John Guy and the Beothuck Indians.

NLP

Newfoundland and Labrador Pilot, 8th edition, 2 vols. (Hydrographic Department, Admiralty, London I 1951, II 1953).

NP

1952 Newfoundland Pilot (Canadian Edition). (Canadian Hydrographic Service, Surveys and Mapping Branch, Department of Mines and Technical Surveys, Ottawa 1953).

NQ

Newfoundland Quarterly, vol. I (St. John's 1901–). Continued as *The New Newfoundland Quarterly*, vol. LXV (1966–).

Noms géographiques de la Province de Québec, 2nd edition (Commission de Géographie de Québec, Québec 1921).

The North-American and West-Indian Gazetteer (Robinson, London 1776).

O'BYRNE, WILLIAM R. *A Naval Biographical Dictionary* (Murray, London 1849).

Electors

Official List of Electors [St. John's 1955]. The following Electoral Districts, as constituted in 1955, are on the Avalon Peninsula: Bell Island, Carbonear-Bay de Verde, Ferryland, Harbour Grace, Harbour Main, Placentia East, Port de Grave, St. John's Centre, St. John's East, St. John's South, St. John's West, St. Mary's, Trinity South (in part).

[OLDMIXON, JOHN]. *The British Empire in America*, 2nd edition, vol. I (London 1741).

PACIFIQUE, Rev. Père. *Le Pays des Micmacs.* (La Réparation, Montréal 1934). Tirage à part du *Bulletin de la Société géographique de Québec*, vols. 21 (1927), pp. 111–7; 22 (1928), pp. 43–55; 25 (1931), pp. 96–106; 28 (1934), pp. 136–47, and map, p. 108.

— *Études historiques et geographiques* (Ristigouche 1935).

PAGE, JOHN LLOYD WARDEN. *The Coasts of Devon and Lundy Island* (Horace Cox, London 1895).

PARKHURST, ANTONY. See Hakluyt, *Voyages*.

PATTERSON, GEORGE. "The Portuguese on the north-east Coast of America," *Proceedings and Transactions of The Royal Society of Canada for the year 1890*, vol. VIII (Montreal 1891), section II, pp. 127–73.

— "Notes on the Dialect of the People of Newfoundland," *Journal of American Folklore*, VIII (1895), pp. 27–40; IX (1896), pp. 19–37; X (1897), pp. 203–13.

PEDDEL, N. *Newfoundland Poems* (first published 1904; republished with additions, Harbour Grace 1908).

PEDLEY, CHARLES. *The History of Newfoundland from the earliest Times to the year 1860*. (Longmans, London 1863).

PERLIN, ALBERT B. (ed.). *The Story of Newfoundland* (St. John's 1959).

PERRET, ROBERT. *La Géographie de Terre-Neuve* (Guilmoto, Paris 1913).

Peters and Burleigh

PETERS, HAROLD S. and THOMAS D. BURLEIGH. *The Birds of Newfoundland*. (Department of Natural Resources, St. John's 1951).

Place-Names of the Province of Nova Scotia (n.p. 1922).

POIRIER, JEAN. *Toponymie Méthode d'Enquête* (Les Presses de l'Université Laval, Québec 1965).

Population Returns [St. John's 1836].

PMC

Portugaliae Monumenta Cartographica. See CORTESÃO, A. and A. TEIXEIRA DA MOTA.

POWELL, J. W. DAMER. "The Explorations of John Guy in Newfoundland," *The Geographical Journal*, LXXXVI, 6 (December 1935), pp. 512–8. See also *The New World*.

POWER, PATRICK. *The Place Names of Decies*, 2nd edition (University Press, Cork; Blackwell, Oxford 1952).

D. W. Prowse

PROWSE, DANIEL W. *A History of Newfoundland from the English, Colonial, and Foreign Sources* (Macmillan, London and New York 1895).

G. R. F. Prowse, CM

PROWSE, GEORGE ROBERT FARRAR. *Cartological Material*. Vol. I *Maps* (Winnipeg 1936); vol. III *Names* (Winnipeg 1942). Mimeograph. Vols. II *Contours* and IV *Voyages* were not published.

PRYS-JONES, A. G. "Lord of poor Cambriol," *Country Quest*, V, 3 (Winter 1964).

PAC

[Public Archives of Canada] *Sixteenth-Century Maps relating to Canada*. (Public Archives of Canada, Ottawa 1956).

PURCHAS, SAMUEL. *Hakluytus Posthumus or Purchas His Pilgrimes*, 10 vols. (MacLehose, Glasgow 1905–7).

QUINN, DAVID BEERS. "The Argument for the English Discovery of America between 1480 and 1494," *The Geographical Journal*, CXXVII, 3 (September 1961), pp. 277–85.

RAND, SILAS TERTIUS. See ANDERSON, W. P.; CLARK, J. S.

READ, ALLEN WALKER. "The Basis of Correctness in the Pronunciation of Place-Names," *American Speech*, VIII, 1 (February 1933), pp. 42–6.

Reaney, *Surnames*
REANEY, PERCY HIDE. *A Dictionary of British Surnames* (Routledge, London 1958).

— *The Origin of English Place Names* (Routledge, London 1960).

Directory 1877
ROCHFORT, JOHN A. *Business and General Directory of Newfoundland* (Lovell, Montreal 1877).

ROGERS, J. D. *A Historical Geography of the British Colonies. Vol. V – Part IV Newfoundland* (Clarendon Press, Oxford 1911).

ROSENZWEIG, M. *Dictionnaire topographique du Département du Morhiban* (Imprimerie Impériale, Paris 1870).

ROSTAING, CHARLES. *Les Noms de Lieux* (Presses Universitaires de France, Paris 1954).

— See also DAUZAT, A.

ROUILLARD, EUGÈNE. *Noms géographiques de la Province de Québec et des provinces maritimes empruntés aux langues sauvages* (Marcotte, Québec 1906).

— *Dictionnaire des Rivières et des Lacs de la Province de Québec* (Département des Terres et Forêts, Québec 1914).

ROULEAU, ERNEST. *Studies on the Vascular Flora of the Province of Newfoundland* (Institut Botanique de l'Université de Montréal, Montréal 1956).

— *A Gazetteer of the Island of Newfoundland based on the Maps (1:50,000) of the National Topographic System.* (Department of Mines and Technical Surveys, Ottawa 1961).

ROUSSEAU, JACQUES. "Les Américanismes du Parler canadien-français," *Le Cahier des Dix*, no. 21 (Les Editions des Dix, Montréal 1956).

ROY, CARMEN. *La Littérature orale en Gaspésie* (Ministre du Nord canadien et des Ressources nationales, Ottawa 1955).

The Royal Gazette and Newfoundland Advertiser (St. John's 1807–1924). Became *Newfoundland Gazette*, 1926– [weekly].

RUDNYCKYJ, J. B. "Classification of Canadian Place Names," *Onomastica*, no. 15 (1958).

SANDS, D. B. "The Nature of the Generics in Island, Ledge and Rock Names of the Maine Coast," *Names*, IV, 4 (December 1959), pp. 193–202.

SEARY, EDGAR RONALD. "The Anatomy of Newfoundland Place Names," *Names*, VI, 4 (December 1958), pp. 193–207.

— "The French Element in Newfoundland Place Names," *Onomastica*, no. 16 (1958); also in *The Journal of the Canadian Linguistic Association*, IV, 2 (Fall 1958).

— *Toponymy of the Island of Newfoundland, Check-List No. 1. Sources I, Maps* (St. John's 1959), mimeograph.

— *Toponymy of the Island of*

Newfoundland, Check-List No. 2. Names I, The Northern Peninsula. (St. John's 1960), mimeograph.

— "Linguistic Variety in the Place Names of Newfoundland," *Canadian Geographical Journal*, LXV, 5 (November 1962), pp. 147–55.

— "The Place-Names of Newfoundland," *The Book of Newfoundland*, edited by J. R. Smallwood, vol. III (St. John's 1967), pp. 257–64.

— G. M. STORY and W. KIRWIN. *The Avalon Peninsula of Newfoundland: an Ethno-Linguistic Study* (National Museum of Canada, Bulletin no. 219, Anthropological Series no. 81, Ottawa 1968).

Sixteenth-Century Maps relating to Canada. See Public Archives of Canada.

SKELTON, RALEIGH ASHLIN. "Captain James Cook as a Hydrographer," *The Mariner's Mirror*, 40, 2 (November 1954), pp. 92–119.

— *Explorers' Maps.* (Praeger, New York 1958).

— *James Cook, Surveyor of Newfoundland* (David Magee, San Francisco 1965).

— T. E. MARSTON and G. D. PAINTER, *The Vinland Map and the Tartar Relation* (Yale University Press, New Haven and London 1965).

— and R. V. TOOLEY, "The Marine Surveys of James Cook in North America, 1758–1768," *Map Collectors' Circle*, IV, 37 (London 1967).

— See also BAGROW, LEO; WILLIAMSON, J. A.

SMALLWOOD, JOSEPH RAMSAY, The Barrelman *pseudonym.* Typescript of radio programme, The Barrelman, 1937–43, in The Library, Memorial University of Newfoundland.

— *Newfoundland 1940. Hand Book Gazetteer and Almanac* (St. John's [1940]).

— *Newfoundland 1941. Hand Book Gazetteer and Almanac* (St. John's [1941]).

— (ed.). *The Book of Newfoundland,* 4 vols. Vols. I and II (St. John's 1937); vols. III and IV (St. John's 1967).

SMITH, CHARLES. *The Antient and and Present State of the County of Kerry* (Dublin 1756).

SMITH, N. *Fifty-two Years at the Labrador Fishery* (Stockwell, London 1936).

Society for the Propagation of the Gospel. Miscellaneous unbound MSS: "Letters from Newfoundland, 1709–1852."

SOUTHWOOD, HENRY. "A True Description of the Course and Distances of the Capes, Bayes, Coves, Ports and Harbours in New-found-land ... between Cape Race and Cape Bonavista," *The English Pilot. The Fourth Book,* 1689 (and later editions).

SPECK, FRANK G. *Beothuk and Micmac.* (Museum of the American Indian Heye Foundation, New York 1922).

SQUIRES, H. J. *Giant Scallops in Newfoundland Coastal Waters* (Fisheries Research Board of Canada, Bulletin no. 135, Ottawa 1962).

STEWART, GEORGE R. "A Classification of Place Names," *Names*, II, 1 (March 1954), pp. 1–13.

— "Names (In Linguistics) Place Names," *Encyclopaedia Britannica*, 1958 edition, 63D–E.

— *Names on the Land*, revised edition. (Houghton Mifflin, Cambridge, [Mass.] 1958).

STORY, GEORGE MORLEY. "Research in the Language and Place Names of Newfoundland," *Journal of the Canadian Linguistic Association*, III, 2 (1957), pp. 47–55. See also SEARY, E. R.

A Summary of Selected Manuscript Documents of Historic Importance preserved in the Archives of the Department (Hydrographic Department, Admiralty, London 1950).

TEIXEIRA DA MOTA, AVELINO. *Topónimos de Origem Portuguesa na Costa Ocidental de África* (Centro de Estudos da Guiné Portuguesa, Bissau 1950).

— *Portuguese Navigations in the North Atlantic in the Fifteenth and Sixteenth Centuries* (Memorial University of Newfoundland, St. John's 1965). See also CORTESÃO, A.

THORESBY, WILLIAM. *A Narrative of God's Love to Wm. Thoresby.* The title-page bears the statement: "This pamphlet is a reprint of those portions of a booklet of that title which deal with the History of Methodism in Newfoundland, 1796–1798." In the Gosling Memorial Library, St. John's. The original work has not been traced.

TOCQUE, PHILIP. *Newfoundland: as it was, and as it is in 1877* (John B. Magurn, Toronto 1878).

TODD, W. E. CLYDE. *Birds of the Labrador Peninsula* (Toronto 1963).

TOMBS, L. C. "Early Portuguese Discovery and Exploration in Canada," *Seaports and the Transport World* (Montreal, April 1963).

VAUGHAN, WILLIAM. *The Golden Fleece* (London 1626).

VERNER, COOLIE. *A Carto-Bibliographical Study of The English Pilot. The Fourth Book* (University of Virginia Press, Charlottesville, Virginia [1960]).

VIGNERAS, L. A. "The Cape Breton Landfall: 1494 or 1497," *Canadian Historical Review*, XXXVIII, 3 (September 1957).

VINCENT, AUGUSTE. *Toponymie de la France* (Bruxelles, 1937).

WHITBOURNE, RICHARD. *A Discourse and Discovery of New-found-land* (London 1622).

WHITBY, BARBARA. "The Beothucks: a Portrayal of their Background from Traditional Sources," *Newfoundland Quarterly* (Summer 1963).

WHITE, JAMES. *Ninth Report of the Geographic Board of Canada 1910*.

Part II *Place-Names in Quebec*; Part IV *Place-Names – Northern Canada* [Ottawa 1911].

WILLIAMS, GRIFFITHS. *An Account of the Island of Newfoundland* ([London] 1765).

WILIAMSON, JAMES A. *The Cabot Voyages and Bristol Discovery under Henry VII.* With The Cartography of the Voyages by R. A. Skelton (Cambridge University Press (Hakluyt Society), Cambridge 1962).

WILSON, WILLIAM. *Newfoundland and its Missionaries* (Dakin and Metcalfe, Cambridge, Mass. and Halifax 1866).

WIX, EDWARD. *Six Months of a Newfoundland Missionary's Journal, from February to August 1835*, 2nd edition (Smith, Elder, London 1836).

WYET, SILVESTER. See Hakluyt, *Voyages*.

YONGE, JAMES. *The Journal of James Yonge [1647–1721] Plymouth Surgeon*, edited by F. N. L. Poynter (Longmans, [London 1963]).

Notes

CHAPTER ONE

1 E. Ekwall, *The Concise Oxford Dictionary of English Place-names*, p. xxvii.
2 Stewart also describes his system in "A Classification of Place Names."
3 See M. F. Burrill, "Toponymic Generics," for an account of some problems in generics.
4 With one exception, Stewart's examples have been replaced by names on the Avalon Peninsula of Newfoundland.
5 G. H. Armstrong, *Origin and Meaning of Place Names in Canada*.
6 W. Kirkconnell, "Canadian Toponymy and the Cultural Stratification of Canada."
7 L. Lacourcière, *Toponymie canadienne*.
8 J. B. Rudnyckyj, "Classification of Canadian Place-Names."
9 J. Poirier, *Toponymie*.
10 See C. Rostaing, *Les Noms de Lieux*; P. H. Reaney, *The Origin of English Place Names*, and K. Cameron, *English Place-Names*.
11 R. Hakluyt, *The Principal Navigations*, VII, pp. 145–6.
12 In *The New World*, p. 61.
13 W. E. Cormack, "Journey across the Island of Newfoundland."
14 M. F. Howley, XXXII, NQ, December 1911.
15 R. A. Skelton, *Explorers' Maps*, p. vii.
16 W. F. Ganong, *Crucial Maps*.
17 G. R. F. Prowse, CM. Prowse coined *cartology* to meet the need for a word to denote the study, as distinguished from the making, of maps. For Prowse's relations with Ganong, see Ganong, *Crucial Maps*, pp. xii–xiii.
18 G. R. F. Prowse, CM, I, p. 1.
19 Skelton, *Explorers' Maps*, p. 78.
20 G. R. F. Prowse, CM, III, pp. xxii–xxiii.
21 Hereafter abbreviated to NTS.
22 H. Harrisse, *Découverte*, p. 283.
23 Harrisse, *Découverte*, p. 344.
24 D. W. Prowse, *A History of Newfoundland*, p. 19.
25 See R. A. Skelton, "Captain James Cook as a Hydrographer," pp. 92–119, and *James Cook, Surveyor of Newfoundland*, p. 19.
26 PRO (Adm. 52/1263).
27 Skelton, "Captain James Cook as a Hydrographer," p. 106.
28 Lane's career is described somewhat inaccurately in L. S. Dawson, *Memoirs of Hydrography*, I, p. 3. The main source of information is in PRO (Adm. 1/470–472), to which Dr R. A. Skelton drew my attention and from which he extracted the foregoing.

344 / *Place Names of the Avalon Peninsula*

29 That these names are not unworthy of study may be seen from some of those at Pouch Cove, near St. John's: Joe Butt's Point, Chimney Gulch, Hauling Point, Blue Madam, Strawberry, The Spout, Red Scrape, Putty Rock. *The Royal Gazette and Newfoundland Advertiser*, CXVI, 10, 6 March 1923. Street names, as in St. John's, might properly form the subject of a separate monograph.
30 R. A. Skelton in a private communication.
31 Stewart, *Names on the Land*, p. ix.

CHAPTER TWO

1 J. P. Howley, *Geography of Newfoundland*, p. 2.
2 B. Whitby, "The Beothucks" pp. 3–6, 24. (The standard work is J. P. Howley, *The Beothuks or Red Indians*.)
3 B. G. Hoffman, *Cabot to Cartier*, pp. 11, 29, 31, 165, 168–9, 169–70, 177–8, 200–1, 215.
4 See p. 8 above.
5 A collection of artifacts, believed to be Beothuck, was found at Old Perlican in August 1962. *Daily News*, 17 September 1962.
6 R. Whitbourne, *New-found-land*, p. 2.
7 J. B. Jukes, *Excursions* II, p. 238.
8 F. G. Speck, *Beothuk and Micmac*, p. 18.
9 Whitbourne, p. 110.
10 T. S. Eliot, *Four Quartets* (London 1944), p. 25.
11 Speck, pp. 25–6.
12 A transliteration of Speck's phonetic spelling of Micmac names.
13 Speck, pp. 26–7.
14 *Ibid*, p. 139.
15 The chief source of Micmac place names in Newfoundland, besides those in Speck and in *Admiralty Chart 232a* (note 21 below) is R. P. Pacifique, *Études historiques et géographiques*, map 282, pp. 310–21. For Micmac names in other parts of Canada (with three references to Newfoundland), see W. P. Anderson, *Micmac Place-Names in the Maritime Provinces and Gaspé Peninsula recorded ... by Rev. S. T. Rand*.
16 R. H. Bonnycastle, *Newfoundland in 1842*, pp. 212–3.
17 A. Murray, and J. P. Howley, *Geological Survey of Newfoundland*, p. 284.
18 Note 2 above.
19 Murray and Howley, p. 282.
20 Information from his daughter, Mrs Ellen Fowler, c. 1873–1967).
21 The chart was published originally in 1870, but the Micmac names, like others, may have been added in later editions. The edition used, the earliest available, was that of 1915.
22 M. F. Howley, XIX, *NQ*, October 1907.
23 *Ibid*, XX, December 1907.
24 C. R. Fay, *Channel Islands and Newfoundland*, p. 17.
25 CO, Misc. 199.18, from data gathered 1702–1807.
26 J. Rousseau, "Les Américanismes du Parler canadien-français."
27 *The Daily News*, St. John's, 16 January 1962.
F. W. Hodge, "Abnaki," *Handbook of American Indians*, I, 2. Rousseau has also *Wabano*, signifying "une manifestation bruyante": "Les Têtes-de-boule ont des jongleurs spécialisés, nommés *wabanos*. La cérémonie de la tente tremblante nécessite une autre sorte de jongleurs. Pour les forestiers du Saint Maurice, *wabano*, devenu le nom de cette cérémonie, signifie toute

réunion tumultueuse." This interpretation does not appear to have any relevance to the present context.

For an account of the ceremony of the Shaking Tent, see R. S. Lambert, *Exploring the Supernatural*, chaps. I and II.

28 G. H. Armstrong, *Origin and Meaning of Place Names in Canada*, p. 222.
29 See p. 8 above.
30 Hoffman. See p. 10 above.
31 J. A. Williamson, *Cabot Voyages*.
32 See chap. I, note 18.
33 T. E. Layng in W. F. Ganong, *Crucial Maps*, p. 472.
34 R. A. Skelton in Williamson, p. 298.
35 Layng in Ganong, *Crucial Maps*, p. 473. R. A. Skelton, however, in a private communication has maintained that the Day letter is by no means irreconcilable with the evidence of the La Cosa map.
36 D. B. Quinn, "The Argument for the English Discovery of America," and Williamson, chap. II.
37 R. Blome, *The Present State of His Majesties Iles and Territories in America*, 1687, cited by G. R. F. Prowse, CM, I, p. 228.
38 G. R. F. Prowse, CM, III, pp. i, iii.
39 *Ibid.*, p. 128. In this context Foreland head (Popple 1733, Kitchin 1762) may be noted.
40 *Ibid.*, p. 129.
41 *Ibid.*, p. 131.
42 Skelton in Williamson, pp. 313–8.
43 *Ibid.*, p. 318.
44 A. Davies, "The Last Voyage of John Cabot," relates Cauo de la spera to the place where a consort ship in John Cabot's second expedition to Newfoundland in 1498 waited in vain for the return of Cabot's ship from her explorations. This interpretation, however, runs counter to Skelton's argument on pp. 40–1.
45 Printed map in Bonnycastle.
46 *NLP* 1951, I, p. 95.
47 G. R. F. Prowse, CM, III, pp. 135–6.
48 W. F. Ganong, *Crucial Maps*, p. 54.
49 A. Dauzat, *Noms de Famille*, pp. 585–6.
50 See p. 54.
51 Ganong, *Crucial Maps*, p. 39.
52 Williamson, *Cabot Voyages*, p. 216.
53 *Ibid.*, p. 201.
54 De la Borderie, "Les Bretons à Terre-Neuve en 1510," cited in A. Anthiaume, *Cartes Marines*.
55 Ch. de la Morandière, *Histoire de la Pêche française*, I, p. 219.
56 *Ibid.*, and Innis, H. A., *The Cod Fisheries*, p. 14.
57 Innis, p. 26.
58 See pp. 30 and 31 above.

CHAPTER THREE

1 H. A. Innis, *The Cod Fisheries*, p. 15.
2 *Ibid.*, p. 26.
3 E. R. Seary, *Toponymy of the Island of Newfoundland*, Check-List No. 2.
4 Quoted in H. P. Biggar, *Voyages of Jacques Cartier*, pp. 239–40. See above, p. 31.

346 / *Place Names of the Avalon Peninsula*

5 Innis, pp. 18–9.
6 A. Dauzat, *Noms de Famille*, p. 127.
7 *Sixteenth-Century Maps*, pp. 98 and 102.
8 G. Lanctot (ed.), *The Oakes Collection: New Documents by Lahontan.* For an account of Lahontan, see *Encyclopaedia Canadiana*, VI, 49.
9 Ch. de la Morandière, I, 220 and Innis, p. 23 and note.
10 D. W. Prowse, *A History of Newfoundland*, p. 103.
11 Quoted *ibid.*, p. 126.
12 See p. 35 above.
13 M. F. Howley, XXVII, NQ, September 1908.
14 Imray, *Sailing Directory*, pp. 71–2.
15 Four, if CARBONEAR, pp. 38–9 above, is taken as French and not Spanish.
16 John Guy, in *The New World*.
17 la Morandière, I, p. 405.
18 D. W. Prowse, pp. 99, 110.
19 la Morandière, I, pp. 225–6.
20 J. Beaudoin, "Journal d'une Expédition de D'Iberville," in Gosselin, A., (ed.), *Les Normands au Canada*. For an account of Beaudoin, see Baudoin, Jean, *Dictionary of Canadian Biography*, I.
21 M. F. Howley, VI, XVII, NQ, March 1903, March 1907.
22 R. de Loture, *Histoire de la Grande Pêche de Terre-Neuve*, p. 242.
23 la Morandière, I, pp. 173–4.
24 L. A. Anspach, *History of the Island of Newfoundland*, p. 301.
25 M. F. Howley, IV, XX, NQ, June 1902, December 1907.
26 A. Dauzat, *Noms de Lieux*, p. 130.
27 W. Blathwayt (c. 1649–1717) held various public appointments including those of secretary-at-war and secretary-at-state. See *DNB* and G. R. F. Prowse, *CM*, I, 39 [48].
28 Dauzat, *Noms de Famille*, p. 406.
29 M. F. Howley, VI, NQ, March 1903.
30 J. Yonge, *The Journal of James Yonge*, p. 120. See pp. 66–70 below.
31 M. F. Howley, XXII, NQ, July 1908.
32 M. Harvey, "Etymology of the Name 'Quidi Vidi.'"
33 See pp. 25–6 above.
34 Letter to the Archbishop of Canterbury 10 February 1742–3, in Society for the Propagation of the Gospel, Miscellaneous unbound manuscripts: Letters from Newfoundland, 1709–1852.
35 Communicated to the *Daily News*, St. John's, 28 January 1959, by N. C. C[rewe].
36 H. Harrisse, *Découverte*, p. 50.
37 Dauzat, *Noms de Famille*, pp. 502, 504.
38 C. R. Fay, *Channel Islands and Newfoundland*, pp. 27, 29.
39 O. Jespersen, *A Modern English Grammar*, I, pp. 212, 213.
40 Bodleian Library MS Rawlinson. A183 f. 101.
41 *CSP, Colonial Office, America and West Indies, 1661–1668*, p. 558, 1730, 1731, pp. 560–1, 1732; and D. W. Prowse, *A History of Newfoundland*, pp. 174, 175, 202–3.
42 The fullest account of the French at Placentia is in la Morandière, I, pp. 403–507.
43 G. R. F. Prowse, *CM*, III, p. 118.
44 Loture, p. 243.
45 Dauzat, *Noms de Famille*, pp. 305.
46 la Morandière, I, pp. 169–70.

Notes: Chapter Three / 347

47 *Petit Larousse*, Paris, [1959], is the only one of several French dictionaries which cites *barachois*.
48 J. B. Jukes, *Excursions*, I, p. 89.
49 R. H. Bonnycastle, *Newfoundland in 1842*, p. 219.
50 *Gazetteer of Canada, Nova Scotia, and New Brunswick*. Of its use in Nova Scotia, Thomas J. Brown writes in *Place-Names of the Province of Nova Scotia*, p. 15: "BARRASOIS or BARACHOIS – A descriptive name found in many places throughout Nova Scotia. The word is from Acadian French 'Barre à cheoir,' and means lagoon or pond. It is generally applied to ponds separated from larger bodies of water by necks of land or sand bars.
   In Pichon's History (1760) he refers to the name 'Barachois' thus 'They give names in this country to small ponds near the sea from which they are separated only by a kind of causeway. There is no possibility of travelling even the distance of a league along the coast of Cape Breton without meeting with some of these pieces of water.'"
51 Dauzat, *Noms de Famille*, p. 493.
52 A. Murray and J. P. Howley, *Geological Survey of Newfoundland*, p. 179.
53 J. F. Imray, *Sailing Directory*, p. 82.
54 M. F. Howley, XXIX, *NQ*, March 1910.
55 Dauzat, *Noms de Famille*, p. 474.
56 See above, p. 47.
57 Imray, *Sailing Directory*, p. 91.
58 Dauzat, *Noms de Famille*, pp. 450–1 under Nicolas. The Sieur Collinet "second et maître de grave du navire" at Conche (NTS Groais Islands) in 1765. la Morandière, II, p. 898.
59 Dauzat, *Noms de Famille*, p. 444.
60 See Chapter 5, note 25 below.
61 See M. F. Howley, IV, *NQ*, June 1902.
62 Dauzat, *Noms de Lieux*, p. 217.
63 *The English Pilot. The Fourth Book*, 1716, p. 17.
64 Anspach, pp. 325–6. Cow and Calf is the name of a sloping stack of rock near Hartland Point, Devon (J. L. W. Page, *Coasts of Devon*, p. 167) and Bull, Cow and Calf of rocks off the coast of Kerry (Charles Smith, *The Antient and Present State of the County of Kerry*, p. 350, communicated by Dr W. Kirwin).
65 See pp. 39–40 above.
66 *The English Pilot. The Fourth Book*, 1716.
67 Dauzat, *Noms de Famille*, p. 299 under Goret.
68 *Ibid.*, p. 361.
69 A. Longnon, *Les Noms de Lieu de la France*, p. 548.
70 A. Rostaing, *Les Noms de Lieux*, p. 98.
71 Dauzat, *Noms de Famille*, p. 162.
72 M. F. Howley, XVII, *NQ*, March 1907.
73 H. M. Mosdell, *When was That?*, p. 16.
74 *NLP*, 1951, I, p. 103.
75 M. F. Howley, XVII, *NQ*, March 1907.
76 Dauzat, *Noms de Famille*, p. 280 under Gasc.
77 la Morandière, II, p. 822.
78 Dauzat, *Noms de Famille*, pp. 418, 419.
79 See p. 48 above.
80 M. F. Howley, XXX, *NQ*, March 1911.
81 Loture, p. 254.
82 *NLP*, I, 104.

348 / *Place Names of the Avalon Peninsula*

83 E. MacLysaght, *IF*, p. 258.
84 *Electors, Placentia East*, pp. 60–1.
85 M. F. Howley, xxviii, *NQ*, December 1909.
86 Dauzat, *Noms de Famille*, p. 63.
87 M. F. Howley, xi, xxviii, *NQ*, June 1904, December 1909.
88 See A. Davies, "The Last Voyage of John Cabot." Davies identifies Ilha de frey luis with Lewis Island (NTS St. Brendan's), apparently overlooking the error common among early cartographers of mistaking capes for islands and the unlikelihood of an unimportant island, rather than a prominent headland, being named at this early date. Lewis Island does not appear to have been recorded before Jukes 1840 and is probably a transferred family name.
89 *OED* Freel, frill. It should be noted, however, that although scallops and clams have been known in Newfoundland coastal waters for many years, as Glam (i.e. CLAM) Cove (Yonge 1663) (NTS Trepassey) witnesses, recent surveys have not discovered scallop beds in the vicinity of CAPE FREELS. See H. J. Squires, *Giant Scallops*.
90 Dauzat, *Noms de Famille*, p. 481.
91 CO Misc. 199.18, "Return of Possessions held in Conception Bay."
92 M. F. Howley, xxi, *NQ*, March 1908.
93 Minute Book, Gower Street Church, St. John's.
94 P. Chapuy, *Origines des Noms patronymiques français*, Paris, [1934], p. 192. Reaney, *Surnames*, p. 258, cites Pouch, but presumably with the pronunciation [paUtʃ].
95 Dauzat, *Noms de Famille*, p. 536.
96 *Electors, St. Mary's*, pp. 10–11, 24.
97 Dauzat, *Noms de Famille*, p. 320.
98 M. F. Howley, xxviii, xxxiv, *NQ*, December 1909, November 1912.
99 Gushue is discussed above, pp. 25–6. Hawco derives from Hautcœur (Dauzat, *Noms de Famille*, p. 322).
100 See p. 5 above.
101 L. Lacourcière, *Toponymie canadienne*, pp. 16-8.

CHAPTER FOUR

1 See D. W. Prowse, *A History of Newfoundland*, pp. 40–1.
2 In Richard Hakluyt, *Principal Navigations*.
3 *Ibid.*
4 See p. 27 seq. above.
5 H. S. Peters and T. D. Burleigh, *The Birds of Newfoundland*, pp. 258–9. George Cartwright, *Transactions* I, [ix], has an entry in the Glossary: "Bull. A small sea bird. I believe it is called the ice-bird." *OED* does not cite this usage. H. Horwood, *Evening Telegram*, St. John's, 26 July 1966, states that BAY BULLS was "named for the walrus (bulls) which were once hunted there."
6 In R. Hakluyt, *Principal Navigations*.
7 M. F. Howley, xvii, *NQ*, March 1907.
8 G. R. F. Prowse, *CM*, III, p. 114.
9 John Mason, *A Briefe Discourse of the New-found-land*, p. 5. Leigh's recording of the name anticipates Mason's, the earliest cited in *OED*, by twenty-three years.
10 R. Hakluyt, *Principal Navigations*, VIII, p. 12.
11 M. Lane, *Directions, 1775, 1810*.

Notes: Chapter Four / 349

12 See pp. 28, 30 above.
13 See p. 33 above.
14 See p. 8 above.
15 *Discoverie made by John Guy in Newfoundland in anno 1612 in and about 48: degrees of Latitude towards the pole Artike: A Iournall of the voiadge of discoverie made in a barke builte in Newfoundland called the* Indeavour, *begunne the 7 of October 1612, & ended the 25th of November following: By John Guy of Bristow:* Lambeth MS. 250 ff. 406–12, transcribed in *The New World*. Excerpts from the *Journal* had been edited and annotated by J. W. Damer Powell, in "The Explorations of John Guy in Newfoundland."
16 See pp. 30, 33 above.
17 See p. 56 above.
18 See p. 34 above.
19 See p. 33 above.
20 See pp. 28–30 above.
21 See p. 40 above. The fort was probably built either by the pirate Easton or for protection against him. See *The New World*, note 13, p. 91.
22 See p. 31 above.
23 See p. 41 above.
24 From its similarity to Heart's Desire: "Mason gallantly captured a Sallee pirate called the *Heart's Desire* or *Good Fortune* at Crookhaven in Ireland [in 1625]" (D. W. Prowse, p. 108 note) and to Heart's Ease: "William Baffin was Pilot (?) in the *Heart's Ease* in voyage, 1612, to west coast of Greenland" (James White, *Ninth Report, Part* IV, pp. 272 and 304). Of the related names in TRINITY BAY, Harts Easse, Heart's Ease Inlet (NTS Random Island) occurs as early as Blaeu c. 1630; the others later: HEART'S DELIGHT (NTS Heart's Content) (Lane, *Directions*, 1775, 1810); HEART'S DESIRE (NTS Heart's Content) (Lane, *Directions*, 1775, 1810); Little Heart's Ease (NTS Random Island) (Lane, *Directions*, 1775, 1810). The later names may have been modelled ? facetiously on HEART'S CONTENT or Heart's Ease.
25 Powell's tentative identification of Avon with AVONDALE (NTS Holyrood) (Powell, p. 514, note 2) is wide of the mark since AVONDALE replaced the original name, Salmon Cove, only about 1906. Similarly, its identification with AVALON (*The New World*, p. 91, note 22) falls away since AVALON dates only from the foundation of Baltimore's colony in 1621–3. See p. 57 above.
26 See pp. 41, 49 above.
27 See p. 38 above.
28 H. Harrisse, *Découverte*, p. 325.
29 J. F. Imray, *Sailing Directory*, p. 61. There does not seem to be any citation to justify a derivation from Port. *abrolho* – a pointed rock in the sea, as proposed by A. B. Perlin, *The Daily News*, St. John's, 29 May 1963.
30 L. A. Anspach, *History of the Island of Newfoundland*, p. 85.
31 G. R. F. Prowse, CM, III, p. 122. See Williamson, J. A., *Cabot Voyages*, p. 62.
32 M. F. Howley, XXII, *NQ*, July 1908.
33 M. F. Howley, XIX, *NQ*, October 1907.
34 *CSP. Colonial Series. America and West Indies*, XXXIX, no. 57, p. 43.
35 *The New World*, p. 54. Identified as SPREAD EAGLE BAY by D. W. Prowse, p. 133, and as Chapple Bay, i.e. CHAPEL ARM by Powell, p. 514; not Bay Bulls, i.e. BULL ARM, as in *The New World*, p. 91, note 24.
36 *The New World*, pp. 55–6. Identified by Powell; not "the extreme NW inlet of Bull Arm" as in *The New World*, p. 91, note 30.
37 *The New World*, p. 56. Identified by Powell.
38 *Ibid.*, pp. 56–7.
39 *Ibid.*, p. 61. Identified by Powell. See note 8 above.

40 *Ibid.*, pp. 57–60. Identified by Powell.
41 W. Falconer, *An Universal Dictionary of the Marine*, ed. 1776, cited in *OED*.
42 *OED*.
43 P. K. Devine, *Folk Lore*, p. 39.
44 *OED*.
45 N. Smith, *Fifty-two Years at the Labrador Fishery*, p. 68.
46 Imray, *Sailing Directory*, p. 37.
47 G. Cartwright, I, p. xv. Blathwayt's use anticipates the citation in *OED* by one hundred and forty years. Havre chatouilleux (Vion 1699) is a ludicrous mistranslation. The change of name of the settlement from Tickle Harbour to BELLEVUE seems to have been made without official sanction in the early 1900's. See pp. 141–2 below.
48 *CSP, Colonial Series, America and West Indies*, 1706–08, pp. 221, 489. For Major Lloyd, see D. W. Prowse, chap. x.
49 See p. 63 below.
50 See p. 56 above.
51 See *Capt. John Mason*, for a memoir of Mason, his "Briefe Discourse of the New-found-land" and other documents; D. W. Prowse, pp. 104–9; and note 24 above.
52 See pp. 40–1 and 58–9 above.
53 *Capt. John Mason*, pp. 12, 142.
54 D. W. Prowse, 109–14. See pp. 39–40 above.
55 See pp. 58–9 above.
56 R. H. Bonnycastle, *Newfoundland in 1842*, I, p. 74.
57 For Vaughan, see *DNB* and A. G. Prys-Jones, "Lord of poor Cambriol." Prys-Jones remarks that Newfoundland "some years ago ... denoted a farm or two in the lower Tywi Valley." There is at least one farm still so called.
58 M. F. Howley, xxvi, *NQ*, July 1909.
59 D. W. Prowse, p. 119.
60 See pp. 58–9 above.
61 See D. W. Prowse, p. 110; M. F. Howley, xviii, *NQ*, July 1907; J. D. Rogers, *A Historical Geography of the British Colonies. Newfoundland*, p. 56; *DNB*.
62 E. Ekwall, *The Oxford Dictionary of English Place-Names*, p. 237; *OED*. J. E. B. Gover et al., *The Place-Names of Devon*, p. 308 notes of Hope, Devon: "This is probably the OE *hop*, though it is tempting to derive the name from ON *hóp*, 'bay, inlet', were there other evidence of Scandinavian place-names in the neighbourhood. Hope is a little fishing hamlet and small harbour sheltered by Bolt Head."
63 D. W. Prowse, p. 130.
64 R. Whitbourne, *New-found-land*, p. 109. See also D. W. Prowse, pp. 117–8.
65 M. F. Howley, xvii and xviii, *NQ*, March and July 1907. For CARBONEAR, see pp. 38–9 above.
66 Ch. de la Roncière, "Le premier routier-pilote de Terre-Neuve (1579)."
67 D. Lloyd, *State Worthies*, 1665, cited in *DNB*.
68 D. W. Prowse, pp. 109–10, 131–2.
69 J. B. Jukes, *Excursions*, II, p. 220. The first description of the BUTTER POTS (NTS Biscay Bay River) in J. Yonge, *Journal* 1663 is somewhat different: "The land we saw was two hommits [i.e. hummocks], or craggy hills which (before the land near the sea appeared) seemed like islands, and these they call the BUTTER POTS." (Yonge, p. 55). Yonge's "two hommits" may account for the plural form of the name.
70 M. F. Howley, xxvi, *NQ*, July 1909.

Notes: Chapter Four / 351

71 See p. 42 above.
72 See pp. 60 and 39 above.
73 See pp. 51–2 above.
74 Insurance Policy dated 2 May 1891 in the possession of Mr Cyril Flynn of AVONDALE.
75 See pp. 30–1 above and M. F. Howley, xx, *NQ*, December 1907.
76 H. A. Innis, *The Cod Fisheries*, pp. 64, 69, 73.
77 See p. 49 above.
78 M. F. Howley, xx, *NQ*, December 1907.
79 C. W. Bardsley, *English and Welsh Surnames*, p. 450; Reaney, P. H., *Surnames*, p. 190; and R. M. N[ance], "Killigrew." W. Kirwin has traced Kelligrew in Paignton and Torquay in 1811.
80 Communication from Mr. G. E. Higgins; P. K. Devine and M. J. O'Mara, *Notable Events*, p. 73.
81 Jukes, *Excursions*, I, p. 17.
82 G. R. F. Prowse, *CM*, III, p. 124.
83 M. F. Howley, xxiv, *NQ*, December 1908. E. Rouleau, *Vascular Flora*, pp. 39, 40, identifies the plant as *Viburnum cassinoides* L. It is described in N. L. Britten and A. Brown, *An Illustrated Flora*, III, p. 272.
84 H. B. Guppy, *Homes of Family Names*, pp. 168, 176.
85 Imray, *Sailing Directory*, p. 59.
86 See p. 58 above.
87 Imray, *Sailing Directory*, p. 60.
88 M. F. Howley, xxiv, *NQ*, December 1908.
89 EDD.
90 Guppy, pp. 403, 404.
91 Reaney, *Surnames*, p. 20.
92 *NLP*, I, p. 89.
93 G. R. F. Prowse, *CM*, III, p. 130.
94 *The Journal of James Yonge (1647–1721)*, edited by F. N. L. Poynter (London 1963).
95 Yonge, pp. 11, 120. "It is clear from the manuscript that Yonge intended to do a great many more of the Newfoundland harbours, as the maps [of FERRYLAND, RENEWS and FERMEUSE] are followed by several blank leaves ... Elsewhere in the volume there are occasionally blanks of this kind, which were obviously left for the illustrations or maps he intended to draw later" (Private communication from Dr Poynter, 24 November 1965). Not all Yonge's maps are of Newfoundland harbours, since his travels took him from England to France, Portugal, Spain and the Mediterranean, and the *Journal* includes maps of Torbay, Portsmouth, St. Malo, Cadiz, Lisbon, Genoa, Messina, The isle of Mayo and Sicily.
96 *Ibid.*, p. 55. See p. 52 above.
97 *NLP*, I, p. 89. M. F. Howley, xxvi, *NQ*, July 1909.
98 Yonge, p. 67. Other descriptions of THE SPOUT are in *The English Pilot. The Fourth Book 1716*; E. Chappell, *Voyage of his Majesty's Ship* Rosamond, p. 23; J. F. Imray, *Sailing Directions*, p. 13; and Imray, *Sailing Directory*, p. 59.
99 Yonge, p. 117.
100 E. G. Gudde, "Sugarloaf."
101 Lane, *Directions*, 1775, 1810, [3].
102 *NLP*, I, p. 74.
103 D. B. Sands, "The Nature of the Generics in Island, Ledge, and Rock Names of the Maine Coast."
104 M. F. Howley, xvi, *NQ*, October 1906.
105 OED.

106 See p. 31 above.
107 Yonge, pp. 119–20.
108 D. W. Prowse, pp. 176, 194.
109 Yonge, Plate 4, facing p. 81.
110 See D. W. Prowse, p. 272: "Sir N. Trevanion's Orders and Fishery Scheme" refers to a "tenement formerly in possession of Sir David Kirk."
111 Yonge, Plate 8, facing p. 177.
112 *Ibid.*
113 M. F. Howley, xxvii, *NQ*, July 1909.
114 For names of Basque origin on the West Coast of Newfoundland, see p. 13 above.
115 The form Amboral(l) may have developed from Amiral, cited in *OED* as late as 1561, with an intrusive b, as in chimley, chimbley.
116 "Regulations for the Newfoundland Fishery" February 10, 1634 ... Chancery Warrants, Series II, File 2106 No. 525 in *In the Privy Council*, Vol. IV, Part IX, no. 712, p. 1720.
117 "Statutes Relative to Newfoundland and the Government of the Fishery ... Act 10 & 11 Wm. III., Cap. 25 (Imperial). An Act to Encourage the Trade to Newfoundland" in *In the Privy Council*, Vol. I, Part III, No. 45, pp. 251–2. For French legislation similar to the English, see *ibid.*, Vol. v, pp. 2171–80.
118 For citations of complaints against the Admirals, see Innis, pp. 156–7.
119 See p. 46 above.
120 Reaney, *Surnames*, p. 126.
121 Anspach, p. 308.
122 Harrisse, *Découverte*, pp. xxviii–xxix.
123 PRO, Adm. 52/1263.
124 See p. 31 above.
125 Devine, *Folk Lore*, p. 35.
126 EDD.
127 Reaney, *Surnames*, p. 299.
128 "An Extract taken out of the Map of Sebastian Cabot, cut by Clement Adams, concerning his Discovery of the West Indies," in Hakluyt, *Principal Navigations*, VII, pp. 145–6.
129 M. F. Howley, xvii, *NQ*, March 1907. Howley has both Split Cape and Split Point.
130 See p. 49 above.
131 G. R. F. Prowse, *CM*, I, p. 297.
132 Harrisse, *Découverte*, p. 340–1.
133 *Ibid.*, p. 345. See note 47 above.
134 *OED* and Peters and Burleigh, pp. 53–4.
135 Imray, *Sailing Directory*, p. 40.
136 Jonathan Couch, *History of Polperro*, ed. T. Quiller Couch, 1871, p. 31, cited in *OED*, article *drang*.
137 *NLP*, I, 1951, p. 71.
138 *Ibid.*, p. 72.
139 *OED*; R. A. Bartlett, *The Log of Bob Bartlett*, p. 136.
140 M. F. Howley, xxii, *NQ*, July 1908.
141 R. M. Nance, "Cornish Names of the Seal."
142 See p. 42 above.
143 See p. 49 above.
144 M. F. Howley, xxiv, *NQ*, December 1908; Barrelman, 15 July 1950.
145 *NLP*, I, 1951, p. 85.
146 *NP*, pp. 27, 34, 55, 136, 292, 336.
147 See pp. 70, 72 above.

148 Dauzat, *Noms de Famille*, p. 122, and Reaney, *Surnames*, p. 67.
149 *NP*, p. 39.
150 See pp. 62–3 above.
151 See p. 69 above.
152 W. F. Ganong, *Crucial Maps*, p. 54.
153 See p. 68 above.
154 See p. 39 above.
155 Guppy, pp. 150–1, 169.
156 See p. 57 above.
157 Guppy, p. 463.
158 *The New World*, p. 60.
159 See p. 69 above.
160 Imray, *Sailing Directory*, p. 54.
161 Imray, *Sailing Directions*, p. 14.
162 M. F. Howley, XXII, *NQ*, July 1908.
163 CO Misc. 199.18.
164 G. R. F. Prowse, *CM*, III, p. 114.
165 *EDD*.
166 G. A. England, "Newfoundland Dialect Items": "Scurwink – A kind of seabird. Also haigdown." Peters and Burleigh, pp. 53–7.
167 See p. 21 above.
168 See p. 46 above.
169 See p. 51 above.
170 See p. 31 above.
171 *OED*.
172 Admiralty Chart 296.
173 M. F. Howley, XXX, *NQ*, March 1911.
174 See p. 68 above.
175 Bardsley, p. 506.
176 See p. 68 above.
177 D. W. Prowse, pp. 241, 249, 263, 265.
178 See p. 68 above.
179 Communicated by Mr Gilbert Higgins, St. John's, and Mrs K. H. A. Marshall.
180 "La prononciation a longtemps balancé entre molue et morue qui a prévalu" Littré). See p. 87 below.
181 Harrisse, *Découverte*, pp. 313–4.
182 J. Beaudoin, "Journal du Voyage que j'ay fait avec M. D'Iberville, Capitaine de Frégate, de France en l'Acadie et de l'Acadie en l'Isle de Terreneuve. Du 26 juin 1696 jusqu'en May 1697" in A. Gosselin (ed.), *Les Normands au Canada. Journal d'une Expédition de D'Iberville*.
183 Beaudoin, pp. 68–9.

CHAPTER FIVE

1 See R. A. Skelton, *James Cook, Surveyor of Newfoundland*, and pp. 12–14 above. For COME BY CHANCE, so named in 1706, see pp. 59 and 60 above.
2 Skelton, *ibid.*, p. 28.
3 See p. 50 above.
4 *CSP, Colonial Office, America and West Indies*, 1722–23, p. 354, 730.i.
5 *Ibid.*, 1724–5, p. 226, 373.
6 G. Cartwright, *Transactions*, I, p. 14. Communicated by G. M. Story.
7 See p. 52 above.
8 Skelton, *James Cook, Surveyor of Newfoundland*, p. 28.

354 / *Place Names of the Avalon Peninsula*

9 J. F. Imray, *Sailing Directory*, p. 84.
10 *Ibid.*, and M. F. Howley, xxix, *NQ*, March 1910.
11 M. F. Howley, xxx, *NQ*, March 1911.
12 *OED*. See p. 13 above.
13 M. F. Howley, xxviii, *NQ*, December 1909.
14 See p. 77 above.
15 See p. 68 above.
16 D. W. Prowse, *A History of Newfoundland*, p. 295.
17 *Ibid.*, pp. 203, 223, 268, and 261–271.
18 Lord Dartmouth's Report, 1706, in D. W. Prowse, p. 267.
19 See p. 74 above.
20 See pp. 38, 51, 53 and 78 above.
21 *OED*.
22 J. Yonge, *Journal*, p. 48.
23 *NLP*, I, 145–6.
24 M. F. Howley, xxviii, *NQ*, December 1909.
25 Specific references to the infestation of Newfoundland waters by Turkish pirates are: "Unless measures are taken, the Newfoundland fleet of 250 sail ... will be surprised by the Turkish pirates" (Mayor of Poole to Privy Council, 8 August 1625, in *CSP, Colonial Series, America and West Indies, 1574–1660*, p. 75), and "The Turks have not visited these coasts for six or eight years" (Warden of Trinity House to Privy Council, 23 February 1637, *ibid.*, p. 246).
26 *NLP*, I, p. 138.
27 M. F. Howley, xxx, *NQ*, March 1911. Ram, Rameau are also French family names (Dauzat, *Noms de Famille*, p. 508).
28 D. W. Prowse, pp. 403–4 note.
29 R. L. Lounsbury, *The British Fishery at Newfoundland*, p. 249.
30 See p. 53 above.
31 See p. 49 above.
32 See p. 48 above.
33 See p. 85 above. The form Tickles, however, may denote a possessive from Tickle – an English family name especially of Cheshire (H. B. Guppy, *Homes of Family Names*, pp. 99, 560), though it is not current in Newfoundland.
34 See pp. 69–70 above.
35 See p. 53 above.
36 See p. 50 above.
37 See pp. 30 and 64 above.
38 See pp. 35–8 above.
39 See p. 53 above.
40 See p. 74 above.
41 See p. 84 above.
42 See pp. 76–7 above.
43 M. F. Howley, xxv, *NQ*, March 1909.
44 M. F. Howley, xxviii, *NQ*, December 1909, and p. 78 above.
45 Imray, *Sailing Directory*, p. 77.
46 *OED* rode^2; G. Patterson, "Dialect of the People of Newfoundland."
47 Imray, *Sailing Directory*, pp. 76–7.
48 M. F. Howley, xxviii, *NQ*, December 1909.
49 M. F. Howley, xxviii, *NQ*, December 1909.
50 J. B. Jukes, *Excursions*, II, p. 185; H. S. Peters, and T. D. Burleigh, *The Birds of Newfoundland*, p. 69.
51 See p. 31 above.
52 *OED* Cold III, p. 16.
53 J. E. B. Gover et al., *The Place-Names of Devon*, vol. IX, part II, p. 475.

54 CO Misc. 199. 18.
55 C. W. Bardsley, *English and Welsh Surnames*, p. 672.
56 *Ibid.*, p. 667.
57 O. Jespersen, *A Modern English Grammar*, I, Sounds and Spelling.
58 See p. 70 above.
59 Peters and Burleigh, pp. 250–1.
60 See p. 30 above.
61 *NLP*, I, 1951, p. 80; M. F. Howley, XXIV, *NQ*, December 1908.
62 L. A. Anspach, *History of the Island of Newfoundland*, p. 299.
63 E. Gosse, *Philip Henry Gosse*, p. 49.
64 See pp. 30 and 77.
65 See p. 63 above.
66 See p. 80 above.
67 See p. 31 above.
68 *NP*, 1952, p. 24.
69 *OED*; *Glossary of Words in Use in Cornwall*, EDS, no. 27 (1880), pp. 6, 78. See also HARE'S EARS, p. 87 above.
70 *NP*, 1952, p. 261.
71 M. F. Howley, XX, *NQ*, March 1908. But see p. 41 above.
72 *NP*, 1952, p. 261.
73 M. F. Howley, XXI, *NQ*, March 1908.
74 Jukes, II, p. 260.
75 M. F. Howley, XX, *NQ*, November 1907.
76 See pp. 64–5 above.
77 W. F. Ganong, "The Origin of the East-Canadian Place-names Gaspé, Blomidon, and Bras d'Or."
78 G. Patterson, "The Portuguese on the north-east coast of America."
79 *OED*, Blow- in combinations.
80 CO Misc. 199.18.
81 Reaney, *Surnames*, p. 176.
82 CO Misc. 199.18.
83 Imray, *Sailing Directory*, p. 49.
84 See p. 80 above.
85 *Electors, Carbonear–Bay de Verde*, p. 131; *Trinity South*, pp. 70–71.
86 *Electors, Carbonear–Bay de Verde*, pp. 144, 147.
87 Guppy, especially p. 447.
88 *Electors, Carbonear–Bay de Verde*, p. 61.
89 M. F. Howley, XVIII, *NQ*, July 1907.
90 See pp. 20 and 70 above.
91 *The Royal Gazette and Newfoundland Advertiser*, V, p. 250, 11 June 1812.
92 See pp. 20–1 above.
93 Imray, *Sailing Directory*, pp. 44–5.
94 Citations are from the second edition of 1810.
95 See p. 83 above.
96 Anspach, pp. 44–5.
97 See D. W. Prowse, pp. 307, 412–6.
98 See pp. 76–7 above.
99 I am indebted to Mr David Webber, sometime Curator of the Naval and Military Museum, St. John's for the foregoing information, culled from CO 194. If the name Frederick's Battery was bestowed only in 1777, it must have been an addition in the second edition of the *Directions*. Tocque 1878 has Fort Frederick.
100 Communicated by Mr C. Day Lewis.
101 Jukes, I, p. 66.

356 / *Place Names of the Avalon Peninsula*

102 For Admiral, see pp. 68–70 above.
103 J. S. Hobbs, *Sailing Directions for the Island and Banks of Newfoundland*, p. 10.
104 M. Lane, *Directions*, 1775, 1810, p. 8.
105 See p. 57 above.
106 Imray, *Sailing Directory*, p. 33.
107 See pp. 56, 59 and 60 above.
108 See p. 58 above.
109 M. F. Howley, x, NQ, [? March 1904]. See DILDO, p. 206 above for an earlier citation than Lane's.
110 Communicated by Miss K. George, New Harbour.
111 *Ibid.*
112 E. Wix, *Newfoundland Missionary's Journal*, p. 14.
113 Jespersen, p. 212; Bardsley, p. 396.
114 Communicated by Miss K. George, New Harbour.
115 See p. 65 above.
116 See p. 58 and chap. 4, note 24.
117 See p. 80 above.
118 Bardsley, pp. 354–5; *Place-Names of the Province of Nova Scotia*, p. 64.
119 For Ragged see p. 35 above.
120 See p. 90 above.
121 For COLLIERS BAY (NTS Holyrood and Harbour Grace) see p. 39 above.
122 W. Thoresby, *Narrative of God's Love*.
123 See pp. 76, 92 above.
124 See pp. 70, 92 above.
125 See p. 92 above.
126 See pp. 70, 76, 92 above.
127 See p. 93 above.
128 See p. 93 above.
129 See pp. 6, 94 above.
130 See p. 92 above.
131 CO Misc. 119.18.
132 Imray, *Sailing Directory*, p. 49.
133 M. F. Howley, XIX, NQ, October 1907.

CHAPTER SIX

1 *The Royal Gazette*, 6 February 1812, cited in Mosdell, *When Was That?*, p. 141.
2 *The Royal Gazette*, 12 March 1812. The poem was reprinted in the *Daily News*, St. John's, 30 May 1967, with the following commentary by M. P. Murphy: "The above poem was written in the year 1812, and descendants of the Tom Kearsey (or Kersy) mentioned in some of the verses are still living close to Twenty Mile Pond or Windsor Lake as it is now known. William Kearsey informs me that the family removed from the old house on the side of the lake to their present home about fifty years ago. Back in the early 1800s Tom Kearsey, as the poem says, kept a sort of halfway house for stage coach passengers and passengers from the packet ships going across the Bay to Carbonear and Harbor Grace and other points. This was back in the days of Coughlan's Coach, the days when a bit of romance (and often downright discomfort) was added to travel."
3 J. B. Jukes, *Excursions*, I, p. 25.
4 OED.

Notes: Chapter Six / 357

5 DNB.
6 E. Chappell, *Voyage of His Majesty's Ship* Rosamond, p. 43.
7 D. W. Prowse, *A History of Newfoundland*, p. 368; and for a short account of Wallace, p. 370.
8 See pp. 46 and 61 above.
9 L. A. Anspach, *History of the Island of Newfoundland*, p. 302. The Rev. Lewis Amadeus Anspach came to Newfoundland from England in October 1799 to take charge of the new Grammar School in St. John's. In 1802 he was appointed by the Society for the Propagation of the Gospel to the Church of England mission of Conception Bay with headquarters at Harbour Grace where he became a Justice of the Peace, deputy governor, and a judge of the Court of Civil Judicature of Newfoundland, and founded schools at Harbour Grace, Bay Roberts and Brigus. He returned to England in 1812. (H. M. Mosdell, *When Was That?*, p. 2; D. W. Prowse, p. 377.)
10 Anspach, p. 368. The mine was reopened in 1839 by Sir James Pearl.
11 *Ibid.*, p. 302.
12 J. Banks, *Journal of a Voyage to Newfoundland*, p. 10.
13 G. Cartwright, *Transactions*, I, p. ix.
14 Anspach, p. 294.
15 Jukes, *Excursions*, II, p. 216.
16 Edward Wix, born in England; MA King's University, Windsor, NS; ordained 1826; chaplain to the Bishop of Newfoundland, 1827; archdeacon of Newfoundland, 1829; left Newfoundland, 1837; died at Stanmore, IOW, 1864. (Mosdell, p. 142.)
17 See pp. 90–1 above.
18 See p. 39 above.
19 E. Wix, *Newfoundland Missionary's Journal*, p. 17.
20 *Ibid.*, p. 18.
21 H. B. Guppy, *Homes of Family Names*, pp. 23, 48, 168, 344.
22 Wix, p. 18.
23 See p. 84 above.
24 Wix, p. 19.
25 George Patterson, "Notes on the Dialect of the People of Newfoundland."
26 Wix, p. 19.
27 OED.
28 Wix, p. 25.
29 *Ibid.*
30 See pp. 51 and 82 above.
31 Wix, p. 26.
32 See p. 52 above.
33 Wix, p. 30.
34 See p. 84 above.
35 Wix, p. 31. See p. 82 above.
36 *Ibid.*; see p. 66 above.
37 *Ibid.*; tradition communicated by Miss J. Linegar, Placentia.
38 Wix, p. 31.
39 P. H. Reaney, *Surnames*, p. 77.
40 Wix, p. 31; Guppy, pp. 346, 355.
41 See p. 76 above.
42 Wix, p. 32.
43 *Ibid.*
44 NP, p. 78.
45 Wix, p. 33.
46 See p. 74 above.

47 Wix, p. 34.
48 See pp. 59-60 above.
49 Wix, p. 34.
50 Guppy, pp. 353, 521.
51 Wix, p. 34.
52 C. W. Bardsley, *English and Welsh Surnames*, p. 634; Reaney, *Surnames*, p. 267.
53 Wix, pp. 34, 35.
54 Ibid., p. 34.
55 Ibid., p. 36.
56 Ibid.
57 Jukes, *Excursions*, II, pp. 225-6.
58 Reaney, *Surnames*, p. 281.
59 Wix, p. 36; see pp. 59, 60 above.
60 Copy in the Gosling Memorial Library, St. John's.
61 To avoid cumbersome repetition, the shift names, which have been previously considered in the context of their first recording, are disregarded here.
62 See p. 69 above.
63 M. F. Howley, xx, *NQ*, December 1907.
64 Guppy, p. 467.
65 See pp. 51-2 above.
66 See p. 64 above.
67 See pp. 49, 85 above.
68 See p. 60 above.
69 See pp. 56-7 above.
70 co Misc. 199.18.
71 See p. 78 above.
72 See p. 79, 94 above.
73 See p. 77 above.
74 After Daniel Broderick of GRATES COVE, *Daily News*, 27 December 1969. As family name, Guppy, p. 476.
75 Anspach, p. 407. The earliest citation of the word in OED is from R. Whitbourne, *New-found-land* 1620 (1623).
76 See pp. 49, 85 above.
77 Communicated by Miss K. George, New Harbour.
78 See pp. 104-5 and 105 above.
79 OED. A common Newfoundland pronunciation indicated by swoil, as in Swoilers Cove (NTS St. Anthony).
80 See p. 83.
81 Reaney, *Surnames*, p. 76; E. MacLysaght, *MIF*, p. 84 n; H. S. Peters, and T. D. Burleigh, *The Birds of Newfoundland*, pp. 164-6. See also Howley, M. F., xxviii, *NQ*, December 1909: "Coot's Point. This is the name of a bird of the duck species. Still I do not think the name is known in Newfoundland, and, moreover, I found a great uncertainty about the pronunciation of the word among the settlers, some calling it Cook's Point, some Goose Point, some Coors Point, &c. This latter seems to give the cue. The word is Course Point, pronounced by the people Coorse, and it is a sailing direction for taking the correct course on entering [St. Mary's] harbour."
82 See p. 68 above.
83 E. MacLysaght, *IF*, pp. 23, 303.
84 See pp. 8-9 above.
85 Peters and Burleigh, pp. 86, 61.
86 G. Cartwright, III, p. 15 and Glossary. Rattle, rattling in this sense is not cited in OED.

87 Jukes, *Excursions*, II, p. 136.
88 See D. W. Prowse, Supplement, chap. II, and p. 153 below.
89 Guppy, p. 473.
90 See p. 54 above.
91 Imray, *Sailing Directory*, 1873, pp. 78–9.
92 Guppy, p. 509.
93 Bardsley, p. 90.
94 *Ibid.*, p. 593, entries Peattie and Peddell. Both names occur in Newfoundland.
95 M. F. Howley, XXVIII, *NQ*, December 1909.
96 Guppy, p. 514.
97 *Electors, Port de Grave*, pp. 85–6; *Harbour Main*, pp. 84–5.
98 M. F. Howley, XXIX, *NQ*, March 1910.
99 In H. P. Biggar, *Voyages of Jacques Cartier*, p. 300.
100 J. F. Imray, *Sailing Directory*, p. 82.
101 M. F. Howley, XXIX, *NQ*, March 1910.
102 *DNB, OCEL*.
103 See pp. 42 and 107 above.
104 M. F. Howley, XXIX, *NQ*, March 1910.
105 In, for example, such a study as E. Rouleau, *Vascular Flora*.
106 See p. 42 above.
107 See pp. 46, 48–9 and 52 above.
108 See p. 104 above.
109 Reaney, *Surnames*, p. 102.
110 For -ville in the U.S.A., see G. R. Stewart, *Names on the Land*, pp. 195–7.
111 MacLysaght, *IF*, pp. 100, 305.
112 See pp. 104 and 49.
113 M. F. Howley, XXVIII, *NQ*, December 1909.
114 J. B. Jukes, *Excursions*. Joseph Beete Jukes (1811–69), fellow of St. John's College, Cambridge; geological surveyor of Newfoundland, 1839–40; naturalist with HMS *Fly* in the survey of the northeast coast of Australia, 1842–6; director of the Irish survey, 1850–69; member of the royal commission on the coalfields, 1866. DNB.
115 *General Report of the Geological Survey of Newfoundland, during the years 1839 and 1840*, London, 1843.
116 Jukes, *Excursions*, I, pp. 14, 22. See p. 54 above.
117 *Ibid.*, especially p. 45. See p. 64 above.
118 *Ibid.*, p. 47. See p. 63 above.
119 *Ibid.*, p. 57. See p. 31 above.
120 See p. 105 above.
121 *Ibid.*, II, pp. 15, 220. See pp. 63–4 above.
122 *Ibid.*, pp. 14, 220. See p. 78 above.
123 *Ibid.*, p. 30. See p. 54 above.
124 *Ibid.*, pp. 32, 35. See p. 49 above.
125 *Ibid.*, p. 39. See p. 87 above.
126 *Ibid.*, pp. 39, 43.
127 *Ibid.*, p. 46. See pp. 39, 105 above.
128 *Ibid.*, p. 261. See pp. 49, 85 above.
129 *Ibid.*, I, p. 74. See pp. 59, 60 above.
130 *Ibid.*, II, p. 46. See pp. 59, 60 above.
131 *Ibid.*, I, p. 9.
132 Mosdell, p. 163.
133 Jukes, *Excursions*, I, p. 6. He makes a similar comment on "the western (or as it is called in Newfoundland the northern) shore of Conception Bay" (*ibid.*, p. 41).

134 *Ibid.*, p. 16. See p. 106 above.
135 *Ibid.*, pp. 28–9. See p. 102 above.
136 *Ibid.*, II, p. 344. Mosdell, p. 108.
137 Jukes, *Excursions*, II, p. 344. See p. 102 above.
138 *Ibid.*, I, p. 32.
139 *Ibid.*, p. 39.
140 P. W. Joyce, *Irish Names of Places*, I, p. 527.
141 J. F. Imray, *Sailing Directions*, p. 15n and communication from Mr E. Russell.
142 Jukes, *Excursions*, I, p. 42.
143 *Ibid.*, p. 44.
144 See M. F. Howley, XXIII, *NQ*, October 1908.
145 Rouleau, p. 62; N. L. Britten and A. Brown, *An Illustrated Flora*, II, p. 85; *OED*, Gold.² Britten and Brown give some twenty-five popular names for this plant.
146 Communicated by Mr George Makinson, grandson of George Makinson of Liverpool and Harbour Grace, who purchased the farm from the estate of Charles Cozens. See A. Murray and J. P. Howley, *Geological Survey of Newfoundland*, p. 285.
147 Jukes, II, p. 46.
148 CO Misc. 199.18.
149 Jukes, II, p. 68. See p. 76 above.
150 W. Percy of Brigus had a fishing room and stage on the island in 1801 (*Description of Fishing Rooms* in the possession of Mr John Hearn, Brigus).
151 The story was told by H. F. Shortis to W. G. Gushue of Brigus, who reported it to The Barrelman, a radio programme conducted by J. R. Smallwood which dealt largely with Newfoundland history and traditions. It was broadcast originally on 25 July 1945; the second version on 14 July 1950.
152 Jukes, I, p. 75.
153 *Ibid.*, II, p. 58.
154 *Ibid.*, p. 15.
155 *Ibid.*, p. 223.
156 *Ibid.*, pp. 223–4. See pp. 5, 22–5 above.
157 *Ibid.*, 224. Guppy, pp. 109, 142.
158 Jukes, *Excursions*, II, pp. 211–44.
159 *Ibid.*, II, pp. 220–1. See pp. 63–4 above.
160 See p. 78 above.
161 See p. 104 above.
162 Jukes, *Excursions*, II, p. 221. "At the present time the American Oyster catcher is not known to breed north of Virginia on the Atlantic coast, but in Audubon's time it must have ranged much farther north, even to the Canadian Labrador, where he found it near Cape Whittle on July 6, 1833. He writes that it was breeding in the month of July, and he describes its nesting. It is possible that Cartwright's notice of his 'Pied-bird' taken at White Cove, Labrador, October 6, 1773, may have referred to this species, although the late date would argue against it." W. E. Clyde Todd, *Birds of the Labrador Peninsula*, p. 283.
163 Jukes, *Excursions*, II, pp. 39, 222.
164 *Ibid.*, p. 45.
165 *Ibid.*, p. 222.
166 *Ibid.*, p. 267.
167 Jukes, Map.
168 Jukes, *Excursions*, II, p. 266. Tradition communicated by Miss J. Linegar.
169 Jukes, *Excursions*, I, p. 11; and also II, p. 217.
170 D. W. Prowse, p. 114.

Notes: Chapter Six / 361

171 See pp. 12–13 above.
172 See pp. 99–101 above.
173 Map printed with W. E. Cormack, "Journey across the Island of Newfoundland," *Edinburgh Philosophical Journal*.
174 R. H. Bonnycastle, *Newfoundland in 1842*, I, p. 197.
175 Murray and Howley, p. 369–70.
176 Sir Richard Henry Bonnycastle (1791–1847), military engineer, *DNB*.
177 *Ibid.*, p. 111.
178 *Ibid.*, II, p. 259.
179 *Ibid.* See p. 85 above.
180 See p. 95 above.
181 Census 1857. Copy in the Gosling Memorial Library, St. John's. Shift names have again been disregarded.
182 Two later important sources of names, however, are J. P. Howley's Survey of Rocky River – 1872 for Micmac lake names, considered in Chap. 2, pp. 22–5, and the National Topographic Series of maps, issued from 1954 to 1959, for names of inland features.
183 See W. Kirwin, "Lines, Coves and Squares."
184 See p. 171 above.
185 See p. 49 above.
186 Guppy, p. 519; Reaney, *Surnames*, p. 211; M. F. Howley, XXIII, *NQ*, October 1908.
187 Guppy, p. 466.
188 Bardsley, p. 512; *Electors, Carbonear-Bay de Verde*, pp. 9, 105; M. F. Howley, XX, *NQ*, December 1907; XXI, *NQ*, March 1908.
189 *Electors, Harbour Main*, p. 114 seq.
190 Tradition from Mr R. Tilley of Manuels; *OED*; Wix, pp. 124–5.
191 Samuel Codner (1806–1858), b. Devonshire. In business in Newfoundland for twenty-five years until his retirement in 1844. Formed the Newfoundland School Society in England in 1823, which founded the Central School, St. John's, in 1824. (Mosdell, p. 24; D. W. Prowse, Supp. "A History of The Churches in Newfoundland," pp. 7–9.)
192 For Lance, see p. 107 above.
193 Guppy, p. 508; MacLysaght, *MIF*, p. 97.
194 *NLP*, II, pp. 90, 111.
195 See pp. 48, 113 above.
196 Banks, p. 10.
197 See p. 117 above.
198 See p. 112 above.
199 See pp. 116–7 above.
200 See p. 78 above; Guppy, p. 457; *Electors, Harbour Grace*, p. 44.
201 CO Misc. 199.18.
202 See pp. 89, 104 and 112 above.
203 See pp. 64, 71 and 95 above.
204 OED Folly sb2.^{5} and as cited in P. K. Devine, *Folklore*, p. 22.
205 Tradition communicated by Mrs A. C. Hunter; *Electors, Carbonear-Bay de Verde*, p. 173; OED. Folly sb2; *EDD*.
206 See pp. 56–7 above.
207 See pp. 112–3 above.
208 See pp. 51–2 above.
209 See p. 63 above.
210 Mother Ixx cove in Imray, *Sailing Directory*, p. 77; *NLP*, 1951, I, p. 97; M. F. Howley, XXVIII, *NQ*, December 1909; Guppy, p. 500; *Electors, St. Mary's*, p. 5.
211 See pp. 22–5 above.

362 / *Place Names of the Avalon Peninsula*

CHAPTER SEVEN

1 See J. Jordan, "Induction to Dialect."
2 M. Harvey, *Text-Book of Newfoundland History*, p. 54.
3 See pp. 79–80 above, and Chap. 4, note 182.
4 J. Beaudoin, *Journal*, pp. 54, 57, 58, 59, 61, 63.
5 Cited in D. W. Prowse, *A History of Newfoundland*, p. 263.
6 *CSP, Colonial Office, America and West Indies,* 1719–1720, p. 178, item 260, ii.
7 R. G. Lounsbury, *The British Fishery at Newfoundland*, pp. 300–4. Statements on Irish immigration in Newfoundland are to be found in Lounsbury, A. H. McLintock, *Constitutional Government in Newfoundland*, and W. F. Adams, *Irish Emigration to the New World*.
8 Statistics from the Scheme of the Newfoundland Fishery, contained in CO 194/9; 221–2 and CO 194/13; 152, communicated by Mr C. Grant Head, of the Department of Geography, University of Wisconsin, Madison, Wis., USA.
9 Lounsbury, p. 303.
10 McLintock, p. 88.
11 *Ibid.*, pp. 89, 126–7, 129.
12 J. D. Rogers, *Historical Geography of ... Newfoundland*, p. 240.
13 Census 1794–5, MS copy in Gosling Memorial Library, St. John's.
14 The dates are based on the entry "Years in Country." The Irishness of the names is based on E. MacLysaght, *GIS*.
15 Information extracted at random from replies to a questionnaire submitted to students of the Memorial University of Newfoundland in December 1966. The questionnaire, which asked for information on Family names, Mummering, Christmas customs, Frightening figures, Games, riddles and rhymes, and Newfoundland words and sayings, elicited about 1200 replies which, when analysed, should reveal a wealth of information about Newfoundland, much of it previously unrecorded.
16 E. MacLysaght, *GIS*, p. 105, of Waterford, Tipperary and Clare.
17 H. M. Mosdell, *When was That?*, p. 54; D. W. Prowse, pp. 341, 424, 427, 433, 434.
18 See p. 109 above.
19 See p. 64 above.
20 Tradition related by Miss D. O'Toole. E. MacLysaght, *GIS*, p. 110, *MIF*, p. 140. Electors 1955.
21 P. W. Joyce, *Irish Names of Places*, II, p. 42.
22 *USHO Newfoundland Sailing Directions 1942; Irish Coast Pilot*, p. 80.
23 *Lovell's Gazetteer of British North America.*
24 Joyce, *Irish Names of Places*, III, pp. 597–8.
25 *Ibid.*, I, p. 315. For St. Bride, see p. 109 above.
26 Joyce, *Irish Names of Places*, I, pp. 286–7.
27 P. Power, *Place Names of Decies*, pp. 371, 410. Tradition related by Mr R. Bursey, Topsail.
28 P. H. Reaney, *Surnames*, p. 240; M. F. Howley, XXXI, *NQ*, November 1911; XXXIII, *NQ*, November 1912; R.-M. S. Heffner, *General Phonetics*, Madison, 1964, pp. 180–1. The problem of the change of the final vowel from [i] to [aI] remains open, however.
29 D. W. Prowse, p. 201; P. K. Devine, *Ye Olde St. John's*, p. 47. See pp. 77, 102 above.
30 See p. 77 above.
31 Joyce, *Irish Names of Places*, I, p. 374.
32 J. B. Jukes, *Excursions*, II, p. 354.
33 Joyce, *Irish Names of Places*, III, pp. 460, 575, 595.

Notes: Chapter Eight / 363

34 E. Rouleau, *Vascular Flora*, p. 83.
35 Joyce, *Irish Names of Places*, II, pp. 272, 285.
36 *Ibid.*, I, p. 364.
37 *Ibid.*, I, p. 368.
38 See p. 112 above.
39 Joyce, *Irish Names of Places*, II, p. 282.

CHAPTER EIGHT

1 See pp. 4-5 above.
2 See p. 62 above. For cove as street in ST. JOHN'S, see below.
3 The use of gulch for a narrow cove appears to be restricted to Newfoundland. See G. A. England, "Newfoundland Dialect Items."
4 See p. 68 above.
5 But see Chap. 5, note 33, above.
6 G. Cartwright, *Transactions*, I, p. xv. See p. 60 above and note.
7 J. P. Howley, *Geography of Newfoundland*, p. 19.
8 J. B. Jukes, *Excursions*, II, p. 31.
9 G. Patterson, "Dialect of the People of Newfoundland," p. 32.
10 N. Peddel, *Newfoundland Poems*, pp. 4-5. Communicated by Mrs C. S. Vavasour.
11 M. F. Howley, XXI, *NQ*, March 1908.
12 *OED* after Patterson.
13 *OED* Narrow. B.2. spec.
14 See pp. 48 and 112 above.
15 See pp. 115-6 above.
16 J. Banks, *Journal*, p. 44.
17 R. Bonnycastle, *Newfoundland in 1842*, I, p. 197.
18 G. Cartwright, I, p. xv.
19 *Ibid.*, III pp. 16-7.
20 Jukes, *Excursions*, II, p. 93.
21 A. Murray and J. P. Howley, *Geological Survey of Newfoundland*, p. 301.
22 P. K. Devine, *Folk Lore*, p. 49.
23 See p. 105 above.
24 *OED* Side 15b.
25 See p. 84 above.
26 See p. 88 above.
27 See pp. 114, 118 and 119 above.
28 See p. 114 above.
29 See pp. 102-3 and 104 above.
30 See R. A. Skelton, T. E. Marston, and G. D. Painter, *The Vinland Map and the Tartar Relation* (New Haven and London, Yale University Press, 1965).
31 Colonial Secretary to Secretary of the Nomenclature Committee [i.e. Board], 15 September 1913.
32 *EDD*. Not in *OED* in these senses.
33 The first and second meanings are illustrated, for example, in J. G. Millais, *Newfoundland and its Untrodden Ways*, pp. 339 and 12; the third and fourth meanings reflect BELL ISLAND usage as recorded in Newfoundland Dialect Archives, Memorial University of Newfoundland.
34 *OED*. See p. 72 above.
35 See p. 140 above.
36 J. Guy, *Journal*, p. 60. See Chap. IV, note 13, and p. 75.
37 D. W. Prowse, *A History of Newfoundland*, p. 272.

38 *Ibid.*, p. 99. For the relation between rooms and coves in ST. JOHN'S, see W. Kirwin, "Lines, Coves, and Squares."
D. W. Prowse, p. 450 note, writes on cook rooms in ST. JOHN'S in the earlier years of the nineteenth century:

"On every large mercantile establishment the cook-room was a necessary institution. All the planters and servants were boarded and lodged on the premises during their stay in the capital; the men slept in bunks ranged round the cook-room like the berths in a ship; generally an ancient retainer of the house, with an assistant, often a man and his wife, cooked for all ...

A great institution on the merchant's premises, always called in the vernacular "The Room," was the periodical serving out of grog; morning, eleven o'clock, noon, and in the afternoon, all employed in the room had a glass of rum; on the Jersey and on Newman's place this continued up to my own time. Various attempts were made by reformers to alter this practice. A most worthy Scotchman – Mr Johnson, familiarly known as Wullie Johnson (managing partner of the old firm of Baine Johnson) – tried to improve it by watering the grog; he went on diluting it until he raised a rebellion. Mr Robert Job was the first man to make a firm stand against the practice; he was execrated at the time, but he stood steadfast, and lived to see his example followed by all of his brother merchants."

39 See p. 107 above.
40 After W. Kirwin, "Lines, Coves, and Squares."
41 *Ibid.*

Index

The index does not include place names on the Avalon Peninsula, and their documentary citations, listed in the Gazetteer and Index of Place Names.

Abnaki Indian place names, 26
Adam (Eng. fam. name), 156
Adams, Clement(e) (? 1519–87), Eng. schoolmaster and author, owner of copy of Sebastian Cabot's world map, 11
Admiral Cove (NTS Grand Bank), 70
Admiral Island (NTS Trinity), 70
Aertsz, cartographer, map of 1631, 43
Aguathuna (NTS Stephenville), 20, 93
Ahwachanjeesh Brook (NTS Harrys River), 22
Ahwachanjeesh Pond (NTS Cold Spring Pond), 22
Alemand, Pierre, Fr. cartographer, map of 1687, 33
Alexander, Sir William (c. 1577–1640), Scottish poet, courtier and colonizer, 59
Alfonse, Jean, Fr. or Port. navigator and cartographer, *Cosmographie 1544*, 31, 34–8, 109, 267
American Name Society, 3
Amherst, Colonel (*later* General) William (d. 1781), commemorated in Fort Amherst, 94
Anderson (Eng. fam. name), 156
Andrews (Eng. fam. name), 103
Annieopsquotch Mountains (NTS Puddle Pond, Howley Lake, Star Lake), 22
Annguachar [now Ignorachoix Bay] (NTS Port Saunders), 13
Anspach, Lewis Amadeus (fl. 1799–1812), schoolmaster, missionary and judge: on mixture of Fr. and Eng. names, 50; on Torbay, 58; on Mistaken Point, 71; defines North Shore, 90; on The Narrows, 94; names in *History of ... Newfoundland*, 102–3; defines barrens, 103; on Hopewell, 226; on jigging, 230; on tilt, 289
Apphorportu [now Port au Port] (NTS Stephenville), 13
Armstrong, George Henry (1858–?), Canadian toponymist: classifies Canadian place names, 6, 7; identifies Penetanguishene, 26
Arnold (Eng. fam. and bap. name), 110; 156
Aske (Eng. fam. name), 157
Avondale (Ireland), 64
Ayles (Eng. fam. name), 157

Bacalhao Island (NTS Twillingate), 33
Baie des Trépassés (France), 39
B. ederra [now Bonne Bay] (NTS Skinner Cove, Lomond, Gros Morne), 13
Baird, James (1828–1915), Nfld. resident, 172
Baker (Eng. and Ir. fam. name), 88–9, 129, 136, 157
Baldwin (Eng. fam. name), 157
Baldwin, Harry, Nfld. resident, 157
Ballyhack (Ireland), 126
Baltimore, Lord, *see* Calvert, Sir George
Banks, Sir Joseph (1743–1820), Eng. scientist and traveller: on Glams (clams), 66–7; on barrens, 102; on gully, 143; on caplin, 192; on jigging, 230; on lords and ladies, 240

366 / *Place Names of the Avalon Peninsula*

Bannerman, Sir Alexander (1788–1864), governor of Nfld., 173
Bantry Bay (Ireland), 89
Barbary pirates commemorated in place names, 49, 85
Bardsley, Charles Wareing Endell 1843–98), Eng. anthroponymist, 109, 152, 156–67 *passim*
Barker, Matthew Henry (1790–1846), Eng. writer of sea-tales, 214
Barrens Pond (NTS Hodges Hill), 103
Barrett (Eng. and Ir. fam. name), 129, 157
Barry (Ir. fam. name), 129
Bartlett, Captain Robert Abram ["Bob"] (1875–1946), Nfld. explorer, 24, 73
Basques: in Placentia area, 38; ? on East Coast, 69; maps, 13; place names, 13, 38, 69, 267
Bastable [Barnstaple], 122
Bateau Barrens (NTS Blue Mountain), 103
Batten (Eng. fam. name), 157
Batton, William (fl. 1798), property-owner at Salmon Cove, 106
Bay Despair [Bay d'Espoir] (NTS Gaultois, St. Albans, Facheux Bay), surveyed by J. Gilbert, 15; 105
Bay of Islands (New Zealand), 14
Beaudoin (or Baudoin), Jean (c. 1662–98), French missionary: on foundation of Harbour Grace, 40–1; settlements named in *Journal*, 79–80, 97; first mention of Irish in Nfld., 121–2
Beckford (Eng. fam. and place name), 109, 157
Bedfordshire: family names from, 156–67 *passim*
Bell Island (NTS Groais Island, Grey Islands Harbour), 41, 49
Belle Isle (NTS Belle Isle), 12
Bellin, Jacques Nicolas (1703–72), French cartographer: map of 1744, 35, 38, 42, 52, 89; map of 1754, 38, 41, 72
Bennet, Goodman, Nfld. planter, 68, 77
Beothuck Indian place names, 19–20, 44
Berkshire: family names from, 119, 156–67 *passim*
Bestowed names, defined, 8; by Cormack, 8; by Guy, 8, 57–9
Biddeford [Bideford], 122
Biggar, Henry Percival (1872–1938), Canadian archivist and historian: on Cauo de ynglaterra, 191; on Renews, 266, 267
Bishop (Eng. fam. name), 118–9, 157
Blackmore, Martin (fl. c. 1865), Nfld. clergyman, on Bay Roberts, 177
Blaeu, Joan, Dutch cartographer: map of 1659, 42; map of 1662, 73
Blaeu, Willem Janszoon (1571–1638), Dutch cartographer, chart of c. 1630, 58
Blake, Sir Henry Arthur (1840–1918), governor of Nfld., 129, 181
Blathwayt, William (c. 1649–1717), English politician: "Blathwayt" map of c. 1630–40, 39, 42, 42–3, 51, 59, 60, 63; Eng. names in, 64–6; 130, 158
Blome, Richard (d. 1705), Eng. publisher and compiler, on changing of early Eng. names in Nfld., 27
Bloody Point (NTS St. Brendans), 20
Bonavist (citations of name), 96
Bonavista Bay and Cape (NTS Bonavista etc.), 13, 26–7, 32, 58, 94, 96, 105
Bond, Sir Robert (1857–1927), Nfld. politician, 297
Bonfoy, Hugh (d. 1762), governor of Nfld., orders erection of gallows, 215
Bonne Bay (NTS Skinner Cove, Lomond, Gros Morne), 13
Bonnycastle, Sir Richard Henry (1791–1847), Eng. soldier: on Micmac Indians, 22; defines barachois, 48; on ponds and brooks, 115, 143; names in *Newfoundland in 1842*, 15, 30, 44, 61, 115–6
Boone (Eng. fam. name), 157
Bowen, Emanuel (fl. 1752), Eng. map-engraver, map of 1747, 42, 46, 48, 52
Bowes (Ir. fam. name), 129
Boyle, Sir Cavendish (1849–1916), governor of Nfld., 195
Boyne, River (Ireland), 128
Bradley (Eng. fam. name), 157
Branscombe, William (fl. 1806), resident of St. John's, 111
Brazil (Ir. fam. name), 129
Bread Island (NTS Harbour Buffet), 78
Breakheart Point (NTS Marystown, Merasheen, Exploits), 51
Bremigen [?Branigan] (Ir. fam. name), 129
Brennan (Ir. fam. name), 129
Breton place names, 34, 39, 41, 42, 49, 53, 55, 58, 267

Bridges (Eng. fam. name), 157
Brien (Ir. fam. name), 124, 129
Brierl(e)y (Eng. fam. name), 157
Briggs, Henry (1561–1630), Eng. mathematician and student of navigation, map of 1625, 12
Bristol, 63, 122
British acts, bills, etc: An act to encourage the trade to Nfld. 1699, 69–70
British Admiralty Hydrographic Department, 14, 15, 16, 76; retains Famishgut, 84
Brock (Eng. fam. name), 157
Broderick, Daniel, Nfld. resident, 107 note 74
Bronte (Ir. fam. name), 47
Brooking, Thomas, Nfld. resident, 262
Brown (Eng. fam. name), 107, 157
Brown, Thomas J. (1867–?), Canadian mining engineer and toponymist, 44
Browns Cove Barrens (NTS Hampden), 103
Bruce (Eng. and Scot. fam. name), 85–6, 157
Bryan (Ir. fam. name), 124
Bryant (Eng. fam. name), 74, 157
Buache, Philippe (1700–73), Fr. geographer, map of 1736, 30, 31, 52
Buckinghamshire: family names from, 156–67 passim
Burin Bay (NTS Marystown), 86
Burke (Ir. fam. name), 124, 129
Burn [?Byrne] (Ir. fam. name), 129
Butler (Eng. and Ir. fam. name), 124, 130, 136, 157–8
Butler, Jas. (fl. c. 1760), Nfld. resident, 158
Byrne (Ir. fam. name), 129

Cabo de boa venture, 12
Cabo Raso (Portugal), 30
Cabot, John (d. ?1498), Italian explorer, 8, 26–7; lost sea-card, 11; 45, 53, 57
Cabot, Sebastian (c. 1475–1557), Italian explorer and cosmographer, lost world map, 11
Cabotia, 102
Cacciola, Francis J. (1870–1957), priest in Nfld., 246
Caein, River (Ireland), 112
Cahill (Ir. fam. name), 130
Calvert, Sir George, 1st Baron Baltimore (?1580–1632), Eng. colonizer, 57; purchases territory in Nfld. from Sir W. Vaughan, 61; 62; names Avalon, 63; 121; biographical note on, 189
Cambridgeshire: family names from, 156–67 passim
Canadian Board on Geographical Names, 9, 43
Canadian gazetteers and maps, 15–6
Canadian place names: classifications of, 6–7; North Atlantic coast, 9–10
Cantley, Thomas (1857–1945), names Wabana, 26
Cantwell (Ir. fam. name), 130
Cape Anguille (NTS Codroy), 14
Cape Breton (Nova Scotia), 27
Cape Degrat (NTS Quirpon), 41 (see also Degrat Harbour)
Cape Freels (NTS Cabot Islands, Musgrave Harbour), 53, 96
Cape Palliser (New Zealand), 14
Cape Ray (NTS Port aux Basques), 63
Cape St. Vincent (Portugal), 30–1
Cape Saunders (New Zealand), 14
Caplin, 56–7, 107, 192
Carlow (Ireland): family names from, 126, 129–36 passim
Carter (Nfld. family), 194
Cartier, Jacques (1491–1557), Fr. explorer: lost maps, 11; imposes Fr. names, 12; 16, 31, 34, 35, 41
Cartwright, George (1739–1819), Eng. soldier, writer and settler in Labrador: defines tickle, 60, 141; cites salmonier, 82; defines barrens, 102–3; defines rattle, 108, 265; defines steady, 143
Cartwright, John (1740–1824), Eng. naval officer and political reformer: map of 1768, 15; account of expedition of 1768, 16
Cary, Sir Henry, 1st Viscount Falkland (d. 1633), purchases territory in Nfld. from Sir W. Vaughan, 61; sends Irish settlers to Nfld., 121
Cashin, Sir Michael P. (1864–1926), prime minister of Nfld., 194
Castors River (NTS Castors River), 102
Castries, Charles, Marquis de (1727–1801), French statesman, 52
Cat Cove (NTS Englee), 41
Catalina (NTS Bonavista), 57
Cayley (? for Cyley), ? Tirwit, Eng. naval officer, 82
Chamberlain (Eng. fam. name), 116, 158

368 / *Place Names of the Avalon Peninsula*

Champlain, Samuel de (c. 1570–1635), Fr. geographer, explorer, founder of Quebec, map of 1612, 41–2, 73
Chapel, Chappell, Chapple (Eng. fam. name), 106, 158
Chappell, Edward (fl. 1813), Eng. naval officer: on out-harbour, 101; names recorded in *Voyage of His Majesty's Ship* Rosamond *to Newfoundland*, 101–2; on The Spout, 285
Charts, *see* Maps
Chaviteau, Jacques, Fr. cartographer, chart of 1698, 12, 35, 48
Cheshire: family names from, 116, 156–67 *passim*
Chute, Newton Earl (b. 1907), American geologist, 234
Clare (Ireland): family names from, 129–36 *passim*
Clarenville (NTS Random Island), 115
Clark(e) (Eng. fam. name), 158
Clark (or Clerke), Adam. ? first settler at Adams Cove, 92
Clark, John and Isaac (fl. 1770), property owners at Brigus, 113
Clear (Eng. and Ir. fam. name), 68–9, 130, 158
Clement(s) (Eng. fam. name), 158
Clerke (or Clark), Adam, 92
Cloghan, Cloghans, Cloghaun (Ireland), 128
Clown (? Eng. fam. name), 68, 158
Cochrane, Sir Thomas John (1789–1872), governor of Nfld.: builds roads, 19; Cochrane Dale named after, 112; 125; biographical note on, 197–8; 246–7
Cod Fishery: Fr. and Eng. rivalry, 13; early pursuit of, 32–3, 34; Fr. ships engaged in, 35; *dégrat*, 41; maps of, 45, 78; *grave*, 47; fishing-stages, 49; Fishing Admirals, 69–70; pronunciation of *molue*, *morue*, 78; boats used in, 86; rote, 87–8; *bacalao*, 171–2; jig, jigging, 230
Codner, Samuel (1806–58), Nfld. philanthropist, 117
Collier (Eng. and Ir. fam. name), 98, 118, 130, 158
Commemorative names: defined, 6; 30; French, 54; 72, 74, 97; religious, 108, 109, 119, 120, 139, 153–4
Commission Nationale de Toponymie et d'Anthroponymie, 3

Connacht: family names from, 129–36 *passim*
Conne River (NTS St. Albans etc.), 96
Connolly (Ir. fam. name), 124
Connor(s) (Ir. fam. name), 130
Conway (Ir. fam. name), 130
Cook, James (1728–79), Eng. hydrographer and explorer, 10; Nfld. surveys, 13; nomenclature in charts, journals of *Grenville* and directions, 14; 15, 71, 81; traditional connection with Cooks Cove, 201; surveys and charts of 1762 (all but one possibly by Gilbert 1768), 13, 53, 77, 82–4, 107; map of 1763, 39, 43, 44, 45, 71, 75, 84, 96; chart of 1764, 99; Cook and Lane 1770 [1775]A, 39, 75; Cook and Lane 1770 [1775]B, 35, 39, 141, 158
Cooper, Cowper (Eng. fam. name), 58, 158
Coote (Eng. and Ir. fam. name), 107–8
Corbin (Eng. and Ir. fam. name), 105, 130
Cork: family names from, 53, 124, 129–36 *passim*; place names from, 126, 128
Cormack, William Epps (1796–1868), Nfld. traveller: on naming places, 8; names Mount Misery, 8, 246; map of 1822, 15; use of lake, 115
Cornwall, Cornish: family names from, 65, 107, 108, 114, 120, 156–67 *passim*; place names from, 65, 72, 73, 242
Corte Real, Gaspar (b. c. 1450/5–1501) and Miguel (b. c. 1450–? 1502), Portuguese explorers, 28, 45, 117, 191
Cortesão, Armando (b. 1891), Portuguese cartologist, 11
Costello (Ir. fam. name), 125
Courage (Eng. fam. name), 158
Couch, Jonathan (1789–1870), Eng. naturalist and physician, 72
Courcelle, Sieur de, French naval officer and hydrographer: chart of 1675, 35, 41, 50; names recorded by, 50; 58, 86
Cox (Eng. fam. name), 108, 158
Cozens, Charles (d. 1863), Nfld. resident, owner of Cochrane Dale, 112, 209
Crawley (Eng. and Ir. fam. name), 110, 130
Crocker (Eng. fam. name), 74, 158
Crowe, Joseph (fl. 1711), Commander-in-chief Nfld., cites room, 147; cites Dildo Island, 206

Cullen (Ir. fam. name), 130
Cumberland: family names from, 156–67 passim
Curren (Ir. fam. name), 130
Cuslett (? Eng. fam. name), 159

Dalton (Ir. fam. name), 124, 130
Daniel (Eng. fam. name), 107, 159
Danielle, Charles Henry (1830–1902), American dancing-master and *restaurateur*, builds Octagon Castle, 253
Dauzat, Albert (1877–1955), Fr. onomatologist, 4; defines Grave(s), 47; on Crèvecoeur, 51
Davey, ? early settler at Coleys Point, 159
Davidson, Sir Walter Edward (1859–1923), governor of Nfld., 280
Davidsville (NTS Carmanville), 9
Davi(e)s (Eng. and Ir. fam. name), 131, 136, 159
Decouagne, cartographer, map of 1711, 51
Dee, John (1527–1608), Eng. astrologer and cosmographer, 32, 57
Degrat Harbour (NTS Quirpon), 41 (*see also* Cape Degrat)
Dennis (Eng. fam. name), 159
Dépôt Hydrographique de la Marine: map of c. 1680, 42, 44, 48, 50–1; map of 1706, 48, 51 (*see also* Decouagne, Detcheverry)
Derry (Ireland): family names from, 129–36 passim
Desceliers, Pierre (1487–1553), Norman cartographer: map of 1542, 12; map of 1550, 38
Descriptive names, defined 5; 52; Fr. 54; 65, 72–3, 87, 89, 97, 104, 105, 106, 109, 115, 117, 119; Irish, 129; 139; 150–1
Detcheverry, Pierre, Basque cartographer, map of 1689, 13, 35, 51, 58, 63
Dethick, Isaac (fl. c. 1633), settler in Nfld., 176
Devine, Maurice A., Nfld. antiquarian, 169, 215
Devine, Patrick Kevin (1859–1950), Nfld. journalist and antiquarian: on steady, 143; on Leamy, 235; on Mount Pearl, 247
Devon(shire): skirwink, 75; family names from, 74, 89, 92, 106, 107, 108, 109, 111, 114, 116, 156–67 passim; place names from, 87, 89; ponds, 115; 241, 296
Dildo, citation of name (Jamaican), 206
Dildo Pond (NTS Gander River, Comfort Cove), 96
Dildo Run (NTS Comfort Cove, Twillingate), 96
Dixon (Eng. and Ir. fam. name), 131, 136, 159, 206
Donegal (Ireland), family names from, 128; 129–36 passim
Donovan (Ir. fam. name), 131, 139, 208
Dorrill, Richard (d. 1762), Eng. naval officer, governor of Nfld., orders deportation of Irish, 124
Dorset: family names from, 70, 74, 104, 105, 108, 119, 156–67 passim; place names from, 70, 73, 83, 253–4
Downing (Nfld. family), 59, 68, 76, 295
Doyle (Ir. fam. name), 131
Drake (Eng. and Ir. fam. name), 131, 159
Drake, Sir Francis (c. 1540–1595/6), Eng. navigator, 56
Drogheda (Ireland), 126, 128
Dry Salvages (Rocks) (USA), 21
Dual element names, defined, 5
Dublin (Ireland): family names from, 129–36 passim
Duckworth, Sir John Thomas (1748–1817), governor of Nfld., 100
Dudley, Sir Robert (1574–1649), Eng. naval commander, inventor and writer, map of 1646, 43, 58, 119
Duff (Ir. fam. name), 131
Dun, River (Ireland), 112
Dunmanus Bay (Ireland), 89
Dunn(e) (Ir. fam. name), 110, 131
Dunscomb, John, Nfld. resident, 262
Durham: family names from, 156–67 passim
Dutch maps, 33

Earl, William (fl. 1760), Nfld. resident, 98
East Side West Branch East River of Pictou (NS), 156
Easton, Peter (fl. 1610–20), Eng. pirate, 209, 279
Ebbegunbaeg Lake (unnamed in NTS Cold Spring Pond), 22
Edinburgh (Scotland), 64
Edwards, Richard (fl. 1740–94), Eng.

370 / Place Names of the Avalon Peninsula

naval officer, governor of Nfld., on number of Irish in Nfld., 124
Ekwall, Bror Oscar Eilert (1877–1964), Swedish toponymist, 4
Eliot, Hugh (fl. 1480–1510), Bristol merchant, ? discoverer of Nfld., 32
England, English
- fam. names: 58, 65, 66, 69, 70, 72, 74, 77, 89, 92, 94, 96, 97, 98, 104, 105, 106, 107, 108, 110, 116, 119, 125, 152–3, 156–67 passim
- maps: loss of, 11; cartography of Nfld., 12–15; 27–8; Fr. names in, 42, 45–50, 52–4; of 17th cent., 60–79 passim; of 18th cent., 81–98 passim; 99, 102, 110, 116
- place names: G. R. F. Prowse on, 27–8; 30, 31; for Nfld., 31–2; 35, 39, 42–3; from Fr. 35–54 passim; of 16th and 17th cent., 56–80; of 18th cent., 81–98 passim; of 19th cent., 99–120
- settlements in Nfld., 40, 57, 60–3, 79–80; population figures for 1732 and 1754, 122–3
English (Ir. fam. name), 118, 131
English Pilot. The Fourth Book: on Bull and Cow, 49–50; on Cape Neddick, 71; on Deadmans Bay and Point, 71–2, 205; on Burnt Point, 74, 188; Southwood's "Description," 74; on Shoe Cove (Southwood), 75; 76–7; Gaudy's chart, 81; St. John's, 139; on Admiral's Cove, 169; on The Spout, 285
English Place-Name Society, 3, 4
Enniscorthy (Ireland), 126
Essex: family names from, 156–67 passim
Euphemistic names, defined, 6; 154
Evolved names, defined, 8
Ezekiel (Eng. fam. name), 159, 209

Falkland, Lord, *see* Cary, Sir Henry
Falmouth, 73
Family names, *see under* English and Irish counties, West Country, France, Newfoundland, Portugal, Scotland, Wales
Farewell (Eng. fam. name), 97
Fa(i)ry (Ir. fam. name), 131
Fay, Charles Ryle (1884–1961), historian, 26
Feeney, Finny (Ir. fam. name), 131
Fenelon (Ir. fam. name), 131

Fenelon, Maurice (1834–97), Nfld. resident, 210
Fergus (Ir. fam. name), 131
Fermanagh (Ireland): family names from, 129–36 passim
Ferryland Head (NTS St. Lawrence), 57
Fisher (Eng. fam. name), 159
Fishing Admirals, 69–70
Fitter (Eng. fam. name), 159
Fitzgerald (Ir. fam. name), 124
Fitzhugh, Augustine, Eng. cartographer, map of 1693, 13, 38, 65, 72, 78
Fitzpatrick, T. (?1857–1917), master of coastal steamer, on rote, 88
Flaherty (Ir. fam. name), 124
Flinn (Ir. fam. name), 131
Förstemann, Ernst Wilhelm (1822–1906), German toponymist, 3
Fogo Island (NTS Fogo etc.), 12, 33
Folk-etymology, defined, 6, 126–7, 154
Fortune Bay (NTS Marystown), 105
Fortune Tolt (NTS Grand Bank), 104
Fouleau (Ir. fam. name), 124
Fowler (Eng. fam. name), 159
Fox (Eng. and Ir. fam. name), 131, 213
France, French
- fam. names: 31, 35, 39, 42, 45, 47, 48, 48–9, 51, 52, 53, 54, 74, 83, 96, 106, 108, 110, 152; as ethnic possessive, 152; 192, 248
- maps: loss of, 11; 12; 34–55 passim
- place names: 12, 27, 30, 31; for Nfld., 32; 33, 34–55 passim, 56, 78, 85, 96, 97, 109, 141
- rivalry for St. John's, 94–5
- settlement in Nfld., 38–41
- support of Irish, 121–2
Franquelin, Jean-Baptiste Louis, Fr. cartographer, map of 1681, 42
Frederick, Thomas Lenox (d. 1799), Eng. naval officer, governor of Nfld., 95
French (Eng. fam. name), 159
French, Ed. (fl. 1775), resident of Bay Roberts, 159
Freneuse (France), 42
Friend, Hilderic (1852– ?), Eng. botanist, on bread-and-cheese, 183
Friend, John, Eng. hydrographer, chart of 1713, 35, 107
Fromes (Eng. fam. and place name), 70
Funk Island, 33
Funnell (Eng. fam. name), 215
Fursey, Mrs, Nfld. planter, 68, 76, 77
Furze, Mr, Nfld. planter, 68, 76

Gaff Topsail (NTS The Topsails), 91
Gallows Harbour (NTS Baines Harbour), 9
Galway (Ireland): family names from, 128; 129-36 passim
Ganong, William Francis (1864-1941), Canadian botanist and cartologist: "Crucial Maps," 10; 30; on the name Newfoundland, 31-2; on Blow Me Down, 91-2; on Cauo de ynglaterra, 191; on Motion Head, 246; on Cape St. Mary, 272; on St. Mary's Keys, 272
Garnish Tolt (NTS Marystown), 104
Gaudy, John, Eng. cartographer, chart of 1715, 31, 35, 50, 51, 81-2
Gaul (Ir. fam. name), 131
Gaul, Kitty, Nfld. resident, 233
Gear (Eng. fam. name), 159
Generics, defined, 5; 42, 44, 48, 60, 62, 84, 88, 91, 92, 103, 104, 105, 106, 108, 112, 115, 116, 117, 119, 125; in single-element names, 138, 140; of hydrographic features, 140-3; of topographic features, 144-6; of man-made objects, 146-8; in multiple-element names, 154-6
George III, King (1738-1820), 97
Gibson, Sir John (1637-1717), Eng. soldier, 94
Gilbert, Sir Humphrey (c. 1537-83), Eng. explorer: Letters Patent, 61, 213
Gilbert, Joseph (fl. 1768-75), Eng. hydrographer, 13, 15, 82
Giles (Eng. fam. name), 159
Gladney (Eng. fam. name), 159, 217
Gleeson (Ir. fam. name), 108
Gloucestershire: family names from, 107, 109, 116, 156-67 passim
Godden (Eng. fam. name), 159
Godden, Thomas (fl. c. 1877), shopkeeper at Harbour Grace, 159
Goff, George (fl. c. 1812), ? innkeeper at Portugal Cove, 100
Golden Grove (Wales), 61
Goobie, Gooby (Nfld. fam. name), 160
Gosling, William Gilbert (1863-1930), Nfld. scholar and philanthropist, on jigging, 230
Gosse, Philip Henry (1810-88), Eng. zoologist, defines North Shore, 90
Gover, John Eric Bruce (b. 1894), Eng. toponymist, 89
Grace (Ir. fam. name), 131
Granny (Ir. fam. name), 131

Grattan, Gratton (Ir. fam. name), 131
Graves, Sir Thomas (? 1747-1814), governor of Nfld., 13
Green (Eng. fam. name), 97, 160
Grenville Rock (unnamed in NTS Flowers Cove), 13
Groais Island (NTS Groais Island), 49
Gröhler, Hermann (1862- ?), German toponymist, 4
Guernsey Island (NTS Bay of Islands), 13
Guppy, Henry Brougham (1854-1926), Eng. naturalist and anthroponymist, 156-67 passim, 298
Gushue (Nfld. fam. name), 25-6, 54
Gushue, George, Nfld. politician, 216
Guy, John (d.c. March 1629), colonizer, explorer, governor of first Eng. colony in Nfld.: 8, 16, 19, 31, 38, 39, 40, 41, 44; records and imposes names during "voiadge of discoverie," 57-9; 60, 61, 62, 63, 70; tilt, 75, 147; 95, 97, 111; cites room, 147; settlement at South River, 282

Hack, William (fl. 1680-1710), Eng. chartmaker: map of c. 1677, 42, 76; map of c. 1690 ?, 35, 42, 44, 65, 66, 78
Hakluyt, Richard (? 1552-1616), Eng. geographer: on first naming of Nfld., 8, 26, 57; refers to lost maps, 11; 16; on beavers, 178; on caplin, 192; on foxes, 213
Hall (Eng. fam. name), 160
Hall, Isaac (fl. c. ? 1840), naval deserter, 118, 160
Haly, W. (? 1772-1835), soldier and pioneer farmer in Nfld., 125
Hamilton, —— (fl. c. 1860), Nfld. resident, 222
Hampshire (England), reflected in place name, 97; family names from, 156-67 passim
Hanrahan (Ir. fam. name), 124
Hants County (NS), 97
Harrisse, Henry (1830-1910), Fr.-Amer. cartologist, 9-10, 45, 58, 71
Harvey, Moses (1820-1901), Presbyterian minister and historian, on Quidi Vidi, 44; on Donovans, 207-8
Hawco (Nfld. fam. name), 54
Hawke (Eng. fam. name), 160
Hawke(s) Bay (New Zealand and NTS Port Saunders), 13, 14
Hayden (Ir. fam. name), 126

Hayes, Edward (c. 1550–c. 1613), Eng. explorer, writer and colonial promoter: records names in English, 56; on beavers, 178; on foxes, 213
Hayman, Robert (1575–1629), Eng. poet, colonizer and governor of Harbour Grace, 62
Heal(e)y, Hely (Ir. fam. name), 131
Hearn (Ir. fam. name), 124
Heart's Ease Inlet (NTS Random Island), 80
Hedges, Sir Charles (d. 1714), Eng. politician and lawyer, 60
Helluland, 145
Hennessey (Ir. fam. name), 132
Herefordshire: family names from, 70, 116, 156–67 passim; place name from, 70
Herwick, Abraham van (fl. c. 1597), 226
Hibbs (Eng. fam. name), 92, 160
Hickey (Ir. fam. name), 132
Hicks (Eng. fam. name), 120
Higgins, W. J. (1880– ?), Nfld. resident, 225
Hodge (Eng. fam. name), 114, 160
Hodges Hill (NTS Hodges Hill), 15
Hoffman, Bernard Gilbert (b. 1925), American cartologist, 10, 27
Hogan (Ir. fam. name), 132
Holly (Ir. fam. name), 132
Homem, Lopo (fl. ?1497–?1572), Port. cartographer, map of 1554, 31, 89
Hood, Thomas (fl. 1577–96), Eng. geographer, map of 1592, 56, 85
Hopewell (Eng. baptismal, ? family, place and ship name), 97, 160, 226
Horse Chops (NTS Trinity), 58
Horton (Eng. fam. name), 160
Hoskin(s) (Eng. fam. name), 160
Howlett (Eng. fam. name), 160
Howley, James Patrick (1847–1918), Nfld. scientist, 19; records Micmac names of ponds, 22–5; 48, 120; defines tickle, 141
Howley, Michael Francis (1843–1914), Nfld. divine and historian: on Kitchuses, 25–6; on Grates Point, 41; on Bell Island, 41; on Harbour Main, 42; on Quidi Vidi, 44; 48; on Gaskiers Bay, 51–2; on Latine Point, 52–3; on Cape Freels, 53; on Perlican, 56; on Torbay, 58; on Cupids, 59; on Vaughan's names, 62; on Bristol's Hope, 62; on Mosquito and Carbonear, 63; on Butter Pot, 64; on Witless, 65; 66; on Cuckold, 67; on Clear, 69; on Logy Bay, 73; on Tors Cove, 73; on Greens Cove, 75; 76; on Pinchgut Tickle, 85; on Ram, 85; on pronunciation of Hare's Ears, 87; on Mall Bay, 87; on Double Road Point, 87–8; on Peters River, 88; on Topsail Head, 91; on Adams Cove, 92; on dildo, 96; on Bareneed, 98; defines South Shore, 106, 282; on Golden Bay, 109; on Distress, 109; on St. Bride's, 109; on Gooseberry Cove, 109–10; cites Arnold Cove, 110; on Maddox, 116; on Manuels, 116–7; on Reginaville, 120; Cappahayden, 125–6; on tickle, 142; on Argentia, 170; on Whaleback, 175; lays cornerstone of Cabot Tower, 189; on Corte Real, 191; on Castle Hill, 194; on Coalpit Point, 197; on Colinet Islands, 199; on Conception Bay, 200; on settlers at Coley's Point, 205; on Frenchmans Cove, 214; on gallows, 215–6; on Graven Beach, 219; on Isaac Heads, 228; on Langley Cove, 235; on Lansecan, 235; on The Motion, 246; on Powles Head, 263; on Renews Rocks, 267; defines Southern Shore, 283–4; on Spear Island, 284–5
Hughes (Eng. fam. name), 25, 160
Humber, River (England and NTS Corner Brook, Pasadena), 13
Huntingdonshire: family names from, 156–67 passim
Hutton, R. (Nfld. resident), 262

D'Iberville, see Le Moyne d'Iberville, Pierre
Imray, James Frederick (?1829–91), Eng. compiler: on Trepassey Bay, 39; records Bay Roberts, 42; records Western Bay Head, 47; records Cross Point, 48; records La Perche Harbour, 49; records Rantem Cove, 59; limits Salmon Cove, 64; on Ship Cove, 75; records Sgeir Islet, 76, 277; on Mall Bay, 87; records Cold East Point, 89; on Distress Cove, 109; on Big Barachois, 173; on Little Barachois, 174; on Castle Hill, 194; on Cavendish Bay, 195; on Centre Hill, 195; on False Cape, 210; on Freshwater Point, 215; on Half Island, 222; records Niagara

Point, 222; on Placentia Sound, 259; on Salmon Cove, 274; records Shoal Bay, 279; records Spare Point, 284; on The Spout, 285; records Spurwink Island, 286; records Stanton Point, 286
Incident names, defined, 5; 20, 30, 54, 59, 87, 96, 139-40, 151-2
Indian Burying Place (NTS Nippers Harbour), 20
Indian place names, 19-26, 50, 152
Ingornachoix Bay (NTS Port Saunders), 13
Innis, Harold Adams (1894-1952), Canadian historian and economist, 32; on arrival of Fr. in Nfld., 34
International Centre of Onomastics, 3
Ireland, Irish
- fam. names, 47, 53, 104, 107, 108, 110, 118, 124-5, 128, 129-36 passim, 152, 153
- place names, 64, 89, 90, 112, 121-9 passim, 148
- emigration to Nfld., 121-4, 127
- population on Avalon Peninsula 1732 and 1754, 122-3
- trade with Nfld., 127
Irvine (Eng. and Scot. fam. name), 160
Isaac (Eng. fam. name), 160
Italian origin of place name, 44, 45

James (Eng. and Ir. fam. name), 118, 161
Jansson, Jan (d. 1664), Dutch cartographer, map of 1636, 42
Jersey (Channel Islands), 144, 153; association with Carbonear, 254
Jervis, John, earl of St. Vincent (1735-1823), Eng. admiral, 31
Jespersen, Otto (1860-1943), Danish linguist, 89
Job (Eng. fam. name), 94
Job (St. John's family), 94, 230
Joe Jeddore's Pond, 22
John(s) (Eng. fam. name), 108, 161
Johnson, D. W., Canadian Methodist minister, on Brownsdale, 187; on Victoria, 294
Johnstone, Wm., Nfld. resident, 262
Jonas (Eng. fam. name), 161
Jones (Eng. fam. name), 161
Jones, Dr, on Kitchuses, 25
Joy (Eng. fam. name), 161
Joyce, Patrick Weston (1827-1914), Irish historian and toponymist: on Vinegar Hill, 126-7; on *tochar*, 127-8; on *clochan* and *droichead*, 128
Jukes, Joseph Beete (1811-69), Eng. geologist: map of 1840, 15, 54, 59, 74, 78, 90; defines barachois, 48; 60; distinguishes two Butter Pots, 63-4; on otter-burrows, 95; records outport, 102; defines barrens, 103; on Centre Hill, 105; defines rattle, 108; names recorded by, 110-15; on South Side Hills, 111; on pond, 115; on road-making (*tochars*), 128; on tickle, 141-2; cites steadies, 143; records Downs, 145; on Aquaforte, 170; on jigging, 230; on rattle, 265; on South River, 282; on tilt, 289-90

Kaegudeck Lake (NTS Mount Sylvester), 22
Kearn(e)y (Ir. fam. name), 132
Kearsey, Thomas (fl. 1812), Nfld. resident, 100-1
Keating (Ir. fam. name), 124
Kelligrew (Eng. fam. name), 65, 161
Kelligrew, John (d. 1853), Nfld. resident, 65
Kelly (Eng. and Ir. fam. name), 132, 161
Kelly, Eng. pirate, 65
Kenna (Ir. fam. name), 132
Kennedy (Ir. fam. name), 132
Kenny (Ir. fam. name), 124, 132
Kenny, Robert, Nfld. resident, 232
Kent (Nfld. family), 132, 232
Kent: family names from, 156-67 passim
Kepenkeck Lake (NTS Kepenkeck Lake), 22
Keppel Harbour (NTS Port Saunders), 13
Kerry (Ireland): family names from, 129-36 passim
Keulen, Johannes van (fl. 1678-96), Dutch chart publisher, chart of 1682-4, 33
Kilbride (Ireland), 127
Kilclooney (Ireland), 127
Kilkenny (Ireland): family names from, 129-36 passim
Killigrew (Eng. fam. name), 161
King (Eng. and Ir. fam. name), 124, 132, 161
King, William (1663-1712), Eng. writer, on dildo and bonavist, 96
"King-Hamy" map of 1504-6, 12, 28, 30, 32

Kirkconnell, Watson (b. 1895), Canadian scholar, classifies Canadian place names, 6
Kirke, Sir David (c. 1597–1654), colonizer and governor of Nfld., 46
Kirwan (Ir. fam. name), 132
Kirwin, William James, Jr. (b. 1925), American linguist: on square in St. John's, 148; on pronunciation of Dennis Point, 205
Kitchin, Thomas, Eng. cartographer: map of 1758, 39; map of 1762, 15, 39, 46, 72
Knight, Stephen, Nfld. resident, 262
Knockoura (Ireland), 128
Kohl, Johann Georg (1808–78), American cartologist, 9, 191
"Kunstmann No. 2" chart of 1503–6, 45
"Kunstmann No. 3" chart of 1506, 30, 32, 53

L'Anse à Barque, 54
L'Anse à Cane, 54
L'Anse à l'Eau (NTS Marystown), 54
L'Anse au Diable (NTS St. Lawrence), 54
La Cosa, Juan de (d. 1509), Span. navigator and cartographer, map of 1500, 27, 28
Lacourcière, Luc (b. 1910), Canadian folklorist and toponymist, classifies Canadian place names, 7; on naming process, 8
Laddan (Ireland), 128
Laet, Jan de, Dutch cartographer, map of 1630, 33, 42, 43
Lahontan or La Hontan, Louis Armand de Lom d'Arce, baron de (1666–1715), Fr. soldier, on Placentia, 38
Lake Michel (NTS Indian Lookout etc.), 22
Lamb, William, second Viscount Melbourne (1779–1848), Eng. statesman, 249
La Morandière, Charles de, Fr. historian, 32; on early Fr. fishing settlements, 40; on *dégrat*, 41; on *grave*, 47; 48–9
Lanahan (Ir. fam. name), 124
Lancashire: family names from, 156–67 *passim*
Lane, Michael (d. 1794 or 95), English hydrographer: Nfld. surveys, 14, 81; Cook and Lane 1770 [1775]A, 39, 75; Cook and Lane 1770 [1775]B, 35, 39, 141, 158; chart of 1772, 31, 38, 52, 53, 76, 84–6; chart of 1773, 35, 43, 48, 53, 86–90, 141; chart of 1774, 65, 70, 90–4; *Directions* 1773, 87; *Directions* 1775, 1810, 57, 64, 83, 94–7, 119; map of 1790, 98
Langley (Eng. fam. name), 235
Lansey Bank Cove (NTS Lamaline), 54
LaPoile (NTS La Poile), 117
Lark Island (NTS Belle Isle), 13
La Scie (NTS Nippers Harbour), 114
Latin Point (NTS Groais Island), 52
Lawler (Ir. fam. name), 132
Lawrence (Eng. fam. name), 161
Layng, Theodore E., Canadian cartologist, 27
Leahy (Ir. fam. name), 132
Leamy (Ir. fam. name), 132
Leamy, Nfld. resident, 235
Lear (Eng. fam. name), 109, 162
Leary (Ir. fam. name), 132
Lee (Eng. fam. name), 162
Leicestershire: family names from, 156–67 *passim*
Leigh, Charles (1572–1605), Eng. merchant and adventurer, 56, 226
Leinster (Ireland): family names from, 129–36 *passim*
LeMessurier, Henry William (1848–1931), Nfld. civil servant, on Quidi Vidi, 44; on Jerseymen at Carbonear, 194, 254
Le Moyne d'Iberville, Pierre (1661–1706), Fr. naval officer, invades Nfld., 40, 79, 92, 94
Leonard (Ir. fam. name), 133
Le Testu, Guillaume (c. 1509–72), Norman pilot and hydrographer, maps of 1555, 35, 39
Le Vasseur, Guillaume (d. 1643), Norman pilot and hydrographer, chart of 1601, 12
Lewis (Eng. fam. name), 162
L'Hermite, Sieur, Fr. cartographer, map of 1695, 43, 44, 72
Limerick (Ireland): family names from 118, 129–36 *passim*
Lincolnshire: family names from, 156–67 *passim*
Little Paradise (NTS Baine Harbour), 49
Littré, Émile (1801–81), Fr. lexicographer, defines *en dégrat*, 41; on pronunciation *molue, morue*, 78 note 180

Index / 375

Lloyd, Thomas (d. 1709), Eng. soldier, 60
Loany, or Loney, Dennis, Nfld. planter, 68, 76–7
Locke, see Lok, Michael
Lockyer (Eng. fam. name), 162
Loder (Eng. fam. name), 162
Lok, Michael (fl. 1615), Eng. traveller, possesses old map, 11
London and Bristol Company, 61, 63
Long, Nick, Nfld. resident, 162
Longnon, Auguste (1844–1911), Fr. historian and toponymist: on Crèvecœur, 51; on Charbonnière, 193–4
Lotter, Tobias Conrad (1717–77), German map-engraver and publisher, map of c. 1758, 38, 41, 42, 46, 48, 52, 72, 102
Loture, Robert de, Fr. historian: defines *en dégrat*, 41; on *grave*, 47; defines *voile latine*, 53
Lounsbury, Ralph Greenlee (b. 1896), American historian, on shalloway, 86
Louth (Ireland), 126
Lower Duck Island Cove Brook (NTS Baie Verte etc.), 156
Luc(e)y (Ir. fam. name), 133
Luther (Eng. fam. name), 162
Lynch (Ir. fam. name), 133

McCarthy (Ir. fam. name), 133
McCue (Ir. fam. name), 133
Macdonald (Ir. fam. name), 133
McGrath (Ir. fam. name), 133
McHugh (Ir. fam. name), 133
McKay, A. M. (1834–1905), Canadian engineer, 241
MacLysaght, Edward (b. 1889), Ir. genealogist, 125
McManus (Ir. fam. name), 124
Maddock, Maddocks, Maddox (Eng. fam. name), 116, 162
Maggiolo, Vesconte (fl. 1504–49), Italian cartographer, map of 1527, 71
Maggot (Eng. fam. name), 76–7
Maher (Ir. fam. name), 133
Maiden(s) (Eng. fam. name), 162
Main (Eng. fam. name), 162
Main Topsail (NTS The Topsails), 91
Maker (Nfld. fam. name), 133, 242
Makinson (Eng. fam. name), 112, 162, 242
Maloney (Ir. fam. name), 133
Mann Point (NTS Carmanville), 9

Manuel (Eng. fam. name), 116, 162
Manufactured names, defined, 6
Maps: as sources of Nfld. toponymy, 11–6; limitations as sources of toponymy, 16–7; see also under names of individual cartographers; see also Basque, Canadian, Dutch, English, French, Newfoundland, Portuguese, Spanish
March, Mary (d. 1820), Beothuck woman, 20
Marshall, — (fl. ? mid 19th cent.), Nfld. resident, 119
Mason, John (1586–1635), explorer, cartographer, second governor of first Eng. colony in Nfld., founder of New Hampshire: map of 1626, 12, 15, 42, 59, 60–4, 115; on caplin, 192
Masters (Eng. fam. name), 105, 162
Masters, John (fl. c. 1723), Nfld. resident, 82
Matheson, Sir Robert Edwin (1845–1926), Ir. civil servant, *Surnames in Ireland*, 125
Matthews Pond (NTS Twillick Brook), 22
Maturin (Ir. fam. name), 133
Mawer, Sir Allen (1879–1942), Eng. toponymist, 3, 4
Mayo (Ireland): family names from, 129–36 *passim*
Meath (Ireland): family names from, 129–36 *passim*
Medonnegonix Lake (NTS Hungry Grove Pond, Mount Sylvester), 22
Medway, River (England and unnamed in NTS Bay of Islands), 13
Meelpaeg Lake (NTS Pudops Lake etc.), 22
Melbourne, Viscount, see Lamb, William, second viscount Melbourne
Mercer (Eng. fam. name), 119, 162
Mercer, Jonathan (fl. 1765), property-owner at Bay Roberts, 119
Merasheen Island (NTS Merasheen, Harbour Buffett), 115
Mewstone (Rock) (NTS Raleigh), 13–4
Micmac place names, 21–6, 120
Miles (Eng. fam. name), 162
Millais, John Guille (1865–1931), British naturalist and hunter, 214
Miller (Eng. fam. name), 162, 244
Mistake names, defined, 6; 51, 54, 65, 76, 104, 105, 109, 113, 154
Mitchell (Eng. fam. name), 162

376 / Place Names of the Avalon Peninsula

Mizzen Topsail (NTS The Topsails), 91
Moll, Herman (fl. 1680–1732), Dutch cartographer: map (after Moll) of 1711, 72
Mollyguajeck Lake (NTS Kepenkeck Lake), 22
Moloney (Ir. fam. name), 133
Monday (Eng. and Ir. fam. name), 133, 162
Monmouthshire: family names from, 108, 156–67 passim
Montagnais Indians, 21
Mooney (Ir. fam. name), 104, 133
Moore(s) (Eng. and Ir. fam. name), 133, 163
Moreton (Ir. fam. name), 124
Moriarty (Ir. fam. name), 133
Morley (Ir. fam. name), 124
Morris, Fr., priest in Nfld., changes name of settlement at Gallows Harbour, 9
Mothel Parish (Ireland), 127
Mount, W. and I. (fl. 18th cent.) Eng. booksellers and publishers: Mount and Page map of 1755, 38, 72, 75, 77; Mount and Page map of 1780, 35, 38, 44, 45, 88, 97
Mount Misery (Nfld.), 8
Mulley (Ir. fam. name), 133
Mullock, John Thomas (1807–69), Roman Catholic bishop of Nfld., on lead mine at La Manche, 234
Mumbles (Wales), 66
Mundy (Eng. and Ir. fam. name), 133, 163
Munster (Ireland): family names from, 129–36 passim
Murphy (Ir. fam. name), 124, 133
Murray (Ir. fam. name), 134
Murray, Alexander (1811–84), director of Geological Survey of Nfld., 22; on ponds, 115; defines steady, 143; on gold, 217; on La Manche, 234; on otter, 254

Nagle (Ir. fam. name), 134
Nameless Cove (NTS Flowers Cove), 14
Nancy Bark, see L'Anse a Barque
Nancy Cann, see L'Anse a Cane
Nancy Jobble, see L'Anse au Diable
Nancy Oh!, see L'Anse a l'Eau
Neagle, John, Nfld. resident, 247
Neil (bap. and Ir. fam. name), 134, 136
Neville (Eng. and Ir. fam. name), 134, 163
New Brunswick place names, compared with Nfld., 22, 48, 102
New Ferolle Cove (NTS Ferolle Point), 41
New Zealand place names, 14
Newfoundland
– origin of name, 8, 31–2, 62
– sources of nomenclature, 10–17
– European discovery, 26–31, 34
– government in 17th cent., 45–6
– population statistics 1696–7, 79–80; Avalon Peninsula 1732 and 1754, 122–3
– Irish immigration, 121–4
– family names peculiar to, 25–6, 53–4, 54, 109, 157, 160
– census returns: 1836, 106–10, 116, 117, 118–9; 1857, 116–20; 1874, 84
– maps, 15–6
– Nomenclature Board, iii, 9, 218, 262; see also proclamations of change of name
– Northern Peninsula, 41
– Population Returns 1836; see census returns
– proclamations of change of name: Aguathuna, 20–1; Avondale North, 64, 171; Bell Island, 41, 178; Bristol's Hope, 185; Brownsdale, 107, 187; Calvert, 57, 189; Cappahayden, 125, 192; Cavendish, 195; Codner, 117, 198; Conception Harbour, 64, 200; Fairhaven, 84, 210; Fox Harbour (St. Bernard), 213; Islington, 119, 229; Kingston, 119, 235; Maryvale, 85, 243; Mount Carmel, 108, 246; New Chelsea, 248; New Melbourne, 248; Portugal Cove South, 261; Regina, 120, 266; Riverdale, 117, 268; St. Michaels, 107, 272; St. Philips, 90, 272; St. Thomas, 116, 273; St. Vincent's, 273; Sibley's Cove (Prowsetown), 280; Sunnyside, 287; Thornlea, 145, 288; Tors Cove, 73, 291; Whiteway, 97, 298; Winterton, 9, 72, 299
Newfoundland Hotel (St. John's), 83
Newfoundland and Labrador Pilot, 15, 30, 52, 66, 110, 128; on Argentia, 170; on Bald Head, 173; on Cliff Point, 197; on Cripple Rock, 202; on Hare's Ears, 224; on Hole in the Wall Island, 226; on Horseshoe Cliff, 227; on Island Cove, 228
Newfoundland Pilot, 18, 77, 78, 81–2,

84, 94; on Shuffle Board, 98; on Eastern Head, 209; on Gibraltar Rock, 217
Newhook (Eng. fam. name), 96, 248
Nichol(s) (Eng. fam. name), 163
Nieuhook, Charles, Nfld. resident, 96
Noel Paul's Brook (NTS Snowshoe Pond etc.), 20, 22
Noreen, Adolf Gotthard (1854-1925), Swedish linguist, 3
Norfolk: family names from, 89, 119, 156-67 passim
Norman (Eng. fam. name), 104, 163
Norman, Dan., Nfld. resident, 249
Normandy: place names, 39, 40; family names, 35, 45
Norris, George, Nfld. resident, 163
North American place names, 7-8
North Atlantic Coast, 9
North Harbour (NTS Sound Island), 84
Northamptonshire: family names from, 156-67 passim
Northeast Crouse (NTS Groais Island), 41
Nottinghamshire: family names from, 156-67 passim
Nova Scotia place names, compared with Nfld., 22, 44, 48, 91-2, 97, 102

O'Brien (Ir. fam. name), 125, 129, 134
Ochre (NTS Eastport), 21
Ochre Pit Hill (NTS Sweet Bay), 21
Ochre Pit Island (NTS Point Leamington), 21
Ochre Pit Pond (NTS Little Bay Island), 21
O'Connell (Ir. fam. name), 130
O'Don(n)el, James Louis (1738-1811), first Roman Catholic bishop of Nfld., 108
O'Donnell (Ir. fam. name), 134
Offaly (Ireland): family names from, 129-36 passim
Ogilby, John (1600-76), English cartographer, map of 1671, 42
Old Indian Path (unnamed in NTS Eddies Cove), 21
Oliver (Eng. fam. name), 163
"Oliveriana" map of 1505-8, 12, 30, 71, 77, 90
O'Mara, M.J., Nfld. annalist, 169, 215
O'Reilly, Fr., parish priest in Nfld., attempts to rename Pinchgut Tickle, 85

Orkney place name, 76
Orlebar, John (1810- ?), Admiralty surveyor, 193
Ossory (Ireland): family names from, 129-36 passim
Outport, 102
Oxford English Dictionary: defines flake and stage, 41; gives late citation of glam, 52; on caplin, 57; witless, 65; ballard, 66; cites sugarloaf, 67; gives late citation of logy, 73; whaleback, 73; omits Old Harry (rock), 74; cites Bread and Cheese, 78; omits shalloway, 86; omits Nfld. meaning of hare's ears, 87; cites cold with adj., 89; omits Nfld. and Ir. meaning of brandies, 90; omits blowmedown, 92; omits otter-burrow, 95; cites dildo, 96; cites bonavist, 96; omits outharbour, 101-2; gives late citation of barrens, 102; omits tolt, 104; cites fox-trap, 117; cites rip rap, 118; cites tickle, 141, 142; omits Nfld. meaning of waters, 143; cites bacalao, 172; omits barking-kettle, bark-kettle, bark-pot, 174; on Bedlam, Bethlehem, 179; on bluff, 182; on badger, beaver, 186; on broom v., 187; defines caplin, 192; cites Pepperalley, 199; defines dunnage, 206; defines grave v., 219; defines holy-stone, 226; on jig, jigging, 230; defines kettlebottom (hill), 232; defines Key, 232; defines norther, 251; omits pumbly, 264; defines rind, 268; cites saddle (hill), 270; defines sculpin, 276; defines velvet (of stags), 294; cites wind-gap, 298
Oxley (Eng. fam. name), 163

Pack (Eng. fam. name), 163
Page, John Lloyd Warden (1858-1916), Eng. writer: on dock, 207; on waters, 296
Page, T., see Mount, W. and I.
Palliser, Sir Hugh (1723-96), governor of Nfld., on Irish female immigrants, 124
Parat, Antoine (d. 1696), Fr. governor of Placentia, 51
Pardy (Eng. fam. name), 127
Parker (Eng. fam. name), 163
Parker, William (1743- ?), Eng. hydrographer, 13

378 / Place Names of the Avalon Peninsula

Parker('s) River (NTS St. Anthony), 13
Parkhurst, Anthony (fl. 1561-83), Eng. merchant and explorer: records names in Eng., 56; on smelt, 57; on caplin, 192
Parsons (Eng. fam. name), 163
Passage des sauvages (unnamed in NTS Eddies Cove), 21
Passage of ye Savages (unnamed in NTS Eddies Cove), 21
Path of the Indians (unnamed in NTS Eddies Cove), 21
Patrick (Ir. bap. and fam. name), 134, 136
Patrick's Marsh or Pond (NTS Badger, Gull Pond), 91
Paul (Eng. fam. name), 164
Patterson, George (1824-97), NS Presbyterian minister and writer: on Blow Me Down, 91-2; on tickle, 142; on bark, 174
Pearce (Eng. and Ir. fam. name), 134, 163
Pearcey, Piercey (Eng. fam. name), 164
Pearl, Sir James (?-1840), Eng. naval officer, farmer in Nfld., 102 note 10, 163, 247
Pearl Island (NTS Bay of Islands), 13
Peckford (Nfld. fam. name), 109, 157
Peddell, Peddle (Eng. fam. name), 109, 163
Peddel, N. (fl. c. 1904-8), Nfld. writer, on tickle, 142
Pennell (Eng. fam. name), 205
Pennell, Daniel, Nfld. resident, 205
Penny (Eng. fam. name), 163
Pepperell, Sir William (1696-1759), American merchant and soldier, 259
Percy, Francis (d. 1741), Eng. naval officer, reports on Irish in Nfld., 122
Percy, William (fl. c. 1830-40), sea-captain of Brigus, 113
Perry (Eng. fam. name), 163
"Pesaro", see "Oliveriana"
Peyton (Eng. and Ir. fam. name), 134, 163
Phillips (Eng. and Ir. fam. name), 134, 164
Picardy family and place names, 35, 39, 45
Picco, Piccott (Nfld. fam. name), 53
Piccott, Elias, Nfld. resident, 53
Pickersgill, Richard (fl. 1771), Eng. naval officer, 14

Piercey (Eng. fam. name), 164
Pike (Eng. fam. name), 164
Pilot, W. (1841-1913), Anglican priest and educationalist, names Tilton, 290
Pincher (Eng. fam. name), 164
Pinhorn (Eng. fam. name), 164
Pirates, see Barbary, Easton
Pitcher (Eng. fam. name), 164
Pittman (Eng. fam. name), 164, 258
Place names
- study of, 3-4, 16-7
- classification of types, 4-8
- naming process, 7-8
- change of name, 8-9; see also Newfoundland, proclamations of change of name
- sources for study, 9-17
- See also Abnaki, Basque, Beothuck, Breton, England, France, Indian, Irish, Italian, Micmac, New Brunswick, New Zealand, Normandy, Nova Scotia, Orkney, Picardy, Portugal, Scottish, South African, Spain, Wales, West Country, and English and Irish counties
- See also Bestowed, Commemorative, Descriptive, Dual-element, Euphemistic, Evolved, Generics, Incident, Folk etymology, Manufactured, Mistake, Possessive, Qualifiers, Shift, Single-element, Specifics
Plancius, Petrus (1552-1622), Flemish cartographer and theologian, map of 1592, 31
Point Ferolle (NTS Ferolle Point), 14
Poirier, Jean (b. 1931), Canadian toponymist, classification of Canadian place names, 7
Poole (Eng. and Ir. fam. name), 134, 164
Poole (Dorset), 73, 253-4
Popple, Henry, Eng. cartographer, map of 1733, 38, 42, 43, 52, 72, 82
Porchet (Fr. fam. name), 48
Port au Choix (NTS Port Saunders), 13
Port au Port (NTS Stephenville, Shag Island), 13
Port Saunders (NTS Port Saunders), 13
Portland Cove (NTS Portland Creek), 13, 83
Portugal, Portuguese
- maps: 11, 12, 27, 28-30
- place names: 12, 27-33; names for Nfld., 32; 42, 43, 54, 56, 57, 68, 92,

117; origin of tickle, 142; 153
Possessive names, defined 5–6; 31, 33, 54, 58, 64–5, 88, 97, 125, 129–36 *passim*, 139, 152, 156–67 *passim*
Pouch (Eng. fam. name), 164
Pouch Island (NTS Cabot Islands), 54
Powell (Eng. and Ir. fam. name), 134, 164
Power (Ir. fam. name), 124, 125, 134
Power, Tom, light keeper, 134
Prince (Eng. fam. name), 164
Prosser (Eng. and Welsh fam. name), 94, 164
Prowse, Daniel Woodley (1834–1914), Nfld. judge and historian, 10; on names in Mason's map, 12; on Carbonear, 39; on Vaughan's names, 62; on Bristol's Hope, 62; on South Forte, 77; on shalloway, 86; on Crow's Nest, 102; on ponds, 115; on cook rooms, 147 note 38; on Sir Thomas Cochrane, 198; on juniper, 231; on Mount Pearl, 247; *Niagara*, 249; on Price William Place, 263; Sibley's Cove briefly named after, 280; *Sophia*, 281; on South River, 282; on Virginia Lake, 295; on witch hazel, 299
Prowse, George Robert Farrar (1860–1946), son of the above, Canadian cartologist: his *Cartological Material*, 10–11; on loss of maps, 11; postulates Eng. surveys, 11, 75; on Portuguese names, 27–8; identifies P da cruz, 30; on Western Bay Head, 46; on Perlican, 56; on Witless Bay, 65; on Cape Ballard, 66; on Sherwink, 75; on Biscay Bay, 180; on Cape English, 190–1; on Conception Bay, 200; on Long Cove, 238; on Motion Head, 246; on Petty Harbour, 257; on Portugal Cove, 261; on Robin Hood Bay, 269
Prunty (Ir. fam. name), 47
Pudops Lake (NTS Pudops Lake), 22
Purbeck (? Eng. fam. name), 164
Purchas, Samuel (?1575–1626), Eng. writer, 12, 16
Purdy, John (1773–1843), Eng. hydrographer, map of 1814, 74, 102

Qualifiers, 6, 151, 154, 155
Quédville, Quetteville, Quidville, Quiédeville (Fr. fam. name), 45
Quetteville (France), 45
Quirpon Island (NTS Quirpon), 41

Ragged Cove (NTS Nippers Harbour), 35
Ragged Harbour (NTS Carmanville, Musgrave Harbour), 35
Ragged Head (NTS Eastport), 35
Ragged Islands (NTS Harbour Buffett), 35
Random Head Harbour (NTS Random Sound), 59
Random Island (NTS Random Sound), 59
Random Sound (NTS Random Sound), 57, 59
Raymond (Ir. fam. name), 134
Reade, J., "The Basques in America," 267
Reaney, Percy Hide (1890–1968), Eng. onomatologist, 152
Redman (Eng. fam. name), 164
Reinel, Pedro (fl. 1485–?1535), Port. cartographer: map of c. 1504, 30, 57; map of 1519 with Jorge Reinel (fl. 1510–c. 1540), 28, 31
Rencontre Bay (NTS La Hune), 20
Rennie, J. and W., millers and bakers in St. John's, 112
Ribeiro, Diogo (fl. c. 1520–30), Port. cartographer, map of 1529, 31
Ricketts (Eng. fam. name), 164
Rix (Eng. fam. name), 164
Roach, John (fl. c. 1832), settler at Coley's Point, 124
Roache (Eng. fam. name), 164
Robert de Vaugondy, Gilles (1688–1766), Fr. cartographer, map of 1749, 42, 52, 89
Robin Hood (Robinhood) Bay (NTS Trinity), 11, 46
Robins (Eng. fam. name), 165
Robinson (Eng. fam. name), 165
Robinson, Sir Robert (c. 1624–1705), commodore of Nfld. convoy, 45–6, 83; map of 1669, 35, 38, 39, 42, 44, 45, 46, 48, 49, 58, 63, 64, 66, 70–1, 72, 102, 111
Roche (Ir. fam. name), 53, 134
Roff, Rolfe (Eng. fam. name), 165
Rogers (Eng. fam. name), 165
Rogers, John Davenport (1857–1914), Eng. lawyer and historian, 62
Roope, John (fl. 1705), resident of St. John's, on Irish in Fr. service, 122

380 / *Place Names of the Avalon Peninsula*

Rostaing, Charles, Fr. toponymist, 4; on Crèvecœur, 51

Rotis, Denis de, Fr. cartographer, map of 1674, 13, 50

Rouleau, Ernest (b. 1916), Canadian botanist, 16, 128

Rousseau, Jacques (b. 1905), Canadian botanist and anthropologist, on *Quitouche*, 26

Rowe, (Eng. fam. name), 165

Rowe, Jimmy, Nfld. resident, 165

Rowe, Martin, Nfld. resident, 165, 242

Rudnyckyj, Jaroslav Bohdan (b. 1910), Canadian toponymist, 6; classifies Canadian place names, 7

Rumley (Ir. fam. name), 133

Russell, Lord John (1792–1878), Eng. statesman, 249

Rut, John (fl. 1512–28), Eng. explorer, 34, 56

Rutlandshire: family names from, 156–67 *passim*

Ruysch, Johannes (d. 1533), Dutch cartographer, map of 1508, 30, 32, 89

Ryall (Ir. fam. name), 135

Ryan (Ir. fam. name), 125, 135

Rygh, Oluf (1833–99), Norwegian archaeologist and toponymist, 3

St. Anthony's Bight (NTS St. Anthony), 42

St. Croix (Fr. fam. name), 31, 54

St. Georges Bay (NTS Codroy etc.), 8

St. John, J.J. (1848–1918), Roman Catholic priest, renames Ram Islands, 85–6; names Regina, 120

St. Jones Within (NTS Random Island), 57

St. Joseph's (NTS Baines Harbour), 9

St. Mein Bay [now St. Anthony's Bight] (NTS St. Anthony), 42

St. Ovide, French Soldier, 94

St. Paul, 74

St. Pierre and Miquelon (archipelago), 52

St. Vincent, 30

St. Vincent, *see* Jervis

Sall, Saul (bap. and Ir. fam. name), 135, 136

Saltee Islands (Ireland), 90

Sam(p)son (Eng. fam. name), 165

Sanches, Cipriano (fl. c. 1600), Port. cartographer: map of 1596, 30; map of 1623, 42

Sands, Donald B. (b. 1920), American toponymist, 5

Sanson, Nicolas (1600–67), Fr. cartographer, map of 1656, 42

Santa Cruz, Alonso de (1500–72), cosmographer major of Seville, atlas of 1545, 31, 71

Saunders, (Eng. fam. name), 165

Sawyer(s) (Eng. fam. name), 165

Scroggins (Eng. fam. name), 89, 165

Scottish fam. names, 85–6, 152, 153, 156–7 *passim*; place names, 64, 85–6

Seller, John (fl. 1667–1701), Eng. publisher of sea-charts, charts of 1671, 38, 44, 47, 66, 71–2, 89

Senex, John (d. 1740), Eng. cartographer, map-engraver and globe-maker, map of 1728, 35, 43

Seymour (Eng. fam. name), 165

Shalloway Island (NTS St. Lawrence, Marystown), 86

Shanadithit (d. 1829), Beothuck woman, 20

Shanahan (Ir. fam. name), 124, 135

Shea (Ir. fam. name), 124, 135

Shears, W.C. (1839– ?), Anglican priest, 278

Sheep Head (Ireland), 89

Shift names: defined 6; 30, 31, 34, 35, 38, 41, 46, 50, 51, 52, 65, 73, 74, 78, 82, 84, 89, 90, 91, 92, 95, 97, 98, 103, 104, 105, 106, 107, 110, 111, 113, 116, 118, 119, 128, 155, 156

Shore (Eng. fam. name), 165

Shropshire: family names from, 116, 156–67 *passim*

Sibley (Eng. fam. name), 165

Simms (Eng. fam. name), 165

Single-element names, defined, 4–5; 138–40

Skeat, Walter William (1835–1912), Eng. scholar, 3

Skelton, Raleigh Ashlin (1906–70), Eng. cartologist, 9, 11, 13, 16 note 30, 27, 28

Skerry (Eng. fam. name), 165

Skerwink Head (NTS Trinity), 75

Skibbereen (Ireland), 126

Slaney, John (fl. c. 1600–20), treasurer of the London and Bristol Company, 39

Sleeper (Eng. fam. name), 71
Sligo (Ireland): family names from 128; 129–36 passim
Sloan (Scot. and Ir. fam. name), 135, 165
Smallwood, Joseph Ramsay (b. 1900), Nfld. politician and writer, 52; on Grates Cove, 218; on *Niagara*, 249
Smith, H.P., Eng. writer, on Poole, Dorset, and Nfld., 253
Smith, W.R. (?1845–1921), Anglican priest, re-names Broad Cove, 90–1
Smyth, William Henry (1788–1865), Eng. admiral and scientific writer, defines bluff, 182
Snagge (Eng. fam. name), 165
Snooks Tolt (NTS Terrenceville), 104
Snow (Eng. fam. name), 165, 205
Solebay (unnamed in NTS Ferolle Point), 13
Somerset family names, 70, 74, 105, 106, 156–67 passim; Avalon, 63; place names from, 70
Sooley (Eng. fam. name), 165
South African place names, 49
Southwood, Henry, Eng. cartographer: map of 1675, 38, 42, 43, 44, 49, 50, 60, 63, 66, 68, 72–4, 76; "A True Description" of 1689, 74–5; 157, 158
Spanish maps, 11; place names, 38–9, 56
Spark(e)s (Eng. fam. name), 165
Sparrow (Eng. fam. name), 166
Specifics, defined, 5; classified, 5–6; Indian 20; 35, 42, 54, 56, 59–60, 60, 63, 64, 65, 67, 73, 75, 78, 82, 86, 87, 91, 95, 97, 98, 102, 104, 104–5, 106, 107, 108, 109, 112, 114–15, 115, 116, 120; Ir., 125–36; 140–1, 144; analysed, 149–50, 156–67; in multiple-element names, 154–6
Speck, Frank Gouldsmith (1881–1950), American anthropologist, on Indians in Nfld., 20–22
Spicer (Eng. fam. name), 166
Sprigg (Eng. fam. name), 166
Squibb (Eng. fam. name), 166
Staffordshire: family names from, 156–67 passim
Stanton (Eng. fam. name), 166
Steel (Eng. fam. name), 166
Stephen(s) (bap. and Eng. and Ir. fam. name), 135, 136, 166
Stevens, John (d. c. 1897), Micmac guide and trapper, 24
Stewart, George Rippey (b. 1895), American toponymist, 4; classifies place names, 4–6, 8; 17; on barrens, 174
Stewart, James, Nfld. resident, 262
Stick (Eng. fam. name), 166
Stile(s), Stoyles (Eng. fam. name), 166
Stickle (Eng. fam. name), 166
Stock (Eng. fam. name), 105, 166
Strai(gh)t(s) of Belle Isle (NTS Quirpon etc.), 15
Subercase, Daniel Auger de (1663–1732), Fr. soldier, governor of Placentia, 94; attacks St. John's, 122
Suffolk: family names from, 89, 156–67 passim
Sully (Eng. fam. name), 165
Surrey: family names from, 156–67 passim
Surveys, *see* Maps
Sussex: family name from, 215
Sutton (Eng. fam. name), 166

Tasker, David, Nfld. resident, 262
Thames, River (England, New Zealand and unnamed in NTS Bay of Islands), 13, 14
Thevet, André (1502–90), Fr. cosmographer and historian, 38
Thomas (Eng. fam. name), 166
Thomas, William, Nfld. resident, 262
Thomey (Ir. fam. name), 124
Thorburn, Sir Robert (1836–1906), prime minister of Nfld., 288
Thoresby, William (fl. 1796–8), Eng. methodist minister in Nfld., 43, 44, 94; names in *Narrative*, 98
Thorn(e) (Eng. fam. name), 58; settlers at Colliers Bay Cove, 145, 166
Thorn(e), Robert, the elder (d. 1519), Eng. merchant, 32, 58
Thornton, John (fl. 1679–1704), Eng. hydrographer: maps of 1689, 43, 44, 46, 66, 68, 72, 74, 76, 77–8, 85, 90, 94, 107, 127
Tickle (Eng. fam. name), 166
Tilley (Eng. fam. name), 105
Tipperary (Ireland): family names from, 118, 129–36 passim
Tirlayden (Ireland), 128
Tobin (Ir. fam. name), 135

382 / *Place Names of the Avalon Peninsula*

Tocher (Ir. fam. name), 127–8, 135
Tolt, The (NTS Marystown etc.), 104
Tolt Brook (NTS Gisborne Lake, Meta Pond), 104
Tolt Hill (NTS Random Island), 104
Tolt Point (NTS Random Island), 104
Top (Eng. fam. name), 91
Toponymy, see Place Names
Townshend, George, 4th Viscount and 1st Marquis (1724–1807), Eng. soldier, 102
Trac(e)y (Eng. and Ir. fam. name), 135, 166
Trinity (NTS Trinity), 70, 80, 96
Tucker (Eng. and Ir. fam. name), 135, 166
Turnalayden (Ireland), 128
Tweed Island (NTS Bay of Islands), 13

Ulster (Ireland): family names from, 129–36 passim
Ups(h)all (Eng. fam. name), 166

"Vallard" map of 1547, 38
Vaughan, Sir William (1575–1641), Welsh scholar and colonial promoter, imposes names on Avalon Peninsula, 12, 61–2; 297
"Velasco" map of 1610, 28, 33, 57, 68
Velho, Bartolomeu, Port. chart-maker, map of 1561, 32
Verarzanus, John, see Verrazzano, Girolama da (brother of Giovanni i.e. John)
Verrazzano, Girolama da, Florentine cartographer, 11; map of 1529, 27, 31, 32
Victoria, Queen (1819–1901), 294
Viegas, Gaspar Luis (fl. 1534–7), Portuguese cartographer, map of c. 1537, 31
Vigneras, Louis-André, Spanish historian, 27
Vinegar Hill (Ireland), 126
Vion, Blaise, Fr. cartographer, map of 1699, 72
Visscher, Nicolas, map of c. 1680, 38, 42, 44, 51, 68, 72, 76–7, 92
Vizard (Eng. fam. name), 166
Voisey (Eng. fam. name), 166

Wade (Ir. fam. name), 125
Walbank, Thomas, naval chaplain, on origin of Quidi Vidi, 44–5

Waldron (Ir. fam. name), 135
Wales, Welsh: family names, 94, 108, 116, 156–67 passim; place names 61–2, 66
Wall (Eng. and Ir. fam. name), 135, 166
Wallace, Sir James (1731–1803), Eng. admiral, governor of Nfld., 102
Walsh (Eng. and Ir. fam. name), 135, 167
Walsh, Tom, light-keeper, 291
Warwickshire: family names from, 156–67 passim
Waterford (Ireland): family names from, 129–36 passim; place names from 112, 126, 127
Watson, Charles (d. 1757), Eng. naval officer, governor of Nfld., reports on Irish in Nfld., 122
Watts (Eng. fam. name), 167
Wattson, Phill., Nfld. resident, 82
Webber (Eng. fam. name), 167
Welch (Eng. fam. name), 167
Wells, Richard (fl. 1798), Nfld. resident, 106
Welsh, (Ir. fam. name), 124
West Country (England): fam. names from, 70, 74, 92, 94, 104, 118; place names, 70, 146, 286; see also especially Cornwall, Devon, Dorset
Westmeath (Ireland): family names from, 129–36 passim
Westmorland: family names from, 156–67 passim
Wexford (Ireland): family names from, 124, 129–36 passim; place name from, 126
Whalen, Whelan (Ir. fam. name), 125, 135–6
Whitbourne, Sir Richard (fl. 1579–1628), sailor, merchant, colonizer, writer, governor of Sir W. Vaughan's colony in Nfld., on Indians in Nfld., 19, 20–1; on mosquitoes, 63; map of 1622, 30, 42, 109, 110; place name Whitbourne, 297
White (Ir. fam. name), 124
Whiteway (Eng. fam. name), 167, 298
Whiteway, Sir William Vallance (1828–1908), Nfld. politician, 97, 253, 298
Whitney, Josiah Dwight (1819–96), American geologist, on wind-gaps, 298
Whittle (Eng. and Ir. fam. name), 65, 136

Wicklow (Ireland): family names from 129–36 *passim*; place name from, 64
Wigmore (Eng. fam. name), 167
William IV, King (1765–1837), 263
Williams (Eng. and Ir. fam. name), 136, 167
Williams, John, ? Nfld. resident, 167
Williamson, James Alexander (b. 1886), Eng. historian, 27
Wiltshire: family names from, 74; 119, 156–67 *passim*
Winter (Eng. fam. name), 167
Winter, Sir James S. (1845–1911), prime minister of Nfld., 72
Wix, Edward (d. 1864), archdeacon of Nfld., 54, 84; on Nieuhook, 96; records names, 103–6; cites fox trap, 117; 130, 145, 161, 166; on lords and ladies, 240

Wood, Anthony à (1632–95), Eng. antiquary and historian, 62
Woodford (Eng. fam. name), 167
Worcestershire: family names from, 156–67 *passim*
Wyet, Sylvester (fl. 1594), Eng. sailing master and fisherman, 38
Wynne, Edward (fl. 1621–6), Welsh sea-captain and colonizer, 62

Yonge, James (1647–1721), Eng. surgeon and diarist, 44, 52, 65, 66; names in *Journal*, 66–70; 77, 158; on Admiral, 169; on pinchgut money, 84
Yorkshire: place names from supposed survey of Nfld., 1498, 75; family names from, 156–67 *passim*
Young, Walter (d. 1780), Eng. naval officer, 14

This book

was designed by

ANTJE LINGNER

under the direction of

ALLAN FLEMING

and was printed by

University of

Toronto

Press

www.ingramcontent.com/pod-product-compliance
Lightning Source LLC
Chambersburg PA
CBHW020349080526
44584CB00014B/954